Counseling
LGBTI Clients

Counseling
LGBTI Clients

Kevin Alderson
University of Calgary

SAGE

Los Angeles | London | New Delhi
Singapore | Washington DC

SAGE

Los Angeles | London | New Delhi
Singapore | Washington DC

FOR INFORMATION:

SAGE Publications, Inc.
2455 Teller Road
Thousand Oaks, California 91320
E-mail: order@sagepub.com

SAGE Publications Ltd.
1 Oliver's Yard
55 City Road
London EC1Y 1SP
United Kingdom

SAGE Publications India Pvt. Ltd.
B 1/I 1 Mohan Cooperative Industrial Area
Mathura Road, New Delhi 110 044
India

SAGE Publications Asia-Pacific Pte. Ltd.
3 Church Street
#10-04 Samsung Hub
Singapore 049483

Acquisitions Editor: Kassie Graves
Editorial Assistant: Courtney Munz
Production Editor: Brittany Bauhaus
Copy Editor: Kim Husband
Typesetter: C&M Digitals (P) Ltd.
Proofreader: Theresa Kay
Indexer: Diggs Publication Services, Inc.
Cover Designer: Candice Harman
Permissions Editor: Adele Hutchinson

Printed in the United States of America

Library of Congress Cataloging-in-Publication Data

Alderson, Kevin.

Counseling LGBTI clients / Kevin Alderson.

p. cm.
Includes bibliographical references.

ISBN 978-1-4129-8718-9 (pbk.)

1. Gays–Counseling of. 2. Lesbians–Counseling of. 3. Bisexuals–

Counseling of. I. Title.

HQ76.25.A44 2013362.89'686—dc232011050599

This book is printed on acid-free paper.

SFI Certified Sourcing
www.sfiprogram.org
SFI-00453

12 13 14 15 16 10 9 8 7 6 5 4 3 2 1

CONTENTS

Preface vi

Counselor Reference Guide to the Common Concerns of LGBTI Clients Included in This Text ix

Chapter 1: Introduction 1

Chapter 2: Historical and Contemporary Perspectives Regarding LGBTI Individuals 17

Chapter 3: Gay Boys and Men 34

Chapter 4: Lesbian Girls and Women 66

Chapter 5: Bisexual Boys and Men 97

Chapter 6: Bisexual Girls and Women 121

Chapter 7: Fetishistic Crossdressing Children and Adults 138

Chapter 8: Transsexual Boys and Transwomen 160

Chapter 9: Transsexual Girls and Transmen 187

Chapter 10: Intersex Children and Adults 204

Chapter 11: Conclusions 226

Appendix A: Glossary 231

Appendix B: Handling the Roleplay Situations 235

Appendix C: Sexuality Questionnaire 247

Appendix D: The Sexual Orientation Counselor Competency Scale 253

References 259

Index 319

About the Author 328

PREFACE

Whether you are a student, a mental health practitioner, an LGBTI person, or a person who wants to learn about this community, keep reading. This book is based on more empirical research than any other that exists on the topic of LGBTI individuals. Furthermore, the issues identified in the text that LGBTI clients bring to counselors are based on what we know to be their common concerns. The same holds true for the counseling interventions aimed at ameliorating the distress caused by these issues.

We expect mental health counselors of all backgrounds to be competent in their practice. When it comes to the focus of this book about counseling LGBTI clients, however, this is rarely the case. Most counselors have never received training in working effectively with LGBT clients (Eubanks-Carter, Burckell, & Goldfried, 2005). While counseling students feel ill prepared to work with LGBTI clients, practicing counselors have expressed a lack of adequate levels of self-awareness and knowledge concerning their issues (Dillon et al., 2004).

What Pearson (2003) wrote is still echoed today: Ignorance and prejudice about LGBTI issues are present in the counseling profession yet seldom discussed. Keppel (2006) noted that even in training programs that provide competent training regarding gay and lesbian issues, the training around working with bisexual clients is inadequate.

The American Counseling Association's Code of Ethics under section C.2.a (i.e., Boundaries of Competence section) states, "Counselors gain knowledge, personal awareness, sensitivity, and skills pertinent to working with a diverse population" (American Counseling Association, 2005, p. 9). Yet most counselors today are going to have one or more LGBTI clients on their caseload. Lesbian, gay, and bisexual clients seek out counseling services at five times the rate (i.e., 50%) of heterosexual clients (i.e., 10%; Palma & Stanley, 2002; Rutter, Estrada, Ferguson, & Diggs, 2008). The increased need of LGBTI individuals to receive counseling should come as no surprise: These individuals have been subjected to "marked prejudice and discrimination in society" (Palma & Stanley, 2002, p. 86). The cumulative effects of homophobia, biphobia, transphobia, and heterosexism on one's psychological, emotional, and physical health are often substantial.

The increasing visibility of the LGBTI community as well means that counselors will become more likely to have them as clients, and in turn, they will need to demonstrate competence in working with them. LGBTI training programs can teach counselors to work effectively with this population (Dillon et al., 2004; Eubanks-Carter, Burckell, & Goldfried, 2005; Rutter et al., 2008).

Logan and Barret (2005) recently developed standards for LGBT counseling competency to aid counselors and counselors in training in the examination of biases and values as well as the implementation of appropriate intervention strategies. These standards have been adopted by the

Association for Lesbian, Gay, Bisexual and Transgender Issues in Counseling (ALGBTIC), a division of the American Counseling Association. This textbook incorporates these standards while at the same time paying particular attention to the multicultural competencies of beliefs and attitudes, knowledge, and skills as outlined by several experts in the field (Arredondo et al., 1996; Sue, Arredondo, & McDavis, 1992; Sue et al., 1982; Sue et al., 1998).

Wherever possible, the text incorporates material from evidence-based peer-reviewed journal articles. In some cases, the lack of research in a specific area is indicated. In this regard, this book speaks to what we know based on the available research, and it is relatively silent on those topics that still require empirical study.

You will notice that in Chapters 3 through 10, most of the opening vignettes begin with a counselor who is lacking competence in one or more areas. The intent is to help you begin thinking about appropriate interventions with this particular group within the LGBTI community. After reading the chapter, I recommend you return to the opening vignette to look at where counseling the individual could be improved based on what you have learned. Not even experts are perfect with their interventions; if we were, we would never face the painful realization of our limitations and of our own humanness. People are complex, and even people who believe they have come to understand themselves are still unaware or nonaccepting of some aspects of their *selves*. We are constantly reminded as counselors of how fallible human beings really are, both in who we work with and in ourselves. This alone should humble us as we continually strive to become still better counselors and even better persons.

There are other pedagogical features of this text that will assist you in your learning. These are highlighted in Chapter 1. By the end of Chapter 11, you will have gained an excellent foundation upon which to provide counseling to the LGBTI community.

The groups within the LGBTI community included in this text will be refreshing to many professionals in the field. Chapter 1 provides an introduction to terminology and to some of the ongoing debates within the field of LGBTI studies and, more generally, within all research endeavors.

Chapter 2 provides a brief history of the LGBTI community. The intent is to provide some context for how this community rose in visibility, and in doing so, how it simultaneously began developing its own cultural norms and mores.

Chapters 3 through 10 are the "meat and potatoes" of the text with their focus on gay men, lesbian women, bisexual men, bisexual women, fetishistic crossdressing individuals, male-to-female transsexual clients, female-to-male transsexual persons, and intersex individuals, respectively. Chapter 11 is the conclusions chapter, which offers a brief synthesis and evaluation of where we are and where we are headed.

Throughout Chapters 3 through 10, while the focus is on one particular subgroup of the LGBTI community, the research done sometimes includes more than one subgroup in its sampling. For example, while discussing bisexual men in Chapter 5, some research may have drawn conclusions not just for bisexual men but also for gay men and lesbian women. In these instances, these additional groups (gay men and lesbian women in this example) will be mentioned here as well. To do otherwise would be to dismiss some of the findings of these particular studies.

As a final preface, some American reviewers of an earlier draft of this text wondered why there was a separate section focused on Canada when the two societies are similar in so many respects. The reason is that our Canadian students lament their desire for a text that addresses the contributions made by researchers in Canada. This contribution is particularly salient as we move into Chapters 7 through 9 with their focus on transgender clients. As professor Kathy Lahey and I (and many others, I might add) noted in the title of our book about same-sex marriage, the personal *is* political (Lahey & Alderson, 2004). Part of the political is in acknowledging our neighbors, and part of the personal is in knowing that we stand together in our need to honor universal human rights and to provide equality and protection to all.

I would now like to thank the individuals who helped breathe this book idea into life. First and foremost, I am deeply indebted to Paul Pedersen. I remember the day well when I received his email asking if I knew of anyone who would be well equipped to write a text that would fit his *Multicultural Aspects of Counseling and Therapy* series. After hearing a promising word a day later from Sage, the arduous work behind this text began.

I must also thank my husband, Manuel Mendoza Montes de Oca. When I look in your eyes and see the joy inside, I know that everything I have done in the field of LGBTI studies has been worth it. You remind me of why this work is so important.

I also thank my ex-wife, Bess Alderson, and my two children, Troy and Shauna, who have never stopped believing in me. You inspire me to keep moving forward. Your unconditional love helps me accept the reflection I see in the mirror each day. Thank you.

Without the wonderful support of people working at SAGE, this book would not have come to fruition, either. Kassie Graves helped me to accept the times when I could not meet the deadlines that continually hovered above my head. That meant a great deal to a person who sometimes forgets to smell the flowers when they first bloom. You helped change my spring.

I also thank Eve Oettinger at SAGE for her attention to the details that help move a book from the ordinary to the exemplary. I appreciate your efforts enormously.

—Dr. Kevin Alderson

Counselor Reference Guide to the Common Concerns of LGBTI Clients Included in This Text*

Chapter 3: Gay Boys and Men

1. Internalized homophobia
2. Affectional orientation confusion and self-identifying as gay (i.e., coming out to self)
3. Fragmentation of identity
4. Religious conflicts
5. HIV/AIDS
6. Relationship problems
7. Disclosing to others
8. Managing the consequences of external homophobia

Chapter 4: Lesbian Girls and Women

9. Career concerns
10. Identity concerns
11. Major depression and suicide risk
12. Weight problems
13. Substance abuse problems
14. Relationship problems
15. Parenthood issues

Chapter 5: Bisexual Boys and Men

16. Identity confusion and labeling issues
17. Internalized biphobia
18. Relationship strain and fidelity concerns
19. Finding support networks
20. Invisibility and its sequelae

Chapter 6: Bisexual Girls and Women

21. Identity confusion and fluidity of sexuality
22. Poor mental health and suicidality
23. Drug and alcohol problems
24. Specific relationship strains
25. Lack of community and isolation

**Note:* Not all of the concerns listed below apply to all subgroups within the LGBTI community. Nonetheless, the list is provided here to assist counselors working with LGBTI clients find the section(s) they are looking for quickly.

Chapter 7: Fetishistic Crossdressing Children and Adults

26. Marital discord
27. Ego-dystonic crossdressing and/or compulsiveness
28. Mild to moderate gender dysphoria

Chapter 8: Transsexual Boys and Transwomen

29. Child and adolescent challenges
30. Gender dysphoria
31. Wanting to transition
32. Relationship and family problems
33. Transitioning at work
34. Need for social support

Chapter 9: Transsexual Girls and Transmen

35. Uncertainty about SRS
36. Learning new gender scripts

Chapter 10: Intersex Children and Adults

37. Bereavement
38. Posttraumatic reactions
39. Shame and guilt
40. Loneliness, secrecy, and feelings of isolation
41. Developing an intersex identity
42. Family issues
43. Family support
44. Social support

1

INTRODUCTION

REFLECTIONS

Have you ever watched a gay pride parade (more inclusively known as a "pride" parade) in a large city, especially one like San Francisco, New York, or Toronto? What a spectacle! The most amazing thing is that the majority of spectators are not lesbian, gay, bisexual, transgender, or intersex (LGBTI) individuals themselves. No, they are heterosexual people and their families who are supportive, accepting, inquisitive, and/or they are those who just like to attend a good party. One definition of gay is "keenly alive and exuberant" (Merriam Webster Dictionary, 2011) and the fact is, the LGBTI community knows how to have a good time. Generally speaking, LGBTI people think outside the box,

(Continued)

(Continued)

so ordinary convention does not always apply. Furthermore, they are accommodating of diversity, so everyone is invited! Next time you have an opportunity, attend a pride parade in a large city and experience the plethora of LGBTI identities firsthand.

1. What reservations, if any, would you have about attending a pride parade?
2. Do you believe that people you know would think differently about you if they saw you attend a pride parade? In what way(s)?
3. What does a pride parade teach spectators about diversity? What are the pros and cons of what they would learn?
4. How would you distinguish a transperson from a drag queen or drag king?
5. What percentage of the LGBTI individuals present have always had the sexual identity they espouse right now?

Book Overview

A portion of most modern societies is composed of individuals who differ with respect to some aspect of their sexuality or felt gender. This does not mean, however, that every society allows its members to express these differences—individualism and its expression are not valued in every culture. For example, there is little question that gay and lesbian individuals can be much more open about their lifestyles in individualistic societies (e.g., United States Canada, Western Europe, Australia) compared with collectivistic societies (e.g., Mexico, Southeast Asia, South America).

Furthermore, the form that such expression takes is also dependent on sociocultural and historical factors. Gay identities in the 1950s, for example, look different than today's gay identities. Their expression also depends on a person's culture, religion, and age.

The main focus of this book will be on contemporary lesbian, gay, bisexual, transgender, and intersex (LGBTI) identities primarily in the United States, but also in Canada and in various collectivist societies. Salient research will be included aimed at increasing your understanding of LGBTI individuals and looking at what we know from the published literature about counseling them.

The Problem With Terminology

Collectively, LGBTI are people with nonheterosexual identities (e.g., lesbian, gay, bisexual) and/or those with transgender identities (e.g., fetishistic crossdresser, transsexual, intersex). More specifically, transgender individuals include those who present unconventional gender expressions (e.g., fetishistic crossdresser, transgenderist, gender bender) and/or those who present unconventional gender identities (e.g., transsexual, transwoman, transman). Terminology is often challenging when writing or talking about groups who have been historically oppressed and disenfranchised. Postmodern writers have become very sensitive to the labels used to describe individuals. Within queer theory, for example, labels are avoided altogether. Although some writers use the term *queer* to refer to LGBTI people, the older generation often associates this label with a derogatory term used mainly to describe masculine gay men in the early part of the 20th century (Minton & Mattson, 1998).

The term *sexual minorities* also has disadvantages, as some writers suggest that the word *minority* may imply a lesser-than status compared to those who are "mainstream." One favorable expression could be *persons with nondominant sexualities*; however, it is cumbersome and pedantic. The term *LGBTI* has been chosen for this text instead of the many acronyms that are in usage today, including some that include one Q for *queer* and another Q for *questioning*. Not only does adding further initials make the acronym needlessly cumbersome, terminology remains in flux for some identities, and some individuals chose not to identify with any of the identity labels within the acronym anyway.

Identity labels are used herein as adjectives, not nouns. For example, *lesbian women*, not *lesbians*; *gay men*, not *gays*; and so forth. While the term *lesbian* is considered appropriate usage by the American Psychological Association (APA; 2010, p. 74), *lesbian women* is arguably a preferred term to equalize it with the suggested term *gay men* by APA (2010, p. 74). It is imbalanced and prejudicial to use *gay* as an *adjective* for *gay men* while using *lesbian* as a *noun* for *lesbians*. This book is primarily about identities, and these social constructions do not describe a person's entirety. To imply that a gay male's identity is socially constructed (through adjective usage) while implying that a lesbian female's identity is essentialized (through noun usage) is incorrect and, if anything, is completely backward. Research provides stronger arguments to suggest that most gay men have affectional orientations that are inherently based much more than is the case for most lesbian women.

Identities describe one aspect of a person. A lesbian woman, for example, is more than just her nonheterosexual identity—she is also someone's daughter, someone's neighbor, and someone's friend. She is a lover, a worker, and an inhabitor of earth. Similarly, referring to a transsexual individual as a "transsexual" diminishes this person's existence to this one aspect of self.

Even the term *LGBTI* is limited in that its focus is *only* on identities. People also differ on the continuum called "affectional orientation," for example, and these do not in and of themselves constitute an identity label. *Affectional orientation* is used preferentially over the older term *sexual orientation* throughout this text as it better reflects "the fact that a person's orientation goes beyond sexuality" (Pedersen, Crethar, & Carlson, 2008, p. 136). *Affectional orientation* refers to the attraction, erotic desire, and philia for members of the opposite gender, the same gender, or both (Alderson, 2010).

A recent scale that measures affectional orientation includes six components: sexual attraction, sexual fantasies, sexual preference, propensity to fall in love romantically, being in love romantically, and the extent to which one has sexual partners of each gender (Alderson, Orzeck, Davis, & Boyes, 2011; Brown & Alderson, 2010). This scale, called the Sexuality Questionnaire, incorporates suggestions made by several researchers to measure affectional orientation on two separate scales: one that measures magnitude of interest in males and another that measures interest in females. Factor analytic work has shown that affectional orientation can operationally be defined and measured as a combination of the above six components (Alderson et al., 2011; Brown & Alderson, 2010). A copy of the scale can be found in Appendix C.

Philia is the propensity to fall in love romantically with members of a particular sex or gender (or both, as in the case of biphilia). Consequently, individuals can have a heterosexual, homosexual, or bisexual orientation—regardless of the extent to which they acknowledge or accept it. Most gay men and lesbian women, for example, went through a "coming out" process before they accepted their homosexual orientation (Alderson, 2002).

Identities and affectional orientation do not always match. A gay male, for example, often identifies as having a bisexual or heterosexual orientation before he accepts his homosexual orientation (Stokes, Damon, & McKirnan, 1997). Some marry a woman before later coming out. Likewise, lesbian women often have a similar experience, despite the finding that their affectional orientation is usually much more fluid than men's (Diamond, 2007, 2008). More on that in Chapter 4.

Identity labels—when chosen at all—are picked by individuals themselves to describe some aspect that defines their sense of self. Consequently, they can be transient labels, inaccurate labels, or oversimplified labels. Such is also the case with some LGBTI individuals—our sexuality and gender is so much more than the label we give it.

Defining LGBTI Individuals

Sexual Identity

Sexual identity refers to the label individuals use to define their sexuality (Alderson, 2010). Most people choose a label that coincides with their affectional orientation (i.e., heterosexual or "straight," gay, lesbian, bisexual, or queer), but most transgender or transsexual individuals will also use a sexual identity label that describes their gender expression or gender identity (i.e., transgender or transsexual). Some *intersex individuals*—that is, people with "congenital conditions in which development of chromosomal, gonadal, or anatomical sex is atypical" (Vilain, 2008, p. 330)—will define themselves as intersex and/or as transgender.

Gay, Lesbian, and Bisexual Individuals

Gay men are males who self-identify as having primarily homosexual cognition, affect, and/or behavior and who have adopted the construct of "gay" as having personal significance to them. *Lesbian women* are females who self-identify as having homosexual cognition, affect, and/or behavior and who have adopted the construct of "lesbian" as having personal significance to them (Alderson, 2010).

Bisexual individuals are defined as those who self-identify as having primarily bisexual cognition, affect, and/or behavior. People might define as bisexual if they have sexual attraction, sexual fantasies, a sexual preference, a propensity to fall in love romantically, the actual experience of being in love romantically, and/or the experience of having sex with both genders. In effect, they acknowledge some degree of affectional interest in both sexes. Bisexual individuals have not established a substantive bisexual community (McKirnan, Stokes, Doll, & Burzette, 1995), so many define themselves as gay, lesbian, or heterosexual (McKirnan et al., 1995).

Transgender and Transsexual Individuals

Transgender persons refer to "individuals who do not comply with the either/or, female/male construction in society" (Ormiston, cited in Herring, 1998, p. 162), while *transsexual individuals* are those who believe their gender is dissonant with their morphology (adapted from Vanderburgh, 2009). Generally, transsexualism is viewed as a subset of transgenderism, the overarching category that also includes intersex people, fetishistic crossdressing individuals, and gender benders.

Transgender persons and transsexual individuals present nondominant gender expressions or gender identities, respectively. Consequently, transgender individuals of all kinds transcend gender binaries, and this transcendence is unrelated to their affectional orientation. A transsexual or transgender person may have any of the three affectional orientations (heterosexual, homosexual, or bisexual). A postoperative transsexual male-to-female person is often referred to as a *transwoman*, while a postoperative transsexual female-to-male individual is a *transman*. Note that not all trans people will use the terms *transman* or *transwoman* to define themselves.

A *transgenderist individual* is a male or female who crossdresses most if not all of the time and who may or may not experience gender dysphoria (Brown et al., 1996; Docter, 1988). *Gender dysphoria* means feeling varying degrees of discomfort with one's biological sex and/or one's expression of gender roles. A transgenderist individual with gender dysphoria usually experiences it in a less severe form and has resolved (or has had it decided for him or her) not to proceed with gender reassignment surgery.

Fetishistic crossdressing individuals are men who crossdress, at least during adolescence, because of the sexual arousal and often climatic release it provides. Most of these men define as heterosexual.

Drag queens are gay men who crossdress for fun and/or money, whereas women who crossdress for fun and/or money are *drag kings*. The core element of drag is "performance and parody" (Lorber, 2004, p. xxv). This form of crossdressing is considered a traditional part of LGBTI culture, and its significance is comparable to wearing a kilt, accepted as traditional Scottish attire for men.

There are many terms with a shorter history that are sometimes used by transgender individuals to describe themselves. Just two of the informal ones include *gender bender* and *she-male*. *Gender benders* are people who intentionally "bend," or transgress, traditional gender roles. A *she-male* "refers to men who have achieved a female chest contour with breast implants or hormonal medication but still retain their male genitals" (Blanchard & Collins, 1993, p. 570).

Although the term *queer* has not caught on in general usage (Savin-Williams, 2005), it refers to those people who refuse to be classified on the basis of sexuality (Herdt, 1997). Not labeling one's sexuality is an outgrowth of queer theory. Queer theory is an outgrowth from social constructionism, a paradigm that will be described shortly.

Defining the Terms of Oppression

As you will glean from every chapter in this book, LGBTI individuals have been victim to a great deal of prejudice, discrimination, harassment, violence, oppression, and denigration. The terms that follow are the ones in most common usage today.

Homophobia is the fear, dislike, or intolerance of gay and/or lesbian individuals. A more specific term is *homonegativity*, which refers to having negative views of gay and/or lesbian people, regardless of the reason. *Biphobia* is the fear, dislike, or intolerance of bisexual individuals and/or rendering them invisible by denying their existence.

Transphobia is the fear, dislike, or intolerance of transgender individuals. This may include rendering transsexual individuals invisible by denying the existence of differing gender identities.

Heterosexism is a term related to homophobia and biphobia, but it does not necessarily require the fear and/or dislike of those who define as gay, lesbian, or bisexual be present. Instead, it refers to the many ways individuals in our society consciously or unconsciously minimize gay, lesbian, and bisexual people, either by assuming that they don't exist or by projecting a belief that they are somehow inferior compared with their heterosexual counterparts.

Caveats Regarding Research Conducted With LGBTI Individuals

You can probably infer from the above that LGBTI individuals are a significantly diverse group. Furthermore, terminology is often confused by both mental health professionals and researchers alike. Adding to the confusion is that those who define themselves on the basis of a sexual identity label (gay/lesbian, heterosexual, bisexual) might be referring to their sexual behavior, their affectional orientation, and/or their sexual identity, just as a transsexual or transgender person might be interested sexually in men, women, or both. Due to the confounding of what is meant by the terms in the published literature, it is impossible to answer the question accurately, "What percentage of the population defines as LGBTI?"

Invisibility

Besides problems with definition, there is a larger issue. Much of the LGBTI community remains invisible to researchers (Flowers & Buston, 2001).

Antisodomy laws remained active in some U.S. states until these were all invalidated by a 2003 Supreme Court decision (Fields, 2004), and most states do not have same-sex marriage legislation. How likely are American citizens to reveal their LGBTI status to enumerators or most researchers for that matter?

Despite the fact that Canada has had same-sex marriage in all jurisdictions since July 20, 2005, the 2006 census reported only 45,300 same-sex couples across the nation (Statistics Canada, 2009)—this figure equals 0.6% of all couples in Canada! Clearly most same-sex couples are remaining closeted, given the estimated size of the gay male community alone. The gay male population, according to various "representative" studies, suggests a percentage between 3% and 10% for both adults and adolescents (Frankowski, 2004; Savin-Williams, 2005).

This invisibility that remains for many if not most members of the LGBTI community is not difficult to understand when one considers the pervasive and pandemic effect of homophobia, biphobia, transphobia, and heterosexism. Regardless of where LGBTI individuals live worldwide, there are factions (in some countries, most of the citizens and residents) that display prejudice, discrimination, denigration, and/or oppression toward them.

Nonrepresentative Sampling

To qualify as a representative sample, a study would need to be drawn from a random sample of a population. All samples in the social sciences are biased, even when random sampling of a population has been attempted. While some people answer surveys or participate in experiments, they may constitute an entirely different sample than those who refrain from participating.

This problem is accentuated further when researchers attempt to random sample the LGBTI community because of their increased invisibility. Consequently, researchers studying the LGBTI community are *not* able to get a random sample, so instead, sampling is almost always biased. As a result, research findings provide only a glimpse of the experience of those who want to be known to us. Research reveals that at least with college students, those who participate in sex studies are a certain type of person—they are more sexually experienced, more liberal in their sexual attitudes, and have higher self-esteem compared with nonparticipants (Wiederman, 1999). It seems likely that LGBTI participants are similar to college students who sign up for sex studies. The more traditional and introverted LGBTI individuals are likely poorly represented in published research.

Given the above caveats, most gay and lesbian research—and in fact most psychological research, for that matter—has been based on well-educated Caucasian samples of individuals who are relatively accepting of their homosexual orientation (Croteau, Anderson, Distefano, & Kampa-Kokesch, 2000). Little is known about uneducated gay and lesbian people and those who have not yet come to identify as gay or lesbian. Even less is known about bisexual individuals.

As a group, individuals who self-report as lesbian or gay exist in all age categories and approximate racial mixes as the population as a whole (Degges-White & Shoffner, 2002). Demographics on the percentage of bisexual and transgender people are not as clear, although prevalence information from the Netherlands suggests that transsexuality occurs in about 1 in 11,900 males and 1 in 30,300 females (Meyer et al., 2001).

Bisexuality is currently impossible to estimate because of the many definitions it encompasses. For example, the National Survey of Family Growth was conducted between March 2002 and March 2003 on 12,571 Americans (4,928 men and 7,643 women), ages 15 to 44, with a response rate of 79% (Mosher, Chandra, & Jones, 2005). Participants were asked the question, "Do you think of yourself as heterosexual, homosexual, bisexual, or something else?" Only 1.8% of the males answered bisexual, while 5.9% admitted to having attraction to both males and females.

The Limitation of All Research

Quantitative studies attempt to generalize their results beyond the findings of the current research project. In doing so, the generalizations that result are just that: generalizations. As we know from qualitative research, the actual experience of many people does not fit neatly into the generalizations derived from quantitative studies. For example, the consistent finding that males score higher in mathematics and females score higher in verbal ability is based on large-group studies, yet there are innumerable examples of women excelling in math and men excelling in verbal skills (and the converse: men poor at math and women poor at verbal skills).

Here is a sex research example: Studies done to date suggest that there is a higher percentage of effeminate gay men compared to effeminate heterosexual men (Barber & Mobley, 1999; Chung & Harmon, 1994; Rieger, Linsenmeier, Gygax, & Bailey, 2008; Savin-Williams, 2005). Does that mean that every gay man is effeminate? Walking into a gay bar will quickly dispel that stereotype, particularly those that cater to the leather and denim crowd. Furthermore, many heterosexual men display effeminate behaviors (Baffi, Redican, Sefchick, & Impara, 1991; Levine, 1993).

For the reasons stated above, the cliché that "the more we learn, the less we know" is particularly true regarding the study of LGBTI individuals. In effect, what we know is based on LGBTI individuals who want us to know them—after all, they are the ones who participate in research studies. That leaves a significant gap in our knowledge, as the "typical" LGBTI persons might be the ones who don't give of their time to become participants.

Maintain critical thinking while reading the chapters in this text, as with any text, for that matter. As you read findings from quantitative research, remember that the results do not apply to all people within that subgroup. Similarly, as you read qualitative research, don't lose sight of the fact that there are also communalities that typify the experience of many people within that subgroup.

Furthermore, as soon as we write about something, we are simultaneously creating it (see next section for an explanation). In maintaining a critical stance, also view the research in this area as reflecting our understanding of LGBTI individuals *now*: at this point in history within a psychosocial and political context. People change and identities shift as they interact with an environment that is also shifting on many levels simultaneously. Today's constructed reality is tomorrow's fiction.

Considerations When Conducting Research With LGBTI Individuals

Given all of the above considerations, Logan and Barret (2005) recommend that research questions be formulated in a way that acknowledges that LGBTI individuals may become participants in them. Furthermore, their inclusion should not be based on stereotypes or overgeneralizations. Research design should also ensure that ethical and legal issues that may affect this vulnerable population are considered and addressed. For example, extra precautions may be necessary to ensure their anonymity and confidentiality, especially in smaller communities (e.g., rural, small colleges).

Another important consideration brought forward by Logan and Barret (2005) is recognizing the potential for heterosexual bias when interpreting research results and test results. Most psychological tests of yesteryear assumed heterosexuality, so questions about relationships implied or stated that they were between a man and a woman. Counselors need to ensure that the tests they are using do not make such heterosexual assumptions.

It is also problematic to review research results and interpret them according to existing heterosexual standards. For example, if a sample of same-sex couples is shown in a study to have shorter relationships compared to a sample of opposite-sex couples, some of whom are legally married, there is an immediate bias given that in most American states, same-sex couples cannot marry currently. Another bias would include assuming that couples are supposed to be married with children and then judging negatively same-sex couples who are not, even in those states that permit same-sex marriage. Same-sex marriage is a new consideration for gay and lesbian couples, and not everyone will think it is the final destination of a committed relationship.

Essentialism Versus Social Constructionism

A debate emerges repeatedly throughout the varied factions of psychology, known holistically as the nature–nurture controversy. Are our thoughts, emotions, and behaviors determined through nature (i.e., biologic and/or genetic causes), through nurture (environmental and/or self-created causes), or through both? In sexuality research, the debate is usually conceptualized as between the essentialists and the social constructionists (Stein, 1996).

Essentialists believe, for example, that people with homosexual orientations and/or discordant gender identities have always existed, regardless of whether they could give themselves a sexual or gender identity label. Essentialists usually support their position with evidence from biologic and genetic studies (Ellis & Mitchell, 2000; Roscoe, 1988).

Social constructionists, on the other hand, believe that homosexual orientations and/or gender identities are environmentally determined and that they require certain socio-political-historical conditions to exist in order to find expression. Consequently, a homosexual orientation or gender identity needs to be created within an environment that allows it at some level. Social constructionists usually support their position with evidence from the social sciences (e.g., history, sociology, anthropology, political science).

Researchers like Kitzinger and Wilkinson (1995) have argued that we will never prove whether essentialism or social constructionism is more accurate because "data cannot settle questions of epistemology" (p. 103). Consequently, spending countless research dollars trying to prove one position or the other is untenable and moot.

Many researchers hold the view that behavior is always the result of both nature and nurture. For schizophrenia to find expression, for example, it is thought that one needs to have a biological predisposition toward it but that environmental factors (such as stress) are needed to release it. Certain medical conditions work this way, such as shingles. For shingles to develop, one must first have the herpes roster virus within one's body as a result of having contracted chicken pox earlier. Only then can the dormant virus erupt into the shingles rash if something environmental (often stress) brings the virus out of its dormant state.

One of the important theoretical developments for sexuality studies that has emerged from social constructionism is *queer theory*. One of its basic tenets is that identity labels are themselves oppressive by presumably restricting one's sexual choices (e.g., a lesbian woman might feel guilty if she has sex with a man). Queer theorists also argue that labels allow others to delegate nondominant groups to a less privileged status in society (Gamson, 2000; Minton, 1997).

Another basic tenet of queer theory is that how we language something constructs the very thing that is being languaged (Gergen, 1985, 2009). In other words, there are no LGBTI or heterosexual individuals unless we socially create them by talking them into existence. Similarly, queer theorists argue that homosexual persons did not exist until the word *homosexual* was invented in 1869, meaning that before then, people defined themselves according to neither sexual orientation nor sexual identity labels. This does not mean that queer theorists would argue against the universality of homosexual behavior; instead, they would argue that it doesn't have any social significance or meaning until we label it.

Individualism Versus Collectivism

The concepts of "individualism" and "collectivism" have generated more thinking and research in the field of cross-cultural psychology compared to any other issue since the early 1980s (McCarthy, 2005). The continuum that exists between these concepts involves "the degree to which a culture encourages, fosters, and facilitates the needs, wishes, desires, and values of an autonomous and unique self over those of a group" (Matsumoto, 2000, p. 41). Countries and cultures vary regarding the extent to which they subscribe to the ideals of individualism versus collectivism.

Hofstede (1980), for example, conducted a worldwide study of 116,000 employees of IBM and found that the most individualistic countries include, in rank order, the United States, Australia, Great Britain, Canada, and the Netherlands. The most collectivist countries were Venezuela, Colombia, Pakistan, Peru, and Taiwan. Hofstede (Itim International, 2009) has ranked many countries according to the individualistic–collectivist dimension.

In an individualistic society, members are expected to strive for individuality, and such qualities as independence, autonomy, and personal freedom are espoused (Arthur & Collins, 2010). In a collectivist society, the collective good and reputation of the family unit are held in highest regard, and individuality and most qualities associated with it are of much lesser importance. Instead of striving for independence and autonomy, the quest is for familial interconnectedness, familial responsibility, and family heritage (Arthur & Collins, 2010; Pedersen et al., 2008).

The worldview of people living in the two types of societies can be remarkably different, and those individuals who relocate from one type of society to the other often face huge challenges regarding their acculturation. The expectation of being a well-adjusted, respected person looks different depending on one's worldview.

Most texts looking at the psychology of LGBTI individuals look at those living in our own individualistic society. Consequently, the expression of LGBTI identities is presented in a one-sided manner where striving for individuality is the hallmark of successfully attaining a positive LGBTI identity.

Does such a presentation of identity remain consistent throughout the world? Not at all, as you will discover as the various subgroups within the LGBTI community are looked at in the United States and Canada and then in other societies. The stereotypes you may have already are applicable to neither the majority of LGBTI individuals (at least in most instances) nor to those who primarily identify with a collectivist society.

The Multicultural Framework and This Text's Organization

The Multicultural Framework

A great deal of work has occurred since the 1970s regarding the creation of a framework for developing multicultural counselor competence (Sue et al., 1998). After several revisions and enhancements, the framework most often cited includes the following three dimensions:

1. Beliefs and Attitudes—Counselors need to become aware of their own biases, values, and assumptions toward clients from a particular nondominant group.
2. Knowledge—Counselors need to understand the worldview of their clients.
3. Skills—Multicultural counselors also need to learn appropriate interventions to work effectively with their clients (Arredondo et al., 1996; Sue, Arredondo, & McDavis, 1992; Sue et al., 1982).

This text will adhere to this framework. Chapters 3 through 10 are organized according to the following headings:

1. *Challenging Your Attitudes and Beliefs About This Group*—This section includes reflection questions, assumption questions, and a reflection from the perspective that you are the client belonging to the particular subgroup of LGBTI individuals focused on in the chapter (Multicultural Framework: Beliefs and Attitudes).

2. *Background Information Regarding the Particular Subgroup of LGBTI Individuals*—This section provides comprehensive knowledge about the specific subgroup (Multicultural Framework: Knowledge).
3. *Common Concerns Facing This Group and Counseling Considerations*—This section begins with two roleplays that can be practiced either in or out of class, with a list of ways to handle the situation presented within the roleplay in Appendix B. Following the roleplays is a section called "How Would *You* Help This Person?" This section helps you further focus on concerns that this subgroup may face. Then the common concerns specific to this subgroup are outlined, followed by the skills needed to work with those issues, followed by available information about counseling diverse populations (Multicultural Framework: Beliefs and Attitudes, Knowledge, and Skills).
4. *Resources for This Group*—This section includes some of the national organizations and Internet sites that may prove helpful to counselors working with this particular subgroup (Multicultural Framework: Knowledge).
5. *Limitations, Furthering Research, and Implications for Counselors*—This section looks at the limitations of the current research available regarding this specific subgroup of LGBTI individuals, followed by areas requiring further research. The last section includes implications for counselors (Multicultural Framework: Knowledge and Skills).
6. *Exercises*—Two or three individual exercises followed by two or three classroom exercises are included (Multicultural Framework: Beliefs and Attitudes).
7. *Chapter Summary*—A brief review of highlights pertaining to this specific subgroup of LGBTI individuals (Multicultural Framework: Knowledge).

Elaborating on the Common Concerns Facing This Group and Counseling Considerations Section

In addition to the above multicultural framework, the counseling sections of the text encompass the concept of inclusive cultural empathy (ICE; Pedersen et al., 2008), which results from the lifework of Pedersen, Crethar, and Carlson in the area of multicultural counseling practice. "ICE is a generic counseling perspective that requires a counselor to manage both similarities and differences at the same time" (Pedersen et al., 2008, p. 45). When counselors practice ICE, they recognize that clients present to counselors their own unique multicultural mosaic: that is, they have been influenced by various cultural influences to varying degrees. The problems that clients present to counselors are embedded within these cultural forces. Developing inclusive empathy for clients will only occur by understanding, appreciating, and honoring their unique cultural milieu.

The list of concerns found in Chapters 3 through 10 is not exhaustive; it is only suggestive of the multitude of issues for which the particular subgroup may seek help. Some of the concerns found in Chapter 3 about gay males will also apply to other subgroups, and likewise other chapters will cover some concerns that will also apply to gay males. The intent is be comprehensive *across* the chapters, not within each one. If you have a gay male client with a different problem that is germane to the LGBTI community but not found in Chapter 3, look in either the end of the Preface or in Chapter 11 (the conclusions chapter) to find out if that problem is covered in a different chapter in this text.

Furthermore, there are many generic issues that clients bring to counselors. Each subgroup also seeks help for the same reasons as the dominant culture, whether for substance abuse problems, sexual difficulties, intimate partner violence, feelings of isolation, or whatever. Counselors need to have a good understanding of a plethora of human conditions to do their jobs effectively.

A Note Concerning Including LGBTI Clients in Groups

One of the competencies (Logan & Barret, 2005) concerning when LGBTI individuals are included in groups is for counselors to have sensitivity to their special needs. Due to their oppression and marginalization, it is important that counselors ensure that LGBTI clients will have allies in the groups they attend. Counselors need to be conscious of this when screening and selecting group members. It is also important that group norms are established and interventions are implemented that are inclusive of LGBTI members. For example, group norms need to be created that allow members to share personal details without judgment or ostracism. LGBTI participants should feel safe to let others know in the group about their sexual and/or gender identity without negative repercussion following such disclosures. Counselors are expected to intervene when overt or covert disapproval of an LGBTI member occurs in the group. To not step in is to neglect the importance of both human dignity and group dynamics.

Beginning to Challenge Your Attitudes and Beliefs

Before concluding this chapter, take two steps to begin your assessment of some beliefs and assumptions that might prove a hindrance in counseling LGBTI clients. First is a change-model approach and second is a test of heterosexist thinking.

A Change-Model Approach

Tyler, Jackman-Wheitner, Strader, and Lenox (1997) used the transtheoretical model of change (Prochaska, Norcross, & Diclemente, 1994) to raise awareness of LGB issues (modified here to include LGBTI) among graduate students in counseling. In the model of change, *precontemplation* refers to the stage in which people are not intending to take action in the foreseeable future and likely are unaware that a problem even exists. In contemplation, the person begins to see that a behavior is a problem while he or she begins to look at the pros and cons of this behavior. In the preparation stage, the person plans for taking action and may begin to take some small steps toward change. The action stage is where the plan becomes implemented and the person moves toward making positive change. During maintenance, the person works actively at preventing relapse, and for some, this stage lasts indefinitely. Finally, the termination stage occurs when the person is no longer tempted to return to the problem behavior and is sure he or she will not begin the unhealthy behavior again. An underlying premise of the transtheoretical model is that the person must be ready to move to the next stage if change is to occur and become permanent. For example, a person who doesn't recognize that alcohol abuse is a problem (i.e., precontemplation) is not going to take steps to reduce or stop consumption (i.e., action).

To get a sense of where you are currently in your attitudes toward LGBTI individuals, refer to Table 1.1 and indicate below your current level of readiness to adopt an affirmative counseling stance toward members of this community.

What level of readiness are you at (i.e., note Tyler et al., 1997, only included the four stages of precontemplation, contemplation, action, and maintenance) in relation to:

1. Your **statements** regarding LGBTI individuals: __________________________________
2. Your **thoughts** about LGBTI individuals: __________________________________
3. Your **feelings** toward LGBTI individuals: __________________________________
4. Your **behavior** toward LGBTI individuals: __________________________________

You may want to return to this self-assessment after you have finished reading the chapters in this text and working through the exercises. Are you ready yet to work effectively with LGBTI clients?

Table 1.1 Characteristics of Individuals at Each Stage of the Transtheoretical Model of Change With Regard to LGBTI Issue

	Precontemplation	*Contemplation*	*Action*	*Maintenance*
Statements	"It's fine with me if someone is gay. I don't understand the need to talk about LGBTI issues."	"I guess I treat LGBTI people differently than straight people."	"I'm going to change the way I've done things in the past."	"I'm glad I've made changes to become more supportive of LGBTI people."
Thoughts	People are people.	LGBTI people have been treated unfairly in the past.	LGBTI people deserve to be treated with dignity and respect.	My life is enriched by my relationships with and the contributions made by LGBTI individuals.
Feelings	Confusion about need to discuss or receive training.	Embarrassed and ashamed about past statements or behavior.	Excited about new attitudes and experiences. Fear about others' reactions.	Pride in personal accomplishment and efforts to be an ally.
Behavior	No extended contact or association with LGBTI individuals. Has never attended LGBTI-oriented activities.	Seeking out opportunities to expand knowledge or gain new perspectives.	Choosing to more closely affiliate with LGBTI individuals and deepening relationships.	Nurturing relationships with LGBTI individuals. Attending P-FLAG, support groups, and other LGBTI activities as an ally.

Table 1.1 is reproduced with written permission from the authors. It is modified from p. 42 in their article:

Tyler, J. M., Jackman-Wheitner, L., Strader, S., & Lenox, R. (1997). A change-model approach to raising awareness of gay, lesbian, and bisexual issues among graduate students in counseling. *Journal of Sex Education & Therapy, 22*(2), 37–43.

A Test of Heterosexist Thinking

On the next page is an enlightening revision—reprinted here with permission—of a popular questionnaire by Dr. Martin Rochlin. The test is entitled, *Are My Attitudes Heterosexist?* Before turning to Chapter 2, complete this test and then find the answers to it at the end of Chapter 2.

ARE MY ATTITUDES HETEROSEXIST?

Designed by former editor of *The Heterosexism Inquirer,*

LORI YETMAN

Take This Test and Find Out!!!

The first step towards change is to find out where it's needed. This test was designed to give you some things to consider about the ways our everyday, often heterosexist, assumptions impact our behaviors and interactions with others. It's not for research purposes and we will not know the results. It's merely food for your thought . . . Please be advised that this test is for heterosexuals . . . and for those who may have internalized homophobic stereotypes . . .

The "Are My Attitudes Heterosexist?" Test

Check the answers that most resemble yours. The scoring instructions can be found at the end of the questionnaire. When you have completed the test, total your score, and find out where your attitudes fit on the heterosexism scale.

1. At what age did you realize that you were heterosexual?
   a. Infancy to age 4.
   b. Age 5 to age 9.
   c. Age 10 to age 12.
   d. Age 13 to age 18.
   e. What do you mean? I was always this way!

If you have asked, or wanted to ask, a similar question to someone who is not heterosexual, check. ☐ *(3)*

2. How do you think you became heterosexual?
   a. Genetics.
   b. Socialization.
   c. Pressure received from heterosexual parents.
   d. A traumatic sexual experience with a member of the same sex.
   e. What do you mean? I was always this way!

If you have asked, or wanted to ask, a similar question to someone who is not heterosexual, check. ☐ *(3)*

3. Is it possible that your heterosexuality is just a phase you may grow out of?*
   a. This is who I am, it isn't a phase.
   b. Yes, possibly.

If you have asked, or wanted to ask, a similar question to someone who is not heterosexual, check. ☐ *(6)*

4. Is it possible that your heterosexuality stems from a neurotic fear of others of the same sex?*
   a. Yes, I am a woman and I fear women.
   b. Yes, I am a man and I fear men.
   c. No, I'm heterosexual because of who I love, not who I hate.

If you have asked, or wanted to ask, a similar question to someone who is not heterosexual, check. ☐ *(6)*

5. If you have never slept with a person of the same sex, is it possible that all you need is a good Gay lover?*
   a. Yes, that's possible.
   b. No, definitely not—I know my sexuality, it's part of who I am.

If you have asked, or wanted to ask, a similar question to someone who is not heterosexual, check. ☐ *(6)*

6. Do your parents know that you are straight?*
    a. Yes, of course they do—I've already come out to them.
    b. Yes, of course they do—they automatically assumed it.
    c. No, I fear what they may say and do if they know. It's so unacceptable in my family, I fear that I'll be ostracized.
    d. This is a stupid question!

If you have asked, or wanted to ask, a similar question to someone who is not heterosexual, check. ☐ *(3)*

7. Why do you insist on flaunting your heterosexuality? Can't you just be who you are and keep it quiet?*
    a. I'm not flaunting it. It's just who I am. And sometimes I like to be spontaneous.
    b. I try not to be obvious about the love I feel for my partner—but sometimes we do get caught showing affection—I'm sorry.

If you thought or made a similar statement about someone who is not heterosexual, check. ☐ *(6)*

8. Why do heterosexuals place so much emphasis on sex?*
    a. We don't really. It just seems that way because of the presence of heterosexual porn on the Internet, in magazines, and in every major city—as well as the number of bars dedicated to either sex as a theme or getting sex. But it is a very important and meaningful way of expressing intimacy.
    b. Well, sex is pleasurable! It should be emphasized. We shouldn't feel ashamed about enjoying it.

If you have asked, or wanted to ask, a similar question to someone who is not heterosexual, check. ☐ *(6)*

9. Why do heterosexuals feel compelled to seduce others into their lifestyle?*
    a. It's necessary! We have to ensure the propagation of the species.
    b. It isn't a lifestyle. It's an identity. And you either have it or you don't. Our society, however, does present heterosexuality as the only possible identity—and that discourages many people from recognizing or acknowledging their own identities.

If you have asked, or wanted to ask, a similar question to someone who is not heterosexual, check. ☐ *(6)*

10. A disproportionate majority of child molesters are heterosexual. Do you consider it safe to expose children to heterosexual teachers?*
    a. This isn't true—the fact is, most homosexuals are child molesters. ☐ ***(9)***
    b. Most of the time I feel safe—child molesters make up a small segment of the population and we, as a society, are beginning to take better care of children by putting mechanisms in place for children to recognize inappropriate behavior and to report it.
    c. Most of the time I do feel unsafe, but just about teachers. Historically, our society hasn't had a good track record in terms of recognizing or preventing child sexual abuse.

If you have asked, or wanted to ask, a similar question to someone who is not heterosexual, check. ☐ *(9)*

11. Just what do men and women do in bed together? How can they truly know how to please each other, being so anatomically different?*
    a. What we do is private—as in all sexualities! And how we please each other doesn't depend so much on anatomy as it does individual expression.
    b. Men and women fit together like a puzzle—we naturally know how to please each other because we are the ones to reproduce. ☐ ***(9)***

If you have asked, or wanted to ask, a similar question to someone who is not heterosexual, check. ☐ *(9)*

12. With all the societal support marriage receives, the divorce rate is spiraling. Why are there so few stable relationships among heterosexuals?*
    a. Wow! This is true—but I can't state one cause—there are multiple reasons.

b. Well, the divorce rate may be high but we're more stable than homosexuals! ☐ ***(9)***

If you have asked, or wanted to ask, a similar question to someone who is not heterosexual, check. ☐ *(9)*

13. Considering the menace of overpopulation, how could the human race survive if everyone were heterosexual?*

    a. Good question! It would be quite frightening if everyone on the planet reproduced.
    b. At least the continuation of the species is guaranteed with heterosexuality! ☐ ***(6)***

If you have asked, or wanted to ask, a similar question to someone who is not heterosexual, check. ☐ *(6)*

14. Could you trust a heterosexual therapist to be objective? Don't you feel she/he might be inclined to influence you in the direction of her/his own leanings?*

    a. I don't believe that people of any sexuality seek recruits—sexuality isn't a social club.
    b. Because there's so few of them, only homosexuals seek recruits. ☐ ***(9)***

If you have asked, or wanted to ask, a similar question to someone who is not heterosexual, check. ☐ *(9)*

15. There seem to be very few happy heterosexuals. Techniques have been developed that might enable you to change if you really want to. Have you considered trying aversion therapy?*

    a. Giving me electric shocks after viewing naked pictures of the sex to whom I'm attracted is not going to change me. My sexuality is part of who I am and is not open to change, like all sexualities.
    b. Heterosexuality is natural, homosexuality is not. Heterosexuality cannot be changed by aversion therapy whereas homosexuality can. ☐ ***(9)***

If you have asked, or wanted to ask, a similar question to someone who is not heterosexual, check. ☐ *(9)*

16. Would you want your child to be heterosexual, knowing the problems that she/he would face?*

    a. I would want my child to be happy and would worry about any relationship he/she entered into . . . I wouldn't want their heart broken.
    b. Rather my child be heterosexual and have problems than be homosexual and happy. ☐ ***(9)***

If you have asked, or wanted to ask, a similar question to someone who is not heterosexual, check. ☐ *(9)*

17. Do you think that people of the same sex should have the right to marry?

    a. Yes.
    b. No. ☐ ***(9)***

18. Do you think that people of the same sex could make good parents, whether they have their own children or choose to adopt?

    a. Yes.
    b. No. ☐ (9)

19. Do you feel uncomfortable in the presence of people whom you think (or know) may be gay/lesbian/bisexual/transgendered?

    a. Yes. ☐ (9)
    b. No.

20. Do you feel that homosexuality is acceptable but only if homosexuals refrain from public displays of affection?

    a. Yes, it's ok if they refrain from showing affection in public. ☐ ***(6)***
    b. No, it's never ok. ☐ ***(9)***
    c. It depends on what kind of affection. ☐ ***(3)***
    d. It's acceptable whether or not affection is displayed publicly.

21. If you answered "a" or "c" in question 20, which activities would you restrict to make homosexuality acceptable? Check all that apply.

    a. kiss on the cheek in the driveway, while partners are going their separate ways. ☐ ***(9)***

b. holding hands walking through a park. ☐ ***(9)***
c. dancing together in any dance bar or at any event where people dance. ☐ ***(9)***
d. holding hands in a romantic restaurant while celebrating an anniversary. ☐ ***(9)***
e. being affectionate while Christmas shopping or at a movie (e.g. light kisses, arms around each other, holding hands, prolonged eye contact). ☐ ***(9)***
f. use of terms of endearment (e.g. honey, sweetheart, etc.) ☐ ***(9)***
g. passionately kissing during a slow dance at any bar downtown. ☐ ***(9)***

22. Have you ever harassed someone that you believed to be gay or lesbian?

a. Yes. ☐ ***(9)***
b. No.

23. If yes to question 22, how? Check all that apply.

a. Name calling. ☐ (9)
b. Staring and laughing. ☐ (9)
c. Ostracizing. ☐ (9)
d. Denying someone a membership, job, student placement, or a place to live. ☐ (9)
e. Physical assault. ☐ (9)

24. Do you tell derogatory jokes about gays, lesbians, bisexuals, or transgendered?

a. Yes. ☐ ***(9)***
b. No.

25. Do you laugh at such jokes when you hear them?

a. Yes. ☐ ***(9)***
b. No.

26. Would you tell racist jokes or laugh at them?

a. Yes. ☐ ***(9)***
b. No.

27. Do you assume that all of your co-workers, colleagues, clients, or peers are heterosexual?

a. Yes. ☐ ***(6)***
b. No.
c. Never gave it any thought. ☐ ***(3)***

28. Do you organize social events in a manner which welcomes people of all sexualities?

a. Yes.
b. No. ☐ ***(3)***
c. Never gave it any thought. ☐ ***(3)***

29. When having conversations with co-workers, colleagues, clients, or peers, do you make that discussion inclusive of everyone?

a. Yes.
b. No. ☐ ***(3)***
c. Never gave it any thought. ☐ ***(3)***

30. Do you equally acknowledge the relationships of your co-workers, colleagues, clients, or peers by ensuring, for example, that anniversaries, births, and marriages/union ceremonies, are celebrated in the same way or that all partners are acknowledged?

a. Yes.
b. No. ☐ ***(3)***
c. Never gave it any thought. ☐ ***(3)***

*Please note that those questions marked with an asterisk are from *The Heterosexual Questionnaire*, created by Dr. Martin Rochlin in 1972. The multiple choice options and those questions that are not marked by an asterisk were designed by Lori Yetman in 2000.

How do your attitudes rate?

To discover whether your attitudes rate as nonheterosexist, somewhat heterosexist, or heterosexist/homophobic, add the numbers that appear next to the answers you've chosen. An explanation of the totals can be found at the end of Chapter 2.

*Dr. Martin Rochlin, age 75, passed away Monday, Oct. 20, 2003, after a short struggle with cancer. *The Heterosexual Questionnaire* he developed is well-known by many in the LGBTI field.

2

Historical and Contemporary Perspectives Regarding LGBTI Individuals

Reflections

*Imagine you are a 22-year-old woman living in Atlanta, Georgia, in 1855. The city was incorporated only a few years ago, and the population is just over 6,000. You have issues like other young women, but the one that most concerns you must be kept quiet. Despite your strongest attempts to overcome your passionate feelings for other women, you are finding it increasingly difficult to do so. How long

(Continued)

(Continued)

can you contain your feelings? Worse, you fall in love with Gladys, and you sense it is reciprocated, although such words are never spoken. Gladys comes into your dad's bakery every day and spends more time talking to you than seems necessary or appropriate. You know that if you could, you would spend every living moment with her. Naturally, you are constantly on the ware for anyone who might notice how you are beginning to look at Gladys and behave in her presence. What on earth will you do? What about your deep yearnings?

It doesn't matter what you want. You will keep working in your dad's bakery–simple. You will not attend college because few schools across the United States will admit women, and your parents couldn't afford it anyway–simple. You will eventually get married and bear children–simple. You will (and must) suppress your feelings for Gladys and get on with your life–*not* so simple.

1. To what extent do you believe that women have a choice over who they fall in love with? What is your basis for believing that?
2. Was life *simpler* 150 or more years ago or more difficult? What is your view?
3. How would you feel about marrying someone that you will never fall in love with?
4. What do you see as the advantages and disadvantages of being a single woman and remaining celibate throughout your life span, both then and in the present?
5. How much would it bother you if others viewed you as a "failed heterosexual" when in fact you simply experience strong homosexual attraction but can't express it–ever?

**Note:* The above is a fictitious account. Atlanta demographics from Avery (1985).

The history of LGBTI individuals has been rife with conflict, prejudice, discrimination, oppression, subjugation, condemnation, persecution, and violence. Unlike Jewish history, however, LGBTI individuals have also lived mostly invisible lives and/or they have been rendered invisible by the dominant culture. "The love that dare not speak its name" (Douglas, 1894, page unspecified) remained unspoken in most cultures throughout world history. Consequently, much of the history of LGBTI individuals remains lost: unheard, unwritten, and uncelebrated. Many cultures and societies around the world continue to keep LGBTI individuals hidden, persecuted, or even murdered under the auspices of morality, criminality, or both. The brief history provided in this chapter is cursory at best. Other books that provide a comprehensive look at LGBTI history include Bronski's (2011) *A Queer History of the United States* and Warner's (2002) *Never Going Back: A History of Queer Activism in Canada.*

The intent here is threefold: (a) to increase your awareness about some of the more interesting and/or misunderstood aspects of LGBTI history in ancient times and in the United States and Canada; (b) to introduce you to some of the different cultural manifestations of gay and lesbian identities (note: cultural differences regarding bisexual, transgender, and intersex individuals will be included in Chapters 5, 6, 7, 8, 9, and 10); and (c) to help you understand the cumulative effects of conflict, prejudice, discrimination, oppression, subjugation, condemnation, persecution, and violence on LGBTI individuals.

If you had asked college students in 1970 if they knew any gay individuals—particularly as friends—the majority would have replied "no." Today's reality is that most college students in the United States and Canada know at least one gay and/or lesbian person, and many know someone from another subgroup of the LGBTI community as well.

Why has everything changed? What happened? Let's take a look.

Historical Perspectives

Before we look at modern-day history, let's spin the clock back to the beginning of recorded history, a history that includes reference to homosexuality. Same-sex practices were recorded on papyrus more than 4,500 years ago in Egypt (Blumenfeld & Raymond, 1993). Historians agree that homosexual behavior, in some form, has always existed. What is hotly debated, however, is the meaning behind the behavior at various times in history and in different cultures.

We all think we know about the ancient Greeks and Romans. The thought of unbridled orgies is disturbing to many if not most of us. Without doubt, some of this did occur back then. Some people today, however, believe that it was the only time in history when homosexuality was encouraged and accepted by the majority of its citizens. That, however, is simply not the case.

What happened in ancient Greece for about 1,000 years before the arrival of Christianity was what could best be described as sequential bisexuality within a class structure (Percy, 1996). Available records suggest it was only in the upper class that homosexual behavior occurred in any systematic and socially acknowledged way. Note that the writing through this period (and through most of history, for that matter) was exclusively by men (this is true of the entire old and new testaments of the Bible as well). In the case of ancient Greece and Rome, these writers were all highly educated aristocrats (Blumenfeld & Raymond, 1993). Consequently, we cannot infer that their writings reflect the perspectives of the "common folk" of that time.

Even the philosophers of the day were in disagreement regarding the virtues of pederasty. Several wrote harshly about it (Karlen, 1980), and "there is no evidence that homosexuality met with any social approval. . . . The Greeks never 'canonized' the physical act of sodomy" (Flacelière, 1962, pp. 195–196). Heterosexuality has been the norm in every society, both past and present (Karlen, 1980).

Pederasty (as it existed in ancient times) was the practice whereby a man took a boy under his tutelage for purposes of educating him in exchange for sexual favors of one sort or another. In ancient Greece, this expectation was placed on upper-class men between ages 21 and 30. The boy, approximately age 12 or 13, was taught the art of warfare while also acting as the man's sexual surrogate.

Most authorities believe the man would have primarily or exclusively intercrural sexual intercourse (rubbing the penis between the legs until ejaculation) with the boy, or it might involve anal intercourse (Herdt, 1997). This was expected behavior, but even then, it is widely believed that preserving the honor of the boy was sacrosanct and that his consent was required for all homosexual activities (Herdt, 1997). To give the reader some idea of how different these times were from today, boys often entered competitions to see who could take the most lashings (Percy, 1996)!

Halperin (2002) insisted that some boys found same-sex behavior so enjoyable back then that they wanted to keep experiencing it as adults. Percy (1996) commented that there was little question that adolescent athletes and other males were sexually aroused by male nudity. If both of these interpretations are correct, it supports the idea that male sexuality is socially constructed, or at least that we are all born inherently bisexual, as argued by Sigmund Freud (Cabaj, 1998) and many others.

After boys developed beard growth, their pederasts were expected to release them from their training and sexual obligations (Herdt, 1997). In any event, by the time they reached age 30, these upper-class Greek men relinquished their boy lovers and/or other male lovers of any age. Following the tradition further, they then married a woman and had children.

Giving up male lovers was particularly important for those who were the passive recipients in the sex act: "Utter scorn was heaped on the free-born adult male who was a homosexual of the passive variety. . . . Passive homosexuals were thrown out of the army" (Veyne, 1985, p. 30).

This was a macho culture, and even cunnilingus was unacceptable (Percy, 1996). Also noteworthy is the evidence suggesting that fellatio was never considered acceptable (Herdt, 1997; Percy, 1996; Veyne, 1985), and anyone caught in the act would be disgraced and ridiculed.

There have been few societies in the past in which homosexuality was accepted by the majority of citizens. One notable exception is that traditionally, many if not most American Indian and Canadian First Nations LGBTI individuals—who now commonly refer to themselves as *two spirited* (Gilley, 2010)—were accepted and revered within their tribes. Most tribes did not classify the world into simple binary categories (e.g., gay/heterosexual, male/female) but instead categorized according to degrees of appropriateness and inappropriateness (Tafoya, 2003). Garrett and Barret (2003) explained that viewing native LGBTI individuals from a psychosexual perspective was incorrect according to most native worldviews. Instead, the two-spirited person was seen as walking in the two worlds of the physical and spiritual, and this gave the person the special power to learn and teach others about balance. Consequently, the two-spirited were often viewed as the "medicine persons, leaders, and intermediaries" (Garrett & Barret, 2003, p. 134).

Sadly, the history for most LGBTI individuals has been fraught with heterosexism, homophobia, biphobia, and transphobia, resulting in prejudice, discrimination, and oppression toward them. Homosexual behavior had historically been considered a sin since Christian ideology became prevalent. Only 300 years ago, homosexual behavior was punishable by death in most western countries (Herdt, 1997), despite its continued prevalence.

Cabaj (1998) claimed that same-sex relationships had existed throughout recorded history, despite the various condemnations and varying degrees of acceptance that they garnered. In New England during the late 19th and early 20th centuries, there were women living together with other women without the financial support of men—an unusual occurrence at this time in history. While it remains unknown and debatable whether these dual-household women engaged in sexual relations, these arrangements came to be known as "Boston marriages."

Even if such relationships included having sex, it is doubtful that these women would have referred to themselves as lesbian. The same would be true for men engaging in homosexual behavior around this time. Defining oneself as "gay" or "lesbian" gradually evolved only since the 1920s, but it was not until the 1960s and 1970s that they became popular and commonly used identity constructs.

The word *homosexual* itself did not enter the English vocabulary until 1869 when K. M. Benkert (under the pseudonym Kertbeny) coined the term (De Cecco, 1981). Kertbeny's term *homosexual* eventually caught on, and as it did, homosexual behavior transformed into an identity, thereby creating the "homosexual person." In turn, this led homosexual behavior to become known as something homosexuals did, not only sinful but also deviant (Brickell, 2006).

Ross, Paulsen, and Stalstrom (1988) claimed that a homosexual identity usually only exists in societies that are condemning of it. Regardless of this claim's accuracy, homosexuals became known as mentally disordered individuals, similar to psychopaths, over the next 100 years. Although Sigmund Freud did not believe that homosexual individuals were either sick or demented toward the end of his career (Sullivan, 2003), he did believe that their sexual development was inferior compared to that of heterosexual individuals. It was Freud's followers that pathologized them (Drescher, 2008). When the American Academy of Psychoanalysis and Dynamic Psychiatry was founded in 1956, for example, attitudes toward homosexuality were simply described as "hostile" (Drescher, 2008, p. 443).

World War II is considered to mark the beginning of gay history today (D'Emilio, 1993). Nonetheless, *real* changes only began occurring in the United States and Canada in 1969.

Contemporary Perspectives

United States

History Snapshot

June 27, 1969, New York City

*My friends and I often frequented the Stonewall Inn, a bar at 55-53 Christopher Street in Greenwich Village. The place has only been open for a little over two years, and the night began as any other Friday.

As usual, we dressed in drag so that we wouldn't be recognized by anyone. You might think that people here are open-minded, but the truth is, gay bashings are not uncommon and several acquaintances have lost their jobs because their employers found out about their homosexuality. Safety is number one in my books, so why take any chances?

After arriving, it didn't take long until we see the usual police vans pull up to give the bar manager and the patrons a hard time. Sometimes they enter mostly to gawk at us, but usually they want to haul a few of us away because we are in drag, or just because we are gay. Either way, you get used to it. I haven't been out that long so I don't know if it's mostly because of the rumors I've heard: Maybe this bar really is owned by the Mafia and that's why we always get harassed. I don't know and I don't really care–so long as I am not outed at work, I will survive this bullshit.

It's now about 1:30 am or so and the same old crap is happening. A few queens are being dragged out of the bar by police and I hear a ruckus stirring outside. First time I've heard so much commotion actually since I started frequenting this place. I went outside to soon become the lucky recipient of getting a baton stabbed into my gut. As I collapsed forwards, another blow–this time across my head–left me unconscious on the pavement. When I woke up, I was at the station again. What just happened back there? It took years to find out the full impact that weekend was to have on all of us.

**Note*: The above is a fictitious account based on factual sources.

Sources:

Outhistory. (2009, October 7). *Stonewall Riot police reports, June 28, 1969. Newly obtained documents reveal name of woman arrestee and names of three men arrestees: Marilyn Fowler, Vincent DePaul, Wolfgang Podolski, and Thomas Staton*. Retrieved from www.outhistory.org/wiki/Stonewall_Riot_Police_Reports,_June_28,_1969 and several other Internet sources.

You can watch a YouTube video that shows still photos telling the story of gay pride in the United States. It is available at www.youtube.com/watch?v=XeLwQCBNmec.

Also, if you want to read some eyewitness accounts of Stonewall, go to http://wasm.us/stonewall.htm. If you prefer instead to watch some eyewitnesses talk about the Stonewall Riots, visit www.youtube.com/watch?v=mTujTI8rGBg. To look at the progress that has been made in the 40 years since Stonewall, visit www.youtube.com/watch?v=LDAGF5WHpmc.

Although many young people believe that the gay movement began with Stonewall, many large American cities had a sizeable gay presence before the turn of the 20th century. Gay individuals in New York City (NYC) lived collectively in several neighborhoods and had businesses that catered to them as early as 1890 (Chauncey, 1995). Chauncey's (1995) work revealed that a highly visible and vibrant gay culture existed in the 1920s and early 1930s in NYC amid a culture of tolerance. Nonetheless, he may have downplayed the lifestyle whereby many gay men lived "double lives": respectable family men by day and gay partiers by night. Chauncey maintained that the "closet" developed during the 1930s as the Great Depression unfolded.

The Roaring Twenties also applied to gay men in other large American cities. Some restaurants, saloons, and bathhouses were their near-exclusive domain (Sullivan, 2003). Prohibition created a backlash, and this continued throughout the 1950s. For example, it was illegal to serve known gay men liquor in New York until 1970 (Sullivan, 2003). In 1951, the Mattachine Society was founded by Harry Hay, which was the first national gay rights organization.

Before the 1950s, a common treatment for lesbianism and other "female deviances" in the United States was female genital mutilation (Koso-Thomas, 1987). While this practice was ending, a stronger voice was emerging. Organizations such as the Daughters of Bilitis (DOB) helped bring sanity to the plight of lesbian women nationwide by challenging the silence of homophobia and heterosexism. It became the first national lesbian political and social organization in the United States. The DOB was founded in 1955 in San Francisco by four lesbian couples, including Phyllis Lyons and Del Martin. Del became its first president while Phyllis became editor of the organization's monthly lesbian magazine, *The Ladder*.

When Dwight D. Eisenhower became President in 1952, within a year he provided the Civil Service Commission the power to deny employment to gay and lesbian individuals in all U.S. government jobs. Concurrently, J. Edgar Hoover, first director of the FBI, kept close tabs on the Mattachine Society and the Daughters of Bilitis, in addition to his surveillance of many others speculated to be threats to the United States (Gallo, 2006).

The Stonewall Riots/Rebellion occurred throughout the weekend of June 27, 1969, a time when police frequently raided bars and other gathering places of gay and lesbian individuals (Bernstein, 1997). While many were in mourning a week after the death of Judy Garland on June 22, 1969, considered an icon within the gay community (Dyer, 2003), patrons had had enough with police harassment and brutality. The pivotal moment occurred after a lesbian woman, Stormé DeLarverie, was clubbed by police. This spurred the protesters to fight back, beginning the modern gay liberation movement throughout the United States and throughout much of the world.

Notable changes occurred after the Stonewall Riots. Due to the efforts of researchers like Evelyn Hooker (1957), who demonstrated that gay men are as psychologically healthy as heterosexual men, progay psychologists, and many political activists, the American Psychiatric Association (APA-1) finally declassified homosexuality as a mental disorder in 1973, based on a vote of 5854 to 3810 (Bayer, 1981).

Before then, APA-1 had earlier first classified gay men as having an antisocial disorder in their book of mental disorders (known as *DSM-I*), followed by labeling them as having a "perversion" in *DSM-II* (Drescher & Merlino, 2007). After the 1973 vote, APA-1 retained "ego-dystonic homosexuality" in *DSM-III* (O'Donohue & Caselles, 1993). It was a catch-all phrase for those who were unhappy being gay. Given that many gay individuals and mental health professionals alike argued that being happy as gay would *itself* be crazy given the negative social climate out there, this fact was later appreciated by APA-1, and they removed any mention of homosexuality in *DSM-III-R* in 1986 (Cabaj, 1988). The World Health Organization, following the lead of APA-1, withdrew homosexuality from its diagnostic system (the *International Classification of Diseases*) in 1992 (Dreschler & Merlino, 2007). Still, it wasn't until 1991 that APA-1 permitted gay and lesbian psychoanalysts into their association (Blumenfeld & Raymond, 1993).

About 2 years following APA-1's 1973 decision, the American Psychological Association (APA-2) got on board and proclaimed that in addition to no longer viewing homosexuality as a disorder, mental health professionals should work at helping to remove the stigma surrounding it (Conger, 1975). In other words, they took a proactive stance, similar to what they more recently did with their proclamation supporting same-sex marriage in 2004 at their annual general meeting.

In 1976, Harvey Milk was appointed to the Board of Permit Appeals by San Francisco Mayor George Moscone, making Milk the first openly gay city commissioner in the United States. Approximately 2 years later, both were assassinated by Dan White, another commissioner who had resigned but was unsuccessful in getting his job back because he was not seen as the best fit.

All accounts suggest that the 1970s were the time when sexual freedom for gay men reached its crescendo (Dowsett, 2005), again occurring mostly in larger cities. Frequent and indiscriminant sex was rampant, and condoms were seldom worn. The gay sexual revolution was heatedly underway, only soon to come to a crashing halt as acquired immune deficiency syndrome (AIDS) struck the gay community with force after first being recognized in 1981. The HIV virus took an average of 10 years or so to incubate before the symptoms of AIDS appeared. To date, the first recorded case of AIDS is a Bantu man living in the Belgian Congo who died of an unidentified illness in 1959 (CNN Interactive, 1998). The onset of AIDS as a pandemic has been insidious and devastating.

The stigma of having AIDS combined with the pervasive oppression already felt by LGBTI individuals left many infected people with a double whammy: Not only had they become very sick, but few others wanted to care for them. The lesbian community stepped up to the plate to care for those afflicted. The AIDS crisis brought the gay and lesbian communities together, creating a common front during this time of need. Besides caregiving, organizations such as ACT UP, formed in March 1987 in New York City by Larry Kramer, arose. ACT UP soon became an international political action group dedicated to improving the lives of people with AIDS. While the HIV pandemic has continued throughout the world, the introduction of highly active antiretroviral therapy (HAART) in 1996 has proven lifesaving and life enhancing to many individuals who have become HIV infected.

In 1992, Colorado voters approved Amendment 2 by a narrow margin (54%). In effect, Amendment 2 would have repealed antidiscrimination laws in several Colorado cities and prohibited the passage of such ordinances in the future (Ward, 1995). The amendment was not dismissed until it was overturned by the U.S. Supreme Court in 1996 (*Romer v. Evans*). The message behind such legislative attempts echoed to the LGBTI community that they are perceived as being less-than in worth and dignity compared to the dominant culture. As you will read throughout this text, the impact of such actions continues to negatively affect the mental health and well-being of LGBTI individuals.

Smith (2005) claimed that the legalization of sodomy in the United States has been the most important policy issue over the last 20 years. Although such laws had been repealed in many states before then, it wasn't until 2003 that the Supreme Court decision *Lawrence v. Texas* repealed all such laws across the United States (Fields, 2004).

Although this is a great beginning, the fight for same-sex equal rights is far from over. As of 2005, "only 11 U.S. states prohibit[ed] employment discrimination against lesbians and gay men at the state level and anti-gay ordinances are often used to forestall discrimination protection in cities and states across the U.S." (Smith 2005, p. 225). High-profile gay murders, such as that of Matthew Shepard in 1998 (Noelle, 2002), remind us that prejudice and discrimination lurk somewhere in the background of one's daily living.

Gay murders have not ended since the Shepard case, either. Parkfor (2011) recently wrote that a gay pride activist was murdered in Elmira, New York. Chibbaro (2011) reported in the *Washington Blade* that a gay man had been stabbed at least 15 times in the back and police reported that the assailant referred to the victim as a "faggot." These are only two examples among countless others.

The current ongoing debate around same-sex marriage is further testimonial that many Americans would still not support its legal recognition. Even in liberal California, the legalization of same-sex marriage has ridden the roller coaster several times. You will recall that Del Martin and Phyllis Lyon were founders of the social and political organization called the Daughters of Bilitis. Del and Phyllis had been together for more than 50 years when they became the first to receive a marriage license on February 12, 2004, after the mayor of San Francisco began issuing same-sex marriage licenses (Gallo, 2006). Their license, along with those of several thousand other same-sex couples, was voided by the California Supreme Court on August 12, 2004. They were then married again on June 16, 2008. Sadly, Del died 2 months later at age 87. In November 2008, a ballot known as Proposition 8 was voted on, and this restored the ban on same-sex marriages. While this did not annul same-sex marriages already performed in California, it did prohibit further issuing of licenses. On August 4, 2010, a federal judge in San Francisco struck down the state's voter-approved ban, creating again a temporary "window" for same-sex couples to marry (McKinley & Schwartz, 2010). Opponents challenged this on June 13, 2011, arguing that the judge was biased because he identifies as gay (Shafer, 2011). The opponents lost (Leff, 2011).

Reflection

The back and forth of California legislation regarding same-sex marriage is notable. California has a sizeable LGBTI population, and the state is often viewed as the west-coast sanctuary of libertarianism.

1. What does California's tumultuous struggle regarding same-sex marriage represent?
2. To what extent is it okay to deny some groups equal legal rights? On what basis?
3. Del Martin and Phyllis Lyon were not allowed to get married despite being committed to each other for more than 50 years. What reaction do you have to this?

In the United States, the legalization of same-sex marriage is both a federal and a state concern, and many states reacted to Canada's and Massachusetts's same-sex marriage laws by passing Defence of Marriage Acts (DOMAs). It will likely be some time before same-sex marriage is recognized throughout the United States (Herek, 2006; Lahey & Alderson, 2004; Smith, 2005).

Nonetheless, we are witnessing LGBTI history in the making at a rate unsurpassed in previous generations. As of this writing, President Obama has repealed the law commonly known as "Don't Ask, Don't Tell," thus ending the ban on gay men and lesbian women serving openly in the military (Associated Press, 2010). Obama will also no longer defend the constitutionality of the 1996 Defense of Marriage Act, which banned federal recognition of same-sex marriages (Froomkin, 2011). These changes are themselves monumental. The future is encouraging for the legal recognition of LGBTI persons and their relationships.

Before ending this section, some important history regarding transgender and intersex individuals follows. Dressing in the clothing of the opposite gender was either illegal or pathologized through most of the last 100 years in the United

States (Martin & Yonkin, 2006). While the first instance of crossdressing was never documented (Dzelme & Jones, 2001), it is believed that people have crossdressed and displayed cross-gender behavior since the beginning of recorded history (Bullough & Bullough, 1993; Docter, 1988; Steiner, 1982), albeit for differing reasons perhaps than today. The term *transvestite* entered the English language when Magnus Hirschfeld first used it in 1910 (Buhrich & McConaghy, 1977). At that time, it was used to include both transsexual and crossdressing individuals. It was not until the 1950s that transvestism became a distinct diagnostic category from transsexual, thanks largely to the work of Harry Benjamin (Docter, 1988). Today, most crossdressing individuals do not like the term *transvestite* due to its association with pathology, the psychiatric profession, and the term's overemphasis on sexual arousal being the defining feature of it.

Surgery for transsexual individuals made its appearance in the 1920s. Magnus Hirschfeld coined the term *transsexual* in 1923 (Zucker & Bradley, 1999), and it is believed that the first transsexual surgery occurred around that time as well (Docter, 1988). Transsexual studies, however, did not flourish until several years after the media sensationalized the case of George Jorgensen, who became Christine Jorgensen, in 1952 (Docter, 1988).

The first sex reassignment surgery in the United States was by performed by Dr. Elmer Belt in 1956, through the encouragement of Dr. Harry Benjamin, the most significant individual in the 20th century regarding the care and treatment of transsexual persons. While receiving his training in Germany, he immigrated to the United States at the beginning of World War I. In 1979, the Harry Benjamin International Gender Dysphoria Association (now called the World Professional Association for Transgender Health) developed the International Standards of Care, outlining a treatment protocol that is still used today (Fontaine, 2002).

Zucker and Bradley (1999) reported that Evelyn Hooker, a well-known psychologist who conducted studies of nonpatient gay men in the late 1950s, coined the term *gender identity* in the early 1960s, while Robert Stoller, a psychoanalyst, named a similar concept, *core gender identity*, in 1964. While the modern gay movement began in 1969, the transgender movement did not develop and grow until the Internet became a tool for activists to mobilize and strategize (Shapiro, 2004).

Since John Money theorized that gender identity is malleable until a child is 18 months of age, intersex individuals were routinely assigned a gender (i.e., either male or female) at birth. Their own activism, beginning with intersex adults and later parents and clinicians, began in 1993. Activists have challenged Money's treatment paradigm and controversy over their diagnosis and treatment continues (Karkazis, 2003).

Canada

History Snapshot

May 14, 1969, Ottawa, Ontario

*I still couldn't believe that the Supreme Court of Canada dismissed the appeal made by Everett Klippert on December 11, 1967, a guy sentenced two years earlier to an indefinite prison term for being gay. If memory serves me well, it was only 10 days later that our Prime Minister, Pierre Trudeau, announced that what goes on in the bedroom ought to be a private matter. After my own coming out, I was frankly tired of being mistreated by so many people at all levels of society. Not unlike in the United States, police would occasionally raid gay bars and haul gay men out for no good reason. We had to be so secretive back then. I was sick of it.

(Continued)

(Continued)

Finally, I drive home after finishing my two-bit job for the day and I hear something that makes me stop dead on the road, cars honking behind me and drivers giving me the finger. I couldn't care less because of what I was hearing: under a Conservative government with Robert Stanfield as our Prime Minister, the lower house passed bill C-150, meaning that Trudeau's initiative was finally going to be a reality–homosexual behavior would become decriminalized!

I shrieked with joy as drivers began leaving their cars to approach my car window. I snapped back to the moment and sped away, not wanting any more unfavorable attention.

Maybe now I could begin to live as a free man. Maybe now I could let others know who I am.

Bill C-150 passed in the upper house on August 26, 1969, forever changing the Canadian social landscape for people engaging in homosexual behavior. Klippert, however, was not released from jail until July 20, 1971.

**Note: The above is a fictitious account based on factual sources.*

Sources:

CBC News. (2007, March 1). *Same-sex rights: Canada timeline.* Retrieved from www.cbc.ca/news/background/samesexrights/timeline_canada.html.

Rothon, R. (2006, August 31). *In hindsight: The decriminalization of homosexuality.* Retrieved from www.xtra.ca/public/Vancouver/The_decriminalization_of_homosexuality-2057.aspx.

If interested, you can see and hear the original CBC broadcast when Trudeau delivered his speech on December 21, 1967, as follows: CBC. (2009). *Trudeau's Omnibus Bill: Challenging Canadian taboos.* Retrieved from http://archives.cbc.ca/politics/rights_freedoms/topics/538/.

Similar to in the United States, a gay culture existed before 1969, but it was underground and largely secretive. Grube (1990) noted a study by Maurice Leznoff that revealed that gay individuals in Montreal, Quebec, in the early 1950s felt a strong pressure to "pass," meaning that they attempted to be seen by others as heterosexual. Although some were openly gay then, they were in stereotypically gay occupations such as artist, hairstylist, or interior decorator or in low-status occupations like bellhop.

The decriminalization of homosexuality in Canada was only the beginning of the fight for equal rights. Svend Robinson was a Member of Parliament (MP) with the New Democratic Party for Burnaby, a suburb of Vancouver. He introduced bills in 1983, 1985, 1989, and 1991 to include same-sex couples in the Income Tax Act and Canada Pension Plan Act, but his bills were defeated.

On February 5, 1981, more than 300 men were arrested in bathhouse raids in Toronto, Ontario (CBC News, 2007), an event to be repeated in Calgary, Alberta, in December 2002 when 17 men were charged with being found in a common bawdy house (CBC News, 2002). Similar to the United States, police raids of gay establishments were also not uncommon in Canada, occurring in the 1950s (Paré, 2009), the 1970s (Pride Library at the University of Western Ontario, n.d.), and even as late as 1990 in Montreal (Burnett, 2009).

In 1991, a lab instructor in Edmonton, Alberta, was fired for being openly gay in a Christian college, and after winning at the provincial level in 1994, the provincial government successfully won an appeal in 1996—the decision was then overturned (CBC News, 2007). The case was then heard at the Supreme Court of Canada. Even after they ruled that the exclusion of gay and lesbian individuals went against the Canadian Charter of Rights and Freedoms (Department of Justice, Canada, 2011), the Alberta government pondered whether to use the notwithstanding clause, which would have effectively meant that they would not have to act on the decision for a 5-year period. After a week of turbulence and hate mail, the Premier decided not to invoke the clause (Filax, 2006).

The Canadian Charter of Rights and Freedoms, by the way, was also introduced by Pierre Trudeau (who had become Prime Minister for a second time). It became law in 1982. Section 15, which dealt with minority rights, did not become effective until 1985, however. Court decisions concerning LGBTI rights have been won ultimately through reference to this Charter (Lahey & Alderson, 2004).

In 1992, the Supreme Court lifted the ban on gay and lesbian individuals serving in the military. The lifting of the ban followed a court battle by Michelle Douglas and four other soldiers that challenged the Department of National Defense's (DND) policy toward homosexual individuals in separate suits against the Canadian Forces. In preparing its legal arguments against Douglas, the DND concluded that it did not meet the standard of proof needed to challenge the Charter of Rights and Freedoms (Belkin & McNichol, 2000–2001).

In 1996, the federal government added "sexual orientation" to the Canadian Human Rights Act. In May 1999, the Supreme Court again ruled, this time awarding same-sex couples living common law with the same social benefits common-law opposite-sex couples already had (CBC News, 2007). In 2002, Marc Hall, an Ontario teen, was denied permission to take his boyfriend to a Catholic high school prom, and after a short court battle, he won, but perhaps only for himself (Grace & Wells, 2005).

Unfortunately, Hall dropped the court case on June 28, 2005, for two reported reasons: (a) the lawyer representing Hall could no longer represent him as he had been appointed as an Ontario Superior Court Judge, and (b) Hall was in university and he wanted to get on with his life (Grace & Wells, 2005). Consequently, it will require another court case in Canada to ascertain if religious rights will override students' choice of bringing someone of the same sex to their proms if they so desire, or vice versa.

One of the most seminal events in Canadian gay and lesbian history occurred on July 20, 2005, when Bill C-38, the Canadian Civil Marriage Act (Hurley, 2005), received royal assent, making same-sex marriage legal throughout the country (CBC News, 2007). Although the Alberta government had again threatened to use the notwithstanding clause against its legalization, they decided against continuing to fight an already lost battle (Filax, 2006).

Other Societies

Modern Snapshot

2009, Iran

*How much more of this am I expected to endure? I was born here 18 years ago, and little has changed since then. I first knew I was strongly attracted to other guys when I was about 11 years old, but I have managed to keep my feelings to myself. Living in constant fear helps, I guess. There is such a strong push to get married that even kids younger than myself have married!

My parents already suspect that I might not be interested in women, and they are worried. They could have got me married off already, and I cannot tell you how relieved I am that they didn't.

Nonetheless, I am fed up living here, but I can't get out easily. My best hope is getting accepted into college somewhere, but my family is not rich and it will take forever to save up enough money to do this on my own. What do I do?

(Continued)

(Continued)

Gay men are put to death here, and if they are lucky, they get to choose how they will die. Stoning anyone? How about hanging, getting cut in half, or getting thrown off a cliff? Hmm, so many choices and so little time. You don't even have to get caught in the act—accusations are sometimes enough.

I've recently read about their latest torture for gay teens and men. Anti-gay Shiite death squads seal your anus shut with glue and then give you something to cause diarrhea. After suffering incredible stomach pains, you eventually die.

I figure it's only a matter of time until I am found out . . . there is little I can do and no escape.

**Note*: The above is a fictitious account based on factual sources.

Source: Another Islamic scientific gift to civilization. (2009, August 22). Retrieved from http://islammonitor.org/index2.php?option=com_content&do_pdf=1&id=2719.

As an exemplar of how LGBTI identities are expressed differently and how those with these identities are treated differently in other cultures, this section will focus on gay men. In Chapters 4 through 10, different cultural expressions for the particular subgroup will be noted in the section called "Recent Research Focused on Other Societies."

The world is an interesting place when it comes to homosexuality. "Attitudes and beliefs about same-sex sexual orientation vary substantially across cultures" (Parks, Hughes, & Matthews, 2004, p. 243). On the one hand, Ford and Beach (1951) found in their study of 76 societies (many of them small) that in 64% of them, homosexual behavior was considered either normal or socially acceptable for some or all of its members. However, homosexual behavior was never the predominant adult sexual activity, despite being found in nearly all the societies they studied. Heterosexual intercourse was always dominant. On the flip side, homosexual behavior remains illegal in 76 countries around the world. In five countries (i.e., Iran, Mauritania, Saudi Arabia, Sudan, and Yemen) and in some parts of Nigeria and Somalia, homosexual behavior is punishable by death (Bruce-Jones & Itaborahy, 2011).

Whitam (1991) reported that most countries were far more tolerant of homosexuality than the United States and other English-speaking countries. Southeast Asia and Polynesia were considered the most tolerant. For example, in Mangaia, which is one of the Cook Islands that is part of Polynesia, nudity among youth is common and boys and girls are expected to masturbate until about age 10 or 11 (Blumenfeld & Raymond, 1993).

Regarding most parts of Southeast Asia, having sex with a man or being penetrated by one doesn't compromise one's masculinity (Laurent, 2005). Coming out to oneself and disclosing one's gay identity to others is uncommon, however, as it is considered a "White" phenomenon that brings more problems than solutions (Laurent, 2005). Remember that in collectivist societies, identity is more a question of how one fits into the extended family, and engaging in same-sex behavior is usually accomplished through leading a double life, pretending not to know anything about it, and/or by remaining secretive.

Chow and Cheng (2010) compared mainland China and Hong Kong, and they stated that "there is still much prejudice against individuals with same-sex orientation, especially in mainland China" (p. 94). While Hong Kong is the only place in Asia that has legalized homosexual behavior (since 1991) between consenting adults (Laurent, 2005), homosexuality is decriminalized in mainland China (Chow & Cheng, 2010). Furthermore, a gay male social movement began in mainland China in the late 1970s (Kapac, 1998), and several gay Chinese groups and organizations exist.

Laurent (2005) reports that Japan is known as a gay-positive country. Japan had criminalized same-sex behavior in 1873 but then repealed the ban a decade later. Japan has a long history of male homosexuality—especially among the samurai and within some Buddhist sects (Wagstaff, Abramson, & Pinkerton, 2000). There is little overt homophobia in Japan, although homosexuality remains controversial (Herdt, 1997).

Furnham and Saito (2009) found that Japanese people living in Japan held more unfavorable attitudes toward gay individuals than British people do. Furthermore, the British supported the belief that homosexuality was caused by biological factors, while the Japanese supported social, biological, and cognitive explanations. Most same-sex couples keep hidden and silent. Nonetheless, you can easily (and silently perhaps) suck back a few beers in a Tokyo gay bar, because they have more of them there than in New York, San Francisco, and Amsterdam combined!

Homosexuality remains an unspeakable taboo in Vietnam (Dong, 1999), although it has never been illegal there (Laurent, 2005). In South Korea, you can hold hands or even brush a male friend's buttocks or genitals when saying goodbye without people assuming there is something sexual between you (Laurent, 2005).

In Thailand, attitudes toward homosexuality are complex, and it is hardly the vision of a "gay paradise" held by many North Americans (Cardoso, 2009). Although Thailand is considered gay positive, a report by Rattachumpoth (1999) suggests that it is different for outsiders compared to Thai citizens. Many gay citizens feel that their lives are miserable, facing job discrimination and biting gossip. Furthermore, turning a blind eye is often "considered to be a traditional method of 'solving' social issues in Thai society" (Rattachumpoth, 1999, p. xxii).

Homosexuality is considered neither illegal nor immoral in Thailand, and homophobic violence against masculine gay men is virtually nonexistent. Those who crossdress, however, are sexually harassed and sometimes targeted as victims of sexual violence. While feminine gay men are stigmatized, their behavior is tolerated. It is working-class gay men who are much less affected by homonegativity compared to the middle-class and upper-class gay men in Thailand. Essentially, Thais are more accepting of same-sex behavior when it occurs among the lower class. A lower-class man experiences fewer stigmas attached to himself, his family, and his friends. Tops are referred to as "gay kings" in Thailand, while bottoms are "gay queens" (Cardoso, 2009). Similar to traditional Latino sexual scripts, the gay queens are assumed to be feminine and to be the "true homosexuals." In contrast to Latino cultures, however, the gay kings are thought to be heterosexual men going through a phase of experimentation. They are viewed as 100% male. Bangkok, similar to New York and London, has a very active gay life, hosting approximately 12 gay dance clubs, 3 cabaret show houses, 14 gay pubs, 20 go-go boy cocktail lounges, and 11 gay bathhouses.

While Southeast Asia remains relatively tolerant of homosexuality, there are legal punishments in many other countries. In Algeria, for example, the penal code states that homosexual activity shall be punished with 2 months to 2 years of imprisonment and a fine of between 500 and 2,000 Algerian dinars. In Angola, those who "habitually practice" acts against nature will be sent to labor camps. In Singapore, while laws against same-sex behavior between males are rarely enforced, the law does allow for imprisonment for up to 2 years (Bruce-Jones & Itaborahy, 2011). Punishments can be for up to 10 years in jail in Sri Lanka, Brunei, Malaysia, and Bangladesh (Laurent, 2005). Not surprisingly, you won't find any gay clubs or bars in Sri Lanka.

A recent study of 70 secondary schools in Brussels revealed that "second-generation migrants had more prejudice toward homosexuals than pupils from the ethnic majority group" (Teney & Subramanian, 2010, p. 151). The degree of modern sexual prejudice (i.e., homonegativity) was fairly stable across the schools surveyed.

Although Russia has become a postcommunist society, a qualitative study found that old fears die hard for LGBTI individuals. Many continue to feel the repercussions of the "old days" when being perceived as different in any respect could lead to social ostracism or prison sentences. LGBTI people continue to feel uncertain about their future in Russia (Horne, Ovrebo, Levitt, & Franeta, 2009).

The situation in Poland has been tense for LGBTI individuals. In November 2005, the organizers for their pride demonstration (known as the Poznan March of Equality) complied with all requirements yet were denied a permit by the Poznan mayor. The "ban" was supported by local politicians. Well, the organizers did what most activists would under such circumstances: They went ahead with the demonstration. Police violently broke up the peaceful demonstration and arrested 68 people out of about 300 (Gruszczynska, 2009). The 2006 Poznan March of Equality occurred without major disturbances (Gruszczynska, 2009).

Prides have been banned in other central and Eastern Europe cities, including Budapest in 2007, Bucharest in 2005, Chisinau in 2005–2007, Moscow in 2006 and 2007, and Riga in 2005 and 2006. In each instance, the marchers have met with aggressive right-wing protesters. The most extreme case occurred at the Belgrade Pride in 2001, where marchers were met with approximately a thousand protesters (Gruszczynska, 2009).

A study out of Austria found that in a sample of 142 lesbian, gay, and bisexual (LGB) and 148 heterosexual adults, childhood gender role nonconformity (CGNC) and childhood harassment (CH) were the most probable factors that led to elevated levels of current suicidal ideation among the LGB participants (Ploderl & Fartacek, 2009). The researchers concluded that there are enduring effects from CGNC and the resulting CH that results from it.

From the Netherlands—the first country to legalize same-sex marriage (SSM) on April 1, 2001—interviews conducted 2 years later (N = 2,174, 52.6% response rate, age range 18–70) revealed that young people's attitudes toward SSM are strongly influenced by the attitudes of their parents toward homosexuality. A very potent determining factor was their religious socialization. Furthermore, men and women with lower educational levels and/or those from non-Western origins were especially likely to oppose SSM. Overall, 65% of the sample disagreed with the statement that "gay marriage should be abolished" (Lubbers, Jaspers, & Ultee, 2009, p. 1714).

An interesting social construction exists in most Latino countries. According to Jeffries (2009), there remains a traditional model alongside an emerging contemporary perspective. The contemporary perspective is similar to today's Western concept that defines a gay identity. Thing (2010) also views Mexican gay culture from the two perspectives of traditional and modern.

In the traditional model, the cultures' concept of machismo plays a significant role. *Machismo* is "a strong or exaggerated sense of masculinity stressing attributes such as physical courage, virility, domination of women, and aggressiveness" (Answers.com, 2010). Traditionally, men are not considered gay if they are the penetrators in anal and/or oral sex, maintaining both their perceived affectional orientation as heterosexual and their masculine gender role. Judgment and derision are only directed at those engaging in the passive role—the one who is penetrated (Herdt, 1997; Mendes-Leite, 1993; Taylor, 1985).

A consequence of machismo in the traditional model is that Latino men have generally remained anally insertive (tops) or anally receptive (bottoms) over their lifecourse (Jeffries, 2009)—well, at least in their public presentations of self. What actually happens in the bedroom, of course, can be another matter. Given the importance of machismo, many Latino men adhering to the traditional model would prefer to be known as tops. Within Latin societies, same-sex relationships are very common (Cardoso, 2009).

Most Latin countries never criminalized homosexual behavior, following the norm of the Napoleonic code (Whitam, 1980). Homosexuality is generally regarded as an ordinary aspect of human behavior and not something to be feared or condemned. Nonetheless, based on the 2002 National Survey of Family Growth composed of 4,928 men living in the United States, Latino men were more likely than non-Latino Blacks and Whites to refuse to answer questions about homosexual behavior (Jeffries, 2009).

In Brazil, it is reportedly common for boys to engage in same-sex games, like *troca-troca*. In this "innocent" game, the boys place their penis in the anus of another (Herdt, 1997). Today, Brazil also boasts a large and dynamic gay culture. Gay men who take on female mannerisms in Brazil enjoy greater notoriety and are tolerated better than masculine gay men. Interestingly, the feminine gay men experience a greater degree of discrimination, whereas the masculine gay men face more resistance regarding their social acceptability. Essentially, masculine gay men create some degree of social discomfort in Brazil (Cardoso, 2009). Feminine men who have sex with men, however, experience forms of symbolic violence, and when seeking help from health care services, they often try to depict masculine behavior in order to minimize the likelihood that they will be perceived as gay (Araujo, Montagner, da Silva, Lopes, & de Freitas, 2009).

Similar to the Latino cultures, men who have sex with men in the Middle East are admired for their virility and do not suffer harm to their reputations—only the effeminate men suffer ridicule. They face an interesting paradox, however: Although homosexual behavior is punishable and a gay identity is unacceptable, because of the seclusion of men from women, same-sex behavior is common. Such behavior occurs in Lebanon, for example, because men enjoy both anal and oral intercourse, but they are considered dishonorable if practiced with their wives (Halwani, 1998).

A double standard exists in Turkey regarding feminine gay men: While their behavior is generally despised, the population remains fascinated with popular transsexual singers. More than half of Turkey's population lives in towns. Cardoso (2009) described their culture as resembling early 19th century Europe . . . including a total lack of a gay rights movement. In traditional Turkish society, a feminine gay man did not marry because he was viewed as impotent. He was also "the worst thing a man [could] be in this culture" (Cardoso, 2009, p. 467) because he accepts passive intercourse similar to a woman and acts in a feminine manner. Nonetheless, especially in rural areas, sex play with other men is substantial in a young man's life, but following marriage, exclusive heterosexuality is normative. Although Istanbul is a large city, it has a very poor gay nightlife when compared to most European or American cities.

The last culture considered here is interesting because of its sexual rituals, which only stopped toward the end of the 20th century. In Papau New Guinea, a tribe exists known as the Sambia. Boys, usually about 7 years old, were taken from their mothers to become part of an all-male initiation group. The intent was to help them grow into puberty and adulthood; the practice was oral sex on older boys with ingestion of semen. By about age 15, they switched roles and became the inseminators for the younger ones. Herdt (1997) studied the Sambia tribe firsthand. He also reported that societies with boy-inseminating rituals implemented either oral sex or anal sex, but not both within the same society. Like other forms of sequential bisexuality, men were expected to eventually marry women and produce children; some, however, continued these insemination practices (Herdt, 1997).

Several studies of other cultures reverberate a current concern of pandemic proportions being realized throughout the United States and Canada: HIV/AIDS is increasing globally, and prevalence data suggest it is worst in low- and middle-income countries (Adam et al., 2009). A documented increase in HIV infection rates has been reported in China (Feng et al., 2010; Ruan et al., 2009; Xiao et al., 2010) and throughout Asia (Lwin, Stanaland, & Chan, 2010). High rates of HIV infection in men who have sex with men (MSM) have also been documented across Africa (Smith, Tapsoba, Peshu, Sanders, & Jaffe, 2009). Prevention is complicated because homosexuality is illegal in most sub-Saharan African countries, and political and social hostility is endemic as well (Smith et al., 2009). The United Nations has reported that only 33% of countries around the world have access to the antiretroviral therapies, the "drug cocktails" that are effective in increasing life expectancy for most people who are HIV+ (HIV positive; Carael, Marais, Polsky, & Mendoza, 2009).

SCORING FOR THE *ARE MY ATTITUDES HETEROSEXIST?* QUESTIONNAIRE

Designed by former editor of *The Heterosexism Inquirer*, Lori Yetman

Nonheterosexist (Your score was 0). If you score was 0, your attitudes show no evidence of heterosexism. You must be an individual who thrives on diversity, inclusiveness, and acceptance. You actively go out of your way to ensure that you respect and acknowledge everyone no matter what their sexual identity . . . and you may be a social activist.

Somewhat heterosexist (Your score was 10–75). You are somewhat heterosexist if you scored within the range of 10 to 75. If the majority of your answers were those scored as "3", then your heterosexism may simply stem from our society's assumption that everyone is straight—and now that you've given it some thought, then you can readily start acknowledging that this is not the case and begin to act accordingly. Some of those answers that scored as "3" could also indicate that you were not exposed to anyone who was outwardly lesbian, gay, bisexual or transgendered and that you are curious. The important thing to remember about some of the questions you may have always wanted to ask is that sexual orientation is just one component of anyone's identity—and it is such a core component, that some of the questions may be impossible to answer. "I am who I am, I don't know why." Other questions that you may have wanted to ask are deeply personal and/or could be potentially hurtful. For example, by asking someone "if their parents know" could trigger an emotional reaction—many LGBT have been ostracized by their families of origin and have formed families of choice. To avoid conversations that are too personal or potentially hurtful, just ask yourself what you would find intrusive or hurtful if the shoe was on the other foot . . . we are all just human—and really not that different. Overall, your level of heterosexism is not severe. It is not based on homophobia and can easily change through a conscious effort to acknowledge and learn.

Heterosexist, Homophobic (Your score was 80–372). Your attitudes reveal heterosexism and homophobia if you scored between 80 and 372. Generally, those answers that scored as "6" were very heterosexist, while those that scored as "9" were homophobic. The highest possible score is 372 . . . the higher the score, the more heterosexist and homophobic the attitudes. Homophobia, a form of heterosexism, refers to the overt expression of fear, hate, or dislike towards homosexuals. Scoring high in this category doesn't make you a "bad" person—the very fact that you were honest in your answers indicates that you are fine . . . it's the social values that have been taught to you by many of our major social institutions that are problematic. And they may be problematic but they're not irreversible! Many of our social institutions, including the family, school, church, and state have taught us to be heterosexist, and at times, homophobic. We've learned that only heterosexuality is natural and right, that other sexualities are unnatural and wrong. And, many times, our families, our teachers, our spiritual leaders, have looked the other way when, as children, we called someone a "fag" or, as teenagers, bullied someone who was "different." To unlearn heterosexist and homophobic social values is not a difficult process—in fact, you've already begun. Keep learning from this web site, http://www.mun.ca/the/sitemap.html. There are tips throughout our pages on how not to be heterosexist. Live them, practice them. Begin by acknowledging the possibility of diversity and acceptance.

Note: *Before* You Read Chapter 3

Before reading Chapter 3, it is suggested that you now complete the Sexual Orientation Counselor Competency Scale by Markus Bidell in Appendix D. This instrument, republished here with permission from the author, will give you a good idea of how competent you already are to work with members of the LGBTI community. You might also want to retest yourself when you have completed reading this text.

3

Gay Boys and Men

Challenging Your Attitudes and Beliefs About This Group

Reflection Questions

1. Have you ever talked about male homosexuality with family members? If so, was it discussed in a positive or negative light?
2. List as many synonyms as you can for *gay male.*
3. We know that some men define themselves as heterosexual, yet they engage in homosexual behavior while serving time in prison. We also know that the majority of gay men have engaged in heterosexual behavior. What explains this?
4. If you had or have a son and he turned out to identify as gay, how would you react? How would you feel?
5. Would it seem better or worse than if he identified as heterosexual? Why or why not?

Challenging Your Assumptions Questions

1. Were you ever teased as a child? On what basis? How do you wish others had treated you instead?
2. How do you currently view gay men? What is the basis for your views? To what extent do your views apply to *all* gay men? How would your views change regarding gay men when you meet one or more who are very masculine?
3. What is your attitude toward effeminate men, regardless of their affectional orientation? Given that gender expression is on a continuum, with some men being highly feminine and others highly masculine, what difference does it make where others fall on the continuum?
4. How would you react if your best male friend disclosed to you that he now identifies as gay?
5. Should male homosexuality be included as an integral part of sex education curricula? Why or why not?

Reflections

[*Note:* Imagine that *you* are the client in these reflections.]

"What words will I use to describe it?" you ask yourself as you think about your upcoming appointment with the school counselor. God knows it took you more than a year to book it, and you are determined to go through with it, despite the quiver in your hands and the sickening feeling in your gut. The apprehension escalates while sitting in the waiting room.

Mr. Locher is finally ready to see you. You discern that his welcoming smile will make it a lot easier to talk. He begins, "Hello, Nigel, thank you for coming in today. How might I help you?" Stammering, spitting, slobbering, you mutter: "I . . . only like guys—that means . . . I'm . . . gay."

"Nonsense, Nigel, that just means you are confused! It's a phase many teens experience. Raging hormones is all." The rest of the session is spent listening to the counselor try to reassure you. At the end you thank Mr. Locher, not sure if you feel any better at all. It is what you want to hear, mind you. You don't want to be different.

From a Client's Perspective

1. What do you think of Mr. Locher's advice? Why?
2. What else should a counselor find out from you before offering reassurance that you are just confused?
3. What difference, if any, would it make if Nigel was an African American, Asian, or Latino?

From a Counselor's Perspective

1. Is having homosexual attraction a phase for some adolescents? If so, how would you know if you need to take it seriously or not?
2. If Nigel later decides he will self-identify as gay, is Mr. Locher the right counselor for him to see? Why or why not? If not, what qualities should Nigel look for in an appropriate counselor?
3. If caught early enough, can homosexual desire and attraction be converted to heterosexual desire and attraction? If so, how would you accomplish it?

Background Information Regarding Gay Boys and Men

Background information regarding gay boys and men is included in this section. The headings here are common to Chapters 3 through 10 and include the following: development through the life span, race and ethnicity, relationships (family, friendships, intimate romantic/sexual), health (emotional and psychological, physical), career and work, spirituality and religion, and sociopolitical realities.

Development Through the Life Span

The most common developmental pathway for gay boys begins with them feeling different from other boys growing up (Savin-Williams, 2005).

This often occurs for two reasons: (a) they become aware of their sexual attraction toward other males and they know this is not normative, and/or (b) their interests and/or behaviors are more cross-gender typed. It is important to understand that many things can make a boy feel different, and it does not mean he will turn out gay. Savin-Williams (2005) suggested that "childhood feelings of differentness have proven to be at best a poor predictor of future sexual status. Too many homoerotic children did not feel different and too many heteroerotic ones did" (p. 111). A better indicator of eventual homosexual orientation is having same-sex attractions (Savin-Williams, 2005).

The accepted gender role for boys is much more stringent than it is for girls, so any boy who displays a "feminine" characteristic is probably going to be called a "fag" or "faggot" (Brown & Alderson, 2010). Furthermore, some boys do outgrow their attractions to other boys, so although being told "it's just a phase" was a typical answer to boys and men only a few decades ago, it is true for some boys. Lastly, not all gay boys experience cross-gender-typed interests or behavior (Chen-Hayes, 2001).

Studies done to date, however, suggest there is a higher percentage of feminine gay men compared to feminine heterosexual men (Barber & Mobley, 1999; Chung & Harmon, 1994; Rieger, Linsenmeier, Gygax, & Bailey, 2008; Savin-Williams, 2005). Not conforming to gender stereotypes brings consequences. First, the more men value the traditional masculine gender role and worry about not violating it, the more likely they will develop negative feelings about their homosexual orientation (Sanchez, Westefeld, Liu, & Vilain, 2010). Second, Cabaj (1998) wrote that "profound deficits in self-esteem are likely to result from being shunned, humiliated, and derided by their peers" (p. 18). Either consequence is not difficult to understand.

Stability versus fluidity of our sexuality. As Kinsey, Pomeroy, and Martin (1948) noted many years ago, the world is not divided into sheep and goats. Although most of us compartmentalize many qualities that we and others have, affectional orientation is more than just the binary of heterosexual or homosexual: There are many gradients in between. One might be a little more attracted to males at one point and later a little more attracted to females, then vice versa again. Some people do seem to be strongly anchored in one direction or the other and remain that way, but they may be more the exception than the rule.

Some theorists argue that our sexuality is fluid and ever changing (Kimmel, 2007). As mentioned in the introduction, these queer theorists believe that as a result, it is a mistake to give ourselves labels for our sexuality, as it puts us into a box that we may find difficult to get out of later. Their arguments are interesting, despite the fact that their research is primarily based on women who define as already having a sexual minority identity (Diamond, 2007, 2008).

Despite the limited amount of research regarding heterosexual men, we do know that the majority of them do not report some change in affectional orientation over time (Savin-Williams & Ream, 2007), while most gay men report feeling that they were always gay (Garnets & Kimmel, 2003). Adolescents and young adults experience a notable degree of change in their sexual identity and sexual behavior (Savin-Williams & Ream, 2007), but this is more common for nonheterosexual individuals (Kinnish, Strassberg, & Turner, 2005). This instability with nonheterosexual youth was found in a convenience sample of 156 gay, lesbian, and bisexual youth (ages 14 to 21). Of this sample, 67 (43%) changed their identity label over the course of a year (Rosario, Schrimshaw, Hunter, & Braun, 2006).

Does this mean an actual change has occurred, or simply that they have become more aware of their sexual identity over time? Adolescents and young adults are in the process of developing a stable identity (Erikson, 1966, 1968). Consequently, we expect them to experience a period of questioning and instability—sometimes extended—in defining themselves (Marcia, 1966).

James Marcia (1966) theorized that there are four possible intimacy statuses resulting from an intersection of commitment level and exploration level. The four statuses have received empirical support (Marcia, 1994). There are as follows:

1. Identity achievement—You have become committed to an identity after experiencing a sufficient level of personal exploration.
2. Identity moratorium—You are still going through the period of personal exploration and cannot yet commit to an identity.
3. Identity foreclosure—You have committed to an identity without going through the period of personal exploration (this happens when children accept their parents' view of the world without critically examining it).
4. Identity diffusion—You have not gone through a sufficient level of personal exploration and you have not committed to an identity, either.

Given that Western society has become far more complex than it once was, and many more choices are available—including sexual choices—it seems likely that it now takes young people longer to decide on their sexual identity, just as it does to sort out one's career path. Consequently, we should expect young people to feel more diffused on a number of levels for a longer period of time than generations before them.

Research informs us that most people know their sexual attractions from age 10 (Floyd & Stein, 2002; Maguen, Floyd, Bakeman, & Armistead, 2002; Smith, Dermer, & Astramovich, 2005). Obviously, there is a great deal of variation on when this occurs for any individual. Some gay men are unaware of their affectional orientation until into their 30s, while others claim they knew by age 5 or 6 (Alderson, 2000).

The above discussion highlights the continuing schism between psychological paradigms. Is our affectional orientation continually in a dynamic state of flux, or are we in search of finding our *true* identity? The schism exemplifies the social constructionist versus essentialist debate (nurture versus nature). Regardless of which paradigm holds greater truth value, we know that growing up gay is not easy for most youth. Although gay youth have often been emotionally abused by well-meaning societies and spiritually rejected by well-meaning religious belief systems (Alderson, 2002), Savin-Williams (2005) has pointed out that many gay and lesbian youth are resilient. Furthermore, he believes that the regional differences (between the Midwest, the South, and the west and east coasts) that used to exist are shrinking due to mass media (R. C. Savin-Williams, personal communication, November 13, 2009). D'Augelli (2006) reviewed representative American studies that have shown that lesbian, gay, and bisexual (LGB) youths continue to experience adjustment problems, however.

A recent study published in the journal *Pediatrics* (Pathela & Schillinger, 2010) used data from the 2005 to 2007 New York City Youth Risk Behavior Surveys. Of 17,200 high school students who completed the survey, 7,261 ($n = 3,805$ male, 3,456 female) reported that they had had sexual intercourse. Within this sample, 9.3% stated that they had a same-sex partner, a statistic higher than that reported in earlier studies. "Many adolescents with only same- or both-sex partners (38.9%) self-identified as straight" (Pathela & Schillinger, 2010, p. 879). In other words, a sizeable number of youth in this sample continued to define as heterosexual despite their report of having a same-sex partner, regardless of whether they had an opposite-sex partner as well. Self-definitions (e.g., heterosexual) are not always indicative of a person's actual sexual behavior (e.g., same-sex behavior).

Coming out. Without question, the greater acceptance of gay individuals is leading people to come out to themselves at increasingly younger ages than ever before and to disclose their identity to others as well at younger ages (D'Augelli, 2006; Savin-Williams, 2005). But obviously not in all families.

Why not? Because there are many influences that determine when a person can *safely* come out, if ever. *Coming out* can mean one of two things, and usually the context provides the appropriate connotation. First, *coming out* can be used to refer to the process of self-identifying as gay. Second, *coming out* can refer to disclosing one's gay identity to others. For clarity, these will be described as the two processes of *self-identifying* and of *disclosing* when it is important to distinguish them.

The most popular and frequent model of gay *and* lesbian identity acquisition in the literature was developed by Cass (1979, 1996). This model will be described below, followed by the ecological theory of LGBTI identity development (Alderson, 2003). Both models have strengths and weaknesses, but together they offer differing perspectives of the coming-out process. Readers should note that several coming-out models have been published that will not be covered here (e.g., Coleman, 1981–1982; Cooper, 2008; Cox & Gallois, 1996; Dank, 1971; Hencken & O'Dowd, 1977; Lee, 1977; McCarn & Fassinger, 1996; Minton & McDonald, 1983–1984; Plummer, 1975; Troiden, 1979).

Cass's (1979, 1996) model was meant to apply to both gay men and lesbian women. It includes the following six stages:

1. Identity Confusion—Increased awareness of same-sex or bisexual thoughts, feelings, or behaviors. This creates confusion because these thoughts, feelings, or behaviors do not fit into a heterosexual mold.
2. Identity Comparison—Begin exploring the gay world, seeking out further information and contact with gay and lesbian people.
3. Identity Tolerance—Increased contact with gay and lesbian individuals, but still mostly identifying as heterosexual.
4. Identity Acceptance—Conflict begins to surface with heterosexual individuals while simultaneously developing increased comfort with the idea of having a gay or lesbian identity. Most people at this stage continue to use passing as a management strategy. *Passing* includes all attempts made by LGBTI individuals to *not* let others know about their LGBTI identity.
5. Identity Pride—Strong pride in the gay/lesbian community. Possible immersion within the gay/lesbian culture with concomitant anger and isolation from heterosexual individuals.
6. Identity Synthesis—Acceptance of gay/lesbian culture and the heterosexual community. Growing appreciation that sexual identity is only part of one's total identity.

Cass's (1979, 1996) is a stage theory, and a criticism of most stage theories is that not everyone goes through the stages in a linear fashion. Furthermore, Sophie (1985–1986) suggested that the role of anger and pride within Stage 5 of her theory has likely diminished a great deal given the historical changes that have occurred in the gay and lesbian liberation movement.

The ecological theory of LGBTI development (Alderson, 2003) includes three phases: before coming out, during coming out, and beyond coming out. The ecological aspect of the model stresses the influences of the environment both in affecting whether one can come out and in the expression or form that a LGBTI identity takes. Before coming out is greatly affected by *catalysts* juxtaposed with *hindrances*. Catalysts are all of the influences that indicate a person has LGBTI leanings, while hindrances include factors that get in the way of coming out. For gay men, examples of catalysts include having homosexual dreams or falling in love romantically with another male. Examples of hindrances include the influences of their families, their culture and church, their peers, and their society. In Iran, one would find few examples of men overtly defining as gay, as homosexual behavior is a criminal offense punishable by death, while in the United States and Canada, the consequences are not as extreme. Nonetheless, there are consequences just the same, and one's environment is predictive of what disclosing a gay identity will bring. A full description of the catalysts and hindrances is contained in both *Beyond Coming Out* (Alderson, 2000) and in a published article (Alderson & Jevne, 2003).

If one is able to self-identity as gay, the next phase occurs, called *during coming out*. This self-identification is usually based on a gay male's self-assessment regarding the extent of his homosexual cognition (e.g., thoughts, images, fantasies), homosexual behavior, and/or homoaffiliative affect (e.g., erotic and passionate feelings for other males—see the largest triangle in Figure 3.1). Most males who self-identity as gay do so because they believe their homosexual orientation is stronger than their heterosexual orientation. This is not always the case, however (Ellis & Mitchell, 2000; Rosario et al., 1996), as some individuals have not gone through sufficient exploration to make this commitment stick.

The newly self-defined gay person struggles with reducing his internalized homophobia and learning what it means to be gay. *Internalized homophobia* refers to gay and lesbian individuals fearing, disliking, and/or hating themselves. The term also applies to gay and lesbian individuals fearing, disliking, and/or hating other gay/lesbian people or those who they perceive as gay/lesbian. Learning what it means to self-define as gay is about learning the psychosocial roles and cultural norms associated with gay culture. Learning about *camp*, a form of gay humor, and about how to date gay men are examples.

Most people progress to the next phase—*beyond coming out*—and develop a positive gay identity to varying degrees. While this process used to take 16 years on average (Obear &

Figure 3.1 Ecological Model of LGBTI Identity

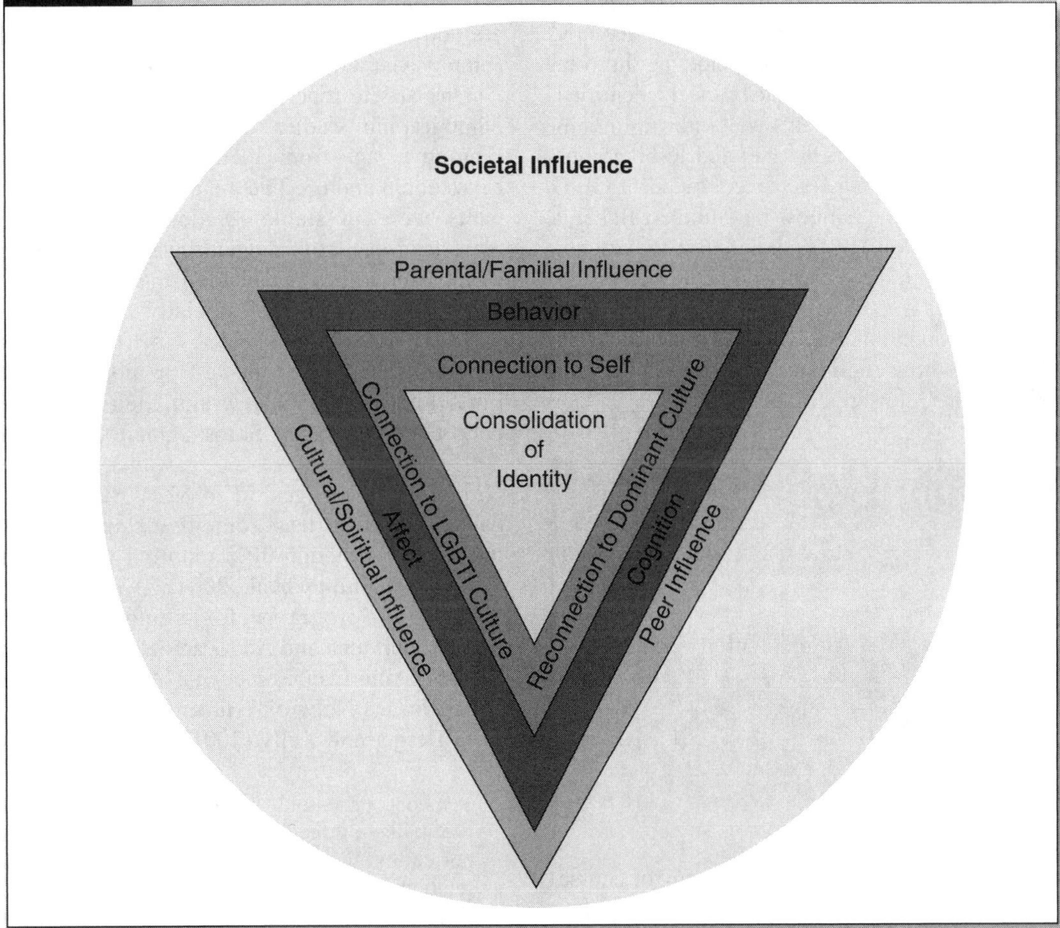

Reynolds, as cited in Pope, Prince, & Mitchell, 2000), Savin-Williams (2005) stated that it only takes most young people a few years now. In the ecological model, a positive LGBTI identity results when individuals begin to feel good about themselves after making connections with self (e.g., becoming self-accepting), after making connections with the LGBTI culture (e.g., developing relationships), and after they find ways to reconnect with the dominant culture (see second smallest triangle in Figure 3.1). A person's unique integration of these three components is then theorized to constitute a positive gay identity (Alderson, 2003).

The smallest triangle in the ecological model is colored pink to represent one of the symbols of gay pride: the inverted pink triangle. The origin of this symbol is that known gay men were required to sew this triangle on their clothing in Nazi Germany as a way for them to be easily identified.

The other symbol that is well known, initially designed to represent the gay and lesbian community but generally accepted by all LGBTI individuals, is the rainbow flag. Gilbert Baker, a friend of Harvey Milk's, designed it for use in a parade in San Francisco about 30 years ago. From there, it caught on and is used in many places throughout the world (Johnson, 2011). The flag is now considered to be within the public domain (Johnson, 2011).

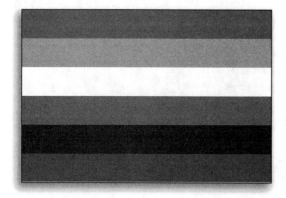

Aging. The other side of development, of course, is aging. Schope (2005) surmised that gay men are perceived as old when they turn 30. While this is highly debatable, it does speak to a North American emphasis on valuing youth disproportionately to the value placed on the aging population. Gay men, compared to lesbian women, are generally more concerned with how gay society will view them as they get older, and they are more concerned about their physical appearance (Schope, 2005).

In actuality, however, research suggests that most aging gay men live successful, satisfying lives. They are socially and psychologically well adjusted and they have good self-esteem (Anetzberger, Ishler, Mostade, & Blair, 2004). However, 27% in another sample said they lacked companionship and 13% reported feeling isolated (Grossman, D'Augelli, & O'Connell, 2001). Other research has shown that gay men are not more isolated than older men in general (Shippy, Cantor, & Brennan, 2004).

One article reported the findings from four ethnographic studies of 69 older gay men, ranging in age from 36 to 79, but with most between 50 and 65. The majority of the participants were in stable relationships, and the majority felt that monogamy was important to them. The authors concluded that the participants had adapted well socially and psychologically to growing older. The participants reported that they spent half or more of their time with gay friends within their own age cohort (Brown, Alley, Sarosy, Quarto, & Cook, 2001). In a sample of 233 gay men living in New York City, ages 50 to 82, 90% reported that they were at least somewhat satisfied with their lives, although 30% reported feelings of depression (Shippy et al., 2004). Two American community programs for aging gay men include Services and Advocacy for Gay Elders and the American Society on Aging's LGBT Aging Issues Network (Haber, 2009). Quoting from Berger and Kelly (2001):

> Someone once told me that every individual's life is like a three-legged stool. Each life is supported by three pillars—health, finances, and relationships. If the individual can keep these three supports firm as he ages, he will grow old successfully. (p. 58)

Race and Ethnicity

Despite their representation in the LGBTI community, gay people of color remain mostly invisible in the psychological literature (Moradi, DeBlaere, & Huang, 2010). Consequently, in this section, the attempt is to provide a *glimpse* of what we know from available research.

A recent study found that gay people of color did not experience significantly greater stress in consequence of their race/ethnicity over that experienced because of their affectional orientation (Kertzner, Meyer, Frost, & Stirratt, 2009). Most studies, however, suggest that ethnically diverse gay individuals struggle with integrating two minority identities.

One recent study of 483 men who have sex with men found that the African and Latino Americans in their sample "were less likely to identify as gay, and to attend gay bars/clubs, and more likely to report self-homophobia" (Flores, Mansergh, Marks, Guzman, & Colfax, 2009, p. 91). Operario, Han, and Choi (2008) interviewed 25 gay Asian Pacific Islander men and found that the way they integrated these two identities was diverse. As postulated by the ecological model (Alderson, 2003), the salience and relevance of identities was situational. Operario and colleagues also state that sexuality is a taboo subject for many Asian Pacific Islanders. Furthermore, stereotypical gay behaviors and gay identities are not typically acceptable, either. Another finding was that they often felt discriminated against and stigmatized by the larger gay community, perpetuated by a common stereotype that gay Asian Pacific Islanders are passive, feminine, and "bottoms" (meaning they prefer to be penetrated: in contrast to "tops").

African American gay men suffer from the opposite stereotype: active, masculine, and tops (Han, 2007). Other Black stereotypes are perpetuated as well (e.g., they are well endowed). Unfortunately, they are also marginalized within the broader gay community and they face multilayered levels of discrimination (Savage & Harley, 2005).

Latino men are treated in two ways: (a) either they are ignored, or (b) they are treated as sex objects and objectified (Han, 2007). They also tend to be oppressed by poverty (Iwasaki & Ristock, 2007). Furthermore, Ramirez-Valles (2007) stated that "Latinos tend to be less supportive of civil liberties for homosexuals than Whites and African-Americans" (p. 303). They are also marginalized from the mainstream gay community (Ibanez, Van Oss Marin, Flores, Millett, & Diaz, 2009).

Han (2007) adds that people of color in the United States are often excluded from leadership positions within gay establishments, and this contributes to a notion that "gay equals white" (p. 51). Han also suggests that people of color experience a unique type of racism and homophobia. The result of this is that they are viewed as belonging to the bottom of the status hierarchy in both the gay and their ethnic communities. Compared to Whites, people of color are also less likely to be out to their parents (Grov, Bimbi, Nanin, & Parsons, 2006).

In more than 100 precolonial American Indian tribes, men who were effeminate and attracted to men enjoyed a special status: They were often revered as religious or spiritual leaders (Herdt, 1997). They were called *berdache* by the French, but a more accurate and respected term is *two-spirited*. They wore women's clothing and lived their lives in feminine roles. They also could take male or female lovers (Ross, Paulsen, & Stalstrom, 1988) without it lowering their status. As these tribes were dominated by Whites with Christian values, the two-spirited became a disenfranchised group and eventually became disrespected by their own people as well. Similar to other people of color, they too are stigmatized by the larger White gay community.

Relationships (Family, Friendships, Intimate Romantic/Sexual)

Developing satisfying relationships is an important aspect of our happiness. Many people view their family and friends as a vital aspect of leading satisfying lives (Prochaska, Norcross, & Diclemente, 1994), not to mention the quest to find a life partner. Unlike heterosexual individuals, gay people have an important question to ask themselves: Whom to tell and whom not to?

In the past, very few students disclosed in high school (Harris & Bliss, 1997). This, however, is changing (Savin-Williams, 2005), but it is difficult to make generalizations, as school environments differ locally and regionally. Not surprisingly, their reluctance is based on good reason: fear of the consequences. Those who do disclose, however, often receive positive feedback from others (Harris & Bliss, 1997). However, those who disclose to their families during adolescence face variable reactions. Savin-Williams (2005) found that with the youth he interviewed, parental reactions to disclosure were far less negative than what the literature suggests. Nonetheless, gay youth who have disclosed to their family compared to those who haven't comparatively experience poorer parental relationships and fear parental harassment and rejection (D'Augelli, Grossman, Starks, & Sinclair, 2010). A moderating factor appears to be the extent to which a family is measurably cohesive and/or adaptable, with those strongest on both measures having the best postdisclosure outcomes (Reeves et al., 2010).

Ryan, Huebner, Diaz, and Sanches (2009) surveyed 224 White and Latino self-identified lesbian, gay, and bisexual young adults (aged 21–25). Those individuals who experienced family rejection had poorer health outcomes compared to families who offered acceptance (e.g., more suicide attempts, depression, drug use, and unprotected intercourse). Many parents are aware at some level that their son is gay, often long before he discloses this to them. This occurs more often when the son is gender atypical in his interests and behaviors (D'Augelli, Grossman, & Starks, 2005). Although a friend is often disclosed to before a parent, it is clear that youths are disclosing to parents more than in the past (Savin-Williams, 2005).

A study by Ann Muller (1987) found that 48% of parents ($n = 111$) reacted with what she called *Loving Denial* (48%), which meant the parents maintained a positive relationship with their gay son or daughter, but they kept the disclosure to themselves. The next most frequent reaction was *Resentful Denial* (36%), whereby the parents did not acknowledge their children's same-sex orientation, but if and when they did so, it was done in a negative manner. *Loving Open* (11%) was the most positive parental reaction. These parents exhibited little denial and they were positive with others about their son's or daughter's sexuality. *Hostile Recognition* (5%) comprised the smallest group, which represented parents who were extremely hostile toward their son's or daughter's homosexuality and consequently estranged them.

Rates of disclosure also vary. D'Augelli and Hershberger (1993) found in their national sample of 15- to 21-year-olds that 81% had disclosed to at least one family member, 66% had disclosed to their mothers, and 44% had disclosed to their fathers. The average age of disclosure to others occurs just after high school (Savin-Williams, 2001).

Nonetheless, disclosure can be a double-edged sword. While nondisclosure can result in several negative consequences, such as feelings of dishonesty, shame, alienation, ulcers, and hypertension, disclosure can also result in various forms of victimization, including physical assault (Carragher & Rivers, 2002). For all of the reasons stated above, some gay individuals find it necessary to postpone romantic relationships until beyond high school or even much later—sometimes never. Not everyone with a strong homosexual orientation can deal with the environment in which he finds himself and/or with his own feelings toward this aspect of self.

Marinoble (1998) wrote that often, gay youth have trouble forming close friendships for fear of being discovered or because they don't relate to typical heterosexual interests. Alternatively, they may feel that they will develop sexual feelings toward heterosexual guys or have to pose as heterosexual when being with the opposite sex (Vare & Norton, 1998). Some friends do not want to be associated with others who define as gay (Flowers & Buston, 2001; Poteat, Espelage, & Koenig, 2009).

Like their heterosexual counterparts, gay men (ages 18 to 79) form close friendships with others who are similar to themselves in gender and race (Galupo, 2007). They also form the majority of their friendships from the LGBTI community. Gay men, whatever their age, rely on friendships more than on family for social support, while the converse is true for heterosexual men (Nardi, 1999; Shippy et al., 2004).

Contrary to popular heterosexual stereotypes, contemporary gay men do establish enduring intimate relationships (Peplau & Fingerhut, 2007). It is also the case that the more committed one is in a relationship, the better one's sense of well-being (Kamp Dush & Amato, 2005). Studies of heterosexuals have shown that the married are the happiest group (obviously not including the 50% who have divorced), followed by cohabiting heterosexual couples, followed next by those who are dating, finally leaving singles as the least happy group (Kamp Dush & Amato, 2005). Is it any different for gay individuals who are in relationships?

No, their story is pretty much the same. A recent study compared a large sample of heterosexual individuals with gay and lesbian ones. The happiest group was the married opposite-sex couples (there were no married gay/lesbian couples in this sample). Cohabiting (although not married) gay and lesbian couples were as happy as cohabiting opposite-sex couples, but not as happy as the married opposite-sex couples. The least happy were the single people, regardless of their affectional orientation (Wienke & Hill, 2009). Marriage seems to offer people psychological insulation from daily stresses.

According to one American survey, the majority of gay and lesbian individuals (74%) would like to get married at some point (Kaiser Family Foundation, 2001). A recent survey reveals that having legalized same-sex marriage helps gay and lesbian individuals see their relationships as more real and that it enhances their search for finding an ideal partner (Lannutti, 2007). Essentially, there is no difference between the relationship quality of same- and opposite-sex relationships at comparable levels of commitment (Kurdek, 2005, 2006; Roisman, Clausell, Holland, Fortuna, & Elieff, 2008).

One American estimate suggests that approximately 28% of gay men are living with a same-sex partner (Black, Gates, Sanders, & Taylor, 2000). Regardless of affectional orientation, men are more likely to look for an attractive partner, whereas women place greater emphasis on their partner's personality (Peplau & Fingerhut, 2007; Townsend, 1998).

Same-sex partners are more likely than opposite-sex partners to remain friends after relationship dissolution (Peplau & Fingerhut, 2007; Rothblum, 2009). Another interesting finding is that lesbian, gay, and bisexual individuals are not as likely as opposite-sex couples to find same-sex partners who are demographically similar to themselves, meaning they are less likely to seek partners of similar age, race, or socioeconomic status (Rothblum, 2009). Furthermore, same-sex relationships do not have a long history of legitimization, and consequently, there are not clear traditions or guidelines associated with what they should look like. This means same-sex couples have greater freedom to construct their relationships in a way that is mutually satisfying (Wienke & Hill, 2009).

Gay men in relationships have the most sex, lesbian couples the least, and heterosexual couples are somewhere in between (Rothblum, 2009). The amount of sex diminishes over time for all of the relationship types, but in contrast to lesbian and heterosexual couples, gay couples become less monogamous over time (Adam, 2006; Rothblum, 2009).

Research has also shown that same-sex relationships have a higher likelihood of ending compared to opposite-sex relationships (Kurdek, 2004). This finding is based on research comparing cohabiting gay and lesbian couples with cohabiting opposite-sex couples (Rothblum, 2009). It also occurs in countries (Norway and Sweden) that have had registered domestic partnerships (not marriages) since the 1990s (Andersson, Noack, Seierstad, & Weedon-Fekjaer, 2006).

One likely explanation is that most gay and lesbian couples are not raising children, and this remains a major reason why unhappy heterosexual couples stay together. Also, registered domestic partnerships and civil unions are not the same as marriage, particularly in regard to their status within society. Researchers do not currently know the longevity of same-sex marriages compared to opposite-sex marriages.

A familiar nemesis raises its ugly head when we look at one of the major obstacles to having a good same-sex relationship: internalized homophobia. Recent studies have implicated it in affecting relationship quality (Frost & Meyer, 2009; Otis, Rostosky, Riggle, & Hamrin, 2006). Furthermore, some research finds that gay men are especially sensitive to interpersonal rejection (Pachankis, Goldfried, & Ramrattan, 2008), and this is a hindrance when building a solid relationship.

By studying 216 partners of 108 same-sex couples that had been together an average of 30 years, Mackey, Diemer, and O'Brien (2004) found that two factors were particularly important that predicted relationship satisfaction: keeping conflicts contained (keeping them minimal) and having psychologically intimate communication. Other studies have shown that gay individuals are most satisfied in their relationships when partners believe they have fairly equal power and decision-making ability (Peplau & Spalding, 2000).

Health (Emotional and Psychological, Physical)

Although most gay youth are resilient and they come through their adolescence unscathed (Savin-Williams, 2005), they are nevertheless affected by many of the same problems that affect marginalized groups, such as American Indians. It is estimated that gay adolescents are at least three times more likely to attempt suicide than heterosexual youth (Cooley, 1998; Morrison & L'Heureux, 2001; Radkowsky & Siegel, 1997). Through several decades of research, gay individuals have been shown to be at high risk for substance use and substance use disorders, and a recent meta-analysis found that this usage pattern often begins in adolescence (Marshal, Friedman, Stall, & Thompson, 2009). Furthermore, when LGBTI individuals seek treatment for addictions, their problems are usually worse than those of heterosexual clients, and they are more likely to have comorbid psychological disorders, too (Cochran & Cauce, 2006). Between 40 and 60% of street youth are estimated to have homosexual orientations (Kunreuther, 1991).

Riggle, Whitman, Olson, Rostosky, and Strong's (2008) research focused on the positive aspects of being a gay or lesbian individual. From their online survey of 203 men and 350 women, they found themes of (a) having greater empathy and compassion for others who are oppressed (most common theme mentioned by gay men), (b) sense of belonging to a community, (c) forming strong relationships with people other than immediate family, (d) feeling more connected to their true selves, (e) freedom from societal norms regarding relationships and gender-typical roles, and (f) having the ability to role model to others and be involved in social justice issues.

Self-identifying as gay and disclosing this identity to others is very much associated with having better physical health and mental health. Cole, Kemeny, Taylor, and Visscher (1996) tracked the incidence of cancer, pneumonia, bronchitis, sinusitis, and tuberculosis in a sample of 222 gay and bisexual men over a period of 5 years. Overall, the incidence of these diseases was higher among the men who hid their gay identity from others.

Gay men also smoke at a higher prevalence compared to the general population (Pachankis, Westmaas, & Dougherty, 2011). A recent study found that those who were more gender nonconforming in boyhood were more likely to smoke, and those who concealed their sexual identity were more likely to smoke on a given day compared to those who disclosed (Pachankis et al., 2011). This study adds further to our understanding that *minority stress* (i.e., the emotional stress experienced by being a member of a disenfranchised minority group) is positively correlated with indulgence in unhealthy habits.

HIV/AIDS and other sexually transmitted infections remain a sizeable risk for men who have sex with men. As this may be a presenting issue for gay men, its discussion is presented later in this chapter.

Regarding mental health, several studies have found that gay men and lesbian women who disclose to others about their identity are healthier (see Garnets & Kimmel, 2003). Again, however, disclosing is not an option for everyone, and some will face dire consequences if they do so.

The evidence supporting the mental health of gay individuals is voluminous (e.g., Brady & Busse, 1994; Chang & Block, 1960; Garnets, Herek, & Levy, 1990; Gonsiorek, 1982a, 1982b; Haldeman, 1994; Hammersmith & Weinberg, 1973; Hooker, 1957; Leserman, DiSantostefano, Perkins, & Evans, 1994; Miranda & Storms, 1989; Morin & Rothblum, 1991; Ross, Paulsen, & Stalstrom, 1988; Rothblum, 1994; Schmitt & Kurdek, 1987; Watters, 1986; Weinberg, 1970). Nonetheless, it has also been shown that gay men are more prone to depression, anxiety, and substance abuse disorders (Cochran, 2001; Mays & Cochran, 2001). In turn, this increased prevalence is based on the antihomosexual bias that remains in society and the resulting prejudicial attitudes and treatment that members of the LGBTI community experience from nonaccepting others (Cochran, 2001). A powerful insulator from the effects of homophobia and heterosexism is being in a committed or legal same-sex relationship (Riggle, Rostosky, & Horne, 2010).

Generally speaking, a psychologically healthy gay individual has achieved a positive gay identity (Alderson, 2002). What does a *positive gay identity* look like?

> Individuals who have attained a positive gay identity have developed a high self-regard for themselves as gay persons. They view their gay status as equal to heterosexual status. If given a choice, they would not prefer to be heterosexual over gay, for they have come to value their uniqueness, and the richness of life that comes from being themselves. They have integrated their gay identity with their other identities, and having accomplished this, they are "out" in most areas of their lives, wherever and whenever it is not highly disadvantageous to do so. They have largely overcome their own internalized homophobia, which frees them to fully love others of the same gender. (Alderson, 2000, p. 189)

Getting to that place is not easy, however, although it is becoming easier for younger people as society becomes increasingly supportive of diversity. A lot will likely change over the next 10 years.

Career and Work

> The issue here is not that I need to come out and expect everyone to love the idea—after all, most heterosexuals don't feel the need to declare their sexuality in the workplace. However, in a sense most heterosexuals do come out by talking about their families and significant others in their lives at the workplace. I cannot comfortably talk about my significant other without some people getting uncomfortable. I love this person in an infinite sense, and each time I hide the fact that I am gay, I feel like I am further perpetuating the myth that this is shameful. (33-year-old male, quoted from Sailer, Korschgen, & Lokken, 1994, p. 40)

While many gay individuals would choose careers in which they can be honest, others would want jobs where most would not suspect they are gay. It becomes a form of "passing," which allows LGBTI individuals to remain highly closeted (Croteau, Anderson, Distefano, & Kampa-Kokesch, 2000). Those who pass deceive others into believing they are heterosexual. The other possible strategies include "covering," which involves attempting to be seen as heterosexual, but not trying to fake heterosexuality. Being "implicitly out" involves being honest about one's life, but not using the label of LGBTI. The final strategy is being "explicitly out," which involves directly telling other people one's sexual identity.

The degree to which LGBTI individuals disclose their sexual identities at work depends upon two factors: their developmental stage regarding identity formation and the perceived level of heterosexism in their work environment.

These two factors play a significant role in the career development of LGBTI individuals (Chojnacki & Gelberg, 1994).

Individuals who are aware of their gay or lesbian identity but not accepting of it (e.g., stage 3, Identity Tolerance, in Cass, 1979, model) would more likely pick a career that is less represented by gay individuals, such as so-called traditional "masculine" and "feminine" jobs, thus allowing them greater ability to remain closeted. Those in the identity pride stage (i.e., stage 5) desire significant contact with the LGBTI community, and they are more likely to pick a career that allows them to self-disclose their sexual identity to others and perhaps one that is often chosen by others who define as gay or lesbian. A career choice made by those in the identity synthesis stage (i.e., stage 6) might also look different because they have integrated their gay identity as only one part of their self-definition. The integrated individual in stage 6 in Cass's model may be in the best place to pick a career on the basis of genuine career interest.

The other factor affecting the career decisions of gay and lesbian individuals is the perceived and actual work environment. Chojnacki and Gelberg (1994) suggested the following four levels of work environment heterosexism as applied to LGB individuals:

1. Overt Discrimination—Work environment has both formal and informal policies that discriminate against LGB individuals (e.g., the American armed forces before "don't ask, don't tell").
2. Covert Discrimination—These work environments do not have a formal policy against hiring or firing LGB individuals, but there remains informal discrimination at the work setting. An open LGB person would not be hired or promoted by the employer or manager. This was the "don't ask, don't tell" policy in the United States military.
3. Tolerance—These employers have formal antidiscrimination policies protecting those with different affectional orientations. They do not provide any additional support for LGB persons, such as insurance coverage for same-sex partners.
4. Affirmation—Work environment has formal antidiscrimination policy and other forms of support for LGB employees. LGB employees are valued for their diversity. Some examples include having same-sex partner benefits, offering a LGB support group or club, and providing training for employees about sexual diversity.

In some companies, it may appear *safe* to disclose a LGBTI identity, but by doing so, the individual is overlooked for further career advancement. This is referred to as the "lavender ceiling" (Conklin, 2000), meaning the same thing the "glass ceiling" means for women who are overlooked for promotion. Will a gay man ever become President of the United States? Not surprising that most LGB individuals do not disclose their sexual identities at work (Nauta, Saucier, & Woodard, 2001). Another finding is that gay men either feel that they should downplay their homosexuality in their jobs or else they end up feeling that they need to conform to stereotypes of how they are to look, act, and work (Williams, Giuffre, & Dellinger, 2009). The Human Rights Campaign publishes many resources that will be helpful to LGBTI individuals in assessing their work environments, such as the annual Corporate Equality Index (the latest version of the Index can be found through a link at www.hrc.org/resources/ for a list of workplace resources).

Spirituality and Religion

There's a T-shirt that I love that says, *I am what I am*. If only gay people could truly believe it—if they could only believe that God truly loves them as they are. There's a song that I sing off and on called, "Since God Is For Us, Who Can Be Against Us?" You know, if you're a spiritual person, just believe God is for you, because if God is for you, who can be against you? (quote from participant Bob Peacock, Lahey & Alderson, 2004, p. 179).

Most major religions prohibit homosexuality (Grant & Epp, 1998). One study reported that 72% of the churches and organizations surveyed condemned both gay people and homosexuality in general (Rodriguez & Ouellette, 2000). Consequently, gay individuals and the Church are often at loggerheads. This can produce deep feelings of shame, depression, and suicidal thoughts within the religious nonheterosexual person (Schuck & Liddle, 2001). A study by Rowen and Malcolm (2003) found a correlation between those men who have sex with men at a lower stage of homosexual identity formation (i.e., as measured by a test based on Cass's [1979] six-stage theory) and higher levels of internalized homophobia. Rowen and Malcolm also found that those with a religious affiliation were more likely to experience internalized homophobia compared to those who identified as nonreligious.

Faith in God is of great importance in many people's lives, and gay individuals are no exception. In fact, history has indicated that many gay and transsexual men have occupied roles as spiritual leaders, such as priests, ministers, faith healers, shamans, and witch doctors. One report issued in 1983 estimated that 30% of Roman Catholic priests, nuns, and brothers have homosexual orientations (Blumenfeld & Raymond, 1993). One of the main theses of Clark's (1997) book, *Loving Someone Gay*, is that what defines gay people is their loving spirits. This is, of course, itself a positive stereotype—LGBTI individuals are raised in families of every known faith (Schuck & Liddle, 2001), and many are also atheists.

One study published in 2002 revealed that in a sample of 565 nonheterosexual Christians living in the United Kingdom, 464 (82.1%) of them believed that "all sexualities are created by God and [are] to be fully accepted" (Yip, 2002, p. 203). Furthermore, most of these individuals (454, or 80.3%) attended local churches at least once per week. In this sample, 389 were gay men, 131 were lesbian women, 24 were bisexual women, and 21 were bisexual men with an age range of 18 to 76. The author concluded that the "vast majority of respondents held progressive views on human sexualities and relationships" (Yip, 2002, p. 202), which stood in contrast to the traditional views espoused by their religious leaders. One approach, then, to dealing with spiritual conflict is to believe that at least in this area concerning loving same-sex relationships, the church is wrong. A recent study of six gay Muslims found similar results (Minwalla, Rosser, Feldman, & Varga, 2005).

In a survey of 43 lesbian, gay, and bisexual individuals who experienced religious conflicts, the following results were found [note: percentages don't equal 100 because respondents were asked to check all that apply]: (a) 53% considered themselves spiritual rather than religious; (b) 40% reinterpreted previous religious teachings; (c) 33% changed religious affiliations; (d) 33% left their previous religion and currently did not identify with any religion; (e) 23% kept their religious beliefs intact but stopped attending a religious institution; and (f) 16% remained in their religion and attempted to change existing attitudes of their religion (Schuck & Liddle, 2001).

Sociopolitical Realities

One inflation of statistics with a speculated political motive was the often-cited statistic in the past that 10% of men were gay. Although this figure is usually credited to Alfred Kinsey and colleagues (1948), neither he nor his colleagues suggested it. It is possible that some activists within the gay and lesbian community overinflated the numbers to further their cause of gaining recognition, credibility, and equality (Herdt, 1997).

A major sociopolitical reality that still exists is homophobia and heterosexism. The Southeastern and Mid-south states have been known as the least tolerant regions in the United States toward gay and lesbian individuals (Sullivan, 2003). In Arkansas, for example, the 2005 poll included several questions aimed at assessing citizens' reactions to gay and lesbian individuals, including topics like morality of same-sex relations, same-sex partner legal recognition, gay and lesbian adoption, foster parenting, serving in the U.S. military, and expansion of civil rights for them. A regression logistic analysis based on these poll results revealed that Arkansans remain uncomfortable with homosexuality, but they are "hesitant to prescribe state-sanctioned discrimination" (Barth & Parry, 2009, p. 309). Perhaps it is the case that most Americans are experiencing a form of future shock, not surprising given that much has changed in the LGBTI landscape over just 40 years.

In September and October 2010, a rash of five suicides by gay teenagers occurred across the United States. These suicides were highly publicized and a common thread was that these youth were teased, taunted, and/or had revealing videos of them posted on the Internet because of their affectional orientations (Hubbard, 2010). Research of 28 random school shootings that occurred in the United States between 1982 and 2001 revealed that all of the assailants had been repeatedly teased and bullied with homophobic epithets, and in most cases, these teens did not define as gay (Kimmel & Mahler, 2003).

Sullivan (2003) remarked that homophobia is harmful to both gay and heterosexual men. One study focused on heterosexual men and found a direct relationship between homophobia and difficulties in creating close friendships with other men (Devlin & Cowan, 1985).

Positive changes in the sociopolitical landscape are also occurring. Governor Jerry Brown recently signed a landmark bill requiring California public schools to include the historical contributions of LGBTI people in their social studies curriculum (Lin, 2011), the first legislation of its kind in the United States. While homophobia is still very prevalent, tolerance and support for LGBTI individuals is slowly increasing (Sullivan, 2003). Even Archie comics launched its first gay character, Kevin Keller, in fall 2010 (Goellner, 2010).

Today, the gay and lesbian communities have become increasingly embracing of other sexual and gender diversities. Along with the growing popularity of postmodernism and queer theory that evolved from it, a contemporary struggle focuses on the notion that all sexualities should be respected and that the actual number of those who define as LGBTI is irrelevant and sidetracks us from what is really important: that LGBTI individuals are worthy of being accepted and respected, and equality should be for all and not just for those enacting the dominant discourse (i.e., heterosexuality). According to a postmodern perspective, the LGBTI discourse is subjugated. Instead, queer theory suggests that all discourses should be affirmed.

The most publicized struggle of the 21st century to date has been the issue of same-sex marriage. Due to space limitations here, same-sex marriage will be discussed in the Sociopolitical Realities section of Chapter 4.

Recent Research Focused on Canada

Aside from the different economies and political ideologies between the United States and Canada, the published literature does not reveal differences between the development and presentation of gay identities in these two countries. Instead of attempting to focus on unobserved differences, this section will focus on some of the recent contributions researchers in Canada have made to our understanding of gay men.

A substantial amount of research has focused on gay men living with HIV/AIDS. Recent research has reported increases in HIV infections among men who have sex with men (MSM) in both Canada (Gastaldo, Holmes, Lombardo, & O'Byrne, 2009) and the United States (Halkitis, 2010). Shuper and Fisher (2008) found in their computer-based experiment that sexually aroused HIV+ MSM are more likely to engage in unprotected sex compared with HIV− MSM. Furthermore, they are more likely to engage in unprotected sex when the partner (a) is attractive, (b) is HIV+ himself, (c) is a long-term lover, or (d) prefers not to use condoms.

In a study of 123 HIV+ gay and bisexual men in Ontario, participants were recently asked about stressful life events during the time they were mostly likely infected (Burchell et al., 2010). The researchers concluded that gay and bisexual men are more likely to become infected during stressful periods.

Research has shown that the percentage of Asian men in Toronto who use gay Internet chat rooms is increasing (Poon, Ho, Wong, Wong, & Lee, 2005), a finding that is likely representative of changes occurring elsewhere. These Asian men were often socially isolated and highly marginalized with intense needs for social connection, thus leaving them potentially open to sexual exploitation. They rarely used condoms in oral sex, and they had a number of misconceptions about HIV and AIDS.

HIV– MSM in a Montreal study coped with the HIV/AIDS epidemic most often using escape/avoidance coping strategies and least often through more constructive confrontive coping methods (Watson, 2003). Another study found that with young MSM, social anxiety is associated with unprotected insertive anal sex, depression, smoking, alcohol use, and drug use (Hart, James, Purcell, & Farber, 2008). These are important findings given that, as noted earlier, the rates of HIV infection are on the increase in both the United States and Canada (Dowsett, 2009; Natale, 2009; Public Health Agency of Canada, 2006).

The motivations for why some MSM consume drugs during sex has been studied. Their reasons include (a) wanting to enhance the sexual experience, (b) enhancing sexual arousal, (c) facilitating a sexual encounter, (d) improving their capacity for sexual behavior, (e) prolonging their sexual experience, and (f) a combination of the above five reasons if involved in sex trade (Myers et al., 2004). Gay-identified escorts use a number of strategies to reduce the stigma associated with their work, including believing that (a) escorting is volitional, (b) escorting is a profession, (c) the escort controls the exchange, and (d) escorting is better than street prostitution (Morrison & Whitehead, 2005).

Circuit parties, which are large raves frequented mostly by gay men, are known for their drug use and sometimes unprotected sex that occurs when minds have been altered and numbed (Adam, Husbands, Murray, & Maxwell, 2008; Westhaver, 2005). Gay bathhouses have also contributed to the spread of the HIV virus (Godin et al., 2008). Relevant counseling considerations for gay men living with HIV/AIDS have also been published (Harris & Alderson, 2006, 2007).

A study done in Toronto found that in their sample of gay men (N = 70), there was a noted hierarchy regarding their search for sexual partners. The highest-status (i.e., most-often-sought) sex partners were those who were Caucasian, middle class, and/or in their 20s up to their early 30s. The lowest-status sex partners were Black, Asian, poor, and/or over 40 years of age (Green, 2008).

Walton (2006) looked at how his gay and lesbian participants integrated their affectional orientation with their Christian ideologies, while Schnoor (2009) looked at the difficulties that Jewish gay men face. Schnoor noted several barriers that arise because of the emphasis on traditional gender roles, the importance of the nuclear family, the ideal of procreation, and conservative religious values within the Jewish faith and culture, rendering their experience similar to that of gay men who are Black, Latino, Asian, Greek, and Italian. Where the experience of Jewish gay men differs, however, is that the Jewish community generally has a particular dislike of same-gender relations due to a preoccupation with ethnic survival and continuity, an engrossment that became amplified after the Holocaust. Also, Jewish gay men have a harder time keeping their sexual orientation private because Jewish communities are commonly intertwined and enmeshed (e.g., friendships, social networks).

Barry Adam (2006) has looked at how men in Toronto have constructed relationships that include nonmonogamy, while Bartholomew, Regan, Oram, and White (2008) have studied partner abuse in gay male relationships. Bartholomew and colleagues found that the reasons partner abuse occurs in some gay male relationships are the same when compared to opposite-sex relationships. However, some additional factors unique to same-sex partner abuse included HIV status, degree of public outness, and internalized homophobia. Chan and Cavacuiti (2008) developed an eight-question scale that family physicians can use to assess for abuse in gay male relationships.

An interesting line of research conducted in Canada concerns the question as to what extent a homosexual orientation is biologically determined. Along this line are the studies conducted by

Simon LeVay (1991, 1993) that focused on the smaller size of the hypothalamus found in a few gay men who had died from HIV/AIDS. The findings from this research have been rebuked (Byne, 1997). Nonetheless, researchers in Canada have continued their search in other biological areas. Witelson and colleagues (2008) have focused on the corpus callosum anatomy of gay men compared to heterosexual men, while Blanchard and colleagues have studied the influence of birth order and left and right handedness in gay men compared to heterosexual men (Blanchard, 2008a, 2008b; Blanchard & Lippa, 2008).

Two other studies include one by Aveline (2006), who interviewed 80 parents. Aveline found that parents retrospectively made sense of their sons' gay identification by recalling many atypical gender behaviors in childhood and their low interest in sports. He saw their constructive process as one that included revelations, confirmations, and/or justifications. Lastly, an interesting study revealed that women who befriend gay men experience more positive body esteem and feelings of sexual attractiveness when compared to what they derive from their friendships with heterosexual men and women (Bartlett, Patterson, VanderLaan, & Vasey, 2009).

Recent Research Focused on Other Societies

As an exemplar, this research was already included in Chapter 2. Please read the section called Other Societies for research looking at how gay identity looks different in selected other cultures and how gay people are treated.

Common Concerns Facing This Group and Counseling Considerations

Roleplay Scenarios

[*Note:* Suggested assessment and intervention strategies for the four roleplays below can be found in Appendix B. Before going there, roleplay in dyads with one of you acting as the counselor and the other as the counselee. If a roleplay is not possible, work individually in writing out a list of your suggestions.]

Roleplay #1, Chapter 3. Counseling Gay Men

John, age 36, has come to see you for help. John has been out for 12 years and everyone knows he is gay. He has become entirely comfortable with himself and who he is. He has been dating Marco, age 32 from Mexico, for the past 2 years, and they have lived together for a year. Marco has only been out to himself for 3 years. Marco has not disclosed his identity to anyone, including his family. Now his mother and father have decided to visit for 6 weeks, and they will be staying with John and Marco. John is beside himself not knowing what to do. He respects Marco but does not respect his dishonesty in not disclosing his identity to others. John will need to hide a lot of things at their home, especially his feelings and attachment to Marco.

Roleplay #2, Chapter 3. Counseling Gay Men

Roger, age 45, has come to see you for help. He has been married to Jane for 20 years and they have two children, ages 15 and 13. Jane recently found him in their garage trying to asphyxiate himself by keeping the car running. After spending several weeks in a psychiatric ward, Roger has since been released. He hates himself because he has always had very strong attraction to men, and now he is aware these feelings are getting stronger. He has already decided to leave Jane and the kids but wants to feel better about himself.

Roleplay #3, Chapter 3. Counseling Gay Male Youth

Peter, age 14, has come to see you for help. Peter has been sexually active with other boys for the past year. Although he has had a great time sexually, he wonders if he is prematurely settling down sexually with guys and wonders if he might also have interest in girls. Peter tells you that he had tried to ask girls for sex last year, but none of them felt either ready for it or they wanted something more than casual sex. Peter is only interested in casual sex right now.

Roleplay #4, Chapter 3. Counseling Gay Male Youth

Donald, age 18, has come to see you for help. Although Donald is aware that his interest is almost exclusively in men, he finds that whenever he gets together with men for sex, he has trouble maintaining an erection during anal sex and never seems able to cum. Donald doesn't want to assume the passive role in anal intercourse but wonders if he will need to if this problem is not soon resolved. There is nothing wrong with Donald physiologically.

How Would *You* Help This Person?

Mark came out at age 35 and soon started spending many nights at the local gay bar. He felt most attracted to the 18- to-20-year-olds, cool kids with slender bodies. They became his role models, and before long, Mark shaved off most of his body hair and bleached what remained. Next came the body piercings, first both ears and later a nipple ring. Then the clothes changed. From a distance, Mark now looked like he was 19, and inside, he felt even younger. Before long, the young gay bar patrons were smitten with Mark's demeanor—he oozed raw sexuality. Mark was like the new kid in town, having as much sex and enjoying as much dating as he wanted. It seemed he had found exactly what he was looking for, yet deep down, he knew something was missing.

Mark felt like an imposter: Whatever he said or did seemed fake to him. This wasn't anything new, though, for he had felt that way long before coming out. The disappointment was in realizing that it had only diminished and not ended completely since coming out. Sometimes others would say to him, "Mark, just be yourself." That seemed so easy for others, but for Mark, it always sounded like an empty cliché.

Mark's life seemed like an endless web, but one with strands that didn't connect. With one friend, he might come across as prudish, yet with another, he would accompany him to the bathhouse and enjoy the very activities he told his other friend that he despised. Similarly, Mark would tell his friends exactly what they each wanted to hear. Behind their backs, however, Mark would occasionally say what he really thought or felt to a different friend. He didn't worry about the contradictions because to his knowledge, each friend didn't know the others. Mark wanted to keep it that way, partly because

(Continued)

(Continued)

they were so different. Each friend brought out a different aspect of his personality, which to Mark seemed like very different parts.

Eventually he told his best friends that he was gay, which was uneventful. Some said they had already suspected, especially since he had adopted this new boyish appearance. Coming out to family then was not the right time, however. This meant that he had to repeatedly lie to them about why he had changed his appearance, why he never told them about his dates, why this, and why that. A year later, Mark finally told them, but by then they had already pieced it together for themselves.

The lying, however, continued, and not just with family, either. Mark had lied so convincingly for so long that it was an ingrained habit. Whenever an untruth would suffice, or whenever it would lead to a more appealing consequence, Mark lied and rarely questioned his reason for doing so. The trouble was, he couldn't always remember what he had said to whom. While his best friends began pulling away, new friends took their place, each sharing some of the same dishonest qualities that Mark had perfected.

Now at age 39, Mark remains primarily attracted to younger guys. He is beginning to feel some attraction to men closer to his own age, but having a relationship with anyone remains elusive. He still can't answer the question, "Who am I?" and therefore doesn't know what kind of person he would want in his life. Perhaps he hasn't just lied to others all these years—perhaps it's deeper than that. Although he came out 4 years ago, he still feels like an incomplete person, and he doesn't understand why.

Note—Remember to view clients within their environmental contexts, keeping in mind societal, parental/familial, cultural/spiritual, and peer influences. Specifically, become aware of the impact that the following influences had? and continue to have in your clients' lives: race, language, religion and spirituality, gender, familial migration history, affectional orientation, age and cohort, physical and mental capacities, socioeconomic situation and history, education, and history of traumatic experience.

1. What defines this person's environment, past and present?
2. Who is this person sitting in front of me, taking into account environmental and personal characteristics?
3. What defines the problem that he or she is presenting within his or her multicultural milieu?

Before working with gay men, therapists need to ensure that they can provide competent care. Most psychologists received little to no training or exposure to gay and lesbian issues while they were graduate students (Alderson, 2004; Buhrke, Ben-Ezra, Hurley, & Ruprecht, 1992; Dillon et al., 2004; Eubanks-Carter, Burckell, & Goldfried, 2005; Pearson, 2003).

The model of multicultural competence presented in this text (see Chapter 1) emphasizes the importance of self-awareness as a foundation for competent practice (Arredondo et al., 1996; Pedersen, Crethar, & Carlson, 2008; Sue, Arredondo, & McDavis, 1992; Sue et al., 1982; Sue et al., 1998). By virtue of living in a society that is strongly heterosexual, even gay-positive therapists must carefully examine their beliefs, values, and assumptions for the ways in which they have internalized these heteronormative biases. Therapists need assistance in overcoming their own homophobia and heterosexism if they are to work effectively with gay persons (Dworkin & Gutierrez, 1989; Malyon, 1982b; Richardson, 1993; Russell, 1989).

A second competency area includes understanding the client's worldview. To work with LGBTI individuals successfully, you need to become a LGBTI-affirmative therapist. LGBTI-affirmative therapists *view LGBTI status as equal to heterosexual status* and they emphasize a nonpathological view in their work with these clients (Pixton, 2003). The gay-affirmative therapist needs to be familiar with the oppression that gay males have experienced and how this invisible minority has suffered psychologically and spiritually, first from learning to hide their feelings from themselves and then how most continue to hide their identities from many who know them. The same is true if you are planning to work with LGBTI clients of all varieties—if you do not feel they are equal to others, do them and yourself a favor and refer them to someone else who *is* affirming.

LGBTI clients have learned to become highly sensitive of any sign that they are being judged. At times this is transference, but other times it is because they are picking up what the counselor is feeling or believing inside through subtle nuances of speech or behavior.

Why would LGBTI clients become so sensitive? Again, many if not most fear negative consequences if they reveal themselves to nonaccepting others. No one likes to be the recipient of prejudice or discrimination—it hurts to know someone wants to dispense with you before they know anything about you. Every person from a minority group has experienced it before.

Let LGBTI clients know you are accepting of them, that you are affirmative in your beliefs and in your actions. First of all, be sure to use verbal and written language that is inclusive and nonheterosexist. Ask the question, "How would I talk about this differently if I knew this client was lesbian or gay?" (Morrow, 1997, p. 10).

Ensure that you have visible signs of your acceptance in your office as well. Remember that the best symbol of LGBTI inclusivity is the rainbow flag, so consider having a small one in your office. The inverted pink triangle is good, too, but it only represents acceptance of gay men (and possibly lesbian women, although they have a separate identity from gay men and would respond better to an inverted black triangle). Another way to do this is to have books or posters from local or national gay organizations visible in your office (Croteau & Thiel, 1993).

As several references already cited have revealed, times are changing for LGBTI individuals, particularly in the Western world. Effective counseling is most likely to occur when you understand that various age cohorts have experienced their LGBTI identities quite differently. For example, many young gay men in Canada are out to everyone or almost everyone, and they talk about someday getting married to another man, a discussion that would have never occurred a few years ago. They have experienced an entirely different social landscape than what older men in Canada and the United States endured.

Remember that homosexuality was considered a mental disorder in the United States until 1973, and homosexual behavior was illegal in some states until only a few years ago. Hillary and Julie Goodridge experienced a lot of prejudice and discrimination before they won the right to marry in Boston, consequently leading the way for Massachusetts to become the first U.S. state to legalize same-sex marriage (Lahey & Alderson, 2004).

Cook-Daniels (2008) prepared a wonderful resource for understanding LGBTI people in the United States who are 50 years of age and older. Cook-Daniels provides a history timeline to show what our elders experienced at various points through recent American LGBTI history. In working with LGBTI clients, keep the individual's age cohort in mind, as this will also reveal some of the struggles they have needed to contend with in self-identifying.

This section now moves into looking at eight common concerns that bring gay men into counseling. These include (a) internalized homophobia,

(b) affectional orientation confusion and self-identifying as gay, (c) disclosing to others, (d) identity fragmentation, (e) relationship problems, (f) religious conflicts, (g) HIV and AIDS, and (h) managing the consequences of external homophobia (including gay bashing).

Internalized Homophobia

As everyone gets exposed to the cultural mores of a society growing up, internalized homophobia results for most gay and heterosexual youth. No one is immune. *Internalized homophobia* refers to gay and lesbian individuals fearing, disliking, and/or hating themselves. The term also applies to gay and lesbian individuals fearing, disliking, and/or hating other gay/lesbian people or those who they perceive as gay/lesbian. More typical problems of gay youth and men will be reviewed in the section looking at Common Concerns Facing This Group and Counseling Considerations in this chapter.

Gay boys grow up learning the same social and sexual scripts as the dominant culture, and they internalize these beliefs like their heterosexual counterparts. Internalized homophobia results to varying degrees (Allen & Oleson, 1999; Fassinger, 1991), and it is strongly associated with psychological distress, especially depression and anxiety (Igartua, Gill, & Montoro, 2003). Recent research has also shown that internalized homophobia is associated with greater relationship problems in lesbian, gay, and bisexual individuals (Frost & Meyer, 2009).

Those who deviate from the heterosexual script spend their lives attempting to overcome the psychological damage created by varying degrees of intolerance. It was for this very reason that the American Psychiatric Association eventually deleted ego-dystonic homosexuality from *DSM:* decades of research had shown that it was society that needed to become more tolerant, not gay-unhappy men who needed to change. School-age children levy antigay slurs at one another (Russell, Seif, & Truong, 2001; Sapp, 2001), and everyone who hears them knows that these words do not describe a sought-after and respected affectional orientation. Working through internalized homophobia is a lifelong process for many gay people (Malyon, 1982b).

How do you help gay men overcome internalized homophobia? Whatever your approach, the central dynamic is that the gay person must come to believe that gay is equal to heterosexual: no better, no worse. For gay people, obviously it is better that they identify as gay and seek out a same-sex lover and perhaps life partner. Most research has shown that affectional orientation is something men cannot change—you are who you are (Drescher, 1998; Gonsiorek, 2004; Haldeman, 1994, Murphy, 1992).

Interventions focused on helping the individual develop self-love and a respect for others who define as gay (which is essentially about learning to appreciate and value the various aspects of one's own gay self) will likely prove most fruitful. If you want to follow a cognitive behavioral approach, ask your client questions like, "What proof do you have that you are less than heterosexual people because you define as gay?" (Answer: Just because some other people believe this doesn't make it true).

In *Breaking Out*, Alderson (2002, p. 16) suggested that gay men and lesbian women challenge their beliefs with the following 12 questions (these can easily be incorporated into one's work with all LGBTI clients):

1. What proof do I have that this is true?
2. Do I have any evidence that indicates it is not true?
3. Are there any competing "truths"? Is another belief just as valid?
4. Does everyone think this way? Why not?
5. Does agreeing with the majority on this make it necessarily correct?
6. Where did I learn this message? Is it possible that the messenger was wrong?
7. What purpose is served in continuing to believe this?
8. What price do I pay for continuing to believe this?

9. What will be the advantages of believing something different?
10. Are my feelings about this providing an accurate gauge of what I should believe?
11. If I were helping someone else deal with this, what would I want him to believe?
12. If I knew I would be dead tomorrow, would I be happy believing this?

Affectional Orientation Confusion and Self-Identifying as Gay (i.e., Coming Out to Self)

Am I *really* gay? This is a common question during the early stages of self-identifying as gay (Jones & Gabriel, 1999). Although more youth are self-identifying as gay than ever before (Savin-Williams, 1998, 2005), the process can create great turmoil for some individuals (McFarland, 1993), particularly for those who are older (Alderson, 2000). Isay (1996), for example, expressed concern that middle-aged married men who begin to self-identify may pose a seriously suicide risk.

Self-identifying is painful for many people, and the decision is generally not taken lightly. Sexuality is complex, and as discussed under the ecological model, an individual needs to consider his cognitions, affect, and behavior in making this assessment. Sexual behavior itself is a relatively poor predictor of one's eventual sexual identity (Hewitt, 1995; Richardson, 1993; Vare & Norton, 1998).

Most gay men and lesbian women have experienced sexual intercourse with the opposite gender (Betz & Fitzgerald, 1993), and many male adolescents and prisoners have had same-gender sexual relations without identifying as gay (Blumstein & Schwartz, 1993; Green, 1998; Vare & Norton, 1998). Sex is just sex, particularly for men (Townsend, 1998), and by itself says very little about one's identity.

Research has shown that particularly for young people, identity labels can change. Most gay people define themselves as heterosexual before they self-identify as gay. Some may first consider themselves to be bisexual and later identify as gay (Rosario et al., 2006), or they may think they are gay and later identify as heterosexual.

Most people with a strong heterosexual orientation never questioned their sexuality much. Not surprisingly, the more one is somewhere in the middle (the majority of people), the more one is likely to question. Young people who choose not to define themselves may simply be in the exploration phase during which they are enjoying sexual activities with both males and females. So what? Well, it just means it may take a little longer to sort things out.

In working with individuals who are confused and/or are having trouble self-identifying as gay, one should focus on assessment before looking at an appropriate intervention. A few ideas follow.

Assessment. Some clients are not certain that a gay identity is appropriate for them (Dworkin, 2000). Affectional orientation confusion occurs when there is perceived disparity and felt conflict (cognitive dissonance and/or outside influences) among sexual affect, cognition, and behavior. The ecological model of LGBTI identity development will prove helpful in assisting both you and the client in making this assessment (refer to Figure 3.1).

Taking a complete history. A complete appraisal of affectional orientation will include taking a history of the following, including information from both the past and the present: (a) relevant *cognitions*, including sexual fantasies (both those that are conscious and those that occur during sleep) and erotic or sexual attraction; (b) relevant *affects*, including crushes or infatuations and the propensity to fall in love romantically or the actual experience of falling in love with males, females, or both; (c) relevant *behaviors*, including whether the preference is for male or female sexual partners and male or female emotional partners.

If you are male and sexually fantasize about both men and women (a cognitive component), you only fall in love with women (an affective component), and you enjoy sex only with other men, you are likely going to feel some internal conflict (Alderson, 2003). Such a lack of consistency between cognitions, affects, and behaviors is not uncommon in the sexual arena (Laumann, Gagnon, Michael, & Michaels, 1994).

Measuring affectional orientation. Some counselors may find it helpful to use an established scale measuring affectional orientation in their assessment. According to Sell (2007), the main scales used to measure affectional orientation are the Kinsey Scale (Kinsey et al., 1948), dichotomous measures (which simply ask the person to identify himself as gay or heterosexual), the Klein Sexual Orientation Grid (Klein, Sepekoff, & Wolf, 1985), and the Shively and De Cecco (1977) Scale. Sell concluded that each measure is unsophisticated and inadequate. He created his own measure of affectional orientation (Sell, 2007), which also has limitations due to its focus on only three factors and its limited time frame in asking respondents only about the past year.

A new measure is the Sexuality Questionnaire (Alderson, Orzeck, Davis, & Boyes, 2011). This measure has excellent reliability (internal consistency and test-retest), and indications are that it also has excellent validity (construct, face, and content). A copy of this questionnaire is found in Appendix C.

Cautions in using other psychological measures. Counselors trained in the use of psychometrics must be cautious when using some of the available measures with gay clients. The Edwards Personal Preference Schedule, which is still widely used in career assessment (Prince, 1997), contains examples of heterosexism. Two of the items on the test are "I like to kiss attractive members of the opposite sex" and "I like to be in love with members of the opposite sex." Other tests that have been found to contain some form of heterosexist bias include the Social Readjustment Rating Scale, the Minnesota Multiphasic Personality Inventory-2, the Sexual Addiction Screening Inventory, the Symptom Checklist Revised, and the Multimodal Life History Inventory (Prince, 1997). Although the Strong Interest Inventory is exemplary in not containing heterosexist bias, the test relies on Holland's theory of occupational choice, a theory based on the concept of congruence between self and environment (Prince, 1995). Because it takes many gay men years to achieve an integrated identity, and some never achieve one, Holland's theory may not apply to all gay men (Prince, 1995).

Clinicians should also remain skeptical of the Myers-Briggs Type Indicator (MBTI). Many individuals respond to the questions with how they wish to be seen by themselves or others (their *ideal* self) rather than with traits that actually define them (their *real* self). Before gay men develop a positive gay identity, many wish they were or could have been heterosexual (Alderson, 2000). Consequently, there may be even less congruence between the real self and the ideal self of gay men as compared to heterosexual men, thus calling into question the validity of using the MBTI with gay men.

Intervention. Remember that *gay* and *lesbian* are identity labels (i.e., sexual identity), while *bisexual* might refer to identity, behavior, or affectional orientation. Most clients who are unsure about their sexual identity are really asking whether their affectional orientation is consistent with their chosen label. The ecological model (Alderson, 2003) predicts that self-identifying as gay will occur when the individual perceives that the catalysts outweigh the hindrances. Once this occurs, either through the client coming to terms with this himself or through counseling interventions focused on increasing self-awareness, counseling focused on helping him affirm his feelings and working through cognitive dissonance will prove helpful.

Fragmentation of Identity

The primary issue for gay men is arguably the need to achieve an integrated identity (Cornett, 1995; Hanley-Hackenbruck, 1988; Malyon, 1982a). Especially in the past, gay individuals relied on defense mechanisms to avoid facing unwanted thoughts and feelings, such as homoerotic attraction. Denial was common (Beane, 1981; de Monteflores & Schultz, 1978; Malyon, 1982a) and so were other defenses, including compartmentalization, overcompensation, repression, reaction formation, and rationalization (Coleman, 1981–1982; Gonsiorek, 1993; Malyon, 1982a). The defense mechanisms serve to shut off or fragment the parts of identity that are considered unacceptable, which is the very essence that defines a homosexual orientation.

A substantial proportion of men who have sex with men define as heterosexual. Some ways they maintain their heterosexual identity are to consider their same-sex activities as recreational, accidental, infrequent, or due to financial need (Reback & Larkins, 2010). Behavioral ways of keeping this separation include depersonalizing the sexual encounter by limiting gestures (e.g., no hugging, no eye contact) and by keeping their distance from gay venues (Reback & Larkins, 2010). For those men who have a strong homosexual orientation, this fragmentation will be difficult to maintain indefinitely.

Splitting off libido—or sexual drive—reduces energy, enthusiasm for life, and passion, not to mention it leaves the conflicted gay person especially vulnerable to depression (Helminiak, 1994; Isay, 1996; Napier, 1990; Vargo, 1998). Becoming whole is an important aspect of developing a positive gay identity (Alderson, 2000, 2002).

It is important to help gay men reconnect the fragments of their identity that became repressed or denied due to guilt and shame (Cornett, 1995). As in creating all therapeutic alliances, it is essential that you practice the three core conditions as advanced by Carl Rogers (Corey, 2009): unconditional positive regard, empathy, and congruence. Beyond that, it is up to you which therapeutic approach to use, depending on your preference and your training. The important thing is that you practice as a gay-affirmative therapist, regardless of your theoretical orientation and your actual practice. I favor the cognitive-behavioral and existential approaches, but that is merely my anchor.

Underlying much of the fragmentation is internalized homophobia. Helping gay men accept their fragmented parts, which have been ego dystonic to this point, will significantly reduce internalized homophobia. Helping them to love themselves fully as gay persons will reduce it still further.

Religious Conflicts

Religion is central in many people's lives (Lease, Horne, & Noffsinger-Frazier, 2005), and having answers to existential questions is strongly related to healthy adjustment (Tan, 2005). Religious conflicts are common for gay individuals (Dworkin, 2000), despite the finding that a substantial number of gay men remain committed to religious and spiritual life (Halkitis et al., 2009). It doesn't help that most world religions are disapproving of homosexual behavior (Birken, 1997; Dobinson, 2004). Consequently, gay individuals need to find ways to successfully deal with religious conflicts, derivatives of the belief that they are sinful if they experience homosexual attraction, fantasies, or behavior.

The Qur'an does not condemn homosexuality per se and does not recommend specific punishments (Blumenfeld & Raymond, 1993). Jesus of Nazareth did not reportedly say anything about homosexuality that would affect his followers, either (Helminiak, 1994). Nonetheless, there are some letters published in the New Testament and some references in the Old Testament that speak against homosexual acts between two heterosexual individuals, particularly when sex occurs out of lust or as an act of domination and power (Helminiak, 1994).

Referring gay men to gay-affirmative clergy or books on this topic can be helpful. Dworkin (2000, p. 172) recommended the following books: "*Twice Blessed: On Being Lesbian, Gay, and Jewish*, *Coming Out Within: Stages of Spiritual Awakening for Lesbians and Gay Men*, and *Just as I Am: A Practical Guide to Being Out, Proud, and Christian*." Another suggested reading is *What the Bible Really Says About Homosexuality* (Helminiak, 1994).

Spiritual conflicts are often particularly disturbing to gay clients who are religious. Often, individuals feel that they need to reject their religion in its entirety. This is certainly an option, but not necessarily the best one. Other options include helping them:

1. Focus more on spirituality than religion (Shannon & Woods, 1991).
2. Accept that some parts of their faith will remain in conflict with others within their religious community.
3. Understand that the written word is often different from people's interpretations of it. The religion may have adopted some beliefs and practices that are not actually contained in the sacred text.
4. Appreciate that although a text may be perceived as sacred, it may still contain errors or omissions, particularly as it applies to modern life. People of earlier times did not understand that some people have a strong homosexual orientation or gender identity that conflicts with their body morphology that remains immutable.
5. Attempt to change attitudes within the church. This is an approach that Bob Peacock and Lloyd Thornhill have been using for years. As born-again Christians, legally married and together for about 37 years when interviewed, they have made it a practice to teach others about God's love for nonheterosexual individuals (Lahey & Alderson, 2004).

There is research that indicates that having a positive image of God is related to having good self-esteem. On the other hand, having a view of God as wrathful, rejecting, and impersonal is related to having negative self-esteem and having feelings of loneliness (Grant & Epp, 1998). "Being well-adjusted does not entail being reconciled with a traditional religion or with a theistic belief" (Tan, 2005, p. 142).

HIV/AIDS

> Globally, around 11% of HIV infections are among babies who acquire the virus from their mothers; 10% result from injecting drug use; 5–10% are due to sex between men; and 5–10% occur in healthcare settings. Sex between men and women accounts for the remaining proportion—around two thirds of new infections. (AVERT, 2009, para. 4)

The Centers for Disease Control and Prevention in the United States estimated that approximately 56,300 Americans were newly infected with HIV in 2006. About 53% of these infections occurred in gay and bisexual men, and the incidence rates for African American men and women were estimated to be seven times higher than among Whites (Divisions of HIV/AIDS Prevention, 2009).

The rate of HIV infection in both the United States and Canada since 2000 has been increasing among men who have sex with men (Dowsett, 2009; Natale, 2009; Public Health Agency of Canada, 2006), and gay men have been the primary victims of the virus (Birken, 1997; Jones, 1997). Counseling related to HIV/AIDS is an area of focus with infected gay men.

Counseling related to HIV/AIDS and other sexually transmitted infections is an area that should be included with all men who have sex with men, regardless of their sexual identity label. After all, it is sexual behavior that is the risk factor, not the self-definition. HIV infection can be transmitted through various means, including (a) sexual intercourse (vaginal and anal); (b) oral sex (mouth-penis, mouth-vagina); and through nonsexual means, such as shared needles between intravenous drug users and through other bodily fluid contact between individuals (saliva excluded). Although the mouth is considered an inhospitable environment for the HIV virus, there are documented cases in which HIV was transmitted orally (SF AIDS Foundation, 2010).

Although the available drug cocktails prolong life for those who are candidates for their usage, they do not kill the HIV virus. If you are not thoroughly familiar with HIV/AIDS and how to prevent it, detailed information is available from the Centers for Disease Control and Prevention (2009) and the SF AIDS Foundation (2010).

Working with gay men living with HIV/AIDS will depend on their level of acceptance of their serostatus, their knowledge of HIV/AIDS, and the stage of their infection. Expect that those in the early stages following diagnosis will experience stages similar to Kubler-Ross's stages of dying (Kubler-Ross, 1969). One HIV-positive individual interviewed for *Beyond Coming Out* (Alderson, 2000) described his disclosure of his serostatus as a third form of coming out: first one comes out to self, then one comes out to others as a gay man, and then one comes out as a gay man who is HIV positive.

Similar to the process of disclosing to others, individuals with HIV/AIDS need to make decisions about whom to disclose their status to, when, and how. The result of doing so is often emotionally difficult for both the infected person and the one receiving the news. Individuals who have developed symptoms of AIDS have concerns about diminishing health, and some develop diminished mental abilities, which makes it more difficult for them to cope with the physical changes that are occurring (Kalichman, 1998).

Relationship Problems

Relationship problems are often the most frequent presenting concern for individuals seeking counseling. Gay men often face a few extra barriers to developing successful, harmonious relationships compared to other relationship types. Males have been largely socialized with scripts that are not conducive to developing intimacy. Instead of learning to be cooperative, they are raised to be competitive, a stance often unhelpful in relationships (Weiten & Lloyd, 2000). Furthermore, the traditional male script is about being strong and emotionless—sensitivity is seen as feminine.

Additionally, gay couples who publicly display physical affection toward one another run the risk of harassment and assault (Garnets & Kimmel, 1993; Klinger, 1995; McKirnan & Peterson, 1989). Gay bashings occur the most frequently in gay neighborhoods or villages (Janoff, 2005) that perpetrators know are hang out spots for many gay men.

Gay male relationships often follow different rules than heterosexual relationships. Dating someone of the same sex is not as clearly defined as opposite-sex dating. Who pays, who initiates advances, how you respond to advances, and similar questions are not delineated. We know that gay men often become sexual very early on in dating (Garnets & Kimmel, 1993; Slater, 1988), but this is not a predetermined eventuality. Perhaps this will change as same-sex marriage becomes possible for ever-increasing numbers of gay couples around the world.

Most heterosexual relationships have a clearly defined trajectory, with possible marriage and childbearing as clear demarcations of commitment. Even many gay men and lesbian women are opposed to same-sex marriage (Lahey & Alderson, 2004), fearing that they will lose some of their identity by following a heterosexual script, especially marriage.

Nonetheless, the vast majority of gay men want to be in a committed relationship (Rothblum, 2009; Troiden, 1979), and approximately half are already in such relationships (Peplau, 1993). About 28% of gay men and 44% of lesbian women are currently living with a same-sex partner (Black et al., 2000). Research indicates that having relationships is good for gay men's psychological health (Simonsen, Blazina, & Watkins, 2000).

Many if not most gay male couples eventually develop sexually open relationships (Bell & Weinberg, 1978; LaSala, 2004a, 2004b; McWhirter & Mattison, 1996). This may create special challenges for how the couple preserves integrity and commitment within their primary relationship. Career challenges and relocation possibilities for one or the other are other potential strains, including possible emigration problems for those who are citizens of different countries.

A positive gay identity does not occur in a vacuum—associating with other gay men is important (Frable, Wortman, & Joseph, 1997). Connection with others of similar ilk helps gay people reduce internalized homophobia, shame, and guilt, and it begins the transformation process of helping them begin to celebrate their uniqueness and their diversity (Alderson, 2002).

The first step in helping gay men with relationships is to first understand what underlies their presenting concern. Interventions will vary tremendously based on this. A man who lacks social skills and cannot initiate or sustain a date has different needs than someone who finds he soon becomes bored in relationships and ends up moving quickly to the next one. Some of the unique aspects that affect gay men in their relationships are varying degrees of internalized homophobia, varying levels of outness between the partners, different stages of identity development (e.g., at different stages in Cass's [1979] model), HIV status, and cultural considerations.

Disclosing to Others

Disclosing to others is difficult for some gay people (Alderson, 2000), but hiding one's affectional orientation can also lead to feelings of isolation (Cooley, 1998). Half of the gay bashing that occurs is at the hands of family members (Bohan, 1996), and the number of street youth who have homosexual orientations speaks volumes to the nonacceptance that many receive at home. The loss of friendships and family ties is also a real threat for many gay individuals.

Most gay men do not disclose their sexual identities at work for fear of retribution (Nauta et al., 2001). Harassment in the workplace is pervasive for gay individuals (Croteau et al., 2000).

A major issue for LGBTI individuals concerns disclosing to family of origin. Helping a client decide whether to disclose to family members requires focusing on all of the pros and cons of doing so. Consequences are inevitable, but the eventual outcome is not entirely predictable. Besides helping clients explore all possible scenarios and the ones that are most likely, it is imperative that the client can also answer the question, "What if it doesn't go the way you expect it will?" A focus in counseling ought to include discussion of the who, what, when, why, and how of disclosure.

Especially important when working with those who are dependent on their families is to consider the worst-case scenario: "If you are rejected by one or more family members, what will result?" Many minors would be ill advised to disclose while they remain dependent on their parents. The literature is replete with examples of gay youth who disclose and are then thrown out of their parental homes. Be sure to establish a backup plan for those adolescents who insist on disclosing to their families, whatever the cost.

Managing the Consequences of External Homophobia

Despite the progress being made in the United States, the 2007 national survey of how grade schools are doing regarding treatment of LGBTI youth suggests that many improvements are still needed. The survey was conducted with 6,209 LGBTI students, ages 13 to 21 (grades 6 to 12) across all 50 states and the District of Columbia. They reported the following:

1. 86.2% of LGBTI students reported being verbally harassed.
2. 44.1% reported physical harassment.
3. 73.6% heard pejorative remarks such as "faggot" and "dyke" frequently or often at school.
4. 60.8% reported feeling unsafe at school because of their affectional orientation.
5. 38.4% felt unsafe because of their gender expression.
6. Nearly a third missed a class or a day of school because of feeling unsafe in the past month (compared to about 5% of a national sample of secondary school students).
7. Those who were harassed reportedly suffered academically because of it (Kosciw, Diaz, & Greytak, 2008).

Indications suggest that the situation in Canada is not significantly different. Research has clearly established that schools (i.e., kindergarten to grades 12, or 13 in some jurisdictions) remain among the most heterosexist and homophobic institutions in Canada (Totten, Quigley, & Morgan, 2004; Williams, Connolly, Pepler, & Craig, 2003).

Adolescents and males who are perceived as having a homosexual orientation are also at risk of being severely beaten or killed (Bartlett, 2007; Dunbar, 2006; Janoff, 2005). Unfortunately, anti-gay attitudes and behavior continue to be commonplace in the United States (Baunach, Burgess, & Muse, 2010). Most research suggests that about 20 to 25% of gay men have been physically assaulted because of their perceived affectional orientation (Carragher & Rivers, 2002; Herek, 2009; Ratner, 1993; Wells & Tsutsumi, 2005), and such assaults leave emotional scars (Dworkin, 2000). More than 10% of gay adults have faced employment and housing discrimination.

When working with individuals who are just coming out with a gay, lesbian, bisexual, or transgender identity, counselors should bring up the issue of physical safety and ensure their client remains aware and suitably cautious when out in public. Prevention is the goal. A counselor might ask the client, "In what ways will you help ensure your safety when you leave home?" Help your client verbalize and commit to concrete ways this will look (e.g., only hold hands with a same-sex partner when no one else is around, go out to the city's party district in groups and never alone).

The treatment of posttraumatic stress disorder is not an uncommon counseling need for those who have been gay bashed (Dworkin, 2000). Consequently, managing the consequences of external homophobia is also a problem for which some gay individuals seek help.

A gay person needs to be properly armed with the skills required to cope with external homophobia. Dealing with people who have been gay bashed is similar to dealing with other victims of violence. A longitudinal study looking at hate crimes committed against lesbian, gay, and bisexual individuals (Herek, Gillis, & Cogan, 1999) provided evidence that anger, stress, and depression can last for up to 5 years following the attack. Doubts about one's sexual identity can also occur following an attack (Bridgewater, 1992).

COUNSELING DIVERSE POPULATIONS

Counseling Individuals With Multiple Nondominant Identity Statuses

It is difficult enough for many people to identify as gay, but a whole new layer is added when one has multiple nondominant identities to navigate. For example, gay men who are non-Caucasian, non-Christian, physically challenged, or mentally challenged face other obstacles.

Which identity status will have the greatest significance (Garnets & Kimmel, 1993)? A recent study with Asian gay men found that situational factors (i.e., familial, cultural, societal influences) determined the importance and relevance of their minority identities (Operario et al., 2008).

Gay men of color generally receive little support from others of their racial/ethnic background, whether Asian (Han, 2006, 2007; Mao, McCormick, & Van de Ven, 2002; Operario et al., 2008), Black (Crawford, Allison, Zamboni, & Soto, 2002; Savage & Harley, 2005), or Latino (Ramirez-Valles, 2007). When Asians, Blacks, and Latinos are cruised sexually, they are often pursued by others because of a stereotypical view that they hold of them. There are no easy solutions to these problems, but therapists can provide support and encourage clients to look at ways to best manage their various identities.

Counseling Aging Gay Men

Research indicates that aging gay men are as well-adjusted psychologically as their heterosexual counterparts (Bohan, 1996). Consequently, their concerns are similar to those of other older people (Garnets & Kimmel, 1993). However, the stereotypes held by heterosexual individuals regarding gay men and lesbian women persist into late adulthood, notably the inversion theory (i.e., that lesbian women and gay men are inverted females and males; Wright & Canetto, 2009).

Aging gay men may have skills that will help them better cope with the increasing possibility that they may be alone someday. For example, because most have not had women who helped take care of them, they have learned to "cook, clean iron, shop, do their own laundry, [and] make their own social arrangements" (McDonald & Steinhorn, 1990, p. 110). Nonetheless, one can speculate that those who are forced to live in nursing homes may face special challenges if they encounter prejudice and discrimination from other residents or nursing staff (Kean, 2006).

Counseling Gay Men Living in Rural Communities

Gay men often feel isolated living in rural communities (Cody & Welch, 1997). Rural areas are generally more homophobic and heterosexist compared to urban living (Bohan, 1996). Consequently, most gay individuals migrate to cities to find greater acceptance and a sense of community (Bagley & Tremblay, 1998). For those who remain in rural settings, a counseling goal may be to help them establish a community network with other rural gay men, similar to what some did in northern New England (Cody & Welch, 1997).

Counseling Gay Students

Common presenting concerns for school counselors include depression, poor self-esteem, social isolation, and suicidal ideation (Birkett, Espelage, & Koenig, 2009; Fontaine, 1998). Many if not most schools continue to be homophobic environments (Kosciw, Greytak, & Diaz, 2009; Russell et al., 2001). Furthermore, LGBTI students continue to be underserved and rendered invisible in most schools (Goodrich & Luke, 2009). University settings also remain largely homophobic and heterosexist (Wills & Crawford, 2000), including programs focused on continuing adult education (Hill, 2006).

Counseling Gay Adolescents

Feeling confused, misunderstood, angry, afraid of negative reactions from others, and having concerns for the future is common with gay youth (Omizo, Omizo, & Okamoto, 1998). A common concern brought to counselors is dealing with a sense of isolation (Hetrick & Martin, 1987). Whereas those 21 years of age and older can frequent gay bars in the United States, which is still a common meeting place for gay people (Shannon & Woods, 1991), minors cannot. Most gay adolescents are not out in high school (Savin-Williams, 2005), so meeting other gay youth is nearly impossible. Most large cities have a gay youth group offered by a gay information resource service, but any particular gay adolescent may not connect to those who attend it.

Another common problem concerns dealing with family members (Hetrick & Martin, 1987). Both individual and family therapy may help a gay adolescent with family conflicts.

Resources for This Group

1. Three excellent resources that can help you design appropriate interventions for gay men and lesbian women are *Breaking Out* (Alderson, 2002; note the second edition of this book will be published winter 2012), the *Handbook of Affirmative Psychotherapy with Lesbians and Gay Men* (Ritter & Terndrup, 2002), and the *Handbook of Counseling and Psychotherapy with Lesbian, Gay, Bisexual, and Transgender Clients* (Bieschke, Perez, & Debord, 2006). *Breaking Out* is designed as a self-help, how-to book for lesbian women and gay men using a cognitive behavioral approach. The topics and exercises within it are very helpful in designing treatment plans. The remaining two books contain highly referenced coverage regarding affirmative counseling practice.
2. The UCLA Lesbian, Gay, Bisexual, Transgender Campus Resource Center provides links to an array of national LGBT resources www.lgbt.ucla.edu/nationalresources.html).

3. The Human Rights Campaign is an organization that works for LGBTI equal rights. Their website contains a wealth of good information www.hrc.org/).
4. AVERT (AVERTing HIV and AIDS) lists many helpful resources for gay people that extend beyond a focus on HIV/AIDS. They also list several American phone-in hotlines www.avert.org/gaylesbianhelp.htm).
5. GLSEN is the Gay, Lesbian and Straight Education Network in the United States www.glsen.org/cgi-bin/iowa/all/home/index.html).
6. Egale Canada is Canada's LGBT human rights organization: advancing equality, diversity, education, and justice www.egale.ca/).
7. The International Lesbian, Gay, Bisexual, Trans and Intersex Association (ILGA). Founded in 1978, ILGA is now an association of more than 700 groups in more than 110 countries campaigning for lesbian, gay, bisexual, trans and intersex (LGBTI) rights (http://ilga.org/ilga/en/article/1161).

Limitations, Furthering Research, and Implications for Counselors

Limitations of the Research With This Group

The biggest limitation with researching gay men and other LGBTI individuals was discussed in Chapter 1: There has never been a representative sample because there has never been a desire for most individuals to be known to researchers. "Poor sampling designs can result in biased results that will mislead other researchers, policymakers, and practitioners" (Meyer & Wilson, 2009, p. 23). Most of the LGBTI community can be invisible whenever needed. LGBTI individuals have learned to pass, and they have learned to be dishonest when authenticity may lead to being further punished or rejected.

Societal change will be needed before most LGBTI individuals feel safe. Call it self-preservation, or call it instinctual survival. Given that most LGBTI individuals cannot change—even if they wanted to—they have little option but to wait for a time when they are at least tolerated wherever they happen to live.

The other limitation of research is that what was studied 10 years ago might already be invalid. The changes that are occurring are happening in many Western countries at a phenomenal rate. No doubt, by the time you read this, several more changes will have occurred. The fairies and queers of yesteryear are slowly becoming respectable human beings. In reference to the title of a book by Lahey (1999), *Are We Persons Yet?*, in Canada, it appears her dream has now segued into reality. Many more positive changes are on the horizon in the United States today as well.

Areas Requiring Future Research

It is amazing how Sir Isaac Newton's famous third law applies not only to motion but also to LGBTI psychology. "To every action, there is an equal and opposite reaction." A backlash occurs when major societal change erupts. Same-sex marriage in Canada arguably helped foster the election of a minority conservative government (in contrast to a liberal government), and perhaps even today where that conservative government has recently won a majority. In the United States, Barack Obama has indicated that although he supports civil unions for same-sex couples, he is not comfortable considering same-sex marriage.

As LGBTI individuals attain greater acknowledgement, understanding, rights, and privileges, an undercurrent exists that may serve to undermine the positive changes that are occurring in American and Canadian society. Conversion therapy remains alive and well in the United States (Alexander, 1999; Associated Press, 2001; Gonsiorek, 2004; Nicolosi, Byrd, & Potts, 2000a, 2000b), and it remains to be seen whether this movement will surface in Canada.

Along with social constructionism has evolved *queer theory*, a philosophy that questions and challenges the identity constructs of gay, heterosexual, or bisexual. There are no identity labels in queer theory (Eardley, 2002), only the indefinite label of "queer." Of course, this word itself is a label, one that many reject entirely. It was derogatory, and it remains so to some individuals. It tells us nothing about the sexuality of those individuals that the word was meant to encapsulate.

Eardley (2002) indicated that queer theory has been criticized because its meaning constantly shifts, along with other social constructs, and the term therefore has little meaning. Consequently, the word cannot be all that freeing or radical. Eardley also suggested that the word *queer* was and is generally applied to gay men, not women, thereby ignoring gender politics.

If there is no immutable quality to affectional orientation, conversion therapy can be argued as an ethical therapeutic practice. In fact, some have already argued that conversion therapy is ethical (Nicolosi et al., 2000a, 2000b; Throckmorton, 1998). The result of ongoing conversion therapy based on social constructionist philosophy will likely only produce one societal effect: the ongoing emotional abuse and spiritual rejection of those who are gay and those who are attempting to come out. As this chapter has clearly articulated, there are many aspects to human sexuality, and *affectional orientation* as a term has been poorly defined, if defined at all, in research that supposedly addresses it and its conversion, whatever it is.

The cutting edge of research, therefore, needs to more clearly define the construct of affectional orientation and further investigate the aspects that change naturally, the aspects that can change through intervention strategies, and the aspects that are immutable. Likewise, it is difficult to do research on a construct until a good measure of it exists. The Sexuality Questionnaire (Alderson et al., 2011) holds promise in this area.

We do not know about the success of same-sex marriage. What began as a social movement is also a societal experiment in interpersonal relationships. Does it work? If so, does it work better, worse, or no differently than opposite-sex marriage? There is no better time to be doing psychosocial research on LGBTI individuals than now.

Implications for Counselors

There is a burgeoning literature regarding gay males, the group within the LGBTI community that boasts the largest numbers and that has become the most visible. Counselors need to be adept at working with the presenting concerns common to all individuals, and in addition to this, their gay clients may have issues dealing with (a) internalized homophobia, (b) affectional orientation confusion and self-identifying as gay, (c) disclosing to others, (d) identity fragmentation, (e) relationship problems, (f) religious conflicts, (g) HIV and AIDS, and (h) managing the consequences of external homophobia. While gay men are capable of establishing and maintaining relationships, a major difference between their relationships and other relationship types is that many become sexually nonmonogamous either initially or over time. Research suggests that open relationships do not detract from relationship quality in gay male relationships when honesty and boundaries are honored and maintained.

The critical factor in working with all LGBTI clients is to ensure that you have developed LGBTI-affirmative attitudes and beliefs so that you can offer affirmative counseling. Most LGBTI individuals have faced numerous occasions on which they felt marginalized and rejected, and they become sensitive to the nuances that indicate this might be true in your case.

Exercises

Individual Exercises

1. If you are a male, clip or staple an inverted pink triangle on your shirt or jacket so that it is visible to everyone who sees you (Chesler & Zuniga, 1991). Alternatively, attach a small rainbow flag to yourself. Wear it for a day and note your reactions. Depending on your community, do not be naïve and remember to maintain awareness of safety issues when and where relevant.
2. If you are a male, during daytime hours, walk hand-in-hand with a male friend on campus or

elsewhere. Again, depending on your community, do not be naïve and remember to maintain awareness of safety issues when and where relevant.

3. Tyler, Jackman-Wheitner, Strader, and Lenox (1997) suggested watching two feature-length videos that portray gay men in a positive light: *Love! Valor! Compassion!* and *Long Time Companion.*

Classroom Exercise

1. In dyads, one student plays the role of a gay man. Begin by introducing yourself to the other student by saying, "My name is . . . , and I self-identify as gay." Either the other student decides to ask his or her own questions, or instead uses the following. If you are playing the gay man, you have the option of not answering any questions you do not want to answer by saying "pass."
   a. How long have you identified as gay?
   b. How many people have you disclosed your gay identity to?
   c. How do you decide who to tell and who not to?
   d. What is it like to tell someone you are a gay man?
   e. Do you plan to have children someday? If yes, how will you make this happen? If no, how do you feel having decided not to have children?
   f. What is the hardest part about being a gay man?
   g. What is the happiest part about being a gay man?
   h. Have you ever felt afraid because you are a gay man?
   i. How do you protect yourself from homophobes?
   j. What else would you like to tell me about your experience of being a gay man? (This exercise is adapted from Finkel, Storaasli, Bandele, & Schaefer, 2003.)
2. "Continuum Activity"—The instructor begins by creating a scale from 1 to 10 on the floor. The easiest way to do this is to use 8 × 11 sheets of paper, each marked from 1 to 10. The instructor then reads out a question that requires you to reflect on your values, beliefs, or attitudes regarding LGBTI individuals. For example, your instructor might ask, "How important is it to have friends with varying affectional orientations?" Then everyone moves to the number that corresponds to their response with 1 meaning *not at all* and 10 representing *critically important.* Participants are provided time to comment briefly on their choice before another question is asked and people again move to the number that best represents their answer (adapted from Tyler et al., 1997).

Chapter Summary

The LGBTI social climate, particularly in Western cultures, is changing rapidly, and gay individuals are beginning to secure equal rights and privileges. The psychological and spiritual damage that has been done through years of global homophobia and heterosexism, however, remains a problem for many who are trying to attain a positive gay identity. The cold dark place of the closet still feels safer for many than the open space of today and especially tomorrow.

Gay youth need our help. As counseling professionals, we ought to be their guiding light as others fade under the pressure of conformity. We cannot be effective counselors while sitting in our offices filing our nails. Sorry, but we need to also act. Today's counseling professional is both a therapist and an activist. To believe otherwise is to discount today's professional movement that encourages the promotion of equality and the push in counseling psychology and social work that believes social justice for all is more than just an ideology.

Regardless of age, religion, gender, or locale, gay individuals continue to live in societies throughout the world, including the United States and Canada, that do not fully accept them. Our job as therapists is to give voice to those who have had their voices diminished. But our job as citizens is to end the prejudice and discrimination once and for all.

4

Lesbian Girls and Women

Challenging Your Attitudes and Beliefs About This Group

Reflection Questions

1. Have you ever talked about female homosexuality with family members? If so, was it discussed in a positive or negative light? How do you think they would react if you disclosed to them that you were a lesbian woman?
2. List as many synonyms as you can for *lesbian woman*.
3. We know that some women define themselves as heterosexual, yet they engage in homosexual behavior while serving time in prison. We also know that the majority of lesbian women have engaged in heterosexual behavior. What explains this?

4. If you had or have a daughter and she turned out to identify as lesbian, how would you react? How would you feel? Would it seem better or worse than if she identified as heterosexual? Why or why not?
5. It is often believed that lesbian women are masculine. What is your attitude toward masculine women, regardless of their affectional orientation? Given that gender expression is on a continuum, with some women being highly masculine and others highly feminine, what difference does it make where others fall on the continuum? How would your views change when you meet one or more who are very feminine?

Challenging Your Assumptions Questions

1. Should female homosexuality be included as an integral part of sex education curricula? Why or why not?
2. Should a girl or woman define as a lesbian if she has one or more sexual encounters with one or more other females? Why or why not? What factors do you think should be considered in making such a self-definition? What difference do you think age makes in this assessment?
3. Some lesbian women continue to have sex with men even after they come out. In what ways does that challenge your views about lesbian women?
4. Given that you would not be able to identify most lesbian women if you met them, how does that challenge whatever stereotypes you currently hold about them?
5. If you had to give up your newborn daughter for adoption and you found out that the new parents were a lesbian couple, what thoughts and feelings would this evoke in you? What is the likelihood that lesbian parents will raise psychologically healthy children?

Reflections

[*Note:* Imagine that *you* are the client in these reflections].

You and your husband, Sean, have two children from your 20-year marriage. It has been a positive experience for you. Sean is easy to be with, he is funny, and he is playful. Having sex with Sean is good as well. You remember the infatuation period, however, even more fondly. Back then, having sex was like having fireworks in your backyard! Over the years, both of you do not feel the same toward each other sexually, but your love has grown into something very deep and meaningful.

At a baseball practice for your son, you meet Sonya. Something about her eyes enraptures you, and your intuition tells you the feeling is mutual. While the boys play ball, you sit together on the bleachers and talk. You feel yourself getting excited sexually as you talk. Foreign to the sense you have of yourself, you set up a time to get together at Sonya's house. You cannot stop thinking about what this will turn into. What you know is that you get stimulated every time you think about what could ensue.

As a Mormon, you believe your feelings are completely wrong, so you book an appointment with a counselor, Tanya. In Tanya's office, you notice many symbols of LGBTI affirmation—so many, in fact, that it scares you! Your mouth suddenly becomes dry as you tell the story about your attraction to Sonya. You notice Tanya smile before she utters the words, "Claire, you are a lesbian: This is something to feel very good about!"

You feel yourself going into shock. Your head is exploding, wanting to deny what Tanya has just said to you. "Tanya," you say carefully, "I cannot be a lesbian. I am happily married with two children. It is also against my faith. You must be mistaken!"

"No, I am not mistaken, Claire. I have seen this many times over the years in my practice. I guess this is more of a shock to you than I had anticipated. We will have to take this very slow."

From a Client's Perspective

1. What do you think of Tanya's proclamation?
2. How would you feel if you were Claire?
3. What impact do you believe religious affiliation would have on someone who defines as lesbian? What impact would it have on her opposite-sex marriage?

From a Counselor's Perspective

1. What else should a counselor find out from you before making such a proclamation?
2. Perhaps more importantly, is it ever appropriate for a counselor to offer an identity label or identity status to a client? Why or why not?
3. What considerations were provided for this client's religion, marital status, and personal attitudes regarding homosexuality?

Background Information Regarding Lesbian Girls and Women

Background information regarding lesbian girls and women is included in this section. As was the case with Chapter 3, the focus is primarily on American research.

Development Through the Life Span

Sexual identity development of lesbian, gay, and bisexual (LGB) youths may follow a variety of patterns. Using a cluster analytic technique, Rosario, Schrimshaw, and Hunter (2008) found that LGB youth self-identify at various times and the extent to which their sexual identities are integrated vary as well (low, medium, and high integration). This is unsurprising given that people self-identify when they believe the catalysts indicating a LGB identity outweigh the hindrances of adopting one (Alderson, 2010). LGB individuals may adopt their minority identity at any age, and it is usually harder the older one gets (Alderson, 2000; Johnston & Jenkins, 2004). Women who come out in midlife, for example, are often in the awkward position of having to convince others that their identity is in fact bona fide (Rickards & Wuest, 2006).

The developmental pathways for lesbian women are considerably more variable than they are for gay men (Diamond & Savin-Williams, 2000) for several reasons. Here is why:

1. Lesbian women's affectional orientation is more often experienced as fluid and freely chosen compared to gay men's. Albeit with many exceptions, sexual minority women's affectional orientation is often experienced as freely chosen (Diamond, 2008; McElwain, Grimes, & McVicker, 2009; Peplau, Spalding, Conley, & Veniegas, 1999). The vast majority of gay men, on the other hand, believe that they have always had a strong homosexual orientation (Barber & Mobley, 1999; Flowers & Buston, 2001; Savin-Williams, 2005). A lesbian identity might be adopted as a choice based on political reasons and/or based on shifting attractions (supporting a socially constructed position), whereas for men, the affectional orientation underlying a gay identity is usually experienced as having always been there (as though it were inborn, supporting an essentialist perspective).

The dichotomy between essentialism and social constructionism, as mentioned in Chapter 1, is a moot point (Kitzinger & Wilkinson, 1995). Most heterosexual women and heterosexual men do not report a change in their affectional orientation over time (Diamond, 2007; Savin-Williams & Ream, 2007), while sexual minority women often make changes to their self-chosen sexual identity labels (Diamond, 2008).

Many teenage women adopt sexual identity labels that do not reflect their sexual behavior (Hollander, 2008). Young lesbian and bisexual women have sex with men, too, leaving them at risk of becoming pregnant (Hollander, 2008). American lesbian baby boomers have also described sexual identities that shift and change across different settings (Read, 2009). A larger percentage of men compared to women experience congruence between their affectional orientation, their sexual identity, and their sexual behavior (Laumann, Gagnon, Michael, & Michaels, 1994).

Consequently, compared to gay men, sexual minority women experience their sexuality as fluid and changeable to a greater extent. Skerven and de St. Aubin (2006) provided evidence that lesbian development occurs through person–environment interactions, thus supporting a perspective that is both essentialist and social constructionist.

2. Girls are raised with greater freedom to express affection in their relationships. Girls are raised to be far more demonstrative—both emotionally and physically—with their female friends and acquaintances compared to boys. Beginning from a young age, girls are taught to develop emotional connections with others, to communicate openly and articulately, and to express their feelings, while boys have traditionally been taught to hold back tears and to suppress other "soft" emotions. For some males, this conditioning is so great that it results in alexithymia, a condition whereby a person has a difficult time identifying and/or actually feeling a plethora of emotions. Girls are also permitted to show physical affection to one another (e.g., having pajama parties and sleepovers, holding hands in public, giving massages to each other, kissing each other's cheek), while boys are more restrained in their expression of physical contact, often limited to aggressive behaviors (e.g., fighting, wrestling, boxing) or quick gestures (pats on the back or buttocks when scoring points in a sport).

Girls have generally been taught to repress sexual desire, and they are therefore more likely to self-identify as lesbian in the context of relationship as opposed to articulating and acting out of sexual desire (McCarn & Fassinger, 1996). Since girls have been raised generally to develop physical connections out of emotional ones, while for boys, this is usually reversed (Townsend, 1998), two girls engaging in affectionate physical contact may find this mutually enjoyable, and thus begin a same-sex relationship for a period of time. This connection, however, may occur without consideration of the degree of same-sex attraction compared to opposite-sex attraction or of the identity politics usually associated with assumption of a lesbian identity.

There has been a lack of research regarding the development of adult lesbian women (Wheeler-Scruggs, 2008), and researchers have tended to assume that the development of lesbian women is the same as that for heterosexual women. Using Levinson's (1978, 1990) theory that purports four life stages (i.e., pre-adulthood—ages 0–22; early adulthood—ages 17–45; middle adulthood—ages 40–65; and late adulthood—ages 60–death), Wheeler-Scruggs (2008) interviewed 10 lesbian women (ages 35–45) and concluded their stages were similar to those of heterosexual women, but the tasks associated with each stage were different. For example, separating from family of origin was not contingent on getting married or having a significant life partner. The lesbian women had more difficulty with maintaining stable relationships and careers during early adulthood compared to heterosexual women in Levinsonian studies. Another difference was that the lesbian women always mentioned their partners when they spoke about future plans, whereas at least in one study (Furst, as cited in Wheeler-Scruggs, 2008), heterosexual women did not mention their husbands.

Elder lesbian and gay male individuals learned over many years to hide their identities to avoid discrimination and epithets thrown at them. This had led to their invisibility, and the result is often poor health and problems with accessing services (Butler, 2004). Neither aging gay men nor lesbian women exercise at recommended levels, and particularly aging lesbian women have increased risk of alcohol problems and experience obesity levels that are twice the American national average (Masini & Barrett, 2007).

An insulating factor for lesbian individuals is the amount and quality of social support they have in their social networks (Masini & Barrett, 2007). Older lesbian women do tend to focus their social lives around a network of friends while also maintaining close family ties (Goldberg, Sickler, & Dibble, 2005).

Gay men often hold more negative views of growing older compared to lesbian women (Schope, 2005). Regardless of age, aging lesbian women are stereotyped as being more similar to heterosexual men regarding gender-stereotypic traits, while aging gay men are viewed as more similar to heterosexual women (Wright & Canetto, 2009).

> . . . the psychosocial factors that have been identified in the existing research as affecting successful aging in older LGB adult populations include a positive identity, socioeconomic resources, access to health care and other formal services, and informal and community-based social support. (Fredriksen-Goldsen & Muraco, 2010, p. 402)

Race and Ethnicity

While the research base regarding women of color grew between 1998 and 2007, particularly in comparison to the previous two decades, there remains a dearth of research in this area. This is especially true regarding lesbian women of color (Huang et al., 2010; Parks, Hughes, & Matthews, 2004). Furthermore, most participants of color were recruited through convenience samples or random sampling of convenience samples. During the 1998 to 2007 decade, Huang and colleagues (2010) noted that only two nationally representative studies were undertaken regarding LGB individuals (Butler, 2000; Cochran, Mays, Alegria, Ortega, & Takeuchi, 2007).

Butler's (2000) study did not focus on people of color per se. Instead, it focused on eight waves of the General Social Surveys conducted between 1988 and 1998. Butler found that the number of Americans reporting having a same-sex partner increased each year, likely representing the greater safety that these people felt in reporting this information.

Cochran and colleagues (2007) used data from the National Latino and Asian American Survey ($N = 4,488$) to look at whether this group has increased risk of mental health and substance abuse disorders. Of those interviewed, 4.8% identified as LGB and/or reported recent same-gender sexual experience. Few differences related to affectional orientation were noted. The Latino and Asian lesbian and bisexual women were more likely to report recent and lifetime histories of depressive disorders compared to others in the sample.

The level of morbidity in this nationally representative sample of Latino and Asian LGB individuals was less than that found in population-based studies of LGB adults (Cochran et al., 2007). Furthermore, Asian, Asian American, and Asian immigrant LGB individuals (60 women, 254 men) report that compared to their countries of residence, those living in the United States were generally more open regarding their affectional orientation (Kimmel & Yi, 2004).

Often working-class, older, religious, and/or lesbian women of color "feel marginalized, rendered exotic or even unwelcome" (Mitchell, 2008, p. 119). A prevalent theory has suggested that LGB people of color experience greater stress related to higher levels of heterosexist stigma (Moradi et al., 2010). Meyer (2010) suggested that while research supports this theory, LGB people of color also have greater resilience to cope with this stress. Meyer encouraged further research in this area.

In a recent dissertation, Nelms (2007) found that Black lesbian women perceived themselves as having moderately high stress and negative effects from experiencing this stress. The Black community and familial reactions to their lesbianism were also moderately negative. Another study (Bowleg, Huang, Brooks, Black, & Burkholder, 2003) found that Black lesbian women ($N = 19$) experienced *triple jeopardy*, meaning that they experienced stress in consequence of race/ethnicity, lesbian identity, and gender.

Generally speaking, African American and Latina American lesbian women have strong bonds to their culture and race/ethnicity, and they tend to view these as primary. Tolerance for their sexual identities "is often gained at the price of silence" (Parks et al., 2004, p. 243). Interestingly, African American and Latina American lesbian women were more likely to question their affectional orientation earlier than their White counterparts, but they took more time to label themselves as lesbian. Furthermore, they disclosed their identity more quickly than White women to family but were less likely to disclose to nonfamily (Parks et al., 2004).

In a qualitative study of 13 interracial same-sex couples, Rostosky, Riggle, Savage, Roberts, and Singletary (2008) found that most of the couples experienced stress because of both race and sexual identity. Nearly half found that the stress from their sexual identities was greater than that related to race. The couples used five coping strategies to cope with these stressors: (a) seeking support, (b) meaning making, (c) using humor, (d) using active problem solving, and (e) avoidant behaviors.

Relationships (Family, Friendships, Intimate Romantic/Sexual)

Researchers often look at various factions of the LGBTI community together in their studies instead of in isolation. These research projects provide us deeper insights into lesbian women as well. They are included first.

Lesbian, bisexual, and questioning (LBQ) women are known to engage in same-sex passionate friendships (SSPF; Glover, 2009). An *SSPF* is an intense friendship that does not include sexual contact. While heterosexual females also develop intimate friendships in adolescence and young adulthood, for LBQ women, it also serves as a means by which they can explore and integrate their affectional orientation (Glover, 2009).

Similar to their heterosexual counterparts, lesbian, gay, and bisexual (LGB) individuals tend to form friendships with others who are similar to themselves in sex and race. Where they differ, however, is that they are more likely to report having cross-orientation compared to same-orientation friendships (e.g., more likely to have heterosexual friends than they are to report having LGB friends; Galupo, 2007). Most gay and lesbian individuals develop their friendships with other LGB people, while most bisexual individuals form their friendships with heterosexual individuals. In grade school, some heterosexual youth will end their friendships with a peer after finding out that she or he identifies as LGB (Poteat, Espelage, & Koenig, 2009).

Current studies find few differences in relationship quality between individuals involved in same-sex as compared to opposite-sex relationships (Balsam, Beauchaine, Rothblum, & Solomon, 2008; Kurdek, 2006, 2008). In Balsam and colleagues' (2008) 3-year follow-up study of same-sex couples and opposite-sex married couples, they found that the same-sex couples reported higher relationship quality, compatibility, and intimacy, and less conflict. Similarly, Kurdek (2006) found that the relationships between heterosexual, gay, and lesbian cohabiting couples work in similar ways, but his most recent 10-year longitudinal study found that cohabiting lesbians had the highest relationship quality compared to gay and heterosexual cohabiting couples (Kurdek, 2008).

Regardless of affectional orientation, women place greater emphasis on their partner's personality than do men (Peplau & Fingerhut, 2007; Townsend, 1998). Further support for this was found in a longitudinal study by Gottman and Levenson (2010). Gottman and Levenson studied same- and opposite-sex couples over a 12-year period. They found that women are more expressive in relationships compared to men, and that both gay and lesbian couples use fewer controlling or hostile emotional tactics during periods of conflict. Furthermore, the same-sex couples displayed more affection and humor during conflictual periods and demonstrated more ability to soothe one another.

According to one American study, approximately 44% of lesbian women live with a same-sex partner (Black, Gates, Sanders, & Taylor, 2000). Usually women construct positive intimate relationships with other women. Lesbian couples report greater relationship satisfaction than either gay or heterosexual couples, for example (Beals & Peplau, 2001; Kurdek, 2008; Spitalnick & McNair, 2005). Several reasons explain this, including (a) the desired and achieved levels of equality established in their relationships, (b) the high value that women attribute to emotional intimacy, (c) the attachment styles of the partners, (d) conflict resolution styles, (e) having positive self-esteem, and (f) the social support they establish in their partnered lives (Rose, 2000; Wienke & Hill, 2009). Roisman, Clausell, Holland, Fortuna, and Elieff (2008) found that in their laboratory observations, lesbian couples were more effective at working together harmoniously compared to gay male and heterosexual couples.

Because lesbian women cannot legally marry in most parts of the world, they construct intimate relationships that have their own code of ethics without having boundaries as "fixed" as those of opposite-sex relationships (Burch, 2008). While most lesbian couples choose to be monogamous, some do negotiate open relationships. But the "possibility of an affair still has to be settled, not assumed" (Burch, 2008, p. 146). The code of ethics is about honoring the commitment that has been established, whatever it happens to look like.

A sizeable percentage of lesbian women have been heterosexually married in the past (Boon & Alderson, 2009). Some women are able to maintain their heterosexual marriages after they self-identity as lesbian (Buxton, 2004; Strock, 2008). Some have children born either before or after self-identifying as lesbian (Neville & Henrickson, 2009).

While it is commonly reported that same-sex couples receive less familial support than opposite-sex couples (Kurdek, 2004, 2006), lesbian couples appear to receive support from friends if it is not available from family (Goldberg et al., 2005). Belonging to a lesbian community is helpful, as it fosters self-confidence, self-esteem, and an enhanced sense of well-being (Heath & Mulligan, 2008).

Belonging to a lesbian community is also helpful with regard to dating. In a study of 38 lesbian women, friendship was the most widely used courtship script across the age groups represented (ages 22–63). Other courtship types included sex-based and romance scripts. The most preferred for dating purposes were friendship and romance scripts. Some aspects of dating women unique from dating men included a sense of not being locked into gender roles, a heightened sense of friendship and intimacy, a more rapid pace of relationship development, and an awareness of prejudice (Rose & Zand, 2002).

Two common myths regarding lesbian couples are the ideas of "fusion" and "bed death." *Fusion* is the idea that lesbian couples enmesh with each other to an unhealthy extent, while *bed death* is hypoactive sexual desire whereby lesbian women experience either a greatly reduced or extinguished sex life together (Spitalnick & McNair, 2005). The idea of fusion has little support in the published literature (Rothblum, 2009). Ackbar and Senn (2010) recommended that counselors distinguish between healthy and unhealthy types of closeness between lesbian women. These researchers also advised counselors to stop pathologizing deep closeness simply because lesbian relationships differ from heterosexual ones.

While bed death does occur in some couples, regardless of relationship constellation, it is not inevitable (Nichols & Shernoff, 2007). In closely examining bed death, van Rosmalen-Nooijens, Vergeer, and Lagro-Janssen (2008) concluded that when it does occur, it is more about gender than about one's affectional orientation.

Another myth common to both lesbian and gay relationships is that one assumes the "husband" role and the other the "wife" role: This stereotype does *not* apply to most contemporary same-sex couples, although this relationship construction has been important at times in the past (Peplau & Fingerhut, 2007). Some lesbian couples do assume the roles of "butch" and "femme," and this relationship construction does have some similarities to traditional opposite-sex couples. In such relationships, the woman who defines as butch embraces masculinity and likely takes on the more masculine-gender-typed roles in the household, while the woman who defines as femme embraces femininity and the feminine-gender-typed roles. Lev (2008) reports that there has been an absence of scholarly work looking at this type of lesbian relationship.

Health (Emotional and Psychological, Physical)

A recent sample derived from 33 health care sites across the United States ($N = 1,304$ women) found that having either a bisexual or a lesbian identity increased the likelihood of experiencing emotional stress compared to identifying as heterosexual. As teenagers, both bisexual and lesbian girls experienced more emotional stress. Lesbian women who were mostly "in the closet" (this means disclosing one's sexual identity to few if any people) were 2 to 2.5 times more likely to have felt suicidal in the past 12 months, and they were more likely to have made a suicide attempt compared to heterosexual women. Interestingly, lesbian women were more likely to have sought psychotherapy for depression than did either the heterosexual or bisexual women in the sample (Koh & Ross, 2006).

Overall, LGBTI individuals report lower levels of positive mental health compared to heterosexual people (Owens, Riggle, & Rostosky, 2007). The most impressive review and meta-analysis looking at the mental health of LGB individuals was conducted by King, Semlyen and colleagues (2008), looking at articles from January 1966 to April 2005. Of the 13,706 articles they identified, only 28 articles (based on 25 studies) met their strict inclusion criteria for the meta-analysis. Even these 25 studies represented 214,344 heterosexual and 11,971 nonheterosexual individuals. The researchers found that LGB people face twice the incidence of suicide attempts compared to their heterosexual counterparts, with lifetime prevalence rates especially high for gay and bisexual men. The risk for depression and anxiety disorders was at least 1.5 times higher over both a 12-month period and lifetime prevalence, while risk for substance dependence was 1.5 times higher over a 12-month period. The meta-analysis also revealed that lesbian and bisexual women were the most at risk for substance dependence.

The greater suicidality of LGBTI individuals is well documented. Precipitants include internal factors, such as internalized homophobia (Igartua, Gill, & Montoro, 2003) and the presence of mental disorders (Haas et al., 2011). There is also a consensus among researchers that external factors play a role as well, including social stigma, prejudice, and discrimination toward those with an LGBTI identity (Haas et al., 2011).

Meyer, Dietrich, and Schwartz (2008) also looked at lifetime prevalence of mental disorders and suicide attempts in 388 LGB individuals who were Black, Latino, and White. They found that Black lesbian women, Black gay men, and Black bisexual individuals had a lower prevalence of disorders compared with Latino and White individuals. The youngest participants had fewer mood disorders compared to older participants.

Using data from the California Quality of Life Survey ($N = 2,272$ adults), Cochran and Mays (2007) found that women who had sex with other women reported a greater variety of health problems compared to exclusively heterosexual women, but these differences disappeared when distress levels were considered. Regarding physical health, both lesbian and bisexual women are more likely than heterosexual women to have poorer physical health, including problems with asthma or diabetes (bisexuals only), to be overweight, to smoke, and to drink alcohol excessively (Dilley, Simmons, Boysun, Pizacani, & Stark, 2010). The literature indicates that many lesbian women feel that health care professionals are sometimes discriminatory and noninclusive of them (Seaver, Freund, Wright, Tjia, & Frayne, 2008).

Results from a recent meta-analysis reported that LGB adolescents report higher rates of substance use: nearly twice that compared to heterosexual teenagers (Marshal et al., 2008). Rates of alcohol abuse with lesbian women are higher when compared to heterosexual women (Dilley et al., 2010; Rosario, 2008; Wilsnack et al., 2008), but the highest rates of alcohol abuse appear to occur with those who define as bisexual (Wilsnack et al., 2008).

In one sample, young women who have sex with women engaged in more risky behaviors compared to non–sexual minority youth in a national dataset. These behaviors included anal intercourse with men, regular binge drinking, pregnancy risk, and smoking (Herrick, Matthews, & Garofalo, 2010).

Despite the increased prevalence of mental disorders, Dahan, Feldman, and Hermoni (2008) and Selvidge, Matthews, and Bridges (2008) argue that lesbian women are resilient, having faced double and triple levels of oppression throughout history. This positive psychology view is not unlike the arguments that Savin-Williams (2005) makes about gay and lesbian adolescents. Dahan and colleagues (2008) also recognize that they have suffered, too, and oppression takes its toll on one's mental and physical health.

An insulating factor for lesbian adolescents against developing eating disorders is that they are happier with their bodies and they are not as affected by media images compared to heterosexual girls (Austin et al., 2004). Another study found that lesbian women are, on average, just slightly more satisfied with their bodies compared to heterosexual women (Morrison, Morrison, & Sager, 2004).

Feldman and Meyer's (2007) study found that while gay and bisexual men had an increased prevalence of eating disorders compared to heterosexual men, there were no differences in prevalence among the lesbian, bisexual, and heterosexual women in the sample ($N = 126$ hetero and 388 LGB men and women). Further to this and based on two large online studies (Ns = 2,512 and 54,865) comparing men and women with varying affectional orientations, Peplau and colleagues (2009) found that heterosexual men report the most positive levels of body satisfaction, while few differences were found among the gay men, lesbian women, and heterosexual women. A high percentage of gay men (42%) reported that the negative view they held toward their bodies negatively affected their sex lives. Comparable figures for lesbian women, heterosexual women, and heterosexual men were 27%, 30%, and 22%, respectively.

Lesbian women are less concerned about their weight compared to men and other women. They have a higher prevalence of being overweight and/or obese compared to other women, placing them at greater risk for morbidity and mortality related to excess weight (Boehmer, Bowen, & Bauer, 2007; Bowen, Balsam, & Ender, 2008). While men often prefer thin attractive partners, regardless of affectional orientation, the same is not true of lesbian women (Legenbauer et al., 2009). Even when compared to heterosexual women, lesbian women often prefer partners who are relatively heavier (Swami & Tovee, 2006).

Lesbian women do not generally get sufficient physical exercise to achieve the optimal physical or psychological benefits from it (Brittain, Baillargeon, McElroy, Aaron, & Gyurcsik, 2006). Several barriers to getting sufficient exercise are reported, including common barriers felt by many women (e.g., too tired, no workout partner) and a few that were specific to identifying as lesbian (i.e., lack of lesbian-focused exercise groups, lack of same-sex family memberships available at fitness facilities; Brittain et al., 2006).

A recurring finding is that lesbian women and others who comprise the LGBTI community face "health care disparities and barriers to treatment" (Coren, Coren, Pagliaro, & Weiss, 2011, p. 66). Due to the continuing discrimination against and marginalization of LGBTI individuals in society, many choose not to disclose their nondominant identity in medical settings. Many health care professionals continue to hold prejudicial views toward LGBTI patients, and this is compounded by their lack of training in LGBTI health (McNair & Hegarty, 2010). Lack of disclosure of one's sexual identity and/or sexual practices can result in less diagnostic accuracy and in less helpful recommendations (Coren et al., 2011).

The above is particularly disturbing when one realizes that lesbian women have unique health care needs. They are more likely to experience behavioral health risks factors for breast and gynecological cancers, smoking, and alcohol abuse (Steele, Tinmouth, & Lu, 2006). On the flip side, they are "less likely to receive preventive health care, including clinical breast exams, pap smears and mammography" (Steele et al., 2006, p. 631). Among other reasons, many lesbian women are hesitant to seek health care because of having had negative interactions with health care providers in the past (see Hutchinson, Thompson, & Cederbaum, 2006, for a thorough look at these barriers to receiving health care). Lesbian women are also less likely to receive needed health care because of experiencing greater financial barriers (Diamant, Wold, Spritzer, & Gelberg, 2000).

Career and Work

Using a subsample of 1,365,145 individuals from the 2000 Census Public Use Microdata Sample, Prokos and Keene (2010) compared the differing poverty chances for cohabitating gay, lesbian, and heterosexual (some married) families. The researchers found that gay and lesbian couples fared worse economically than married opposite-sex couples but better than cohabitating opposite-sex couples.

Although "work is extremely important to most lesbian women" (Hook & Bowman, 2008, p. 93), they continue to feel discriminated against there (Hook & Bowman, 2008). While federal law prohibits discrimination based on sex and race, it remains legal to fire someone for identifying as gay or lesbian in many states (Hook & Bowman, 2008).

When organizations do acknowledge the worth of LGBTI people, there is often a backlash (Embrick, Walther, & Wickens, 2007; Hill, 2009). LGBTI employees are subjected to varying degrees of sexual harassment (Ryniker, 2008). "Negative attitudes and barriers against gay men and lesbians in workplaces still remain" (Embrick et al., 2007, p. 757).

While the supportiveness of a work environment is one factor in helping LGB people decide if they should disclose or not, another factor, according to heterosexual colleagues, is that the timing of when their LGB coworker discloses should also be considered (King, Reilly, & Hebl, 2008). A worker who is already known for having a good work ethic and who has positive personality qualities will have an easier time continuing to be accepted in an organization after disclosure, for example.

Black lesbian workers continue to face a triple whammy brought on by displays of heterosexism/homophobia, racism, and sexism (Bowleg, Brooks, & Ritz, 2008). Some occupations are known for having less accepting settings as well. For example, lesbian and gay police officers continue to face barriers to equal employment opportunities (Colvin, 2009).

As noted in Chapter 3 and applicable here as well, gay and lesbian employees are sometimes able to disclose their sexual identities at work in the United States today, but there is a price: They either downplay their homosexuality at work or they experience the constraints imposed by stereotypes about how they are supposed to look, act, and work (Williams, Giuffre, & Dellinger, 2009). Many gay and lesbian employees continue to present a heterosexual façade at work (Button, 2004).

Lyons, Brenner, and Lipman (2010) found, using cluster analysis, that there are three groups of LGB young adults who differ regarding the conflict they feel between their sexual identities and their career development: (a) the career conflict group, (b) the sexual identity conflict group, and (c) the group that only feels low levels of conflict in both domains. The career conflict group indicated that career-related tasks left them little energy for exploring their sexual identity—they, in turn, felt little sexual identity conflict. On the other hand, the sexual identity conflict group reported that exploring their sexual identity interrupted their career development. The largest cluster was the low-conflict group: They experienced low levels of both varieties of conflict. This research addresses the varying strategies that today's LGB employee is using at work to cope—successfully or unsuccessfully—with the demands of being a sexual minority in the career marketplace.

Spirituality and Religion

Rodriguez (2010) has recently provided a review of the psychological research regarding gay and lesbian Christians, beginning from a theoretical paradigm that considers gay and lesbian individuals as fundamentally spiritual and religious beings. Experts believe that LGBTI individuals would be especially likely to benefit from spiritual practices because of the ongoing oppression they encounter (Tan, 2005). After all, a substantial number of LGBTI individuals remain committed to religious and spiritual life despite the intolerance they experience with some people or within some faith communities (Halkitis et al., 2009).

Tan (2005) found in a study of 93 gay and lesbian individuals that they experienced high levels of spiritual well-being. Included in the concept of spiritual well-being were the notions of *religious well-being* (how one relates to God) and *existential well-being* (how one feels about life). While existential well-being was related to depression, religious well-being did not predict any measure of psychological adjustment. Consequently, Tan concluded that focusing on existential well-being was the important factor in improving psychological adjustment. Also interesting to note is while religiosity generally increases as heterosexual individuals enter the latter years of life, this was not found in a recent qualitative dissertation that focused on 20 lesbian women 60 years of age and older (White, 2009).

A substantial amount of empirical literature links conservative religiosity with the endorsement and perpetuation of negative attitudes toward gay and lesbian individuals (Veenvliet, 2008). Three strategies that gay and lesbian churchgoers use to cope with this in the South include (a) some Black lesbian women place their sexuality in second place compared to their Christian identity; (b) most Black and White gay and lesbian members normalize their sexuality by adopting Christian morals (e.g., monogamy); or (c) a small number use their sexuality to challenge homophobia within the church (McQueeney, 2009).

Jewish lesbian women also find ways to bridge their sexuality with their faiths (Glassgold, 2008). A good review looking at the impact of Judeo-Christian beliefs and their impact on lesbian women can be found in Morrow (2003). Same-sex couples are more likely to involve themselves in private forms of religious practice (e.g., prayer, meditation) rather than attend public forms (e.g., attending church; Rostosky, Otis, Riggle, Kelly, & Brodnicki, 2008).

Sociopolitical Realities

Lesbian and bisexual women continue to be targeted for victimization because of their sexuality. In a nationally representative study of 662 LGB adults (152 lesbian women, 159 bisexual women, 241 gay men, and 110 bisexual men) conducted in 2005, 12.5% of the lesbian women in the sample and 12.7% of the bisexual women reported experiences of person or property crimes based on their sexual orientation (Herek, 2009). Balsam (2003) reported the results from two studies that differentially found between 6% and 19% of lesbian women reported at least one incident of physical assault because of their sexual orientation.

The biggest debate and controversy surrounding gay and lesbian couples as of late has centered on the legalization of same-sex marriage. As of this writing, same-sex marriage is legal in several countries and states (see Table 4.1 for timelines).

Table 4.1 Same-Sex Marriage Timelines—Countries and American States

1.	The Netherlands	April 2001
2.	Belgium	January 2003
3.	Massachusetts	May 2004
4.	Spain	July 2005
5.	Canada	July 2005
6.	South Africa	November 2006
7.	Connecticut	November 2008
8.	Norway	January 2009
9.	Iowa	April 2009
10.	Sweden	May 2009
11.	Vermont	September 2009
12.	New Hampshire	January 2010
13.	Washington, DC	March 2010
14.	Mexico City	March 2010
15.	Portugal	June 2010
16.	Iceland	June 2010
17.	Argentina	July 2010
18.	New York	July 2011

The domino effect has indeed begun (Lahey & Alderson, 2004). Same-sex couples living anywhere in the world can marry in Belgium and Canada, which are the only two countries offering same-sex marriages that do not have restrictions regarding nationality (Stritof & Stritof, 2009).

The state of California granted 18,000 same-sex marriages between June 2008 and November 2008, but voters overturned the law by requiring that the state's Constitution be rewritten to recognize only marriages between a man and a woman. Although California's Supreme Court heard arguments regarding the ban on March 5, 2009 (Associated Press, 2009), the court had 90 days to rule in the case (McKinley & Schwartz, 2009). On May 26, 2009, it ruled: It upheld the voter-approved ban on same-sex marriages. The court decided not to annul the 18,000 marriages that were performed before the ban took effect (Schwartz, 2009). Governor Schwarzenegger remarked that although he believed same-sex marriage was inevitable, he would take no action against the Supreme Court ruling. Thankfully, a California federal judge determined on August 4, 2010, that the ban was unconstitutional (Dwyer, 2010). However, attorneys opposed to the overturn of the ban promised that "the verdict will now be appealed to the Ninth Circuit Court of Appeals and may ultimately reach the U.S. Supreme Court, where experts say a decision could transform social and legal precedent" (Dwyer, 2010, para. 9). Opponents of gay marriage were set to challenge this in San Francisco on June 13, 2011, on the basis that the judge might have been biased because he himself identifies as gay (Shafer, 2011).

While forward momentum continues, since same-sex marriage became legal in Massachusetts and throughout Canada, more than half of the American states hastily passed amendments to their constitutions, known as Defense of Marriage Acts, or DOMAs. The intent was to exclude same-sex couples from becoming legally married (Riggle, Rostosky, & Horne, 2009).

Public opinion polls conducted between 1977 and 2004 have shown that Americans' attitudes toward same-sex couples marrying have become more liberal (Avery et al., 2007). Perhaps this greater awareness of and respect for diversity has led to the legislative challenges occurring within nearly every state that has not already legalized same-sex marriage (Avery et al., 2007). What many people may not realize is that it is ordinary gay men and lesbian women that are turning to courts to deliberate on same-sex marriage (Peel & Harding, 2008). Sometimes these fights are tremendously expensive (Lahey & Alderson, 2004).

Same-sex marriage has been shown to have positive emotional effects on LGBTI people (Herdt & Kertzner, 2006). A recent national study compared results for LGB individuals from the National Epidemiologic Survey on Alcohol and Related Conditions ($N = 34{,}653$) during wave 1 (2001–2002) and wave 2 (2004–2005). Wave 2 was chosen, as it was the timeframe during which several states enacted bans on same-sex marriage. The survey found a significant increase between wave 1 and wave 2 for psychiatric disorders (as defined by the *DSM-IV*) in states that had banned gay marriage. Mood disorders had increased by 36.6%, substance abuse disorders by 41.9%, and generalized anxiety disorders by a walloping 248.2%! Comparatively, these disorders did not increase significantly among LGB respondents in states that did not enact constitutional amendments (Hatzenbuehler, McLaughlin, Keyes, & Hasin, 2010).

In Massachusetts, Hatzenbuehler et al. (2011) compared health care use of sexual minority men a year before same-sex marriage became legal in that state with comparable data a year after its legalization. Their results provided evidence that same-sex marriage may improve the mental health of sexual minorities and decrease health care usage and cost.

The American political situation is unique in that there is a "distinction between 'conduct' and 'status,' a distinction that is unknown elsewhere and that led to stigmatizing policies such as 'don't ask, don't tell'" (Smith, 2005, p. 225). For example, despite the finding that the overall majority of Americans favor antidiscrimination policies concerning employment and housing for LGBTI individuals, only 11 states by 2002 had enacted such policies (Smith, 2005). Many societal changes are underway, and it seems imminent that LGBTI people will likely receive equal legal rights within the next generation—not everywhere, but throughout the Western world at least.

Lesbian women continue to experience at least a dual minority status by virtue of their gender and their affectional orientation. In consequence of the discrimination targeted at both statuses, many lesbian couples experience much greater financial stress compared to both opposite-sex couples and gay male couples. This and other factors result in substantial health care disparities when compared to other marginalized groups. Their experiences are also minimized, as researchers appear generally more interested in focusing on gay men's experience and less so on lesbian women's experience.

Recent Research Focused on Canada

A recent article has reviewed developments in Montreal's lesbian Jewish community, including a history of lesbian Jewish groups between the 1970s and 1990s (Margolis, 2005). Another study from Montreal found that sexual minority Francophone women competing in team sports preferred to refer to themselves as "gaie," a French word for *gay* but with a different connotation (at least as used by the women in the study). They constructed the word to mean something more feminine, thus softening the connotation of the word and the positive valence of it as well (Ravel & Rail, 2006).

A study of 197 LGB participants (90 female, 107 male; age range = 18–63) found that internalized homophobia was positively related to measured depression and anxiety scores (Igartua et al., 2003), adding to our knowledge of the destructive effects internalized homophobia has on the LGB community. For those sexual minority women who require psychological help from psychiatric and mental health settings, some experience a negation of their sexual identities, an avoidance of concerns that affect them, and/or they experience their sexuality as a source of stress in help seeking (Daley, 2010).

Other health conditions have been studied as well, including the sometimes contradictory ways that the lesbian community deals with those living with cancer. While most lesbian women experience tremendous community support, others do report instances of isolation and disconnection linked to fear of cancer and/or exclusion patterns adopted in some lesbian communities (Sinding, Grassau, & Barnoff, 2007). Some lesbian women with cancer experienced homophobia in the medical community, including being denied standard care or having aspects of their sexual identity and the social context of their illness dismissed (Sinding, Barnoff, & Grassau, 2004).

There are also strong links between the stigma that LGB youth experience and their likelihood of becoming involved in teen pregnancy (Saewyc, Poon, Homma, & Skay, 2008). A study from British Columbia found that rural sexual minority girls were less likely to experience dating violence but were more likely to have early sex and to abuse substances, while the rural sexual minority boys were more likely to report suicidal behaviors and pregnancy involvement compared to their urban peers (Poon & Saewyc, 2009). Acting out is often viewed in psychology as a response to stress that is not being managed well.

Boon and Alderson (2009) looked at sexual minority women who were married to men in the past. Other research by Peters (2009) found that the representation of lesbian characters in the television series *Queer as Folk* was rated by some viewers as an embarrassment and like a parody, while other viewers commented on the accuracy and realism of the portrayals. One interpretation of these divergent opinions is in realizing that there is not *one* lesbian identity—instead, there are *lesbian identities*. All people construct their own identities based on many conscious and unconscious factors.

Nelson (1999) found that of those female same-sex couples who are raising children, there are differences between their experiences of family building and family life, depending on whether the children were conceived within a prior heterosexual relationship or during the lesbian relationship, generally through donor insemination. Perinatal depression may be more common among sexual minority women, although replication of these findings is needed (Ross, Steele, Goldfinger, & Strike, 2007). One possible explanation of these findings is that compared to heterosexual women, sexual minority women are more likely to lack social support, particularly from their families of origin, and they may experience increased stress due to homophobic attitudes and discrimination from others (Ross, 2005). For those female same-sex couples who decide to adopt, it is experienced as a stressful process that may have long-term mental health effects (Ross et al., 2008).

An interesting study by Poulin, Gouliquer, and Moore (2009) found with sexual minority women who were discharged from the Canadian military for reasons of homosexuality before 1992 (note: In 1992, being openly gay or lesbian identified became legal in the Canadian military), their reports of relentless military surveillance, risk assessments, and need to hide their identities led to psychological, physical, and social effects. These were described by the researchers as similar to the sequelae caused by torture.

A recent book chapter described the development beginning in 1997 of a community-building program for LGBTI youth in Toronto called *Supporting Our Youth* (Lepischak, 2004). Another interesting study looked at the physical features of two bathhouses in Canada that open themselves up periodically for women who have sex with women (Hammers, 2009).

There are two books that may be of interest to students interested in reading more about the lesbian experience in Canada. The titles include *The Romance of Transgression in Canada* (Waugh, 2006) and *Lesbians in Canada* (Stone, 1990).

Recent Research Focused on Other Societies

Chow and Cheng (2010) commented that little is known about Asian lesbian women. Their study compared a sample of lesbian women living in mainland China ($N = 244$) with another sample living in Hong Kong ($N = 234$). Results indicated that there continues to be cultural stigma attached to homosexuality, and the cultural practice is for parents to shame their children for having a homosexual orientation. To come out as lesbian in China (and, to a lesser extent, in Hong Kong) is to bring dishonor to both themselves and their families. Chow and Cheng stated that "there is still much prejudice against individuals with same-sex orientation, especially in mainland China" (Chow & Cheng, 2010, p. 94). The lesbian women who had the weakest and most negative lesbian identities were also the most likely to *not* disclose their identities in both China and Hong Kong (Chow & Cheng, 2010).

In mainland China, most lesbian organizations operate secretly, they are not strong, and they are highly dependent on the Internet to sustain themselves (Chen & Chen, 2006). Shanghai has perhaps the most vibrant lesbian communities in China, but the situation there remains conflictual. Lesbian women often have problems with family, and they face a continuing expectation to marry and bear children, examples of the continuing hegemonic heterosexuality expected of Chinese individuals (Kam, 2006).

While the tolerance level for same-sex-oriented individuals has increased in Hong Kong over the past 10 years, it "remains far from ideal" (To, 2004, p. 65). Nonheterosexual individuals there have higher rates of depression, generalized anxiety disorder, eating disorders, alcohol problems, and attention deficit hyperactivity disorder compared to their heterosexual counterparts (Frisell, Lichtenstein, Rahman, & Langstrom, 2010).

Lesbian communities remain invisible in Japan (Kamano, 2005), and so do lesbian women in general (Horie, 2006), despite Japan's portrayal of being tolerant toward homosexuality (Horie, 2006). There is strong activism occurring there to make lesbian women visible (Horie, 2006). Suicidality and self-harm are serious problems among sexual minorities in Japan, particularly adolescents and those in their early 20s. This has also been linked to both the homophobic environment there and the economic decline (DiStefano, 2008).

Most Singaporeans have negative attitudes toward lesbian women and gay men, and they are rather intolerant of media portrayals of homosexuality (Detenber et al., 2007). In Jakarta, Wieringa (2007) reported that lesbian couples continue to ascribe to the butch–femme pattern, a relationship configuration that has become much less popular in the West. Lesbian women and gay men contend with a country in which both Muslim fundamentalism and economic liberalism are growing.

In Thailand, lesbian studies in universities seem to be flourishing, yet most Thai people reject the words *lesbian* and *lesbian studies* because these words are seen as Western constructions that oversexualize the lives of women in same-sex relationships (similar to why the LGBTI community does not like the word *homosexual* when used as a noun). Thai scholars, when they write or speak about lesbian women, refer to those women who love women (WWLW) in countries (such as the United States) other than Thailand! Consequently, it is more often the case that non–Thai scholars write about WWLW in Thailand (Enteen, 2007).

For WWLW in Thailand, there are many resources available, including several bars in Bangkok that have special nights dedicated just for them. There are at least three social/activist organizations. Enteen (2007) suggests that Thai WWLW will develop their own language, community, and identity—one that may look a little different from the Western construction.

Whitam and his colleagues (Whitam, Daskalos, & Mathy, 1994; Whitam, Daskalos, Sobolewski, & Padilla, 1998; Whitam & Mathy,

1991) compared female homosexuality among four countries: the United States, Peru, Brazil, and the Philippines. These researchers concluded that of the four countries, the United States was likely the least tolerant of homosexual men and women, while the Philippines was the most tolerant. Whitam and his colleagues also found evidence that while lesbian sexuality often began in childhood, this was least obvious in the United States and most noticeable in the other three countries.

Internationally, the central theme of the published research is that prejudice, discrimination, homonegativity, homophobia, marginalization, and/or oppression are alive and well to varying degrees throughout the world. Hegemonic heterosexuality has also been written about in Chile, and lesbian women there continue to face the never-ending fear of discrimination (Herrera, 2009). Many LGB adults in a study from Mexico (Ortiz-Hernandez & Granados-Cosme, 2006) report that they suffered violence during their childhood and adolescence, but mostly because they failed to live up to prevailing gender norms. University students in Turkey also hold negative attitudes toward lesbian women but especially toward gay men (Gelbal & Duyan, 2006).

LGB individuals experience high levels of mental disorders in the United Kingdom, and discrimination is speculated to be a causal factor (Warner et al., 2004). Similar findings have been found in the Netherlands from data derived from the Dutch National Survey (Sandfort, Bakker, Schellevis, & Vanwesenbeeck, 2006), although these researchers note that further exploration is needed to explain why. This is surprising given that Europe boasts a reputation for holding more tolerant attitudes toward gay and lesbian individuals than does the United States (Watzlawik, 2004). Children in the Netherlands raised by 78 planned lesbian families were more open about growing up in a lesbian family, reported less homophobia, and experienced fewer emotional and behavioral problems compared to children from 74 planned lesbian families in the United States (Bos, Gartrell, van Balen, Peyser, & Sandfort, 2008).

The development of lesbianism in India has had much in common with the West, but with a couple of differences. First, India has seen examples of same-sex-couple suicide. Nearly all the couples are female, lower-middle-class, young, and without any contact with lesbian or women's organizations. Some attempted to get marriage licenses and failed. India's first national gay-lesbian magazine was printed in 1990, and around 1993, a group in Delhi began organizing annual film festivals. The Internet has served to boost communications, linking South Asian lesbian women across the world (Vanita, 2007).

Polders, Nel, Kruger, and Wells (2008) demonstrated that hate speech in Gauteng, South Africa, is linked with reports of lower self-esteem with lesbian individuals. The extent of hate speech is also a significant predictor of depression in lesbian people there. Black lesbian women in South Africa also experience stress and trauma from fearing that they will become victims of rape and violence (Arndt & Hewat, 2009).

More lesbian women are making a choice and becoming parents in Australia (Rawsthorne, 2009). A sample of children (ages 8 to 12) raised in the Netherlands by two moms reported low levels of stigmatization (Bos & Van Balen, 2008). While boys more often reported that they felt excluded by peers, girls more often reported that other children gossiped about their family constellation. Bos and Van Balen (2008) concluded that children raised by two moms would benefit from meeting other children raised in similar families.

Another study from the UK found that 18 students (ages 12–16) raised by two moms did not differ significantly from those with opposite-sex parents or the general student population in terms of (a) reported victimization, (b) psychological health, (c) their general life concerns, and (d) their use of familial and peer supports (Rivers, Poteat, & Noret, 2008). However, these 18 participants were less likely to use school-based supports compared to the other students (Rivers et al., 2008).

A study out of New Zealand found that LGB individuals ($N = 2{,}269$) who report not having a religion experienced more support from their families and their same-sex partners compared to those raised by Christians. Furthermore, those reporting no religion were also happier about their sexual identity (Henrickson, 2007).

Unsurprisingly, LGB people with disabilities also want to develop sexual and intimate relationships. In a United Kingdom study, participants expressed their need and desire to be loved by a significant other; however, their accounts were mostly ones of isolation, loneliness, and depression (Abbott & Burns, 2007).

Lastly, there is growing awareness in Australia of the aging gay and lesbian population (Hughes, 2009), although services for aging lesbian women investigated in a study in Victoria, Australia, found that their identities and needs were not addressed by service providers (Phillips & Marks, 2007). Fokkema and Kuyper (2009) used data from two sources in the Netherlands and found that LGB elders did report higher levels of loneliness and lesser levels of social connectedness compared to heterosexual elders. They were less involved with their families and they were less likely to attend church as well.

Common Concerns Facing This Group and Counseling Considerations

Roleplay Scenarios

[*Note:* Suggested assessment and intervention strategies for the four roleplays below can be found in Appendix B. Before going there, roleplay in dyads with one of you acting as the counselor and the other as the counselee. If a roleplay is not possible, work individually in writing out a list of your suggestions.]

Roleplay #1, Chapter 4. Counseling Lesbian Women

Debbie, age 25, has come to see you for help. She started dating guys when she was 16 and, since then, has probably dated and slept with more than 40 guys. Her boyfriends have lasted anywhere from 2 weeks to 9 months, and she has usually been the one to end it. She is concerned that despite liking many of these guys, she has never felt a special connection or feeling of romantic love for any of them. Recently she has met Karen, and she notices that her heart seems to beat faster every time they get together. She can hardly keep her mind from thinking about Karen, and she is beginning to wonder what sex would be like with her. Although the idea of being intimate with a woman is not frightening to Debbie, she is surprised by her feelings and questions whether she could develop an actual relationship with another woman.

Roleplay #2, Chapter 4. Counseling Lesbian Women

Susan, age 46, has come to see you for help. She has been in a relationship with Ellen, age 42, for the past 10 years. Susan was previously married to a man, and she has two teenage boys (Mark and Shane) from that marriage, ages 14 and 16. The boys live with Susan and Ellen, and it has become difficult for them to take Mark and Shane out with them. Mark and Shane feel embarrassed to be seen with them. Many people assume Susan and Ellen are a lesbian couple because they fit many of the stereotypes, not to mention they are somewhat demonstrative in public. In addition to this, Susan tells you that she has not been sexually intimate with Ellen for 2 years, and she wants to re-establish a sex life with her.

Roleplay #3, Chapter 4. Counseling Lesbian Youth

Kyla, age 15, has come to see you for help. Her mother has recently become aware that Kyla is having a sexual relationship with Sharon, a 22-year-old open lesbian woman. Kyla tells you that her mom hasn't told her dad because she is concerned about his reaction. Kyla's mom believes Sharon has "recruited" Kyla into this lifestyle, and she wants their relationship to end immediately. If Kyla doesn't act, she will be told to leave home. Although Kyla could live with Sharon, she doesn't want to because of what her peers at school will think. Kyla hasn't told anybody at school about her relationship.

Roleplay #4, Chapter 4. Counseling Lesbian Youth

Malani, age 16, has come to see you for help. She is really struggling with her deep attractions to girls and her absence of attraction to boys. Malani is Muslim, and her faith is not accepting of homosexual activity. Malani's parents have already got eyes on Ahmed, a guy they want her to marry eventually. Malani has met him, but she is not attracted to him. She is attracted to Ellen, a Caucasian 16-year-old in her class at school. Ellen has already shown interest in Malani and wants her to come over to her home when her parents aren't there. Malani is pretty sure that Ellen wants sex because she has told Malani that she has had sex with girls before. Malani's feelings of guilt are eating her up, and she feels desperate.

How Would *You* Help This Person?

You are working as a professional counselor. Becky, age 24, comes to see you alone at first because of several problems she is experiencing. She tells you that she struggles with fully accepting herself as a lesbian woman, despite the fact that she has always had strong sexual attractions for young women and is simply not attracted to guys. As you collect her history, you find out that she was raised within a strict Catholic family. Her mother and father have disowned her and have told her she is not welcome back at home unless she renounces her homosexuality and her female partner, Sara, whom she has been involved with for the past 4 years. Becky and Sara have lived together now for about 18 months.

Becky has a lot to unload on you. You find out that through her adolescence, she was prone to cutting herself, which on two occasions led to hospital visits for slashed wrists. Thankfully, you discover that this behavior ended shortly after meeting Sara. Becky's bigger concerns right now are twofold: (a) She is deeply bothered by her estrangement from her family and her spiritual community, and (b) she doesn't believe Sara is happy with their sex life. You ask Becky which concern she wants to begin working on first, and she tells you her relationship with Sara is most important because she is afraid she will lose her if something doesn't change. Consequently, you ask Becky to bring Sara with her to the next session if possible.

A week later, you bring both of them into your office. Sara is a beautiful young woman, and you find out she just turned 22. Sara tells you that they used to have a fairly active sex life, but everything

(Continued)

(Continued)

seemed to change after they began living together. Increasingly, Becky rebukes Sara's advances, and Sara has become reticent about even trying anymore. Sara tells you that it was never easy to be the one who always had to make the approach in the first place. After all, she never learned to be sexually assertive from her family of origin, either.

You ask, "How often do the two of you have sex?" Becky retorts, "I guess that depends on what you mean by sex. We are physically intimate every single day." Sara chimes in, "Yeah, that's true, but I want more than just back rubs and endless kissing. When was the last time we got into tribbing (a form of sex involving a woman rubbing her vulva against her partner's body for sexual stimulation) or had oral sex, for that matter? I'm sure it has been at least 6 months, Becky. That saddens me because I love you so, so deeply."

As you listen carefully to Becky and Sara, you are impressed by how connected they are in every other aspect of their lives. Their communication is deep, meaningful, and reflective, they do not struggle much with power issues, and aside from Sara's angst in wanting more sex, you observe that there appears to be no tension between the two of them. Quite the contrary, in fact—these two seem like perfect mates that never argue!

The story deepens. You also discover that Sara is polyamorous, and Becky appears to be completely fine with this. Sara has two other women she sees periodically. Although Sara maintains that these connections are mostly friendships, you are also told that Sara does enjoy engaging in sexual activity with both of them.

There you have it: Becky has become largely asexual with Sara, Sara wants more sex than Becky is providing, and although Sara is having sex with two other women with Becky's awareness, tolerance, and possibly even acceptance of this, Becky remains afraid that Sara will leave her if her asexuality continues. Sara is playing it cool and is giving you the impression that although she would like more sex with Becky and that she is frustrated by this, she is okay with getting sex from her two outside relationships. Sara tells both of you that she is seriously contemplating ending her relationship with Becky.

Note—Remember to view clients within their environmental contexts, keeping in mind societal, parental/familial, cultural/spiritual, and peer influences. Specifically, become aware of the impact that the following influences have and continue to have in your clients' lives: race, language, religion and spirituality, gender, familial migration history, affectional orientation, age and cohort, physical and mental capacities, socioeconomic situation and history, education, and history of traumatic experience.

1. What defines this person's environment, past and present?
2. Who is this person sitting in front of me, taking into account environmental and personal characteristics?
3. What defines the problem that he or she is presenting within his or her multicultural milieu?

Lesbian women seek out counseling services more often than heterosexual women (Eubanks-Carter, Burckell, & Goldfried, 2005; Twist, Murphy, Green, & Palmanteer, 2006). Consequently, it is likely that counselors will have lesbian women as clients throughout their careers.

This does not mean, however, that lesbian women are inherently more disturbed psychologically. Most psychological research—particularly until recently—has focused on the weaknesses of various groups instead of on their strengths (Collins & Oxenbury, 2010). Researchers look for differences more than similarities between groups of people. When researchers compare one group to another group, the ones with the marginalized voice (in this case, LGBTI persons) often appear less functional and/or less healthy than those who share the dominant discourse (i.e., the dominant culture).

It is important to keep in mind that when lesbian women do experience psychological pain, it is more often the result of socio-political pressures (i.e., the homophobic and heterosexist environments in which they live) than from intrapsychic conflicts (Collins & Oxenbury, 2010). Lesbian women carry an added minority stress compared to gay men: They also face sexism. Consequently, they belong to at least two minority groups (Walker & Prince, 2010) and sometimes more (e.g., a woman of color with a disability).

Furthermore, many problems are the result of several dynamics occurring simultaneously in a client's life. For example, a woman who develops a substance dependency problem may also experience deep levels of self-loathing because of her internalized homophobia, and the two working together lead her to develop relationship problems, inhibited sexual desire, and depression. They may also experience a fragmented identity, given that fewer lesbian women self-disclose their sexual identities at work compared to gay men (Fassinger, 1995). The more places one is expected to pass as heterosexual, the more likely one's identity will feel and/or be fragmented.

The theories and intervention methods focused on heterosexual individuals have, for the most part, simply been applied to LGBTI individuals without a great deal of consideration for their appropriateness and/or efficacy. This is also true for gay and lesbian couples counseling (Iasenza, 2000; Spitalnick & McNair, 2005). Further to this, studies of gay male relationships have also been generalized to lesbian relationships (Rivett, 2001). Counselors need to be both affirming and sensitive to LGBTI clients, and those working with lesbian women also must have a good understanding of women's needs in general and their unique needs as well.

Some general suggestions, according to Pixton's (2003) research, are that affirming and sensitive counseling to LGB clients will include the following:

1. The counselor communicates a nonpathological view of homosexuality.
2. The counselor provides a space that allows full exploration of sexuality.
3. The counselor has specific knowledge and awareness of the issues that affect LGB individuals and is comfortable with exploring sexuality.
4. The counselor does not experience prejudice that compromises his or her ability to fully connect with LGB clients.
5. The counselor acts as a positive role model for his or her own sexuality group and enables LGB clients to be themselves fully in the relationship.
6. The counselor is fully himself or herself in the relationship. (adapted from p. 214)

More specifically, Browning, Reynolds, and Dworkin (1991) recommended feminist therapy as an excellent approach to use with both lesbian and bisexual women. The central tenets of feminist therapy include (a) the notion that the personal is political, (b) a deep valuing and respect for creating equal relationships, and (c) the acceptance that there are multiple realities (Lalande & Laverty, 2010).

Like LGBTI-affirmative therapy, feminist theory is more an approach to counseling people than it is a well-formulated set of constructs. It questions many of the traditional counseling approaches by placing an emphasis on the societal oppression of women in general (and of other minority groups as well) and the power differential that is always present between the counselor and the client. LGBTI affirmative counseling and feminist therapy can easily be integrated in working with LGBTI clients, as the two approaches are complementary and compatible with each other.

This section now moves into looking at common concerns facing this group and counseling considerations for lesbian women. These include (a) career concerns, (b) identity concerns, (c) major depression and suicide risk, (d) weight problems, (e) substance abuse problems, (f) relationship problems, and (g) parenthood issues.

Career Concerns

While many lesbian women choose careers in which they can be honest, others want jobs at which most would not suspect their sexual identity. It becomes a form of *passing*, which allows LGBTI individuals to remain secretive (Croteau, Anderson, Distefano, & Kampa-Kokesch, 2000). Three other strategies are possible: (a) *covering*, which means attempting to be perceived as heterosexual without trying to "fake" it; (b) *implicitly out*, which means being honest while still withholding the label of LGBTI; and (c) *explicitly out*, which involves directly disclosing one's sexual identity to others.

The degree to which LGBTI individuals disclose their sexual identities at work depends upon two factors: their developmental stage regarding identity formation and their perceived level of heterosexism in their work environment. These two factors play a significant role in the career development of queer individuals (Chojnacki & Gelberg, 1994).

Regarding the stage of identity development according to Cass's (1979, 1996) model, a lesbian woman may be at any of her six stages: (a) identity confusion, (b) identity comparison, (c) identity tolerance, (d) identity acceptance, (e) identity pride, and (f) identity synthesis. Someone at the identity tolerance phase will likely want to keep her sexual identity secretive, while someone in the identity pride stage may be inclined to disclose whatever the cost, while someone at the identity synthesis stage will likely discern the actual work environment before making an informed decision.

Regarding work environment, Chojnacki and Gelberg (1994) suggested four levels of work environment heterosexism that can be applied to all LGBTI individuals:

1. *Overt Discrimination*—The work environment has both formal and informal policies that discriminate against LGBTI individuals. The American military before "don't ask, don't tell" is a good example of this level.
2. *Covert Discrimination*—While these organizations do not have a formal policy against hiring or firing LGBTI individuals, there remains informal discrimination at the work setting. An open LGBTI person would not be hired or promoted by the employer or manager. The best example here is the "don't ask, don't tell" policy that existed in the U.S. military for several years.
3. *Tolerance*—These employers have formal antidiscrimination policies protecting those with different sexual orientations. They do not provide any additional support for LGBTI persons, such as insurance coverage for same-sex partners.
4. *Affirmation*—These organizations have implemented formal antidiscrimination policies and other forms of support for LGBTI employees. LGBTI employees are valued for their diversity. Some examples include having same-sex partner benefits, offering a LGBTI support group or club, and providing training for employees about sexual diversity.

Encourage lesbian clients to assess a potential work environment before considering employment. Three practical methods include:

1. Seek out resources that identity lesbian affirmative work environments. As mentioned in Chapter 3, the Human Rights Campaign publishes many resources that will be helpful to LGBTI individuals in assessing their work environments, such as the annual Corporate Equality Index (the latest version of the Index can be found through a link at www.hrc.org/resources/ for a list of workplace resources).

2. Talk with other lesbian women about their experience with a specific employer.
3. If appropriate, ask the employer about support for open lesbian employees (Croteau & Hedstrom, 1993).

If the third choice is appropriate, suggest that your client consider asking the following questions:

1. Do you have open LGBTI individuals working here? How do others, especially the management, receive them?
2. Do open LGBTI employees bring their partners to work socials?
3. At your employer's Christmas party, do LGBTI individuals dance with their partners?

Does that mean LGBTI individuals should avoid choosing careers because they will likely face an unfriendly work environment? Given that career satisfaction is one of the most important factors that create happiness and provide meaning to a person's life, and also given that greater tolerance and acceptance of LGBTI individuals appears to be steadily increasing, the decision may be more of to what extent should a LGBTI person disclose his or her identity in a particular work environment than not considering a career choice at all. Nonetheless, LGBTI clients must be the ones who ultimately decide on weighing the many factors to be considered before choosing a career and then ultimately working in it somewhere.

Another helpful suggestion when working with LGBTI individuals is to point out LGBTI role models who have been successful. This can be particularly helpful if you are able to find a role model(s) within the field(s) your client is considering. A helpful list with photographs of some such role models can be found at www.queerattitude.com/society/famous.php. A Google search may reveal individuals who identify as LGBTI regarding specific career choices.

Identity Concerns

Current research offers strong support for the idea that women's sexuality is much more "fluid" and malleable than men's (McElwain et al., 2009). This seems particularly true for sexual minority women (Diamond, 2008). Consequently, the confusion that women may confront in attempting to understand their sexualities may be more difficult than it is for sexual minority men. While not labeling one's sexuality may suffice for some clients who are comfortable with the ambiguity this may create in their lives (Ohnstad, 2009), this may not be a soothing place for people who like to have decisions settled in their lives, including that of their sexual identity.

While Savin-Williams (2008) has found in his research that many young people have adopted the postmodern view and now refuse or resist giving themselves sexual identity labels, Russell, Clarke, and Clary (2009) analyzed data from 2,558 California secondary school students (collected over a 3-year period). In the sample, 1,581 defined as heterosexual/heterosexual, 858 defined as nonheterosexual, and 119 did not answer this question (62.7% female, 34.6% male, 0.7% unspecified gender). Of the 858 who defined as nonheterosexual, 71% of these youth preferred to give themselves traditional sexual identity labels, despite being given the choice to provide themselves an alternate label like "queer." Furthermore, another 13% of the nonheterosexual students reported that they were still "questioning" their sexuality. In effect, the vast majority of LGBTI youth would appear to still prefer to use traditional labels to define themselves. While some lesbian and bisexual women still define themselves by the traditional labels of "butch" and "femme," few differences have been found in the sexual identity formation process of women who identify as butch or femme. Differences have been found between women who identify as lesbian or bisexual (Rosario, Schrimshaw, Hunter, & Levy-Warren, 2009).

Another point worth mentioning is that the LGBTI identities of an individual often become a defining feature ascribed to them by others (e.g., "He is gay," "She is lesbian"). Due to the difficulty of self-identifying as LGBTI, a consequence of societal homophobia and heterosexism, LGBTI people themselves may come to overemphasize this one identity over all others that they possess (Reynolds, 2003). Even within the most popular model of gay/lesbian identity development—that by Cass (1979, 1996)—overemphasizing one's gay/lesbian identity was hypothesized to occur during stage 5 (identity pride). One still had another step to achieve before getting to a place of having a positive gay/lesbian identity: stage 6 (identity synthesis).

Being aware of the Cass (1979, 1996) model may be helpful to counselors working with lesbian clients who are struggling with identity issues. It is also important to be aware that not all women follow the stages in a linear fashion: There may be back-and-forth movement at any stage in a sexual minority women's life, and while these changes occur, sexual identity labels may change as well.

One should encourage sexual minority women to maintain flexibility regarding their sexual identity labels, particularly when they are young and/or in a period of sexual exploration. It may also mean helping some to live with a degree of ongoing ambiguity (Ohnstad, 2009).

Like most men, many lesbian and bisexual women will embrace an identity label and stick with it so long as life circumstances (such as falling in love with a man) don't threaten it. These will not likely be the clients who end up in your office trying to answer the question, "Am I a lesbian woman?" For counselors who want to use a psychometrically sound scale to measure the extent that their clients have achieved a solid identity status, the Measure of Sexual Identity Exploration and Commitment scale is recommended (see Worthington, Navarro, Savoy, & Hampton, 2008).

Major Depression and Suicide Risk

Women are more prone to developing major depressive disorder compared to men, and LGBTI individuals are more likely to develop mood and anxiety disorders compared to the heterosexual majority (King, Semlyen, et al., 2008). Women, whether self-identified as lesbian or bisexual, have histories more commonly associated with childhood maltreatment and attempted suicide (Corliss, Cochran, Mays, Greenland, & Seeman, 2009). African American women who are sexually active with women report levels of psychological distress, including major depression, that greatly exceed population norms for African American heterosexual women (Mays, Cochran, & Roeder, 2003). The results from the Mays and colleagues (2003) study underscore the vulnerability of African American women who are facing the triple stigma of their ethnicity, their affectional orientation, and their gender.

Evidence from several countries reveals that LGBTI youth have elevated rates of suicide (McDermott, Roen, & Scourfield, 2008), and the rates are particularly high with Aboriginal (e.g., American Indian) gay and lesbian youth (Wilson, 2007). Interestingly, it appears that adolescents with LGB identities and those who are still questioning are at greater risk for suicidality compared to youth who define as heterosexual, but youth who experience same-sex attraction and/or engage in same-sex behavior but maintain a heterosexual identity do not (Zhao, Montoro, Igartua, & Thombs, 2010).

Many factors can lead to a major depressive episode. The causes of depression are vast, including intrapsychic (e.g., coping resources, perceptions of stress, reliance on defense mechanisms, psychological conflicts), interpsychic influences (e.g., unresolved and ongoing relationship difficulties, homophobic and heterosexist environment, living with other depressed individuals), and biological and genetic factors (e.g., hypothyroidism, hypertension medication side effect, genetic predisposition).

Arnow and Post (2010) stated that although the median length of a depressive episode is 2 to 5 months, a significant percentage experience an episode for 2 years or longer. In fact, major depressive disorder (MDD) is now seen as being a recurring condition that is also chronic in some sufferers.

The Canadian Network for Mood and Anxiety Disorders carefully reviews and evaluates ongoing research that is occurring worldwide concerning the clinical guidelines for depression in adults. Most recently (Parikh et al., 2009), their report concludes that cognitive behavior therapy (CBT) and interpersonal therapy (IPT) continue to have the most evidence for their efficacy (i.e., they have Level 1 status), and both during the acute and the maintenance phases of MDD. Several therapies (i.e., acceptance and commitment therapy, motivational interviewing, mindfulness-based cognitive therapy, and psychodynamic therapy) do not have sufficient evidence as acute treatments for depression.

In working with lesbian clients, counselors trained in CBT will likely focus on the beliefs that underlie varying depths of internalized homophobia that may be triggers for major depression. Those trained in IPT will likely focus on coping with the dysfunctional relationships that are created when others treat lesbian individuals homophobically and unfairly. If the client is in an intimate relationship, her style of communicating and externalizing internalized homophobia will likely need exploring as well.

There is usually a building-up period before a person attempts or commits suicide (Sanchez, 2001). As it is commonly stated, while three times more women attempt suicide, three times as many men actually die from it (McWhirter, McWhirter, McWhirter, & McWhirter, 2004). The suicide rate for children between the ages of 10 and 14 increased by 196% in the 15 years leading up to 2002 (Poland & Lieberman, 2002). This is especially disturbing given the results of the meta-analysis reported earlier that established that LGBTI individuals are twice as likely to make suicide attempts compared to their heterosexual counterparts (King, Semlyen, et al., 2008). Also troubling is knowing that even today, there do not exist empirically supported interventions to help prevent suicidal behavior (Linehan, 2008).

Sanchez (2001) has developed an easy-to-use risk factor model for assessing suicide risk. It is based on the premise that suicidal behaviors emerge through an interaction of risk factors (e.g., experiencing major mental illness, substance abuse) and protective factors (e.g., familial and social support, satisfying social life). His guidelines are published in Sanchez (2001; see his Appendices A and B).

Weight Problems

On the surface, the finding that lesbian women are generally more satisfied with their bodies compared to heterosexual women (Morrison et al., 2004) is encouraging. Despite this, however, it does not appear to lead to appreciable differences between the prevalence of eating disorders between lesbian, bisexual, and heterosexual women (Feldman & Meyer, 2007; Share & Mintz, 2002). Only heterosexual and bisexual men have low rates of eating disorders.

Lesbian women have been found in most studies (Bowen, Balsam, & Ender, 2008) to have a higher prevalence of being overweight and/or obese compared to other women, placing them at greater risk for weight-related health problems (Boehmer et al., 2007; Bowen et al., 2008). Lesbian women tend to exercise less than heterosexual women as well (Brittain et al., 2006).

The American College of Preventive Medicine issued a practice policy statement in 2001 that stated,

> there is conclusive evidence that obesity is associated with increased morbidity and mortality . . . Weight reduction, at least in the short term, has been shown in small prospective cohort and randomized controlled trials to confer beneficial health effects. However, there is no convincing evidence for the consistent effectiveness of any single, currently used weight-loss method. (Nawaz & Katz, 2001, p. 73)

For most people, much of the above is obvious. What is also obvious is that to lose weight, one needs to reduce the amount of daily calories consumed and/or increase the number of calories needed burned each day through exercise. What is not so obvious to counselors working with overweight lesbian clients is whether they should introduce weight-loss strategies if the client doesn't make the request.

Chrisler (1989) argues that feminist counselors should not generally offer weight-loss counseling. Evidence-based weight-loss programs are behavioral (Krukowski, Harvey-Berino, & West,

2010), and consequently the methods represent highly directive interventions offered by a counselor in the "expert" role. These two aspects of behavioral counseling are both antithetical to feminist practice. Consequently, if considering using behavioral methods with lesbian clients, it is imperative that this is something they want and they collaborate throughout its execution.

Buckroyd and Rother (2007) found that 80% of obese women who attended their weight-management groups were unable to maintain weight loss. They also acknowledged that between 30 and 50% overeat because they are emotionally and psychologically distressed. Given that many LGBTI individuals suffer the added burden of minority stress (Kelleher, 2009), one might hypothesize that the reason many lesbian women are overweight is a consequence. The actual reasons may be far more complex than this. Given that most lesbian women are also feminists and it is generally men who expect their sexual partners to be suitably thin, losing weight may be negatively viewed as "buying into" a patriarchal structure.

Substance Abuse Problems

Lesbian women tend to abuse alcohol at higher rates than heterosexual women (Dilley et al., 2010; Rosario, 2008; Wilsnack et al., 2008). While bisexual individuals have the highest rates of alcohol abuse (Wilsnack et al., 2008), alcohol abuse will be covered in this chapter, as it also affects lesbian women disproportionately. A study of 2,011 lesbian and bisexual women found that both groups also reported elevated levels of illegal drug use that caused them several difficulties (Corliss, Grella, Mays, & Cochran, 2006).

A study by Amadio and Chung (2004) found that internalized homophobia in sexual minority women was related to lifetime use of alcohol, marijuana, and cigarettes, as well as monthly use of marijuana. Also, when LGBTI individuals enter substance abuse treatment programs, they tend to have more severe substance abuse problems and greater psychopathology compared to heterosexual individuals entering treatment (Cochran & Cauce, 2006).

A qualitative study found that many lesbian and gay individuals do not perceive that their needs are met in addiction treatment programs (Matthews, Lorah, & Fenton, 2006). LGB clients who seek treatment for addiction have reported that the most successful rehabilitation experiences have occurred in settings in which they felt the programs were LGBTI affirmative (Matthews & Selvidge, 2005). A more recent study found that when LGB clients could be open and honest about their sexual identities, more positive treatment outcomes generally followed, including higher program completion rates, higher satisfaction ratings, enhanced feelings of support, and greater connectedness to the program (Senreich, 2010).

Kasl (2002) stated that in comparison to working with heterosexual women with substance abuse problems, there are additional dynamics and concerns that need to be considered when working with lesbian women. Kasl's suggestions focus on material that has been covered elsewhere in this chapter (e.g., basic knowledge of lesbian issues, internalized homophobia, lack of societal support). Essentially, treating lesbian women with addiction problems is best implemented by people with expertise in substance abuse treatment who also have the requisite attitudes/beliefs, knowledge, and skills to work effectively with lesbian women.

Relationship Problems

As noted earlier, a relationship problem that is sometimes experienced by lesbian couples is hypoactive sexual desire (i.e., *bed death*). Hall (1987) wrote that hypoactive sexual desire (HSD) and discrepancy between the sexual desire of the partners are the problems most commonly reported by lesbian couples.

The concept of HSD is commonly mentioned in the literature, and it does have empirical support (Spitalnick & McNair, 2005). Although the frequency of sex usually diminishes over time in relationships, with most married opposite-sex couples having sex on average about seven times a month (Laumann et al., 1994), lesbian couples experiencing HSD may stop having sex altogether (Nichols, 1982).

Iasenza (2000) suggested, however, that counselors be careful about overinterpreting sexual phenomena. It is imperative that counselors refrain from looking at lesbian (and gay) couples through a heterosexual lens (Igartua, 1998). The average amount of sex married heterosexual couples have has little bearing on anything. It is important to not look at LGBTI couples and believe their sex lives ought to look the same as those of heterosexual couples. Even with heterosexual couples, the amount of sex the partners have varies tremendously both within their own relationships and in comparison to other heterosexual couples.

Furthermore, as Trotter and Alderson (2007) demonstrated, along with other researchers before them, what constitutes "having sex" varies between individuals. Many young people would not include oral sex in their definition of having had sex. Compared to other couple types, lesbian couples engage in more nongenital contact, such as cuddling and hugging (Laumann et al., 1994). Additionally, HSD is not an inevitable outcome for any relationship type (Boon & Alderson, 2009; Nichols & Shernoff, 2007). Generally speaking, lesbian couples who experience high levels of relationship satisfaction also experience increased sexual arousal for each other, greater pleasure and orgasm, greater sexual satisfaction, and better sexual functioning overall (Tracy & Junginger, 2007). Nonetheless, a recent qualitative study found that 23 of 30 lesbian participants reported that they experienced HSD either in a past or present same-sex relationship (van Rosmalen-Nooijens et al., 2008).

Instead of judging the amount of sex that couples engage in, it is far more important to listen to and collaborate with clients to establish appropriate treatment goals and problems that require intervention. Empowering LGBTI clients is a critical undertaking of counselors (Walker & Prince, 2010). When HSD is a focus of counseling, Hall (1987) stressed that the primary effects of homophobia must be addressed, including the sense that one or both have failed or are fundamentally flawed. Hall then suggested sex therapy that includes four stages: (a) a beginning, (b) a middle during which the problem becomes reframed, (c) inclusion of sensually focused assignments, and (d) termination. Laird (2000) offered more contemporary suggestions regarding how couples and family counseling can be adapted for lesbian couples, including ideas for merging cultural, constructionist, narrative, and feminist approaches.

Another consideration that affects most LGBTI individuals is that when their relationships end, they will likely continue to see this individual again repeatedly in different venues (Reynolds, 2003). In most locales, the LGBTI community is small enough that there is a limited number of social circles, community activities, and bars or nightclubs. Although this eventuality may not be a presenting concern, it does affect the grieving process for many LGBTI clients.

Parenthood Issues

An extensive research base concludes that lesbian women make excellent parents (Goldberg, 2010). A sizeable percentage of lesbian couples are already raising one or more children from previous sexual experiences or relationships with men. Increasingly, lesbian women are becoming impregnated through other means, such as sperm donation and sperm recipiency (Horowitz, Galst, & Elster, 2010). A recent national study found that fewer lesbian couples (and even fewer gay male couples) compared to heterosexual couples state a desire to become parents (Riskind & Patterson, 2010). Of course, this may change dramatically once same-sex marriage becomes legalized throughout the United States.

Regardless of how children are conceived, raising them tends to "out" lesbian women—it is hard to not be noticed by family and friends, at the supermarket, or at the child's school, for example. Being highly visible also brings with it greater exposure to homophobia, discrimination, and minority stress. Furthermore, lesbian mothers may also need help in determining best parenting practices and decision making (e.g., does a male child need adult male role models to grow into a healthy adult?).

When a single lesbian woman or a lesbian couple is raising a child(ren), issues may arise that center on appropriate parenting skills, external homophobia or internalized homophobia of one or more parents or children, and/or concern for the impact that lesbian parenting may have on a child(ren)'s treatment outside the home. As Erwin (2007, p. 99) notes, "lesbian mothers are often excluded from the experiences, wisdom, and folklore shared by heterosexual mothers." Furthermore, they may not receive their own "mothering" and information sharing from *their* mothers if they have been rejected by their family of origin. Consequently, current or future mothers may lack information and support. Erwin's article is recommended reading for providing research-based answers to many of the questions that lesbian women may have regarding parenthood—it is an excellent resource. Another helpful resource, based on a critical ethnography of lesbian mothers' experiences of childbearing, is Renaud (2007).

COUNSELING DIVERSE POPULATIONS

Counseling Individuals With Multiple Nondominant Identity Statuses

Black lesbian women do experience varying degrees of "triple jeopardy" for their statuses of color, gender, and affectional orientation (Bowleg et al., 2003), and they sometimes seek counseling for help with the challenges of managing this (Bridges, Selvidge, & Matthews, 2003). Parks and colleagues (2004) recommended that counselors help lesbian women of color to function effectively within both the lesbian community and the Black community. They suggested six ways of assisting with this: (a) help clients develop positive attitudes toward both groups, (b) encourage them to enhance their knowledge of both groups, (c) enhance their sense of bicultural efficacy, (d) improve their communication ability, (e) teach skills to improve their ability to function in both roles, and (f) encourage them to become grounded within systems of social support.

Counseling Aging Lesbian Women

Regardless of whatever counseling modality is used, counselors must have an awareness of the common concerns of aging lesbian women and couples (Neustifter, 2008). Neustifter (2008) provided several of these in her article. First, many (20–25%) elderly gay and lesbian people are living with a long-term partner. However, many of the social and economic structures are not available to long-term couples who are unmarried (keeping in mind that same-sex couples cannot marry in most U.S. states currently). For example, when one partner dies, the remaining partner is not entitled to federal survivor benefits (i.e., the Social Security income of the higher-benefiting partner) that applies to married heterosexual couples. Other forms of tax relief, such as that from inheritances, are also unavailable to the surviving partner.

Older lesbian couples are likely to have reduced incomes and limited access to government services compared to their heterosexual counterparts. Many lesbian women fear that their money will not last through their lifetime, and Neustifter (2008) provides evidence that this is often true.

As many lesbian women experience homophobic responses from medical providers (especially male doctors), aging lesbian women do not feel that they have the same access to health care services. Elderly lesbian women and gay men have often created close ties to *fictive kin*, which are close friendships that have become like family members. In offering couples or family counseling, elder lesbian women should be asked if they want fictive kin to join them in session (Neustifter, 2008).

Counseling Lesbian Women Living in Rural Communities

Little is known about the experience of LGB individuals who live in rural areas. Research participants state that they value rural living but lack community-based resources (Leedy & Connolly, 2007). Some lesbian women have in fact congregated in rural areas because of their love for the lifestyle (Whitlock, 2009). Rural lesbian youth face several obstacles in their development of a positive identity (Cohn & Hastings, 2010), and results from a Canadian study found that rural sexual minority girls were especially likely to report substance use (Poon & Saewyc, 2009).

Counselors working with rural lesbian girls and women will likely find that feelings of isolation are common (Hastings & Hoover-Thompson, 2011). Lesbian women in rural communities will experience a lack of a visible gay community, a lack of resources and services, and often a heightened degree of stigma due to a conservative political climate and a greater emphasis on fundamentalist religious beliefs (Hastings & Hoover-Thompson, 2011). Recommending networking via the Internet will prove helpful, and depending on many contextual factors, the client may decide eventually to move to a larger center. The counselor may be called upon to help in this decision making.

Counseling Lesbian Students

The two suggestions here apply to LGBTI students in general. Gay–straight alliances (GSAs) are clubs established in grade schools (usually high schools) where students, heterosexual and nonheterosexual, can hang out and receive social support in a safe environment, usually proctored by a school staff member. GSAs are becoming increasingly prevalent across the United States (Fetner & Kush, 2008). Another method that has increased the rate of involvement in postsecondary schooling of LGBTI students is having a mentor system. These have been found to be especially helpful in increasing the educational "resilience" of sexual minority women of color (Gastic & Johnson, 2009). There is no obvious reason why having teacher mentors would not also be helpful at the high school level.

Counseling Lesbian Adolescents

Adolescence is a time of identity development, and those who feel that their identity is marginalized experience worse mental health, have poorer academic performance, and engage in riskier behaviors at higher rates than those who develop "acceptable" identities (Marks, Powell, & Garcia Coll, 2009). For most adolescent girls, the teenage years are a time when they are involved in developing friendships, experiencing sexual feelings, and doing "girl talk." For girls who have disclosed their sexual identities, however, isolation and peer exclusion become likelier possibilities (Bedard & Marks, 2010). Not surprisingly, there is empirical evidence that gay and lesbian adolescents are "especially vulnerable to loneliness" (Martin & D'Augelli, 2003, p. 486).

Lemoire and Chen (2005) contend that person-centered counseling is especially well suited for LGBTI adolescents. They provide six reasons for this:

1. Counselors demonstrate unconditional positive regard, congruence, and empathy.
2. Counselors adopt the subjective view of the client.
3. They encourage the client to focus on her or his own system of evaluation.
4. They emphasize the importance of developing a positive self-concept.
5. They believe in the client's potential to grow.
6. They ensure that the counseling process is client directed.

Lemoire and Chen (2005) also reframed what they saw as the three limitations of person-centered counseling for LGBTI clients. To overcome or at least minimize these limitations, Lemoire and Chen recommended that counselors (a) ensure that they explicitly validate the LGBTI person's identity, (b) conduct a guided risk assessment regarding possible reactions to the client's disclosure, and (c) recommend to LGBTI clients that they become involved in the LGBTI community in an age-appropriate manner.

Resources for This Group

In addition to the resources listed in Chapter 3, some additional ones include the following:

1. The National Gay and Lesbian Taskforce. They are a politically active group that deals with many issues facing the LGBTI community, including advocacy for lesbian women www.thetaskforce.org/).
2. A list of lesbian health resources can be found on the website of the American College of Obstetricians and Gynecologists (http://classic.acog.org/departments/dept_notice.cfm?recno=18&bulletin=4848).
3. The Lesbian Health and Research Center also provides helpful links for lesbian, bisexual, and transgender women (www.lesbianhealthinfo.org/community/resources.html).
4. The University of Washington also lists many national and international organizations and publications that concern LGBTI issues (http://faculty.washington.edu/alvin/gayorg.htm).
5. Several resources are listed under lezpride.tripod.com, including a list of films that will have appeal to many within the LGBTI community (http://lezpride.tripod.com/indexus.html).
6. Several resources for lesbian women living in Canada can be found at windsorpride.com (www.windsorpride.com/cms/Content/lesbian-resources.html).

Limitations, Furthering Research, and Implications for Counselors

Limitations of the Research With This Group

Two tier-1 journals have recently devoted special issues to the problems of conducting research with LGBTI individuals—the *Journal of Lesbian Studies* (*JLS*; 2009, volume 13, issue 2) and the *Journal of Counseling Psychology* (*JCP*; 2009, volume 56, issue 1). *JCP* is the flagship journal of the American Counseling Association. As Mallinckrodt (2009) reported in his introduction to the special issue, the first article published in *JCP* about any LGBTI individuals was about gay men, published in 1956 (3 years after *JCP* was founded). Remarkably, however, it took another 25 years before the second empirical article about LGB persons was published in 1981. Looking through a still larger lens, Mallinckrodt found that in the 40 years between 1956 and 2006, *JCP* had published a mere five articles in total.

The *Canadian Journal of Counselling and Psychotherapy* (*CJCP*) is the flagship journal of the Canadian Counselling and Psychotherapy Association. *CJCP* also publishes LGBTI empirical studies and will soon have a special issue devoted to this topic.

The special issue of *JLS* reminds us that working in the area of sexuality moves us into sensitive issues. Given that sexual minority adolescent girls and women experience a fluid and malleable sexuality, what then defines a lesbian woman (Weston, 2009)? If a woman defines as lesbian today and bisexual 6 months later, and somewhere along the way she participates in an empirical study, where should her results get placed? Also, if we construct a lesbian woman as possessing certain characteristics and traits while not possessing certain other ones, are we not doing the community a disservice by perhaps precluding others from becoming a part of this community who do not fit neatly into the identity boxes that we have created by doing research on the part of their community that researchers can grasp and induce into participating in their studies (Ryan-Flood & Rooke, 2009)? It is a postmodern challenge to conceptualize and define sexual minority populations when labeling is antithetical to its very ideology (Moradi, Mohr, Worthington, & Fassinger, 2009).

Areas Requiring Further Research

The research regarding lesbian youth has suffered from an overemphasis on their pathological characteristics (Kulkin, 2006). Similar to Savin-Williams's (2005) perspective, Kulkin (2006) believes we now need to focus our research endeavors on understanding young lesbian women's resiliency—after all, most are not breaking down emotionally and psychologically in front of us as we see them walk the hallways of our schools and city streets. No, a new ethos has developed, and it is the ethos of identity pride—not in the Cass-ian (1979, 1996) sense, but in this regard: Having a lesbian identity is something to be proud of even when it does not become the only identity status that defines you.

Research with lesbian women will need to remain open to the plethora of possible lesbian sexualities conceivable. Clearly there is not one lesbian identity, assuming that even this identity status is not already overly restrictive. Perhaps researchers would be more accurate to call them sexual minority women and thus provide greater space for the identity diversity and the fluidity that defines them.

Even that may be too restrictive. Are sexual minority women really that much different from heterosexual women? If female sexuality is indeed as fluid and flexible as researchers are now suggesting, does it mean that such fluidity is reserved only for those who, through whatever means, are able to get the special status of "sexual minority" ascribed to their identities? It would seem that a more accurate interpretation is that likely all women have the potential for intimate and sexual same-sex relationships of a deep, meaningful kind. How do we even begin to research that?

Implications for Counselors

Counselors need to be aware that most lesbian women subscribe to a feminist ideology, so counseling approaches that emphasize equality among counselor, client, and others will be most respected and likely assist in creating a positive therapeutic alliance. Female sexuality and male sexuality are vastly different, and generalizations made from working with gay men will not stand up in your work with lesbian women. Women, lesbian and heterosexual, are generally monogamous and prefer to maintain fidelity in this manner. Women often develop same-sex passionate friendships, and for those exploring their sexuality, such friendships often provide a safe medium for doing so. This, however, may also confuse some women given that women's sexuality is much more flexible and fluid than men's.

Research reveals very positive results regarding lesbian relationships, and often lesbian couples report greater relationship satisfaction than do either gay or heterosexual couples. However, many struggle with maintaining an active sex life, an outcome commonly referred to as "lesbian bed death." Counselors need to be sensitive to this topic and discuss as appropriate with lesbian couples.

While lesbian women are less concerned about their weight than men and other women, the drawback to this is that more struggle with being overweight and/or obese compared to other women. Counseling interventions aimed at helping lesbian women become more aware of the health hazards of being overweight followed up by weight-management strategies are sometimes indicated. Lesbian women and especially bisexual women are at increased risk for substance dependence, and assessment and intervention targeted at use of drugs and alcohol may be important.

Exercises

Individual Exercises

1. If you are a female, clip or staple an inverted black triangle on your blouse or jacket so that it is visible to everyone who sees you (Chesler & Zuniga, 1991). Alternatively, attach a small rainbow flag to yourself. Wear it for a day and note your reactions. Depending on your community, do not be naïve and remember to maintain awareness of safety issues when and where relevant.

2. If you are a female, during daytime hours, walk hand-in-hand with a female friend on campus or elsewhere. Again, depending on your community, do not be naïve and remember to maintain awareness of safety issues when and where relevant.

Classroom Exercise

1. In dyads, one student plays the role of a lesbian woman. Begin by introducing yourself to the other student by saying, "My name is . . . , and I self-identify as lesbian." Either the other student decides to ask his or her own questions or instead uses the following. If you are playing the lesbian person, you have the option of not answering any questions you do not want to answer by saying "pass."

a. How long have you identified as lesbian?
b. How many people have you disclosed your lesbian identity to?
c. How do you decide who to tell and who not to?
d. What is it like to tell someone you are a lesbian?
e. Do you plan to have children someday? If yes, how will you make this happen? If no, how do you feel having decided not to have children?
f. What is the hardest part about being a lesbian woman?
g. What is the happiest part about being a lesbian woman?
h. Have you ever felt afraid because you are a lesbian woman?
i. How do you protect yourself from homophobes?
j. What else would you like to tell me about your experience of being a lesbian woman? (this exercise is adapted from Finkel, Storaasli, Bandele, & Schaefer, 2003).

Chapter Summary

As our understanding of sexual minority adolescent girls and women deepens, we are beginning to witness revelations of a most significant order. Lesbian women are women first, and women have developed an uncanny ability to be strong even when they are expected by traditional societal scripts to appear weak. Despite their gender conditioning, women throughout millennia have needed to become resilient in order to cope with patriarchal systems that have tried to subjugate them and still do today throughout most parts of the world.

A lesbian woman navigates a landscape of needing to develop the strength to embrace the finest qualities of androgyny and the contrasts that emerge from this nexus of opposites. In other words, the lesbian woman epitomizes someone who is strong yet nurturant and egalitarian; tough yet deeply loving and profoundly insightful.

Transcending one minority status is more than enough for most people to bear, referring now to the experience of gay men in the previous chapter. But in this chapter, the closets have been opened wider so that you can see how two minority statuses can actually create an individual who is stronger, deeper, and more loving within a gestalt that is greater than the individual parts.

Lesbian women are more likely to experience problems with weight control than other women and men. Together with bisexual women, they also have a higher likelihood of developing substance abuse problems.

Lesbian women usually develop egalitarian relationships with other women, and their relationship quality is generally very high. They are often excellent communicators, and research indicates they often do a better job of parenting than either gay men or heterosexual couples. Women's sexuality is much more flexible and fluid compared to men's, and this can create greater confusion for those who never expected they could develop such strong affinity for another woman.

5

BISEXUAL BOYS AND MEN

CHALLENGING YOUR ATTITUDES AND BELIEFS ABOUT THIS GROUP

1. Have you ever talked about male bisexuality with family members, friends, or both? If so, was it discussed in a positive or negative light?
2. Do you believe that bisexual men really exist, or are they simply gay men who have not come to accept themselves or heterosexual men who want more sex than women care to provide them? What is the basis for your views?
3. If you had or have a son and he turned out to identify as bisexual, how would you react? How would you feel? Would it seem better or worse than if he identified as gay? Why or why not?
4. If a bisexual man was married to a woman, what do you believe would pose difficulties for the couple?
5. How would you react if you were or are male and became aware that you have a strong bisexual orientation? What would be the hardest part for you in discovering this?

Challenging Your Assumptions Questions

1. How do you currently view bisexual men? What is the basis for your views? To what extent would you apply your views to all bisexual men?

2. Do you believe that bisexual men would be more masculine or more feminine compared to gay men? What do you think would account for that?

3. According to the six components of affectional orientation included in the Sexuality Questionnaire (i.e., sexual attraction, sexual fantasies, sexual preference, propensity to fall in love romantically, being in love romantically, and the extent to which one has sexual partners of each gender; see Appendix C), what components do you believe a person should have before a self-definition of bisexual makes sense to you? What is the basis for your belief? Is a male in your definition a bisexual if he has had a few sexual encounters with both genders, either at the same time (a ménage à trois) or on different occasions?

4. How can you tell if a male adolescent or adult defines as bisexual?

5. If you define as heterosexual (reverse this question if you define as gay or lesbian), have you ever had some kind of sexual activity with a member of the same gender?

   (a) If your answer is "yes," what was that experience like for you, considering both the positive and negative aspects of the experience? Would you consider doing this sexual activity again or perhaps other sexual activities with a member of the same sex? Why or why not?

   (b) If your answer is "no," have you ever considered doing so? What has prevented you from pursuing it?

Reflections

[*Note:* Imagine that *you* are the client in these reflections.]

You are a good-looking guy who is popular with women. While you never have a shortage of potential dates, you are confused. Although you find women attractive and sexually desirable, you have also been checking out several guys in college. Naturally, you have kept that strictly to yourself because you don't want to be thought of as gay. But you are 21 years old, and your mind is often gravitating toward sexual themes and imagery.

You finally break down and make an appointment at the student counseling center. This is more difficult than you had imagined. Are you *really* going to share this secret with a complete stranger? You almost renege on going to the scheduled appointment, but this really is driving you crazy and it is affecting deeply your emotional health.

After a short wait, you hear your name called by the counselor. As she greets you, she says, "Hello, Sean, my name is Amanda. Please follow me to my office." As you walk down the hall, you wonder if you are doing the right thing. After all, maybe these feelings will subside on their own with a little more time.

Amanda asks, "What brings you here today, Sean?" You stammer a bit, but manage to utter, "Well, I am confused. Too much of my attention seems to be focused on sexual interest right now. I can hardly focus on getting my school work done." Amanda replies, "Having a strong sex drive is common at your age, you know. But how do you think it is getting in the way of staying focused on your studies?" "I guess it's not just that I am preoccupied . . . it's more than that. I am not just checking out girls anymore . . . I am also checking out some of the guys here at school. This has to stop." Amanda's composure doesn't shift at all when she says, "That's not unusual either at your age. It is easy to feel confused while your sex drive is near its peak."

"That might be easy for you to say, but I am a guy." Amanda comes back, "I know. How long have you been feeling these homosexual desires?" "Thanks for calling it that, Amanda. That really makes me feel better already!" "Sorry, Sean, perhaps I am going too fast with you, but I am interested in knowing how long you have noticed this occurring." You reply, "At least for the past 5 years."

Amanda takes a deep breath and says, "I know it is not easy to accept these feelings, Sean, yet it is important that you do not deny what this means." If you were anxious before, you now feel yourself nearly hitting the roof with panic. "What do you mean, Amanda?" "Sean, all this says is that you are probably gay." "But I also have interest in women, Amanda!?"

"I realize that, but I think with some counseling, you will come to know yourself better. That will help you decide the right course regarding your emerging interests." The session finally ends, and you leave feeling more dazed and confused that when you entered. You begin wondering, "Am I really a gay man who hasn't come to accept himself? Is that what this is really about?" Amanda's comments were more than you were ready to hear.

From a Client's Perspective

1. If you were Sean, how would you feel about being classified as "probably gay" in the first session? Why?
2. Would you want to come back for a second session with Amanda—why or why not?

From a Counselor's Perspective

1. What other approach could Amanda have taken that would have helped Sean to feel safe and understood?
2. In what ways is labeling Sean's experience potentially helpful? In what ways will it hurt him?
3. What else does Amanda need to explore with Sean? What is more important than labeling him?
4. Is having bisexual attraction a phase for some people? If so, how would you know if you need to take it seriously or not?

Background Information Regarding Bisexual Boys to Men

An actual classified ad posted in September 2010 reads, Header: "Discreet 18 year old—m4m—18." Ad: "I am a 18 year old inexperienced guy with a girlfriend. I just wanna experiment a little bit and it has to be very discreet only reply with pictures otherwise no response . . . I'm 6' 2", 7" uncut."

This type of posting is becoming increasingly common in most metropolises. As explained in Chapter 3, the greater tolerance and acceptance of homosexuality over the past several decades has led to an extended moratorium period for young people regarding their sexuality, regardless of whether they decide at some point to label it. All we know from the teenager in the classified ad above is that he is curious and interested in having sex with another guy.

When people share that they are "bisexual," one does not know whether they are referring only to their sexual behavior, their sexual identity, and/or their affectional orientation. Potoczniak (2007) indicated a related usage of the word *bisexual* to describe those who develop romantic feelings for both genders.

A recent study found that between 29 and 32% of female and 12 and 19% of the male college students in two large empirical studies across three regions of the United States reported same-sex feelings (Hoburg, Konik, Williams, & Crawford, 2004). The majority of these young adults will neither act on their feelings (same-sex behavior) nor will they assume a bisexual identity. In a survey of 6,982 men who have had sex with both men and women, 29% defined as bisexual, 2% as homosexual (i.e., gay), and 69% as heterosexual (Lever, Kanouse, Rogers, Carson, & Hertz, 1992).

As Potoczniak (2007) has noted, there is great variation regarding the percentage of men who have experienced sex with another guy. An estimate provided by Rust (2000) is a lifetime prevalence of 20.3%, since puberty 9.1%, and somewhere between 4.9% and 9.1% since age 18 or 20. Interestingly, a recent study found that White heterosexual-identified men report that having sex with other White men "bolsters their heterosexual masculinity" (Ward, 2008, p. 414).

When does having same-sex feelings or engaging in same-sex behavior (often referred to as being *bi-curious*) become more than just that? When does it, if ever, become part of a person's self-identity?

As you ponder this question, a more salient one arises: Is it only because of social conditioning that most of us do not either acknowledge and/or act on same-sex attractions? In other words, are we *all* fundamentally bisexual?

Keep in mind that before the 20th century, people were not defined by their sexuality (Chauncey, 1994). It was likely assumed that everyone was the same: We were all heterosexual individuals and we did not question this because it did not define us. In a sense, it was similar to saying we are human. Given that we are all human, the identity of "human" does little to differentiate us. If you happened to enjoy having sex more with the opposite gender than the same, or both to some extent, that was fine, because in addition to people believing you were heterosexual, they also believed that what goes on in the bedroom is no one's business. It was seen as a private affair, so much so that what we would now define as spousal and child abuse was normative back then.

The ideology was different back then, too, of course. In early Judeo-Christian times, a wife was seen as a man's property (Singer, McLaughlin, Schechter, Greenstone, & Jacobs, 2002), African Americans were property in the United States before the Civil War (Public Broadcasting Service Online, n.d.), and children have been abused physically and sexually across many societies and cultures throughout recorded history (deMause, 1998). When you *own* something (so the theory goes), you can do whatever you want to it.

When the word *homosexual* was coined by Benkert (under the pseudonym Kertbeny) in 1869 (Money, 1993), what was once an act now became for some an identity status, and an underprivileged and oppressed one at that. Before long, despite the cautions of people like Alfred Kinsey, who wrote that the world is not divided into sheep and goats (i.e., heterosexuals and homosexuals), people's need to polarize much of the human condition into binaries once again emerged and predominated.

Binaries have a long history, and they are everywhere. Here are a few examples:

1. Life comes in twos—either a plant or an animal.
2. Most body parts come in twos—we have two eyes, two arms, two legs, two breasts, two ovaries, or two testes.
3. There are two genders—male or female.
4. There are two gender roles—masculine or feminine. This one even got built into Latin languages (e.g., Spanish, French).
5. Take two!—Noah was purported to have filled his ark with a male and female of every animal species to repopulate earth.

No wonder bisexuality has been even more controversial than homosexuality. At least people are used to seeing the world in binaries, but a *third* sexual orientation? That is almost as frightening as believing that we have a *third* gender, a transgender one if you will (the subject of Chapters 7, 8, and 9).

Fox (1996) indicated that early theorists used the notion of bisexuality as a springboard to explain homosexuality—bisexuality itself did not have its own identity status. Even Sigmund Freud (1925/1959) believed we were all constitutionally bisexual and that this could and would be uncovered in psychoanalysis; however, one wouldn't want to remain on the homosexual side of the dichotomy, as this would be viewed by Freud and other psychoanalysts as a sign of developmental arrest. Fox (1996) also noted that famous anthropologist Margaret Mead (1975) believed that likely most people, male and female, were bisexual in their ability to love. It is generally believed that "most people have some bisexual potential" (Shechter, 2004, p. 271).

Kinsey and his colleagues (1948, 1953) were perhaps the first researchers to acknowledge that bisexuality could be a stable and enduring affectional orientation. Nonetheless, he saw it as the "midpoint of a continuum with exclusive homosexuality at one end and exclusive heterosexuality at the other" (Oxley & Lucius, 2000, p. 117). Kinsey's view, however, has never been entirely accepted.

Storms's (1980) research supported the idea that a bisexual orientation exists, however. Although his study relied on small sample sizes of heterosexual, bisexual, and gay/lesbian participants ($N = 185$), Storms found that the overall differences between groups regarding masculinity and femininity were not significant. In other words, one could not predict who was homosexually and/or heterosexually inclined based on scores measuring masculinity and femininity. He did find strong support, however, for the notion that sexual orientation was primarily about sexual fantasies toward one or both genders. The bisexual group scored high on sexual fantasies toward both men and women, which was not characteristic of the homosexual and heterosexual samples.

Besides self-report measures as used in Storms's (1980) study, the existence of bisexuality has been strongly supported in new research indicating that bisexual men do elicit sexual arousal (as measured by increased blood flow to the penis) to sexual imagery (i.e., 3-minute pornographic videos). The videos depicted two men having sex and two women having sex (Rosenthal, Sylva, Safron, & Bailey, 2011).

Nonetheless, the credibility and validity of a bisexual identity is often questioned (Cochran & Heck, 2008). Consequently, research in this area remains scant (Cochran & Heck, 2008). Often, bisexual individuals (and transgender people) are included in research focused primarily on gay men and lesbian women in order to create the appearance of inclusion (Dworkin, 2006). The regrettable side of this is that these individuals remain largely invisible in research (Barker & Langdridge, 2008). Inadvertently, their identities are relegated to an inferior status by the fact that they become the "tagalongs," thus remaining marginalized in research projects.

Consequently, many if not most of the studies cited in this chapter and the next are about lesbian, gay, and bisexual (LGB) individuals. Where distinguishing characteristics of bisexual men from the other two subgroups can be filtered out, this will be done. Otherwise, they will be lumped together, which informs you that there are also commonalities among the groups that are important to note.

On the surface, those who define as bisexual compared to those who relegate their status to that of "queer" have much in common (Horner, 2007). The difference lies mostly in the politics (refusing to buy into identity statuses), in the paradigm (i.e., modernist or postmodernist), or in the extent of commitment (i.e., identity moratorium or achievement) that one is prepared to make to a label, however transient that label might be in the person's life. One might assume that a teenager calling himself queer is using this word differently than someone middle-aged, for example. Becoming overfocused on words will offer little in understanding a person's sexuality either now or in the future.

In the ecological model (Alderson, 2003), it was hypothesized that people who experience the least congruence between sexual cognition, sexual affect, and sexual behavior will in turn experience the greatest amount of cognitive dissonance. Research supports this hypothesis regarding bisexual individuals (Moore & Norris, 2005). As you will see in the sections that follow, bisexual individuals "are at elevated risk for difficulties above and beyond those experienced by gay men and lesbians" (Cochran & Heck, 2008, p. 597).

This chapter will discuss bisexual individuals who are male, from childhood to adulthood. The discussion at times will be incomplete. This is in consequence of the limited research base. The reader will learn about what we know—and don't know—based on findings from empirically informed research.

Development Through the Life Span

From retrospective studies, most LGB individuals questioned their sexuality beginning in childhood (Carver, Egan, & Perry, 2004). Carver and colleagues (2004) studied 182 children in the fourth through eighth grades and found that participants who were less confident in their heterosexuality experienced more impaired self-concepts, expressed less satisfaction with their social relationships, and were less satisfied with their gender. However, it affected neither their feelings of self-worth nor their perception of acceptance from peers.

Recent research from Minnesota and British Columbia in Canada found that bisexual adolescents reported having fewer protective factors (i.e., less family support, less connectedness in school) compared to heterosexual youth. Furthermore, the teens with sexual partners of both genders had lower levels of protective factors compared to those with only same-sex partners (Saewyc et al., 2009). In another study, heterosexual and LGB youth differed neither on measures of friendship quality nor in their perception of school climate (Busseri, Willoughby, Chalmers, & Bogaert, 2006).

Few bisexual individuals experience equal attraction to both genders (i.e., *bi-bi*) (Weinberg, Williams, & Pryor, 2001). Instead, the majority are either more attracted to the same gender (i.e., *bi-gay*) or the opposite gender (i.e., *bi-straight*; Weinrich & Klein, 2002).

Dworkin (2006) concluded that the study of bisexual development remains largely unresearched, but some theories have nonetheless been advanced. On the basis of their seminal study, Weinberg, Williams, and Pryor (1994) suggested four phases of development that would permit some back-and-forth movement: (a) initial confusion, (b) labeling oneself as bisexual, (c) settling into the label, but (d) maintaining uncertainty. Based on subsequent further study with bisexual individuals in midlife, they later modified their phases (Weinberg et al., 2001) to reflect their finding that many had adopted stable bisexual identities. Brown (2002) also created a model that was the same as Weinberg and colleagues' (1994) for the first three stages, but similar to their later model. The final stage in Brown's model was called "identity maintenance." Based on her research with bisexual individuals, Bradford (2004) also advanced a theory of bisexual identity development that included four stages: "questioning reality, inventing the identity, maintaining the identity, and transforming adversity" (p. 7).

Weinberg and colleagues (1994) found that bisexual men and women self-identified in their early to mid-20s on average, which was later than for gay men and lesbian women. Other studies have supported this later acquisition of a bisexual identity when compared to homosexual self-identification (Matteson, 1996). Further, Weinberg and colleagues found that similar to gay men self-identifying earlier than lesbian women, the same was true regarding bisexual men compared to bisexual women. Another notable comparison is that while bisexual women generally experience opposite-sex attraction before same-sex attraction, bisexual men in general experience same-sex attraction either before or around the same time as opposite-sex attraction.

"Research indicates that the LGBT community is more ageist than the general public" (Kimmel, Rose, Orel, & Greene, 2006, p. 13), and consequently, LGBTI elders do not feel welcome in their own community. Another consequence of this is that most bisexual elders are invisible (Dworkin, 2006). Those with children generally view them as the most important part of their lives (Dworkin, 2006), which is no different from aging heterosexual parents.

Race and Ethnicity

Collins (2004) noted that by the year 2050, about 50% of the U.S. population is expected to be composed of people of color, a percentage that is already true or nearly true in several cities and states. Collins remarked that bisexual identity development has received little attention in the research to date, and that this is especially true for bisexual individuals of color. The focus has been either on bisexual identity development separately or on ethnic identity development separately, but not on both together. Collins (2000) developed a model that focuses on how a bisexual person of color establishes a dual identity. His model includes four phases: (a) Questioning/Confusion, (b) Refusal/Suppression, (c) Infusion/Exploration, and (d) Resolution/Acceptance.

In Phase 1, Collins's (2000) model recognizes that bisexual persons of color must endure the developmental milestones of both minority identities, a process that is complicated, as they do not feel fully affiliated with either identity. In Phase II, self-identification occurs, but here one identity is valued while the other is suppressed or denied. In Phase III, individuals may find a reference group to identify with (e.g., African American community or bisexual group), but often confusion and occasionally guilt is felt. As Phase IV unfolds, individuals move toward accepting the rejected identity while simultaneously recognizing that both identities are of equal importance.

According to Collins (2004), few researchers have carefully studied bisexual African Americans, Asian Americans, Hispanic Americans, or Native Americans, again neglecting to look at the intersection of race/ethnicity and bisexuality. Wilson (1996) looked at how Canadian First Nations peoples and Native Americans construct an identity that interconnects sexuality, race, and gender. Alluded to in Chapter 3, many LGB indigenous Americans and Canadians use the term *two-spirited* to describe an identity that integrates sexuality, culture, and community.

The phenomenon called "the down low" has received much media attention (Boykin, 2005). The *down low* has several definitions, and a common one refers simply to African American men who have sex with men but who do not identity as gay. Boykin (2005) believes that ultimately, the down low is not about bisexual men at all: It is simply about "cheating" on one's partner, and such behavior extends to men and women of *every* race/ethnicity.

Pitt (2006) concluded that the media pathologizes Black bisexual behavior (their behavior is seen as a threat to Black masculinity), while it either ignores or displays sympathy toward White bisexual behavior (their behavior is seen as being constrained by society). That harsher judgments are launched at bisexual men of color compared to White men is not surprising in both the media and in society, given that they need to navigate two stigmatized identities instead of only one.

Meyer and Ouellette (2009) remarked on the trouble that many Black LGB individuals have trying to deal with both their sexual identities and their racial/ethnic identities.

Jamil, Harper, and Fernandez (2009) studied gay, bisexual, and questioning adolescent males of color (i.e., Latino and African American) and concluded that their ethnic identity and sexual identity development occurred simultaneously (in contrast to the model proposed by Collins, 2000). Although the two processes were different, they seemed to occur independently of one another because the participants did not refer to one process (e.g., ethnic identity development) while describing the other (e.g., sexual identity development).

Relationships (Family, Friendships, Intimate Romantic/Sexual)

Concomitant with homosexual desire are the societal taboos surrounding it. Consequently, as bisexual individuals confront this together with societal and familial expectations that one will marry and follow a heterosexual relationship script (i.e., monogamy), many bisexual individuals enter heterosexual commitments long before they have explored their same-sex interests (Matteson, 1996). Bisexual men who marry did not deceive their wives but instead did not identify as either gay or bisexual when their relationships began (Matteson, 1995). It is far more typical that bisexual men marry heterosexual women than the opposite (i.e., that bisexual women are married to heterosexual men; Matteson, 1999). Richard Isay (1996) stated that most bisexual men are happy with their heterosexual marriages, which is the opposite of gay men who are married to women.

A study of 26 married couples that included a bisexual husband found that most were satisfied with their marriages despite the husband's homosexual behavior. Nonetheless, they did report experiencing intense conflict to get to a place where wives could accept the open marriage concept (Wolf, 1985). While bisexual individuals would prefer to have more than one sexual partner, a gender difference arises for approximately

80% of bisexual men and women. Bisexual men report that having more than one sexual partner is about fulfilling sexual needs, while bisexual women report how each gender provides something different emotionally (Matteson, 1996). Nonetheless, fewer than 20% of bisexual individuals are involved with men and women simultaneously (Matteson, 1996). Rust (2001b) concluded from her large-scale study of 917 bisexual individuals from the United States and seven other countries that both bisexual men and women are more emotionally attracted to women but more sexually attracted to men.

A common myth is that bisexual people cannot maintain faithfulness in relationships. Many bisexual men do maintain monogamous, happy marriages (Edser & Shea, 2002). Matteson (1995) maintains that faithfulness is actually about being honest and following through on commitments—he does not equate it with monogamy. Some bisexual individuals are *polyamorous*, meaning that they reject the value-laden construct of monogamy and instead believe that having more than one sexual/romantic partner is acceptable so long as all individuals consent to it (Rust, 2003; Weitzman, 2006). This is different than *infidelity*, where consent is not provided or likely even requested (Weitzman, 2006).

In a study of 217 bisexual individuals, 33% were currently living a polyamorous lifestyle, while 54% of the sample believed polyamory was their preferred relationship style (Page, 2004). A well-known supporter of polyamory was Dr. Albert Ellis, who wrote his book about the virtues of open marriage in the 1940s, despite not being successful in finding a publisher until the more liberal 1960s unfolded (Weitzman, 2006).

Unlike the gay and lesbian community, a substantial bisexual community does not exist (Matteson, 1995). Consequently, many bisexual men and women feel a sense of community isolation (Rust, 2001a). One of the pressures that bisexual individuals encounter is feeling torn between fitting into the heterosexual community while involved with someone of the opposite sex and then needing to relinquish much of this to become part of the gay and lesbian community while involved with the same sex. Many if not most gay, lesbian, and heterosexual individuals continue to mistrust bisexual people, believing they are either "fence-sitters," hedonists who are taking the best of both worlds, or that they really have a homosexual orientation but don't want to take the stigma that coincides with the label (Mohr & Rochlen, 1999).

While even college students do not agree on what constitutes "having sex" (Trotter & Alderson, 2007), Mexican, Nicaraguan, and Brazilian men who have sex with men view oral sex and masturbation as foreplay. Unless anal penetration occurs, it is not viewed as having had sex (Long, Burnett, & Thomas, 2006).

While it is often believed that LGB youth establish better friendships with other LGB individuals than with heterosexual friends, a recent study from Indianapolis found that LGB youth had comparable friendships with both groups on measures of contact frequency, emotional closeness, and hassles (Ueno, Gayman, Wright, & Quantz, 2009). On the other end of the age spectrum, elder bisexual men and women construct many different relationship styles, including monogamous opposite-sex or same-sex relationships and polyamorous relationships (Dworkin, 2006).

Health (Emotional and Psychological, Physical)

Studies have typically shown that LGB youth are at greater risk of suicidality compared to heterosexual youth (Zhao, Montoro, Igartua, & Thombs, 2010). Similar to gay and lesbian youth, bisexual youth also experience more mental health symptoms compared to heterosexual youth (D'Augelli, 2002). In one study, those youth who were questioning or who felt less certain about their sexuality generally reported the highest levels of victimization, substance abuse, and suicidal ideation (Poteat, Aragon, Espelage, & Koenig, 2009). Using data from the National Longitudinal Study of Adolescent Health ($N = 11,153$, 50.6% female, $M = 21.8$ years), Needham and Austin (2010) found that LGB youth generally experience less support from their parents compared to heterosexual youth, but when parental support is present, it acts to mediate negative health-related outcomes (e.g., suicidal thoughts, depression, heavy drinking, and drug use).

A nationally representative study found that bisexual men and women experienced more conflict regarding their sexual orientation and were less open about it compared to those who exclusively identified as either gay or lesbian, respectively. On the positive side, they reported experiencing less minority stress resulting from violence and discrimination (Lewis, Derlega, Brown, Rose, & Henson, 2009).

Numerous studies show that when compared to gay and lesbian individuals, bisexual men and women tend to experience worse mental health (Barker & Langdridge, 2008; Dilley, Simmons, Boysun, Pizacani, & Stark, 2010; Jorm, Korten, Rodgers, Jacomb, & Christensen, 2002; Rosario, Schrimshaw, & Hunter, 2008). They experience worse problems with anxiety, depression, and negative affect (Jorm et al., 2002; Mills et al., 2004), higher levels of identity diffusion (Balsam & Mohr, 2007; Dworkin, 2006), and lower levels self-disclosure and community connection (Balsam & Mohr, 2007). A recent study found that approximately one-third of individuals diagnosed with borderline personality disorder experience conflicts with same-gender attraction (Reich & Zanarini, 2008).

Bisexual drug users are at higher risk for contracting HIV compared to heterosexual drug users (Logan & Leukefeld, 2000). Compared to HIV-positive gay men, HIV-positive bisexual men report higher levels of internalized homophobia and less involvement in the gay community (O'Leary, Purcell, Remien, Fisher, & Spikes, 2007). Using results from the 2002 cycle of the National Survey of Family Growth, behaviorally bisexual men reported higher levels of condom use with women than did other homosexually or heterosexually active men (Jeffries & Dodge, 2007), suggesting that bisexually active men are generally taking the necessary steps to protect their partners from sexually transmitted infections.

A large-scale national probability study from Britain (N = 18,876, aged 16–59 years) reported on when men and women first became involved in sexual activity. They found that women with same-sex interest had an earlier first sexual experience compared to heterosexual women, while men with same-sex interest (especially bisexual men) became sexually involved earlier compared to heterosexual men (Bogaert & Friesen, 2002).

The physical health of bisexual men is an area that is grossly understudied. Cochran and Mays (2007) used population-based data from the California Quality of Life Survey, and from their sample of 2,272 individuals, only 29 bisexual men were identified. The bisexual men did not differ from men who were exclusively heterosexual (n = 946) in their reports of physical health or disability. Given the small sample size, these results must be viewed as tentative at best.

Career and Work

Datti (2009) recently commented that the literature regarding career issues for LGBTI individuals is limited with empirical studies to date. Datti recommended utilizing available resources, including LGBTI websites along with networks of LGBTI-positive employers and educational institutions (e.g., www.outforwork.org/), community groups, and professional organizations like the Association for Lesbian, Gay, Bisexual, and Transgender Issues in Counseling (n.d.). Chung (2003) noted that literature regarding career issues for bisexual individuals is almost totally ignored, and when they are studied, they are lumped together with other members of the LGBTI community. There is no empirical research regarding bisexual persons' vocational behavior (Chung, 2003).

Counselors will want to be aware of a scale with good psychometric properties that measures organizational characteristics for LGBTI individuals called the Lesbian, Gay, Bisexual, and Transgendered Climate Inventory (workplace climates range from *actively supportive* to *openly hostile* (Liddle, Luzzo, Hauenstein, & Schuck, 2004). Bisexual individuals often have an easier time "passing" than do gay men and lesbian women because of their heterosexual interests (Matteson, 1996), and this may facilitate better ease at working in unsupportive environments so long as their bisexuality remains invisible.

Spirituality and Religion

Gallup polls in the United States consistently reveal that about 96% of the population believes in God, and 90% say their belief is important in their lives (Rosario, Yali, Hunter, & Gwadz, 2006). While earth-spirited spiritualities (e.g., Pagan and Wiccan faiths) are generally affirming of LGBTI individuals (Smith & Horne, 2007), many mainstream religions and sects continue to exclude them (Morrow & Tyson, 2006). Walls (2010), however, reminds us that while some spiritual communities are not supportive of same-sex marriage, some religious communities may not embrace fully the doctrine of their denomination of faith, and certainly there are some individuals in every congregation that are supportive despite objection based on doctrine. Unfortunately, LGB individuals with conservative religious beliefs are more likely to experience shame, guilt, and internalized homophobia compared to those with more liberal spiritual beliefs (Sherry, Adelman, Whilde, & Quick, 2010).

Only one reference specifically about bisexual men and spirituality could be found in the literature, and its focus is specific to African American men (i.e., Jeffries, Dodge, & Sandfort, 2008). Interviews with 28 men living in New York City revealed that although they faced rejection because of their bisexuality, some participants did report that they found some religious individuals who accepted them. Others discussed how the church acted as a meeting place with other non-heterosexual individuals, sometimes with the purpose of meeting sexual partners.

Sociopolitical Realities

Herdt (2001) wrote about how over the past three decades in the United States, tolerance for bisexuality has increased substantially. Nevertheless, as previous sections in this chapter have shown, bisexual individuals often choose to be and/or are rendered more invisible compared to gay and lesbian individuals. A bisexual community does not exist in most places (except in some major cities), and both heterosexual and gay/lesbian individuals judge them for not fitting into the glove of their own community. We have become accustomed to placing much of the human condition into binaries of "either-or." The place "in-between" is generally misunderstood, misaligned, and subjugated under the dominant discourses of "heterosexual" or "gay/lesbian." As bisexual individuals can often pass if they want, they carry a "secret" that carries negative connotations throughout many factions of society. Their love life can be complicated as they navigate a world that pushes a monogamy script within opposite-sex relationships; however, their experience may be one of polyamory, providing yet further opportunity for judgmental curiosity to surface from others. The bisexual individual is viewed with a similar suspicion as those with borderline personality disorder: Somehow, others may view them as simply not well developed psychologically.

Recent Research Focused on Canada

A recent study from Ontario, Canada, focused on looking at why bisexual individuals experience mental health disparities compared to their heterosexual counterparts. The researchers led focus groups and conducted interviews with 55 bisexual people. Participants reported that experiences of discrimination contributed to mental health problems, findings that are similar for other members of the LGBTI community (Ross, Dobinson, & Eady, 2010). Referred to earlier under the Health section was the study by Zhao and colleagues (2010), conducted in Montreal, Quebec, that found that LGB youth are at increased risk for suicidality compared to heterosexual youth.

Another study from Ontario found community-level HIV prevention efforts can be effective in lowering the incidence of unprotected anal intercourse in bisexual men with both casual and regular sex partners (Leaver, Allman, Meyers, & Veugelers, 2004). Comparing White men who have sex with men with those of color, both those born in Canada and those born elsewhere, George and colleagues (2007) found that the most likely group to have unprotected sex were the White men born outside of Canada, while the White men born in Canada were the most likely to have ever sold sex or to have had their bodies pierced.

Despite the fact that Canada has removed many of the social and legal barriers faced by LGBTI individuals, Dysart-Gale (2010) recently concluded that the literature continues to find that many Canadian LGBTI adolescents report feeling excluded, isolated, and fearful. Canada still has a long way to go before LGBTI individuals are treated as and can feel like equal members of society.

Recent Research Focused on Other Societies

A random sample of 5,000 Norwegians living in Oslo (aged 18–49) in 1997 was drawn, and 45% responded to the survey. Participants were asked about their sexual behavior, including sexual fantasies, sexual attraction, sexual conduct, and falling in love. Interestingly, the researchers found that "exclusive homosexuality was rare in the population" (Traeen, Stigum, & Sorensen, 2002). Those respondents who reported having sex with both genders had a higher number of lifetime sexual partners than those who had opposite-gender sex only. They also reported an earlier age of debut into orgasm and masturbation.

In a study from Thailand, 1,725 vocational-school youth between ages 15 and 21 were self-interviewed using computer-assisted software. The researchers found that 9% of males (HBM) and 11.2% of females (HBF) in their sample identified as either gay/lesbian or bisexual. Drug use was more common among HBF but less so among HBM compared to their heterosexual counterparts (HC), while HBM were more likely to show signs of social isolation and depression (van Griensven et al., 2004). The interesting finding here is that the HBM were less likely to use drugs than the HC males—the direct opposite finding compared to North American studies. In rather sharp contrast, Ventegodt (1998) found in his sample of 2,460 Danish citizens (aged 18–88 years) that only 1.2% and 0.9% reported they identified as bisexual or homosexual, respectively.

Traeen, Martinussen, Vitterso, and Saini (2009) compared male and female students in Havana (Cuba), Tromso (Norway), Hisar (India), and Cape Town (South Africa). Traeen and colleagues found that in Hisar and Cape Town, few people reported having a LGB identity. In all the cities studied, the heterosexual men and women scored higher on all quality-of-life measures, although quality of life was higher in cultures with accepting attitudes toward homosexuality compared to cultures with restrictive attitudes.

In Britain, Barker, Bowes-Catton, Iantaffi, Cassidy, and Brewer (2008) reflected on their bisexual community and concluded that British media continue to portray sexualities as binary (gay/lesbian or heterosexual). They also quoted Meg Barker as surmising that bisexual people in Britain want to have a choice about (a) quality and quantity of sexual activity; (b) relationship type (e.g., monogamy, polyamory); (c) gender expression and whether to have sex with men or women; (d) exploring their spirituality; (e) to have fun; and (f) for bisexual individuals to be recognized as diverse.

Several leaders in African countries have denounced same-gender sexual activity as "un-African," thereby reducing the likelihood that homosexuality or bisexuality will be freely discussed. But Africa—like everywhere else—has people of differing affectional orientations. Bisexual individuals experience prejudice and hostility from both gay and lesbian individuals, thus compounding the animosity directed at them by both the heterosexual and gay/lesbian community in Africa (Stobie, 2003).

In a sample of 60 bisexual men and women in Australia, several participants reported that they were not active in the gay and lesbian community because they believed they would be rejected or discriminated against. Those who did participate in the community tended to keep their bisexuality secret for fear of not being welcome. McLean (2008) concluded "that bisexual men and women have an ambivalent and complex relationship with the gay and lesbian community in Australia" (p. 63).

Mathy's (2002) study looked at suicidality and sexual orientation in Asia, Australia, Europe, North America, and South America. The sample included 38,204 participants who responded to an online survey. Mathy found that male sexual orientation was related to suicide attempts in four continents but not in Europe. Likewise, a relationship was found between female sexual orientation and suicide attempts everywhere except in North America. This study provides some evidence that there is variation between continents in the relationship between suicidality and sexual orientation.

A study of 1,019 New Zealanders found that both men and women who experienced same-sex attraction (SSA) had higher risks of hurting themselves. Compared to those who claimed not to experience same-sex attraction (NSSA), men and women with SSA were about three times more likely to experience suicidal ideation in the past year (Skegg, Nada-Raja, Dickson, Paul, & Williams, 2003).

HIV/AIDS continues to be studied throughout the world. Aggleton's (1996) edited book looked at bisexualities and AIDS in several countries, including Britain, Canada, Australia, France, Mexico, Costa Rica, the Dominican Republic, Peru, Brazil, India, China, New Guinea, and the Philippines. Recent research on 831 men who have sex with men (MSM) who attended voluntary counseling and testing in Mumbai, India, revealed HIV prevalence among MSM at 12.5% (Kumta et al., 2010). The researchers concluded that the men accessing this service were at high risk of STI and HIV infection. In Russia, 45% of a community sample of 434 Russian MSM reported engaging in unprotected anal intercourse with their male partners (Kelly et al., 2002). Researchers from Rio de Janeiro, Brazil, found that despite their sample of 295 gay and bisexual men (aged 18–49) having sound knowledge about how to protect themselves from HIV infection, knowledge and awareness did not readily translate into behavior change: A substantial proportion of these men continued to practice unprotected sex with both primary and secondary partners (Vieira de Souza et al., 1999).

Common Concerns Facing This Group and Counseling Considerations

Roleplay Scenarios

[*Note:* Suggested assessment and intervention strategies for the two roleplays below can be found in Appendix B. Before going there, roleplay in dyads with one of you acting as the counselor and the other as the counselee. If a roleplay is not possible, work individually in writing out a list of your suggestions.]

Roleplay #1, Chapter 5. Counseling Bisexual Men

Robert, age 28, has come to see you for help. He has been in a relationship with Sara, age 24, for the past 4 years, and although he loves her, he craves sex with men periodically and goes out and gets it. Sara believes they are monogamous, as this has always been their understanding. Robert doesn't want to lose Sara, but he knows she will not accept his outside sexual behavior. The longest

Robert has been able to hold off on having sex with men is about 2 weeks. If he doesn't get it, he starts feeling depressed and deprived.

Roleplay 2, Chapter 5. Counseling Bisexual Men

Adam, age 45, has come to see you for help. He has been with James for 6 months, a 40-year-old gay man who has been out for nearly 20 years. Adam used to be married to Nancy, but their marriage ended 8 years ago after Adam told Nancy that he wanted to start having sex with other people, including both men and women. As Adam dealt with his issues in a mature, responsible, and honest manner, Nancy and he maintained a good friendship following their marriage dissolution.

James, however, has started telling Adam how jealous he is of the time he spends with Nancy and some of his other female friends. James believes Adam will have sex with these women because Adam defines himself as bisexual. In fact, there are times when he has had sex with women behind James's back. You find out that Adam does want an open relationship with James but doesn't know how to broach the subject.

HOW WOULD *YOU* HELP THIS PERSON?

Jake has been married to Susan for 21 years. Together they have three adult children, ages 18, 19, and 20. Jake knew he was attracted to guys from about age 13 but never acted on these feelings. Thankfully, he thought, he was also attracted to several women in his school. Susan was his high school sweetheart, and a year after graduation, they married. Jake and Susan are both 40 years old now. Like many married couples, the amount of sex diminished over time to a point where now, they only have intercourse about once a week on average. Jake wants more, but Susan is uninterested in increasing the frequency.

About 8 months ago, Jake began placing ads on the Internet looking for oral sex. As he did not specify gender, he was actually surprised by how many men e-mailed him, while no women at all responded. Several of the respondents specified that they did not want reciprocation. This suited Jake, as he did not see this as cheating behavior.

When Susan walked into his home office and inadvertently saw one of his e-mails on the computer screen, however, she did not see it the same as Jake! The argument that ensued left Susan hysterical and Jake quivering from the accusations that he was really gay and that she would not stay married to a gay man. Susan felt he had cheated on her by not confiding in his desire to have extramarital sex.

At that point, Jake asked, "Would you be willing to let me have some oral sex on the side then?" Susan screamed back at him, "OF COURSE NOT—ARE YOU CRAZY?!" Feeling hurt, defeated, and embarrassed, Jake booked an appointment with you. He is now in your office asking for help.

He honestly doesn't think he can stop pursuing outside sex but is dreadfully afraid of losing Susan. Jake tells you that he does not believe Susan will give him more sex because this has been an ongoing issue for them for several years. Once a week even seems to be pushing her limits. The other thing is, Jake tells you that now that he has began fulfilling his long-denied sexual desire for men, he does not believe he can stop this activity without feeling that his sexual life will never be satisfactory again.

Note—Remember to view clients within their environmental contexts, keeping in mind societal, parental/familial, cultural/spiritual, and peer influences. Specifically, become aware of the impact that the following influences have and continue to have in your clients' lives: race, language, religion and spirituality, gender, familial migration history, affectional orientation, age and cohort, physical and mental capacities, socioeconomic situation and history, education, and history of traumatic experience.

1. What defines this person's environment, past and present?
2. Who is this person sitting in front of me, taking into account environmental and personal characteristics?
3. What defines the problem that he or she is presenting within his or her multicultural milieu?

When bisexual individuals seek counseling, it is often because of either or both of two issues: (a) identity issues and (b) difficulty in managing a bisexual lifestyle (Matteson, 1996). Bisexual identity development is challenged as, similar to gay/lesbian individuals, bisexual men and women have to also deal with the societal taboos against homosexuality. Related to this, they often need to overcome their own homophobia and biphobia (Matteson, 1996). Due to pressure to marry and have children from outside influences (e.g., family, peers, church/culture, society), many bisexual individuals commit to a member of the opposite gender before they have explored their same-gender sexuality sufficiently. According to Matteson (1996), those who desire having sex with men and women concurrently do so out of longing, and generally not out of choice.

If you receive even a few hours devoted to counseling bisexual individuals in graduate school, consider yourself fortunate. Belanger (2008) surveyed 117 students from APA-accredited professional psychology doctoral programs in the United States and deemed their current training on bisexual issues to be "unacceptable." This is especially problematic when you consider that working with bisexual individuals is often difficult.

Guidry (1999) stated that many counselors are challenged to work with bisexual clients because of the complexity that may surface as they navigate a culture that prefers to place sexuality into binaries. Unquestionably, bi-positive counselors need to think "outside the box" and be themselves capable of not judging that which resides outside the norm. Page (2007) found in her study of 217 bisexual men and women that six themes emerged as important to them regarding their experiences of counseling:

1. Did the counselor validate their sexual orientation and/or help them achieve greater acceptance of their bisexuality?
2. Did the client perceive the counselor as "healthy" or "unhealthy" overall?
3. Did the counselor have adequate knowledge of bisexual issues?
4. Was the counselor skillful in assisting the client with bisexual issues?
5. Did the counselor intervene in proactive ways to support bisexual issues?
6. Participants also discussed generic counseling skills that were helpful to their ongoing identity development and bisexual lifestyle.

Deacon, Reinke, and Viers (1996) wrote about the application of cognitive behavioral therapy to couples in which one or both of the partners define as bisexual. Their approach utilized communication training, emotional expressiveness training, and cognitive restructuring. Earlier, Wolf (1987) encouraged the use of group psychotherapy, as it provides a supportive framework (i.e., a support network) for couples to work through their issues with one another. Two excellent resources (i.e., books) for counselors who work with bisexual clients are edited by Firestein (2007) and Fox (2006).

Remember that bisexual men seek out counseling for many of the same reasons as gay men, and for those concerns, refer to Chapter 3. The focus here is on those issues that are generally more specific to bisexual men. They include (a) identity confusion and labeling issues, (b) internalized biphobia, (c) relationship strain and fidelity concerns, (d) finding support networks, and (e) invisibility and its sequelae.

Identity Confusion and Labeling Issues

For gay men, the issue with identity is often one of fragmentation, while for bisexual men, it is more commonly about the confusion created by desiring both male and female sexual partners. The awareness of this confusion may occur at any of three junctures: (a) an early awareness that one is attracted to both genders before settling into a relationship with either, (b) while dating or being committed to a woman (and defining as heterosexual), the bisexual man becomes aware of his interest in men, or (c) while dating or being committed to a man (and defining as gay), he becomes aware of his interest in women. Each juncture brings with it different issues.

Regardless of when one becomes aware of bisexual interests, deciding whether to act on these desires is complicated by one's internalized beliefs (e.g., familial, spiritual, societal). Those who first define as gay need to give up one stigmatized identity, along with the requisite identity politics of belonging to the gay community, for another identity that is stigmatized by both gay/lesbian- and heterosexual-identified individuals. Because of the binary expectation (i.e., interest in only males or females) that most individuals expect, it can create substantial confusion when the man who thought he was gay now finds himself sexually excited by a woman (Matteson, 1996). For those who first defined as heterosexual, they need to consider taking on a stigmatized identity—the homosexual component—and deal with the fallout from this should they decide to self-identify as bisexual.

Perhaps it is not surprising that many people with a bisexual orientation never elect to take on a bisexual identity. It is also likely that many with bisexual desire will simply refuse to label themselves with a sexual identity label. However, as Arbaugh (2002) indicated, many bisexual individuals adopt a label in order to solidify their sense of self.

Other issues that may surface regarding the acquisition of a bisexual identity are that some clients believe that having a bisexual identity means they will remain unsettled and that they are condemned to remain unhappy (Oxley & Lucius, 2000). Another complication is that it is sometimes true that bisexual behavior is transitional as one moves toward identifying and accepting a gay or heterosexual identity. For many of the reasons stated here, it is not surprising that it generally takes longer for individuals to self-identify as bisexual compared to gay and lesbian people, with men generally acting on their homosexual desires earlier than women (Matteson, 1996).

In counseling bisexual clients, Arbaugh (2002) stressed the importance of not placing too much importance on categories or labels. Instead, it is far better to focus on the various aspects of sexuality that relationships with men and/or with women fulfill. Such areas include sexual behavior, affect (feelings, emotions), and other intimacy needs. Furthermore, as reflected in the Klein Sexual Orientation Grid (Klein, Sepekoff, & Wolf, 1985), other life areas that may be fulfilled differentially include social preference (i.e., with whom does the client prefer to socialize—men or women?) and whether the client prefers the heterosexual or gay/lesbian lifestyle (e.g., hanging out with gay men and/or lesbian women may be perceived by some clients as more fun and entertaining than spending time with their heterosexual friends). Counseling then is about helping clients accept that different people fulfill different roles in their lives and that gender is not the most important determinant of this for bisexual individuals.

Another helpful assessment device that can be used for exploring the various components of a bisexual orientation is the Sexuality Questionnaire (see Appendix C). After completion, the counselor can use the questionnaire as a springboard for asking questions about what these components mean to the client.

Many clients do need to adopt an identity label to feel a sense of completion (Arbaugh, 2002), and the counselor may need to help the client work through the barriers to doing this. One of the barriers may well be internalized biphobia.

Internalized Biphobia

Internalized biphobia refers to bisexual individuals fearing, disliking, and/or hating themselves. The term also applies to bisexual individuals fearing, disliking, and/or hating other bisexual people or those who they perceive as bisexual. Dworkin (2001) surmised that "for gay men and lesbians, this [internalized biphobia] manifests as heterophobia, and for heterosexuals, this manifests as homophobia" (p. 673). While this idea makes intuitive sense, there does not appear to be a research base to support it. Researchers do not know if internalized biphobia—and externalized biphobia, for that matter—is about disdain for the same-sex attraction aspect (i.e., homophobia), the opposite-sex attraction component (i.e., heterophobia), or because of the bisexual aspect, or "nature," of the bisexual person. The answer to this question awaits further research.

Similar to internalized homophobia, internalized biphobia can be crippling for bisexual individuals, and more commonly and intensely for bisexual men. Bisexual men could avoid dealing with biphobia if they only acted on their heterosexual interests; however, many either cannot or choose not to restrict themselves in this way. In a qualitative study based on interviews with 18 clients and 16 counselors, Bowers, Minichiello, and Plummer (2010) concluded that many of the clients in their study were experiencing a lifelong recovery from religious-based homophobia (i.e., "homophobia in the context of organized religion," p. 77).

Besides internalized biphobia, there is also biphobia that is felt by nonbisexual individuals. Some research suggests that disdain for bisexual men may be higher than for any other sexual minority group. Eliason (2001) collected data from 229 (170 females, 59 males) college students, all of whom self-defined as heterosexual. As a group, 26% of the sample found bisexual men "very unacceptable," compared to 21%, 14%, and 12% for gay men, lesbian women, and bisexual women, respectively.

Many heterosexual individuals experience varying degrees of biphobia toward bisexual people (Israel & Mohr, 2004). A recent dissertation (Dengel, 2007) found that from an online survey of 1,338 participants of mixed genders and orientations, the heterosexual men and the lesbian women had the highest biphobia scores. The overall sample, however, experienced biphobia scores in the mild range.

As noted earlier, the gay and lesbian community has also maintained negative attitudes toward bisexuality (Weiss, 2003). Ochs (2001) advanced the possibility that gay males have generally embraced an essentialist view of their own affectional orientation and perhaps react negatively toward bisexual men for fear of losing political power within the ongoing gay rights movement. Another possibility is that bisexual attraction is threatening to some gay males' own identity (Ochs, 1996). The threat would be that some gay men might also wonder if they have attraction to women and would wonder if they need to again question their sexual identity.

It should not be surprising that like gay men, bisexual men also have much internal work to do. Furthermore, Herek's (2002) study found that in his survey of 1,335 participants using random-digit dialing, likeability ratings were the lowest for bisexual men and women than for all other groups (including gay/lesbian individuals) except for ratings toward injecting drug users. The heterosexual women in the sample rated bisexual men and women less favorably compared to gay and lesbian women, respectively, while heterosexual men rated both gay and bisexual men as less favorable compared to all female targets. It is difficult to love and accept yourself when so many others are looking down on you.

Potoczniak (2007) believes it will be helpful if counselors understand what causes and maintains internalized biphobia (IB) and what effect it has on bisexual individuals. One problem is that there are few role models due to their invisibility. An important strategy then for reducing IB is to help bisexual clients increase their social network (discussed below). Furthermore, as it is easier for most bisexual individuals to simply pass and avoid having others know them as bisexual, it is easy to relegate their same-sex interests to a lesser position of status and acceptability. Part of the work with bisexual clients with IB is to help them accept all parts of themselves and not to value their opposite-sex interests (or partner) over their same-sex interests (or partner): Both must be validated and accepted equally. To diminish either interest is to diminish the person's overall sense of self-worth.

Relationship Strain and Fidelity Concerns

The majority of married bisexual men did not deceive their wives before marrying them. Studies have consistently shown that only a minority self-identified as gay or bisexual when their relationships with women began (Matteson, 1995). Consequently, the realization and/or acceptance of one's bisexuality often create strain in a committed relationship. One of the issues that arises is fidelity (Long, Burnett, & Thomas, 2006). While much of society equates fidelity with monogamy, maintaining intimacy is more about faithfulness in a relationship. For many couples, and perhaps especially bisexual couples in which one or both partners define as bisexual, faithfulness is equated with "being honest . . . and following through on the covenants and commitments the couple has made" (Matteson, 1995, p. 148).

A common outcome is that the nonbisexual partner feels threatened by the bisexual partner's desires and sexual behaviors. Jealousy may become rampant if the nonbisexual partner is unable to understand and experience his or her relationship as primary. This is not to suggest, however, that all bisexual individuals decide to have sex outside the committed relationship, with or without endorsement from their partners. Instead, it acknowledges that many bisexual individuals will desire concurrent sexual experience with both genders. Even in polyamorous relationships in which the female partner knows and has provided consent to outside sexual activity with men, adjustments are required to reduce and perhaps eliminate the jealousy and fear of losing one's intimate connection with the bisexual man (Weitzman, 2007).

When nonbisexual partners are unaware of their partner's outside sexual activity (i.e., "cheating"), this usually results in major feelings of betrayal if the behavior is discovered or eventually disclosed. Myers (1991) discussed counseling practice with HIV-infected men who are married to women and the processes they go through in coming to some kind of resolution. For both, there are feelings of mourning and grief. For the woman, there may be guilt if she was aware of the outside sexual activity, and reactions to infidelity if this activity was not previously known. There is also the fear of contracting the virus herself. For men, acknowledging and accepting their bisexual behavior may be challenging if they lived with denial and rationalization for years.

In cases in which bisexual men do not tell their female partners about their bisexuality, research has shown that they generally protect the women by not engaging in high-risk sexual activities (Lever, Kanouse, Rogers, Carson, & Hertz, 1992; Stokes, McKirnan, & Burzette, 1993). Research using a convenience sample has also provided preliminary evidence that men who do not identify as either gay or bisexual but who have sex with other men are less likely to inform their wives of their outside sexual activity (Earl, 1990).

Encouraging couples to clearly communicate their expectations, needs, and level of commitment in the relationship is essential if the presenting issue is fidelity, including whether any of these are now changing (Long et al., 2006). Wherever possible, it helps if the couple can agree on the ground rules at the early stages of dating. Questions as to whether the couple will be monogamous, polyamorous, or open to other sexual partners are best managed before the couple has already invested a great deal of time, energy, and devotion in constructing the relationship in a given manner. If the disclosure of a bisexual identity does not occur until well into the relationship, the partner is likely going to experience many conflicting feelings, including a sense of betrayal, anger, fear, suspicion and/or distrust, jealousy, confusion, and questioning regarding his or her level of commitment.

If the couple is to move toward having an open relationship from a previously monogamous one, the counselor will need to encourage very open communication in which both agree and act in a manner that reflects primacy of their relationship over all other outside involvements (Matteson, 1996). Similar to gay male couples who have constructed open relationships, the ground rules regulating outside involvement must be negotiated and agreed upon by the partners.

Here are a few examples of what has been negotiated by some couples:

- Only have outside sex when travelling.
- Only see the same person once or twice.
- Only engage in threesomes so that both you and your partner are involved.
- Practice safer sex with outside partners.
- For those who cohabitate, don't bring anyone home for sex—do it elsewhere.
- Tell the outsider that you are in a relationship, and if an emotional connection begins to develop, don't see the person again.
- Agree not to provide information with or without details regarding outside involvements (i.e., turn a blind eye), or do the opposite (i.e., provide information with or without details).
- For polyamorous relationships, decide how the primary relationship will be protected while the bisexual partner(s) becomes sexually and emotionally involved with another person(s).

The above should give you a good sense of the array of possibilities, and for many of you, the list will also stretch your own sense of what a relationship "should" look like. To work successfully with a couple in which one or both define as bisexual, the counselor must be willing to help the couple negotiate any arrangement that leads to consensus.

In reality, any relationship construction can work successfully if there is agreement and both find ways to cope with the feelings and emotions that may arise. Often there is a difference between what we believe we can handle intellectually and what our feelings tell us once the actual behavior occurs. This too is the work of the counselor.

Counselors should be aware that most polyamorous couples seek counseling for problems or issues unrelated to polyamory (Weitzman, 2006). More commonly, they seek counseling for typical presenting concerns such as anxiety and depression. A special instance of counseling occurs if either partner becomes HIV positive in consequence of outside sexual activity. This is especially challenging if the partner who seroconverts did not negotiate this outside activity (i.e., he or she was "cheating"). The feelings and emotions that arise can be overwhelming even for the counselor. The counselor, however, must encourage the couple to express and vent all of their feelings to provide the couple the opportunity to return to a satisfactory place (Myers, 1991).

Finding Support Networks

Several writers have stressed the importance of bisexual individuals receiving social support, especially from other bisexual people (Auerback, 1987; Matteson, 1996; Wolf, 1985). The reality, however, is that bisexual individuals are usually challenged to find support networks where they live. Often this means deriving support either from Internet groups or from supportive friends and family.

Sheets and Mohr (2009) found that bisexual young adult college students were less likely to experience depression if they had general support from family and/or friends. Those who had support related specifically to their bisexuality were less likely to experience internalized biphobia (referred to in this research as internalized binegativity).

As described earlier, friends and family members usually do not understand bisexuality, and they are often judgmental of it. While larger cities may have several clubs and organizations specifically targeted at bisexual persons, other cities and smaller communities will have nothing available. Most cities have a gay information service (usually found by looking in the white pages under "gay"), and they may be able to provide information on potential support groups. Some bisexual individuals will be comfortable attending groups primarily aimed at gay and lesbian people. Many today are inclusive and advertise to the LGB community.

Hutchins (2007) wrote about erotic communities that combine social and friendship aspects with sexual activity, and this may be a viable option for some bisexual individuals. An excellent referral is the Bi Men Network, the largest free worldwide social and support network for bisexual, bi-curious, and gay men, and bisexual couples (visit www.bimen.org/). They claim they are the largest association for bisexual individuals on earth.

Invisibility and Its Sequelae

While many gay men will not disclose their sexual identity to others (called "passing") who may be harmful to them in some way (Alderson, 2000), bisexual men are even less likely to reveal their identities, not only to avoid dangerous repercussions but also to avoid confusion or having to provide explanations (Arbaugh, 2002). Matteson (1996) also noted that while bisexual individuals belong to an invisible minority just like gay and lesbian individuals, bisexual people can more easily pass by maintaining a public identity that is heterosexual.

While on the surface, passing may appear to be ideal as a form of identity management, keeping one's sexual identity a secret can increase internalized biphobia (i.e., if you feel good about something, why would you keep it a secret?). Furthermore, the "secret," if ever discovered, can create huge psychosocial problems in a person's life. Living with the risk of discovery can turn something as harmless as one's sexuality into a major source of anxiety and concern, turning the secret into something akin to not getting caught while committing a crime.

The societal cost is also huge: When bisexual individuals make themselves invisible, no one gets to learn about their experience. Researchers have a harder time finding bisexual individuals who will participate in their studies, and the everyday person has a harder time understanding something that, on the surface, appears to be extremely rare because it is not spoken about openly. Compounded with the ignorance based on invisibility is that when bisexuality does get spoken about, people assume they must be conflicted gay or lesbian individuals who simply cannot accept themselves!

It will not be prudent for every bisexual male to make himself visible, just as it is contraindicated for gay men under certain circumstances (Alderson, 2000). This becomes a choice that the bisexual individual must make given his or her unique situation. Questioning whether to "out" oneself might be the presenting concern, but more typically, the counselor will be dealing with the sequelae from clients demeaning the side of themselves that is attracted to the same sex. Self-loathing is a serious problem for people who have not embraced important parts of themselves. Bisexual individuals who are living closeted lives also risk exposure to their partners, families or friends, employers, and the public at large.

Counseling will focus on helping bisexual clients accept the many parts of themselves that have been fragmented, disenfranchised, and/or disregarded. After self-acceptance occurs, clients can then decide the extent to which they wish to be visible to others. Counselors should encourage their clients to look at the potential advantages (benefits) and disadvantages (harms) that will likely arise by taking different actions.

COUNSELING DIVERSE POPULATIONS

Counseling Bisexual Men With Multiple Nondominant Identity Statuses

Much research reveals the rampant homophobia within African American life, often resulting in the relegation of one of their identities (African American or LGB identity) to "exile" (Arbaugh, 2002, p. 121). Scott (2007) acknowledged the complexity that bisexual individuals of African descent encounter when attempting to create an identity that respects both their racial/ethnic heritage and culture and their bisexual interests. Scott's approach to helping clients achieve this is through narrative reauthoring of a client's life. The following narrative themes are suggested: (a) discussion of the various aspects (i.e., sociocultural, political) that affect their development of a biracial identity; (b) discussion of their experiences of invalidation, oppression, and marginality; (c) exploration of the costs and benefits of promoting their mental health and sense of well-being through accepting their identities; and (d) use of narrative therapy to reauthor their marginalized stories and life experiences.

Counseling Latino bisexual men also poses special challenges based on the need for Latino men to present machismo in all circumstances (Ferrer & Gomez, 2007). Unlike African American culture, however, remember that Latino men are often not judged negatively so long as they assume the active role (i.e., dominant penetrative role) in sexual activity. Refer to Ferrer and Gomez (2007) for greater discussion in this area.

Counselors working with bisexual Asian/Pacific Islanders will also encounter a context in which communication styles, values, and family structure will likely conflict with bisexual interests (Collins, 2007). Each situation is unique, and counselors are reminded to review the ecological model (Appendix D and the section following the "How Would You Help This Person?" section of this chapter) to ensure that the environmental context is considered together with the individual dynamics of this particular client. An excellent resource for working with Asian American men is Ming Liu, Kenji Iwamoto, and Chae (2010).

Counselors working with bisexual Native Americans also require special knowledge of their culture. Arbaugh (2002) reminds us that Native Americans place "great emphasis on harmony" (p. 122). In indigenous communities in which two-spirited individuals are accepted, conflict is less likely. Unfortunately, since the arrival of White settlers, fewer bisexual Native Americans experience appreciation and reverence for their identities.

Counseling Aging Bisexual Men

Aging bisexual men continue to have sexual needs, regardless of whether they live independently or in supported housing (Keppel & Firestein, 2007). Most literature focuses on the needs of aging gay and lesbian individuals, and the needs of aging bisexual individuals include the possible integration of both male and female intimate and/or sexual partners. While most navigate this well when living independently, problems may arise if living in circumstances in which caregivers knowingly or unwittingly deny them their freedoms. Keppel and Firestein (2007) recommend both individual and systemic interventions to assist aging bisexual individuals in coping with their circumstances.

Counseling Bisexual Males Living in Rural Communities

A survey of 527 rural LGBTI individuals revealed both positive and negative aspects of living in nonurban areas. On the plus side, some LGBTI participants noted that they enjoyed close relationships, a high quality of life, involvement in LGBTI social networks and organizations, and self-acceptance. On the negative side, some participants reported experiencing weak and fragmented LGBTI resources, homophobic environments, and lacking equal rights (Oswald & Culton, 2003).

A national study of LGBTI high school students ($N = 5{,}240$) found that those living in rural communities and in areas in which the adults had lower educational attainment experienced the greatest likelihood of facing particularly hostile school climates (Kosciw, Greytak, & Diaz, 2009). A qualitative study of LGB adolescents living in rural settings uncovered three themes: (a) feeling different from their heterosexual counterparts, (b) experiencing a limited social life in high school, and (c) perceiving that they are avoided by peers and staff in their high school (Jackson, 2010).

Counseling Bisexual Male Students

In light of the invisibility and internalized biphobia characteristic of most bisexual students, interventions may need to first provide a safe place for them to congregate. Snively (2004) recommended building community-based alliances (like gay–straight alliances discussed in Chapter 3). These could operate in schools or in communities. Counselors working in grade schools should consider establishing gay–straight alliances. These are always considered inclusive (this openness may need to be advertised, of course) of all members of the LGBTI community and those who are still exploring their sexualities and/or gender.

Counseling Bisexual Male Adolescents

A study by Saewyc and colleagues (2009) found that bisexual teenagers were less likely to receive family support and feel connected at school compared to heterosexual and mostly heterosexual adolescents. Teens with attraction to both sexes are at somewhat higher risk for substance abuse and abuse compared to heterosexual youth (Russell, Driscoll, & Truong, 2002). Compared to gay/lesbian and heterosexual youth, bisexual youth also appear to be at greatest sexual risk (including HIV) based on reported condom use (Rotheram-Borus, Marelich, & Srinivasan, 1999). As most bisexual youth are part of an invisible population (Thomas & Larrabee, 2002) that is unlikely to bring up the topic of bisexuality (Arbaugh, 2002), counselors need to ask carefully constructed questions within the context of a caring environment to provide a safe place for youth to disclose and work through aspects of their bisexuality. An outstanding resource for counselors working with LGBTI adolescents is edited by Sears (2005a, 2005b).

Resources for This Group

1. The Bi Men Network is the largest free worldwide social and support network for bisexual, bi-curious, and gay men, and bisexual couples. They claim they are the largest association for bisexual individuals on earth (www.bimen.org/).
2. The American Institute of Bisexuality contains many links and information about bisexual individuals (www.bisexual.org/resources.html).
3. The Bisexual Resources Center has a special section for bisexual youth (http://biresource.net/biyouthresources.shtml).
4. The LGBT Community Service Directory is a database containing information about member LGBT Community Centers and member Affiliates in the United States and around the world (www.lgbtcenters.org/Centers/find-a-center.aspx).
5. PFLAG New York City contains many links to LGBT resources available online (www.pflagnyc.org/links). PFLAG is an acronym for Parents, Family and Friends of Lesbians and Gays. Their national organization's website follows (http://community.pflag.org/Page.aspx?pid=194&srcid=-2).

Limitations, Furthering Research, and Implications for Counselors

Limitations of the Research With This Group

The newness of this identity and its continued barriers in receiving widespread acceptance have created a scenario wherein bisexual individuals are "thrown into the heap" with studies that primarily focus on gay and lesbian people. As you have witnessed in this chapter, most studies have not focused strictly on bisexual individuals. The entire field of bisexuality awaits further study by those employing both quantitative and qualitative methodologies.

While it has been noted that it is difficult to find representative studies of gay and lesbian individuals, the difficulty is magnified when we consider bisexual males and females. Bisexual individuals often "hide," and they hide well. Researchers have a difficult time finding them. The hide-and-seek of today will hopefully give yield to what has occurred to a much greater degree in the gay and lesbian community. To be out, one needs to feel safe, accepted, and respected. Unfortunately, none of these prerequisites have occurred yet for most bisexual individuals.

Areas Requiring Further Research

The most fascinating question of all is one that has never been answered: Is everyone, male and female, inherently bisexual, and if so, in what ways? If we could get people to be *absolutely* honest, would everyone admit to some degree of having bisexual (a) sexual attraction, (b) sexual fantasies, (c) sexual preference (a desire to have sex with both genders), and/or (d) love interests? If our society displayed absolutely no judgment toward homosexuality, what would change? How would relationships look different in a world already overcrowded, a world in which it has become increasingly expensive to have children and send them through college?

Another research question concerns comparisons between bisexual individuals who remain monogamous with a partner and those who seek out multiple partners. How is it that some bisexual men can live happy lives with sexual/romantic involvement with one gender or the other while others insist on having both simultaneously? What similarities and differences exist between the two groups?

Given the dearth of research in this area, the study of bisexuality is ripe with opportunity. Virtually any topic is worthy of exploration or further study.

Findings in psychology, like other social sciences, are ideally based on replication of studies. The more often similar results are found, the greater our trust level in that which is discovered. This is from a positivist paradigm, mind you. From a postmodern perspective, there is equally a great need to uncover the various ways that males construct bisexual identities in today's world and the ways in which these are negotiated in the majority of places where they are misunderstood and maligned.

Implications for Counselors

Bisexual men are usually no more effeminate than heterosexual men, and consequently, counselors may not have any idea of a man's bisexual proclivities. When sexual behavior is relevant to a client's presenting issue, it is important to inquire and not assume same-sex sexual activity is or is not occurring. Many men who have sex with other men do not define as gay or bisexual. When clients report that they are bisexual, the counselor needs to ask about whether this refers to sexual behavior, sexual identity, and/or affectional orientation.

As few bisexual individuals experience equal attraction to both genders, it may be important—depending on the presenting issue—to look at whether the client has more interest in other males or in females. A common presenting issue involves the complexity of maintaining a relationship if the bisexual man feels the need to be sexual with both genders simultaneously. While some partners can accept outside sexual activity, for others it is a bottom line. Some bisexual men develop polyamorous relationships, with or without the knowledge of their partners or spouses.

Given that bisexual men and women tend to have worse mental health than gay and lesbian individuals, counselors should be cognizant of this and be alert to signs of failing or failed mental health. Furthermore, many bisexual individuals do not feel much support from their environments, and assisting them with connecting to an online bisexual community may be helpful.

Exercises

Individual Exercises

1. Take yourself to a busy place where there are plenty of men (e.g., shopping mall, dance club, bar). As you look around, which ones do you think define as gay, heterosexual, or bisexual? After spending some time doing this, on what basis did you find yourself making these discernments?
2. Talk to a guy you know who defines as bisexual and ask him the same questions that are found below under *Classroom Exercise*.

Classroom Exercise

1. In dyads, one student plays the role of identifying as a bisexual male. Begin by introducing yourself to the other student by saying, "My name is . . . , and I self-identify as bisexual." Either the other student decides to ask his or her own questions, or instead uses the following. If you are playing the bisexual male, you have the option of not answering any questions you do not want to answer by saying "pass."

   a. How long have identified as bisexual?
   b. How many people have you disclosed your bisexual identity to?
   c. How do you decide who to tell and who not to?
   d. What is it like to tell someone you are a bisexual male?
   e. What is the hardest part about being a bisexual male?
   f. What is the happiest part about being a bisexual male?
   g. Have you ever felt afraid because you are a bisexual male?
   h. How do you deal with heterosexual people and gay or lesbian people wanting to pull you into their "club," so to speak?
   i. How do you protect yourself from biphobics?
   j. What else would you like to tell me about your experience of being a bisexual male? (this exercise is adapted from Finkel, Storaasli, Bandele, & Schaefer, 2003).

Chapter Summary

Despite Kinsey et al.'s (1948) warning that the world cannot be divided into sheep and goats, most researchers, counselors, and laypersons have done exactly that. The hegemonic scripts of masculinity and femininity have wielded incredible power throughout every world culture, both past and present. Wherever bisexuality has existed within a culture, it has been for a specified period of time in a man's life—until now. Today, people can create and embrace bisexual identities throughout most of their life span if they so choose.

Both male and female bisexuality have been understudied. Bisexual individuals are more invisible than their gay and lesbian counterparts. Generally, they can pass more readily as heterosexual, as they emphasize these aspects in their public presentation of self. Due to the greater questioning that occurs in assuming a bisexual identity, bisexual individuals usually adopt these identities later than do gay and lesbian people.

The greater degree of questioning required to identify as bisexual may also underlie one of the consistent findings in this area: Bisexual men and women generally experience worse mental health compared to gay and lesbian individuals (who in turn experience generally worse mental health compared to their heterosexual counterparts). Bisexual individuals are also at higher risk of suicidality.

Many bisexual men have been or still are married to women. Research has revealed that most did not deceive their spouses; at the time they married, they did not identify as bisexual. While most bisexual men would prefer more than one sexual partner, the majority do not construct their relationships with women this way. Some research suggests that both bisexual men and women prefer emotional relationships with women and sexual ones with men.

Regarding counseling implications, five main common problems with counseling applications were noted in this chapter: (a) identity confusion and labeling issues, (b) internalized biphobia, (c) relationship strain and fidelity concerns, (d) finding support networks, and (e) invisibility and its sequelae. Readers are reminded that issues typical of other LGBTI individuals may also surface for bisexual individuals, and these are explained in the chapters in which these problems are most commonly presented to counselors.

6

Bisexual Girls and Women

Challenging Your Attitudes and Beliefs About This Group

Reflection Questions

1. If you were a bisexual woman, what challenges would you face in today's society? Given that being in a relationship with a woman brings with it outside homophobia and negative reactions from others, why not simply stay solely focused on being in a relationship with a man?
2. If a drug was developed that could eliminate the attraction toward others of the same sex, would you encourage bisexual women to take it? Why or why not?

(Continued)

(Continued)

3. We know that some women define themselves as heterosexual, yet they engage in homosexual behavior while serving time in prison. We also know that the majority of lesbian women have engaged in heterosexual behavior. What explains this?
4. Given that women can be more physically demonstrative in public than men without facing negative reactions from others, do you think this increases the likelihood that women will become bisexual? To what extent would this affect their capacity to fall in love romantically with a member of the same gender?
5. What would you see as the advantages and disadvantages of being a bisexual woman?

Challenging Your Assumptions Questions

1. Do you believe that bisexual women would be more masculine or more feminine compared to lesbian women? What do you think would account for that?
2. Do you concur with Sigmund Freud's view that we are all inherently bisexual? If this were true, why do so few people identify as bisexual?
3. Should bisexuality be included as an integral part of sex education curricula? Why or why not?
4. How can you tell if a female adolescent or adult defines as bisexual?

Reflections

[*Note:* Imagine that *you* are the client in these reflections.]

By everyone's standards, you are considered physically beautiful—and you know it, too. Your name is Jenine, and you define yourself as exclusively heterosexual. You give little thought to a classmate named Becky who is constantly hanging around you, vying for your attention.

Becky is also very attractive and popular, so you decide to start spending time together. After a few weeks of getting to know each other and having fun, Becky asks, "Hey, are you free Saturday night? I was thinking it would be fun to have a slumber party at my house. Watch some flicks, have a few drinks, that sort of thing."

You are free Saturday night and ask Becky, "What should I bring?" "Just bring yourself—I will have everything, including sleepwear, drinks, and snacks." Saturday arrives and you arrive at Becky's. Becky greets you, "Right on time, Jenine! Come to my room so we can get changed. I have a couple of new comedies for us to watch."

After you both get changed, Becky starts the movie and begins pouring drinks. After four, you feel half drunk already. About half way into the movie, Becky begins cuddling up to you in a way that makes you uncomfortable. Nonetheless, your curiosity is aroused, and as the night progresses, the two of you begin making out and exploring each other's bodies.

You are feeling bothered the next day, however, as you leave for home, nursing a mild hangover. The night with Becky was more enjoyable than you had expected, and this disturbs you. You are heterosexual, after all, yet the sensitivity Becky showed you was unsurpassed by any man you have yet dated. You make an appointment with a college counselor. Barbara is a woman of about 45 years of age, and she immediately makes you feel welcome with her beaming smile. You tell her about your experience and the feelings it has left inside you.

Barbara seems like the perfect counselor. Her smile is unwavering as you pour out the emotions attached. After your tears subside, Barbara says, "Hey, you really are being hard on yourself. It sounds like Becky set the stage and then hit on you in a respectful manner." "Yeah, I have to agree with that. I let her continue because it made me feel sensual. It was overly pleasant—that is what bothers me actually."

"So you are bothered because you had more fun than you have had in a long time?" "Well, more than that, Barbara. I had more fun with her than I have ever had with a guy! The guys I have dated have just wanted one thing and have given very little back to me. Also, I really like her: we have a lot in common. I feel that I crossed the line by becoming sexual with her. I enjoyed it, but it bothers me at the same time."

"Do you feel bad because the experience was with a woman and not with a man?" "Well, I guess so. I just don't see myself as a bisexual—that's all." "Jenine, you don't have to define as bisexual to acknowledge and accept that you simply enjoyed the physical company of being with another woman on this occasion. It doesn't matter if you ever repeat this experience again or not. What matters is that you accept that you enjoyed yourself and helped someone else feel good, too. What can be wrong with that?"

"Nothing, Barbara. Thank you!" you reply as your session ends. You leave there feeling heard, appreciated, and respected. You have also given this experience a healthy perspective.

From a Client's Perspective

1. If you were Jenine, how would *you* feel about your experience of counseling? Why?
2. Would you want to come back for a second session with Barbara if something else came up for you? Why or why not?

From a Counselor's Perspective

1. What do you think of Barbara's interpretation that it was really a harmless experience?
2. Barbara did not label Jenine's behavior, thereby not challenging Jenine's heterosexuality. Do you agree with this approach? Why or why not?
3. If you were Barbara, what else would you want to explore in your session with Jenine (e.g., spiritual beliefs, family of origin)?
4. Would the depth of feelings that Jenine has for Barbara make any difference in counseling her? Why or why not?
5. Is having bisexual attraction a phase for some women? If so, how would you know if you need to take it seriously or not?

Background Information Regarding Bisexual Girls to Women

Dr. Paul Gebhard was one of the original Kinsey researchers listed as author in the classic *Sexual Behavior in the Human Female* (Kinsey, Pomeroy, Martin, & Gebhard, 1953). Gebhard recently said that Kinsey would have been

> disheartened that so little emancipation seems to have been granted to bisexuals, that they continue to be viewed as "the unhappy minority," and that our society expects people to be exclusively straight or gay and that we still tell people to "make up your mind." (Dodge, Reece, & Gebhard, 2008, p. 184)

As mentioned in Chapter 5, researchers struggle to find financial support for studies concerning human sexuality, particularly when its focus is on sexual minorities (Fairyington, 2008).

What we do know, however, generally does support the "unhappy minority" view of bisexual men and women that would have displeased Kinsey if he were still alive. Williams (1999), however, concluded that bisexual individuals have achieved a higher level of personal self-development.

Bisexual women are disproportionately overrepresented compared to men in their reporting of bisexual attractions (Diamond, 2006), and bisexual attractions are more common than exclusive same-sex attractions (Laumann, Gagnon, Michael, & Michaels, 1994). Hoburg, Konik, Williams, and Crawford (2004) studied bisexuality among self-identified heterosexual college students. In their two studies with a combined sample size of 730 participants, 29 to 32% of the females and 12 to 19% of men reported having same-sex feelings. The more recent study by Vrangalova and Savin-Williams (2010) found that in their sample of heterosexually identified young adults (n = 203; 47% female), 84% of the women reported having some degree of same-sex interest in one or more of sexual attractions, fantasies, and behaviors, compared to 51% of the men.

Based on Rust's (2001) large-scale study of 917 bisexual men and women, she described that most individuals who define as bisexual see their bisexual identity as meaning they are "sexually, emotionally, and/or romantically attracted to both women and men, but many also mention their sexual experiences or connections to the bisexual community or politics" (p. 58). Compared to bisexual men who are married, bisexual women are less likely to have been aware of their same-sex interests before marriage and are less likely to try and eliminate these interests through counseling (Coleman, 1985).

Burrill (2002) wrote that queer theory would likely be of benefit to bisexual individuals. The hope was that it would lead to greater bisexual visibility. However, theorists are divided on whether they should be favorable toward bisexuality because queer theory does not embrace categorical labels.

A recent study by Moore and Norris (2005) did not find that the bisexual individuals in their sample scored higher on their flexibility measures than did the heterosexual and gay/lesbian individuals. Instead, they found that the bisexual individuals were simply more conflicted about their sexuality than the others.

Overall, however, studying women is the ideal population for queer theorists. Voluminous amounts of research indicate that women are far more flexible and fluid regarding their affectional orientation compared to men (Diamond, 2006, 2007, 2008; Diamond & Savin-Williams, 2000; Kinnish, Strassberg, & Turner, 2005).

Development Through the Life Span

One cannot write about the development of bisexual women as a separate entity. Rust (1993) found in her study of almost 400 lesbian and bisexual women that 75% of bisexual respondents once identified as lesbian, while more than 40% of lesbian participants reported once identifying as bisexual. Diamond's (2008) 10-year longitudinal study of sexual minority women also revealed that over the 10-year span, two-thirds of the women changed their identity labels from what they were at the beginning of the study. In fact, one-third changed their labels more than once!

These results were not supported, however, in the first and second waves of the National Longitudinal Study of Adolescent Health (NLSAH; Russell & Seif, 2002). Russell and Seif's (2002) study had a sample size of more than 20,000 7th- to 12th-grade students (ages 12–19) in wave 1. In wave 2 conducted 18 months later, more than 70% of the participants were reinterviewed. The researchers found that of the 3.88% (n = 397) of females who reported bisexual attractions at wave 1, only 5% reported only same-sex attractions in wave 2. Russell and Seif concluded that their results did not support the idea that female bisexuality is a transitional period to identification as lesbian. In fact, they concluded that exclusive same-sex attraction was less stable than bisexual attraction among the young women in their study.

A study of 60 sexual minority youth (ages 15–23) by Diamond and Lucas (2004) found that compared to heterosexual youth, they had comparable self-esteem, sense of mastery, and perceived stress. But they also reported greater negative affect. Furthermore, regardless of their age, sexual minority youths had higher worries about losing friends, experienced less sense of control in their romantic involvements, and expressed greater fear of never finding the type of love relationship they wanted.

Needham and Austin (2010) used results from wave 3 of the NLSAH (n = 11,153, 50.6% female, mean age = 21.8 years). Lesbian and bisexual women reported that they had lower levels of parental support compared to heterosexual women. In comparison to heterosexual women, lesbian and bisexual women were more likely to have suicidal thoughts, recent drug use, and heavy drinking and were more likely to experience depressive symptoms. With the exception of heavy drinking, all other negative effects were mediated by parental support. This study clearly indicates that parental support can act as an insulation against many of the problems that befall young lesbian and bisexual women.

Bisexual females take longer to self-identify compared to lesbian women (Matteson, 1996). Bisexual women also report desiring a partner of each sex, as each fulfills different emotional needs (Matteson, 1996).

The study by Weinberg, Williams, and Pryor (2001) included 28 bisexual middle-aged women (ages 35–67). The results, which included the 23 men and 5 transgender persons in their research, suggested that bisexual individuals at midlife move toward (a) less sexual involvement, (b) only having sex with one gender, (c) less involvement in the bisexual subculture, and (d) less perceived importance of having a bisexual identity. More recent research reveals that when midlife LGB individuals perceive daily discrimination, are female, and/or have less education, these factors are associated with feeling a lower sense of well-being (i.e., less sense of personal growth and feeling that life is purposeful and meaningful; Riggle, Rostosky, & Danner, 2009).

Bisexual identity appears to remain stable through the middle and older years for both men and women (Dworkin, 2006). For some midlife and older bisexual women, feelings of "restlessness, reassessment, and regeneration" occur (Dworkin, 2006, p. 42).

Race and Ethnicity

Research specifically focused on bisexual women of color is scant, as most researchers have focused instead on gay and lesbian participants (Collins, 2004). Steinhouse (2001) concluded that bisexuality is a politically hot topic, and perhaps this too has led to the paucity of research in this area.

Balsam, Lehavot, Beadnell, and Circo (2010) recently completed an online study of 669 LGB adults, 21% of whom were persons of color. They found that the Latina/o and Asian American participants reported the highest levels of physical abuse, while Latina/o and African American participants reported the most sexual abuse. They further found that "childhood emotional abuse was the strongest predictor of psychopathology symptoms for all participants" (Balsam et al., 2010, p. 459). The authors concluded that ethnicity might be an important variable when looking at childhood abuse and mental health.

While we might hypothesize that the issues concerning bisexual women of color are similar to those affecting lesbian women of color, they likely face some unique stresses. Bisexual individuals usually face pressure to fit into one community or the other (heterosexual or gay/lesbian), and bisexual women of color may face this sense of being forced into this dichotomy more than their White counterparts. Furthermore, their triple minority status (i.e., race/ethnicity, gender, and affectional orientation) may make their lives more difficult than most. The answers to these questions are currently unknown.

Relationships (Family, Friendships, Intimate Romantic/Sexual)

Qualitative findings based on interviews with 10 bisexual women found that dissimilar to what happens with gay men and lesbian women, bisexual women often experience discrimination and bias from their sexual partners because of their affectional orientation, including a sexualization of their identities (Samji, 2008). Samji (2008) also concluded that many bisexual women are content to live monogamously with their partners.

In another study with a sample size of 26 male–female couples in which the women defined as bisexual, Reinhardt (2002) found that half maintained sexual relationships with other women while committed to their opposite-sex relationship. These women reported feeling happy in their sexual relationships with both genders. These results replicated similar findings in a study by Dixon (1985). Women in Dixon's study were married before beginning sexual "swinging" with other couples, and from this experience, these women changed their self-definition to bisexual while continuing to enjoy sexual activities with both genders.

While many bisexual women will maintain monogamous relationships, those who establish open relationships need to deal with the same issues that other couples face when creating non-monogamous arrangements. Issues such as dealing with jealousy, setting boundaries, and maintaining open communication are vital (McLean, 2004).

As Thompson (2007) indicated, young women often develop physically and emotionally close friendships with other women that serve as a safe place for some to explore flexibility in their sexual identity. Having sexual experiences with same-sex friends can serve an important role in the eventual construction of a bisexual identity (Morgan & Thompson, 2007).

Regarding friendships, some research suggests that heterosexual women view bisexual women as more similar to themselves compared to lesbian women (Galupo, Sailer, & St. John, 2004). Interestingly, the two of them (i.e., the heterosexual and the bisexual woman) perceive a shift in their friendship dynamics in response to the particular sex of the bisexual woman's partner (i.e., a shift occurs depending on whether the woman is involved with a man as opposed to another woman).

Health (Emotional and Psychological, Physical)

Compared to heterosexual women, both bisexual and lesbian women report having less parental support. They also have a higher likelihood of experiencing suicidal thoughts, depression, and heavy drinking (Needham & Austin, 2010).

Bisexual and lesbian women are more likely than heterosexual women to have poor physical and mental health (Case et al., 2004; Dilley, Simmons, Boysun, Pizacani, & Stark, 2010). They are more likely to have asthma, to drink excessively, to be overweight, and to smoke. Bisexual women specifically are more likely to have diabetes compared to lesbian and heterosexual women (Dilley et al., 2010).

Compared to lesbian and heterosexual women, bisexual women have a more difficult time integrating all aspects of their lives, and consequently, many experience poorer mental health (Rothblum & Factor, 2001). Compared to lesbian women, bisexual women experience more conflict regarding their affectional orientation, they are less open about it, and they report less minority stress (Balsam & Mohr, 2007; Lewis, Derlega, Brown, Rose, & Henson, 2009).

While Koh and Ross (2006) found that bisexual women were twice as likely to experience eating disorders compared to lesbian women, Feldman and Meyer (2007) did not find a difference between bisexual women compared to either lesbian or heterosexual women. In interpreting these results, Feldman and Meyer suggested that lesbian and bisexual women might not be immune to the standards of beauty that the dominant culture has set for women, thereby leaving them at the same risk for eating disorders as heterosexual women. Taub's (1999) research, based on 77 bisexual women, further adds to our understanding of the importance of gender in setting beauty standards. Taub found that when romantically involved with men, bisexual women become more concerned with their appearance than when they are involved with women.

Adding still further to these findings, Meyer, Blissett, and Oldfield (2001) tested 100 students (20 lesbian women, 20 gay men, 30 heterosexual women, and 30 heterosexual men) and found that eating problems were not associated with having a homosexual identity but instead were correlated with femininity scores on the Bem Sex Role Inventory. Masculinity scores, on the other hand, were not. Meyer and colleagues surmised that masculinity might act as a protective factor against eating psychopathology. These results should be viewed as tentative, however, given that these participants were not chosen on the basis of having a diagnosed eating disorder.

Career and Work

While the 1980s saw the beginning of a career counseling focus for women with nondominant sexualities (Farmer, 2006), there remains an absence of research specifically focused on bisexual women. As noted in the previous section, bisexual women are less open about their sexuality compared to lesbian women (Lewis et al., 2009). Consequently, it seems likely that most would pass as heterosexual in work settings, unless they are perhaps in a committed long-term relationship with another woman.

Spirituality and Religion

Lease, Horne, and Noffsinger-Frazier (2005) sampled 583 LGB individuals who were identified with a faith group. Lease and colleagues found a positive relationship between being part of an affirming faith community and psychological health. This finding is important in that research suggests that spirituality is associated with psychological health (Lease et al., 2005). LGB individuals, however, have generally experienced negative effects from religious experiences (Gage Davidson, 2000). Consequently, they tend to be less inclined than heterosexual individuals to attend organized religion (Ellis & Wagemann, 1993).

Sociopolitical Realities

Women are frequently victims of sexism, including acts of rape and sexual assault (Moradi & DeBlaere, 2010). In addition to this generic finding regarding the treatment of women, bisexual women also face greater stigma within the lesbian and gay communities compared to what they face in the heterosexual community (Beaber, 2008). The reasons for this were stated in Chapter 5: In effect, most gay and lesbian individuals mistrust bisexual people of both sexes (Mohr & Rochlen, 1999).

On a positive note, bisexuality has continued to become increasingly accepted in American society over the past 30 years (Herdt, 2001). There is a growing recognition and exploration of bisexuality emerging in today's youth and a continuing redefinition of what it means to assume a bisexual identity (Herdt, 2001).

Recent Research Focused on Canada

Antigay attitudes were assessed among adolescents in both Belgium (n = 6,330) and Canada (n = 3,334). The analysis revealed that negative feelings toward LGBTI rights are especially prevalent among boys; the effects of socioeconomic status and parental education are limited. Several religious denominations were found to have a strong negative impact on tolerance, with particularly high scores for Islam (Hooghe, Claes, Harell, Quintelier, & Dejaeghere, 2010).

While same-sex marriage has legally equalized the playing field for the LGBTI community in Canada, as Onishenko and Caragata (2010) noted, "one only has to scratch the surface to realize that discrimination and exclusion are still very much part of the social order" (p. 106). For example, lesbian and bisexual mothers experience more challenges in adopting children compared to heterosexual mothers (Ross et al., 2008).

Heterosexual students can become allies to the LGBTI community, however, and Ji, Du Bois, and Finnessy (2009) explored ways that this can occur. Alderson (2004) provided a curriculum that instructors can use to teach counselors how to work with sexual minority clients.

A cross-sectional analysis of data from the Canadian Community Health Survey (Steele, Ross, Dobinson, Veldhuizen, & Tinmouth, 2009) included 354 lesbian women, 424 bisexual women, and 60,937 heterosexual women. Steele and colleagues (2009) found that bisexual women were the most likely group to report poor or fair mental and physical health, anxiety or mood disorders, lifetime prevalence of STD diagnosis, and especially lifetime suicidality.

Compared to lesbian women, data from the American 2002 National Survey of Family Growth revealed that bisexual women are not at increased risk of becoming overweight or obese (Boehmer, Bowen, & Bauer, 2007). Canadian lesbian and bisexual women do experience barriers to basic health care and accessibility to medical services, however (Mathieson, Bailey, & Gurevich, 2002). Canadian research is clearly showing that while same-sex marriage has contributed a great deal to the legal equality of LGBTI individuals, our society still has a long way to go to realize psychosocial acceptance.

Recent Research Focused on Other Societies

Fox, Goetstouwers, and Pallotta-Chiarolli (2008) wrote that whether researchers are looking at bisexuality or sexuality more generally, there are many aspects that are specific to particular cultures. For example, research from Australia (McLean, 2008) and France (Welzer-Lang, 2008) reveal that they are dichotomous in their thinking about sexuality, resulting in an impact on bisexual individuals in both countries. This, of course, is not unlike what we experience in both the United States and Canada. Rigidity in dichotomous views of sexuality (i.e., you are either heterosexually or homosexually inclined) is also true in Turkey (Bereket & Brayton, 2008).

Indigenous individuals who define as two-spirited in the United States and Canada, on the other hand, often view all aspects of their identity (e.g., sexuality, race, gender) as interconnected. In this manner, sexuality becomes inseparable from their culture and their community (Wilson, 1996).

One dissertation study found that in comparing a sample of college students in the United States to a sample in Taiwan, heterosexual participants were more likely to experience congruence between their sexual identity and their sexual preferences when compared to nonheterosexual participants (Roberts, 2003). Furthermore, Taiwan students were far more likely to be celibate compared to American students.

While even early cross-cultural studies found that homosexual behavior is found in virtually every culture, past and present (Ford & Beach, 1951), the concept of adopting a bisexual identity is new. Cross-cultural studies specifically focused on women who define as bisexual currently do not exist.

Common Concerns Facing This Group and Counseling Considerations

Roleplay Scenarios

[*Note:* Suggested assessment and intervention strategies for the two roleplays below can be found in Appendix B. Before going there, roleplay in dyads with one of you acting as the counselor and the other as the counselee. If a roleplay is not possible, work individually in writing out a list of your suggestions.]

Roleplay #1, Chapter 6. Counseling Bisexual Women

Maggie, a Black woman aged 20, has come to see you for help. She has been aware of her interest in both men and women for several years, and she has had sexual relations with both sexes as well. Her heterosexual friends and lesbian friends alike are threatened by her middle position, and they pressure her to take one side or the other. Most of her lesbian friends they tell her she is really a lesbian and that she is just trying to hang on to some remnant of a heterosexual identity. On the other hand, she finds that most of her Black heterosexual friends refuse to believe her interest in women is real, and they tell her to grow up and find a man. Mostly, Maggie is confused by her dual attractions. She is also seeing you because she feels rejected by both the heterosexual community and the lesbian community. She rarely gets invited to anyone's home.

Roleplay #2, Chapter 6. Counseling Bisexual Women

Janis, age 35, has come to see you for help. She has been an active member of the lesbian community for the past 15 years. Her 12-year relationship with Emma (age 43) has been fairly positive and fulfilling, but like several long-term relationships, it has had its ups and downs. While Emma was away on a 2-week business trip, Janis went out dancing to a mixed (both gay and heterosexual) club and found herself being seduced by Clint, a handsome 40-year-old businessman. The two of them spent some time together every night together during Emma's absence, having sex following the third date. Shocking to Janis, she found herself developing strong feelings of attachment for Clint and craving more and more sex. After Emma returned, Janis has found herself making excuses about why she is out some nights, spending that time secretively with Clint. She is seeing you because she doesn't know what to do.

How Would *You* Help This Person?

Sylvia, age 39, comes to see you at your office. You are struck by how youthful she appears! Many people would probably see her as closer to age 25. She tells you that she has been living the good life, enjoying sex with several individuals. Both her identity and her behavior are bisexual. In the past year, Sylvia has had 10 male lovers of varying durations, and she is sexually involved with 3 women she has known for a long time. Having children has become important to her, and she wants to bear a child but is afraid of the economic repercussions.

Sylvia begins: "You know, I never thought I would get to this age without having children by now. I work at a local retail store and barely earn enough money to make ends meet. The trouble is, I haven't met either a man or a woman with whom to make a serious commitment."

You ask, "To what extent then are finances blocking you from achieving your goal of having a child?"

"This is a huge factor," Sylvia replies. "I cannot afford to keep a child, and I do not see my situation changing anytime soon. Furthermore, I really would prefer having a committed relationship with a woman. I cannot find a lesbian who is attracted to me who also accepts me. On two occasions, I did meet a suitable female partner, but both of them wanted an exclusive monogamous relationship. I do not see myself living in a monogamous way perpetually, so I will not commit to someone who insists on keeping me from ever having sex with a man again!"

Where would you take it from here if you were counseling Sylvia?

Note—Remember to view clients within their environmental contexts, keeping in mind societal, parental/familial, cultural/spiritual, and peer influences. Specifically, become aware of the impact that the following influences have and continue to have in your clients' lives: race, language,

(Continued)

(Continued)

religion and spirituality, gender, familial migration history, affectional orientation, age and cohort, physical and mental capacities, socioeconomic situation and history, education, and history of traumatic experience.

1. What defines this person's environment, past and present?
2. Who is this person sitting in front of me, taking into account environmental and personal characteristics?
3. What defines the problem that he or she is presenting within his or her multicultural milieu?

As previously mentioned, lesbian and bisexual women are more likely than heterosexual women to seek counseling services. However, besides those who do feel understood and supported, many bisexual women feel invalidated and dissatisfied with their counseling experience (Zook, 2002). As Firestein (2007) noted, many counselors have difficulty understanding and validating the bisexual experience, embracing the same myths and stereotypes as many laypersons. Firestein believes that many counselors are uncomfortable with bisexual clients, especially around the topic of polyamory.

Before we begin looking at concerns that are most specific to bisexual women, it is important to provide a caveat that applies to members of the LGBTI community: The majority are living well without a need for counselors. While a book about counseling is going to create a problem-focused narrative, it is important to be reminded periodically that most people learn to cope with their challenges, and strength of character and hardiness are more normative than exceptional. Nonetheless, remember what was written in Chapter 1 about the bias that research creates: When group differences are found, they are based on large sample sizes and calculated using statistical procedures. When we look at the LGBTI community as a group, they do experience mental health difficulties to a greater extent when compared to the heterosexual community as a group.

Scales Rostosky, Riggle, Pascale-Hague, and McCants (2010) completed an online survey of 157 bisexual participants (67% female) where they asked about the positive aspects of identifying as bisexual. The following themes emerged: (a) sense of freedom from labels, (b) living honestly and with authenticity, (c) feeling unique, (d) perceiving that they have increased insight and awareness, (e) freedom to love either gender, (f) freedom to create unique relationships, (g) freedom in sexual expression, (h) acceptance of diversity, (i) feeling a sense of belonging to a community, (j) deeper appreciation for understanding privilege and oppression, and (k) becoming an advocate and/or an activist. Paradoxically, it is the flip side of these positive aspects that often propels individuals into counseling for reasons related to their bisexuality.

As Page (2004) noted, most bisexual clients do not seek counseling for reasons related to their bisexuality. Instead, they pursue counseling for the same reasons as most everyone else: relationship issues, anxiety, and depression. The counselor working with bisexual women needs to become "both an educator and a fellow explorer" (Horowitz & Newcomb, 1999, p. 154). Lourea (1985) suggested that the counseling process for bisexual women include helping them develop support systems, examining their internalized homophobia and sex-role stereotyping, and helping them deal with the issues that arise in opposite-sex relationships when one or both members define as bisexual. Smiley (1997) added a few other competencies, including (a) understanding their feelings, beliefs, and behaviors regarding the bisexual experience; (b) providing voice to their invalidation in society (i.e., a social justice agenda); (c) seeing bisexuality as healthy and embracing an affirmative stance toward it; (d) staying abreast of the positive aspects of a bisexual identity; and (e) assessing the client's identity using appropriate developmental models.

Bradford (2006) offered several recommendations for counselors. These include (a) acknowledging and working at reducing the effect of homophobia and biphobia; (b) making no assumptions about a client's sexual identity; (c) recognizing that the problems faced by bisexual people are culturally constructed (i.e., there is nothing inherently wrong with belonging to a sexual minority); (d) practicing affirmative counseling; and (e) becoming familiar with available resources.

Bradford (2006) also provided what she believed would be a helpful four-step process in counseling bisexual women. Her considerations included:

1. Questioning Reality—the counselor can offer a safe place for her to explore her feelings that do not fit into the binary system of gay/lesbian or heterosexual.
2. Inventing Identity—The client may need help in searching for language and understanding that reflect her experience.
3. Maintaining Identity—Maintaining a bisexual identity requires effort, a lifelong quest for many bisexual individuals.
4. Transforming Adversity—Similar to what other LGBTI individuals need to do, Bradford encourages counselors to help their clients cope with adversity and transcend it as much as possible.

Israel, Gorcheva, Walther, Sulzner, and Cohen (2008) sampled 14 psychotherapists to identify their perceptions of what is helpful and unhelpful in working with LGBTI clients. The variables identified included the importance of fostering the working alliance, their response to working with clients of differing sexualities, and the type of presenting concerns brought forward by the client. Other factors they believed needed to be addressed included the clients' ethnicity, gender identity, therapy needs, and their socioeconomic status. The participants believed that clients dealing with multiple layers of marginalization (e.g., female, bisexual, disabled) would be particularly difficult for practitioners.

This section now moves into looking at five concerns that are pertinent to counseling bisexual women. As in previous chapters, remember that most of these issues will also pertain to other members of the LGBTI community. The concerns raised in this chapter include (a) identity confusion and fluidity of sexuality, (b) poor mental health and suicidality, (c) drug and alcohol problems, (d) specific relationship strains, and (e) lack of community and isolation.

Identity Confusion and Fluidity of Sexuality

As noted in Chapter 5, bisexual individuals generally come out later than do either gay men or lesbian women. Most bisexual women view their affectional orientation as fluid and instead are more likely to focus on the person, not the gender (Brooks & Quina, 2009). In Bradford's (as cited in Firestein, 2007) doctoral research, 30% of her interviewees first identified as lesbian or gay before changing their self-definition to bisexual. Most first identify as heterosexual. When compared to lesbian and gay peers, bisexual participants often report higher levels of identity confusion (Balsam & Mohr, 2007).

Regardless, changing self-definitions is stressful. Most people prefer to label their behavior and their feelings in order to make sense of them and to provide closure so that they can focus their attention on other matters.

Whether the client will want to own an identity label eventually is not the main concern here, however. Embedded with same-sex interests is usually a degree of homophobia and biphobia. Both need to be addressed if these factors are holding back the client from accepting her same-sex interests in the context of bisexual experience. Alderson (2002) recommended a cognitive behavioral approach in helping sexual minorities to accept their feelings and their inclinations. As many LGB individuals do not experience integration between their sexual affect, sexual behavior, and affectional orientation (Laumann et al., 1994), encouraging a client to seek out same-sex sexual experiences may be completely unnecessary, and contraindicated if the client is a legal minor. Many individuals define as bisexual, but they have not yet had a sexual experience with someone of either or both genders.

As belief in the binary system is pandemic throughout most societies, the counselor may need to educate the client about the sexual continuum, perhaps most readily exemplified by the 7-point Kinsey Rating Scale (Kinsey, Pomeroy, & Martin, 1948). On the Kinsey Scale, 0 represents absolute heterosexuality, while 6 represents absolute homosexuality. Obviously most people lie somewhere in the middle on the Kinsey Scale, suggesting varying degrees of bisexual interest.

Another suggestion is to have the client complete the Sexuality Questionnaire (see Appendix C). Her responses will indicate the current extent of her same-sex interests alongside her opposite-sex interests for comparative purposes.

Poor Mental Health and Suicidality

When compared to heterosexual and lesbian individuals, bisexual women as a group appear to experience an increased incidence of mental health problems (Lieppe, 2006; Volpp, 2010). Bisexual women who seek counseling may experience an array of mental health concerns, but especially mood and anxiety disorders. A critical appraisal of the literature is needed, however, in making such sweeping generalizations. Researchers themselves do not agree on a definition of bisexuality, so what they focus on and what they do not may well produce different results.

Lieppe (2006) included participants who self-identified as bisexual. On what basis did these participants create their self-definition (recall the six components of affectional orientation)? Volpp (2010) wrote about this confounding variable when she began her conclusions with the statement, "Clearly, multiple measures of sexual orientation need to be used in our research to gain a better understanding of these differences and how each construct of sexual behavior, identity, and desire is associated with markers of mental health" (p. 48).

Bisexual participants often report lower levels of self-disclosure and less involvement in the LGBTI community compared to their lesbian and gay counterparts (Balsam & Mohr, 2007). They are also at higher risk of being physically assaulted compared to heterosexual women (Horowitz, Weis, & Laflin, 2003).

McLaughlin, Hatzenbuehler, and Keyes (2010) used the results from the National Epidemiologic Survey on Alcohol and Related Conditions ($N = 34{,}653$), a large sample that included a sizeable number of Black, Hispanic, female, and LGB individuals. McLaughlin and colleagues found that "Psychiatric disorders are more prevalent among individuals reporting past-year discrimination experiences. Certain responses to discrimination, particularly not disclosing it, are associated with psychiatric morbidity" (p. 1477). In other words, LGB individuals, when they experience discrimination, are best off talking about their experience and/or working through it with an understanding significant other or counselor.

It is critical that counselors assess for suicidality with all clients experiencing mood disorders and intervene appropriately. A new structured clinical interview has been developed by Nelson, Johnston, and Shrivastava (2010) that assesses suicide risk. The assessment tool was able to successfully categorize 74% of the participants tested. For counselors requiring practical strategies to deal with suicidal clients, Granello (2010) has provided a list of 25 interventions with proven effectiveness.

Drug and Alcohol Problems

Bisexual women appear to be at higher risk for experiencing drug and alcohol problems (McCabe, Hughes, & Boyd, 2004; Tucker, Ellickson, & Klein, 2008; Wilsnack et al., 2008). However, this finding is not replicated in every study (Bostwick et al., 2007). Counselors should be aware of this possibility, however, as many people with substance abuse problems deny that their use is causing them difficulties in various aspects of their lives. Substance abuse problems were covered in Chapter 4, and readers are encouraged to re-read that section.

Specific Relationship Strains

Before self-identifying as either lesbian or bisexual, many women report that they feel distant from important people in their lives (Reynolds, 2003). Alternatively, there are also many risks that LGBTI individuals face when they begin disclosing their identities. Disclosure to one's family of origin often brings varying degrees of dissention, for example. Disclosure issues are discussed in Chapter 3.

In contrast to heterosexual men, heterosexual women, lesbian women, and bisexual men, bisexual women sometimes surrender their bisexual identities when they are involved with lesbian women (Firestein, 2007). This is largely due to how controversial bisexuality is considered within the lesbian community (Rust, 2000).

It is unlikely that bisexual women will find themselves in relationships with other bisexual women (Firestein, 2007). Unless they live in a large urban area that provides access to an organized bisexual community, they are unlikely to meet other women who identify as bisexual.

Counselors need to be aware that bisexual women have many relationship options open to them, and they create a variety of relationship styles (Firestein, 2007). Consequently, they must be open to varying lifestyle choices. The counselor may be faced with issues arising from the gender of the client's partner (e.g., it is likely easier to be involved with a man so that passing as heterosexual can occur) and the type of relationship they have constructed (e.g., monogamous, polyamorous). The specific relationship strains that a bisexual woman experiences will need to be openly discussed within an atmosphere of acceptance.

Today, many lesbian and bisexual women, whether single or involved, are choosing to have children (Morris, Balsam, & Rothblum, 2002). This may raise many issues regarding parenthood, conception, adoption, and parenting. See Chapter 4 for a discussion of parenthood issues.

Lack of Community and Isolation

As Bradford (2006) noted recently, many bisexual women have no community to which they belong, despite its importance in helping bisexual women develop positive identities (Fox, 1991). As Firestein (2007) noted, most community involvement occurs via the Internet, at bisexual gatherings, or in the few large urban centers that have an organized bisexual community. Firestein indicated that physical bisexual communities exist in some cities, including Boston, San Francisco, Chicago, Seattle, New York City, Minneapolis, St. Paul, and Los Angeles.

For bisexual women living in areas in which a visible bisexual community exists, the Internet may serve as a source of support and belonging. Several pertinent websites are included in the Resources section of this chapter and in Chapter 5.

COUNSELING DIVERSE POPULATIONS

Counseling Bisexual Women With Multiple Nondominant Identity Statuses

Brooks, Inman, Malouf, Klinger, and Kaduvettoor (2008) interviewed 14 ethnic minority bisexual women ($M = 30$, age range 25 to 53). Findings revealed that these women needed to manage a bisexual and a community identity. They faced challenges and pressures from family and within their social environments. Managing multiple identities was also a salient theme, as well as a concern that counselors would not understand them. An earlier study

(Stanley, 2004) reported results similar to those of Brooks and colleagues.

Counseling Aging Bisexual Women

Dworkin (2006) acknowledged that a bisexual identity is stable throughout middle age and the older years with those who earlier accepted this identity label. Nonetheless, the emphasis on youth culture, particularly in the gay male community (which remains the largest of the LGBTI subcultures), often makes LGBTI elders invisible, including bisexual women.

Although a stable bisexual identity is normative in aging bisexual women, Dworkin (2006) commented that for women of all affectional orientations, "midlife and older ages sometimes are times of restlessness, reassessment, and regeneration" (p. 42). This realization may bring some women into counseling as they begin examining existential and spiritual issues. Most no longer have caregiving responsibilities, freeing them to have time and energy to focus more on themselves.

Dworkin (2006) also reported on research showing that fewer lesbian and bisexual women see their physicians for breast exams and Pap smears compared to heterosexual women. This is disconcerting because as women age, they have greater need for these exams if early detection is to be realized.

Counseling Bisexual Women Living in Rural Communities

There is currently no research looking specifically at this group. As research continues to lump bisexual individuals in with studies focused primarily on gay and lesbian participants (Dworkin, 2006), findings have not differentiated bisexual women and their experience in rural areas.

Counseling Bisexual Female Students

Kennedy and Fisher (2010) wrote about the needs of bisexual students in school settings. Their recommendations parallel those that would apply to all sexual minority students. Nonetheless, they indicate that the research they reviewed does suggest that both individual and group counseling needs to be tailored to this group. Kennedy and Fisher note that bisexual youth do pose a high risk for suicidal ideation, so assessment and intervention need to address this important concern. Furthermore, counselors also need to be aware of the other risk factors for bisexual youth, including (a) substance abuse, (b) academic and behavioral school problems, (c) marginalization and victimization, (d) social and familial rejection and/or isolation, (e) religiosity, and (f) gender nonconformity in some instances.

Counseling Bisexual Adolescent Females

In one study, sexual minority females had more extremely close friends than did their heterosexual counterparts. Sexual minority youths of both genders, however, worry about losing friends and about never finding a suitable romantic relationship (Diamond & Lucas, 2004). Concerns about friendship may well be a presenting issue within a counselor's office.

Russell and Seif (2002) reviewed results from the National Longitudinal Study of Adolescent Health, a comprehensive study that included more than 20,000 adolescents in the United States. The adolescents were all between 12 and 19 years of age. Wave 2 of the study occurred 18 months after wave 1. In wave 1, 3.88% of the females reported romantic attractions to both males and females, while only 1.45% reported attraction to the same sex only. Their findings are revealing:

> Given their heterosexist culture, it is perhaps not surprising that more than half of the sexual minority women in the study reported other-sex attractions or relationships 18 months after the first wave. Nevertheless, approximately one quarter of the females who reported bisexual attractions in Wave I reported similarly in Wave II. Of the remaining bisexually attracted females at Wave I, approximately 60% reported other-sex only attraction at

> Wave II, while approximately 5% reported same-sex only attraction. A majority of females who report bisexual attractions in Wave II reported other-sex only attractions in the first survey. (p. 87)

Ford and Jasinski (2006) analyzed results from the 1999 Harvard School of Public Health College Alcohol Study, a study with 14,000 students at 119 4-year postsecondary schools in 39 states. Their analysis was based on approximately 9,400 of the respondents. They found that compared to heterosexual men, heterosexual women, gay men, lesbian women, and bisexual men, bisexual women were the most likely to have used both marijuana and other illegal drugs!

Consequently, counselors may face several presenting concerns with bisexual adolescent females. As denial is a common defense mechanism for those abusing substances, counselors will need to work hard at creating a strong working alliance before opening up this conversation. As the Russell and Seif (2002) study reveals, the percentage of bisexual adolescent females is small, and many will later enmesh themselves in opposite-sex relationships. This means that for many bisexual adolescent females, romanticizing and dating other females will be a short passage through their adolescence. Others, however, will develop a lifetime bisexual identity.

Resources for This Group

In addition to the resources listed in Chapter 5, here are several other websites that pertain to bisexual women:

1. The Bisexual Resource Center used to produce the *Bisexual Resource Guide*, an international listing of bisexual groups. They are currently moving their listing to the Internet (www.biresource.net/biresources.shtml).
2. Bi Women Boston, home of the Boston Bisexual Women's Network and *Bi Women*, a quarterly newsletter produced in Boston for women everywhere. This is the longest-lived bi women's group in the world (http://biwomenboston.org/).
3. Several excellent links, including recommended films, can be found at Robin Och's website (www.robynochs.com/resources/Bisexual.html).
4. Another excellent resource, including many links for both lesbian and bisexual women, is hosted by Pierre Tremblay (people.ucalgary.ca/~ptrembla/gay-lesbian-bisexual/2p-lesbian-resources.htm).
5. The Toronto Bisexual Network contains many useful links for bisexual women (www.torontobinet.org/resources.htm).
6. The Centers for Disease Control and Prevention provides several links focused on health concerns of lesbian and bisexual women (www.cdc.gov/lgbthealth/women.htm).

Limitations, Furthering Research, and Implications for Counselors

Limitations of the Research With This Group

The research regarding bisexual women is currently scarce, as they continue to be lumped together with other sexual minority individuals in studies, usually in consequence of their small numbers (Dworkin, 2006). Research in this area suffers a great deal from extrapolating results from studies primarily focused on lesbian women and assuming the same holds true for bisexual women.

What complicates our understanding further is knowing that in some cases, this is entirely correct (extrapolating research results from lesbian women)! As discussed in Chapter 4, young sexual minority women often change their identity labels during their developmental years (Diamond, 2008). The bisexual woman of today may well develop into the lesbian or heterosexual woman of tomorrow.

Consequently, in many instances, research focused on younger bisexual females, from ages 12 to 25 approximately, will be describing a sample of women in identity flux: a transient label that merely describes how a young woman currently sees herself. Interestingly, despite this likelihood, as this chapter has shown, there remain some distinguishing features regarding bisexual girls to women.

Areas Requiring Further Research

Any area of research in this area is ripe to assist in furthering our understanding of bisexual girls and bisexual women. Firestein (2007), one of the world's experts regarding bisexual women, posed several questions that she finds particularly salient:

> What constitutes a healthy developmental trajectory for a bisexual woman, man, or transgendered person coming of age in a culture that is still largely dichotomous with respect to gender identity and sexual orientation? How might a bisexual young person being urged to constructively explore his or her authentic interest in bisexual expression, polyamory, or alternative sexuality? What constitutes optimal psychological and social functioning for a polyamorous bisexual woman? For single bisexual women? For older, African-American bisexual women in a racist society? For a bisexual woman coming out in a bi-phobic lesbian community? Or for a transgendered individual who's recently discovering her or his bisexual desires? (p. 110)

Implications for Counselors

As noted throughout the above sections, working with bisexual girls and bisexual women requires that you, as a counselor, have a deep understanding and appreciation for the ambiguity that defines many of these clients. For many bisexual girls, exploring bisexuality will become mostly that: an exploration within a limited time span. For those who move on to maintaining a bisexual identity, counselors need to be mindful that some will construct many varieties of relationships. An open and accepting mind will become your best attitude to begin your work with this population. But what will define you as a counselor is your ability to truly relate to women who are sometimes struggling immensely to make sense of living outside the binary system of lesbian versus heterosexual.

It is never easy to be different, and empathic counselors will feel some of the pain created when their clients attempt to live successfully outside the box of the binary, outside the box of conformity, and outside the box of usual social restraint. If our clients do not stretch us to grow, then we probably chose the wrong field for ourselves. They too become our teachers.

EXERCISES

Individual Exercises

1. Take yourself to a busy place where there are plenty of women (e.g., shopping mall, dance club, bar). As you look around, which ones do you think define as gay, heterosexual, or bisexual? After spending some time doing this, on what basis did you find yourself making these discernments?

2. Talk to a teenage girl or woman you know who defines as bisexual and ask her the same questions that are found below under Classroom Exercise.

Classroom Exercise

1. In dyads, one student plays the role of identifying as a bisexual female. Begin by introducing yourself to the other student by saying, "My name is . . . , and I self-identify as bisexual." Either the other student decides to ask his or her own questions, or instead uses the following. If you are playing the bisexual female, you have the option of not answering any questions you do not want to answer by saying "pass."

a. How long have identified as bisexual?

b. How many people have you disclosed your bisexual identity to?

c. How do you decide who to tell and who not to?

d. What is it like to tell someone you are a bisexual female?
e. What is the hardest part about being a bisexual female?
f. What is the happiest part about being a bisexual female?
g. Have you ever felt afraid because you are a bisexual female?
h. How do you deal with heterosexual people and gay or lesbian people wanting to pull you into their "club," so to speak?
i. How do you protect yourself from biphobics?
j. What else would you like to tell me about your experience of being a bisexual female? (this exercise is adapted from Finkel, Storaasli, Bandele, & Schaefer, 2003).

Chapter Summary

This chapter has explored an area that remains understudied: bisexual girls and bisexual women. The research currently available suggests that bisexual teenagers (not bisexual by definition but by having romantic attraction to both sexes) outnumber girls who are only attracted to the same gender. Over time, a good percentage of bisexual females gravitate toward having relationships with males. However, some will also define as bisexual, and this self-definition may remain throughout their lifespan.

Research is showing that defining as bisexual is difficult when living in societies around the world that prefer to keep our sexualities more simplified than reality actually dictates. Many people engage in bisexual behaviors, and for those who define as bisexual, there are few supports within the environments in which most bisexual women live. Thankfully, via the Internet, bisexual individuals can build communities of support and belonging—a reality that too few experience in their own locale.

In consequence of the difficulties of defining as bisexual, there appears to be an increase in mental health issues, substance abuse, and suicidality when compared to even those who define as gay or lesbian. While it has been a difficult journey for many gay and lesbian individuals, bisexual men and women appear to have an even more challenging road to traverse. Neither the gay/lesbian or heterosexual communities embrace them. They remain outcasts in a world of marginalization and isolation.

Counselors can play a significant role in helping bisexual women adjust to their affectional orientations. While society slowly evolves around us, counselors can help bisexual women develop the inner strength—the hardiness, as some researchers have called it—to stand strong and be themselves. After all, we are only diminished as people when we pretend we are someone we are not.

Remember that most bisexual clients will see counselors for issues unrelated to their bisexuality. This chapter focused on five issues that may arise for bisexual clients that are specific to their affectional orientations. These problems included (a) identity confusion and fluidity of sexuality, (b) poor mental health and suicidality, (c) drug and alcohol problems, (d) specific relationship strains, and (e) lack of community and isolation.

7

Fetishistic Crossdressing Children and Adults

Challenging Your Attitudes and Beliefs About This Group

Reflection Questions

1. Do you know or have you known someone who fetishistically crossdresses? If so, what reactions did you share with this person(s), and what reactions did you keep to yourself? If you haven't ever known someone who fetishistically crossdresses, what would be your reaction if one of your friends told you that he does?
2. If you had a 10-year-old son and you caught him crossdressing, how would you react? If you wanted him to stop this behavior but he would not or did not, what action would you take?

3. What emotions would you experience if you were a fetishistic crossdressing male living a closeted life (e.g., you only crossdress at home without anyone else knowing)? How would you feel if someone found out?
4. What emotions would you experience if you were a male crossdressed in public and a stranger knew you were actually male and made a comment that others could overhear? How would that change if you knew the person who recognized you and he or she was shocked?
5. What other barriers do you imagine you would face if you were a man crossdressing most of the time (i.e., a transgenderist individual) as you interface with others in your daily life? Include areas of life such as employment and career; spiritual and/or religious life; family and home life; friendships and social life; physical health, including interactions concerning it with a family physician and dentist; and leisure.

Challenging Your Assumptions Questions

1. Is crossdressing a normal variant of human behavior? Why or why not? If you consider it to be normal, why do most partners of fetishistic crossdressing men have a negative view of it?
2. Do you believe that fetishistic crossdressing men have control over their crossdressing behavior? If they are, why do so many have trouble stopping this behavior indefinitely?
3. Most individuals who fetishistically crossdress are heterosexual and very masculine in their gender role presentation. What do you believe explains this?
4. What are your views regarding transgender individuals in general? How would you need to change your views, beliefs, attitudes, or values to become more effective in working with them as a counselor?
5. Many drag queens become paid female impersonators. Does it change your view of crossdressing if it is for money? Why or why not?

Reflections

[*Note:* Imagine that *you* are the client in these reflections.]

You couldn't imagine a worse day in your life. You get home from work and the first thing your wife of 20 years tells you, "Sergio, I need to talk to you about something that is killing me right now!" Judith is really upset—in fact, you have never seen her this distraught. You hesitate but momentarily mutter, "Of course—let's sit down and talk."

She begins, "Sergio, I was looking for some old magazines in the basement and found this box beside them. I thought it maybe had some of my magazines in it, so I opened it. I found these instead [Judith pulls out several pair of panties, bras, skirts, dresses, a wig, and high heels]. WHAT IS GOING ON HERE?"

Shocked, you search desperately for the right words, but at first nothing comes out and nothing makes sense. After all, you have been baffled by this yourself ever since you can remember. After the moments that feel like hours, you begin: "Uh, okay, I will tell you the truth, Judith. I have been a crossdresser since even before I reached puberty. I knew you would be freaked out by it so I chose to never tell you but instead, kept it a secret all these years. Please don't leave me over this—I am not ruled by it, but occasionally the urge to crossdress becomes so strong that I do it when you leave the house."

Judith screams back, "SO YOU WANT TO BE A WOMAN?"

"No, Judith, I don't. I love you and I am happy being a guy—well, for the most part anyway. What I am saying is that I don't want anything to change in our marriage."

With resignation in her voice, she replies, "You should have thought of that before. You have lied to me for more than 20 years, and that is unforgiveable. I need time to think about this. In the meantime, I will be staying at Mom's. Bye for now." She leaves with her two suitcases, and all you hear is the car backing out of the driveway.

During that week, you feel the worst internal misery. You wonder, in fact, if this will put you over the edge. You never felt good about crossdressing, but you could not stop it, either. As you dwell on this and eat yourself up inside, the phone finally rings and it is Judith. You wait desperately to hear her first words and she says, obviously crying: "Sergio . . . I love you so much. I can't stop thinking about you. I don't know what to do about this. Mom suggested we see a counselor. Are you willing to see someone with me? I want to save our marriage."

Overwhelmed with emotion, you cry out, "Judith—thank God you are in my life. I will do everything to save the marriage. I cannot live without you. The past week has been a hell like I have never experienced before. I will do anything for you."

A week later, you meet Dr. Parsons, a psychologist with experience in this area. You tell her you want to stop crossdressing once and for all. You also want to get rid of the thought that creeps up periodically that makes you wonder if you should become a woman. As part of taking a complete history, she asks you a few questions in front of Judith:

1. "At what age did you begin crossdressing?"
   "I think I was 7 or 8. I would sneak into my sister's room when she was out and I would put on her skirt or dress, sometimes a bra. I got caught once by my mom and she scolded me severely."
2. "Did your crossdressing look any different following puberty?"
   "Hum. Yes, I did find it sexually stimulating and I would sometimes masturbate."
3. "How often do you think you want to become a woman?"
   "Well, mostly when I am under a lot of pressure at work. Maybe once a month or so, sometimes for a few days?"
4. "Okay. While you masturbate, how often do you imagine that you are the woman in your imagery?"
   "Quite often, I suppose. Actually, I almost always have that fantasy."
5. "How would you feel about losing your penis?"
   "My God, what a question! But yes, I have occasionally wondered what it would be like to have a vagina instead."

Toward the end of the first session, Dr. Parsons tells you both that it is highly unlikely that you will ever stop crossdressing. She also tells you that you may end up becoming a woman if you keep on feeding the sexual fantasy of yourself being one.

You and Judith leave, both looking and feeling horrified. The questions inside are overwhelming.

From a Client's Perspective

1. How would *you* feel after hearing such news at the end of your first session?
2. In what way do you believe Dr. Parsons's conclusion will affect your marriage?

From a Counselor's Perspective

1. How likely is it that a client will stop crossdressing?
2. If caught early enough, can crossdressing be stopped? If so, how would you accomplish it?
3. Is it possible that crossdressing can actually transform into transsexuality?
4. If you need to provide information that will potentially have a huge effect on a marriage, how and when would you provide it so that the result is not devastating?

Background Information Regarding Fetishistic Crossdressing Children and Adults

"Whereas the transvestite suffers from the castration anxiety that all men experience (Freud, 1926), the

transsexual does not—in fact he energetically seeks castration." (Glasser, 1992, p. 52)

Recall from Chapter 1 that transgender individuals include those who present unconventional gender expressions (e.g., fetishistic crossdresser, transgenderist, gender bender) and/or those who present unconventional gender identities (e.g., transsexual, transwoman, transman). In this and the next two chapters, the focus is on three types of transgender individuals: fetishistic crossdressing, male-to-female (MTF) transsexual, and female-to-male (FTM) transsexual people. *Fetishistic crossdressing (FC) individuals* are men who crossdress, at least during adolescence, because of the sexual arousal and often climatic release it provides. Most of these men define as heterosexual, but not all. While the term *transvestite* is sometimes used as a synonym, this word has fallen out of favor with the LGBTI community and some mental health professionals due to its association with pathology, the psychiatric profession, and the term's overemphasis on sexual arousal being the defining feature of it.

One highly contested and controversial aspect regarding FC, MTF, and FTM individuals is that each appears in the two most commonly known and used diagnostic systems in the world: the *Diagnostic and Statistical Manual of Mental Disorders Fourth Edition* (Text Revision) (*DSM-IV-TR*; American Psychiatric Association, 2000) and the *ICD-10 Classification of Mental and Behavioural Disorders System* (*ICD-10*; World Health Organization, 1992). *DSM-IV-TR*, published by the American Psychiatric Association, is the current system used primarily in the United States and Canada, while *ICD-10*, published by the World Health Organization, was designed as an international system to be used for both the classification and research of mental disorders throughout the world.

Task forces are currently reviewing each section of the *DSM* system, and they will be providing revised criteria before *DSM-V* is published in May 2013 (American Psychiatric Association, 2010b). The revisions that are proposed to the diagnosis of transvestic fetishism include renaming the diagnosis to transvestic disorder with the following criteria: (a) duration of at least 6 months, (b) intense and recurring feelings of being sexually aroused while crossdressed (through fantasies, urges, or actual behaviors), and (c) acknowledgment that it causes significant distress or impairment in important life areas (American Psychiatric Association, 2010a). The diagnostician then also specifies if one or more of the following is involved: (a) fetishism—attraction to materials, clothing, or fabrics; (b) autogynephila; and (c) autoandrophilia. *Autogynephilia* is "a male's propensity to be sexually aroused by the thought of himself as a female" (Blanchard, 1989, p. 616). *Autoandrophilia* is a male's propensity to be sexually aroused by the thought of himself as a male.

Another classification scheme from the past proposed that FC individuals could be sorted into two types: nuclear/periodic transvestites and marginal transvestites. Periodic transvestites were viewed as being satisfied with crossdressing alone. Marginal transvestites were seen as wanting to be feminized by hormones and/or by gender reassignment surgery. They were also less likely to report becoming sexually aroused by crossdressing and more likely to have a stronger sexual interest in the same biological sex (Docter & Prince, 1997). Other classification schemes have also been proposed, and these will be mentioned where appropriate.

Many have questioned whether crossdressing in any of its forms ought to qualify as a mental disorder (Brierley, 1979; Gert, 1992; Pomeroy, 1975; Rosario, 2004). The problem with pathologizing fetishistic crossdressing and transsexuality is that it implies to both the legal profession and to social service agencies (such as child custody) that those who display the respective characteristics are mentally ill (Wright, 2010). Furthermore, there is no statute of limitations on a mental diagnosis: once it is given, it "appears to apply for the lifetime of the individual" (Wright, 2010, p. 1230).

While crossdressing itself includes fetishistic crossdressing and other forms of female and male impersonation (e.g., drag queens, drag kings), the latter—similar to men who wear kilts—are not pathologized but are instead viewed as traditional parts of LGBTI culture. This chapter only focuses on fetishistic crossdressing (FC), which is currently called "transvestic fetishism" in *DSM-IV-TR*. They are included as a separate chapter because fetishistic crossdressing men are sometimes targeted for treatment, sometimes through their choice but more typically because someone else has discovered it and is reacting to it (Dzelme & Jones, 2001).

While a few instances of FC have been acknowledged to occur in some women (Stoller, 1982), their numbers are few, and rarely would FC become the focus of intervention. Consequently, most of this chapter is about FC men.

As Cairns (1997) concluded, research focused on FC individuals seeking help from mental health professionals reveals some negative outcomes from crossdressing, while research focused on FC individuals attending social clubs and gatherings for crossdressing individuals reveals mostly positive outcomes. Sample bias is very important when we are looking as outsiders into a population of individuals who are not well understood. More recent research by Lentz (2004) supports the conclusion that some FC individuals demonstrate good mental health, some are conflicted regarding their FC and report dissatisfaction with their lives, while others are somewhere in the middle.

The bias in this chapter, and in this book for that matter, is one in favor of promoting affirmative practice in working with sexual and gender minorities, including those who are transgender and those who are transsexual. Perhaps what is most remarkable is how unremarkable transgender people are. They are just like the rest of us, with the exception that they are more willing or more in need of stretching the gender binary in one way or another. Consequently, transgenderism is *not* seen as a mental disorder. Instead, transgender people are viewed as belonging to a minority group who have experienced tremendous amounts of misunderstanding and oppression.

As in previous and in future chapters, although it is simpler to write *fetishistic crossdresser*, the term will be used only as an adjective to ensure that the reader remembers that this identity is one of many that a person owns. Furthermore, using it as a noun suggests something essentialist in nature, and that is not intended because, like most psychological phenomena, our behavior is largely socially constructed. This does not imply, however, that something socially constructed can be easily changed—or changed at all, for that matter.

Research has found, for example, that very few FC individuals ever cease crossdressing altogether, even after abstaining for months or years (Brown, 1996). Most get married and eventually have children (Docter & Prince, 1997; Zucker & Blanchard, 1997), and most will continue crossdressing either secretly or with varying degrees of awareness and approval from their spouses. Pomeroy (1975) suggested that FC is on a continuum; those on the lowest end occasionally or rarely wear a bra or female panties, while those on the highest end will dress completely as a woman constantly or whenever possible.

Langstrom and Zucker (2005) used a random sample from Sweden (N = 2,450; 1,279 male, 1,171 female; age range = 18–60) and established that 2.8% of men and 0.4% of women reported at least one incident of FC. These researchers also found that some of these men were more likely to engage in becoming sexually aroused by pain, exhibitionism, and voyeurism. These results should be viewed cautiously, however, as 2.8% of 1,279 men is only 35 individuals, and only some of these men reported some of these additional experiences.

In the discussion of crossdressing that follows, it is important to note that the motivations for crossdressing often or usually change over time. A boy may begin crossdressing for several reasons or a combination of reasons, including but not limited to the following: (a) imitative behavior of a sister or his mother (i.e., modeling); (b) desire to be a girl (most will outgrow this desire later; Money & Russo, 1981); (c) transformative fantasy of being a woman, similar to dressing up like Batman or Superman (Person & Ovesey, 1984); (d) expression of a second or feminine self (Larsson & Bergstrom-Walan, 1999); and (e) crossdressing to experience pleasure and comfort (Wheeler et al., 2008). When crossdressing is discussed in the sections that follow, the underlying motivations for it are *not* implied or indicated unless it is referred to specifically as FC.

Development Through the Life Span

Regardless of the underlying motivation, most males who crossdress begin before or during puberty (Buhrich & Beaumont, 1981; Croughan, Saghir, Cohen, & Robins, 1981; Wheeler, Newring, & Draper, 2008). Whether they are feminine or masculine in their gender role presentation, most grow up without gender dysphoria. Researchers have studied the development of some highly feminine boys, both cross-sectionally and longitudinally, and the most common outcome is that they develop homosexual interests. Consequently, only in a small percentage of boys does early crossdressing or effeminacy lead to continued crossdressing or the development of transsexuality (Bailey & Zucker, 1995; Davenport, 1986; Green, Roberts, Williams, Goodman, & Mixon, 1987; Money & Russo, 1979, 1981; Zuger, 1978).

During puberty, adolescents vary in the extent of their crossdressing behavior, and they also vary in how much they acknowledge that sexual arousal is associated with it (Zucker & Blanchard, 1997). The clothing feels good to wear as it becomes increasingly eroticized. Frequently the adolescent will masturbate and orgasm while crossdressed (Wheeler et al., 2008). The original reasons for crossdressing may remain as well, but either way, a fetish is in the making. For some FC individuals, excitement is also derived from the potential for discovery when they leave their home crossdressed (Bolin, 1988). Passing as a woman is fun for these individuals (Bolin, 1988).

The erotic and fetishistic properties are often reported by FC individuals to subside as one ages (Buhrich & Beaumont, 1981; Zucker & Blanchard, 1997). As the fetishistic aspects diminish, the most commonly reported continuing motivation is that FC makes the individual feel self-soothed, less stressed, and more comfortable as a result (Buhrich, 1978; Wheeler et al., 2008; Zucker & Blanchard, 1997). Consequently, FC in men is often seen as primarily a coping strategy to deal with stress: the more and greater the stress, the more crossdressing occurs. For others, however, FC is about (or also about) wanting to emulate women and wanting to express their love of feminine things (Prince, 1967; Prince & Bentler, 1972). As should be clear from the above, despite the finding that FC usually begins as a fetish, the meanings and purposes for continuing the behavior often change over time.

Most FC men have purged themselves of their opposite-gender clothes, sometimes more than once (Prince & Bentler, 1972). However, again mostly while experiencing stress, the powerful drive to crossdress returns and a new wardrobe is acquired. Interestingly, most FC individuals are heterosexual males who demonstrate masculine or hypermasculine gender roles and overall presentation in most areas of their lives (Freund, Steiner, & Chan, 1982; Prince, 2005/1957; Zucker & Blanchard, 1997). On the contrary, homosexually oriented crossdressing individuals, including drag queens, tend to be feminine or hyperfeminine in their gender roles and overall presentation (Person & Ovesey, 1974b, 1984).

Several researchers have written about the notion that some fetishistic and homosexually inclined crossdressing individuals will develop gender dysphoria to varying degrees, and some to the extent that they later become candidates for cross-sex hormones and gender reassignment surgery (Adshead, 1997; Bancroft, 1972; Benjamin, 1966; Person & Ovesey, 1974b). Most will find these desires to be intermittent and situationally based, however, often increasing at times of stress and turmoil. Those who become candidates for surgery have become preoccupied with their desire to become female, a desire that has become overwhelming and nearly constant.

Blanchard (1989) developed a popular theory explaining why this crossover to transsexuality occurs in the fetishistic male. He coined the term *autogynephilia*, which as noted earlier is "a male's propensity to be sexually aroused by the thought of himself as a female" (Blanchard, 1989, p. 616). For some FC men, autogynephilia becomes a major precipitating factor that leads to their later request for gender reassignment surgery.

It is not understood currently if autogynephila can create transsexuality or whether the propensity to see oneself as a woman was there all along, but perhaps denied by the male who has tried very hard all his life to ignore transsexual longings. Regardless of etiology, which continues to be debated and researched for nearly every psychological condition, the autogynephilic men (including homosexual-crossdressing individuals) were traditionally referred to as secondary transsexuals (Person & Ovesey, 1974b).

The label of *primary transsexuals* was reserved for those transsexual males or females who had a deep conviction that they were the wrong gender since early childhood (Person & Ovesey, 1974a). Such men tended to be very feminine through their lifespan, while such girls tended to be very masculine. Both were most often sexually attracted to members of their own biological sex (Person & Ovesey, 1974b; Stoller, 1996).

Race and Ethnicity

The literature is replete with references to the North American Indian individuals who were referred to as *berdache* by White settlers, but who, at least in modern day, prefer to be called two-spirited by indigenous peoples themselves (Herdt, 1997). The berdache were usually male, anatomically normal individuals who dressed, behaved, and worked as members of the opposite biological sex (Callender & Kochems, 1983). Accounts of the berdache go back to the 16th century (Katz, 1976). Their numbers disappeared soon after settlers took control of their lands and their culture (Callender & Kochems, 1983). It is incorrect to refer to these people by any of our modern-day constructs of transgender because of the distinct cultures of these indigenous peoples and the unique roles held by berdache. Many of the berdache were highly revered by their tribe or First Nation, some assuming the highest roles of spiritual leadership and healer (Herdt, 1997). This was not the case in all tribes, however; in some, they were ridiculed and scorned (Greenberg, 1985). Their sexual partners were always nonberdache individuals (Callender & Kochems, 1983). While most berdache engaged in homosexual activity, not all berdache were homosexually oriented, "and not all individuals who engaged in homosexuality were berdaches" (Greenberg, 1985, p. 183).

No research to this writer's knowledge has focused specifically on FC individuals of differing ethnicities. Nonetheless, it seems doubtful that FC men would be better received in the Black and Latino communities compared to Black or Latino gay men. Caceres and Cortinas (1996) wrote about the frequent tension that arises between the dichotomy of *hombre* (a man) and *maricón* (insulting word for gay male) in Latin cultures. Recall from Chapter 2 that at least in traditional Latino sexual scripts, judgment and the label of "gay" were only heaped on men assuming the passive role. It would appear that at least to some extent, this negative judgment was a consequence of these sexually passive gay men not fitting the stringent role of hegemonic masculinity. Similarly, FC men, despite the finding that they are mostly heterosexual, would likely be viewed unfavorably for transgressing gender roles as well.

Relationships (Family, Friendships, Intimate Romantic/Sexual)

Brown (1994) surveyed 106 women involved with FC men over a 6-year period. Participants came from both monthly discussion groups for spouses or girlfriends of FC men and national conventions for transgendered men and their partners. As one might expect, the degree of acceptance toward their mates' FC varied. A quarter of the sample revealed that they occasionally found their mates' FC to be sexually arousing. The lowest acceptance of FC behavior was found with married women who did not know about their husband's fetishistic crossdressing before marriage. Another finding was that the women generally developed greater acceptance of FC over time. More than two-thirds of the women never seriously considered divorce or separation because of their partner's fetishistic crossdressing, despite receiving strong advice from friends and family to do so.

Reynolds and Caron (2000) found some positive results in their study of 21 FC men. Most of the married men had wives who were either tolerant or accepting of their fetishistic crossdressing.

Weinberg and Bullough (1988) surveyed 70 wives of FC husbands and found that the higher a wife's self-esteem, the happier she rated the marriage. Those with lower self-esteem believed they had failed as spouses and were worried about public exposure. Weinberg and Bullough (1988) wrote, however, that many of these women felt hostility and resentment toward their husbands, and most did not support the FC behavior. Nonetheless, most still felt that their marriages were happy.

While some studies suggest that FC men had impaired relationships with one or both parents or experienced separation from them during childhood (Buhrich & McConaghy, 1978; Langstrom & Zucker, 2005), other studies suggest that most were raised by both parents and that they had good parental relationships (Bullough, Bullough, & Smith, 1983; Docter & Prince, 1997; Prince & Bentler, 1972). Research has *not* demonstrated that fathers who fetishistically crossdress have an effect on the sexual development of their sons (Chapman & Teed, 1990).

From the research available, it appears difficult to make sweeping generalizations regarding the effect that FC will have on family members. Most married FC men will likely keep this behavior secret from their children, and many will also attempt to keep it secret from their wives. If the behavior is kept secretive but is later discovered, the shock combined with the dishonesty can create serious rupture to the trust so important to maintaining a solid foundation within a relationship. That rupture may well require the work of a counselor to help repair.

Health (Emotional and Psychological, Physical)

Goodwin and Peterson (1990) surmised, based on their study of 1 female and 50 FC males, that early childhood abuse is often a causal factor in FC behavior. They further added their belief that FC fits criteria for addiction, given the finding that the behavior often continues throughout a person's life.

Reports from around the world suggest that crossdressing sex trade workers—who may be either MTF transsexual or FC individuals—are often at risk of HIV infection, largely in consequence of inconsistent condom use while involved in receptive anal intercourse (Boles & Elifson, 1994; Gattari, Spizzichino, Valenzi, Zaccarelli, & Rezza, 1992; Grandi, Goihman, Ueda, & Rutherford, 2000). Boles and Elifson (1994) report that crossdressing sex trade workers have higher rates of HIV infection compared to other sex workers and suggested that they experience the lowest status in the hierarchy of prostitution.

Buhrich (1981) compared 24 nonfetishistic MTF transsexual men with two groups of crossdressing men. One of the crossdressing groups was what we refer to here as FC (n = 20), while the other group was closer to what we call he-shes

($n = 14$). Buhrich concluded that all three groups reported greater psychological stress, neuroticism, and introversion on the Eysenck Personality Inventory compared to men in general.

In contrast, Beatrice (1985, p. 358) did not find "clinically significant dysfunction" in her sample of 10 crossdressing males. As mentioned earlier, Lentz (2004) found that some FC males were psychologically healthy, others were mentally unwell, while others were in between. Brown and colleagues (1996) tested 188 nonpatient FC men and found that they were nearly indistinguishable from noncrossdressing men on personality, sexual functioning, and psychological distress measures.

As Lovitt (2004) wrote in the *British Medical Journal*, now that homosexuality is no longer viewed as a mental disorder, those who fetishistically crossdress are the new societal outcasts, given diagnoses and treatments aimed at curing them of something that society does not approve of. "Most transsexual, transgendered, and crossing persons are mentally healthy. . . . Some transgendered clients have psychopathology that has come about because of the way they have been treated by an intolerant society" (Cole, Denny, Eyler, & Samons, 2000, p. 170).

While FC behavior may be statistically unusual, the behavior itself causes no harm and no dysfunction (Newring, Wheeler, & Draper, 2008). Newring and colleagues (2008) suggest that it be viewed as a sexual *variation*, not as a sexual *deviation*. More accurately, however, FC ought to be viewed as a *gender* variation.

Career and Work

FC men are generally not effeminate in childhood; they are usually heterosexual and masculine in their leisure interests and in their career choices (Zucker & Blanchard, 1997). Career choices usually fall within traditionally male-dominated occupations, such as blue-collar work and business (Zucker & Blanchard, 1997). They almost never choose occupations that are considered typical of feminine gay men. It would be uncharacteristic for FC men to come to work crossdressed because of their adherence to traditional masculine scripts.

Transgender men who do crossdress at work are usually very feminine, placing them at increased risk for both economic discrimination and violence (Lombardi, Wilchins, Priesing, & Malouf, 2001). "Workplace discrimination is so rampant that it is the norm among transgendered people, while outside the workplace visibly transgendered people are harassed, intimidated, and assaulted in public places" (Lombardi et al., 2001). As crossdressing at work is more typical for MTF transsexual individuals while going through the real-life experience, dealing with issues resulting from this will be covered in the next chapter.

Women who crossdress have often done so for instrumental reasons. For example, throughout history, women dressed as men have served in the military (Wheelwright, 1989). Bullough (1991) reported that at least 30 women who became saints within the Catholic faith lived as men while they were alive and were only discovered to be women on their deathbeds. Women dressed as men have also successfully lived as sailors, pirates, businessmen, politicians, and physicians (Bullough, 1991).

Spirituality and Religion

Smith and Horne (2007) surveyed LGBTI individuals (2.1% reported having a transgender identity, while 8.5% were unsure) from the United States and Canada, comparing those who had always adhered to an earth-spirited faith (e.g., Pagan, Wiccan; $n = 45$) with those who began in a Judeo-Christian faith and then converted to an earth-spirited one ($n = 49$). The researchers found that participants reported that the earth-spirited faith communities were more affirming of LGBTI individuals. Furthermore, those who once affiliated with Judeo-Christian faiths reported greater conflicts with their faith than the group not brought up in Judeo-Christianity. While many of the LGBTI individuals did not feel affirmed in their earlier Judeo-Christian communities, others did report positive experiences. The researchers concluded that counselors should not assume that LGBTI individuals who are religious are not accepted by their faith.

The only published research accessible through PsycINFO that specifically addresses spirituality and crossdressing pertains to drag queens performing Black gospel at a bar in Chicago. McCune's (2004) writing makes clear the continuing "contradictions, complications, and complexities of the relationship between the Black church and the Black gay community" (p. 151).

Sociopolitical Realities

Transgender people, including those who are transsexual, are at increased risk of experiencing discrimination, prejudice, and violence (Lombardi et al., 2001). In their survey of 402 transgender individuals, Lombardi and colleagues (2001) found that more than half were victims of some form of harassment or violence during their lifetimes. Furthermore, about 25% reported experiencing a violent incident.

A recent report from Serbia found that violence, including fear of violence by police, was a primary concern of crossdressed sex trade workers (Rhodes, Simic, Baros, Platt, & Zikic, 2008). Coerced sex was routinely expected by police in exchange for not being detained, arrested, or fined. The researchers concluded that preventing violence toward this vulnerable group should be a priority in Serbia.

While a PsycINFO search did not reveal any research specifically focused on the sociopolitical realities of crossdressing individuals, those who crossdress need to remember that there is danger if one does not pass well in public or if a given situation reveals their biological sex. The danger factor is likely no different than it is for those who are transsexual who are "discovered," but research to date has not explored this hypothesis.

Recent Research Focused on Canada

Much of what has already been reported in this chapter is, in fact, stemming from research based at the Centre for Addiction and Mental Health (CAMH) located in Toronto, Ontario. Besides the main facility, it also has 32 community locations throughout Ontario. Information gleaned from the website (www.camh.net/) indicates that it is Canada's largest mental health and addiction teaching hospital. Furthermore, it is one of the world's leading research centers in these areas. CAMH was formed in 1998 after a merger occurred between the Clarke Institute of Psychiatry, the Addiction Research Foundation, the Donwood Institute, and Queen Street Mental Health Centre.

Two notable researchers from CAMH already cited for their works in this chapter include Kenneth J. Zucker and Ray Blanchard. Dr. Zucker is currently the chair of the American Psychiatric Association (2010c) taskforce for undertaking revision to the upcoming *DSM-V* section, "Sexual and Gender Identity Disorders."

Recent Research Focused on Other Societies

Crossdressing is practiced in many cultures around the world. Crossdressing men in Samoa are called *fa'afafine*, or *teine pepelo*, which translates to "a lying girl" (Mageo, 1996, p. 590). Crossdressing men in Tonga, Polynesia, are referred to as *fakafefine*, while in Tahiti they are *mahu* (Heinemann, 2000). In Thailand, their "third gender" is referred to as *kathoey*, although today in urban centers they are usually called *lady boys* or *tomboys* (Balzer, 2004). Crossdressing males have been studied in Java, Thailand, Guatemala, Peru, and the Philippines (Whitam, 1997; Whitam & Mathy, 1986). Crossdressing male sex trade workers (CMSTW) in Jakarta, Indonesia, are called *waria*. There, they reportedly have the highest rates of HIV prevalence among groups studied to date (Joesoef et al., 2003).

CMSTW in Jakarta report frequent, unprotected anal intercourse (Joesoef et al., 2003). Similar reports come from Rio de Janeiro (Inciardi, Surratt, Telles, & Pok, 1999) and Rome (Gattari, Spizzichino, Valenzi, Zaccarelli, & Rezza, 1992).

In Brazil, male crossdressing sex trade workers are referred to as *travesties* (Kulick, 1997). Travesties not only crossdress, they also transform their bodies, beginning as young as age 10 or 12. These boys begin ingesting or injecting large quantities of female hormones. The hormones create rounded features, larger buttocks, breasts, and broad hips. These hormones are very inexpensive in Brazil. Besides hormones, silicone is also injected so that by age 17, most travesties in Salvador have some silicone inside them. Most will have this silicone within their buttocks, hips, inner thighs, and knees, but not in their breasts as (a) they believe this could cause cancer, and (b) they are aware that the silicone can shift its position quite easily (Kulick, 1997).

The *hijras* of India are biological men or intersex individuals who crossdress, many of whom have had their penises and scrotums cut off by a clan member with some experience in this rudimentary castration (Bakshi, 2004; Sifuentes-Jauregui, 2006). Not all hijras survive this procedure. Bullough (1991) reported that the majority of their sects center around Mumbai.

Similar to the berdache or two-spirited individuals, it is inaccurate to think of hijras in the same way FC men are described in this chapter. They are believed by some to have special spiritual powers to give blessings at births and weddings. If money is not provided, they often curse the spectators and display their mutilated genitals (Jani & Rosenberg, 1990). Individually, most are involved in prostitution. Jani and Rosenberg (1990) reported that some young boys are either coerced or convinced to join the hijras.

Nanda (1985) reported that the central feature of their culture is devotion to Bahuchara Mata, who is one of the Mother Goddesses worshipped across India. It is through this allegiance that hijras claim their special place in Indian society. According to Sifuentes-Jauregui (2006), the hijras today are losing their special place in Indian culture and increasingly are being viewed with dislike and disrespect. They are being seen as public nuisances.

Hijras are also found in Pakistan (Baqi, Shah, Baig, Mujeeb, & Memon, 1999). In fact, most male sex trade workers there are hijras. Of 300 studied by Baqi and colleagues (1999), only 45 (15%) had their penises and scrotums removed. The researchers also found that more than two-thirds of the hijras had left home from a young age.

While China today is a very repressive society in many ways, including sexually, it was different in ancient times (Ruan & Matsumura, 1991). For the first 4,000 years of their recorded history, the philosophy of yin-yang established positive attitudes toward sexuality. Yin and yang work together, with yin representing negative, weak, and destructive energy, while yang is positive, active, and constructive. Ruan and Matsumara (1991) reported that the first recorded case of crossdressing in China was that of Meixi, the concubine of a king around 1600 B.C.

While traditionally, transgender individuals of all kinds were involved in the entertainment world in Japan, today, many have distanced themselves from entertainment and instead have sought mainstream status (McLelland, 2003). McLelland (2003) stated that the often moral and social condemnation heard in English media is largely absent in Japan.

In Berlin, there are two types of crossdressing gay individuals: the Tunten and the drag queens. The Tunten are a community of gay crossdressers who generally wear trashy clothing as a political protest or statement. On stage, they perform as the "woman next door," in contrast to the drag queens, who generally impersonate famous divas (Balzer, 2004).

Cross-culturally, it has been reported that drag is on the increase in Argentina, Brazil, Colombia, Japan, South Korea, Thailand, and in some European countries (Balzer, 2004). Furthermore, drag is represented differently in several cultures. Drag performances appear to be gaining in popularity worldwide.

Common Concerns Facing This Group and Counseling Considerations

Roleplay Scenarios

[*Note:* Suggested assessment and intervention strategies for the two roleplays below can be found in Appendix B. Before going there, roleplay in dyads with one of you acting as the counselor and the other as the counselee. If a roleplay is not possible, work individually in writing out a list of your suggestions.]

Roleplay #1, Chapter 7. Counseling Crossdressing Individuals

George, age 48, has come to see you for help. George has crossdressed since he was 12 years old. No one has ever caught him doing this, despite the fact that he used to go out in public when he was single. The problem began 4 years into his marriage with Claire (age 41) after she discovered his female clothing in their basement closet. That was 6 years ago. Although Claire got her head around the fact that George would dress up when she was away from home, George began insisting that he wear female clothing whenever he is at home and that she would have to get used to it. Claire did, and for the past 2 years, George often dresses as a woman at home.

George tells you that he has taken this a step further. For the past year, he has insisted that he have sex with Claire while dressed as a woman. Claire reluctantly complied but declared 2 weeks ago that she married him as a man and that she only wants to have sex with him as a man from now on. She will not tolerate any more of his crossdressing at home or while they have sex. He is quite distraught about her "change of heart."

Roleplay #2, Chapter 7. Counseling Crossdressing Individuals

Herb, age 39, has come to see you for help. He is having terrible feelings of guilt because he finds that he only gets sexually aroused when he is dressed as a woman. Herb is disgusted by this, but he feels compelled to dress up nonetheless before he masturbates. He is single and would love to be in a relationship with a woman but fears that he could not get involved with someone while this is going on in his life. Besides this, he wonders if he should consider getting a sex change to "make things right."

How Would *You* Help This Person?

Your next client of the day comes in to see you at your counseling office. Jake, a divorced 45-year-old, is looking overwhelmed and very anxious. You begin:

You: Jake, nice to meet you. You are looking very distraught right now. Tell me about what is happening.

(Continued)

(Continued)

Jake: My God, I have been living alone for the past 10 years. My job is causing me incredible stress and I can't cope. I am doing things that make me feel terrible, and it is getting worse.

You: You sound overwhelmed. Please carry on.

Jake: I *am* overwhelmed and really depressed and anxious. I work as a bricklayer and my boss is always on my back. He tells me I am not working fast enough and if I don't pick it up, he will fire me. I cannot afford to be unemployed—I am still paying huge child support.

You: I understand your need to work. You also mentioned you are doing things that make you feel . . . [Jake interrupts]

Jake: I CAN'T GO THERE RIGHT NOW!

You: No problem, I don't mean to upset you more than you already are.

Jake: Sorry, I'm so embarrassed. I'm sure you've never had someone like me in your office before. Listen . . . I'm a crossdresser. It's getting worse . . . I can't stop it. It's eating me up. As soon as I get home, my work clothes come off and the lingerie comes on. God, I'm ready to go to bed even before I have dinner. Once I get into bed, I play with myself over and over again. It's driving me crazy.

You: It looks like we have a lot to talk about. Hey, I don't want you to feel embarrassed around me—okay? I don't understand much about crossdressing but I do know a lot about helping people. Plus, no one is perfect. I want you to feel safe here. I will do my best to help you explore this and do something about it. Okay?

Jake: [now looking visibly calmer than before] Thank you. I mean THANK YOU! You are the first person I have ever felt safe with talking about this. It all began . . .

Note—Remember to view clients within their environmental contexts, keeping in mind societal, parental/familial, cultural/spiritual, and peer influences. Specifically, become aware of the impact that the following influences have and continue to have in your clients' lives: race, language, religion and spirituality, gender, familial migration history, affectional orientation, age and cohort, physical and mental capacities, socioeconomic situation and history, education, and history of traumatic experience.

1. What defines this person's environment, past and present?
2. Who is this person sitting in front of me, taking into account environmental and personal characteristics?
3. What defines the problem that he or she is presenting within his or her multicultural milieu?

From an LGBTI-affirmative counseling perspective, counseling focused on eliminating FC behavior is contraindicated for at least two reasons. First, it is not unto itself a harmful behavior. Second, there are no controlled outcome studies for treating FC men (Newring, Wheeler, & Draper, 2008) and, consequently, no empirically supported treatments have been published for it, either (Newring et al., 2008).

Few researchers or clinicians today believe that FC behavior can be "cured" (Newring et al., 2008). Instead, the goal is to help FC men integrate this behavior into their lives in a way that lowers or eliminates the interpersonal and occupational risks (Stayton, 1996). This stance *is* congruent with affirmative counseling.

In the past, however, several approaches at curing crossdressing were attempted. The following treatments attempted in the past are included to provide examples of how behavior that is not understood in a society is often targeted for intervention, thus perpetuating the oppression and silencing of those who are different.

Stoller (1971) stated that psychoanalysis has not been successful in treating FC. Anecdotal reports with one to three patients included aversive techniques, including electric shock (Blackmore, Thorpe, Barker, Conway, & Lavin, 1963), use of apomorphine or emetine (both induce vomiting; Barker, 1965), and watching an aversive video (Wolfe, 1992). While these case studies reported positive outcomes, a long-term follow-up of two cases using aversion therapy found total relapse in both cases (Rosen & Rehm, 1977). Faustman (1976) raised ethical concerns regarding the use of aversive techniques to reduce crossdressing behavior.

Hypnosis has been used, but also on very few cases (Beigel, 1965; Wright & Humphreys, 1984). In another application, biofeedback was used over 12 treatment sessions while the 45-year-old male was hospitalized. While the patient maintained the treatment was a success over a 2-year period, his wife reported that he had resumed fetishistic crossdressing. These clinicians highlighted how this case constituted "a dramatic example of the unreliability of self-report" (Rosen & Kopel, 1977, p. 908).

Various medications have also been used, again with very few cases: (a) buspirone hydrochloride ("Buspar"—an antianxiety agent; Fedoroff, 1988); (b) fluoxetine hydrochloride ("Prozac"—an antidepressant; Masand, 1993); and (c) Depo-Provera (an antiandrogen that blocks testosterone production; Tsang, 1995). Newring and colleagues (2008) concluded that the limited data suggest that these medications may be effective at reducing the desire and actual behavior of FC.

Another controversial treatment is aimed at stopping FC in childhood and adolescence. Several researchers and clinicians believe this is possible. As Zucker and Blanchard (1997) indicated, however, most adolescents are in denial of FC, even when there is abundant evidence that it is occurring. With adolescents, they recommend attempting to re-train the client to become sexual aroused in alternate ways. The example they provided is teaching him to masturbate to imagery that does not involve the thought or the wearing of female clothing. The authors conceded that there is little information regarding the long-term success of this treatment when the client is already an adolescent.

The approach taken by Rekers, Rosen, Lovaas, and Bentler (1978) in treating children was to reinforce "masculine" aspects of behavior and to extinguish behaviors that are sex-typed as "feminine." In the clinic, the child was shown videotaped feedback to teach him how to distinguish masculine from feminine behaviors. The parents were also taught to use behavior-shaping techniques. In the same breath, however, these authors suggested that society needs to become more tolerant of individuals in the way they express their sex roles!

The controversial aspect of treating minors becomes especially salient when working with prepubescent boys. A child sent for treatment generally fits the *DSM* criteria for gender identity disorder. The criteria for children do not require that the child state a desire to become the opposite gender. Instead, it is sufficient to give the diagnosis and treat if there are enough indicators of cross-gender interests, which may include crossdressing behavior. Yet all of the longitudinal research done to date finds that boys with feminine interests and who might also be effeminate turn out in the majority of cases to become gay or bisexual, not transgender (Green et al., 1987; Money & Russo, 1979; Wallien & Cohen-Kettenis, 2008). The boys that are at risk of becoming fetishistic crossdressers are not the effeminate ones who enjoy feminine interests! Instead, they are the masculine-identified boys that will grow up to be heterosexual—entirely the wrong group such clinicians (and, perhaps, more commonly, the parents of these children) are seeking for their witch hunts. Wallien and Cohen-Kettenis (2008) concluded that "most children with gender dysphoria will not remain gender dysphoric after puberty. Children with persistent GID [gender identity disorder] are characterized by more extreme gender dysphoria in childhood than children with desisting gender dysphoria" (p. 1413).

Children grow up best in a nurturing home, not one that is judgmental toward their individual differences. In the study by Money and Russo (1979) of nine boys with gender identity disorder followed up to young adulthood, they concluded that an attitude of nonjudgmentalism had "a strongly positive therapeutic effect on the boys' personal development" (p. 29). Acceptance in a loving home is central to raising healthy children.

While no standard approach to assessing FC exists in the literature (Adshead, 1997), Newring and colleagues (2008) recommend collecting the following information as part of a comprehensive intake assessment: (a) demographic information; (b) reason for referral; (c) family of origin information; (d) developmental history; (e) history of erotic fantasies, interests, and sexual behavior; (f) educational background; (g) occupational history; (h) relationship history; (i) substance abuse history; (j) relevant medical background; (k) mental health history and diagnoses; (l) administration of intelligence, achievement, and personality tests as required; (m) interviews with relevant others; and (n) possibly physiological assessment (e.g., biofeedback, plethysmography—measures blood flow in the penis). Adshead (1997) stresses the importance of assessing the "patient's" ability to establish and sustain relationships.

A reading of the assessment and treatment literature makes one thing clear: both as described follow the medical model of pathologizing this behavior. The word *patient* above is in quotation marks to emphasize that they are talking about a person who is, in the minds of these researchers and clinicians, "sick" and in need of treatment. The parallels between the treatment of FC individuals both in the past and in the present compared to those who were given the diagnosis of "homosexual" in the past is remarkable and uncanny.

As in previous chapters, this one will only review concerns that tend to be more commonly experienced by FC individuals. This list would look different in a culture that has fewer hang-ups about what is considered appropriate attire for either biological sex. Gender expression in a culture can either be rigid or fluid. It is the social system or culture that decides whether the behavior is abnormal (Shaffer, Barclay, & Redman, 1989). Adshead (1997) commented that "many different cultures tolerate or encourage transvestic behavior, at least in men" (p. 280). While Americans and Canadians are often relatively accepting of female impersonators, FC individuals are not well tolerated or accepted in our cultures.

Mostade (2006) concluded that FC clients seek counseling for one of three issues, including wanting to preserve their marriage or relationship, wanting to improve their self-esteem and self-worth, and/or believing that their FC behavior is becoming compulsive and wanting to control it. Brown (1996) created a more comprehensive list, including the following potential issues: (a) legal problems, (b) threat to one's military career, (c) problems at work related to cross-dressing, (d) strong guilt, (e) co-occurring alcohol problems or depression, (f) feelings of gender dysphoria, (g) deciding on whether to tell the children, and (h) discovery by one's spouse or family member.

The three most common presenting issues, according to the literature, that FC men bring to counseling include (a) marital discord, (b) ego-dystonic crossdressing and/or compulsiveness, and (c) mild to moderate gender dysphoria. The following section begins this discussion regarding suggested counseling interventions.

Marital Discord

Two large-scale surveys of crossdressing men were conducted by Prince and Bentler (1972; *N* = 504) and by Docter and Prince (1997; *N* = 1032). In the 1997 study, 87% of the participants described themselves as heterosexual, while the remaining 13% described themselves as bisexual, asexual, or homosexual. While 83% of the sample had married, only 60% were married at the time of the survey. In 1972 and 1997, 24% and 45% of the sample had received counseling, respectively. Prince and Bentler found that 36% of those who were divorced had reported that FC was a cause of their marital discord. In the Docter and Prince study, the participants reported that 28% of their wives were completely accepting of their FC, 47% had a mixed view, and 19% reported antagonism toward it. Within the married group, 32% reported that their wives were told about their FC before marriage. To summarize, FC behavior is often not revealed to wives before marriage, and when it is known or becomes known, the majority of wives harbor negative or ambivalent feelings toward it. Nonetheless, most wives do not leave their husbands as a result of FC (Woodhouse, 1985).

Wise (1985) investigated the coping styles of 20 wives living with FC husbands. The sample was biased in that the participants were drawn from a clinical sample in a hospital setting. As one might expect, the women "coped" with the FC behavior through negative means, such as becoming depressed, hostile, sadistic, and/or drunk. Such a reaction is obviously in contrast to those who accept their husbands' FC, some of whom accompany their husbands to national crossdressing conferences.

Zucker and Blanchard (1997) postulated that some FC men develop impaired relationships because the fetish aspects become more important to them than their partners. They qualified their conclusion by noting that it was based on anecdotal findings and not on systematic empirical study. Stayton (1996) suggested that the partner's first reaction is to suspect that the FC individual is gay.

Cairns (1997) noted that women who read the academic literature may feel "inadequate, frightened, and further stigmatized" (p. 303). As noted earlier, Cairns commented on the dichotomy between clinical studies that pathologize the behavior and studies based on participants attending crossdressing social groups and conventions who normalize it. Regardless of sample biases and sample characteristics, Cairns's observations from her clinical practice (again, note these are her anecdotal conclusions) are that wives will tend to move away from fear and grief to feelings of resentment regarding the time and money spent on the fetish.

The presenting client may be the husband, the wife, or both (Bullough & Bullough, 1993). The most motivated men who arrive at the counselor's doorstep usually do so under pressure from the wife or partner as a condition for maintaining the relationship (Docter, 1988). In this instance, crisis counseling may be sufficient until the feelings and values around this behavior are worked through (Mostade, 2006).

Brown (1996) cautioned that for some FC men, they are merely patronizing their partners by attending counseling. Consequently, such men may be more interested in having the counselor collude with them instead of taking the concerns of their partner seriously.

Bullough and Bullough (1993) concluded that "the wife needs to realize that her husband will probably continue to cross dress, and the husband needs to realize that he will have to accept some limits if the marriage is to survive" (p. 356). It is important for the partner to understand that

FC does not influence one's affectional orientation (Stayton, 1996).

Mostade (2006) recommended that counselors do the following when working with FC individuals:

1. Ask the client to be specific regarding what is causing inter- and/or intrapersonal stress.
2. Encourage the partner (if applicable) to become involved in the counseling.
3. Work at understanding the complexity of the two expressions of gender (i.e., both masculine and feminine aspects).
4. Normalize the behavior for both client and partner (if applicable), and help both understand that the behavior will likely continue.
5. Help the couple (if applicable) establish appropriate compromises regarding the behavior.

Stayton (1996) elaborated on some of the questions that can be asked of FC men in helping them (and their partners, if applicable) define boundaries:

1. What will be the limits, if any, on the crossdressing behavior?
2. Will the client be satisfied with only crossdressing at home, or will he want to also go out in public?
3. Will he want to crossdress more often when it seems reasonable (will need to define what "reasonable" is if there is a partner involved)?
4. Will crossdressing have a bearing on his gender identity (i.e., movement toward transsexuality)?

If the partner is unwilling to accept some degree of FC behavior, the couple will need to look at whether their marriage is salvageable (Stayton, 1996). Weinberg (as cited in Mostade, 2006) found that wives often bring the following concerns regarding their FC husbands: (a) is my husband gay? (b) will others find out about the FC? (c) will it affect the children? (d) have I failed as a woman? (e) have I failed as a wife? and (f) is he mentally ill?

Ego-Dystonic Crossdressing and/or Compulsiveness

Langstrom and Zucker (2005) found in their nationally representative study from Sweden that more than 50% of the FC men did not see this behavior as acceptable to themselves. In other words, they experienced the crossdressing as ego-dystonic. Wysocki (1993) noted the strong feelings of guilt often experienced by FC men. Bullough and Bullough (1993) suggested that if FC becomes too frequent or intense, it can interfere with one's lifestyle and one's relationships. Similar to other fetishes, in some individuals, FC can become the principal outlet for a person's sex life, replacing sexual activity with another human being (Adshead, 1997).

Albert Ellis and Russell Grieger (1977) believed that guilt was not a rational emotion: Unlike regret or remorse, guilt did not arguably stop or diminish the behavior from recurring, and it also lowered self-esteem. It would seem counterproductive for an FC individual to continue harboring guilt over a behavior that will likely be chronic and reoccurring. Better instead to help the person develop relapse-prevention strategies (i.e., intervention aimed at decreasing the likelihood of reoccurrence) and harm-reduction strategies (when the behavior does reoccur, keeping the negative consequences to a minimum or to none at all; Newring et al., 2008).

Regarding guilt reduction, cognitive behavioral (Alderson, 2002) or rational emotive behavior therapy is an appropriate intervention (Ellis & Grieger, 1977). Pastoral counseling may be best suited for those with religious convictions (Shields & Bredfeldt, 2001; Vanderwall, 1986). Alternatively, one could work from a narrative, humanistic, existential (Richert, 1999), or emotion-focused perspective (Greenberg, 2002). In any instance, the client is helped through normalizing the behavior and through understanding the chronic relapsing nature of it. If the client can appreciate that the behavior unto itself is harmless to self and others, this too can be helpful. Two other approaches suggested by Newring and colleagues (2008) regarding treatment of the ego-dystonic aspects of FC are acceptance and commitment therapy, founded by Steven Hayes (Hayes, Strosahl, & Wilson, 1999), and dialectical behavior therapy, founded by Marsha Linehan (Swales, 2009).

Sometimes FC behavior is symptomatic of obsessive-compulsive disorder (OCD). The current treatment of choice for OCD is cognitive behavioral therapy with exposure and response prevention (Freyer et al., 2011). Pharmacotherapy is also indicated in severe cases (Fineberg & Craig, 2010).

Mild to Moderate Gender Dysphoria

All 1,032 crossdressing men in Docter and Prince (1997) self-defined as periodic in their crossdressing behavior with an age range between 20 and 80. Some in the sample were no doubt transsexual individuals, whether or not they were aware of this at the time. In the sample, 17% believed they were women trapped inside a man's body. Regarding gender identity, 11% saw themselves as masculine, 28% as feminine, and 60% equally. Docter and Prince predicted that between 15 and 20% of periodic crossdressers that attend crossdressing clubs will eventually live full-time as women (i.e., transgenderists) or become secondary transsexuals. Crossdressing men are more likely to report gender dysphoria during times of stress (Ellis & Eriksen, 2002; Person & Ovesey, 1974b). Steiner, Satterberg, and Muir (1978) had noted that several FC men had requested gender reassignment surgery while they were experiencing midlife crises.

Given that it appears rare for gender dysphoria to dissipate in most adolescents and in almost all adults, the dysphoria needs to be either managed or embraced in FC individuals who do not fulfill the criteria for gender identity disorder and the later gender reassignment surgery that some transsexual individuals will pursue. One can work with FC clients with some degree of gender dysphoria in either an individual or group format (de Vries, Cohen-Kettenis, & Delemarre-van de Waal, 2007; Lothstein, 1979).

Benestad (2010) wrote recently about working with clients to help them move from gender *dysphoria* to gender *euphoria*. Gender therapy, as prescribed by Benestad, is focused on helping individuals move toward greater happiness through self-acceptance and through educating significant people in the client's life. Many individuals with milder or moderate forms of feeling uncomfortable with their gender can integrate their masculine and feminine aspects of self, thereby creating a more androgynous or bi-gendered identity (de Vries et al., 2007). Thus, the clients learn to express the transgender part of their identities through activities like FC and gender bending (Carroll, 1999). As Devor (1996) has also stressed regarding females with gender dysphoria, it is helpful to remind clients that it is society that is deficient in its low acceptance of gender diversity and not the individual that is defective in any way.

COUNSELING DIVERSE POPULATIONS

Counseling FC Individuals With Multiple Nondominant Identity Statuses

A PsycINFO search did not produce any research that has specifically focused on FC individuals with a nondominant ethnicity. A few reports have been published of people with intellectual disability who crossdress and have gender dysphoria (Parkes & Hall, 2006). The authors concluded that gender identity disorder might be more prevalent in those with intellectual disabilities but offered this only as a hypothesis. In a later study, Parkes, Hall, and

Wilson (2009) conducted a retrospective review of 13 participants with learning disabilities who crossdressed, 12 of whom were male, at least one of whom was reportedly transsexual. They concluded that individuals with learning disabilities experience a range of gender identities comparable to those of the general population.

Counseling Aging FC Individuals

Wise (1979) described the case of a 43-year-old married man who had secretly been wearing women's clothing for 20 years. After a period of intense stress from having lost his son in an automobile accident, he developed the idea that he wanted gender reassignment surgery. Wise wrote about how the news of this was an incredible shock to his wife and friends. Wise described how he successfully worked with this man until his desire for surgery subsided.

Wise and Meyer (1980) compared 10 younger cases (M = 35.9 years) with seven older cases (M = 51.1 years) of FC men who requested surgery following a period of major life stress. The younger cases were more likely to report marital discord as a precipitating event, while the older cases were more likely to experience illness, separation, and physical loss stressors as precipitators.

There currently appear to be no studies that specifically focus on FC individuals who are elderly. The limited literature that exists suggests that with those who began crossdressing for fetishistic reasons are the most likely subgroup of crossdressers to request gender reassignment surgery during or soon after experiencing undue stress. Counselors need to assess such individuals carefully and help them cope with the life stressors while attending to the deepening feelings of gender dysphoria.

Counseling FC Individuals Living in Rural Communities

While the study by Oswald and Culton (2003) first mentioned in Chapter 5 focused on 527 LGBTI individuals living in rural communities, only three were included that were transsexual. It appears there are no studies that specifically focus on FC individuals who live in rural areas.

An excellent resource for crossdressing individuals of all kinds and their families, whether urban or rural, is the largest support group called the Society for the Second Self (Tri-Ess). Contact information for Tri-Ess can be found at www.tri-ess.org.

Counseling FC Students

Most FC students do not feel an urgency to crossdress while at school, but those who do may find comfort in attending a gay–straight alliance, mentioned in earlier chapters as a social club that celebrates sexual and gender diversity, often found today in high schools. Most colleges and universities in the United States and Canada have a social club as well for LGBTI individuals. Evans (2002) described a LGBTI Safe Zone project at Iowa State University that has resulted in increased visibility of LGBTI people at their campus and greater awareness of their issues. In turn, Evans reported this has led to increased support and tolerance or acceptance of LGBTI students on campus.

Counseling FC Adolescents

This topic was covered earlier in this chapter. Some clinicians, such as Zucker and Blanchard (1997), have recommended attempting to alter the fetishistic aspects of crossdressing (where these are present) by encouraging boys to masturbate without using autogynephilic fantasies or while crossdressed. Several clinicians have also recommended teaching feminine crossdressing boys and adolescents to become more masculine in their gender-role presentation. Such approaches are controversial, as stated earlier.

Resources for This Group

1. An excellent resource for crossdressing individuals of all kinds and their families, whether

urban or rural, is the largest support group called the Society for the Second Self, Tri-Ess (www.tri-ess.org).

2. Crossdresser Heaven provides tips regarding fashions, makeup, and body movements (www.crossdresserheaven.com/category/advice-and-encouragement/crossdresser-resources/).
3. The Transgender Support Site offers several useful support materials (http://heartcorps.com/journeys/).
4. The National Transgender Advocacy site provides links to many of the transgender advocacy groups in the United States (www.genderadvocates.org/links/national.html).
5. Transgender Zone's mission is to educate, communicate, and inform. It also provides an online support group (www.transgenderzone.com/features.htm).

Limitations, Furthering Research, and Implications for Counselors

Limitations of the Research With This Group

Controversy mars the opinions and research regarding transgender individuals of all varieties. There is ongoing debate regarding whether FC individuals and transsexual individuals experience a "mental disorder" at all. If not, why are they included in the *DSM* diagnostic system? The research tends to be biased, as researchers and clinicians find what that they are looking for. Those with a medical and clinical orientation generally view these as bona fide mental disorders that require treatment, but even these professionals are not in agreement regarding what should constitute the diagnosis and whether these conditions even warrant one (Newring et al., 2008). They focus on clinical samples to prove their points, individuals who are either distressed enough with their crossdressing behavior or who request help because they have other presenting issues.

Those with a humanistic, postmodern, or counseling perspective tend to view these conditions as variations of normal gender development and presentation. The samples are usually drawn from social clubs and conventions attended by crossdressing individuals who embellish their crossdressing behavior and who tend to be well adjusted in other domains of their lives.

Consequently, the research with this group is divided, and the reader's opinion can be swayed depending on which literature is considered. Research focused on representative samples, such as in the study by Langstrom and Zucker (2005), is needed to shed better light on what differentiates those who find this behavior troubling from those who do not.

Areas Requiring Further Research

Wheeler and colleagues (2008) recommended further research concerning the development of "transvestic fetishism" and its development over the life span. As noted earlier, there appears to be no study that has focused exclusively on aging FC men. Longitudinal studies are needed to identify those children who begin crossdressing and continue it into adulthood from those who do not continue the behavior. Further understanding is also needed regarding how the function behind FC moves from self-soothing to sexual gratification to creation of fantasies and then back to self-comforting (Wheeler et al., 2008).

Furthermore, of great importance is the need for longitudinal studies that track how some FC men eventually become transsexual and successfully end up fulfilling requirements to begin the real-life test with gender reassignment surgery as the final outcome. Also, why is it that gay men rarely if ever crossdress for fetishistic reasons? Why are they mostly immune from developing this dynamic?

Another important question is in what ways are gender and sexuality related? Which holds primary importance in the development of a person, or does this vary from person to person? Is there any way to predict which will have the greater salience in any one person's development?

Implications for Counselors

Counselors may find themselves in the same quagmire that researchers have found themselves in: Should one attempt to treat the FC behavior itself, thereby giving it the status of a mental disorder, or should one instead work with whatever other problems FC may be creating for the client while leaving the FC behavior itself alone? How does that change, if at all, if the client is finding the FC is escalating in either importance or frequency? There are no easy answers to these questions.

Counselors, however, would do well to accept that diversity marks the turf in the areas of sexual and gender diversity. Those working in this area need to accept the many differences that clients bring to the table of counseling. Of greatest importance is remembering to keep each problem a client raises as just one of the many petals that make this particular flower a whole entity. Identities are just that: While they help define aspects of a person, they do not define the person himself or herself. Remember to be respectful of a client's terminology. If your client uses language that sounds derogatory, look deeper as to whether the use of language reflects, in fact, a self-denigrating attitude toward his or her FC behavior.

Regardless of our clients' behavioral tendencies, our job as counselors is to help them put the many petals of their existence into perspective. Their need is to integrate their many parts and learn to accept them, whether or not one or more of these parts becomes a target for intervention. For example, it is difficult for obese individuals to lose weight while they continually put themselves down for their weight. Continual put-downs, self-denigration in other words, leads to a negative mental attitude and possibly depression, and depressed people have trouble accomplishing goals due to the inertia and many setbacks depression creates. As they try to move one step forward, their negative mindset brings them two steps back. Happy people who accept their human condition, whatever it looks like in their particular case, are most likely to have the energy, stamina, and positive mental attitude to move forward and accomplish the goals that are reasonable for them to attain.

For the most part, FC is harmless behavior. But like anything, if too much time and energy is devoted to it, it may take on a life of its own (referring here to the possibility that some FC men will become transsexual or compulsive in their FC). As is often said in Buddhist philosophy, all things in moderation. Part of our role as counselors is to help clients lead balanced, healthy lives.

Exercises

Individual Exercises

1. Carroll and Gilroy (2002) recommend that both counselor educators and students explore their attitudes and beliefs about transgender people through the use of biographies, novels, and films. They recommend the following books and resources: *All About My Mother*, *Boys Don't Cry*, *The Brandon Teena Story*, *Confessions of a Gender Defender*, *Ma Vie En Rose*, *My Gender Workbook*, *Outlaw*, *Paris Is Burning*, *Stone Butch Blues Gender Outlaw: On Men, Women, and the Rest of Us*, and *Transgender Warriors: From Joan of Arc to RuPaul*. Periodicals recommended include *Chrysalis Quarterly*, *Gendertrash*, *Hermaphrodites*, *Transgender Tapestry*, and *With Attitude*.
2. Make a point to get to know someone who defines as transgender. Explore the differences and similarities between you and him or her. Note your reaction to the differences: What judgment do you make of these? What do you like and dislike about the differences that you notice? To what extent are these differences the result of him/her having a different perception or way of expressing gender than you?
3. Consider attending a drag show at a local gay bar (Schacht, 2004). What was your reaction to it? What did you observe about other people's reactions?

Classroom Exercises

1. Lead a discussion in class about the various reasons that explain why some men crossdress. Create a hierarchy in terms of the extent that each reason is considered socially acceptable

by the class. What explains why some reasons are considered more acceptable than others?

2. Invite one or more men who crossdress for various reasons (e.g., a drag queen, a drag king, an FC individual, a transgenderist individual) as guest speakers to your class (Lance, 2002). Lead a discussion about the visit at your next class. What did students learn? In what ways did it change their perceptions of crossdressing individuals?

Chapter Summary

This chapter has focused on fetishistic crossdressing (FC) boys and men and who define and/or have defined for them what this means. The discussion makes clear that a great deal of controversy exists with respect to FC individuals: Do they have a mental disorder, or is their behavior merely a variation from the norm? The latter position is upheld by counselors who are LGBTI affirming.

Counselors would do well to remind themselves that not everyone's behavior will fit into the same box: Variety *is* the spice of life. We need to help clients accept themselves, both their good qualities and those they wish they could or will eventually change. When an underlying disorder that requires treatment is presented—such as schizophrenia, obsessive thoughts, or compulsive behaviors—it would be imprudent for us not to ensure these clients get the help they need, whether from us if we are qualified or from other mental health professionals with this expertise.

When a behavior is harmless, however, and it is mostly society's intolerance of diversity that is problematic, this calls for a different response from us. As professional counselors, we are expected to be advocates for our clients and to engage in social justice activities when needed. This is not just lip service, but in fact, it is written into our ethical codes of conduct.

We are neither the conduits of social conformity nor the rebels of a new society. We are, however, expected to work on behalf of our clients and to educate the uninformed. This can only be based on what we know from the research done to date and from maintaining a social consciousness that exalts all people as equal.

8

Transsexual Boys and Transwomen

Challenging Your Attitudes and Beliefs About This Group

Reflection Questions

1. Imagine that you are a male who always thought you should have been born a female. How do you believe this would affect you during your childhood, teenage years, and early adulthood years?
2. If you were a male-to-female (MTF) individual before actually transitioning, what reactions can you imagine receiving from your friends and family when you disclose this to them? How would it affect your subsequent relationships with them?

3. If you were a MTF individual, what effect would this likely have in terms of your chosen career (consider entry into the career and advancement)?
4. What concerns would you have, as an MTF person, when you decide to go out dressed as a woman? Would your concerns be any different during daytime hours as opposed to at night?
5. If you belong to a religion, what beliefs does your faith community have toward MTF individuals? If you are not religious but consider yourself spiritual, how do your spiritual beliefs affect your beliefs regarding MTF individuals?

Challenging Your Assumptions Questions

1. To what extent do you believe MTF individuals make a free choice to be the way they are? On what basis do you believe this?
2. How do you currently view MTF individuals? To what extent do your views apply to *all* MTF individuals?
3. How would you react if your son disclosed to you that he wants to become a woman?
4. If you fell deeply in love with a transsexual individual of either gender but were unaware of this initially, how would you react following the disclosure? What considerations would affect your decision regarding whether you could continue in the relationship?
5. Imagine that you walk into a bar and unknown to you, the bar predominantly caters to the transsexual community. What steps, if any, would you need to take to become comfortable there?

Reflections

[*Note:* Imagine that *you* are the client in these reflections.]

You were always more feminine in your demeanor, mannerisms, and interests than most boys. You preferred playing with girls as a child, and then as a teenager, you preferred to be around boys while most of your peers wanted to hang out with girls. You knew you were sexually attracted to boys despite never sharing this feeling with anyone. What troubled you more than this, however, is how you felt about your body while you were going through puberty. While your male friends were proud of the increasing size of their genitals and their increasing muscularity, you felt the opposite. You were actually disgusted by how everything grew but never shared this with anyone, either. Instead, you craved having breasts and thought constantly about having a vulva.

Now at age 21, you could not stand looking at yourself in the mirror. Nothing seemed right about that reflection. In desperation, you made an appointment with your college counselor, Fran, and poured your story out before she could hardly say anything.

Fran looks at you and says, "Slow down, Roger. This is obviously overwhelming you right now. Take a few moments to breathe while I explain what I think is going on with you."

"Okay, sorry to push through all of this so fast. What do you think so far?"

"Well, I think you have body image problems, Roger, and that you are gay on top of it."

"Hum, that doesn't quite seem like the problem, Fran. Whenever I think about having sex with a guy, I don't picture myself as a guy myself. I am really disgusted with that image actually."

"Roger, that is exactly why I say you have a body image problem. You have never learned to accept the changes that occurred during puberty. Your internalized homophobia is worse than I have ever seen yet in my office! I believe I can help you overcome your denial."

From a Client's Perspective

1. What do you think of Fran's interpretation? Why?
2. What critical part of Roger's story is Fran ignoring or minimizing?

3. Given Roger's desperation, what emotions are likely for him to have at the end of his session with Fran? If Roger feels relieved, what has likely happened?

From a Counselor's Perspective

1. What questions might Fran ask to ascertain if internalized homophobia is an issue with Roger?
2. What is the likelihood that Fran could help Roger feel good about his genitals and his increased muscularity?
3. What questions should Fran be asking to provide a more thorough assessment of what is going on with Roger?

Background Information Regarding Transsexual Boys and Transwomen

> *"I want people to realize that transsexuals are just normal people" (transwoman quoted in Connell, 2010, p. 319).*

The next three chapters focus on individuals who, more than the others already reviewed in this book, have faced not only the most difficult time accepting their reality but who have also faced the greatest challenge in being accepted by others, including the medical community. Currently, the debate rages furiously by those mental health professionals who will ultimately revise the *DSM-IV-TR* criteria for gender identity disorder (Knudson, De Cuypere, & Bockting, 2010).

The most basic questions among the complicated ones continue to be asked: Is gender identity disorder a mental/biological disorder or a natural variant of gender amid a "discourse of intolerance" (Manners, 2009, p. 67)? If it isn't a disorder, how can those requiring surgery be properly assessed and treated? The difficulty in answering even these obvious questions has become complicated by history, the current postmodern conception of gender, and the transgender movement of activists against their antagonists.

Before discussing these three factors, terminology is critical. Terminology is highly controversial currently, as the terms mean many things to different researchers, activists, and transgender people themselves (Cook-Daniels, 2006). For the sake of clarity, *transgender individuals* include those who present unconventional gender expressions (e.g., fetishistic crossdresser, transgenderist, gender bender) and/or those who present unconventional gender identities (e.g., transsexual, transwoman, transman). Generally, transsexualism is viewed as a subset of transgenderism, the overarching category that also includes intersex people, fetishistic crossdressing individuals, and gender benders.

Male-to-female transsexual (MTF) individuals are biological males who believe their gender is dissonant with their morphology (adapted from Vanderburgh, 2009). *Transwomen* will refer strictly to postoperative MTF individuals, whether or not they themselves assume this identity label (note that many postoperative MTF individuals do *not* use this term to refer to themselves). *Gender identity disorder* (GID) is the official diagnosis for those individuals who meet the *DSM-IV-TR* criteria. *Gender dysphoria* means feeling varying degrees of discomfort with one's biological sex and/or one's expression of gender roles. *Core gender identity* is one's sense of being male, female, or indeterminate and is usually established between 18 and 30 months, while *gender identity* can also refer to one's *current* sense of seeing oneself as male, female, or indeterminate (Lawrence, 2008). Consequently, gender identity in the latter regard can change over time and be incongruent with a person's core gender identity (Lawrence, 2008).

It is important to note that gender identity is a different construct from affectional orientation: While gender identity is about viewing oneself as primarily male, female, or indeterminate, affectional orientation refers to a person's attraction, erotic desire, and philia for members of the opposite gender, the same gender, or both. Who you have the propensity of falling in love with romantically—denoting either a heterosexual, homosexual, or bisexual orientation—is entirely different from whether you experience yourself as a male/man, as a female/woman, or as some combination or transcendence of the two genders. In other words, you can have a strong sense of being male or female and be attracted to men, women, or both.

Transitioning refers to the process by which many transsexual individuals begin and continue physical steps to alter their body morphology. For MTF transitioning, this includes cross-sex hormone therapy, top surgery (e.g., breast augmentation), and bottom surgeries (e.g., vaginoplasty—creation of a vagina; clitoroplasty—creation of a clitoris; vulvoplasty—creation of the vulva). It is important to clarify that not all MTR or female-to-male (FTM) transsexual individuals elect to transition, and those that do might only transition in a partial sense (e.g., hormones only, top surgery only, bottom surgery only).

Transsexual individuals have existed throughout history and throughout cultures worldwide (Lev, 2007). The first sex reassignment surgery was performed in Germany in the early 1920s, but these operations did not become well known until an American by the name of George Jorgensen became Christine Jorgensen in 1952 (Docter, 1988).

The transgender movement did not garner much momentum until the 1990s (Broad, 2002), largely in consequence of the Internet allowing the transgender community to organize in substantial numbers for the first time in history (Lev, 2007). The transgender movement has sought to normalize transgender people, partly by promoting the perspective that gender variance is an example of human diversity, not pathology. Bockting (2009) stated that the disease-based model of transgender health is giving way to a model that is identity based, suggesting a less pathological approach is underway.

In regard to the medical community, transsexual individuals were pathologized from the outset in the *DSM* diagnostic system. Some questioned if gender identity disorder (GID) was introduced into the *DSM* in 1980 as a countermeasure to removing homosexuality from *DSM* in 1973. Zucker and Spitzer (2005) disputed this, however, and stated that instead, GID in childhood was introduced as a result of expert consensus by researchers, a process used to introduce many new psychiatric diagnoses.

DSM-III-R listed three disorders: gender identity disorder of childhood, gender identity disorder of adolescence or adulthood, and transsexualism (Zucker & Cohen-Kettenis, 2008). Following a review of existing research, these three disorders were packaged into one in *DSM-IV* and *DSM-IV-TR:* gender identity disorder (Zucker & Cohen-Kettenis, 2008). The current diagnostic criteria for gender identity disorder in children contained in *DSM-IV-TR* include four main components: (a) having a strong and enduring identification to the opposite sex (manifested by at least four of five behaviors), (b) having an enduring discomfort with one's sex or of its appropriateness (manifested by specific criteria for males versus females), (c) not being intersex, and (d) it causes distress or impairment in functioning (Zucker & Cohen-Kettenis, 2008).

The criteria for adolescents and adults in *DSM-IV-TR* are somewhat different and include the following: (a) having a strong and enduring identification to the opposite sex (several examples provided), (b) having an enduring discomfort with one's sex or of its appropriateness (manifested by being preoccupied with it or believing one was born into the wrong sex), (c) not being intersex, and (d) it causes distress or impairment in functioning (Lawrence, 2008).

While estimated prevalence of gender identity disorder in children is estimated at somewhere between 0.9 to 1.7% (Zucker & Cohen-Kettenis, 2008), the prevalence is much lower in adults. *DSM-IV-TR* includes an estimate of 1:30,000 MTF and 1:100,000 FTM individuals in the United States. Research done elsewhere, however, is assumed to provide more accurate estimates. Studies from the Netherlands and Belgium (Bakker, Van Kesteren, Gooren, & Bezemer, 1993; De Cuypere et al., 2007) estimate the prevalence at 1:11,900 or 1:12,900 MTF and 1:30,400 or 1:33,800 FTM, respectively, in a ratio between 2 and 3 men to 1 woman (Lawrence, 2008).

One of the reasons that may explain the difference in prevalence between children and adolescents/adults is that the diagnostic criteria are different. While a child may receive a GID diagnosis for displaying mannerisms and behaviors more characteristic of the opposite sex (e.g., for boys, playing with dolls and avoiding rough-and-tumble play), adolescents and adults must state their desire to either get rid of their primary or secondary sex characteristics or to *be* the opposite sex. Another reason is that most children outgrow GID (Wallien & Cohen-Kettenis, 2008; Zucker, 2006). However, Zucker (2006) concluded that if GID continues from childhood into adolescence, the prognosis for overcoming GID is poor. Research indicates that those children with extreme GID are the least likely to experience desistance (Wallien & Cohen-Kettenis, 2008).

Does GID ever remit in adulthood? While this rarely occurs, Marks, Green, and Mataix-Cols (2000) documented five case reports of MTF individuals where GID remitted, based on follow-ups to the 10-year mark. Marks and colleagues recommended a long real-life experience (RLE, i.e., 1 to 2 years) to minimize the likelihood. The RLE is discussed in this chapter under Common Concerns Facing This Group and Counseling Considerations.

The percentage of transsexual individuals who regret their surgery is extremely low (1–2%; Smith, van Goozen, Kuiper, & Cohen-Kettenis, 2005), and most report much-improved happiness and psychosocial well-being postsurgery (De Cuypere et al., 2005; Johansson, Sundbom, Hojerback, & Bodlund, 2010), suggesting that careful assessment and the staggered transition process works for the vast majority of individuals. A recent meta-analysis based on 28 studies found that sex reassignment surgery together with hormonal interventions in individuals with GID "likely improves gender dysphoria, psychological functioning and comorbidities, sexual function and overall quality of life" (Murad et al., 2010, p. 214).

While several classification schemes have been suggested to make sense of the diversity of transsexual individuals, the one that is arguably most helpful for both sexes is to categorize based on whether one's sexual interests are toward the same biological sex (homosexual) or toward the opposite sex with sometimes co-occurring interest in the same sex (nonhomosexual; Blanchard, 2005; Lawrence, 2008; Lev, 2007). Each type has a different developmental path.

Development Through the Life Span

During the preschool years, gender atypicality does not generally get noticed, as there is sufficient overlap in the sex-typical behaviors for boys and girls (Green, 1996), although Zucker and Cohen-Kettenis (2008) suggested that the atypical behaviors generally begin between ages 2 and 4. By elementary school, however, nonconformity often brings name-calling and rejection, especially toward atypical boys (Green, 1996). It is during the school years that some parents become concerned enough to bring their child to a mental health practitioner. With or without treatment, most children with gender dysphoria will outgrow it after puberty (Wallien & Cohen-Kettenis, 2008).

The homosexual MTF individual used to be the most commonly diagnosed biological male, but today more nonhomosexual MTF individuals are finding their way into clinicians' offices (Lawrence, 2008). Lawrence (2008) summarized the differences between these two groups and their developmental differences.

According to Lawrence (2008), the homosexual MTF person is the one most probably think of when they imagine an MTF individual. Most are very feminine during their childhood years, and this often creates concerns for their parents. Crossdressing may or may not occur, but cross-sex behavior and/or mannerisms are apparent. If parents bring their child to a psychiatrist or psychologist, the boy will likely get a diagnosis of GID. It is important to remember that longitudinal studies have shown that the vast majority of children with GID do not grow up to identify as transsexual, but instead, the majority end up later reporting either primarily homosexual or bisexual interests (Green, 1987, 1996). Homosexual MTF people are only attracted to men sexually. If they have crossdressed and/or do so currently, the behavior was (or is) not experienced as sexually arousing. They usually transition while in their 20s.

Puberty is often difficult for homosexual MTF individuals, as their dislike for the physical changes is often experienced. While very rare, this disdain may be to such an extreme that a percentage of MTF persons have mutilated their genitals. Haberman and Michael (1979) reported two MTF men, aged 23 and 25, who castrated themselves (removal of testes only). Cole, O'Boyle, Emory, and Meyer (1997) found that in 8% of the 318 MTF charts they reviewed, 8% had caused physical damage to their genitals in some way (usually through taping, hitting, and squeezing, but also a few through cutting). Dixen, Maddever, Van Maasdam, and Edwards (1984) reported that 9.4% of the MTF men that been evaluated at their gender clinic over a 13-year period in Palo Alto, California, had self-mutilated their genitals (manner in which this occurred was not reported).

Nonhomosexual MTF persons, according to Lawrence (2008), have a completely different development. They now comprise the largest group presenting to clinicians to transition (Lawrence, 2008). Most appeared to be overtly masculine in childhood. Most have crossdressed, and for them, crossdressing was or is accompanied by sexual arousal. From the last chapter, you will recall that autogynephilia is "a male's propensity to be sexually aroused by the thought of himself as a female" (Blanchard, 1989, p. 616). Nonhomosexual MTF people are sexually attracted mostly to women, to women and men, or to neither. They usually transition while in their 30s.

A substantial percentage of transsexual people do not transition until late into middle age (Cook-Daniels, 2006) or even later (Docter, 1985, wrote about one MTF person who had sex reassignment surgery at age 74). Cook-Daniels (2006) surmised that this is a cohort effect caused by the amount of information on the Internet concerning transsexuality reaching a critical mass.

A controversial aspect of those with differing gender identities concerns sexual identity labels. For example, is a transsexual man who is attracted to other males a gay man or a heterosexual woman? Such questions are unresolvable, as the answer becomes one of definition. While people pick their own sexual identity label based on how they view themselves in relation to the world, other people also provide them labels. If, for example, a man who self-identifies as heterosexual has many mannerisms more typically associated with being female, he may be thought of by others as a gay man who hasn't come out—even if this individual experiences little to no interest in the same gender. The same can be said for trans people.

Presurgically, many homosexual MTF individuals already view themselves as women; consequently, they maintain a heterosexual identity even when involved sexually with men. This becomes more prevalent postsurgically. Alternatively, nonhomosexual MTF individuals may have the opposite experience, although this clinically appears less common (i.e., they may define as lesbian or bisexual before and after surgery).

Gender roles are socially constructed, so what is considered masculine or feminine is really a social convention that is held by the dominant discourse in a society. If we agree that aggressiveness is a masculine trait, we become likely to label a male who appears sensitive and gentle as more feminine than the aggressive-acting male. It is important to keep in mind that our view of what is considered the "proper" behavior for males and females is something created by members of a society.

Cook-Daniels and Munson (2010) reported that relatively little is known about the lives of transsexual people following their transition, and even less about those who are aging. Persson (2009) noted that while transsexual individuals face the same concerns as other aging adults, they also encounter some that are unique. For example, they may encounter fear of rejection by family and their adult children, transphobia, and marginalization from both the gay and lesbian communities and from the heterosexual community. Those who have taken female hormones are at increased risk for breast cancer, prostate cancer, deep vein thrombosis, pulmonary embolism, and osteoporosis (Persson, 2009). Those who have had sex reassignment surgery have greater risk for rectovaginal fistulas (i.e., an abnormal connection between the rectum and the vagina that can cause debilitating symptoms) and urinary tract infections.

Many transsexual seniors are not open about their gender identity, which can lead to feelings of social isolation and self-neglect. Those placed in nursing homes and other assisted-living facilities may be especially challenged if their genitals or other physical features are not congruent with their biological sex (Persson, 2009).

Cook-Daniels and Munson (2010) reviewed the results from three surveys and found that most of the transsexual elders over the age of 50 had experienced sexual abuse (as children and/or as adults) and elder abuse. A majority believed that the perpetrator's motive was partly based on transphobia. In a sample of 34 MTF individuals, the majority recalled experiencing an unwanted sexual event before age 18, and most had been verbally abused and insulted before age 15 (Gehring & Knudson, 2005).

Race and Ethnicity

Erich, Tittsworth, and Kersten (2010) compared 45 transsexual persons of color (38 male, 5 female) with 63 White transsexual individuals (49 male, 9 female, 3 intersex, and 2 were missing this data) and found no significant differences regarding levels of self-esteem or life satisfaction. The transsexual persons of color reported higher levels of support from significant others and from friends. Note that in the Erich and colleagues study, individuals self-identified as transsexual—according to the *DSM* system, intersex individuals are *not* transsexual (although as noted in Chapter 1, they are included under the general umbrella of "transgender"). In another study, Erich, Tittsworth, Meier, and Lerman (2010) found that in their convenience sample of 33 transsexual persons of color, participants reported that the discrimination they faced in consequence of their transsexual status was more aversive than that based on race/ethnicity.

Garofalo, Deleon, Osmer, Doll, and Harper (2006) had 51 MTF transsexual youth (ages 16–25, med = 22 years; 57% African American) complete a questionnaire. High rates of HIV infection (22%), forced sexual activity (52%), difficulty finding work (63%), history of incarceration (37%), sex trade exchanges (59%), and homelessness (18%) were reported. Also reported was a high incidence of substance abuse with alcohol (65%) and marijuana (71%) over the past year. Transwomen of color have high rates of HIV infection and are often involved in sex trade work out of economic necessity (Sausa, Keatley, & Operario, 2007). Interviews with 17 MTF African American individuals revealed that they felt a strong need to be loved by men and they were willing to engage in unprotected sex to help preserve their relationships (Crosby & Pitts, 2007). Selling sex and engaging in unprotected sex were also common (Crosby & Pitts, 2007).

Relationships (Family, Friendships, Intimate Romantic/Sexual)

It is a common experience for family, friends, romantic partners, and others to experience denial, anger, shock, and depression after they discover a transsexual person's gender identity (Zamboni, 2006). If they can deal successfully with their emotions and accept the individual's transsexualism, their support can have a huge impact. Ryan, Russell, Huebner, Diaz, and Sanchez (2010) conducted research looking at how family acceptance was related to the health of 245 LGBTI adolescents and young adults. This retrospective study found that family acceptance was related to having greater self-esteem and social support and better overall health, and it was a protective factor against depression, substance abuse, and suicidality. Bockting,

Huang, Ding, Robinson, and Rosser (2005) found in their study comparing transsexual persons (159 MTF, 48 FTM) with men who have sex with men ($n = 480$) and women who have sex with women ($n = 122$) that the transgender group reported the lowest level of support from family and friends.

A study of eight transgender adolescents in secondary school found that all but one had been bullied in school. While they had difficulty developing friendships, each participant received support from at least one peer (Wilson, Griffin, & Wren, 2005).

When wives find out their husbands identity as MTF, they are usually shocked and angry and feel betrayed (Gurvich, 1992). It also stretches their sexual identity unless they already self-identify as lesbian or bisexual (Gurvich, 1992). More recently, Alegria (2010) studied 17 couples in which an MTF individual had a natal female partner (NF). Alegria found the women were profoundly shocked and confused by their husbands' disclosure. Frequent and open communication was most important if the relationship was to be strengthened. The main challenges included (a) relationship uncertainly and questioning by the wife of her sexual identity, (b) decision making around whether to transition, and (c) how and when the husband would present in public as a woman. The transition experience of partners is impacted by the extent to which they feel isolated and whether support services are available (Joslin-Roher & Wheeler, 2009). While it was once believed MTF-NF marriages would fail, Samons (2009) expressed a view that many marriages can be enriched and maintained following disclosure, even if he transitions.

Most MTF individuals who are not married look for a new partner after sex reassignment surgery (SRS; De Cuypere et al., 2005). A follow-up study 12 months after SRS found that many MTF individuals have difficulty finding regular sex partners (Lawrence, 2005).

A recent study by Factor and Rothblum (2008) surveyed 166 transgender adults, which included 50 MTF, 52 FTM, and 64 genderqueer (neither completely male nor female) individuals. The MTF sample was less likely than the FTM sample to disclose their gender identity to their parents. While there were no differences between the three groups regarding their sense of connection to the transgender community, the genderqueer sample felt more connected to the LGB community than either the MTF or FTM sample did.

White and Ettner (2004) surveyed therapists who had considerable experience working with gender-dysphoric patients. Their focus was to look at the experience of individuals who had children before transition began. White and Ettner found that the children who were preschoolers at the time of the parental transition adapted best both at first and over time, and adult children generally adapted well, while adolescents had the most difficult time dealing with the transition.

An area that has been much understudied is with couples in which both partners are transsexual. Ettner (2008) evaluated 20 such couples. Without exception, all of the couples met through a service focused on gender-related issues, especially support groups, conferences, online chat rooms, and political functions. Most couples reported instant attraction, but most took far longer than nontranssexual couples to begin sexual activity (according to poll results of the sexual habits of Americans). All the couples ranked communication and talking as more important than erotic activity.

Health (Emotional and Psychological, Physical)

The state of research describing the health care needs of transgender and intersex individuals remains in its infancy; much needs to be done that focuses on "effective medical and mental health programs and interventions" (Johnson, Mimiaga, & Bradford, 2008, p. 214). Transgender individuals encounter many barriers in accessing competent health care (Hanssmann, Morrison, Russian, Shiu-Thornton, & Bowen, 2010; Williamson, 2010) and they also experience discrimination from health care providers (Keiswetter & Brotemarkle, 2010). As further research is conducted and our understanding of transgender individuals grows, these barriers will likely diminish.

Currently, the health literature contains few publications related to LGBTI health. Eliason, Dibble, and DeJoseph (2010) reviewed articles published in health-related journals between 2005 and 2009 and found only .16% focused on LGBTI concerns (8 of nearly 5,000 articles).

Several research studies have estimated the rate of HIV infection in MTF individuals to be disproportionately high (Keiswetter & Brotemarkle, 2010; Kosenko, 2011). A meta-analysis based on 29 American studies found that in four of these, 27.7% of MTF individuals tested positive for HIV infection, while 11.8% self-reported being HIV positive in 18 studies (Herbst et al., 2008). Between 27 and 48% reported involving themselves in risky sexual behaviors. Nuttbrock and colleagues (2009) found that White Americans reported fewer risk factors predictive of HIV and STI infection compared to Hispanic and African Americans.

Studies have shown that transgender individuals are at high risk for substance abuse problems (Cole et al., 1997; Lombardi & van Servellen, 2000). They score lower on measures of self-concept (Taher, 2007), and many experience crippling effects from guilt (Schaefer & Wheeler, 2004). Most studies, however, provide favorable reports of mental health, particularly postsurgically.

A recent study of 30 MTF, 17 FTM, and 114 control subjects found that people in the transsexual sample were as psychologically healthy as the control group; however, they were more likely than the control sample to feel isolated and emotionally deprived and to need to meet others' needs (Simon, Zsolt, Fogd, Dora, & Czobor, 2011). The transsexual groups also felt more vulnerable and deficient compared to the control sample. Sanchez and Vilain (2009) demonstrated that MTF individuals who feared how their identity would affect their lives were most likely to feel psychological distress. Similar to other marginalized groups, the stress of feeling stigmatized affects mental health (Sanchez & Vilain, 2009).

Studies have consistently shown that the mental health of MTF and FTM individuals improves postsurgically, and most do not experience continuing psychopathology (Banks, 2002; Caron & Archer, 1997; Cole et al., 1997; De Cuypere et al., 2005; Gomez-Gil, Vidal-Hagemeijer, & Salamero, 2008). While preoperative MTF and FTM individuals are often insecure and feel unattractive because of body image, postoperatively they score high on attractiveness and self-confidence (Kraemer, Delsignore, Schnyder, & Hepp, 2008). Some evidence suggests transsexual individuals are less likely to attempt suicide after they transition (Israel & Tarver, 2001).

Transsexual individuals are more likely to have a stable sexual relationship after SRS compared to before surgery (52.7% vs. 35.3%, respectively; De Cuypere et al., 2005). Most MTF individuals also report improvement of their sexuality (De Cuypere et al., 2005), although some report problems with arousal, lubrication, and pain (Imbimbo et al., 2009; Weyers et al., 2009).

A study by Dhejne and colleagues (2011), however, provides a different picture. Dhejne and colleagues looked at all postsurgical transsexual individuals in Sweden between 1973 and 2003 and compared them to a population-based matched cohort sample. In total, 324 individuals were identified (191 MTF, 133 FTM). Compared to controls, the overall mortality of sex-reassigned persons was higher, particularly death from suicide. They also had a higher likelihood of making suicide attempts and being admitted as psychiatric inpatients. In a recent review by Haas and colleagues (2011), the suicidality specifically of transsexual individuals has been clearly understudied. However, even if continuing psychological problems exist postsurgically, it is unclear whether GID creates these or if they are a response to how transsexual people are treated in society. Evidence exists to support both positions (Fontaine, 2002).

Career and Work

Work is an area that is often very challenging for both transsexual employees and their employers. Preoperative MTF and virtually all FTM individuals work hard at not exposing their undressed bodies to others, and many problems arise in their use of public washrooms and required physical exams (Kessler & McKenna, 2000). During the real-life experience (this will be discussed later under Counseling Considerations), transsexual individuals are expected to live full-time as the opposite sex, including use of opposite-sex washroom facilities. This can create awkward circumstances in which the transsexual person and/or employees at work feel uncomfortable with one another in this private gendered area.

Schneider and Dimito (2010) had 119 LGBTI students complete a questionnaire. The authors concluded that compared to the LGB individuals ($n = 113$) in their study, the six transgender persons were likely the most vulnerable to discrimination in work settings. Kirk and Belovics (2008, p. 29) stated that "transgender individuals experience widespread employment discrimination." Sangganjanavanich and Cavazos (2010) looked at the various implicit and explicit forms of workplace discrimination faced by transsexual employees, including social isolation, physical threats, demotions, and outright termination. Not all states have laws protecting workers from discrimination based on gender identity (Winfeld, 2005). When transitioning at work does proceed without major incident, transsexual individuals often attempt to present an alternative conception of gender, but coworkers create rituals intended to place them back into the rigid binary system (Schilt & Connell, 2007).

Employers are generally ignorant of sex change issues (Barclay & Scott, 2006), and the degree of acceptance that can be achieved in a work setting is guarded (Barclay & Scott, 2006). Research supports the notion that transsexual people are generally hard-working individuals who immerse themselves in work to avoid inner turmoil (Gender Identity Research and Education Society, as cited in Barclay & Scott, 2006).

Budge, Tebbe, and Howard (2010) interviewed 13 MTF, 2 FTM, 2 genderqueer, and 1 male crossdressing individual regarding their experience at work and their career decision-making process. They developed a three-phase model comprised of a pretransition, transition, and posttransition phase, which encompassed five major themes: (a) preparation for transition, (b) disclosing at work, (c) appearance and presentation at work, (d) dealing with others' reactions at work, and (e) use of coping strategies. Regarding their career decision-making process, six major themes emerged that included perceived occupational barriers, prospects, action steps, job satisfaction, and situational influences. Winfeld (2005) wrote about the importance for transitioning individuals and their employers to collaboratively develop a "transition plan," outlining the steps that will be followed in beginning the disclosing process and the real-life experience at work.

It is noteworthy that many U.S. and Canadian businesses have adopted affirming policies and practices for LGBTI individuals. For example, several Fortune 500 companies have formally implemented antidiscrimination policies for transgender and transsexual employees (go to www.tgender.net/taw/goodcomp.html). The Business and Human Rights Resource Centre reports on the positive and negative impacts of more than 5,100 companies worldwide, and their website is also excellent for assessing the climate for LGBTI employees (go to www.business-humanrights.org/Categories/Miscellaneous/Ratingsindexes/HRCCorporateEqualityIndex USA).

Spirituality and Religion

LGBTI individuals face conflicts with many orthodox faiths and faith communities (Levy & Reeves, 2011). Gay and lesbian individuals typically use one of five strategies for dealing with this conflict: (a) rejection of their sexual identity, (b) rejection of their religious identity, (c) integrating the two identities, (d) keeping their identities separate through compartmentalizing them, or (e) living with the conflict (Couch, Mulcare, Pitts, Smith, & Mitchell, 2008). Jones's (2008) dissertation, based on interviews with 15 LGBTI students, echoed these feelings of conflict as participants attempted to bridge their sexual or gender identity with their religion and spiritual beliefs.

A recent dissertation focused exclusively on the spiritual experiences of four transsexual persons using heuristic methodology (Reinsmith-Jones, 2009). Reinsmith-Jones (2009) looked at the inward spiritual changes that accompanied the physical transition process. A movement from feeling abandoned by God and hating self to feeling loved by God and loving self was a challenging process for these participants. This journey was wearying and filled with anguish.

Sociopolitical Realities

Shelley (2009) argued that transsexual individuals are repudiated by both society and the *DSM* system, both of which lead to social marginalization and discrimination. Even debates over whether to include transpeople as part of the feminist movement continue and remain unresolved (Green, 2006).

Taylor (2007) outlined several areas in which transsexual individuals face problems either unique or in a more extreme form compared to LGB individuals. Taylor maintained that there has been a legislative avoidance regarding transsexual concerns, partly because of the small size of the community and the need for politicians to garner votes by avoiding controversial subjects. Some of the areas in which legislation has lagged, at least in many states, is in regard to legal documents, workplace discrimination policies, surgical costs, discrimination in school settings, hate crimes, and prison segregation.

While affectional orientation is mostly a private matter, transsexual identities become public when people request legal changes to their name and birth certificate, passport, and Social Security records. Furthermore, not all states allow postoperative transsexual people to change their birth certificates, and courts have generally not honored amended birth certificates. Compared to LGB individuals, far fewer states and local governments have enacted statutory discrimination protections for transsexual individuals. Sex reassignment surgery can cost up to $100,000, and it is almost always excluded from health care plans. While universities are enacting policies around gender identity and gender expression, this is not universal throughout the United States. Federal hate crime legislation does not protect transsexual people. Lastly, transsexual individuals serving time in prison are segregated on the basis of anatomical sex and not on their gender identity (Taylor, 2007). Brown and McDuffie (2009) found that all states who responded to their survey about treatment of transsexual inmates denied surgical treatments for GID, and there was wide variability in provision of access to cross-sex hormones.

The majority of transsexual individuals have experienced varying degrees of harassment, economic discrimination, and/or violence (Lombardi & Davis, 2006). Transgender people are subjected to violence from early in life and remain at risk throughout their lives (Stotzer, 2009). They also remain at high risk for sexual assault (Stotzer, 2009). Unsurprisingly, transgender individuals have often been traumatized by the treatment they receive from those who are unsympathetic (Mizock & Lewis, 2008). When hate crimes against transsexual individuals occur, they are usually violent, and the perpetrators themselves hold high levels of prejudice toward them (Stotzer, 2008). In recognition of transpeople who were killed because of hatred, a Transgender Day of Remembrance is commemorated in 250 locations worldwide (Lamble, 2008).

Recent Research Focused on Canada

As stated in Chapter 7, the Centre for Addiction and Mental Health (CAMH) in Toronto has produced a prolific amount of research and publication since its inception. CAMH is recognized as one of the main research-intensive gender clinics in the world. Some of the research from this clinic aims to have children become more comfortable with their biological gender. There is great controversy in the field about this practice.

Nonetheless, Canada has been on the leading edge in the study of gender identity disorder, with prominent researchers such as Ray Blanchard and Ken Zucker and his colleagues leading the charge. Their publications are too numerous to list here. Several Canadians have also contributed to the recent discussion about upcoming changes to the *DSM* criteria for gender identity disorder (see April 2010 issue of the *International Journal of Transgenderism*).

Klein and Gorzalka (2009) reviewed the literature regarding the sexual functioning of transsexual individuals following hormone therapy and genital surgery. They concluded that transsexual individuals report adequate sexual functioning and/or they report having a high degree of sexual satisfaction following SRS. Vasey and Bartlett (2007) wrote about the Samoan *fa'afafine*, feminine males who are well accepted in this culture. As these males were not distressed by their gender-atypical behavior or identity, Vasey and Bartlett concluded that changes to the *DSM* criteria for GID should reflect that not all gender-variant individuals are bothered by their diversity.

Dahl, Feldman, Goldberg, and Jaberi (2007) provided protocols for assessment, prescription planning, and endocrine therapy for transsexual patients, while Holman and Goldberg (2007) wrote about ethical, legal, and psychosocial issues pertinent to transgender adolescents. Devor (2004) created a 14-stage model of transsexual identity development. His stages included aspects of anxiety, first questioning one's biological sex and gender before questioning one's experienced sex and gender, and eventually coming to accept a trans-identity both pre- and post-surgery. Integration and pride were the final achievements.

Bauer and colleagues (2009) reported on the results of phase I of the Trans PULSE Project, a community-based research project in Ontario. Qualitative data from focus groups with 85 transsexual individuals revealed that health care institutions lack knowledge of transpersons and they generally lack policies for dealing with them. In this way, transpeople are rendered invisible and "erased."

Another recent Canadian study using focus groups looked at the views of 80 service providers in the Greater Toronto area regarding the needs of LGBTI youth. Some of the highlights included an awareness of the specific needs of both transgender youth and with ethnically and culturally diverse youth with varying affectional orientations (Travers et al., 2010).

The above reflects only a sample of the work being done in Canada that pertains to transgender individuals. Many researchers are involved in furthering our knowledge of this disenfranchised group.

Recent Research Focused on Other Societies

Gender is conceptualized differently in some other world cultures. Much of this discussion can be found in Chapter 7. In South Africa, while laws have been enacted protecting gay and lesbian individuals from discrimination, there has been little progress made with transsexual rights (Vincent & Camminga, 2009). In Serbia (part of former Yugoslavia), a 20-year follow-up of the transsexual population has shown that the sex ratio of surgeries (MTF vs. FTM) is close to 1:1, and most were younger at the time of their first consultation compared to other countries (majority between 18–25 years; Vujovic, Popovic, Sbutega-Milosevic, Djordjevic, & Gooren, 2009). Another study compared Sweden and Australia, where differences were also found between both the frequency and the sex ratio, suggesting an effect from societal differences (Ross, Walinder, Lundstrom, & Thuwe, 1981).

From a survey of 229 transsexual people from Australia and 24 from New Zealand, Pitts, Couch, Mulcare, Croy, and Mitchell (2009) found the sample had poorer health ratings compared to the general population in these two countries. Furthermore, those who reported the most discrimination were also most likely to report being currently depressed. A sample from Spain found that more transsexual people lived with their parents compared to other European countries (Gomez-Gil, Trilla, Salamero, Godas, & Valdes, 2009). In the United Kingdom, recent legislation was passed (the Gender Recognition Act) that Hines (2009) believed reflects the changing attitudes toward transgender people there.

The first case of SRS in mainland China was reported in Ruan and Bullough (1988). It involved the 20-year-old son of a prominent army official. A study of MTF individuals in the Philippines found that the majority were taking hormones but SRS was rare (Winter, Rogando-Sasot, & King, 2008). It was also stated that Filipino society did not have a positive view of transgender individuals. Many reported rejection by parents, especially fathers.

Common Concerns Facing This Group and Counseling Considerations

Roleplay Scenarios

[*Note:* Suggested assessment and intervention strategies for the two roleplays below can be found in Appendix B. Before going there, roleplay in dyads with one of you acting as the counselor and the other as the counselee. If a roleplay is not possible, work individually in writing out a list of your suggestions.]

Roleplay #1, Chapter 8. Counseling MTF Individuals

Scott, age 23, has come to see you for help. Scott is very feminine in his mannerisms and his gender role, and you soon discover he has thought of himself as predominantly a girl since age 10. His sexual interest is in other men. He tells you he wants to become a woman. He confides in you that he always hated his penis and often wishes it was gone. Your inner sense is that Scott is quite unstable at this time and you have concern that he may self-injure.

Roleplay #2, Chapter 8. Counseling MTF Individuals

Tina, age 65, has come to see you for help. Tina had sexual reassignment surgery 10 years ago and soon after discovered she was HIV positive. Now that she has retired, she has decided that she wishes to pursue a long-term relationship with Julio, a 70-year-old man she has known platonically for a few months. She wonders if she should tell him that she is both a transsexual and that she is HIV positive. She believes her chance of giving Julio the virus is very low.

How Would *You* Help This Person?

You are working as a professional counselor. Lorne (age 55) and Twila (age 52), married for 22 years, come to see you. Twila is nearly hysterical as Lorne begins telling you that over the past 5 years or so, he has become increasingly aware of his belief that he should have been born a female. Your observation is that Lorne is much more feminine that most men you have ever met. You wonder if he has sexual interest in men and you ask. Lorne reluctantly admits that he has always had interest in other men, but he does not want to ever have a same-sex relationship. He sadly reflects that his fundamental Christian beliefs have always precluded this possibility. You are relieved that he tells you that he has no intention of having SRS. Instead, he has decided that the best approach is to take a middle position by only taking cross-sex hormones to induce breast growth and several other feminizing features. In this way, he believes he can still satisfy his wife sexually while meeting many of his needs. Twila screams that she is unwilling to live with a man who has female-like breasts! Nonetheless, Twila is also a fundamentalist Christian and does not believe that she should leave Lorne, given the "sickness" he has developed. She asks you to cure him while Lorne asks what is needed so that he can begin taking hormones.

Note—Remember to view clients within their environmental contexts, keeping in mind societal, parental/familial, cultural/spiritual, and peer influences. Specifically, become aware of the impact that the following influences have and continue to have in your clients' lives: race, language, religion and spirituality, gender, familial migration history, affectional orientation, age and cohort, physical and mental capacities, socioeconomic situation and history, education, and history of traumatic experience.

1. What defines this person's environment, past and present?
2. Who is this person sitting in front of me, taking into account environmental and personal characteristics?
3. What defines the problem that he or she is presenting within his or her multicultural milieu?

The practitioner is encouraged to also read Chapter 9, as some of the recommendations made there are also applicable to MTF clients. Transsexual clients see counselors for the same reasons as everyone else, but in addition, they have some needs and problems that are unique (Korell & Lorah, 2007). Counselors are often expected to play a dual role with transsexual clients (if one follows the SOC, explained below), a conflict that has been duly noted in the literature (Fontaine, 2002; Mostade, 2006). On the one hand, counselors are there to be supportive and helpful to their clients, a role that is generic within the counseling profession. On the other hand, however, the counselor (if sufficiently trained for this purpose) may also act as a gatekeeper for those clients who want to physically transition.

Both the American Psychological Association (APA) and the American Counseling Association (ACA) have recently released important reports concerning the treatment of transgender clients. The Report of the Task Force (APA-TF, 2009) provides a succinct overview of research regarding transgender individuals and suggests many recommendations to APA to adopt inclusive policies concerning them.

The ACA recommendations (Burnes et al., 2010) lay out suggested multicultural competencies (i.e., affirmative attitudes, knowledge, and skills) for use in counseling transgender clients. The competencies focus on a wellness, resilience, and strength-based approach as opposed to an illness model. The eight overarching competencies include the following (note that the list of individual competencies is extensive and only a few examples are provided here):

1. *Human growth and development* (e.g., affirm developmental and health needs throughout the life span, understand the factors that affect their development).
2. *Social and cultural foundations* (e.g., use of appropriate language and pronouns, acknowledge their oppression and internalized transphobia, be an advocate where needed).
3. *Helping relationships* (e.g., understand the harm caused by conversion therapies, recognize how your own gender and sexuality affect the counseling relationship, create a welcoming environment).
4. *Group work* (e.g., be supportive and nonjudgmental of all gender expressions, involve members in group treatment plans and goals, be sensitive if only one transgender person is in the group).
5. *Professional orientation* (e.g., be aware of historical heterosexist and gender bias in the *DSM* diagnostic system, address the gatekeeper role and function, seek consultation or supervision to minimize the effect from personal bias).
6. *Career and lifestyle development competencies* (e.g., help with exploring career choices, be aware of bias in career assessment instruments, develop skill in addressing employment issues and challenges).
7. *Appraisal* (e.g., identify reason for counseling during first visit, appreciate the diversity of gender identity and expression, consider how oppression and discrimination contribute to psychological symptoms).
8. *Research* (e.g., consider limitations of existing literature, have knowledge of different types of research processes, formulate research questions collaboratively with transgender people, make research available to the transgender community).

The Canadian Psychological Association has also recently published fact sheets concerning transsexual individuals (Alderson & Cohen, 2011; Cohen & Alderson, 2011) and a policy statement (Canadian Psychological Association, 2010) concerning their treatment as follows:

> The Canadian Psychological Association affirms that all adolescent and adult persons have the right to define their own gender identity regardless of chromosomal sex, genitalia, assigned birth sex, or initial gender role. Moreover, all adolescent and adult persons have the right to free expression of their self-defined gender identity.
>
> The Canadian Psychological Association opposes stereotyping, prejudice, and discrimination on the basis of chromosomal sex, genitalia, assigned birth sex, or initial gender role, or on the basis of a self-defined gender identity or the expression thereof in exercising all basic human rights. (para. 10)

Carroll, Gilroy, and Ryan (2002) wrote that the focus in counseling has shifted from using hormones and surgery to help transsexual individuals within the binary gender system to affirming their unique identities. While this suggestion does represent an important movement, research to date supports transitioning for those with severe gender dysphoria (APA-TF, 2009). Furthermore, many if not most clients requesting counseling for GID are intent on beginning the transition process. Attempting to help clients change their minds about this becomes an ethical question. If they have already suffered greatly in their attempts to live outside the "binary box," how will they perceive your attempts to keep them in this difficult place?

Nonetheless, APA-TF (2009) states that "in reality, there is no single pathway or pathway or protocol for gender transition, and transgender persons must find a way to utilize transitional options to find what is best for them" (p. 38). Furthermore, there is no gold standard regarding what constitutes a "completed transition." Some transsexual individuals opt for hormone treatments only, some for partial surgery or full sex reassignment surgery (SRS), and some for both. Others choose to live without any physical intervention, instead living in a gender-ambiguous or neutral position. However, counselors need to be aware that there is currently little research in the United States regarding the outcome of those transsexual individuals who either live without any physical interventions or who choose either hormone and/or partial surgeries (APA-TF, 2009).

Rachlin (2002) surveyed 23 MTF and 70 FTM individuals about their experience of counseling and found that most sought help early in life for personal growth concerns and later sought specialized help for gender issues. Individuals were consistent in their appreciation for counselors who were flexible in their treatment approach and who demonstrated respect for gender identity.

In their overview of counseling transgender clients, Korell and Lorah (2007) surmised the following:

1. Many counselors will see one or more transgender clients in their careers.
2. Still more counselors will work with one or more family members of a transgender person.
3. Most counselors know very little about how to work with transgender clients.
4. Having a transgender identity does not imply pathology.
5. There is no relationship between transgenderism and affectional orientation (note that APA-TF, 2009, does suggest a link between affectional orientation and gender identity—most feminine MTF boys grow up to have attraction toward their same biological sex).
6. They come for counseling for the same reasons as nontrans clients.
7. SRS is not always appealing to them.

One of the major reasons transsexual clients who wish to transition seek the services of counseling is because it is a required step. This is how it works: Clients who believe they want to transition need to first be assessed that they meet the criteria for gender identity disorder according to *DSM-IV-TR* criteria. Some counselors have the credentials to diagnose, depending on their training. Some conditions can mimic GID or temporarily cause it in otherwise nontranssexual individuals (e.g., schizophrenia, psychosis, dissociative identity disorder; see Borras, Huguelet, & Eytan, 2007; Mizock & Fleming, 2011; Modestin & Ebner, 1995); a differential diagnosis is essential.

Once other potential causes have been eliminated and clients meet the criteria for GID and they desire transitioning, most counselors throughout the world (Long, Burnett, & Thomas, 2006) have followed the sixth edition of the *Harry Benjamin International Gender Dysphoria Association's Standards of Care for Gender Identity Disorders (SOC-6;* Meyer et al., 2001). It is likely that counselors will now, however, begin using the seventh version, referred to as the *Standards of Care for the Health of Transsexual, Transgender, and Gender Nonconforming People (SOC-7;* Coleman et al., 2011). *SOC-7* was developed through extensive consultation with world experts in the field (*SOC-7* is available for free at www.thisishow.org/Files/soc7.pdf).

Compared to *SOC-6, SOC-7* now refers to gender identity disorder as *gender dysphoria. SOC-7* provides "flexible clinical guidelines" (Coleman et al., 2011, p. 35). The increased flexibility regarding treatment provisions for transgender and transsexual clients is one of the most salient changes compared to *SOC-6. SOC-7* is a much larger publication than *SOC-6:* It now contains a wealth of essential information for anyone working with transgender and transsexual clients, including qualified mental health professionals, physicians/surgeons, and voice and communication therapists. According to *SOC-7,* counseling is no longer a requirement for referral for hormonal and surgical treatments for gender dysphoria, although it remains highly recommended.

Some other recommended revisions to *SOC-7* that were adopted include the following:

1. Physician responsibilities clarified, along with more information about cross-sex hormones and the suggested hormone regimens (Feldman & Safer, 2009).
2. Information about disorders of sex development (i.e., intersex conditions) added (Meyer-Bahlburg, 2009).
3. Reproductive options (e.g., semen banking, ovarian tissue freezing, oocyte or embryo freezing) included (De Sutter, 2009).

4. Purpose, duration, assessment, and relationship of the real-life experience to overall happiness clarified (Levine, 2009).
5. Some changes and a shift in emphasis regarding eligibility and readiness for the real-life experience added (De Cuypere & Vercruysse, 2009).
6. Language changed in referring to transpeople, gender variance depathologized, acknowledgment that transprejudice is a health issue, and cultural differences incorporated (Winter, 2009).
7. Information about recent transpositive psychotherapy models and additional sections included (Fraser, 2009c).
8. Content regarding etherapy included (i.e., electronic provision; Fraser, 2009b).
9. Acknowledgment that GID in children is related but not the same as GID in adolescents and adults added (de Vries & Cohen-Kettenis, 2009).
10. Informed consent procedure elaborated (de Vries & Cohen-Kettenis, 2009).

MTF Cross-Sex Hormones and Sex Reassignment Surgery

Not all transsexual individuals will take cross-sex hormones or undergo all of the sexual reassignment surgeries that are available (Mostade, 2006). Cross-sex hormones are contraindicated in some people, while SRS can vary in cost between $6,000 and $100,000, depending on what surgery is being performed (Cook-Daniels, 2006).

MTF individuals who take cross-sex hormones and either a gonadotropin releasing hormone (GnRH) agonist or testosterone blockers will experience softening of their skin, swelling and growing of breast tissue, loss of muscle, shrinkage of the penis and prostate, redistribution of body fat to more characteristically feminine proportions, and a lowering of serum cholesterol. Hair loss is stopped and beard and body hair growth are slowed. The voice does not rise and lost head hair does not regenerate. The individual often feels changes in mood, libido, and attitude. Often, increased feelings of relaxation are reported. Other effects may include weight gain, hypertension, and liver changes (Cohen-Kettenis & Gooren, 1992; Mostade, 2006; Seil, 2004; Wylie, Fung, Boshier, & Rotchell, 2009). Breast enlargement continues for 2 years after commencing cross-sex hormones (Dickey & Steiner, 1990). If further breast enlargement is desired after 2 years, breast augmentation surgery will be required. If hormones are discontinued, most of the effects are reversible, except for the breast growth that has occurred (Lawrence, 2008).

Cross-sex hormones do not cause the voice to rise; consequently most MTF individuals will pursue speech therapy (Cole, Denny, Eyler, & Samons, 2000). Most will also require extensive electrolysis to remove unwanted hair (Cole et al., 2000). It is important for all transsexual persons to stop smoking before beginning cross-sex hormones. For MTF persons, taking estrogen increases the risk of deep vein thrombosis (Cole et al., 2000). Cross-sex hormones can create other health issues, a list of which can be found in Wise and Meyer (1980).

SRS in MTF individuals involves vaginoplasty (i.e., creation of a vagina), clitoroplasty (creation of a clitoris), and vulvoplasty (creation of the vulva). The operation may be performed in either one or in two sessions (Sohn & Bosinski, 2007). SRS for MTF persons has reached a high level of technical refinement (Lawrence, 2005).

Some MTF individuals elect to have their "Adam's apple" shaved to reduce the thyroid cartilage (Dickey & Steiner, 1990). Dickey and Steiner (1990) do not recommend having surgery to shorten the vocal cords to create a higher-pitched voice, as the results may be unsatisfactory or hardly noticeable.

The neovagina created is almost indistinguishable from that of a biological female. The depth can exceed 5.9 inches (15 cm) and functions well during sexual intercourse, including its capacity for orgasm (Wise & Meyer, 1980).

Providing a letter for cross-sex hormones becomes the first gatekeeping function, and for many, the only one that will be requested. Given that some of the effects of cross-sex hormones are not fully reversible should they be discontinued, this is a huge responsibility on the part of the referring counselor. If getting approved for hormones was the sole purpose for clients seeing the counselor, the counseling may end rather abruptly after they get the coveted letter.

Be aware that some individuals take cross-sex hormones that they purchase through the black market. This is a risky practice for at least three primary reasons: (a) cross-sex hormones might be medically contraindicated in an individual's specific case; (b) the individual might not have ever been assessed for GID, and if the hormones are stopped, some changes remain irreversible; (c) the correct dosage cannot be ascertained with hormones purchased illegally, thereby further increasing medical risks at higher doses and not creating the desired effect at lower doses.

Besides assessment, counseling, and hormones, transsexual individuals who desire SRS, according to *SOC-7*, must also complete a minimum 12-month real-life experience (RLE). In this test, the individual must live and work as the desired gender in all life areas (e.g., work and volunteer, school), secure a legal change of first name, and provide documentation from other persons that this test is or has occurred to the qualified mental health professionals who will approve the surgery (requires two signatures; Coleman et al., 2011).

Research identifies SRS as the treatment of choice for transsexual individuals who experience severe gender dysphoria and who want to transition (Lawrence, 2008). Nonetheless, Marks, Green, and Mataix-Cols (2000) discussed a few cases in which GID appeared to remit, albeit returning several years later. Marks and colleagues recommended a long real-life experience (1 to 2 years) to minimize this rather remote possibility.

Counselors should note that the *DSM* diagnostic criteria for GID will change in the fifth edition. A suggested name change for *DSM-V* for GID in children is *gender dysphoria in children*. The proposed criteria include the following: (a) a clearly evident incongruence between one's assigned gender and one's experienced or expressed gender for at least 6 months (one must demonstrate at least six from a list of seven behavioral examples), and (b) it causes significant distress or impairment (American Psychiatric Association, 2010b).

The suggested name change in *DSM-V* for GID in adolescents or adults is *gender dysphoria in adolescents or adults*. The proposed criteria include the following: (a) a clearly evident incongruence between one's assigned gender and one's experienced or expressed gender for at least 6 months (one must demonstrate at least two from a list of six examples, most based on desire or conviction); and (b) it causes significant distress or impairment (American Psychiatric Association, 2010a).

Wester, McDonough, White, Vogel, and Taylor (2010) used gender role theory to create a five-stage model for working with transgender clients. The five stages include (a) awareness (recognizing that one feels different from others), (b) information seeking, (c) exploration (exploring the meaning that transgenderism has in one's life),

(d) disclosure (informing others of one's identity), and (e) integration (includes acceptance and posttransitional resolution). The concerns that are common to transsexual clients can occur at any of these stages. Some of the therapeutic approaches that have been used with gender-dysphoric individuals include behavior therapy, psychotherapy, parental involvement in treatment, setting limits on the expression of cross-gender behaviors and mannerisms, and supportive treatments that are affirmative (Zucker & Cohen-Kettenis, 2008).

The most common reasons that transsexual clients seek counseling are related to gender dysphoria, problems caused by acting on their feelings, or relationship problems resulting from their transgender feelings or behavior (Denny, 2007). These will be discussed below under the following headings: (a) child and adolescent challenges, (b) gender dysphoria, (c) wanting to transition, (d) relationship and family problems, (e) transitioning at work, and (f) need for social support.

Child and Adolescent Challenges

A Dutch study compared 120 children with GID to 47 other children referred for attention-deficit/hyperactivity disorder. Just over half (52%) of the GID group had at least one other diagnosis besides GID (Wallien, Swaab, & Cohen-Kettenis, 2007). Counselors working with children need to be aware of this comorbidity. Another study found that poor peer relations were the strongest predictor of behavior problems in children referred to both the Toronto and Utrecht clinics for gender identity (Cohen-Kettenis, Owen, Kaijser, Bradley, & Zucker, 2003). Children who express more severe gender atypicality and who feel conformity pressure are most likely to develop internalizing problems, such as depression (Yunger, Carver, & Perry, 2004).

Transgender youth report having many issues with discrimination, marginalization, access to support services, lack of family support, and confusion between gender identity and affectional orientation (Grossman & D'Augelli, 2006). Meyenburg (1999) stressed being extremely cautious when working with transgender adolescents and that SRS not be initiated until at least 18 years of age (same as *SOC-7* recommendation).

Counselors may be placed in the awkward position of deciding whether to treat a child or adolescent with GID by attempting to reduce or eliminate the gender atypicality. There is a great deal of controversy surrounding whether GID in children should become the focus of treatment (APA-TF, 2009). While some experts advocate treatments targeted at gender atypicality (Rekers, Rosen, Lovaas, & Bentler, 1978; Zucker & Bradley, 1999), others oppose this view in that it promulgates a view of GID as pathology instead of as a normal variant of gender expression (Hill, Rozanski, Carfagnini, & Willoughby, 2007; Langer & Martin, 2004).

Furthermore, attempting to make children more gender conforming can be harmful to them, creating feelings of shame, inadequacy, and depression. Such treatments are aimed at maintaining gender stereotypes. By perpetuating and supporting this myth of what gender is supposed to look like, counselors inadvertently collude with parents, which in turn may exasperate disruptive relationships between the child and his or her family (Langer & Martin, 2004).

Keep in mind that most children outgrow GID but far fewer adolescents do, and those who do not tend to later identify as gay or lesbian and not as transsexual. A recent dissertation by Bradley (2010) found that parents who were the most rejecting of their child's gender atypicality also reported that their child experienced the most psychological distress and had the most behavioral problems compared to parents who were more accepting.

Those with an affirmative stance view *gender-variant* behavior and mannerisms as simply a form of natural variation. Particularly with young children, the counselor would be more apt to work with the parents than the child to explore whether an intervention is appropriate. Rosenberg (2002) suggested an individual and group program that includes both the parents and their child. The Royal College of Psychiatrists (Di Ceghe, Sturge, & Sutton, 1998) published useful guidelines for working with children and adolescents with GID as well.

Cohen-Kettenis, Delemarrevan de Waal, and Gooren (2008) recently reported, based on their work at the Netherlands gender clinic, that children between ages 12 and 16 suffering from substantial gender dysphoria can be provided gonadotropin-releasing hormone analogs (these block further secretion of sex hormones and their effects are completely reversible if stopped). Cross-sex hormones can begin between the ages of 16 and 18. Cohen-Kettenis and colleagues noted that other clinics in Europe and North American have adopted this policy as well.

Gender Dysphoria

Like most human differences, gender dysphoria can be seen as being on a continuum. Counselors should be mindful that there is not a 100% correlation between one's level of distress and one's desire to transition. Some individuals experiencing low distress from gender dysphoria are convinced they need to transition (Abel, 1979), while others with extreme distress would never consider transitioning.

Schrock, Boyd, and Leaf (2009) noted that MTF individuals first entering the public arena dressed as women are often anxious. They looked at how MTF persons managed their emotions while beginning this necessary step. First, they began by doing preliminary emotional work to help bolster their confidence and reduce anxiety. Second, they worked at transforming their negative emotions while in public. Lastly, they retrospectively reviewed their past public appearances as women and worked at reinterpreting their experiences in a positive way.

As Carroll and colleagues (2002) noted, counselors need to be careful to not perpetuate the commonly held binary systems of male/female and masculinity/femininity. Many gender-dysphoric individuals learn to accept their diversity and live their lives blurring these gender binaries, while others cannot live happily without transitioning to varying degrees. Consequently, counselors need to be flexible in their approach to treatment. They need to build a strong working alliance by creating collaboration between treatment goals and their achievement.

Affirmative counseling can be offered, regardless of one's theoretical orientation. Fraser (2009a) wrote about how depth psychology, using contemporary psychodynamic principles, can be helpful. Livingstone (2008) recommended person-centered counseling as especially indicated given its phenomenological approach (i.e., a focus on the subjective experience of an individual) and because empathy and affirmation are important to help transsexual clients deal with their commonly experienced feelings of shame.

Wanting to Transition

Wanting to transition is a very common reason a transgender person comes to see a counselor. Often, the client has thought about this for some time and many have read more than the counselor about the criteria and what is needed to become eligible for hormones and eventual SRS. Informed clients, of course, can also provide the answers that the counselor is looking for in their desperate attempts to get a diagnosis of GID (Lawrence, 2008). While deception may be difficult to understand at first, many transgender individuals—including some fetishistic crossdressing men and others with lower levels of gender dysphoria—believe that SRS is the only solution to their problems (Abel, 1979). Furthermore, the counselor is often the gatekeeper between them and initiation of the process.

An underlying assumption of affirmative counseling is that individuals have a right to self-determination (Korell & Lorah, 2007). However, there are limits to this assumption. For individuals who insist on transitioning, they still need to meet the criteria for GID and then proceed through the necessary steps, usually the ones suggested by the *SOC*. To do otherwise, quite frankly, is to risk that the individual will later have regrets. Given that SRS is unidirectional, not all effects of hormones are reversible, and there may be other reasons besides GID why someone would want to transition as noted earlier (e.g., schizophrenia and other psychotic conditions), it would be unprofessional and unethical to allow anyone wanting to transition to proceed. Counselors cannot be swayed by the sense of urgency that many transgender individuals experience once they come to believe that transitioning is their only option (Fontaine, 2002), however strongly that may be experienced.

Regarding use of pronouns, it is affirmative to refer to transgender clients based on their current presentation of gender (Carroll & Gilroy, 2002). If the counselor is uncertain, it is important to ask, both in terms of pronouns and in regard to the client's preferred name (some transgender people prefer to be called by a male name when presenting as male and by a female name when presenting as female).

Relationship and Family Problems

Surprisingly little research has been published that focuses on the family issues of adult transgender people (APA-TF, 2009). A huge area of concern for transsexual individuals coming to counseling centers on how they will deal with their current relationships with family, friends, and significant others. Today, many transsexual individuals continue living with their life partners and raising children (Lev, 2004). Samons (2009) wrote that many live together even after they fully transition. As noted earlier in this chapter, however, children's reactions to their parent's transsexualism were correlated with the age the children were when the disclosure occurs. Preschoolers generally adapted well, while adolescents generally had a more difficult time (White & Ettner, 2004).

Family members, spouses, and others are typically shocked and/or in denial when they first learn about a person's transsexualism, and several researchers (see APA-TF, 2009) have compared their process to Kubler-Ross' stages of bereavement theory (e.g., denial, anger, bargaining, depression, acceptance). Many transsexual individuals have heartwrenching stories about the varying degrees of rejection they have felt and experienced.

Family members and partners experience different reactions than the transgender individual (Emerson & Rosenfeld, 1996). In a study by Erich, Tittsworth, Dykes, and Cabuses (2008), 91 transsexual participants (82 MTF, 9 FTM) completed questionnaires assessing the quality of their family relationships. The results revealed that most of their sample reported favorable family relationships. Hegedus (2009) also found that most of the parents (11 mothers, 1 father) she interviewed for her dissertation were accepting of their daughter's decision to transition (note her study focused only on FTM individuals). Nonetheless, all parents worried about rejection, losing connections with others, being cut off from their families and/or their communities, feeling alienated and alone, and/or fear of having others gossip about them.

Parents of transsexual individuals often require counseling to deal with the self-blame, guilt, and shame as they begin searching for explanations as to how their son or daughter developed gender identity disorder. Their response to the gender struggles of their son or daughter "is a deeply moral issue" (Wren, 2002, p. 377). These moral components need to be addressed if the parents are to become truly supportive of their adult child's choices, particularly if this involves transitioning. Family counseling focused on the transsexual person's experience of daily living in their current morphology may help the parents develop empathy for the extent of suffering their child endures. Work focused on helping the parents appreciate their transsexual son or daughter and on strengthening their emotional bond is recommended as well (Zamboni, 2006).

Families, friends, and romantic partners of a transgender person need to mourn whatever losses they perceive will unfold (Zamboni, 2006). Zamboni (2006) suggested many roles counselors can take to help significant others cope, such as encouraging them to take time alone before expressing themselves to the transgender individual, offering social support, validating their feelings, and providing accurate information.

Menvielle and Tuerk (2002) described a support group for parents of gender-nonconforming boys, recognizing that often parents feel shame and stigmatized themselves. Similarly, Wren (2002) described a group for parents of transgender adolescents. The parents formed a story of how their teenagers developed their gender identities as a coping strategy. They also took great care in who they told both within and outside the family.

Transitioning at Work

A sizeable literature has accumulated describing the difficulties that transsexual individuals face when transitioning at their place of work (Barclay & Scott, 2006; Kessler & McKenna, 2000; Kirk & Belovics, 2008; Korell & Lorah, 2007; Winfeld, 2005). Colleagues often experience a significant reaction of their own, and not all become supporters (Barclay & Scott, 2006). Transsexual individuals encounter varying degrees of aggression, hostility, and discrimination in the workplace, with some becoming socially isolated, physically threatened, demoted, and terminated (Sangganjanavanich & Cavazos, 2010).

Transsexual individuals will eventually need to disclose their identities at work if they have chosen to physically transition. Hormones create obvious changes, including breasts growing on an MTF person or a beard growing on an FTM individual (Cook-Daniels, 2006). As the literature has revealed the difficulties transsexual individuals face when their employers and/or colleagues find out, counselors can be instrumental in facilitating this process. An approach based on the following steps is usually helpful (Alderson, 2007):

1. Collaboratively decide on when the client will disclose at work—This is often necessary at the point hormones begin to show their effects.
2. Discuss and collaboratively decide who are the key players—This often includes the immediate supervisor and that person's manager. If there is a human resources (HR) department, find the appropriate person who will become the first contact. Collaborate with her or him, the client, and yourself regarding the transition plan.
3. Assist client in preparing a letter to relevant colleagues (a sample letter can be found at http://destrantalk.blogspot.com/2009/12/open-transition-letter-transgender-life.html).
4. Teach client how to cope with negative and positive reactions to the imminent disclosure.
5. Plan a meeting time with the key players—This meeting is best handled initially with all players present except the client. The goals are to (a) legitimize the gender dysphoria, (b) help the key players understand some of the dynamics of gender dysphoria and provide information, and (c) ensure that they understand that their employee is under both medical and psychological care.
6. Let key players know that you will be monitoring your client's progress in transitioning throughout the process.
7. Have the client join the meeting (if agreeable)—If the client wants to join the meeting (some do not), have this occur toward the end when planning can occur collaboratively.
8. Jointly plan a strategy for disclosure to relevant colleagues. If possible, plan an in-service (i.e., professional development session) at which you meet the colleagues of the client to provide information and field questions. If this is not feasible, encourage some mechanism whereby colleagues can ask questions or gain greater understanding, such as by providing informative websites or encouraging one-on-one discussion between colleagues and the client (in a way that is considered reasonable and appropriate to your client).
9. Have HR person or most senior person at the meeting send out the client's letter to relevant colleagues at the agreed-upon time—In this way, employees will find out simultaneously and it will have greater legitimacy given that it is coming from a person in authority.
10. Ensure that client understands that people will need time to adjust—Some colleagues may gossip in ways that are not predictable. Remind the client that this passes for most people after some time has elapsed.

11. Monitor the client during the first few weeks of the RLT regarding work adjustment and emerging issues.

Need for Social Support

The need for social support has been a recurring theme in every chapter, and this becomes particularly pertinent as we move into discussing the most vulnerable members of the LGBTI community. While the gay and lesbian movement has benefitted from its relatively large population and from their political lobbying efforts, the transsexual community is small, many of its members wish to remain hidden after transitioning (called going "stealth"), nontranssexuals have a harder time understanding them, and they remain pathologized within diagnostic systems that perpetuate the belief that they have a mental disorder.

It is hard for most of us to imagine a life in which being honest about something as basic as our sense of gender and sexuality leads others to want nothing more to do with us. Unfortunately, research shows that transgender people tend to have few social supports (APA-TF, 2009). Those who have disclosed to more people generally have more social supports than those who have disclosed to only a few (Maguen, Shipherd, Harris, & Welch, 2007).

MTF individuals, particularly those from ethic/racial minorities, often suffer psychologically in many different ways as already highlighted in this chapter. Research shows that those who receive support from social networks are helped in alleviating many of these problems (Pinto, Melendez, & Spector, 2008). Those with social support are generally healthier psychologically (APA-TF, 2009).

Several Internet resources are listed under the Resources section found later in this chapter. Larger cities will have services for transgender people—first contact is usually the gay and lesbian information service. Group counseling is another means of offering social support (Mostade, 2006).

COUNSELING DIVERSE POPULATIONS

Counseling MTF Individuals With Multiple Nondominant Identity Statuses

As reported earlier, transsexual individuals of color often experience more aversive discrimination based on their gender identity compared to their ethnicity or race (Erich, Tittsworth, Meier, & Lerman, 2010). Estrada's (2008) dissertation found that Latina MTF individuals face discrimination on many levels, often needing to flee their families of origin. Counselors need to be aware that transgender people of color face more barriers to acceptance than those who are White. Disclosing to family may well lead to rejection. Counselors working with transgender people of color need to consider the additional considerations that ethnicity and race evoke. Also given the finding that transwomen of color have high rates of HIV infection (Sausa et al., 2007) and 59% of ethnic-minority youth in one study engaged in unprotected high-risk sex in the past year (Garofalo, Osmer, Sullivan, Doll, & Harper, 2007), counselors may be instrumental in educating and encouraging their clients to practice safer sex.

Counseling Aging MTF Individuals

Aging individuals are often marginalized to varying extents in societies that are youth oriented, and this is especially true for aging transgender individuals who may be ignored by both the gay and lesbian community and the heterosexual community. They often keep their gender identities hidden as well. Counselors working with this group will find it helpful to teach aging clients to use e-mail and Internet resources (Cook-Daniels, 2006), such as the Transgender Aging Network (www.forge-forward.org/tan/index.php), which has a mandate to help improve the lives of aging transgender people and their significant others.

Counseling MTF Individuals Living in Rural Communities

Willging, Salvador, and Kano (2006) interviewed 20 providers of mental health care in mostly two rural communities in New Mexico. The providers reported that individual and institutional forms of bias were present toward LGBTI individuals in a number of mental health treatment facilities.

The number of transgender people living in rural communities is unknown. Walinsky and Whitcomb (2010) offered some recommendations, including a willingness to take on a larger role of advocate for their transgender clients. Transgender clients in rural areas may need extra help appreciating job market realities and the difficulties they may face (Walinsky & Whitcomb, 2010). Furthermore, counselors will have a more difficult time avoiding dual relationships given the increased likelihood they will encounter clients in their social events.

Counseling MTF Students

The literature concerning the developmental needs and the affirmation of transgender postsecondary students is limited (Lynch, 2011). In a study of 300 Polish college students (153 men, 147 women), the majority of participants believed that transsexual individuals should have the right to change their name (67%), take hormone therapy (70%), and have surgery (63.5%). Most were against funding either hormonal therapy (63.4%) or surgery (65.6%) from insurance plans (Antoszewski, Kasielska, Jedrzejczak, & KrukJeromin, 2007). A similar percentage of individuals believing that SRS should be paid by the transsexual individual (63%) was found in a Swedish national survey (Landen & Innala, 2000).

Two articles were recently published that focus on counseling transgender students using the ACA Transgender Competencies. Lennon and Mistler (2010) advocated an affirmative approach to counseling transgender students in colleges and universities. They recommended that counselors receive training in working with these clients and for the advancement of research in this area. They also recommended colloborating with other mental health settings, hospitals, and on-campus health centers. Gonzalez and McNulty (2010) highlighted the importance of collaboration, but they also recommended that school counselors become familiar with the research regarding transgender youth.

Counseling MTF Adolescents

A Canadian study found that LGBT teenagers continue to experience exclusion, isolation, and fear (Dysart-Gale, 2010). Toomey, Ryan, Diaz, Card, and Russell (2010) reported that gender nonconforming adolescents and young adults are often victimized. In their sample, Toomey and colleagues found that LGBT youth who either perceived or experienced actual victimization reported greater problems with psychosocial adjustment as measured by life satisfaction and depression. Often, adolescents experience intense distress regarding gender dysphoria (Di Ceghe et al., 1998). Counselors will need to carefully assess and recommend appropriate interventions, often working in concert with the parents or legal guardians. A team approach is also recommended wherever possible.

Resources for This Group

1. The World Professional Association for Transgender Health (WPATH) used to be called the Harry Benjamin International Gender Dysphoria Association (HBIGDA). It is dedicated

to understanding and treating gender identity disorder (www.wpath.org/).

2. Dr. Anne Lawrence's website provides excellent information for transsexual individuals. She is one of the noted authorities on this subject (www.annelawrence.com/).
3. Laura's Playground is an excellent resource, listing many of the main support groups throughout the world, including most American states and Canada (www.lauras-playground.com/trans_support_groups.htm).
4. The Gender Education and Advocacy website is a national organization dedicated to the needs, issues, and concerns of gender-variant people (www.gender.org).
5. The National Center for Transgender Equality is dedicated to improving the lives of transgender people. They provide excellent resources and research reports regarding transgender and transsexual individuals (http://transequality.org/).
6. GenderTalk offers a list of suggested readings and many resources regarding transitioning and coming out. (www.gendertalk.com/info/resource/books.shtml).

Limitations, Furthering Research, and Implications for Counselors

Limitations of the Research With This Group

The transsexual community is extraordinarily small (.0000775% MTF, .0000295% FTM, using De Cuypere et al., 2007, stats from Belgium), and this means that research mostly occurs at two of the most known gender clinics in the world: Toronto, Ontario, and Ultrecht, the Netherlands. Consequently, we know a great deal about transsexual individuals who are referred to two clinics in one Canadian and one European city. Both clinics operate according to a medical and/or clinical psychology model: that which is different is abnormal or pathological. Counseling and counseling psychology, on the other hand, focuses more on the strengths of individuals and their resiliency. Instead of seeing the division between *them* (the patients) and *us* (the clinicians), counselors are more apt to view clients from a position of equality and are therefore less interested in diagnosis and labeling. That ideology, however, does not imply that the other position is wrong—it is just different, bringing with it its own strengths and weaknesses in the treatment of other people.

The biggest limitation, then, is that research has been slanted toward pathologizing the differences between one of the most vulnerable groups within the LGBTI community and the rest of the so-called normal people out there. Despite this bias, it is amazing how the majority of MTF individuals have managed to look psychologically normal, despite the numerous psychological tests used on them, mostly designed to highlight difference instead of sameness.

Areas Requiring Further Research

We need more research based on the ideology that underlies counseling and counseling psychology—in other words, research focused more on sameness, resiliency, positive psychology, and coping resources. We also need longitudinal studies that focus on the long-term outcome for those transsexual individuals who decide not to transition and instead decide to live their lives as transgenderist individuals. Is surgery a necessary procedure, and if so, for whom under what circumstances? Would surgery be chosen by few if any transsexual persons if gender transcendence ever became a reality in American and Canadian society (i.e., that we no longer ascribed gender to human traits, mannerisms, or characteristics)?

Implications for Counselors

Transsexual clients bring a myriad of problems to the counseling office, ranging from the common problems most people face at times in their lives to the complex decision making surrounding the transitioning process. Most trans-clients are well informed regarding what is needed to transition before they see a counselor. The community is small enough that word spreads quickly as to which counselors to seek and which ones to avoid. The counselor in demand is the one who provides affirmative counseling and will provide needed letters for those who wish to transition. Particularly given the requirements prescribed by the *Harry Benjamin International Standards of Care (SOC)*, involved counselors play an integral role in the transitioning process of transsexual individuals.

The gatekeeper function puts counselors in a dual role, and one that is fraught with ethical dilemmas. If clients are to be self-directed and self-determined, they ought to play the larger role in deciding the goals of treatment and in how these goals are to be realized. A gatekeeper, however, has the power to override a client's goals and their attainment. This is unlikely to happen for those transsexual clients who have been carefully assessed as having severe and persistent gender dysphoria and who are willing to follow the steps of the *SOC-7* (assuming they wish to transition).

The stress of the dual role only emerges the moment the counselor is not in agreement with the goals and/or method of attainment of the client. This is particularly likely to happen when the counselor does *not* assess that the client has severe and persistent gender dysphoria or that a severe gender dysphoria is evident but that a major contributing factor underlying it is a psychotic process, such as schizophrenia or the very rare condition called dissociative identity disorder (formerly called multiple personality disorder). When clients do not get what they want from a counselor, they usually terminate soon thereafter.

Preoperative transsexual clients have already lived their psychological lives in their biological bodies. Despite a counselor's best intentions, transsexual clients have usually made up their minds already as to what they want from the encounter if transitioning is the issue at hand. Attempting to talk a transsexual client who wants to transition into living instead in their current body—with all of the repercussions they have already experienced—is a bit like telling someone to continue facing their stigmatization and oppression by "sucking it up." The sense of urgency that so many feel is palpable. A real advantage of the *SOC* is that it advocates a system that forces most transsexual clients to slow things down while transitioning occurs in an increasingly irreversible direction.

Transitioning brings with it many psychosocial, emotional, and physical challenges, but so does not transitioning. The alternative to surgery that some transsexual individuals do pursue is to live their lives to the best of their ability in the midst of a societal gender binary system. But while academics create postmodern ideas of a blissful world where everyone is accepted, the reality for most is not that idealistic. Most people make judgments of others based on observable characteristics, and if the person is not deemed to be sufficiently male/masculine or female/feminine, the judgments do not generally fall in a positive direction. Whether one transitions or not, there are significant consequences.

With a caveat, counselors ought not to be the preservers of a social order or the radicals that dramatically deviate from it, either. The caveat is that we must advocate for social justice and social equality when we see that its basic tenets are not being applied. For most counselors, that means ensuring clients find ways to live meaningful lives that are happy and fulfilled. It also, however, means bringing attention to the societal factors that impinge upon their actualization.

Exercises

Individual Exercises

1. Make it a point to meet or chat with at least one MTF individual. If you live in a large city, find out if you can attend a meeting for transsexual persons. If you live somewhere smaller, go to a website that caters to the transsexual community and begin an online chat with someone.

2. Decide on Halloween or at a costume party to present as the opposite sex, both in appearance and mannerisms. As you play out this role for the night, pay attention to the moments during which you feel comfortable and those that feel awkward. What defines these moments? What do your observations tell you about gender and gender expression?

Classroom Exercise

1. In dyads, have a discussion about the costs and benefits of being male, and then do the same for being female. In the larger class, discuss how the world could be better if some of these costs were minimized while the benefits were maximized. What would need to happen to get there?

2. Alternatively, in dyads, do your best to act and talk like a member of the opposite sex. After an allotted time, discuss the challenges you faced in doing this well.

3. Invite a transsexual person to be a guest speaker in your class. Encourage him or her to talk about his or her life and its challenges. Be prepared in advance with plenty of questions that you can ask following the presentation.

Chapter Summary

Transsexual individuals represent a very small percentage of the population. MTF persons come to counseling for similar reasons as most clients. Some may not disclose their transsexual status to the counselor, particularly if this is irrelevant to their reason for seeking help. Some transsexual individuals live their lives going *stealth*, meaning that they live fully in their chosen gender without revealing their biological sex to others.

Not all desire to transition, but those who do are usually very determined and sometimes impatient. Transsexual persons need to be carefully assessed if they do wish to transition. The counselor who adheres to the *Standards of Care (SOC)* plays a dual role, both that of the understanding counselor and that of a gatekeeper. The *SOC*, now in its seventh edition, outlines the role of gatekeeper but is silent regarding how the required counseling component should look. The *DSM* criteria for gender identity disorder are under revision, and the most recent suggested name is to call it *gender dysphoria* instead (note: *SOC-7* has already implemented this name change).

Research indicates that most transsexual people are psychologically healthy in aspects unrelated to their felt sense of gender. The diagnosis of gender identity disorder is hotly contested, particularly regarding the diagnosis of children. Some advocate attempting to diminish gender-variant behaviors and mannerisms, while others strongly encourage others to accept gender-variant children as they are. Whether treatment is initiated or not, most children outgrow the diagnosis, and most eventually grow up to identify as either gay or lesbian. Few eventually identify as transsexual.

9

TRANSSEXUAL GIRLS AND TRANSMEN

CHALLENGING YOUR ATTITUDES AND BELIEFS ABOUT THIS GROUP

REFLECTION QUESTIONS

1. Imagine that you are a female who always thought you should have been born a male. How do you believe this would affect you during your childhood, teenage years, and early adulthood years?
2. If you were a female-to-male (FTM) individual before actually transitioning, what reactions can you imagine receiving from your friends and family when you disclose this to them? How would it affect your subsequent relationships with them?

(Continued)

(Continued)

3. If were an FTM individual, what effect would this likely have in terms of your chosen career (consider entry into the career and advancement)?
4. How would your concerns about going out dressed as an FTM person be similar and different to concerns about going out dressed as an MTF person? Would your concerns be any different during daytime hours as opposed to at night?
5. Men continue to have more societal privileges compared to women. How would you imagine these privileges to be affected if you were a transman (i.e., which ones would likely be forthcoming and which ones would remain elusive)? What factors might affect which privileges are bestowed and which ones withheld from you?

Challenging Your Assumptions Questions

1. To what extent do you believe FTM individuals make a free choice to be the way they are? On what basis do you believe this?
2. How do you currently view FTM individuals? To what extent do your views apply to *all* FTM individuals?
3. How would you react if your daughter disclosed to you that she wants to become a man?
4. You are asked to share a hotel room with a fellow employee (or fellow student) and you are the only one who knows that this individual is a postsurgical transsexual person who is now of the same gender as you. What reaction would you have to sharing the hotel room with him or her (positive, negative, and neutral)? What is the likelihood that you would keep this person's identity to yourself?
5. Do you believe that FTM transsexual individuals "put on" stereotypical gestures and speech? Do some actually have these characteristics in childhood?

Reflections

[*Note:* Imagine that *you* are the client in these reflections.]

Your name is Chris, a 29-year-old FTM individual in a 10-year committed relationship to Wanda. Wanda identifies as a lesbian, but she knew from the outset that you eventually intended to become a transman. While living in New York City 3 years ago, an affirmative counselor, Dr. Clarke, helped you begin the transitioning process. After seeing Dr. Clarke for several weeks, she provided you a letter to begin cross-sex hormones. Taking the hormones at first provided everything you could ever ask for—your sex drive became stronger than ever and Wanda was enjoying the increased attention you provided her. Inside, you felt a sense of calm. That, however, did not last long. Wanda's employer insisted that she transfer to their office in Savannah, Georgia. As her work was far more stable than yours working for a temporary firm, the two of you moved. That's when the nightmare began.

Wanda was becoming less appreciative of the changes you were experiencing. As your musculature increased, your voice deepened, and your desire for sex intensified, Wanda expressed feeling overpowered and overwhelmed. She wanted things to be the way they were. Wanda was never that interested in sex, but more than that, she was never interested in having sex with a man. Wanda said that you were beginning to feel like a man in a way that left her uncomfortable.

Wanda had a great employee assistance plan through work, and the two of you soon headed for your first appointment with a counselor named Charlie. Charlie seemed like a nice enough fellow and was about your age. After you and Wanda explained the troubles you were having as a couple, he began: "Your situation couldn't be any more difficult, could it? But what did you expect, Chris? Wanda has always been a lesbian, and that means she wants to be with a woman, not with a man."

At this point, Wanda speaks up: "You know, Charlie, that is an oversimplification. I have been with Chris for a long time and I knew early on that he would someday transition. It's more that I have noticed Chris is changing into a different person."

Charlie responds, "What do you mean by that?"

"Well, I feel like Chris is becoming less appreciative of me. He seems preoccupied with wanting sex and is looking at other women in a way I find demeaning."

"You know, I have never counseled transpeople before. But seriously, how can your relationship possibly work when you are not interested in being in a relationship with a man, Wanda?" At this point Wanda looks up at Chris and says, "I want to leave—you can stay if you prefer." Chris apologizes to Charlie, and she and Wanda head for home. Wanda becomes silent, looking distraught but unable to find the right words to say. You can barely keep your own composure, fearing that Charlie might be right.

From a Client's Perspective

1. From Chris's perspective, what would you have preferred to hear from Charlie? What about from Wanda's perspective?
2. From Chris's perspective, what feelings are not being either heard or acknowledged by Charlie? What about from Wanda's perspective?
3. To what extent do you think a counselor's reaction and response will vary depending on where you live in the United States?

From a Counselor's Perspective

1. What mistakes has Charlie made in trying to help Chris and Wanda? What would be a better way to conduct this session?
2. Was Charlie "right"? What factors is Charlie not considering?
3. Given that Charlie has never worked with a transperson before, what action(s) should he take to remain ethical in his practice?
4. What messages would an affirmative counselor want this couple to hear?

Background Information Regarding Transsexual Girls and Transmen

Female-to-male transsexual (FTM) individuals are biological females who believe their gender is dissonant with their morphology (adapted from Vanderburgh, 2009). *Transmen* will refer strictly to postoperative FTM individuals, whether or not they themselves assume this identity label (note that similar to many MTF persons, many postoperative FTM individuals do *not* use this term to refer to themselves; Forshee, 2008). Those who go *stealth* (i.e., those who live fully in their chosen gender without revealing their biological sex to others) will likely identify themselves simply as men.

While FTM individuals have not received anything close to the amount of research dedicated to MTF persons (Forshee, 2008), what we do know is that there are substantial differences between these two groups (Fontaine, 2002). A summation of these differences highlights the finding that FTM individuals are psychologically healthier than MTF individuals (Michel, Ansseau, Legros, Pitchot, & Mormont, 2002; Pauly, 1974b), they are more satisfied postsurgically (Smith, Van Goozen, Kuiper, & Cohen-Kettenis, 2005), they establish more stable and enduring relationships (Fleming, MacGowan, & Costos, 1985; Michel et al., 2002), they are better integrated socially (Fontaine, 2002), and their status as men provides them greater status and respect in work settings (Schilt, 2006).

Pauly (1974a) credited Westphal in 1870 as being the first to mention a case of a woman with gender dysphoria, while Hirschfeld reported the first case of FTM surgery in 1922. Many researchers and writers in the past did not believe women experienced GID. Stoller (1971) suggested that females do not crossdress for fetishistic purposes but instead only do so for gender expression and to be accepted as a male in society. Of course, many women today dress more as men for stylistic reasons and also because long pants are warmer to wear in winter.

Pauly (1974a) made an interesting observation regarding the gender ratio of FTM to MTF (about 1:2 or 3; Lawrence, 2008). It is more common for young girls to prefer the male role and behave in typical masculine ways (e.g., climbing trees, playing rough) than the reverse is true for boys. Furthermore, males in general and men in particular enjoy a preferred role in society compared to girls and women. Pauly questioned why, then, are there are so many more MTF individuals prepared to give up their male status by transitioning? Reasons may include the finding that men in general are far more sexually aroused by visual stimulation than women (Townsend, 1998), perhaps leading gender dysphoric men to want to literally see their gender become physically more compatible with their inner sense of gender. Furthermore, most nonhomosexual MTF persons experience autogynephilia (i.e., a male's propensity to be sexually aroused by the thought of himself as a female), a fetishistic mechanism that research has not demonstrated has its opposite counterpart in nonhomosexual FTM individuals.

Green (2005) asked eight transmen six questions at an FTM international meeting about masculinity in 2002. He did not ask whether they were pre- or postsurgical. Green concluded they were all undeniably masculine. He also found that all participants agreed that maleness and masculinity are not the same thing: They did not believe a penis was necessary to say that one had a male body. Vegter and Alderson (2011) found comparable results in their sample of six FTM individuals. Participants believed a penis did not equate to maleness—one could be male without having one. Masculinity and femininity were viewed by participants as a set of traits that vary among all humans, regardless of gender (Vegter & Alderson, 2011).

Comparable to MTF individuals, several schemes have developed to categorize FTM persons. Hansbury (2005) created a taxonomy with three transmasculine identities he called "genderqueers," "transmen," and "woodworkers." Genderqueers were the youngest group (teens to mid-20s). They expressed diverse and fluid identities, embellishing a postmodern sense of not committing to a gender identity per se. The transmen (late 20s to early 30s) did not fully identify as men, as they continued to own their histories as biological females. The woodworkers (late 30s and up) were the group who tended to "fit in with the woodwork" as they engaged in life as male and who went stealth.

The other more popular classification is again based on whether the FTM person is sexually interested in primarily women (homosexual type) or is attracted to men with possible co-occurring interest in women (nonhomosexual type; Blanchard, 2005; Lawrence, 2008; Lev, 2007). Each type has a different developmental path.

Development Through the Life Span

According to Lawrence (2008), homosexual FTM individuals are overtly masculine during childhood. They generally have sexual attitudes more typical of biological males and they have a greater desire for phalloplasty (the surgery that creates a neopenis). They typically have less comorbid psychopathology compared to nonhomosexual FTM individuals. It was believed in the past that almost all FTM individuals were homosexual (attracted to their own biological sex).

Nonhomosexual FTM persons are usually visibly masculine during childhood and are less interested in phalloplasty. They have sexual attitudes less typical of biological males and they are more likely to experience co-morbidity. Both homosexual and nonhomosexual FTM individuals were usually aware they wanted to change sexes by age 8, and both groups usually transition while in their 20s (Lawrence, 2008).

Remember that longitudinal studies have shown that the vast majority of children with GID do not grow up to identify as transsexual, but instead, the majority end up later identifying as gay or lesbian (Green, 2006). A recent longitudinal study first tested a group of 25 girls with GID at the mean age of 8.88 years (range: 3–12) and then again at the mean age of 23.24 years (range: 15–36; Drummond, Bradley, Peterson-Badali, & Zucker, 2008). During their assessment as girls, 60% fully met the *DSM* criteria for GID, while 40% were subthreshold for this diagnosis. At the follow-up age, only three participants (12%) were deemed to still have GID or gender dysphoria, and only two of the three were interested in SRS. Regarding sexual orientation, eight (32%) expressed mostly bisexual or homosexual sexual fantasy and six (24%) were classified as bisexual or homosexual on the basis of their sexual behavior. This is a substantially smaller percentage in comparison to the number of boys with GID who later express homosexual or bisexual interests (most studies show that between 75 and 80% of behaviorally feminine boys followed longitudinally later report primarily homosexual or bisexual interests). Drummond and colleagues (2008) also reported that studies to date, without exception, have shown that both gay men and lesbian women retrospectively report more cross-gender behavior in childhood compared to heterosexual control groups.

Pauly (1974b) concluded, following her literature review, that FTM children manifest cross-gender behavior before age 3 and that the developmental process is complete by age 7 or 8. She also found that by age 20, most have moved permanently into the male role and that FTM persons experience fewer fluctuations in their gender-role behavior compared to their MTF counterparts.

Williams and colleagues (as cited in Green, 1996) looked at parent–child factors in tomboys. They found that tomboys, in comparison to girls who were gender typical, less often imitated their mothers or helped her around the house. They more commonly imitated their fathers and expressed their desire to grow up to be like them. In one study, 21 FTM individuals were compared to 139 female controls. While the FTM sample rated both parents as more rejecting and less emotionally warm compared to the control group, their mothers were rated as more protective (Cohen-Kettenis & Arrindell, 1990). Another study found that the mothers of both MTF and FTM individuals were rated as dominant, emotionally abusive and neglectful, and as making their children feel that they would fail in achievement compared to the control subjects (Simon, Zsolt, Fogd, & Czobor, 2011). Despite this, Simon and colleagues (2011) did not find elevated levels of psychiatric symptoms in the transsexual individuals.

Race and Ethnicity

A recent dissertation reported that FTM people of color in the United States are affected by racism, transphobia, their family members, and their ethnic communities (Mar, 2011). Mar (2011) interviewed 12 FTM individuals of Asian and Pacific Islander (API) descent. The participants reported that there were currently no resources dedicated to FTM-API individuals. Half were out to their parents while half were not. All of the participants noted the ways their parents demonstrated support (e.g., not pressuring them to wear women's clothing, handing down men's clothing).

Discrimination and marginalization are barriers to many ethnic and racial minorities that are attempting to escape poverty (American Psychological Association [APA], 2011). Overall, racial and ethnic minorities in the United States have a lower standard of living compared to their White counterparts (APA, 2011). Such economic disadvantage means that FTM individuals of color will face greater difficulties accessing needed services to even consider transitioning, whether these funds are required for psychological services, medical consults, hormones, and/or surgeries.

Relationships (Family, Friendships, Intimate Romantic/Sexual)

FTM individuals create more stable relationships compared to MTF persons (Fleming et al., 1985; Michel et al., 2002). In Forshee's (2008) Internet sample of 321 FTM respondents, 35% reported being in a significant relationship, 37% were single, 9% were legally married, and 7% were dating. While most MTF individuals look for a new relationship after SRS, the majority of FTM persons stay with their partner post-surgically (De Cuypere et al., 2005). Furthermore, both MTF and FTM transsexuals are more likely to report a stable relationship following SRS (52.7%) compared to before (35.3%; De Cuypere et al., 2005).

The American Psychological Association Task Force on Gender Identity and Gender Variance (2009) reported that there is little research published focused on the family issues of adult transgender individuals. There is no published research looking at the male partners of FTM individuals.

Brown (2010) studied the sexual relationships between sexual minority women and transmen. She interviewed 20 partners involved with transmen and found that that the effect of transitioning "on the couple's sex life were mixed" (Brown, 2010, p. 561). While some reported their sex life was negatively affected, others spoke about the positive aspects of having a partner who felt better integrated and had increased libido.

Mason (2007) interviewed nine lesbian women involved with a FTM partner. The lesbian women reported that most individuals or couples would never have a comparable experience to a change (i.e., the transition process) that was so profound, fundamental, and yet basic at the same time. They also spoke about how the transitioning of their partners led them to question their own sexual orientation, sexual desires, and preferences, similar to what the female partners of MTF transitioning individuals experience. A grief process was also described that included feelings of grief, anger, denial, depression, acceptance, appreciation, and admiration. Six of the nine participants questioned if they would stay.

Fleming and colleagues (1985) compared the relationship quality of 22 FTM individuals with their spouses compared to a control group of 22 nontranssexual couples. Relationship quality was comparable between the two groups. While lesbian couples work hard to create egalitarian relationships, research suggests that the relationships between women and their FTM or transgender female partners are not as likely to be egalitarian (Pfeffer, 2010). In Brown's (2010) research, she also found that as the FTM partner transitioned, their relationships with women became more heteronormative. Another study of nine stable relationships between FTM persons and their female partners compared to nine heterosexual couples also found that there were no differences regarding relational and sexual satisfaction between the two groups (Kins, Hoebeke, Heylens, Rubens, & de Cuypere, 2008).

Health (Emotional and Psychological, Physical)

As already noted, FTM individuals have been shown to consistently be psychologically healthier than MTF individuals (Michel et al., 2002; Pauly, 1974b). FTM individuals are more reliant on using positive coping strategies in stressful situations compared to MTF persons (Matsumoto et al., 2009). They are also less likely to attempt suicide compared to MTF individuals (Korell & Lorah, 2007).

A small percentage of presurgical FTM women mutilate their breasts. One study reported in Seil (1996) reported a 2.4% attempt rate. Transitioning itself has been reported as a time that evokes many emotions, including fear, anxiety, anticipation, and a regenerative view of self

(Forshee, 2008). A study of 446 FTM transsexual and transgender participants (384 from the United States) compared to the U.S. male and female population found that the trans participants reported poorer quality of quality of life, particularly in relation to mental health (Newfield, Hart, Dibble, & Kohler, 2006). The researchers also found that taking cross-sex hormones is associated with improved quality of life.

Regarding HIV risk, FTM individuals in one study were less likely to use protection the last time they had sex and were more likely to engage in high-risk sexual activity compared to the MTF sample (62 vs. 122, respectively; Kenagy & Hsieh, 2005). Another study using existing data sources in San Francisco found that the transmen were behaviorally placing themselves at risk for HIV infection (Chen, McFarland, Thompson, & Raymond, 2011).

Yet another study from San Francisco looked at all visits to an STD clinic between January 1, 2006, and December 31, 2009. Stephens, Bernstein, and Philip (2011) compared all self-identified MTF and FTM patients for STD and HIV infections. Shockingly, they found no differences in STD or HIV infection rates between the two groups. Most studies have found FTM participants to have significantly lower HIV infection rates. The comprehensive meta-analysis of HIV prevalence and risk behaviors of American transgender individuals found that prevalence rates of risk behaviors and HIV rates were low among FTM persons when compared to MTF individuals (Herbst et al., 2008).

Often, FTM individuals have increased needs for housing services, counseling, social services, and health care compared to MTF persons (Forshee, 2008). As reviewed in Chapter 8, transsexual individuals often encounter prejudice and discrimination when seeking out such services. van Trotsenburg (2009) stated that gynecologists lack knowledge of the special needs of the transsexual population. In many countries, physicians have a reserved attitude toward transsexual patients (van Trotsenburg, 2009).

Career and Work

Many FTM persons transition while at the same place of employment (Schilt, 2006).

FTM individuals perceive having greater advantages when they are tall and White as opposed to short and colored, reflecting societal White male privilege (Schilt, 2006). Most can pass successfully due to the masculinizing effects of testosterone. Two-thirds of Schilt's (2006) participants, posttransition, talked about the greater respect they received for their ideas, abilities, and attributes, regardless of whether they were known as transsexual to their employers.

In Forshee's (2008) unrepresentative sample of 321 FTM transgender men, 62% reported full-time employment, 10% part-time work, and 16% were full- or part-time students. Forshee could not conclude if employment discrimination was a factor in her study. Of her sample, 75% were under age 35.

Spirituality and Religion

Kidd and Witten (2008) examined the religious, spiritual, and faith beliefs and behaviors of FTM individuals using the Fetzer Multidimensional Measurement of Religiousness/Spirituality instrument. Many of the respondents found it difficult to complete the survey due to its reliance on Judeo-Christian-Islamic belief systems. Kidd and Witten recommended that future researchers conduct an ethnographic investigation of the nontraditional nature of the belief systems of many FTM individuals.

Sociopolitical Realities

The rights of minority groups often require a fight to gain acknowledgment that they are deserving of equal rights. One only needs to be reminded of the Stonewall Rebellion (see Chapter 2) to know that the modern gay rights movement required a physical confrontation to begin. The FTM community is exceptionally small: between perhaps .0000295 and .0000775% of the population (Bakker et al., 1993; De Cuypere et al., 2007). Given that many of this small percentage prefer to live stealth, how many are left to fight for the community?

According to the Corporate Equality Index conducted by the Human Rights Campaign (2011), 50% of all Fortune 500 companies included gender identity in their nondiscrimination policies. Only 19%, however, provided coverage for transition-related medical services or treatments as well as short-term medical leaves. While companies are becoming more transgender inclusive, the fact remains that most transsexual individuals will not be currently funded to proceed with needed surgeries.

Given that transsexual individuals do not choose their gender identity, and also given that extreme gender dysphoria is associated with high levels of suicidality, should it not be considered a medical necessity to provide their needed surgeries? Besides the medical perspective is an ethical and moral one. Is it right to allow people to suffer needlessly when there are treatments available to alleviate it?

Recent Research Focused on Canada

Plenty has already been written in Chapters 7 and 8 about the contributions of Canadian researchers in the area of transgenderism and transsexualism. One contribution regarding only FTM individuals stems from a needs assessment conducted in Quebec. Namaste (1999) found five important issues regarding FTM persons and HIV: (a) there is a lack of information regarding FTM bodies and sexuality, (b) many FTM persons do not believe they are at risk for HIV infection, (c) poor access to needles to inject hormones places FTM individuals at risk for HIV infection, (d) low self-esteem may keep FTM persons from adopting safer drug use and sex practices, and (e) the administrative aspects of social service agencies exclude FTM individuals.

Recent Research Focused on Other Societies

Nanda's (2008) chapter titled "Cross-Cultural Issues" did not include any information about FTM individuals in other cultures. Not surprisingly, a PsychInfo search does not reveal any references that pertain only to FTM individuals from other than White-dominated societies. Much of the world research regarding both MTF and FTM transsexual individuals is occurring at the gender clinics in Toronto, Canada, and Utrecht, the Netherlands.

A study of 138 transsexual patients (122 male, 16 female) in Brazil (all were diagnosed between March 1998 and September 2005) found that while 17.6% of the MTF sample were HIV infected, none of the FTM sample were (Lobato et al., 2008). A significant percentage of both groups had psychiatric conditions, but given the small size of the FTM sample, any generalizations should be guarded.

In Spain, 252 consecutive applicants for SRS were evaluated with a male-to-female ratio of 2.2:1. The MTF individuals were older than the FTM individuals when requesting SRS but did not differ when they began cross-sex hormone therapy (Gomez-Gil, Trilla, Salamero, Godas, & Valdes, 2009).

A sample of 100 Aravanis, a transgender community in Tamil Nadu in India, found that they supported gender transgressions for both males and females (Mahalingam, 2003). However, while the Aravanis believed in transformation from male to female, they did not endorse female-to-male transition. Mahalingam (2003) explained that in Hindu patriarchal beliefs, masculine gender transformation is part of a male's prerogative but not a female's.

Winter, Webster, and Cheung (2008) examined the attitudes that 121 male and 82 female undergraduates held toward transsexual people, using a scale developed in Canada. Winter and colleagues compared their data to Canadian data from a previous study. Transphobia was higher in Hong Kong than in Canada. Furthermore, men were more transphobic than women, and "gender variance in men was viewed less favorably than in women" (Winter et al., 2008, p. 670).

Common Concerns Facing This Group and Counseling Considerations

Roleplay Scenarios

[*Note:* Suggested assessment and intervention strategies for the two roleplays below can be found in Appendix B. Before going there, roleplay in dyads with one of you acting as the counselor and the other as the counselee. If a roleplay is not possible, work individually in writing out a list of your suggestions.]

Roleplay #1, Chapter 9. Counseling Transmen

Becky, age 31, has come to see you for help. She has felt more like a boy ever since she can remember. However, she has some doubt whether she should pursue sex reassignment surgery. She knows that the surgery to construct a penis is difficult and that many transmen are unhappy with the common complications and the surgical result. She is interested sexually in women only. Nonetheless, she is desperately unhappy as a woman and constantly thinks about how much she hates her breasts and her vagina.

Roleplay #2, Chapter 9. Counseling Transmen

Laura, age 21, has come to see you for help. Laura has always known that she was supposed to be born a boy, but it didn't happen that way. She is desperate to be in a relationship and cannot imagine a life of remaining single. She believes she would rather be dead than spend the rest of her life devoid of a long-term committed relationship. Laura wants to pursue sex reassignment surgery. Her sexual interests are exclusively toward men—heterosexual men, that is.

How Would *You* Help This Person?

You are working as a professional counselor. You greet Al in the waiting room and invite him into your office. When he tells you that he is a transman, you are completely surprised! There are no external indicators that would make you think Al wasn't always male: He has masculine features, broad shoulders, good musculature, and a deep voice. Al recounts, however, the problems he is having in his job. Al has been a petroleum engineer for the past 10 years. After he transitioned, he changed jobs so he could go stealth, hoping that no one would discover he was once a woman. Houston is a big city, he thought, and he expected he could blend in with other engineers. Six months into his new, job, however, a new engineer was hired who recognized him immediately. Al didn't know what to do and hasn't taken any steps so far to deal with the situation or his fear. He asks for your help to decide upon his best option for proceeding. You get the sense that Al is currently stricken with anxiety about this and would likely not conduct himself well to carry out whatever action is decided.

Note—Remember to view clients within their environmental contexts, keeping in mind societal, parental/familial, cultural/spiritual, and peer influences. Specifically, become aware of the impact that the following influences have and continue to have in your clients' lives: race, language, religion and spirituality, gender, familial migration history, affectional orientation, age and cohort, physical and mental capacities, socioeconomic situation and history, education, and history of traumatic experience.

1. What defines this person's environment, past and present?
2. Who is this person sitting in front of me, taking into account environmental and personal characteristics?
3. What defines the problem that he or she is presenting within his or her multicultural milieu?

The practitioner is encouraged to also read Chapter 8, as some of the recommendations made there are also applicable to FTM clients. The brevity of this section does not imply that FTM individuals have an easier time deciding how to proceed as trans persons compared to MTF individuals. FTM persons also face the issues discussed in Chapter 8: child and adolescent challenges, gender dysphoria, wanting to transition, relationship and family problems, transitioning at work, and need for social support.

As children and youth, FTM individuals generally "fit in" better societally. Parents and others are generally more willing to tolerate the antics of a tomboy than of a feminine boy. Consequently, FTM children are less likely to be referred to gender clinics for assessment and treatment. When severe gender dysphoria leads FTM individuals to consider transitioning or to proceed with it, however, reactions from others are comparable to what MTF persons face. Some or all of the stages of bereavement (e.g., denial, anger, bargaining, depression, and acceptance) are felt. Transitioning at work is often somewhat easier for FTM compared to MTF individuals, as most gain the advantages of being a man in general, leaving behind the subordination they experienced as women (Schilt, 2006). A recurring theme that has surfaced in every chapter is the need that LGBTI individuals have for social support. Those who feel the most support are usually the healthiest psychologically.

There has been very little research or scholarly writing focused on the counseling needs of transgender clients (Korell & Lorah, 2007), and that seems especially the case regarding FTM clients. FTM clients are simply "lumped in" with scholarly writing focused on MTF individuals, and few suggestions are actually provided beyond looking at diagnosis of GID and treatment as prescribed by the *Standards of Care (SOC-7;* Coleman et al., 2011). Pazos (1999) focused on issues that FTM youth often experience, and her suggestions will be offered where appropriate.

Wise and Meyer (1980) provided a list of 10 criteria in question format that should be considered by those counseling both MTF and FTM clients, particularly those who are considering SRS. These are summarized as follows:

1. Does the client understand his or her gender dysphoria and the available options for living with it?
2. Has the client had a long history of opposite-gender self-imagery and feelings, together with difficulty suppressing or denying them?
3. Does the client have knowledge of what SRS can and cannot do, including the risks, procedures, and contraindications? Does he or she

understand the implications that this surgery will have in his or her life?

4. Has the client experienced a diminished fear of not passing (either being read or discovered)? Is he or she able to lessen or eradicate guilt feelings and thereby feel a greater sense of legitimacy and genuineness?
5. To what extent does the client believe that SRS is necessary to feel an increased sense of congruence, unity, and safety in both his or her private and public life?
6. Is the counselor convinced that the client is fully aware and understands the SRS option? Have they found a competent surgeon? Are the counselor, the client, and the surgeon in agreement with this choice?
7. Is the counselor sure that the client does not have a thought disorder, psychotic process, or cognitive impairment?
8. Are both the counselor and the client aware of HIV infection and the risks following surgery (recall from Chapter 8 that one theory suggests that SRS renders the tissues more vulnerable to becoming infected with the HIV virus)?
9. Does the client have clear, realistic expectations of the effect that SRS will have regarding occupation and romantic and personal relationships?
10. Do both the counselor and client concur that he or she is fully prepared for living life after SRS?

FTM Cross-Sex Hormones and Sex Reassignment Surgery

FTM individuals who elect not to pursue SRS may bind their breasts, pad them, have a mastectomy, and/or have masculinizing implants placed (Mostade, 2006). As mentioned in Chapter 8, not everyone can take cross-sex hormones, and SRS is expensive, particularly for several of the surgeries associated with FTM persons (Cook-Daniels, 2006).

Hormone treatment for FTM individuals will consist of a gonadotropin-releasing hormone (GnRH) agonist and testosterone (Wylie, Fung, Boshier, & Rotchell, 2009). Ongoing physical monitoring is needed to maximize the benefits and minimize the risks associated with cross-sex hormones (Wylie et al., 2009). When monitored, research has shown that there are no significant serious adverse effects from taking testosterone (Traish & Gooren, 2010).

Hormones deepen the voice, and over the course of a few weeks, it generally moves into the male range. Van Borsel, De Cuypere, Rubens, and Destaerke (2000) reported that not all voice changes are unproblematic, and they recommended that those considering cross-sex hormones first seek out a voice assessment.

The clitoris enlarges from a prehormone average of 0.6 inches (1.4 cm.) to almost 1.6 inches (4 cm.) or even up to 2 inches (5 cm.). Ovarian function becomes suppressed and menses stops within 4 months of taking testosterone. Some FTM individuals report breast atrophy, but most do not report a change in breast size (Dickey & Steiner, 1990). Testosterone also increases muscle size and libido. Over time, testosterone creates receding hairlines, male pattern baldness, coarsening of the skin, body and facial hair growth, and acne (Mostade, 2006; Seil, 2004).

If cross-sex hormones are stopped, face and body hair will not disappear, nor will clitoral growth and vocal changes (Cole, Denny, Eyler, & Samons, 2000). A complete list of possible side effects and complications can be found in Wise and Meyer (1980). On the positive end, FTM individuals report a greater sense of well-being while taking testosterone (Cohen-Kettenis & Gooren, 1992).

(Continued)

(Continued)

Available surgeries for FTM individuals include mastectomy with chest contouring to give it a male appearance, hysterectomy (surgical removal of the uterus), oophorectomy (surgical removal of the ovaries), and for some, either metaoidioplasty (a procedure where the clitoris is released from its hood, providing it greater length) or phalloplasty (construction of a penis using skin grafts from the forearm or elsewhere; Cook-Daniels, 2006; Wise & Meyer, 1980).

Metoidioplasty is a similar procedure to metaoidioplasty. It is a one-stage procedure that lengthens the clitoris (now referred to as a neophallus), lengthens the urethra to enable voiding while standing, and includes scrotal reconstruction. The mean length of the neophallus is 2.2 inches (5.7 cm.) with a range of between 1.6 inches (4 cm.) and 3.9 inches (10 cm.; Djordjevic et al., 2009).

There are different methods of creating a penis, each with advantages and disadvantages. Transmen who have an erectile prosthesis as part of their surgery report greater sexual fulfillment than those who do not, but pain during intercourse is not uncommon (De Cuypere et al., 2005). A scrotum can be created from the labia majora and prosthetic testicles implanted (Cook-Daniels, 2006). Many FTM individuals elect not to pursue any genitoplasty technique, as these surgeries have not been perfected (Lawrence, 2008). Their appearance, their functionality, and/or surgical complications lead many to put this surgery on hold indefinitely.

As mentioned in Chapter 8, very few transsexual individuals regret their surgery (1–2%; Smith et al., 2005), and most report much-improved happiness and psychosocial well-being postsurgery (De Cuypere et al., 2005; Johansson, Sundbom, Hojerback, & Bodlund, 2010). A 30-year review by Pfafflin (1992) found that less than 1% of FTM individuals and between 1 and 1.5% of MTF individuals report regret. FTM individuals report that orgasms become shorter yet more powerful, while MTF persons develop more intense, smoother, and longer orgasms postsurgically (De Cuypere et al., 2005).

One of the most important skills counselors bring to working with transsexual clients is helping them reflect on the various experiences of self and identity as they exist within a postmodern world. There is no one solution to a transsexual person's experience. Any decision made will have both positive and negative consequences. But one cannot live comfortably in a tortuous place, either. It is in working with transsexual clients that a counselor might be most struck by what true suffering looks like. Making life decisions about whether to stay or leave a job or a relationship are challenging, but they pale by comparison to deciding how to live with the deep conviction that one's body and gender do not jibe. If one doesn't transition, one remains at odds with others of the same biological sex, but if one transitions, one is still not fully a member of the opposite sex, either (Green, 1994).

It takes incredible intestinal fortitude to live in a postmodern world, in an ideology not shared by most people worldwide. Binary systems have a strong allure, as they simplify the human condition into either-or categorical structures. Gender pervasively dictates appropriate social behavior, and that which is not masculine is deemed feminine. What about living in the middle somewhere between such a great divide?

Two issues that FTM individuals may seek out counseling for not already covered in Chapter 8 include (a) uncertainty about SRS and (b) learning new gender scripts. These issues are looked at next.

Uncertainty About SRS

Counselors must remain sensitive when dealing with issues related to SRS. For example, it is inappropriate to ask the client if she or he has had surgery. This becomes an invasion of privacy. Furthermore, the answer is usually not relevant. The situation is different, however, when the client brings up the issue of SRS.

While SRS for MTF individuals has arrived at a point at which the appearance of the vulva and neovagina is virtually indistinguishable from those of biological females, this is not the case for FTM persons. Given that sex-reassignment procedures remain in the process of refinement and improvement for FTM bottom surgery, many FTM clients are unsure of whether to proceed with it. If the client does want SRS, given that the procedures are steadily improving, a reasonable question to ask is when to proceed with it?

Think about a decision to purchase a computer: Do you buy this year's model or wait for next year's that has the larger hard drive, a faster processor, and other bells and whistles? People often agonize over whether they should proceed with corrective laser surgery for eyesight, given that these procedures are also steadily improving. Now imagine it being the most private region of the body: your sex organs. Anyone would want the best for themselves when a surgery is to be undertaken that will alter the body permanently.

Counselors can assist FTM clients in gathering the latest information concerning surgical options. The best source of information is contained in the latest journals (particularly medical journals) that include peer-reviewed articles on the subject (e.g., *International Journal of Transgenderism*, *Journal of Sexual Medicine*). Transsexual websites can be rich sources of information. Two that are particularly strong include information provided by the official site of the World Professional Association for Transgender Health (www.wpath.org/publications_standards.cfm) and the Gender Education and Advocacy site (www.gender.org). While the Internet can be particularly helpful, one should cautiously read testimonials, as they are often biased toward those holding strong opinions. A frank discussion with the surgeon is also essential before a surgery is undertaken.

Besides having access to the latest information, the decision remains a difficult one for most FTM individuals: What surgery to pursue, if any, and when? Smith and colleagues (2005) stated that the most important surgery for FTM individuals from an emotional standpoint is breast surgery. Breast binding is a constant reminder that the body betrays the inner sense of gender. For many, binding is both physically and emotionally uncomfortable. Cole and colleagues (2000) mentioned that hysterectomy with ovary removal is generally recommended and performed on FTM individuals taking testosterone for cancer prevention. Counselors can help FTM clients explore all aspects of these important decisions. Decision making about surgery (when and what) often occurs at various junctures for FTM individuals to decide. An affirmative counselor can be instrumental in decision making and then helping FTM clients live successfully and happily with the result of these decisions.

Learning New Gender Scripts

While severe gender dysphoria creates deep distress over and conviction that one ought to be the opposite sex, it does not teach individuals how to present themselves as the opposite gender. Both MTF and FTM individuals need to learn appropriate gender scripts. It is the similar problem that gay and lesbian teenagers often face in attempting to be part of their peer groups. While other boys and girls talk and show interest in the opposite sex and in gender-typical interests, gay and lesbian adolescents often cannot relate to these discussions—at least not with convincing depth or breadth of interest—and thus appear as "outsiders" to their peers. Transsexual individuals, particularly those sexually attracted to their own biological sex, often have an even more difficult time fitting in as children and adolescents. Recall that this group is typically much more gender nonconforming compared to the nonhomosexual type, in addition to having homosexual interests.

Besides the problems of fitting in as children and adolescents, however, their problem continues into adulthood for different reasons. As adults, they will have a difficult time passing as the opposite sex until they master the gender scripts of the opposite biological sex. This will be particularly challenging for those sexually attracted to their opposite biological sex (i.e., the nonhomosexual type).

MTF individuals need to learn how to purchase and wear women's clothing, how to apply makeup, raise the pitch of their voice, and how to act while on a date, for example. The same applies to FTM individuals. But besides the more obvious aspects concerning appropriate attire, speech, and mannerisms, there are the nuances of gender that provide cues to others regarding whether one fits in with a group or does not. Learning to fully think like or express oneself as a man or woman when one has not been indoctrinated into this since being born means a lot needs to be absorbed. This is not unlike learning a second language in which the nuances are missed until later in the language-acquisition process.

Passing is not the goal of all transsexual individuals, and those who maintain a transsexual identity may not be so desirous of learning or mastering opposite-sex gender scripts. The word *trans* does not mean fitting into the binary system at all—instead, it provides room for individuals to define gender (or to not define it) in their own unique ways.

Just as behavioral approaches have been used with children to extinguish gender atypicality while simultaneously rewarding gender-typical behaviors and mannerisms (Meyer-Bahlburg, 2002; Zucker & Cohen-Kettenis, 2008), similar behavioral techniques can be used to help MTF and FTM adults. Hay, Barlow, and Hay (1981) described how they modified a boy's feminine gender behaviors by focusing on five targets: walking, standing, sitting, mannerisms-gestures, and book carrying. Such methods can be useful in teaching adults how to behave in accord with their preferred gender presentation.

Observational learning (modeling) also has great potential to be of help to transsexual clients, and this can be encouraged in numerous naturalistic settings (e.g., restaurants, bars, dances, meetings, baseball games). In larger cities, referring clients to support groups for transgender individuals will be helpful, as other participants either will be needing to learn similar skills or will have knowledge of what proved helpful to them.

COUNSELING DIVERSE POPULATIONS

Counseling FTM Individuals With Multiple Nondominant Identity Statuses

Mar's (2011) dissertation provided a reminder that FTM people of color are affected by multiple sources of prejudice, discrimination, and oppression stemming from racism, transphobia, their families, and their ethnic communities. These factors will play out differentially with each client and will have potentially diverse impacts depending on the reason the client is seeking help. The presenting concern may have nothing to do with one's gender identity. On the other hand, disclosing a transsexual identity to others or deciding to transition can raise insurmountable challenges with some FTM individuals having more than one nondominant identity status.

Counseling Aging FTM Individuals

There are no specific counseling protocols recommended in the published literature addressing needs specific to aging FTM individuals. An excellent resource for all aging transgender individuals is the Transgender Aging Network (www.forge-forward.org/tan/index.php).

Counseling FTM Individuals Living in Rural Communities

There are no specific counseling protocols recommended in the published literature addressing needs specific to FTM individuals living in rural areas. Generic suggestions for transgender people can be found in Chapter 8.

Counseling FTM Students

Many FTM students are verbally taunted by their peers (Pazos, 1999). One coping mechanism has been to excel in some aspect of school (e.g., academics, athletics, drama, computers) or to keep busy to avoid thinking about their inner distress. Another coping strategy used by some is to dissociate, detaching emotionally from their bodies and going through the motions of living (Pazos, 1999). Developing a support system is very helpful, and having even one or two close friends can make a huge difference in preventing feelings of despair, isolation, and depression (Pazos, 1999).

Another issue that may arise is being "outed" in a classroom when the official name on the roster does not match the student's gender identity and presentation (e.g., being identified in class because your legal first name "John" is called in class while you are dressed and presenting as female). Such misfortunes can be avoided if the grade school, college, or university has software that allows both the preferred name and the legal name to be included.

Dating is usually a frustrating experience for FTM individuals in high school. Many who are attracted to their own biological sex are viewed by others as lesbian, while those who want to date boys do not want to relate to them sexually as females. Consequently, many choose not to date or date rarely (Pazos, 1999). Some FTM individuals do first identify as lesbian because of their sexual attraction to other females (Pazos, 1999).

Counseling FTM Adolescents

Pazos (1999) recommended counseling from a strength-based perspective. The counselor is encouraged to view transgenderism as an important part of identity development for FTM teenagers as opposed to taking a pathology perspective. Respect clients' wishes to be called by their preferred name and preferred pronoun. Pazos also recommended that where possible, the transgender individual be provided a safe place to dress in the way that feels most comfortable.

Counseling FTM adolescents and their families will likely require compromises to be made by both parties. Pazos (1999) suggested that this might entail looking at what name the client will be called and the type of clothing that will be tolerated. The families will also require support as they go through their own feelings of shock, denial, anger, guilt, and shame.

It is stressful for people of all ages to face societal stressors, but particularly when one is young (Pazos, 1999). Some individuals succumb to stress by acting out and becoming involved in substance abuse, sexual promiscuity, or prostitution. Paying attention to clients' stress and helping them develop coping strategies can do a lot to help bolster their self-esteem and their confidence.

Resources for This Group

1. FTM International is the largest organization serving the FTM community in the world, and it also has the longest history (www.ftmi.org/).
2. The Transitional Male was established in 1998 and has logged more than 5 million hits (www.thetransitionalmale.com/).
3. Hudson's FTM Resource Guide contains a wealth of information relevant to FTM individuals (www.ftmguide.org/).
4. Transguys.com also offers many helpful resources to the FTM community (http://transguys.com/).
5. Successful Transmen provides links and photos of well-known FTM individuals (http://ai.eecs.umich.edu/people/conway/TSsuccesses/TransMen.html).

6. There is an online Yahoo support group for FTM individuals, established in 1999 (http://groups.yahoo.com/group/FtM-trans/).

Limitations, Furthering Research, and Implications for Counselors

Limitations of the Research With This Group

The limitations mentioned in Chapter 8 also apply to FTM individuals. Substantially more research has focused on MTF persons; consequently, there are huge gaps in our understanding of FTM individuals. We know very little about counseling FTM clients in general, but even less about those who are diverse. While the research done to date is of impressive quality, the biggest limitation is that we need more of it. Our understanding of transmen is in its infancy stages.

Areas Requiring Further Research

We know little about those who choose not to take any steps toward transitioning. What distinguishes those who pursue physical transitioning from those who do not? What strategies do those who do not transition use to cope with everyday life?

Research informs us that FTM individuals are generally healthier psychologically than MTF individuals—why is this the case? Why are they more resilient? They also tend to be more satisfied with their surgeries, yet particularly regarding SRS, FTM bottom surgery is much less advanced than MTF bottom surgery. Why wouldn't MTF persons be the more satisfied group regarding surgical outcomes? We know next to nothing about FTM individuals in other cultures; this is huge area that would be interesting to explore.

Studies have indicated that FTM individuals often do not feel they need a penis to be a man. Most biological men, however, would be horrified if their penis was severed or otherwise mutilated. Is it the case that you don't miss something you never had in the first place? If that were true, one would wonder why transpeople exist at all. Comparative research between transmen and biological men might shed insight regarding the importance of the penis in constructing masculinity and maleness.

Another line of research could explore the differences and similarities between very masculine lesbian women and those who identify as FTM. What developmental process explains why and how some learn to embrace their womanness while others wish to disown it?

Implications for Counselors

The FTM community is especially small, and it is doubtful that most counselors, except those who work specifically with this population, will encounter those who are considering transitioning. When transitioning is the issue, the ideas contained in this chapter and in Chapter 8 will prove helpful. Counselors need to understand that transsexual clients have several options open to them. Some may find ways to deal with their gender dysphoria that do not require surgical intervention. It will be a most difficult challenge to encourage clients to pursue this option if they are already convinced surgery is going to be their only salvation. Furthermore, the bulk of research to date supports physically transitioning as the treatment of choice for transsexual clients.

Does that make it the *best* choice, however, for any given individual? The problems that trans clients bring to counseling remind us of both the importance of gender and the insanity of gender at the same time. Can we not live in a world in which it is acceptable to embrace masculinity and femininity in whatever way it might be expressed by an individual? The trans client's experience goes deeper than that, however. It is not just that they transcend gender; they also uphold a deep conviction that they ought to be the opposite biological sex, and some for as far back as they can remember. It has historically been impossible to change that once it becomes deeply ingrained into the psyche.

Exercises

Individual Exercises

1. If you live in a large enough city, there will be a night when drag kings perform in either a gay bar or an alternative bar. Attend one of their performances. There is usually a contingent of drag kings who define as FTM. If possible, attempt to strike up a conversation with drag kings afterward to find out more about their motivations for becoming a drag king. What does it represent to them? If there is no opportunity to attend a drag king show where you live, search for "drag king" on YouTube and find out how they get ready for a performance. This will provide an introduction into some of what is required to successfully pass as a man.

2. Watch the movie called *Venus Boyz*, produced in 2002. The movie is about drag kings and FTM individuals. Alternatively, watch a different movie with a transgender theme. A list of these can be found at www.superliminal.com/melinda/tgmovies.htm.

Classroom Exercise (1 or 2)

1. Stephanie Goodwin (n.d.) suggested several activities that can be used in the classroom to explore gender. One of her adapted exercises follows. Students are asked to read a magazine of their choice from cover to cover and to flag instances that either support or counter traditional gender roles and stereotypes. The instructor then leads a discussion in class regarding what students found in the magazines and later segues into a discussion about FTM individuals and their experience of gender.

2. Invite a FTM guest speaker, preferably a transman, to your class to talk about his experience.

3. Ask the students to anonymously submit three to four questions that they have about FTM individuals. Either provide the answers to these questions in class or assign each student to find out the answer to one question and then ask them to provide this answer during the next class period. Alternatively, separate the class into groups of three or four. Ask each group to come up with a list of four questions that they have about FTM individuals. Once the lists are compiled, have them give their list to another group in the class, and each group then answers the questions as homework and provides these answers during the next class period.

Chapter Summary

Most girls who display tomboyish behavior outgrow this before adulthood. Likewise, most girls and teenagers with gender dysphoria no longer experience this in adulthood. A sizeable percentage do report homosexual or bisexual interests in adulthood, however, but to a much lesser degree compared to feminine boys. For some, severe gender dysphoria persists.

Female-to-male (FTM) individuals comprise an exceptionally small percentage of the population, and in most studies, are about a half to a third as prevalent compared to MTF individuals. One classification system that has current popularity distinguishes between those FTM persons who have primarily homosexual interests (homosexual type) and those who have sexual interest in the opposite biological sex (nonhomosexual type).

In comparison to MTF individuals, FTM persons generally have better psychological health and report greater satisfaction with the results of sex reassignment surgery (SRS), despite the technical problems that persist in FTM bottom surgery. Many if not most FTM individuals decide not to have bottom surgery as they await improvements in surgical procedures.

Besides the typical problems that bring anyone into counseling, FTM individuals face the same issues as MTF persons. Also highlighted in this chapter are two problems that transsexual individuals encounter—that is, having uncertainly about SRS and the importance of learning new gender scripts.

10

INTERSEX CHILDREN AND ADULTS

CHALLENGING YOUR ATTITUDES AND BELIEFS ABOUT THIS GROUP

REFLECTION QUESTIONS

1. Some intersex conditions, such as Klinefelter syndrome, are fairly common (between 1 in 500 and 1,000 male births). Why do you think most people would report not knowing someone who is intersex?
2. If you were intersex and had both a penis and a vagina, what situations would be difficult for you? What effect would it have regarding how you view yourself (i.e., your self-concept and your self-esteem)?

3. Do you believe that intersex newborns should be assigned a gender at birth? What do you see as the advantages and disadvantages of doing so?
4. What special accommodations should intersex children be provided at school and in work settings?
5. List as many synonyms as you can for an *intersex individual.*

Challenging Your Assumptions Questions

1. Most people believe there are two biological sexes: male and female. How does your concept of biological sex become stretched when you find out that some individuals who have XX sex chromosomes look like males and some with XY chromosomes look like females?
2. Many people feel sorry for intersex individuals: After all, they did not choose to be born this way. How does feeling sympathy for intersex individuals help and hurt them at the same time? How do you currently view intersex individuals? What is the basis for your views? To what extent do your views apply to *all* intersex individuals?
3. How would you react if your best female friend disclosed to you that she is genetically male according to her sex chromosomes?
4. How would you react if your son or daughter was born with ambiguous genitalia? What would your instincts tell you to do about it?
5. In the past, it was common to see photographs of intersex individuals, often with their faces covered but not always. What advantages and disadvantages do you see in showing these pictures for purposes of general education (i.e., *not* as part of a medical curriculum)?

Reflections

[*Note:* Imagine that *you* are the client in these reflections.]

You are 17 years old and have worked out hard in the gym to develop a muscular male body. Your natural good looks have also made you popular with girls in your school. You have been interested in Barb for some time, actually. Other guys have also noticed her, as she is quite stunning with a very gentle disposition. You have always been too shy to approach her, so you are quite shocked the day she asks you out on a date! Even on the first date, Barb is all over you, and you tell her you want to take it slow so she doesn't think your only interest in her is having sex. Inside, your heart is sinking to an all-time low. You decide to talk to the high school counselor about your feelings.

Waiting to see the counselor seems like hours, your hands becoming sweaty and shaky. Ms. Oliver finally calls you into her office. "Wow, I never expected to see you here, Todd. You are one of the most popular boys in the school."

You want to turn around and run, but the issue is too important to defer any longer. You begin, "Ms. Oliver, I am beside myself with anxiety. I have had a crush on Barb for nearly two years, and I had my first date with her Friday night. She was all over me and I had to nearly push her away. She probably thinks I am nuts."

"Todd, that must have taken immense self-control on your part. You have sent her a positive message that you are not just interested in her for her body."

"Well, the truth is I am . . . I mean, I think she is hot. No, the problem is this . . . uh, how do I say this without sounding ridiculous? Uh, I have a very small penis. Um, I mean very small—I mean as small as most infant boys! My parents tell me I was born with micropenis and that, well, says it all. Barb is going to reject me the moment she finds out!!"

"Todd, I am sure you are exaggerating. I know that penis size varies from boy to boy, but the size of an infant? That is taking it a bit far, isn't it? I'm sure Barb or any other young woman is not going to judge you based on your penis size. You are more than what is between your legs."

You leave after 45 minutes, not at all convinced that what Ms. Oliver told you is true. Your anxiety is no better than it was when you entered her office. You feel more confused than ever.

From a Client's Perspective

1. What do you think of Ms. Oliver's advice? Why?
2. What mistakes has Ms. Oliver made in her counseling of Todd? What would you want to hear from Ms. Oliver if you were Todd?

From a Counselor's Perspective

1. What obligation do counselors have when they hear about a condition (micropenis in this example) that they have never heard of before?
2. Given that micropenis is an irreversible condition, what goals would be appropriate for you and Todd to agree upon? What methods can you think of that might help Todd achieve these goals?

Background Information Regarding Intersex Children and Adults

As should be evident by now from your reading of previous chapters, marginalized groups have often been called pejorative names in the past, sometimes unintentionally. It also seems that the names become worse as one moves further from what is considered "socially acceptable." Intersex individuals in the United States, for example, were once referred to as "monstrous, sinister, threatening, inferior, and unfortunate" (Reis, 2009, p. xv). Other terms that have since taken on pejorative meaning include *hermaphrodite* and *pseudohermaphrodite*. The modern term of *intersex* has also been criticized recently because the word implies to some people that these conditions are about sex or that they represent confusion regarding sex that is not felt by the majority of intersex individuals (Reis, 2009).

The newest terminology refers to *disorders of sex development* (DSD; Pasterski, 2008), but some have argued that even this is inappropriate, as it suggests disorder when this is not always the experience of intersex individuals. Reis (2009) suggested use of the term *divergence of sex development* (also DSD) to avoid the implication of disorder, but it is too early to know if this term will become standard terminology. One difficulty with both terms is neither offers an adjective that can be used to describe these people. For that reason, the expression *intersex individuals* will be used henceforth to designate those people with a DSD condition. Perhaps by the second edition, a new adjective will come into common usage that is accepted as respectful by everyone.

Intersex individuals herein will be defined as those with "congenital conditions in which development of chromosomal, gonadal, or anatomical sex is atypical" (Vilain, 2008, p. 330). Some intersex individuals also identity as transgender, but this is not universal (Martin & Yonkin, 2006). *Genotype* refers to the entire genetic constitution of an individual (Ross, St. Dennis-Feezle, & Weber, 2002). Genes are found within the chromosomes. The *karyotype* refers to the individual's chromosomal pattern (Ross et al., 2002). Most people have a karyotype of 46,XY (male) or 46,XX (female), but some *mosaic individuals* have a variety of cells containing XX and XY chromosomes. Most people have 22 pairs of autosomes and an additional pair that determines biological sex, the X and the Y chromosome, within each cell of their body. *Phenotype* refers to the observable characteristics or traits of an individual. *Phenotypic sex* refers to the individual's primary and secondary characteristics. *Gonadal sex* refers to the type of gonads present within an individual (i.e., testis and/or ovary; Vilain, 2008).

The incidence of DSD is estimated to be 1 in 4,500 births, but if minor variants are included (including males with abnormal placements of the urethral opening and those with undescended testes), it jumps to close to 1% (Vilain, 2008). Consequently, the percentage of intersex individuals in the population is far greater than the percentage of transsexual individuals.

To understand these conditions, it is helpful to know about the particulars of many DSDs. The section below is adapted from the writings of O'Neil (2011), Pasterski (2008), and Vilain (2008), with citation exceptions noted.

Sex Chromosome DSDs

Four sex chromosome disorders are included here. Klinefelter syndrome and XYY syndrome occurs in males, while Turner syndrome and Triple-X syndrome occurs in females. Diamond and Watson (2004) reported that both males and females with sex chromosome DSD are at increased risk for behavioral and learning disabilities.

Table 10.1 The Sex Chromosomal DSDs

#	*Name*	*Karyotype*	*Phenotype*	*Characteristics*	*Prevalence*
1	Klinefelter Syndrome (KS)	47,XXY (Note: more X chromosomes can be attached)	Male	Individuals with KS are tall and have delayed puberty and small, dysgenetic (meaning underdeveloped, dysfunctioning, and fibrous) testicles that do not contain sperm. Gynecomastia (i.e., breast enlargement in males) is seen in 30–90% of those with KS, often resulting in great shame and embarrassment for teenage boys (Diamond & Watson, 2004). Some individuals with KS view themselves as transgender, intersex, or transsexual (Diamond & Watson, 2004).	1 in 500 to 1,000 male births
2	Turner Syndrome (TS)	45,X	Female	Individuals with TS are short and have delayed puberty with lack of menses and experience several congenital malformations, including defects with the heart and kidneys. Their underdeveloped ovaries result in infertility and in low levels of estrogens. While most women with TS lead normal lives for the most part, it	1 in 2,500 female births

(Continued)

(Continued)

#	*Name*	*Karyotype*	*Phenotype*	*Characteristics*	*Prevalence*
				is often their infertility that causes them the greatest distress (Sutton et al., 2005).	
3	Triple-X Syndrome	XXX (Note: more X chromosomes can be attached)	Female	As adults, these women are usually an inch or so taller than average with unusually long legs and slender torsos. Other than these characteristics, they appear normal. Sexual characteristics usually develop normally and they are fertile. They may have mild learning disabilities and are typically in the lower range of normal intelligence (especially those who are XXXX and XXXXX).	1 in 1,000 female births
4	XYY Syndrome	XYY	Male	As adults, these men are usually tall (more than 6 feet) and they generally appear and act normal. However, high levels of testosterone are produced. As adolescents, they are typically slender and awkward with severe facial acne. They are usually fertile and lead ordinary lives in adulthood. Some researchers believe their high testosterone levels may leave some of them more vulnerable to violence.	Estimates lie between 1 in 900 male births up to 1 in 2,000.

Nonchromosomal DSDs

If there is not enough androgen in a male fetus or some that enters a female fetus, the result will be some disparity between genetic and phenotypic sex. In the past, intersex individuals with ambiguous genitalia were classified according to whether they were true hermaphrodites (individuals having ambiguous genitalia with both testicular and ovarian tissue) and those who were pseudohermaphrodites (individuals having ambiguous genitalia with either testicular or ovarian tissue). The new terms for female pseudohermaphroditism is *46,XX DSD* and for males is *46,XY DSD*. See Table 10.2 for a list of the more commonly known nonchromosomal DSDs.

There are several outcomes that become likely when the intersex individual is 46,XY

Table 10.2 The More Commonly Known Nonchromosomal DSDs

#	*Name*	*Karyotype*	*Phenotype*	*Characteristics*	*Prevalence*
1	46,XY androgen resistance (complete) OR androgen insensitivity syndrome, complete (CAIS)	46,XY	Intersex	These individuals are born with testes but with female external genitalia and no uterus. They are assigned a female gender soon after birth, they develop a female gender identity with typically feminine behaviors, and consequently they do not later request a sex change.	*1 in 20,400 births
2	46,XY androgen resistance (partial) OR androgen insensitivity syndrome, partial (PAIS)	46,XY	Intersex	These individuals are born with testes and ambiguous genitalia. Most are assigned a female gender soon after birth, most develop a gender identity and sex-typed behaviors as assigned and reared, but some later request a sex change.	*1 in 130,000 births
3	46,XY defect of testosterone biosynthesis	46X,Y	Intersex	These individuals have testes and ambiguous genitalia.	Rare
4	46,XY gonadal dysgenesis	46X,Y	Intersex	These individuals have fibrous gonads and female external genitalia with a uterus. They are assigned a female gender, which is consistent with their identity and their behavior. Consequently, they do not later request a sex change.	Rare
5	46,XY 5 alpha-reductase-2 deficiency (5 alpha-RD-2)	46,XY	Intersex	These individuals are born with testes and ambiguous genitalia. They may be assigned either gender soon after birth. All male-assigned identify as male, while 60% of those female-assigned also identify as male (subsequently leading to requests for a sex change). Their behavior is typically masculine.	Rare

(Continued)

(Continued)

#	*Name*	*Karyotype*	*Phenotype*	*Characteristics*	*Prevalence*
6	46,XY 17 betahydroxysteroid dehydrogenase-3 deficiency (17 beta-HSD-3)	46X,Y	Intersex	These individuals are born with testes and either have female or ambiguous genitalia. Most are assigned as female, but their identity and behavior are typically male, subsequently leading to requests for a sex change.	Rare
7	46,XY micropenis	46X,Y	Intersex	These individuals have testes but an extremely small penis. They are assigned either gender and identify and behave in accord with the gender they are assigned. Consequently, they do not request a sex change.	Rare
8	46,XX congenital adrenal hyperplasia (CAH)	46,XX	Intersex	These individuals are born with ovaries and ambiguous genitalia. CAH accounts for the largest number of cases of ambiguous genitalia at birth in females. The genitalia are masculinized due to prenatal exposure to excess androgens. Many females with CAH present some male-typical behaviors in childhood, including a preference for boy toys, boy playmates, and rough-and-tumble play. They are mostly assigned to the female gender, and while their behavior is masculine, they develop female identities and do not later seek out a sex change. Today it is possible to treat the fetus affected by CAH prenatally by giving the mother steroids, thus preventing the development of ambiguous genitalia.	1 in 15,000 births

#	*Name*	*Karyotype*	*Phenotype*	*Characteristics*	*Prevalence*
9	46,XX fetal exposure to androgens (by tumor or medication)	46,XX	Intersex	These individuals are born with ovaries and ambiguous genitalia.	Rare
10	46,XX testicular DSD	46,XX	Usually male	Individuals coded as 46,XX testicular DSD have normal male genitalia, small testes that do not produce sperm, but no uterus or fallopian tubes. Some at birth also have ambiguous genitalia.	Rare
11	46,XX ovotesticular DSD (formerly known as XX true hermaphroditism)	46,XX	Usually male	These individuals have both testicular and ovarian tissue. The external genitalia may be ambiguous, with about two-thirds raised as males. Most 46,XX ovotesticular DSD results from the two different cell lines developing from different zygotes, but rarely, it results from a Y-to-X chromosomal dislocation (Ostrer, 2009). The 46,XX ovotesticular DSD is the rarest form of intersex in humans (Bostwick & Martin, 2007).	Very rare
12	XY females with gonadal dysgenesis	XY	Usually female	These females have normal female genitalia with a normal uterus but with fibrous streak gonads instead of ovaries. If the dysgenesis is partial, they may have ambiguous genitalia at birth.	Rare

*Prevalence is estimated.

DSD. The normal Y chromosome together with SRY (i.e., a gene that leads to the formation of a male individual; Vilain, 2008) results in normal testicular development. The problem occurs later with the production of testosterone or, more commonly, in its receptor (this results in the most commonly encountered situation in males, called *androgen resistance*). At birth, the infant will have normal testes but without typical masculinization. He may present as a phenotypic female or as intersex.

There are two outcomes that become likely when the intersex individual is 46,XX DSD. Since there is no Y chromosome, the ovaries develop normally. However, androgens become impregnated into the tissues during prenatal development, and the infant is born with masculinized features and ambiguous external genitalia. The source of androgens can be the result of medications taken by the mother, an androgen-secreting tumor, or more commonly, by the overproduction of androgens within the fetus caused by a problem in the synthesis of steroids by the adrenal glands (this results in the most commonly encountered situation in females, called *congenital adrenal hyperplasia*, or CAH).

In very rare instances, individuals with XX chromosomes appear as male at birth because some SRY was transmitted during the prenatal period, while some with XY appear as female at birth if SRY did not get transmitted or was unable to be absorbed. These rare conditions, occurring in about 1 in 20,000 births, are known as *sex-reversed* because the phenotypic sex is opposite to that of the karyotype. These variations include XX male syndrome (now called 46,XX testicular DSD), XX true hermaphroditism (now called 46,XX ovotesticular DSD), and XY females with gonadal dysgenesis.

The DSD Controversy

The most controversial aspect of DSD currently concerns whether surgical intervention should occur soon after birth or whether it should be deferred until the child is able to make his or her own decision regarding it (Creighton, Minto, Liao, Alderson, & Simmonds, 2004; Holmes, 2002; Martin & Yonkin, 2006; Meyer-Bahlburg, 1998). There are groups like the Intersex Society of North America (ISNA; www.isna.org) that advocate for surgery to be avoided on intersex individuals unless it is medically required. Instead, the ISNA supports the view that individuals should make their own choice regarding these surgeries when they reach an appropriate age to do so.

Slijper, Drop, Molenaar, and de Muinck Keizer-Schrama (2000) disagreed with that position, arguing that the literature provides many examples of how harmful delaying surgery is to those with ambiguous genitalia. Slijper and colleagues wrote that delaying surgery prevents these children from developing a clear gender identity, not to mention the increased likelihood of stigmatization they will feel and experience. They suggested that parents take responsibility for the decision about sex reassignment surgery.

Cosmetic genital surgery is performed routinely on infants around the world (Creighton et al., 2004), but several practices surrounding it have raised serious ethical questions. The usual practice in the United States has been to assign the child a sex at birth based on whether the penis is considered an acceptable size (Martin & Yonkin, 2006). If the child is deemed to be female at birth and has an atypically enlarged clitoris, it is often surgically reduced in size or removed. Such procedures can cause scarring. Some children have been later coerced into surgeries regardless of their felt sense of gender, while others have not provided their consent. Furthermore, parents are not always aware of the intersex status of their child, and when they are, physicians have sometimes encouraged them to keep this secret from their child (Martin & Yonkin, 2006). This secretiveness was in sync with Money's theory that a child would grow into whatever gender he or she had been assigned (Creighton & Minto, 2001). That theory has now been proven false: "Neither external genitals nor environment solely determines gender identity" (Bostwick & Martin, 2007, p. 1504).

A case that received a great deal of media attention involved John Money himself (Alderson, 2004). Bruce Reimer and his identical twin were born in Winnipeg, Manitoba, on August 22, 1965. When Bruce was 8 months old, a urologist performed a circumcision on him that did not go as planned: Reimer's penis was burned beyond surgical repair. His parents were persuaded to have an orchidectomy (i.e., removal of the testes) performed on him, and this occurred when he was 22 months old. In Money's (1975, 1991) writings, he reported on Reimer's progress by referring to him as the "John/Joan case." When Money later pressured his parents to have a vagina constructed, the family discontinued follow-up visits because Reimer had experienced these visits as more traumatic than therapeutic. He threatened suicide at age 13 if he had to see Money again. At age 14, Bruce decided to assume a male identity and changed his name to David. Due to unemployment, the death of his twin brother to an overdose of antidepressants 2 years earlier, and his wife requesting a separation on May 2, 2004, Reimer stormed from the house and committed suicide the same day at age 38.

The current consensus among experts is that gender should be assigned to newborn infants, regardless of whether surgical interventions are to be postponed (Pasterski, 2008). Creighton and Minto (2001) recommended that long-term follow-up studies of intersex adults are needed that require the involvement of clinicians, peer support groups, and the intersex individuals themselves. Daaboul (2003) believed that once all the outcome data are eventually collected and analyzed, they will show that there is no single answer or management protocol for DSD, but instead, they will suggest that answers will need to be tailored to each family.

Pasterski (2008) stated that while there have been some reported cases of sex reassignment later in life from intersex individuals, most identify with the gender in which they were raised. The cases that have come forth, however, should give all medical professionals cause for concern. In a follow-up study of 16 males born with cloacal exstrophy (a rare condition resulting in males being born either lacking a penis or with serious penile inadequacy), 14 were assigned the female sex surgically, while the parents of the other two boys did not permit the surgeries. They were then evaluated between ages 5 and 16. Eight of the 14 declared themselves male, along with the two that were not surgically altered (Reiner & Gearhart, 2004). These findings clearly show how reassignment in infancy can result in gender identity difficulties later.

The medical adage to do no harm is not always realized when surgically altering intersex newborns. Unquestionably, some surgical interventions are critical when it concerns saving someone's life, but the intersex child's health is seldom an issue (Martin & Yonkin, 2006). Furthermore, surgery for intersex conditions can and does cause damage to sexual function (Cull, 2002).

Members of the World Professional Association for Transgender Health (WPATH) were recently surveyed to ascertain whether they were providing services to intersex individuals. The response rate was 71%. The majority of the sample ($N = 93$) had worked with only a few intersex individuals. They expressed their desire to receive continuing education on the topic (Mazur, Cohen-Kettenis, Meyer, Meyer-Bahlburg, & Zucker, 2008).

A study of 37 intersex individuals found that many of the participants required surgery to correct the appearance and functioning of their genitalia. Many participants viewed their medical care very negatively, reporting that the worst part was the degree of secrecy, untruthfulness, and concealment demonstrated by medical personnel (Brinkmann, Schuetzmann, & Richter-Appelt, 2007a). It appears that many professionals working with intersex individuals could benefit from an increased understanding of what constitutes responsible and proactive care.

Development Through the Life Span

As should be evident from the preceding discussion, the development of intersex individuals will have much to do with whether they feel concordance between their behavior, their assigned gender, and their gender identity. Many intersex individuals grow up feeling insecure about their gender identity and experience psychological problems related to sexuality (Brinkmann, Schweizer, & Richter-Appelt, 2007b). While transgender individuals often experience a similar disconcordance, intersex individuals may experience the added burden of needing to maintain secrecy about their inadequate or malformed genitals, as well as anger toward parents or others if they had surgeries performed on them in infancy or without informed consent (Witten, 2003). Intersex individuals are often stigmatized by those who are aware of their DSD (Liakopoulou, Keramydas, Dracopoulou, & Dacou-Voutetakis, 2009), and they stigmatize themselves as well, knowing they are different.

The lives of intersex individuals often contain implicit themes of violence and abuse (Witten, 2003). As with transgender individuals, they are often economically disadvantaged, a factor that affects all people as they age (Witten, 2003). Overall, intersex individuals go through a lot to survive throughout their life spans. Those that manage to live long lives have learned significant coping skills (Witten, 2003).

Race and Ethnicity

Perhaps given the secrecy that often surrounds intersex individuals and their small numbers, and the even smaller numbers when we consider those of different race/ethnicity, there are currently no published psychological studies that pertain specifically to intersex people of color. In Chapter 8, the study of 33 transsexual persons of color by Erich, Tittsworth, Meier, and Lerman (2010) revealed that discrimination based on transsexual status was worse than that based on race/ethnicity. One may speculate that the same may be true of intersex individuals of color, but the converse may be true, too, given that people might be less blaming toward those who are intersex. This will be an interesting line of future research.

Relationships (Family, Friendships, Intimate Romantic/Sexual)

Most parents do not consider that their child may be born with a DSD, and when it happens, they often view such a result as inconceivable and they experience emotional pain (Zeiler & Wickstrom, 2009). Unsurprisingly, many will elect to have the ambiguity corrected through surgery. However, unlike the child born with Down syndrome, doctors often advise parents to keep the child's ambiguous sex secretive. This perpetuates the child's divergence as a source of silence and shame (Zeiler & Wickstrom, 2009).

In Estrada Inda's (1983) 2-year longitudinal study of five families with an intersex child, the parents hid the problem, thereby overprotecting or infantilizing the children. They worried that their children would be taunted at school, and some of the mothers feared their child would never get married. Some parents saw their child's condition as stigmatizing and even as a form of divine punishment. This, too, led to feelings of parental guilt and shame.

Rajon (2008) observed intersex infants and their parents during the first few days of life with follow-up over several years. Rajon reported that the absence of a clear gender identity can create obstacles in parent–child bonding. In their sample of 37 intersex women compared to a community sample of women, Richter-Appelt, Brinkmann, and Schutzmann (2006) found that the DSD sample rated their parents as less caring, less warm, and more punitive.

Five women with congenital adrenal hyperplasia (CAH) were asked about several aspects of their lives, one of which included relationships. They reported that they felt isolated and embarrassed to share their condition with others. Shame was also a prominent theme. These women reported few intimate and significant relationships despite their mean age of 27 years (Guth, Witchel, Witchel, & Lee, 2006).

Another study found that individuals with CAH had difficulty establishing intimate relationships, a result of impaired body image and problems identifying as a female (Kuhnle, Bullinger, Schwartz, & Knorr, 1993). Kuhnle and colleagues (1993) concluded that once relationships were established, however, they were reported as stable and satisfying.

Health (Emotional and Psychological, Physical)

Rajon (2008) wrote that in consequence of the disturbed parent–child bond that can occur, some intersex children will develop a pathological self-identity. Schweizer and Richter-Appelt (2010) suggested that intersex individuals might be more at risk of developing borderline personality disorder because of the disturbance in self-identity that can result from having an ambiguous body.

In a study of 15 46,XY individuals with DSD reared as females, Gueniche, Jacquot, Thibaud, and Polak (2008) concluded that they experienced a low quality of life with impaired social relations. The intersex individuals were sexually inhibited, more likely to be homosexually inclined, and doubted their female gender identities, and secrets marked their family lives. All 15 complained about not having a meaningful talk with their parents, especially their mothers, about their development.

In the study by Diamond and Watson (2004), only 51% of their participants reported that their physicians had told them they experienced androgen insensitivity syndrome (AIS). After finding out that they had AIS, most felt depressed, some to the point of emotional breakdown, while others experienced shock or denial.

A intersex child often feels different compared to other children, and combined with secrecy, misinformation, and/or deceit, feelings of isolation, alienation, objectification, and shame can result (Denver, 2005). When the experience is accompanied by honesty, education, and connection, however, the result can be liberating, empowering, and transcendent (Denver, 2005).

In a recent study by MacKenzie, Huntington, and Gilmour (2009), three intersex individuals interviewed talked about the negative impact of societal ignorance, the lack of acceptance of those with body differences, and their personal journeys from silence to disclosure. They eventually learned to accept their individuality and their choice of gender identification.

In comparing clinic-based women with CAH to population data, Morgan, Murphy, Lacey, and Conway (2005) found that the CAH sample was psychologically well adjusted. They did not have elevated incidences of psychiatric disorders or problems with social adjustment.

Johnson, Mimiaga, and Bradford (2008) introduced a special issue of the *Journal of Homosexuality* dedicated to the health issues of LGBTI and intersex individuals. They concluded that especially for transgender and intersex populations, research regarding their health care needs remains in its infancy stages.

Career and Work

There are no published articles focused specifically on career and work with intersex individuals. The same issues that apply to transsexual individuals would likely emerge for those undergoing sex reassignment surgery in adulthood. However, would their experience of transitioning be better received by colleagues if they understood a DSD precipitated the surgery? Will greater empathy be reported by others? Only future research studies will answer questions such as these.

Spirituality and Religion

Kerry (2009) wrote that intersex individuals have struggled with ongoing psychosocial and emotional trauma resulting from a long history of silence, secrets, and scars. He introduced recent findings suggesting that some intersex individuals are turning to traditional discourses of religion to understand the treatments they have received. Looy (2002) and Looy and Bouma (2005) challenged Christians to rethink the theology of gender and to become embracing of the differences and ministering to the needs of intersex individuals.

Sociopolitical Realities

The intersex movement has gained momentum over the past two decades (Kerry, 2009), mostly since the Intersex Society of North America (ISNA) was founded in 1993 and pushed for reform to the diagnosis and treatment of DSD. Cheryl Chase was the founder of the ISNA, and her work has been internationally acknowledged (Morland, 2008; Rosario, 2006). Most movements take significant time to produce the level of social change desired, and perhaps most fall short of what seem like lofty goals: those of equality and the right to self-determination. Such equality has never been fully realized by the women's movement, the African American movement, or the gay and lesbian movement. The research tells us that worldwide, most intersex children today continue to have little choice in deciding what is best for them surgically.

Recent Research Focused on Canada

Ken Zucker at the Centre for Addiction and Mental Health in Toronto is also a notable figure regarding his work and publications regarding intersex individuals (please see Chapters 7, 8, and 9 for more about his important contributions to the treatment of crossdressing and transsexual individuals). Heather Looy's work regarding embracing intersex individuals was mentioned earlier under spirituality and religion. Looy works at the King's University College in Edmonton, Alberta.

Holmes (2008) at Wilfred Laurier University argued against taking a bioethical perspective used to justify extensive pre- and postnatal interventions aimed at eliminating DSD. Instead, he took the position that intersex individuals be viewed as having legitimate bodies and that they be provided the right to self-determination.

Recent Research Focused on Other Societies

While the Bamana and Maninka peoples of Mali (a country in west Africa) believe that intersex individuals result from aberrant parental social behavior, they also believe that both twins and intersex individuals are extraordinary beings with special powers (Imperato & Imperato, 2006). Unfortunately, such a positive view of intersex people is globally rare.

Warne and Raza (2008) reviewed the presentation and management of DSD in different cultures; the bulk of what follows is adapted from their work. Not surprisingly, people with DSD are looked at and treated differently cross-culturally. Even those who are well educated have difficulty understanding these conditions, but in third-world countries where low education and poverty preside, traditional beliefs, folk remedies, and prejudice make the lives of intersex children and adults "extremely difficult and sad" (Warne & Raza, 2008, p. 227). In southern Africa, for example, a DSD is thought to occur because of witchcraft. Due to rumor and discrimination, intersex individuals are often devalued and isolated from their communities. While long-term outcome studies have been published in many countries, the values underpinning their treatment have not been questioned.

In large countries such as India, Pakistan, China, Indonesia, and Vietnam, there are very few pediatric endocrinologists. In developing countries, health care is not provided by government and few people have health insurance. Hospitals are overcrowded and expensive. Children in India born with ambiguous genitalia are sometimes thought to be Hijra. The mere thought of this to parents causes tremendous fear. In Vietnam, the extremely derogatory term *ai nam ai nu* is used to refer to both intersex individuals and gay people without distinction.

In many countries such as India, Turkey, Saudi Arabia, Malaysia, and Thailand, there is a strong preference for male babies. Many parents from Arabic, Chinese, Pakistani, and Indian backgrounds will be resistant to raising a child as female if the child has ambiguous genitalia (e.g., female children with congenital adrenal hyperplasia). Male children, even if infertile, are more likely to achieve economic independence than those who are female.

Warne and Raza (2008) recommended that wealthy countries assist developing countries regarding the treatment of DSD. They advocated for having at least one specialized DSD treatment center in every country, along with several other recommendations aimed at better care.

Nielsen and Stradiot (1987) conducted a transcultural study of 111 girls from Belgium, Canada, Denmark, France, Germany, and Hungary with Turner syndrome. They found that ignorance and secrecy remained prevalent and that better information concerning Turner syndrome was needed in all countries. While participants with Turner syndrome were shown to be happy, active, extroverted, realistic, and talkative, many also experienced anxiety, loneliness, and inferiority feelings.

Common Concerns Facing This Group and Counseling Considerations

Roleplay Scenarios

[*Note:* Suggested assessment and intervention strategies for the two roleplays below can be found in Appendix B. Before going there, roleplay in dyads with one of you acting as the counselor and the other as the counselee. If a roleplay is not possible, work individually in writing out a list of your suggestions.]

Roleplay #1, Chapter 10. Counseling Intersex Individuals

Tabitha, age 18, has come to see you for help. Most of the other grade 12 girls in her school have started dating, and Tabitha feels desperate to start herself. She is very self-conscious, however, as she has tells you she has a significantly enlarged clitoris and is lacking labia because of a "birth defect." She makes it clear that she does not want to talk further about her physical condition.

Roleplay #2, Chapter 10. Counseling Intersex Individuals

Mannix, age 55, has come to see you for help. He tells you that he has never had a relationship before and feels extremely lonely. He blurts out that he is interested in men but that he does not define as gay. Mannix believes he ought to have been born a woman and was even assessed when he was in his mid-20s at a gender clinic for transsexuality. He was told then that he was not a candidate for sex reassignment surgery, although the details were never explained to him. It strikes you that if he did transition, he would likely be a physically unattractive woman. As you ask about his medical history, you find out that he has Klinefelter syndrome.

How Would *You* Help This Person?

You are working as a professional counselor. Matthew Wong (age 39) and his wife of 15 years, Huan (age 38), come to see you at your office. They are very distraught. They tell you the debilitating feelings they had when their first child was born a few weeks ago with ambiguous genitalia. They received the results earlier today that, using the physician's terms, their child is a "true hermaphrodite"—having a 46,XX ovotesticular DSD. Despite the XX sex chromosomes, the child appears more male than female, given the size of what looks more like a penis than a clitoris. While Matthew and Huan are determined to love their child to the best of their ability, they are confused about the physician's advice to assign a female gender. They are also anxious to have surgery to correct the genitalia, but in what direction?

As you begin to get a better sense of Matthew and Huan, you discover that they had both wanted a boy child. While they were born in Seattle, both are first-generation Chinese. Neither consider

(Continued)

(Continued)

themselves religious, although they were raised Buddhist. Huan had had difficulty in becoming pregnant, and they were both nearly ready to stop trying and to adopt a child instead. They were pleasantly surprised when Huan became pregnant, but their joy was completely negated when little Chris was born. Frankly, they were both horrified and devastated when they first set eyes on Chris. Huan couldn't stop crying in the session, and Matthew's eyes frequently swelled up with tears that he tried hard to suppress.

Note—Remember to view clients within their environmental contexts, keeping in mind societal, parental/familial, cultural/spiritual, and peer influences. Specifically, become aware of the impact that the following influences have and continue to have in your clients' lives: race, language, religion and spirituality, gender, familial migration history, affectional orientation, age and cohort, physical and mental capacities, socioeconomic situation and history, education, and history of traumatic experience.

1. What defines this person's environment, past and present?
2. Who is this person sitting in front of me, taking into account environmental and personal characteristics?
3. What defines the problem that he or she is presenting within his or her multicultural milieu?

There are three recent documents recommended particularly for physicians working with intersex individuals, but these also provide counselors with very useful background information regarding best care practices. These include the following: (a) *Clinical Guidelines for the Management of Disorders of Sex Development in Childhood* (Consortium on the Management of Disorders of Sex Development [CMDSD], 2006a); (b) *Handbook for Parents* (CMDSD, 2006b); and (c) the *Consensus Statement on Management of Intersex Disorders* (Lee, Houk, Ahmed, & Hughes, 2006).

The CMDSD (2006a) stated that agreement has not been reached regarding when the various treatments are recommended. Pasterski (2008) reported the consensus among experts is to assign a gender to newborn infants, regardless of whether surgical interventions should be deferred.

Lee and colleagues (2006) compiled the results of a number of working groups that included 50 international experts in the field. They recommended that gender reassignment *must* be avoided before expert evaluation occurs with newborns and that evaluation and long-term management occur at a center with an experienced multidisciplinary team. Most surgeries for intersex children are cosmetic instead of critical (CMDSD, 2006a; Lee et al., 2006).

Discovering that one has a DSD is a highly challenging situation for individuals (Schweizer, Brunner, Schutzmann, Schonbucher, & Richter-Appelt, 2009). Many experience problems adjusting, whether they are transitioning or remaining in their assigned gender (Schweizer et al., 2009). Intersex individuals may have issues with gender similar to those of other transgender persons, but they may also bring very different issues concerning adjustment to sex, gender, and gender presentation (Mostade, 2006). For those who have gender issues, refer to Chapters 8 and 9 for pertinent counseling strategies.

Schweizer and colleagues (2009) recommended that psychological counseling should be offered to all individuals and their families diagnosed with a DSD. Two problems they noted, however, is that there remains a lack of concrete guidelines for counselors and little in the way of training curricula. Furthermore, while a sizeable literature has developed around transsexualism, most textbooks in both clinical and counseling psychology have ignored DSD (Schweizer et al., 2009).

Schweizer and colleagues (2009), Guth and colleagues (2006), and Mostade (2006) offered recommendations to counselors working with intersex individuals. A combined list of these includes the following:

1. Obtain training about DSD.
2. Be empathic, curious, compassionate, and real—admit that you know little about being an intersex individual.
3. Recognize how your own attitudes and knowledge about intersex individuals may affect your work with them.
4. Strive to understand the particular challenges, circumstances, and diversity issues faced by particular clients in the context of their families.
5. Normalize to the client that adjustment during childhood and adolescence is difficult but that becoming healthy and having satisfying relationships and a career are attainable.
6. Advocate for the rights of intersex children.
7. Understand how difficult it is for intersex clients to open up about their conditions due to the many times they have faced stigma.
8. Encourage growth through helping the clients deal with grief and shame they may be experiencing.
9. Help clients acknowledge the isolation and confusion they may be feeling and encourage them to connect to others with similar experiences.
10. Assist clients in finding educational resources related to their DSD.
11. Encourage physicians and clients to explain the medical condition to children as developmentally appropriate at each stage of treatment.
12. Provide counseling, support, and groups to intersex clients and their families.
13. Allow clients an opportunity to discuss their gender identity and sexuality and help them become accepting of these.
14. Encourage other treatment specialists to make you part of the treatment team to provide education regarding the psychosocial effects of DSD and the psychological aspects of the treatment process.
15. Help clients, families, and treatment team members explore the broad range of treatment options available, and then help families make informed decisions based on the best interests of the child.

This section now moves into looking at eight concerns that may bring intersex individuals into counseling. These include (a) bereavement; (b) shame and guilt; (c) posttraumatic reactions; (d) loneliness, secrecy, and feelings of isolation; (e) developing an intersex identity; (f) family issues; (g) family support; and (h) social support.

Bereavement

When intersex individuals find out about their DSD, most go through bereavement that may contain stages of denial, depression, anger, and bargaining before an eventual acceptance. For the majority, intense emotions and cognitive disequilibrium follow a loss for at least a period of time (Currier, Neimeyer, & Berman, 2008). Currier and colleagues (2008) performed a recent meta-analysis based on 61 controlled studies. They found that bereavement interventions are helpful to a small extent over the short term with negligible effects over the long run. This likely suggests that most people will eventually overcome the pain of bereavement on their own (Currier et al., 2008). Nonetheless, intersex individuals can experience first finding out about their DSD intensely, and simply having someone to talk to may be helpful and supportive.

Boelen, de Keijser, van den Hout, and van den Bout (2007) found that cognitive behavioral interventions (i.e., cognitive restructuring and exposure therapy) were more helpful to people suffering from complicated grief than was supportive counseling alone. Piper, Ogrodniczuk, Joyce, Weideman, and Rosie (2007) offered suggestions regarding group composition and group counseling for those with complicated grief.

Posttraumatic Reactions

Hird (2008) wrote that some intersex individuals develop trauma because of repeated surgeries, invasive medical examinations, and required aftercare procedures (e.g., surgically created vaginas require daily dilation with a prosthetic). Individuals may also develop trauma from the surgeries themselves (e.g., some surgeries result in loss of erotic sensation).

A recent review and meta-analysis of 21 studies found that cognitive behavior therapy (CBT) is supported for the treatment of childhood posttraumatic stress disorder (Kowalik, Weller, Venter, & Drachman, 2011). Kowalik and colleagues (2011) concluded that their findings add to the best practices data. CBT was more helpful in reducing anxiety and depression compared to externalizing symptoms (e.g., aggression and rule-breaking behavior).

Shame and Guilt

Schweizer and colleagues (2009) reported that intersex individuals often experience high levels of psychological distress, including insecurity, anxiety, shame, and guilt. Hird (2008) reported several studies, however, that speak to the resiliency of intersex individuals, and most grow up to be psychologically healthy.

Van Vliet's (2008) grounded theory of 13 adults experiencing shame provided a framework for overcoming these feelings. In her framework, an individual needs to rebuild through five processes: connecting, refocusing, accepting, understanding, and resisting. Connecting is about building a supportive social network, a process that begins within the counseling relationship itself. Second, counselors can help clients refocus their energies into positive activities, plans, and interests. The intent here is to help clients use their energies in more positive directions. Third, clients need to confront, feel, and accept their shame, together with accompanying feelings. Van Vliet recommended humanistic-existential and process-experiential approaches as particularly helpful. Fourth, counselors can help clients understand their shame experience with the goal of enhancing their self-concept and sense of control. Why did the event (e.g., the DSD or surgeries) occur and what external circumstances contributed? Fifth, clients need to learn to take back their power. Counselors can help by challenging the judgments that create and sustain the shame. Van Vliet recommended cognitive behavioral techniques to help accomplish this task.

Loneliness, Secrecy, and Feelings of Isolation

All of the seven participants in Schweizer and colleagues' (2009) study spoke about feeling different from others while growing up. Only one participant had someone to talk to about the challenges faced during puberty and adolescence. Most intersex individuals grow up in a vacuum of silence with their DSD being an unspoken taboo, leading them to feel lonely during the critical time of puberty (Schweizer et al., 2009).

Most people turn to family, friends, relatives, neighbors, and coworkers for social support (Andersson, 1998), and counselors can help clients explore to what extent they can use or expand existing resources or improve the quality of those connections to help alleviate loneliness. In addition to Margalit's (2010) suggestions, counselors can help clients break the secrecy surrounding their DSD and encourage clients to become socially connected through Internet and technological resources and/or through live resources available in larger cities. Lonely and isolated clients often do well in group settings in which they get to meet others facing similar problems of stigma and/or rejection. There are also many behavioral approaches that can be used to treat loneliness (e.g., social skills training, shyness groups, depression groups; Rook, 1984).

Margalit (2010) suggested that loneliness and isolation trouble youth in increasing numbers. She maintained that loneliness is not only the lack of social connectedness but it also represents the conflict between opposing needs: to be oneself and to be like one's peers. Her approach encourages youth to become more resilient, less isolated, more empowered, and hopeful.

Developing an Intersex Identity

Most intersex individuals identify as either a man or a woman (Hird, 2008), but some develop what Stoller (1968) called a "hermaphroditic identity." Stoller described this as a rare condition in which a person feels that he or she fits neither gender. In Schober's (2001) pilot study, eight participants described their gender identity as intersex instead of male or female. Preves (2003) also found some intersex individuals who embraced intersex as their identity label.

Potoczniak, Aldea, and DeBlaere (2007) found in their sample of 347 lesbian, gay, and bisexual (LGB) individuals that those who had social support developed stronger ego identity development, both in regard to commitment to an identity and exploration of possible identities. Their findings are in league with what Erikson (1968) proposed when he stated that intimate and trusting relationships facilitate the development of a healthy ego identity.

Furthermore, Potoczniak and colleagues (2007) found that the more LGB individuals withheld information about themselves, the less ego identity development occurred, and the converse was true as well. Consequently, it is likely therapeutic as well for intersex individuals to talk openly about their "secrets" with a counselor in such areas as their surgeries, the outcomes of surgeries, their processes of making sense of their gender identity, their affectional orientation, and their feelings and thoughts about such matters. A positive therapeutic alliance is essential in working with clients, and perhaps more so when working with a group that has customarily been made to feel invisible, shameful, stigmatized, and rejected. Beyond the counseling office, it will likely be helpful for intersex clients to become more open about these matters with other people who are showing indications of being a positive support in their lives.

Family Issues

Parental and familial relationships can be negatively affected by the silence and secrecy around surgery for DSD (Hird, 2008). Decisions made by parents can result in intersex individuals feeling anger, hostility, betrayal, and ongoing trust issues. Counselors, with their clients, can decide what will likely be the most effective method of dealing with the clients' family issues. For some, family therapy may be indicated, while for others, individual work may be sufficient.

Family Support

Parents go through a significant adjustment when their child is intersex. Some will mourn the loss of having a perfect daughter or son (Hird, 2008). They often require support to help them cope and learn to manage an intersex child (Slijper, Drop, Molenaar, & Scholtmeijer, 1994).

Besides the counseling that can be offered to families, a helpful resource is the *Handbook for Parents* (Consortium on the Management of Disorders of Sex Development, 2006b). The Intersex Society of North America also provides tips for both parents and adoptive parents (go to www.isna.org/articles/tips_for_parents).

Social Support

Intersex individuals face many challenges as they deal with intrusive and sometimes painful medical interventions and the repeated feeling of being different from others. Social support is important to help them cope successfully with their challenges. Affiliating with others acts as a protective factor against the harmful effects of stigma (Crocker & Major, 1989).

Counselors can work with clients to help them identify sources of support that affirm their identities and their experience. The Intersex Society of North America (www.isna.org/) is a superb starting place. Larger cities may also have specialized groups for intersex individuals, and contacting the local gay and lesbian information service will be helpful in finding out exactly what is available. Counselors who work with individuals with DSD may also be knowledgeable about available resources.

COUNSELING DIVERSE POPULATIONS

Counseling Intersex Individuals With Multiple Nondominant Identity Statuses

There is no research that addresses intersex individuals with more than nondominant identity status, let alone on how to counsel them. Holmes (2008) stated that disability studies have not focused on people with DSD, which perhaps make sense given that everyone views intersex individuals as "disabled" (Tremain, 2001). Some individuals with DSD are more likely to experience learning disabilities, however. Inozemtseva, Matute, and Juarez (2008) compared 11 girls with congenital adrenal hyperplasia (CAH) with 11 healthy girls and found the CAH group experienced a higher incidence of learning disabilities, which were predominantly reading related.

Counselors should be aware that there are cultural implications that affect intersex individuals of color and their families. Until research clarifies these cultural differences, counselors are reminded that all of us are individuals living within cultural milieus. Chapters 3 through 10 have each included a text box that focuses on the three questions that should be considered when working with all clients:

1. What defines this person's environment, past and present?
2. Who is this person sitting in front of me, taking into account environmental and personal characteristics?
3. What defines the problem that he or she is presenting within his or her multicultural milieu?

Counseling Aging Intersex Individuals

The needs of aging intersex individuals have not been distinguished from other transgender individuals in the published literature. Cook-Daniels (2006) reminded us that aging individuals with noncongruent bodies may find it traumatizing to expose their bodies to health care providers, thus making it awkward for them to live in residential facilities or, in some cases, to seek needed medical help.

Counseling Intersex Individuals Living in Rural Communities

There is no published research focused on intersex individuals living in rural communities. We might speculate that intersex individuals living in rural areas would be less likely to share their DSD with others and, consequently, may find it necessary to keep this more secretive than those living in cities in which they can become more anonymous. This area awaits empirical research.

Counseling Intersex Students

Martin (2008) wrote about the violence that occasionally erupts on college campuses, together with bullying, sexual harassment, and stalking. She argued that all of these represent real dangers to students, but especially to women and LGBTI individuals. It remains uncommon for academic institutions at all levels to include LGBTI curriculum or to adequately consider the needs of LGBTI students (Weinstock, 2003). There are currently no guidelines for counseling intersex students.

Counseling Intersex Adolescents

Adolescence is a difficult time for intersex youth, particularly if their fertility and sexuality are compromised (Sivapalan, 2009). Dating and sexual relations may be delayed, as was the case in a study of girls with congenital adrenal hyperplasia (Hurtig & Rosentha, 1987). Intersex children and teenagers may experience stigmatization if their difference is noticeable, an experience that many find traumatic (Liakopoulou et al., 2009). Disclosing one's sexual ambiguity is always distressing to an intersex person (Michel, Wagner, & Jeandel, 2008), particularly during the adolescent years when peer acceptance is considered so important. Intersex youth may bring to counseling a plethora of issues, many of which have been touched on through the chapters of this text.

Resources for This Group

1. The Intersex Society of North America is an outstanding resource for intersex individuals and others wanting to understand them. They are devoted to advocacy aimed at ending shame, secrecy, and unwanted genital surgeries (www.isna.org).
2. Robin Och provides an excellent list of links for intersex individuals and those interested in knowing more about them (www.robynochs.com/resources/Intersex.html).
3. The Kinsey Institute also has a list of resources helpful to intersex individuals (www.iub.edu/~kinsey/resources/sexlinks.html#InterSex).
4. The Intersex Initiative provides several resources for students (www.ipdx.org/academia/students.html).
5. PFLAG Canada lists several resources for intersex individuals (www.pflagcanada.ca/en/help-frame-e.asp?helpframe=links-e.asp?audience=intersex).

Limitations, Furthering Research, and Implications for Counselors

Limitations of the Research With This Group

Lee and colleagues (2006) reported that the consensus by 50 international experts was that there is a major shortage of long-term outcome studies in DSD, and they recommended that an educational program be provided to ensure the many professionals working with intersex individuals and their families are provided the latest information. What this implicitly says is that countless decisions with long-term consequences have been made (without sufficient understanding of likely long-term impact) that affect the lives of intersex individuals and their families. In the recent past, John Money's theory that children up to 18 months would grow into whatever gender was assigned to them was trusted by clinicians as though it were fact. Is it what they wanted to hear that made his theory so pervasive and believable? Was it the case that nearly everyone concerned was unsettled by the presence of individuals who were sexually ambiguous, not fitting neatly into the binary categories of male or female? Like an oil spill that continues to be cleaned up, the practice of surgically deciding gender at or near birth on the basis of ambiguous genitalia was an epic disaster in the history of caring for people who are different.

Areas Requiring Further Research

There remains a great deal unknown regarding what determines gender identity in intersex individuals (Lee et al., 2006). What is needed are studies with representative sampling to carefully measure and look at the development of gender identity in people with DSD. Studies are needed that look at the timing and content regarding the psychological management of intersex individuals as well. Furthermore, the effects of early versus later surgery need to be carefully evaluated (Lee et al., 2006).

The quality of psychological assessments done on people with DSD has been lacking, and Meyer-Bahlburg (2005) has recommended long-term follow-up data based on standardized psychological instruments is needed. There is little research dealing with diverse populations (e.g., those with multiple nondominant statuses, aging, living in rural areas). Intersex individuals remain an understudied population. As evident from the preceding sections, there is little work done regarding counseling interventions focused on helping intersex individuals live better lives.

Implications for Counselors

The counseling profession has been based on premises of self-determination and self-actualization. Its ideology has regarded all people as equals, and consequently, there is little judgment placed on others who are different in some way. One of the roles that counselors play is that of advocate, and it may be here that they play the most significant part in assisting children who do not have an equal voice regarding their treatment plan. They may also be of significant help to families deeply conflicted by society's hegemonic views of the binary system of sex and gender against those that reflect the best interests of a vulnerable child. It is traumatic to discover one's newborn does not have a typical body, and bad decisions can be made in the midst of trauma. Counselors can help parents to take their time with decisions that are not considered life threatening. After the trauma subsides, a rational decision-making process can unfold.

In working with adolescents and adults, counselors may be called upon to help with any of the concerns raised earlier in this chapter, but in addition to this, they may assist with any of the general concerns that people bring to counseling. When one's intersex status is not related to the presenting issue, it seems doubtful that most counselors would ever know their client has a DSD. Counselors who reflect deep compassion and unconditional positive regard for their clients are most likely to see the true suffering of the person. Unless a genuine and deep therapeutic alliance is formed, information shared by the client will always be screened to one extent or another.

Exercises

Individual Exercises

1. Read the information available on the Intersex Society of North America website (www.isna.org/).

2. Have a discussion with a friend or family member about what it would be like if each of you had been born with a DSD. Consider how it would have been for you in gym class at school, when finding a new physician and asking for an annual physical, when going on a date, when teased by other children, and when wanting to get married and have a family.

Classroom Exercise (1 or 2)

1. Attain a copy (either by purchase or by making a donation) of one of the three videos (*Hermaphrodites Speak!*, *Is It a Boy or a Girl?*, or *Mani's Story*) available from the Intersex Society of North America (www.isna.org/videos) to show in class. Alternatively, download the video *XXXY* from the website above. It is a short documentary about DSD.

2. Invite an intersex individual to be a guest speaker in your class to talk about the struggles faced in everyday life.

Chapter Summary

In parallel with other marginalized groups, the terminology used to talk about intersex individuals has shifted from *hermaphroditism* in the past to the most recent term of *disorders of sexual development*, or, as Reis (2009) recommended, *divergence of sexual development*. People with DSD in this chapter were referred to as *intersex individuals*.

The voice of intersex individuals was largely absent in the literature until the Intersex Society of North America began to give voice to a community of people who have been kept secret, silent, and stigmatized. Painted with the same brush as other members of the LGBTI community, the intersex difference has been met by misunderstanding, prejudice, harsh judgment, oppression, and discrimination. One of the ways that medicine has "normalized" intersex individuals in the past (and in the present in many places worldwide) has been to force them into being either male or female, a decision often made based on the size of what looked like a phallus. Children thus forced to wear the brand of their newly created genitalia were often lied to so that the secret of their early existence could be sheltered from the rest of us.

The new guidelines of care for intersex individuals provide recommendations for greater engagement of the parents and the child before surgical intervention to the genitalia is undertaken. The counselor may encounter intersex clients who were victims of the old regime or those who are now provided some choice in the matter of their sexual futures. In either instance, the problems they bring to counseling need to be heard with an understanding and compassionate ear. While some surgeries may be irreversible, one's psychological health can always be redeemed.

11

Conclusions

"It is better to be hated for what you are than to be loved for something you are not"

André Gide,
French author (1869–1951)

First they came for the communists,
and I didn't speak out because I wasn't a communist.
Then they came for the trade unionists,
and I didn't speak out because I wasn't a trade unionist.
Then they came for the Jews,
and I didn't speak out because I wasn't a Jew.
Then they came for me,
and there was no one left to speak out for me.

Attributed to Pastor Martin Niemöller (1892–1984) about the inactivity of German intellectuals following the Nazi rise to power.

General Conclusions

Exemplified in media by songs such as "Born This Way" by Lady Gaga, not all LGBTI people need to hide any longer. Furthermore, while hiding (i.e., passing) remains necessary for many people throughout the world, her song reminds us that we need to love ourselves despite the ongoing injustices that still prevail. While not all LGBTI people are "born this way" (recall that identity labels are self-chosen, but what lies below them—such as affectional orientation and gender identity—are not), you are who you are, and that person is worth loving.

As the fourth wave of psychology (Pedersen, 1990, 1999) promulgates throughout the modern world, a new sexual and gender revolution is well underway. It is a postmodern version of the 1960s and 1970s revolution that changed the traditional codes of behavior regarding sexuality. We are now seeing nonhegemonic forms of sexuality and gender emerging from the codes of silence that kept LGBTI individuals invisible. Like an earthquake that continues to release aftershocks, our minds are sometimes overwhelmed with the human complexity that exists around us. It is no longer permissible to keep people in tightly contained boxes to preserve a sense of order, stability, and simple understanding. The imprisoned have set themselves free.

Postmodernism and multiculturalism have brought an awareness that there are many truths, making it more difficult for people to know what they should believe and how they should act. Unfortunately, the hope that postmodern thought will flourish globally and that the labeling of others will stop is like expecting humans to see human complexity instead of the neat categories that keep information about others manageable. Judgments are inevitable, but which judgments matter and which ones don't?

What should be clear from reading this text is that LGBTI individuals have experienced unduly harsh prejudice, harassment, discrimination, marginalization, homophobia, biphobia, transphobia, heterosexism, oppression, and violence throughout most of recorded history. They have been viewed as the deviant criminals and sinners that have literally destroyed civilizations (Hetrick & Martin, 1987), but nothing, in fact, could be further from the truth.

Destroying the spirit of a person is the gravest sin of all. Throughout the world, the majority of cultures both past and present have condemned those who have differing affectional orientations and those who have expressed gender in differing ways from the majority. A pandemic worse than the bubonic plaque of the 14th century or the AIDS crisis of today has, until recently, been allowed to spread an illness as crippling as disease itself: hatred.

Look at the list of many of the concerns that were identified in Chapters 3 through 10 in Table 11.1. Place a checkmark beside each issue that, at least to some extent, becomes an issue for LGBTI people because of their treatment by family, friends, church, and society. Then multiply that number by 100 and divide by 30 to get a percentage. What percentage of these concerns result to some degree by the way these individuals are treated today?

Table 11.1 Checklist of Many of the LGBTI Issues Identified in This Text

Place a checkmark to the left of each issue listed below that you believe is partly a consequence of how LGBTI individuals are treated in society today.

√	#	*Issue*
	1	Internalized homophobia
	2	Affectional orientation confusion

(Continued)

(Continued)

√	#	*Issue*
	3	Fragmentation of identity
	4	Religious conflicts
	5	HIV/AIDS
	6	Relationship issues/marital discord
	7	Disclosing to others
	8	Managing the consequences of external homophobia (e.g., harassment, homophobia, violence)
	9	Career concerns
	10	Major depression, poor mental health, and suicide risk
	11	Weight problems
	12	Substance abuse problems (drug and alcohol)
	13	Parenthood issues
	14	Identity confusion and labeling issues
	15	Internalized biphobia
	16	Need for family and social support
	17	Invisibility and its sequelae
	18	Lack of community, secrecy, and feeling isolated
	19	Ego-dystonic crossdressing and/or compulsiveness
	20	Mild to severe gender dysphoria
	21	Child and adolescent challenges
	22	Wanting to transition
	23	Transitioning at work
	24	Uncertainty about sex reassignment surgery
	25	Learning new gender scripts
	26	Bereavement
	27	Posttraumatic reactions
	28	Shame and guilt
	29	Problems accessing psychological and/or medical services
	30	Struggles with self-esteem and self-concept
Multiply total by 100 and divide by 30		

Can you see how the majority of these issues result from others not understanding LGBTI persons and from what, at least on the surface, would appear to be a desire to have everyone look and behave the same? If the rainbow were only one color, it wouldn't be nearly as beautiful. If people were all the same, we would quickly grow bored with one another, and human progress would diminish as we all worked at staying in the box instead of trying to expand it.

Cats are not the only curious observers: people are, too. Spend time in a downtown city or in an urban park close to a metro core. It is likely you will soon begin noticing the differences between people based on height, weight, gender, color, appearance, gait, mannerisms, perceived demeanor, socioeconomic status indicators, and whether one appears to belong to any other nondominant group, such as the LGBTI community. Now pay attention to the valence you give to each difference you observe. Are you the most judgmental toward those that seem the most different from you?

While today, most Westerners are considerate enough to know the proper words to call people to their faces, or at least ask if they don't know, the negative judgment behind differences remains, a judgment that some today call "modern prejudice" (Morrison & Morrison, 2008) to distinguish it from the prejudice of yesteryear that was more blatant. But subtle can still be pervasive, and pervasive still negatively affects the development and psychological health of those who know negative judgments are constantly being made about them.

LGBTI individuals have been designated as *other*, meaning that they have been made to look as though they are inherently so different that some of their perceived humanity is denied to them by the dominant culture. In war times, for example, the enemy is often referred to by a name that places them into the *other* category, creating a "we–they" relationship. The enemy comes to symbolize all that is bad and evil, while the insiders become all that is good and godly. As Boykin (2005) pointed out, "more Americans have died from AIDS than from battle during all the wars of the 20th century combined" (p. 283). It is time we become enlightened enough to see that to oppress, discriminate against, belittle, loathe, or otherwise mistreat the *other* is to create an artificial hierarchy of human worth. It is time to end the symbolic civil war against the *other*. The *other* is among us—the *other* is one of us.

"Be the change you want to see in the world" (Mahatma Gandhi, 1869–1948), and know that your footsteps make a difference. Do you still know whose feet in the sand are looking up at you?

Conclusions for Counseling Practice

If you have embraced more affirming attitudes and beliefs, gained knowledge, and developed skills to work with LGBTI individuals through this text, its goals have been fully realized. Consider yourself fortunate as a counselor if you have the opportunity to work with a LGBTI client. As a result of being forced by stigma to be *other*, LGBTI clients bring a breath of fresh air into the counseling office. To some extent, they are forced to develop an alternate worldview than those upholding the dominant social discourse.

LGBTI clients bring a myriad of potential presenting issues to counselors. Nearly every study that compares them to heterosexual individuals reports higher rates of substance abuse, depression, and suicidal behaviors (Eliason, 2011). The more a group is marginalized, the more it learns to incorporate some of the dysfunction bestowed upon it.

It should be evident by now that there is not one identity that defines any of the groups discussed in this book. Instead, there are identities, and identities look different depending on many factors explained within the ecological model presented in Chapter 3. Identities are created through an interaction between self and environment, and cross-cultural differences add to the richness of the mix.

As mentioned in Chapter 1, Pedersen, Crethar, and Carlson (2008) concluded that multicultural counselors today need to practice inclusive cultural empathy, which they defined as "the learned ability of counselors to accurately understand and respond appropriately to each culturally different client" (p. 44). Each person belongs to at least 1,000 cultures at any point in time (Pedersen et al., 2008), and each affects the individual's perspective and identity. Our cultural identities affect who we are and how we think and act. The identity categories identified by Pedersen and colleagues include race/ethnicity, language, religion/spirituality, family migration history, affectional orientation, age, physical and mental ableness, socioeconomic status and history, education, and traumatic experiences. Just as no two heterosexual men or women are exactly alike, the same is true for diverse clients.

Final Thoughts

The more marginalized a community, the greater the need for caring others who see deeper than the surface of color, sexuality, ableness, sexuality, gender, or what have you. Without pockets of tolerance and acceptance, the holocaust of hate perpetuates, both that which is internalized and that which finds itself rotting in the cavities of a nation's consciousness.

We must move beyond the nature/nurture controversy and come to a deeper understanding of what human rights are *really* about. It is the place where we celebrate the individuality of each person, a philosophy that our nations embrace because we know we do not want to become the same, the same as what Hitler did with his Nazi soldiers, the same that communists did to equalize goods and services.

Human rights are about upholding the highest virtues and realizing that without them, we are diminished as citizens of our country and of our world. We, as the civilized and powerful West, have an obligation to other countries to be leaders. We are the ones who must set the example.

The battle for same-sex marriage that has already concluded in Canada still wages its war of havoc in the United States. Washington, D.C., itself has legalized same-sex marriage, yet it is not legal nationally or in most states. As predicted a few years ago (Lahey & Alderson, 2004), same-sex marriage is here to stay. It is time to legislate justice and equality for all.

Konik and Stewart (2004) found that in a sample of 358 college students, those who had a sexual minority identity (e.g., lesbian, gay, bisexual, or "other" nonheterosexual identity) demonstrated "more advanced global, political, religious, and occupational identity development" (p. 815). The group who identified as heterosexual scored higher on identity foreclosure, moratorium, and diffusion, while the sexual minority group scored higher on identity achievement. The participants included 202 self-identified heterosexual, 100 lesbian or gay, 40 bisexual, and 14 individuals who defined as "other" (e.g., queer). LGBTI individuals have many positive qualities that are often unacknowledged.

Many LGBTI individuals will never make it into a counselor's office. While this text has been problem focused, Savin-Williams (2005) reminded us that most LGBTI individuals have learned to become resilient. There is so much we can learn from the majority that never seek our counseling services. These are the people researchers would benefit from knowing as well. It is difficult to pathologize the *other* when the *other* is yourself. If you think about it, we are all *other* in some way.

Appendix A

Glossary

Affectional orientation: Refers to a person's attraction, erotic desire, and philia for members of the opposite gender, the same gender, or both.

Affectional orientation confusion: A confusion that results when there is perceived disparity and felt conflict (cognitive dissonance and/or outside influences) among sexual affect, cognition, and behavior.

Affirmative therapy: Therapy offered by an LGBTI-affirmative therapist. Such therapists view LGBTI status as equal to heterosexual status and they emphasize a nonpathological view in their work with these clients.

Alexithymia: A condition whereby a person has a difficult time identifying and/or actually feeling a plethora of emotions.

Autoandrophilia: A male's propensity to be sexually aroused by the thought of himself as a male.

Autogynephilia: A male's propensity to be sexually aroused by the thought of himself as a female.

Biphilia: The propensity to fall in love romantically with members of either sex or gender.

Biphobia: The fear, dislike, or intolerance of bisexual individuals and/or rendering them invisible by denying their existence.

Bisexual individuals: People who self-identify as having primarily bisexual cognition, affect, and/or behavior.

Circuit parties: Large raves frequented mostly by gay men. They are known as venues where substantial drug usage and sometimes unprotected sex occurs.

Collectivist society: A society whose members are expected to strive for familial interconnectedness, familial responsibility, and family heritage. Mexico, China, Japan, and India are examples.

Coming out: *Coming out* can mean one of two things, and usually the context provides the appropriate connotation. First, coming out can be used to refer to the process of self-identifying as LGBTI. Second, coming out can refer to disclosing one's LGBTI identity to others.

Conversion therapy: Therapy directed at changing a homosexual or bisexual orientation into a heterosexual orientation. Also known as reparative therapy.

Core gender identity: One's sense of being male, female, or indeterminate; it is usually established between 18 and 30 months.

Crossdressing individuals: People who dress in the clothing of the opposite gender with the intent of displaying cross-gender characteristics.

Disclosing: A more specific term than *coming out*. This refers to telling other people that he or she identifies as LGBTI.

Disorders of sexual development (DSD): An expression that refers to people with "congenital conditions in which development of chromosomal, gonadal, or anatomical sex is atypical" (Vilain, 2008, p. 330). They are referred to as *intersex individuals* in this text.

Drag king: A woman who crossdresses for fun and/or money.

Drag queen: A gay man who crossdresses for fun and/or money.

Ecological model of LGBTI identity: A new holistic theory intended to identify all influences affecting the person's sexual identity development, including internal factors (physical and psychological) and external factors (social and environmental). The development of a positive gay identity represents the final achievement in the model.

Essentialists: People who believe that those with homosexual orientations have always existed, regardless of whether they could give themselves a sexual identity label. Essentialists usually support their position with evidence from biologic and genetic studies.

Female-to-male transsexual (FTM): Biological females who have a male gender identity and who want sex reassignment surgery, whether preoperative or postoperative.

Fetishistic crossdressing (FC) individuals: Men who crossdress, at least during adolescence, because of the sexual arousal and often climactic release it provides. Most of these men define as heterosexual.

Gay identity: An identity status denoting those individuals who have come to identify themselves as having primarily homosexual cognition, affect, and/or behavior and who have adopted the construct of "gay" as having personal significance to them.

Gay men: Males who self-identify as having primarily homosexual cognition, affect, and/or behavior and who have adopted the construct of "gay" as having personal significance to them.

Gender benders: People (male or female) who intentionally "bend," or transgress, traditional gender roles.

Gender dysphoria: Feeling varying degrees of discomfort with one's biological sex and/or one's expression of gender roles.

Gender identity: May refer to core gender identity, but it can also refer to one's current sense of seeing oneself as male, female, or indeterminate.

Gender identity disorder (GID): The official diagnosis for those individuals who meet the *DSM-V* or *DSM-IV-R* criteria.

Genotype: Refers to the entire genetic constitution of an individual.

Gonadal sex: Refers to the type of gonads present within an individual (i.e., testis and/or ovary).

Heterophilia: The propensity to fall in love romantically only with members of the opposite sex or gender.

Heterosexism: This term refers to the many ways individuals in our society consciously or unconsciously minimize gay, lesbian, or bisexual people, either by assuming that they don't exist or by projecting a belief that they are somehow inferior compared with their heterosexual counterparts.

Homonegativity: A more specific term than *homophobia*. This refers to having negative views of gay and/or lesbian people, regardless of the reason.

Homophilia: The propensity to fall in love romantically only with members of the same sex or gender.

Homophobia: The fear, dislike, or intolerance of gay and/or lesbian individuals.

Homosexual orientation: A sexual orientation created through the interaction between affect and cognition such that it produces homoerotic attraction, homoaffiliative desire, and ultimately homophilia.

Individualistic society: A society whose members are expected to strive for individuality, and such qualities as independence, autonomy, and personal freedom are espoused. The United States, Canada, Europe, and Australia are examples.

Internalized biphobia: This refers to bisexual individuals fearing, disliking, and/or hating themselves. The term also applies to bisexual individuals fearing, disliking, and/or hating other bisexual people or those who they perceive as bisexual.

Internalized homophobia: This refers to gay and lesbian individuals fearing, disliking, and/or hating themselves. The term also applies to gay and lesbian individuals fearing, disliking, and/or hating other gay/lesbian people or those who they perceive as gay/lesbian.

Intersex individuals: People with congenital conditions in which development of chromosomal, gonadal, or anatomical sex is atypical.

Karyotype: Refers to the individual's chromosomal pattern. Most people have a karyotype of 46,XY (male) or 46,XX (female).

Lesbian women: Females who self-identify as having homosexual cognition, affect, and/or behavior and who have adopted the construct of "lesbian" as having personal significance to them.

LGBTI individuals: People with nonheterosexual identities (e.g., lesbian, gay, bisexual) and/or those with transgender identities (e.g., fetishistic crossdresser, transsexual, intersex).

Male-to-female transsexual (MTF) individuals: Biological males who have a female gender identity and who want sex reassignment surgery, whether preoperative or postoperative.

Minority stress: The emotional stress experienced by being a member of a disenfranchised minority group.

Mosaic individuals: People that have a variety of cells containing XX and XY chromosomes.

Multicultural framework: A theoretical framework that purports that having culturally sensitive beliefs and attitudes, knowledge, and skills is necessary to become a multiculturally competent counselor.

Passing: Includes all attempts made by LGBTI individuals to *not* let others know about their LGBTI identity.

Pederasty: In ancient times, it was the practice whereby a man took a boy under his tutelage for purposes of educating him in exchange for sexual favors of one sort or another.

Phenotype: Refers to the observable characteristics or traits of an individual.

Phenotypic sex: Refers to the individual's primary and secondary characteristics.

Philia: The propensity to fall in love romantically with members of a particular sex or gender (or both, as in the case of biphilia).

Queer identity: Refers to those people who refuse to be classified on the basis of sexuality.

Queer theory: A theory evolving out of social constructionism. Its basic tenet is that all aspects of our sexuality are socially constructed and therefore flexible and malleable. Queer theorists avoid labeling people regarding their sexuality or gender due to this flexibility.

Same-sex passionate friendship: An intense friendship that does not include sexual contact.

Sexual identity: Refers to the label individuals use to define their sexuality (i.e., heterosexual or "straight," gay, lesbian, bisexual, or queer).

She-male: A man who has achieved a female chest contour with breast implants or hormonal medication but still retains his male genitals.

Social constructionists: People who believe that homosexual orientations are environmentally determined and that they require certain socio-political-historical conditions to exist in order to find expression. Consequently, a homosexual orientation needs to be created within an environment that allows it at some level. Social constructionists usually support their position with evidence from the social sciences.

Stealth: Refers to transgender people, usually transsexual, who live fully in their chosen gender without revealing their biological sex to others.

Transgender individuals: People who present unconventional gender expressions (e.g., cross-dressers, drag queens, drag kings) and/or those who present unconventional gender identities (e.g., transsexual, transwoman, transman).

Transgenderist individual: A male or female who crossdresses most if not all of the time and who may or may not experience gender dysphoria. A transgenderist individual with gender dysphoria usually experiences it in a less severe form compared to transsexual individuals and has resolved (or has had it decided for him or her) not to proceed with gender reassignment surgery.

Transitioning: Refers to the process by which many transsexual individuals begin and continue physical steps to alter their body morphology. This includes cross-sex hormone therapy, top surgery (e.g., chest recontouring for female-to-male, breast augmentation for male-to-female), and bottom surgeries (e.g., vaginoplasty—creation of a vagina; clitoroplasty—creation of a clitoris; vulvoplasty—creation of the vulva; hysterectomy—surgical removal of the uterus; oophorectomy—surgical removal of the ovaries; metaoidioplasty—a procedure in which the clitoris is released from its hood, providing it greater length; phalloplasty—construction of a penis using skin grafts from the forearm or elsewhere). It is important to clarify that not all transsexual individuals elect to transition, and those that do might only transition in a partial sense (e.g., hormones only, top surgery only, bottom surgery only).

Transman: A postoperative transsexual female-to-male (FTM) individual. Not all FTM individuals will use this term to define themselves.

Transphobia: The fear, dislike, or intolerance of transgender individuals. This may include rendering transsexual individuals invisible by denying the existence of differing gender identities.

Transsexual individuals: People who believe their gender is dissonant with their morphology.

Transwoman: A post-operative transsexual male-to-female (MTF) individual. Not all MTF individuals will use this term to define themselves.

Two-spirited: A relatively new term used by many American Indian and Canadian First Nations LGBTI individuals to describe their sense of having both a male and a female spirit. The term has a positive connotation, as many such individuals historically were revered by their tribes.

Appendix B

Handling the Roleplay Situations

Roleplay #1, Chapter 3, Counseling Gay Men

John, age 36, has come to see you for help. John has been out for 12 years and everyone knows he is gay. He has become entirely comfortable with himself and who he is. He has been dating Marco, age 32 from Mexico, for the past 2 years and they have lived together for a year. Marco has only been out to himself for 3 years. Marco has not disclosed his identity to anyone, including his family. Now his mother and father have decided to visit for 6 weeks, and they will be staying with John and Marco. John is beside himself not knowing what to do. He respects Marco but does not respect his dishonesty in not disclosing his identity to others. John will need to hide a lot of things at their home, especially his feelings and attachment to Marco.

- Help John develop empathy—have John remember what it was like before he came out.
- Help John explore his feelings—what is he most concerned about, hiding feelings from family or that Marco is unwilling to disclose their relationship? How does Marco's stance reflect upon John?
- Discuss his concerns and feelings with Marco.
- Multicultural awareness—might not be wise for Marco to come out to his family. John should learn more about culture.
- Learn more from Marco—is it possible that family already knows despite everyone's unwillingness to label it? Is his family typical or unique in Mexican culture?
- Explore options and compromises—parents leave house for an evening, couple rents hotel room periodically or goes out on dates. Might it be appropriate for Marco to disclose to his family after they get to know John?
- Consider couples counseling.
- Look at bottom lines. What if this situation never changes—what will be each partner's response?
- Discuss family/values, supports, their relationship history, discuss the different stages of gay identity development of both parties.
- Consider offering counseling to Marco.
- Do not make assumptions; instead, ask questions.
- Normalize John's feelings.
- Bibliotherapy for John to understand Marco.
- Explore coping strategies with John.
- Explore John's assumptions about Marco—how does he know this to be true?
- Explore the respect aspect (i.e., he says he does not respect Marco's dishonesty).

Roleplay #2, Chapter 3, Counseling Gay Men

Roger, age 45, has come to see you for help. He has been married to Jane for 20 years and they have two children, ages 15 and 13. Jane recently found him in their garage trying to asphyxiate himself by keeping the car running. After spending several weeks in a psychiatric ward, Roger has since been released. He hates himself because he has always had very strong attraction to men, and now he is aware these feelings are getting stronger. He has already decided to leave Jane and the kids but wants to feel better about himself.

- Assess current suicide risk.
- Get history from him. Explore life circumstances—what led him to attempt suicide?
- Assess for reasons underlying internalized homophobia.
- Help client reduce internalized homophobia—bibliotherapy, including Internet resources.
- Help client reduce internalized homophobia—exposure to other gay men and community.
- Help client reduce internalized homophobia—counseling focus, such as challenging his beliefs and normalizing being gay.
- Self-esteem work.
- Explore his affectional orientation and determine if he wants to pick an identity label.
- Impart hope.
- Encourage Roger *not* to make significant life changes at this time—especially do not leave wife until further counseling work is done.
- Defer telling Jane about his attractions to men until he is in a more stable state emotionally. Assess his readiness for change.
- Assess his support system—who is behind him and will be nonjudgmental?
- Suggest couples and/or family counseling.
- Normalize his attractions for men.
- Explore potential marriage consequences.
- Encourage Jane to receive counseling.

Roleplay #3, Chapter 3, Counseling Gay Male Youth

Peter, age 14, has come to see you for help. Peter has been sexually active with other boys for the past year. Although he has had a great time sexually, he wonders if he is prematurely settling down sexually with guys and wonders if he might also have interest in girls. Peter tells you that he had tried to ask girls for sex last year, but none of them felt either ready for it or they wanted something more than casual sex. Peter is only interested in casual sex right now.

- Informed consent—From mom or dad, but if parents are separated or divorced, do parents have joint legal custody? If so, you need permission from both to counsel Peter.
- Normalize his feelings and behavior.
- Avoid labeling his behavior—possibly just sexual release.
- Explore his affectional orientation—is he developing strong feelings for any of these guys?
- Explore his sexual practices. Safer sex? If not, provide education.
- Explore problems he is having becoming sexual with girls. Perhaps he needs assertiveness training or simply needs to change the way he approaches girls.
- Is Peter in denial? Assess if internalized homophobia is operating.
- Empathy assessment—ask him how he would feel if the situation was reversed and he was being used for sex.
- History—what led him to become sexual with boys from such a young age?
- Training may be indicated—(e.g., social skills, assertiveness).
- Bibliotherapy.
- Inquire about sexual identity.
- What type of sex is he engaging in with boys?
- Risk assessment—is he engaging in other risky behaviors when he has sex (e.g., alcohol, drugs)?
- Explore self-concept, self-esteem, body image, and appearance.

Roleplay #4, Chapter 3, Counseling Gay Male Youth

Donald, age 18, has come to see you for help. Although Donald is aware that his interest is almost exclusively in men, he finds that whenever he gets together with men for sex, he has trouble maintaining an erection during anal sex and never seems able to cum. Donald doesn't want to assume the passive role in anal intercourse but wonders if he will need to if this problem is not soon resolved. There is nothing wrong with Donald physiologically.

- Check if he is on antidepressants or other meds that could interfere with sexual performance.

- Inquire about performance with other sexual behaviors, such as oral sex, vaginal sex, etc. Does it look any different regarding erection and ejaculation?
- Inquire about performance during masturbation.
- Assess for reason—internalized homophobia or other psychological reason, such as performance anxiety. Does he have this problem with women as well? Maybe he is just not interested in anal sex? Is he in a relationship or only having one-night stands? (May be that his morals and values are opposed to one-nighters.)
- Will be helpful if he is with a consistent partner who is understanding and willing to assist in overcoming this problem.
- Use behavioral technique called "shaping"—closer and closer approximations to the desired behavior.
- May need more practice with this sexual behavior.
- His views on taking the "passive" role—why the aversion? Probably internalized homophobia.
- Sexual risk assessment—using condoms consistently? If yes, using shaping technique noted above.
- Affectional orientation assessment.
- Sexual identity assessment—how does he define himself?
- Take history of where he is living, relationship with family, and so forth. Cultural, spiritual, and familial influences.
- There are a variety of sexual practices to choose from—anal sex is only one of them.
- Reassure him that many gay men do not enjoy anal sex (about one third).
- Normalize his feelings.

Roleplay #1, Chapter 4, Counseling Lesbian Women

Debbie, age 25, has come to see you for help. She started dating guys when she was 16, and since then has probably dated and slept with more than 40 guys. Her boyfriends have lasted anywhere from 2 weeks to 9 months, and she has usually been the one to end it. She is concerned that despite liking many of these guys, she has never felt a special connection or feeling of romantic love for any of them. Recently she has met Karen, and she notices that her heart seems to beat faster every time they get together. She can hardly keep her mind from thinking about Karen, and she is beginning to wonder what sex would be like with her. Although the idea of being intimate with a woman is not frightening to Debbie, she is surprised by her feelings and questions whether she could develop an actual relationship with another woman.

- History—explore Debbie's past relationships with men. What was missing?
- Affectional orientation exploration—help her examine her feelings for Karen.
- Sexuality for women is often fluid—possible that Debbie will still fall in love with a man someday? Does it matter to her that much?
- Internalized homophobia—To what extent is Debbie homophobic? What would a lesbian identity mean to her?
- Reciprocation—Questions about Karen—does she define as lesbian or bisexual? Will she be receptive to advances?
- Encourage exploration—Lesbian erotica? Bibliotherapy regarding lesbian women or community?
- Associate with lesbian women and community.
- Normalize her experience.
- Assess social support—How much support does Debbie have in her life? Will these individuals support her if she takes on a lesbian identity or if she begins a relationship with Karen?
- No need to label her feelings toward Karen, but certainly an option for Debbie.
- Explore her feelings and the importance she places on relationships in general.
- Explore sexual identity and its meaning.
- Establish her counseling goals.
- Help her explore her options for being in relationship with Karen.
- Are there any cultural differences to consider?

Roleplay #2, Chapter 4, Counseling Lesbian Women

Susan, age 46, has come to see you for help. She has been in a relationship with Ellen, age 42, for the past 10 years. Susan was previously married to a man and she has two teenage boys (Mark and Shane) from that marriage, ages 14 and 16. The boys live with Susan and Ellen, and it has become difficult for them to take Mark and Shane out with them. Mark and Shane feel embarrassed to be seen with them. Many people assume Susan and Ellen are lesbian because they fit many of the stereotypes, not to mention they are somewhat demonstrative in public. In addition to this, Susan tells you that she has not been sexually intimate with Ellen for 2 years and she wants to re-establish a sex life with her.

- Normalize Susan's plight with teenagers' embarrassment.
- Normalize children's reactions to not wanting to be with their parents at their age.
- Empower Susan to talk to her children about how she feels when they do not want to be seen with her and Ellen in public.
- Consider family counseling to deal with Mark's and Shane's embarrassment. How do they feel about mom and Ellen?
- Explore reason behind embarrassment—homophobia or developmental? How did they react in the past?
- Explore possible options or compromises regarding family outings. Perhaps less demonstrative in public?
- For family counseling, ensure biological father does not have joint legal custody (if so, you need his permission to do counseling involving the boys).
- History of what happened to their sex life. Is the chemistry between them still there?
- Consider couples counseling.
- Sex therapy—help them re-establish a sex life. Can do some work with Susan alone if Ellen won't come in for counseling as well.
- Bibliotherapy.
- Explore Susan's feelings about her sons' behavior and her relationship with them. Is she feeling guilty or hurt? Are they close?
- History of how Mark and Shane have reacted in the past. Has this been a consistent problem or is it recent?
- Help Susan to prioritize her issues.
- Clarify what Susan (and Ellen) mean when they refer to "having sex."
- Clarify counseling goals.

Roleplay #3, Chapter 4, Counseling Lesbian Youth

Kyla, age 15, has come to see you for help. Her mother has recently become aware that Kyla is having a sexual relationship with Sharon, a 22-year-old open lesbian woman. Kyla tells you that her mom hasn't told her dad because she is concerned about his reaction. Kyla's mom believes Sharon has "recruited" Kyla into this lifestyle, and she wants their relationship to end immediately. If Kyla doesn't act, she will be told to leave home. Although Kyla could live with Sharon, she doesn't want to because of what her peers at school will think. Kyla hasn't told anybody at school about her relationship.

- Informed consent—From mom or dad, but if parents are separated or divorced, do parents have joint legal custody? If so, you need permission from both to counsel Kyla.
- Is Kyla safe at home right now? Assess for safety.
- Avoid labeling Kyla or her relationship—may well be an exploration.
- Help her explore her relationship with Sharon—what meaning does it have for her?
- Consider family counseling with mom involved at least. Is mom really going to kick her out? Perhaps she can be helped to understand the situation better. If Kyla won't end relationship and mom is adamant, may need to look at other living arrangements for Kyla.
- Assess affectional orientation—look at crushes, attractions, and so forth.
- How does Kyla define herself? Is she aware that her sexuality may be fluid and changeable?
- Legal—Note: The age of consent for engaging in sexual relations in all U.S. states is between 16 and 18. See www.ageofconsent.us/ for state-specific details. Some states and all Canadian jurisdictions also have age gap provisions for those under the age of consent. In Canada, the age of consent is 16. Age of consent in some places is higher for individuals engaging in same-gender as opposed to opposite-gender sexual relations (e.g., age of consent in Canada regarding consensual anal sex is 18). Consult to find out if there is a duty to report. See www.cbc.ca/canada/story/2008/05/01/crime-bill.html.
- Issue of not telling her friends—what does this represent (internalized homophobia, confusion, or anticipated reaction)?
- What social supports does Kyla have outside of immediate family?
- Explore options.

- Look for signs that there may be cultural or spiritual conflicts.
- Normalize that female sexuality is fluid and changeable.
- Find out everyone's bottom lines and help them negotiate.
- Normalize and reassure Kyla's parent(s).

Roleplay #4, Chapter 4, Counseling Lesbian Youth

Malani, age 16, has come to see you for help. She is really struggling with her deep attractions to girls and her absence of attraction to boys. Malani is Muslim, and her faith is not accepting of homosexual activity. Malani's parents have already got eyes on Ahmed, a guy they want her to marry eventually. Malani has met him, but she is not attracted to him. She is attracted to Ellen, a Caucasian 16-year-old in her class at school. Ellen has already shown interest in Malani and wants her to come over to her home when her parents aren't there. Malani is pretty sure that Ellen wants sex because she has told Malani that she has had sex with girls before. Malani's feelings of guilt are eating her up and she feels desperate.

- Informed consent—From mom or dad, but if parents are separated or divorced, do parents have joint legal custody? If so, you need permission from both to counsel Malani.
- Assess physical and emotional safety—Is she potentially suicidal?
- Learn more about her family—What if her parents find out? How traditional are they?
- What does her faith mean to her? Explore this. Perhaps consult with someone of Muslim faith.
- Multicultural sensitivity—Learn more about her culture and its influence in her life.
- Help her to avoid labeling—her attractions may shift. Adolescents are highly impressionable.
- Normalize—Help her accept her feelings regardless of whether she decides she can act upon them.
- Explore her guilt—is it faith based or coming from other sources?
- Exploration of her affectional orientation. Previous crushes/relationships?
- Encourage Malani to defer having sex with Ellen because of the conflict she feels between her opposing values.
- Explain that there are often differences in what the scriptures say and in the adopted practices.
- What is Malani's *bottom line*? Is Malani able to compartmentalize her life and keep her orientation quiet from her family?
- Assess and treat for internalized homophobia.
- Explore options—Look at whether it is best for Malani to wait until she is of age to move out before disclosing.
- How much support does Malani have in her life?
- Explore her sexual identity.
- Encourage Malani to come back for another session regardless of what she does or does not do with Ellen.

Roleplay #1, Chapter 5, Counseling Bisexual Men

Robert, age 28, has come to see you for help. He has been in a relationship with Sara, age 24, for the past 4 years, and although he loves her, he craves sex with men periodically and goes out and gets it. Sara believes they are monogamous, as this has always been their understanding. Robert doesn't want to lose Sara, but he knows she will not accept his outside sexual behavior. The longest Robert has been able to hold off on having sex with men is about 2 weeks. If he doesn't get it, he starts feeling depressed and deprived.

- Cheating—Robert is cheating—should he stay with Sara or leave? When does he intend to tell her about this behavior? Perhaps he needs to end relationship because of "a conflict with his personal values."
- Affectional orientation exploration—what does his sex with men represent? Is it just sex or is it fulfilling other emotional needs? Is being with Sara simply disguising a same-sex affectional orientation? Why isn't he having sex with other women?
- Exploration of his identity—What does he define as? Does the self-definition cause him conflict?
- Explore compulsive nature—emphasize he has choice over his sexual behavior. Help him realize that sex is not a need. Explore his depression in this context.
- Explore his relationship and sexual history. Has he cheated on previous partners? Explore relationship with Sara—what is not working?

- Sexual risk assessment. Explore his sexual practices with men—what type of sex is he engaging in? What precautions is he taking?
- Encourage STD testing and explore risk to Sara re STDs.
- Decide on whether you will continue working with Robert if his intent is to continue cheating.
- Consider couples counseling.
- Normalize bisexuality as an identity and affectional orientation but that behavior is still a choice.
- Empathy assessment—does Robert have empathy for Sara? What would it be like if the situation were reversed?
- What is the bottom line for Robert?
- Values clarification—What does it mean for Robert to be in a committed relationship? What place does monogamy have in what he values about long-term relationships?
- Influences—explore the influence of family and peers (who are the boys he is having sex with; ages)?
- Explore options.
- Education—(e.g., teach Robert that open relationships can work if they are honest and consensual).
- Explore for internalized homophobia.
- What is his goal(s) for counseling?
- What social supports does Robert have?

Roleplay #2, Chapter 5, Counseling Bisexual Men

Adam, age 45, has come to see you for help. He has been with James for 6 months, a 40-year-old gay man who has been out for nearly 20 years. Adam used to be married to Nancy, but their marriage ended 8 years ago after Adam told Nancy that he wanted to start having sex with other people, including both men and women. As Adam dealt with his issues in a mature, responsible, and honest manner, Nancy and he maintained a good friendship following their marriage dissolution.

James, however, has started telling Adam how jealous he is of the time he spends with Nancy and some of his other female friends. James believes Adam will have sex with these women because Adam defines himself as bisexual. In fact, there are times when he has had sex with women behind James's back. You find out that Adam does want an open relationship with James but doesn't know how to broach the subject.

- Sexual risk assessment. Is he practicing safer sex ALL of the time? Emphasize it as he may be putting James at risk.
- Explore Adam's feelings toward his cheating behavior. Does he feel guilty? Help Adam to see James's point of view—is he able to empathize with James?
- Encourage Adam to stop having sex outside the relationship until or unless James agrees with it.
- Explore Adam's previous relationships. Have they been open? Has he cheated in the past?
- Suggest that Adam bring James in for couples counseling.
- Explore James's knowledge of and feelings toward open relationships.
- Explore whether either scenario (open or closed) is a deal-breaker for either Adam or James.
- Options—Explore whether Adam still wants to have a relationship with James.
- What is Adam's goal for counseling?
- Explore Adam's relationship with James.
- Social-skills training may be needed.
- Education—(e.g., teach Adam about open relationships).
- Work with Adam focused on building integrity.
- Help him find a support system (e.g., perhaps a bisexual support network).

Roleplay #1, Chapter 6, Counseling Bisexual Women

Maggie, a Black woman aged 20, has come to see you for help. She has been aware of her interest in both men and women for several years, and she has had sexual relations with both sexes as well. Her heterosexual friends and lesbian friends alike are threatened by her middle position and they pressure her to take one side or the other. Most of her lesbian friends they tell her she is really a lesbian and that she is just trying to hang on to some remnant of a heterosexual identity. On the other hand, she finds that most of her Black heterosexual friends refuse to believe her interest in women is real, and they tell her to grow up and find a man. Mostly Maggie is confused by her dual attractions. She is also seeing you because she feels rejected by both the heterosexual community and the lesbian community. She rarely gets invited to anyone's home.

- Explore sexual identity confusion further. How does she define herself?
- Explore affectional orientation confusion further. What components of affectional orientation go out to men and women (perhaps use Alderson's sexuality questionnaire here)?
- Explore the meaning of her friendships—do none accept her as she is?
- Encourage her to help her friends understand her better. Provide assertiveness training if necessary.
- Reframe her problem as her friends being biphobic and its resultant feelings of isolation and rejection.
- Resources for bisexual people, either in the community or online.
- Help her find a bisexual community nearby or online.
- Bibliotherapy.
- Provide validation for a bisexual identity.
- Romantic partner—Question Maggie about the person she would like to see herself with. Explore the person's characteristics that she falls in love with.
- What supports are there in the Black community? In the lesbian community? What social supports does she have—friends and family—whether inside these communities or external to them?
- Assess for whether there may be other reasons for why this is happening. Maybe Maggie is a very difficult person to be around.
- Get her relationship history and friendship history.
- Assess all influences affecting Maggie.
- Normalize her experience.
- Help her explore her options.
- Discuss malleability/fluidity of female sexuality.
- Explore internalized homophobia.

Roleplay #2, Chapter 6, Counseling Bisexual Women

Janis, age 35, has come to see you for help. She has been an active member of the lesbian community for the past 15 years. Her 12-year relationship with Emma (age 43) has been fairly positive and fulfilling, but like several long-term relationships, it has had its ups and downs. While Emma was away on a 2-week business trip, Janis went out dancing to a mixed (both gay and heterosexual) club and found herself being seduced by Clint, a handsome 40-year-old businessman. The two of them spent some time together every night together during Emma's absence, having sex following the third date. Shocking to Janis, she found herself developing strong feelings of attachment for Clint and craving more and more sex. After Emma returned, Janis has found herself making excuses why she is out some nights, spending that time secretively with Clint. She is seeing you because she doesn't know what to do.

- Sexual identity confusion—how do her feelings for Clint threaten her identity?
- Affectional orientation confusion—what components of affectional orientation are being expressed with Clint? Which ones are not? How would it matter if Clint were a woman instead?
- Explore options—leave Emma or stay with her? If she wants to stay, what will she do about Clint?
- Explore history of her lesbian identity.
- Explore her relationship with Emma, including sex life and their history together. What are the issues that explain why she has sought another relationship?
- Consider couples counseling.
- Cheating and the problem of continuing to deceive Emma. How would she feel if the situation were reversed? What values are in conflict for Janis? Is this a time she should be confiding in her long-term partner?
- Is she practicing safer sex with Clint?
- Normalize that women's sexuality tends to be more fluid than men's. Also that it is common to develop feelings for others.
- In what ways is her identifying as lesbian or being a part of the lesbian community being challenged?
- Gather more information about Clint. Why is he in this?
- Help her find a support network (e.g., bisexual community).
- What are Janis's goals in counseling?
- Normalize bed death as common with lesbian couples.

Roleplay #1, Chapter 7. Counseling Crossdressing Individuals

George, age 48, has come to see you for help. George has crossdressed since he was 12 years old. No one has ever caught him doing this, despite the fact that he used to go out in public when he was single. The problem began 4 years into his marriage with Claire (age 41) after she discovered his female clothing in their basement closet. That was 6 years ago. Although Claire got her head around the fact that George would dress up when she was away from home, George began insisting that he wear female clothing whenever he is at home and that she would have to get used to it. Claire did, and for the past 2 years, George often dresses as a woman at home.

George tells you that he has taken this a step further. For the past year, he has insisted that he have sex with Claire while dressed as a woman. Claire reluctantly complied but declared 2 weeks ago that she married him as a man and that she only wants to have sex with him as a man from now on. She will not tolerate any more of his crossdressing at home or while they have sex. He is quite distraught about her "change of heart."

- Get a history of George's crossdressing behavior. Have any other previous partners known about his desire to crossdress? Does his crossdressing always involve masturbation? Does he crossdress in public?
- Does he have anyone in his life who is supportive of his behavior? If not, encourage involvement in the crossdressing community.
- Normalize his behavior.
- What does George want? Explore if he has ever been interested in ideally being a woman.
- Consider couples counseling.
- Explore relationship history. Is crossdressing about taking control over his partner's wishes?
- Give-and-take. Claire has been supportive of George's desire to crossdress, even while he has escalated his behaviors without any negotiation with her. Present George with Claire's perspective—how does she feel about all of the changes in her husband? Help George have empathy for Claire's feelings.
- What is the bottom line for both George and Claire? Assess if there is a possibility of negotiation of boundaries around crossdressing. Discuss options.
- Help George develop empathy for Claire.
- Assess that George is not a nonhomosexual male-to-female transsexual individual.
- Is he still capable of having sex without crossdressing?
- What are the goals of counseling?
- Education—(e.g., crossdressing behavior increases with stress).
- Bibliotherapy.
- Explore if George's feelings of stress are his own or if they are associated with Claire's demands regarding his crossdressing.

Roleplay #2, Chapter 7. Counseling Crossdressing Individuals

Herb, age 39, has come to see you for help. He is having terrible feelings of guilt because he finds that he only gets sexually aroused when he is dressed as a woman. Herb is disgusted by this, but he feels compelled to dress up nonetheless before he masturbates. He is single and would love to be in a relationship with a woman but fears that he could not get involved with someone while this is going on in his life. Besides this, he wonders if he should consider getting a sex change to "make things right."

- Assess whether there is substance to wanting to transition—more likely that he does not have a stable and persistent desire to become a woman. More a stress reaction to crossdressing. Does he have obsessive-compulsive disorder—if not, why is he "compelled"?
- Educate him about difference between crossdressing and transsexuality. Consider bibliotherapy.
- Explain the behavior is a fetish—it is associated with sexual excitement for him.
- Choice is his—attempt to eliminate fetish or own it? Some women will not mind he has this fetish (important to be honest about it, however).
- Normalize his experience. Reduce guilt about fetish, regardless of what he wants to do about it. This may involve reducing transphobia.
- Take history of his crossdressing behavior. Was it always associated with sexual excitement?

- If eliminating fetish, attempt shaping (perhaps begin with reducing amount of female clothing worn during masturbation, then looking at female clothing while masturbating without wearing it, etc.). Have him work on changing his sexual fantasies (less and less clothing focus). Try sex toys.
- Assess for medication or drug use that may be affecting his sexual ability.
- Consider a support group, online or in person.
- Does Herb have other relationship issues besides crossdressing? One might suspect so given that he is 39. What is his relationship history?
- Diagnose. Does Herb have obsessive-compulsive disorder or another mental disorder? Why does he feel compelled?
- Assess if Herb is a fetishistic crossdressing individual or a nonhomosexual male-to-female individual.
- Bibliotherapy.
- What is Herb's relationship with his penis? Does he want it removed?
- Assess Herb's sexual identity.
- Ask him to explain the consequences of transitioning (e.g., hormones) to you.

Roleplay #1, Chapter 8. Counseling MTF Individuals

Scott, age 23, has come to see you for help. Scott is very feminine in his mannerisms and his gender role, and you soon discover he has thought of himself as predominantly a girl since age 10. His sexual interest is in other men. He tells you he wants to become a woman. He confides in you that he always hated his penis and often wishes it were gone. Your inner sense is that Scott is quite unstable at this time and you have concern that he may self-injure.

- Risk assessment—how likely is he to hurt himself? Is he suicidal?
- Explain process to him: 3 months minimum therapy, hormone therapy (either by your referral to a physician or wait until assessed by psychiatrist), 12 months real-life test, sex reassignment surgery.
- Assess for other possibilities—schizophrenia, bipolar, dissociative identity disorder. Assess that he is not simply gay with extreme internal homophobia.
- Gather a complete history regarding his desire to become female. Check for signs of cross-gender interests and persistent cross-gender identity. To qualify, he needs to show a persistent and stable desire to transition. How often does he masturbate while crossdressed?
- Consider talking to those who know him to confirm a long-stated desire to transition (especially if you are recommending hormone therapy yourself).
- Review relationship history.
- Why does he hate his penis? Explore.
- Recognize that often transwomen are very persistent and want everything to change NOW.
- Bibliotherapy.
- Normalize his feelings. Many others have felt this way.
- Assess psychosocial supports. Regardless of current support, refer to a support group or online resources for transpeople. Community connection is important.
- What does he see his transition looking like when it comes to his feelings, his outward appearance, and his transitioning around friends and family? Does he see that going smoothly? Plan around how he will start the transition.
- Ask him to explain the consequences of transitioning (e.g., hormones).
- Rule out intersex conditions.
- Work within your areas of competence—outsource assessment (i.e., the gatekeeper function) if needed or desired.
- What is his sexual identity?
- What is his affectional orientation?
- Help Scott get in touch with the emotional component of wanting to be a woman.

Roleplay #1, Chapter 8. Counseling MTF Individuals

Tina, age 65, has come to see you for help. Tina had sexual reassignment surgery 10 years ago and soon after discovered she was HIV positive. Now that she has retired, she has decided that she wishes to pursue a long-term relationship with Julio, a 70-year-old man she has known platonically for a few months. She wonders if she should tell him that she is both a transsexual and HIV positive. She believes her chance of giving Julio the virus is very low.

- Normalize her feelings. Many others have not wanted to tell their partners, either.
- Gather a complete relationship history from Tina. Has she been dishonest in major areas of her life with previous partners—why or why not? As a transwoman, does Tina live stealth, or is she honest about being trans with most people?
- Explore with Tina the pros and cons of telling and not telling Julio her transsexual status. Recall that most experts believe it is better to tell the partner.
- Education—Help Tina to see that she still poses a risk to Julio and he can indeed become infected with HIV from her.
- Know the law in this area—in some jurisdictions, it is illegal to *not* inform a sexual partner if you are HIV positive.
- Why is she now looking for a long-term relationship? Has anything changed in her life to make this switch? What is her idea of a long-term relationship, and is being honest part of that? What type of relationship is she wanting to develop: platonic or sexual?
- If the relationship she desires is sexual, what types of sexual activities is she interested in? Why does she believe the chance of giving Julio the virus is low? Discuss safer-sex practices.
- Help Tina develop empathy for Julio. Has he done anything to make her think that she couldn't tell him? How would you feel if you ended up transmitting the virus to Julio? If the situation were reversed, would you want him to tell you if he was HIV positive? What are Julio's values? What kind of culture is he a part of? Sexism, racism, and political leanings may give more insight on how he might react.
- What is Tina's support system like? Will she have people to fall back on if things do not work out the way she is hoping?
- Refer Tina to her HIV clinic or specialist for information about the impact that viral loads and CD4 counts can have on increased/decreased risk of transmission of the HIV virus.
- Explore if Tina's anxiety is partly related to her own internalized transphobia.

Roleplay #1, Chapter 9. Counseling Transmen

Becky, age 31, has come to see you for help. She has felt more like a boy ever since she can remember. However, she has some doubt whether she should pursue sex reassignment surgery. She knows that the surgery to construct a penis is difficult and that many transmen are unhappy with the common complications and the surgical result. She is interested sexually in women only. Nonetheless, she is desperately unhappy as a woman and constantly thinks about how much she hates her breasts and her vagina.

- Explain process to her: 3 months minimum therapy, hormone therapy (either by your referral to a physician or wait until assessed by psychiatrist), 12 months real-life test, sex reassignment surgery.
- Assess for other possibilities—schizophrenia, bipolar, dissociative identity disorder.
- Gather a complete history regarding her desire to become male. Check for signs of cross-gender interests and persistent cross-gender identity. To qualify, she needs to show a persistent and stable desire to transition.
- Consider talking to those who know her to confirm a long-stated desire to transition (especially if you are recommending hormone therapy yourself).
- Review relationship history.
- Bibliotherapy or online resources.
- Normalize her feelings. Many others have felt this way.
- Assess support system—refer to a support group or online resources for transpeople regardless.
- Affirm her concern about the surgery—many are waiting for this reason.
- She could consider hormone replacement therapy and having breast reconstruction (making breasts look like male pecs).
- Suicide risk assessment.
- Explore if Becky ever wants to have a child. Will this affect her desire to transition in any way? Should she consider having her eggs stored?
- Affectional orientation change. This may occur, but it is more commonly experienced by male-to-female transsexual individuals.
- Enhance current comfort—ask what she is doing right now to make her feel more comfortable in her body (for example, binding her breasts, wearing certain clothes).
- Ask her to explain the consequences of transitioning (e.g., hormones) to you.

- "COM": Work within your areas of competence—outsource assessment (i.e., the gatekeeper function) if needed or desired.
- Assess sexual identity.
- Assess affectional orientation.
- Find out is she is currently assuming the male role in aspects of her life—which aspects?
- What is it that she hates about her breasts and her vagina?
- What is her goal(s) for counseling?
- Explore options—look at the pros and cons of having surgery.
- What does she believe her life would be like following surgery?

Roleplay #2, Chapter 9. Counseling Transmen

Laura, age 21, has come to see you for help. Laura has always known that she was supposed to be born a boy, but it didn't happen that way. She is desperate to be in a relationship and cannot imagine a life of remaining single. She believes she would rather be dead than spend the rest of her life devoid of a long-term committed relationship. Laura wants to pursue sex reassignment surgery. Her sexual interests are exclusively toward men—heterosexual men, that is.

- Major problem—she is only interested in heterosexual men, but she will become a man if she transitions! Explore Laura's vision of how it would work to be a man and yet attract a heterosexual man.
- Another major problem—alas, gay men will not be that interested, either.
- Encourage her to get to know gay men, perhaps by going to the gay bar.
- Explain process to her: 3 months minimum therapy, hormone therapy (either by your referral to a physician or wait until assessed by psychiatrist), 12 months real-life test, sex reassignment surgery.
- Assess for other possibilities—schizophrenia, bipolar, dissociative identity disorder.
- Gather a complete history regarding her desire to become male. Check for signs of cross-gender interests and persistent cross-gender identity. To qualify, she needs to show a persistent and stable desire to transition.
- Consider talking to those who know her to confirm a long-stated desire to transition (especially if you are recommending hormone therapy yourself).
- Review relationship history.
- Bibliotherapy or online resources.
- Refer to a support group or online resources for transpeople.
- If she cannot face a life without a romantic relationship, she may not be a good candidate for sex change.
- Suicide risk assessment. Why is she desperate? Why would she rather be dead? How serious is she?
- What is her *bottom line*?—transitioning or a relationship?
- Has she ever wanted children? How will she reconcile this with transitioning?
- Affectional orientation change. This may occur, but it is more commonly experienced by male-to-female transsexual individuals.
- Normalize her experience and her confusion.
- Assess affectional orientation.
- Ask her to explain the consequences of transitioning (e.g., hormones) to you.
- What does she believe life will be like following surgery?
- What will sex look like postsurgery?

Roleplay #1, Chapter 10. Counseling Intersex Individuals

Tabitha, age 18, has come to see you for help. Most of the other grade 12 girls in her school have started dating, and Tabitha feels desperate to start herself. She is very self-conscious, however, as she has tells you she has a significantly enlarged clitoris and is lacking labia because of a "birth defect." She makes it clear that she does not want to talk further about her physical condition.

- Respect Tabitha's desire to not talk about her physical condition.
- Normalize DSD. Explain to her that you are somewhat knowledgeable about DSD and you know that divergent individuals often enjoy stable and enduring adult relationships.
- Normalize the dating experience. Explain that many people, especially when younger, experience many short relationships as they learn about

themselves. Many desire to not settle down with one person early in the dating process.

- Is Tabitha interested in boys, girls, or both?
- Look at her parent's view of dating—are they supportive of her beginning dating?
- Explore her history regarding her reactions to her physical differences. How has she coped up until this point?
- Help Tabitha see the range of potential dating behaviors: which ones would be okay for her in the initial stages of dating?
- As dating progressed to the point where her physical differences would become obvious, roleplay with her ways that she could inform her boyfriend/girlfriend.
- Help her develop coping strategies for whatever the outcome of this conversation.
- Help her develop coping strategies for engaging in sexual activity and the possible outcomes.
- If relevant, explore with her possibilities for plastic surgery eventually.

Roleplay #2, Chapter 10. Counseling Intersex Individuals

Mannix, age 55, has come to see you for help. He tells you that he has never had a relationship before and feels extremely lonely. He blurts out that he is interested in men but that he does not define as gay. Mannix believes he ought to have been born a woman and was even assessed when he was in his mid-20s at a gender clinic for transsexuality. He was told then that he was not a candidate for sex reassignment surgery, although the details were never explained to him. It strikes you that he if did transition, he would likely be a physically unattractive woman. As you ask about his medical history, you find out that he has Klinefelter syndrome.

- Fully explore Mannix's history, including medical. What is the closest he has come to having a relationship? Has he at least dated others, and if so, men, women, or both?
- Look further at his not defining as gay. Is internalized homophobia a factor? If so, it should be worked on in counseling.
- What has prevented him from dating and/or attempting to establish a relationship? Are there behavioral interventions that might help him date and/or establish a relationship?
- Assess for whether Mannix fits the criteria for gender identity disorder. If he does, how severe is the gender dysphoria? Does his GID warrant referral to a gender clinic? Are you qualified to work with individuals who have GID?
- Normalize his feelings. There is evidence suggesting that gender dysphoria is more common with those who have Klinefelter syndrome.
- Has he ever dressed as a woman? How convincing does he believe he looks? How attractive does he view himself to be? What could be done to increase his attractiveness (e.g., makeup, clothing style, hairstyle)? If he qualified for transitioning and wanted to do so, what surgical procedures could improve his attractiveness?
- Can he afford sex reassignment surgery?
- What resources are there in the community?

APPENDIX C

Sexuality Questionnaire

Kevin Alderson, Ph.D. © 2012

1. TODAY'S DATE: ____________________
2. AGE: _____
3. BIOLOGICAL SEX: Male ____ Female ____ Intersex _____
4. GENDER (i.e., aside from your biological sex, this refers to the extent you actually **view** yourself as a male or a female):

5.	Male RATINGS: 0 = Zero or none 1 = Unsure 2 = Low 3 = Moderate 4 = High	NO 0	UNSUR 1	LOW 2	MOD 3	HIGH 4
6.	Female RATINGS: 0 = Zero or none 1 = Unsure 2 = Low 3 = Moderate 4 = High	NO 0	UNSUR 1	LOW 2	MOD 3	HIGH 4

7. GENDER ROLE (i.e., this refers to what extent you see yourself as **behaving** in traditionally masculine and/or feminine ways):

8.	Masculine RATINGS: 0 = Zero or none 1 = Unsure 2 = Low 3 = Moderate 4 = High	NO 0	UNSUR 1	LOW 2	MOD 3	HIGH 4
9.	Feminine RATINGS: 0 = Zero or none 1 = Unsure 2 = Low 3 = Moderate 4 = High	NO 0	UNSUR 1	LOW 2	MOD 3	HIGH 4

10. EDUCATIONAL LEVEL COMPLETED (circle or check whichever answer is closest):

a. Less than high school	b. High school graduate	c. One year full-time post-secondary	d. Two years full-time post-secondary
e. Three years full-time post-secondary	f. Baccalaureate degree completed	g. Master's degree completed	h. Doctoral degree completed

11. RELIGION:

a. Protestant	b. Catholic	c. Christian—Unspecified	d. Jewish
e. Mormon	f. Jehovah's Witness	g. Muslim	h. Hindu
i. Buddhist	j. Native	k. Spiritual, no label	l. Atheist
m. Agnostic	n. Other (please specify)		

12. CITIZENSHIP:

a. American	b. Canadian	c. South American	d. European
e. Asian	f. African	g. Australian	h. Other (please specify)

13. ARE YOU:

a. White/Caucasian	b. African American, African Canadian, or Black African	c. Aboriginal (American Indian)
d. Native Hawaiian or Pacific Islander	e. Hispanic (Latino)	f. Southeast Asian
g. Arab/Middle Eastern	h. South Asian (Indian or Pakistani)	i. Mixed Race
j. Other (please specify)		

Please answer the following two questions **BEFORE** turning the page.

14.	The questions that follow pertain to various aspects of human sexuality, including opposite-gender and same-gender attractions, behaviors, and affections. How comfortable do you think it will be for you to answer these questions? RATINGS: 0 = No comfort 1 = Unsure 2 = Low comfort 3 = Moderate comfort 4 = High comfort	NO UNSUR LOW MOD HIGH 0 1 2 3 4 COMFORT
15.	How confident in ability do you feel about answering the questions that follow? RATINGS: 0 = No confidence 1 = Unsure 2 = Low confidence 3 = Moderate confidence 4 = High confidence	NO UNSUR LOW MOD HIGH 0 1 2 3 4 CONFIDENCE

The following questions pertain to the magnitude of your opposite-gender and same-gender interests. To what extent have you experienced the following during the two time periods indicated?

SEXUAL ATTRACTION—This refers to feeling sexually aroused by someone you find attractive.

		MAGNITUDE [Use the following ratings]: 0 = Zero or none 1 = Unsure 2 = Low 3 = Moderate 4 = High									
		INTEREST IN MALES/MEN					INTEREST IN FEMALES/WOMEN				
#	ITEM	ZERO	UNSUR	LOW	MOD	HIGH	ZERO	UNSUR	LOW	MOD	HIGH
16.	During the past 12 months	0	1	2	3	4	0	1	2	3	4
17.	*During ages 12 to 19 (*NOTE: If you are currently 19 years of age or younger, complete this question from ages 12 to a year ago. Follow this same procedure in all subsequent sections.)	0	1	2	3	4	0	1	2	3	4

SEXUAL FANTASIES—This refers to your sexual fantasies experienced during either masturbation or during sex with a partner.

		MAGNITUDE [Use the following ratings]: 0 = Zero or none 1 = Unsure 2 = Low 3 = Moderate 4 = High									
		INTEREST IN MALES/MEN					INTEREST IN FEMALES/WOMEN				
#	ITEM	ZERO	UNSUR	LOW	MOD	HIGH	ZERO	UNSUR	LOW	MOD	HIGH
18.	During the past 12 months	0	1	2	3	4	0	1	2	3	4
19.	*During ages 12 to 19	0	1	2	3	4	0	1	2	3	4

SEXUAL PREFERENCE—This refers to your preference for having male and/or female **sexual** partners.

		MAGNITUDE [Use the following ratings]: 0 = Zero or none 1 = Unsure 2 = Low 3 = Moderate 4 = High									
		INTEREST IN MALES/MEN					INTEREST IN FEMALES/WOMEN				
#	ITEM	ZERO	UNSUR	LOW	MOD	HIGH	ZERO	UNSUR	LOW	MOD	HIGH
20.	During the past 12 months	0	1	2	3	4	0	1	2	3	4
21.	*During ages 12 to 19	0	1	2	3	4	0	1	2	3	4

PROPENSITY TO FALL IN LOVE ROMANTICALLY—This refers to your natural **inclination** to have crushes and fall in love romantically with males and/or females.

		MAGNITUDE [Use the following ratings]: 0 = Zero or none 1 = Unsure 2 = Low 3 = Moderate 4 = High									
		INTEREST IN MALES/MEN					INTEREST IN FEMALES/WOMEN				
#	ITEM	ZERO	UNSUR	LOW	MOD	HIGH	ZERO	UNSUR	LOW	MOD	HIGH
22.	During the past 12 months	0	1	2	3	4	0	1	2	3	4
23.	*During ages 12 to 19	0	1	2	3	4	0	1	2	3	4

BEING IN LOVE ROMANTICALLY—This refers to how often you have **actually** felt romantic love (liking the person, having chemistry or feelings of lust toward this person, and feeling some degree of commitment toward this individual).

		MAGNITUDE [Use the following ratings]: 0 = none 1 = unsure 2 = rarely 3 = occasionally 4 = frequently									
		INTEREST IN MALES/MEN					INTEREST IN FEMALES/WOMEN				
#	ITEM	NONE	UNSUR	RAR	OCC	FREQ	NONE	UNSUR	RAR	OCC	FREQ
24.	During the past 12 months	0	1	2	3	4	0	1	2	3	4
25.	*During ages 12 to 19	0	1	2	3	4	0	1	2	3	4

SEXUAL PARTNERS—This refers to how often you have had sexual partners who are male and/or female. [NOTE: "sexual partner" refers to anyone you have engaged in penetrative sexual acts with, including oral, vagina, and anal sex.]

		MAGNITUDE [Use the following ratings]: 0 = none 1 = unsure 2 = rarely 3 = occasionally 4 = frequently									
		INTEREST IN MALES/MEN					INTEREST IN FEMALES/WOMEN				
#	ITEM	NONE	UNSUR	RAR	OCC	FREQ	NONE	UNSUR	RAR	OCC	FREQ
26.	During the past 12 months	0	1	2	3	4	0	1	2	3	4
27.	*During ages 12 to 19	0	1	2	3	4	0	1	2	3	4

SELF-IDENTIFICATION—This refers to your own self-identification.

To what extent do you, and did you, think of yourself using the following terms?

Use the following ratings for the next seven questions:

0 = Zero or none 1 = Unsure 2 = Low 3 = Moderate 4 = High

		DURING THE PAST 12 MONTHS					*DURING AGES 12 TO 19				
Please answer each question.		ZERO	UNSUR	LOW	MOD	HIGH	ZERO	UNSUR	LOW	MOD	HIGH
28.	Heterosexual	0	1	2	3	4	0	1	2	3	4
29.	Bisexual	0	1	2	3	4	0	1	2	3	4
30.	Gay or Lesbian	0	1	2	3	4	0	1	2	3	4
31.	Queer	0	1	2	3	4	0	1	2	3	4
32.	Transsexual	0	1	2	3	4	0	1	2	3	4
33.	I do *not* (or did *not*) use a label	0	1	2	3	4	0	1	2	3	4
34.	Other (please specify)	0	1	2	3	4	0	1	2	3	4
Use the following ratings for the next question: 0 = unsure 1 = very uncomfortable 2 = uncomfortable 3 = comfortable 4 = very comfortable											
35.	To what extent are you, and were you, comfortable with your self-identification label(s) [Q. 28–34 above]?	0	1	2	3	4	0	1	2	3	4
Identity Labels		**PRIMARY**					**SECONDARY**				
36.	If you could only use one primary label and up to one secondary label to define your **present** sexuality to another person, which label(s) would you choose? Please fill in the blanks to the right. →						[NOTE: Only fill in this blank if you **actually use** a secondary label to define your sexuality.]				

Graphing Affectional Orientation

Place an "X" in the appropriate squares below [i.e., "Sexual Attraction + Sexual Fantasies + Sexual Preference + Propensity to Fall in Love + Being in Love + Sexual Partners" (out of 24 max.)]:

Opposite-Sex Interests	**Past**	0	1	2	3	4	5	6	7	8	9	10	11	12	13	14	15	16	17	18	19	20	21	22	23	24
	0 – 12 = LOW Opposite-Sex Interests														**13 – 18 = MODERATE Opposite-Sex Interests**						**19 – 24 = HIGH Opposite-Sex Interests**					
	Present	0	1	2	3	4	5	6	7	8	9	10	11	12	13	14	15	16	17	18	19	20	21	22	23	24
Same-Sex Interests	**Present**	0	1	2	3	4	5	6	7	8	9	10	11	12	13	14	15	16	17	18	19	20	21	22	23	24
	0 – 12 = LOW Same-Sex Interests														**13 – 18 = MODERATE Same-Sex Interests**						**19 – 24 = HIGH Same-Sex Interests**					
	Past	0	1	2	3	4	5	6	7	8	9	10	11	12	13	14	15	16	17	18	19	20	21	22	23	24

Place an "X" in the appropriate squares for the most fitting primary and secondary labels for the two constructs below. *Affectional Orientation* refers to the clinician's or researcher's assessment of it from the present scores (from above chart), whereas *Self-Identification Label* refers to the respondent's own label(s) from question 36.

For the *Confidence and Comfort Scores*, write what their score means in the box to the right.

(e.g., for Q. 15, 0 = No confidence 1 = Unsure 2 = Low confidence 3 = Moderate confidence 4 = High confidence**).**

Affectional Orientation (From Above)				**Self-Identification Label (Question 36)**			
Primary		**Secondary**		**Primary**		**Secondary**	
Heterosexual		Heterosexual		Heterosexual		Heterosexual	
Bisexual		Bisexual		Bisexual		Bisexual	
Homosexual		Homosexual		Gay or Lesbian		Gay or Lesbian	
Confidence and Comfort Scores				Queer		Queer	
Confidence in Responding (Question 15)				Transsexual		Transsexual	
Comfort in Responding (Question 14)				No Label		No Label	
Comfort with Self-Identification (Question 35)				Other		Other	

Appendix D

The Sexual Orientation Counselor Competency Scale

Markus P. Bidell

The need for mental health professionals to provide culturally competent psychotherapeutic services is now well established. Multicultural counselor competency (MCC) initially focused on defining and assessing awareness, skill, and knowledge competencies specific to ethnic/racial minority populations (Sue, Arredondo, & McDavis, 1992). Drawing on the tridimensional MCC model, Bidell (2005) developed the Sexual Orientation Counselor Competency Scale (SOCCS) to assess the attitude, skill, and knowledge of counselors working with LGB clients. The SOCCS focuses on sexual orientation and *not* gender identity. Because sexual orientation and gender identity present important differences, counselors and psychologists need to develop distinctive competencies regarding transgender clients. To date, no instrument has been published specifically focusing on transgender counselor competency, and the lack of such research is a serious problem (Bidell, 2005; Carroll & Gilroy, 2002).

Sexual orientation counselor competency includes attitudinal, knowledge, and skill competencies needed to work effectively with LGB clients. The attitudinal component consists of personal beliefs about LGB individuals that include heterosexist, biased, and stereotypic assumptions regarding individuals that are LGB. Knowledge competencies include social, political, and legal issues facing this minority group. LGB clinical skills include experience with assessment and LGB-affirmative supervision and counseling as well as case conceptualization and treatment planning. The establishment of the SOCCS addresses the relative absence of LGB theory-based research and instrumentation (Bidell, 2005).

Development and Psychometric Assessment of the SOCCS

Examining previous multicultural counselor competency instrumentation literature (see Dunn, Smith, & Montoya, 2006), the sampling procedures and psychometric evaluations of the SOCCS were developed. More than 300 ($N = 312$) mental health professionals were included in the sample (235 women, 77 men, mean age = 31.9 years). Participants included counseling and psychology students (64.5 %) as well as doctoral-level counselor educators and psychologists (35.5%) recruited from 13 public and 3 private universities across the United States. Recruiting participants across the United States ensured a diverse sample with regard to sexual orientation (12.2% identified as LGB), and more than 30% were ethnic/racial minorities. All participants were given a demographic questionnaire, three instruments (Attitudes toward Lesbians and Gay Men Scale [ATLG], Multicultural Counseling Knowledge and Awareness Scale [MCKAS], and Counselor Self-Efficacy Scale [CSES]), and the initial 42-item SOCCS.

The original item pool for the SOCCS was developed from a comprehensive review of LGB and multicultural research and literature utilizing the rational-empirical approach (Dawis, 1987). A pool of 100 test items was produced that measured various competencies of counselors working with LGB clients. In addition, a focus group and two separate card-sort procedures were also conducted to develop and sort test items. This process reduced the original pool of 100 test items to 42 questions. Factor analysis and reliability testing, as well as criterion, convergent, and divergent validity assessment, were used to assess the standard psychometric properties of the SOCCS.

An exploratory factor analysis was conducted on the 42 original SOCCS items using principal-axis factoring procedures and oblique rotation. A priori decision rules included a minimum .35 item loading to be included in a factor, and each factor needed a minimum of four items. The factor analysis with the a priori decision rules yielded 29 questions and a three-factor solution that accounted for 40% of the total variance. The initial factor consisted of 11 test items that dealt with specific LGB counseling skills. It was labeled Skills and accounted for 24.91% of the variance (eigenvalue = 11.21). Comprising 10 items, the second factor was labeled Attitudes and examines a counselor's biases about LGB clients; it accounted for 9.66% of the variance (eigenvalue = 4.34). The final factor consisted of eight items and examined specific issues regarding LGB clients and mental health care. It was labeled Knowledge and accounted for 5.41% of the variance (eigenvalue = 2.43).

The factor analysis produced a final SOCCS instrument consisting of 29 questions, of which 11 are reverse scored. The SOCCS uses a seven-point scale ranging from 1 (*Not At All True*) to 7 (*Totally True*), with higher scores indicating greater levels of sexual orientation counselor competency. The overall SOCCS mean score (of the final 29 items) was 4.64 (SD = 0.89), with scores ranging from 2.52 to 6.90. The Skills subscale had a mean score of 2.94 (SD = 1.53), ranging from 1.00 to 6.91. The Attitudes subscale had scores ranging from 3.10 to 7.00 and an overall mean score of 6.49 (SD = 0.79). For the Knowledge subscale, the mean was 4.66 (SD = 1.05), with scores ranging from 1.63 to 6.88. The intercorrelations between subscales were relatively weak (.29 between Attitudes and Skills, .29 between Knowledge and Attitudes, and .45 between Knowledge and Skills). The coefficient alphas for the overall SOCCS as well as the Attitude, Skills, and Knowledge subscales were .90, .88, .91, and .76, respectively. Test–retest reliability (1-week) correlation coefficients were .84 for the overall SOCCS, .85 for the Attitudes subscale, .83 for the Skills subscale, and .84 for the Knowledge subscale.

Criterion validity for the SOCCS was established using participants' education level and sexual orientation, as these criteria would be expected to correlate with scores on the SOCCS. Compared with heterosexual respondents, LGB participants scored significantly higher on the overall SOCCS, $F(1, 301) = 30.14, p < .001$; on the Attitudes subscale, $F(1, 301) = 8.27, p < .005$; on the Skills subscale, $F(1, 301) = 29.12, p < .001$; and on the Knowledge subscale, $F(1, 301) = 8.80$, $p < .005$. The mean score for LGB respondents on the overall SOCCS was 5.33 (SD = .96) compared to 4.53 (SD = .82) for heterosexual participants. Education levels also established criterion validity. Compared to those with less education, participants who had higher levels of education scored significantly higher on the overall SOCCS, $F(3,308) = 75.10, p < .001$; on the Attitudes subscale, $F(3, 308) = 5.33, p < .001$; on the Skills subscale, $F(3, 308) = 107.82, p < .001$; and on the Knowledge subscale, $F(3, 308) = 25.62, p < .001$.

The overall mean SOCCS score was 4.03 (*SD* = .39) for undergraduates, 4.63 (*SD* = .74) for master's-level students, 4.85 (*SD* = .72) for doctoral-level students, and 5.84 (*SD* = .61) for doctoral-level psychologists and counselors.

The three subscales on the SOCCS demonstrated excellent convergent validity through strong correlation coefficients with established psychology instruments assessing similar constructs. The ATLG (Herek, 1998) assesses LGB bias and was used to validate the Awareness subscale of the SOCCS. Of the three subscales, the Attitudes subscale correlated the strongest with the ATLG scale, $r(312) = -.78$, $p < .01$. The MCKAS (Ponterotto et al., 2002), a scale that measures multicultural counselor competency with an emphasis on knowledge competencies, correlated the strongest with the MCKAS Knowledge subscale, $r(312) = .63$, $p < .01$. To validate the SOCCS's Skills subscale, the CSES (Melchert, Hays, Wiljanen, & Kolocek, 1996) was used, which measures counselors' perceptions regarding specific skills needed to be effective counselors. The SOCCS's Skill subscale correlated the strongest with the CSES, $r(312) = .65$, $p < .01$. In addition, divergent validity was explored by including three social desirability questions that examined impression management (see Paulhaus, 1991). A bivariate correlation between SOCCS scores and the mean social desirability cluster questions ($M = 1.19$, $SD = .59$) showed a weak association between the social desirability cluster and total SOCCS scores ($r = .27$).

The Utilization and Limitations of the SOCCS

Since its publication in 2005, the SOCCS has been utilized in plentiful dissertation research as well as national and international peer-reviewed studies. Doctoral students have utilized the SOCCS to examine the LGB competency of college counselors (Day, 2008), school counselors (Andrews, 2004), and graduate counseling students (Graham, 2009; Roberts, 2005), as well as examined the efficacy of counselor training programs (Frank, 2004) and LGB mental health professional workshops (Lewis, 2008). Graham's (2009) dissertation research explored LGB competency using the SOCCS with an impressive sample of 235 counseling and psychology graduate students from across the United States.

The reliability data reported by Graham (2009) is consistent with Bidell's (2005) coefficient alphas. The researcher reported Cronbach's Alpha for the overall SOCCS and the Awareness, Skills, and Knowledge subscale as .87, .91, .86, and .71, respectively. Graham (2009) reported mean scores on the overall SOCCS, Attitude, Skill, and Knowledge subscales (5.01, 6.52, 3.88, 4.67, respectively) that were consistent with those reported by Bidell (2005). Also similar, Graham (2009) found participants' Skill subscale scores to be the lowest overall. Bidell (2005) noted "skill competencies were over one third lower than knowledge and one half lower than awareness competencies" (p. 277). Graham's (2009) data support the beneficial role of education and training regarding sexual orientation counselor competency. She reported that students in her study reporting higher education levels or attendance at LGB workshops had significantly higher SOCCS scores. Also noteworthy, Graham (2009) found that counseling psychology students had higher SOCCS scores compared to counselor education participants.

The SOCCS is also gaining use as an outcome variable in peer-reviewed research. The SOCCS has been utilized to show the effectiveness of various forms of training, including LGB workshops for postgraduate psychology students (Fell, Mattiske, & Riggs, 2008); a British integrative counseling program (Grove, 2009); a counselor education program in the United States (Rutter, Estrada, Ferguson, & Diggs, 2008); and a study comparing school and community/agency counselors (Bidell, 2012). Utilizing the SOCCS, Henke, Carlson, and McGeorge (2009) explored the connection between homophobia and counselor competency. The researchers examined more than 700 couple and family clinicians, concluding that counselors with higher self-reported levels of LGB bias and prejudice had lower levels of sexual orientation counselor competency. In another study (Rock, Carlson, & McGeorge, 2010), 190 couple and family therapy students reported receiving limited to no LGB training and felt only somewhat competent to work with this population of clients. The SOCCS is also elucidating how counselor specialization can impact GLB competency. A recent study (Bidell, 2012) showed that school counseling students had significantly lower SOCCS scores compared to general community/agency students.

Limitations are being identified with multicultural counselor competency self-report instruments that include the tri-component model, reliance on self-report answers, and assessment of explicit attitudes versus implicit bias, as well as their lack of attention to clinical outcome, case conceptualization, and client perspective (Dunn, Smith, & Montoya, 2006). Since the SOCCS is fashioned on the MCC scales, it is probable that similar issues apply. Despite these limitations, the SOCCS has been shown to be a psychometrically sound assessment of LGB attitude, knowledge, and skill competencies and is increasingly being utilized as an outcome variable in social science research.

References

Andrews, B. V. (2004). An examination of the factors affecting school counselors' competency to address the needs of children of same-sex parented families. *Dissertation Abstracts International: Section A. Humanities and Social Sciences, 65*(12A), 4471.

Bidell, M. P. (2005). The Sexual Orientation Counselor Competency Scale: Assessing attitudes, skills, and knowledge of counselors working with lesbian, gay, and bisexual clients. *Counselor Education and Supervision, 44*(4), 267–279.

Bidell, M. P. (2012). Examining school counseling students' multicultural and sexual orientation competencies through a cross-specialization comparison. *Journal of Counseling and Development, 90*, 200–2007.

Carroll, L., & Gilroy, P. J. (2002). Transgender issues in counselor preparation. *Counselor Education & Supervision, 41*(3), 233–242.

Dawis, R. V. (1987). Scale construction. *Journal of Counseling Psychology, 34*, 481–489.

Day, S. W. (2008). College counselors' self-perceived competency in counseling lesbian, gay male, and bisexual college students. *Dissertation Abstracts International: Section A. Humanities and Social Sciences, 69*(03A), 884.

Dunn, T. W., Smith, T. B., & Montoya, J. A. (2006). Multicultural competency instrumentation: A review and analysis of reliability generalization. *Journal of Counseling & Development, 84*(4), 471–482.

Fell, G. R., Mattiske, J. K., & Riggs, D. W. (2008). Challanging heteronormativity in psychological practice with lesbian, gay and bisexual clients. *Gay & Lesbian Issues & Psychology, 4*(2), 127–140.

Frank, D. A. (2004). Relationships among queer theory pedagogy, sexual orientation competency, and multicultural environment in counselor education training programs. *Dissertation Abstracts International: Section A. Humanities and Social Sciences, 65*(06A), 2097.

Graham, S. R. (2009). *Counseling competency with lesbian, gay, and bisexual clients: Perceptions of counseling graduate students* (Doctoral dissertation, Auburn University). Retrieved from http://etd.auburn.edu/etd/handle/10415/1762.

Grove, J. (2009). How competent are trainee and newly qualified counsellors to work with lesbian, gay, and bisexual clients and what do they perceive as their most effective learning experiences? *Counselling & Psychotherapy Research, 9*(2), 78–85.

Henke, T., Carlson, T. S., & McGeorge, C. R. (2009). Homophobia and clinical competency: An exploration of couple and family therapists' beliefs. *Journal of Couple & Relationship Therapy, 8*(4), 325–342.

Herek, G. M. (1998). The Attitudes Toward Lesbians and Gay Men (ATLG) scale. In C. M. Davis, W. L. Yarber, R. Bauserman, G. Schreer, & S. L. Davis (Eds.), *Handbook of sexuality related measures* (pp. 392–394). Thousand Oaks, CA: Sage.

Lewis, J. D. (2008). The effects of the workshop, sexual orientation 101: A guide for mental health professionals who do not specialize with sexual minorities on the knowledge, skills and competency levels of participants. *Dissertation Abstracts International: Section B. Sciences and Engineering, 69*(05B), 3270.

Melchert, T. P., Hays, V. L., Wiljanen, L. M., & Kolocek, A. K. (1996). Testing models of counselor development with a measure of counseling self-efficacy. *Journal of Counseling & Development, 74,* 640–644.

Paulhaus, D. L. (1991). Measurement and control of response bias. In J. B. Robinson, P. R. Shaver, & L. S. Wrightsman (Eds.), *Measures of personality and social psychological attitudes* (pp. 17–59). San Diego, CA: Academic Press.

Ponterotto, J. G., Gretchen, D., Utsey, S. O., Rieger, B. P., & Austin, R. (2002). A revision of the Multicultural Counseling Awareness Scale. *Journal of Multicultural Counseling and Development, 30,* 153–180.

Robertson, P. K. (2005). A comparison of counseling competency and attitudes toward gay, lesbian, and bisexual individuals held by beginning and advanced counseling students. *Dissertation Abstracts International: Section A. Humanities and Social Sciences, 66*(04A), 1284.

Rock, M., Carlson, T. S., & McGeorge, C. R. (2010). Does affirmative training matter? Assessing CFT students' beliefs about sexual orientation and their level of affirmative training. *Journal of Marital & Family Therapy, 36*(2), 171–184.

Rutter, P. A., Estrada, D., Ferguson, L. K., & Diggs, G. A. (2008). Sexual orientation and counselor competency: The impact of training on enhancing awareness, knowledge and skills. *Journal of LGBT Issues in Counseling, 2*(2), 109–125.

Sue, D. W., Arredondo, P., & McDavis, R. J. (1992). Multicultural counseling competencies and standards: A call to the profession. *Journal of Multicultural Counseling & Development, 20*(2), 64–88.

SEXUAL ORIENTATION COUNSELOR COMPETENCY SCALE

Using the following scale, rate the truth of each item as it applies to you by circling the appropriate number.

1	2	3	4	5	6	7
Not At All True			Somewhat True			Totally True

1. I have received adequate clinical training and supervision to counsel lesbian, gay, and bisexual (LGB) clients.
2. The lifestyle of a LGB client is unnatural or immoral.
3. I check up on my LGB counseling skills by monitoring my functioning/competency via consultation, supervision, and continuing education.
4. I have experience counseling gay male clients.
5. LGB clients receive "less preferred" forms of counseling treatment than heterosexual clients.
6. At this point in my professional development, I feel competent, skilled, and qualified to counsel LGB clients.
7. I have experience counseling lesbian or gay couples.
8. I have experience counseling lesbian clients.
9. I am aware some research indicates that LGB clients are more likely to be diagnosed with mental illnesses than are heterosexual clients.
10. It's obvious that a same sex relationship between two men or two women is not as strong or as committed as one between a man and a woman.
11. I believe that being highly discreet about their sexual orientation is a trait that LGB clients should work towards.
12. I have been to in-services, conference sessions, or workshops, which focused on LGB issues in psychology.

13. Heterosexist and prejudicial concepts have permeated the mental health professions.

14. I feel competent to assess the mental health needs of a person who is LGB in a therapeutic setting.

15. I believe that LGB couples don't need special rights (domestic partner benefits, or the right to marry) because that would undermine normal and traditional family values.

16. There are different psychological/social issues impacting gay men versus lesbian women.

17. It would be best if my clients viewed a heterosexual lifestyle as ideal.

18. I have experience counseling bisexual (male or female) clients.

19. I am aware of institutional barriers that may inhibit LGB people from using mental health services.

20. I am aware that counselors frequently impose their values concerning sexuality upon LGB clients.

21. I think that my clients should accept some degree of conformity to traditional sexual values.

22. Currently, I do not have the skills or training to do a case presentation or consultation if my client were LGB.

23. I believe that LGB clients will benefit most from counseling with a heterosexual counselor who endorses conventional values and norms.

24. Being born a heterosexual person in this society carries with it certain advantages.

25. I feel that sexual orientation differences between counselor and client may serve as an initial barrier to effective counseling of LGB individuals.

26. I have done a counseling role-play as either the client or counselor involving a LGB issue.

27. Personally, I think homosexuality is a mental disorder or a sin and can be treated through counseling or spiritual help.

28. I believe that all LGB clients must be discreet about their sexual orientation around children.

29. When it comes to homosexuality, I agree with the statement: "You should love the sinner but hate or condemn the sin."

Thank you for completing this scale.

Scoring the SOCCS: Instructions: First, reverse score those questions in parentheses (so 1 = 7, 2 = 6, 3 = 5, 4 = 4, 5 = 3, 6 = 2, 7 = 1). **Note. Scoring information was not provided to research study participants.**

Total SOCCS Scoring

To calculate total SOCCS scores, add up all items (remembering to add the reverse score for questions in parentheses) and divide by 29. So, 1 + (2) + 3 + 4 + 5 + 6 + 7 + 8 + 9 + (10) + (11) + 12 + 13 + 14 + (15) + 16 + (17) + 18 + 19 + 20 + (21) + (22) + (23) + 24 + 25 + 26 + (27) + (28) + (29) = Your Raw Score/29 (Divide Your Raw Score by 29 – number of SOCCS questions)

Subscale Scoring

For each subscale, add up the scores of the question listed (remembering to add the reverse score for questions in parentheses) and divide by the number of questions in each subscale.

Awareness: (2) + (10) + (11) + (15) + (17) + (21) + (23) + (27) + (28) + (29) = Your Raw Score/10 (Divide Your Raw Score by 10 – number of Awareness questions)

Skills: 1 + 3 + 4 + 6 + 7 + 8 + 12 + 14 + 18 + (22) + 26 = Your Raw Score/11 (Divide Your Raw Score by 11 – number of Skills questions)

Knowledge: 5 + 9 + 13 + 16 + 19 + 20 + 24 + 25 = Your Raw Score/8 (Divide Your Raw Score by 8 – number of Knowledge questions)

Author Note

Markus P. Bidell, Associate Professor in the Department of Educational Foundations & Counseling Programs, Hunter College, 695 Park Ave. W1017, New York, NY 10065. E-mail: **mbidell@hunter.cuny.edu**; (212) 772-1474 (O); (212) 650.3198 (F).

References

References for Preface

American Counseling Association. (2005). *ACA code of ethics 2005*. Retrieved from www.counseling.org/resources/codeofethics/TP/home/ct2.aspx.

Arredondo, P., Toporek, R., Brown, S. P., Sanchez, J., Locke, D., Sanchez, J., & Stadler, H. (1996). Operationalization of the multicultural counseling competencies. *Journal of Multicultural Counseling & Development, 24*(1), 42–78.

Dillon, F. R., Worthington, R. L., Savoy, H. B., Rooney, S. C., Becker-Schutte, A., & Guerra, R. M. (2004). On becoming allies: A qualitative study of lesbian-, gay-, and bisexual-affirmative counselor training. *Counselor Education and Supervision, 43*(3), 162–178.

Eubanks-Carter, C., Burckell, L. A., & Goldfried, M. R. (2005). Enhancing therapeutic effectiveness with lesbian, gay, and bisexual clients. *Clinical Psychology: Science and Practice, 12*(1), 1–18.

Keppel, B. (2006). Affirmative psychotherapy with older bisexual women and men. *Journal of Bisexuality, 6*(1–2), 85–104.

Lahey, K. A., & Alderson, K. (2004). *Same-sex marriage: The personal and the political.* Toronto, ON: Insomniac Press.

Logan, C. R., & Barret, R. (2005). Counseling competencies for sexual minority clients. *Journal of LGBT Issues in Counseling, 1*(1), 3–22.

Palma, T., & Stanley, J. (2002). Effective counseling with lesbian, gay, and bisexual clients. *Journal of College Counseling, 5*(1), 74–89.

Pearson, Q. M. (2003). Breaking the silence in the counselor education classroom: A training seminar on counseling sexual minority clients. *Journal of Counseling and Development, 81*(3), 292–300.

Rutter, P. A., Estrada, D., Ferguson, L. K., & Diggs, G. A. (2008): Sexual orientation and counselor competency: The impact of training on enhancing awareness, knowledge and skills. *Journal of LGBT Issues in Counseling, 2*(2), 109–125.

Sue, D. W., Arredondo, P., & McDavis, R. J. (1992). Multicultural counseling competencies and standards: A call to the profession. *Journal of Counseling and Development, 70,* 477–483.

Sue, D. W., Bernier, J. E., Durran, A., Feinberg, L., Pedersen, P., Smith, E. J., . . . Vasquez-Nutall, E. (1982). Position paper: Cross-cultural counseling competencies. *Counseling Psychologist, 10*(2), 45–52.

Sue, D. W., Carter, R. T., Casas, J. M., Fouad, N. A., Ivey, A. E., Jensen, M., . . . Vazquez-Nutall, E. (1998). *Multicultural counseling competencies: Individual and organizational development.* Thousand Oaks, CA: Sage.

References for Chapter 1

Alderson, K. (2002). *Breaking out: The complete guide to building and enhancing a positive gay identity for men and women.* Toronto, ON: Insomniac Press.

Alderson, K. G. (2010). From madness to mainstream: Working with gay men today. In N. Arthur & S. Collins (Eds.), *Culture-infused counselling: Celebrating the Canadian mosaic* (2nd ed., pp. 395–422). Calgary, AB: Counselling Concepts.

Alderson, K. G., Orzeck, T. L., Davis, S., & Boyes, M. (2011). Sexual orientation: Defining and measuring it. *Manuscript in preparation.*

American Psychological Association. (2010). *Publication manual* (6th ed.). Washington, DC: Author.

Arredondo, P., Toporek, R., Brown, S. P., Sanchez, J., Locke, D., Sanchez, J., & Stadler, H. (1996). Operationalization of the multicultural counseling competencies. *Journal of Multicultural Counseling & Development, 24*(1), 42–78.

Arthur, N., & Collins, S. (Eds.). (2010). *Culture-infused counselling: Celebrating the Canadian mosaic* (2nd ed.). Calgary, AB: Counselling Concepts.

Baffi, C. R., Redican, K. J., Sefchick, M. K., & Impara, J. C. (1991). Gender role identity, gender role stress, and health behaviors: An exploratory study of selected college males. *Health Values: Health Behavior, Education & Promotion, 15*(1), 9–18.

Barber, J. S., & Mobley, M. (1999). Counseling gay adolescents. In A. M. Horne, M. S. Kiselica, et al. (Eds.), *Handbook of counseling boys and adolescent males: A practitioner's guide* (pp. 161–178). Thousand Oaks, CA: Sage.

Blanchard, R., & Collins, P. I. (1993). Men with sexual interest in transvestites, transsexuals, and she-males. *Journal of Nervous and Mental Disease, 181*(9), 570–575.

Brown, G. R. (1996). Transvestism. In G. O. Gabbard & S. D. Atkinson (Eds.), *Synopsis of treatments of psychiatric disorders* (2nd ed., pp. 829–836). Washington, DC: American Psychiatric Association.

Brown, T. L., & Alderson, K. G. (2010). Sexual identity and heterosexual male students' usage of homosexual insults. *Canadian Journal of Human Sexuality, 19*(1–2), 27–42.

Chung, Y. B., & Harmon, L. W. (1994). The career interests and aspirations of gay men: How sex-role orientation is related. *Journal of Vocational Behavior, 45,* 223–239.

Croteau, J. M., Anderson, M. Z., Distefano, T. M., & Kampa-Kokesch, S. (2000). Lesbian, gay, and bisexual vocational psychology: Reviewing foundations and planning construction. In R. M. Perez, K. A. Debord, & K. J. Bieschke (Eds.), *Handbook of counseling and psychotherapy with lesbian, gay, and bisexual clients* (pp. 383–408). Washington, DC: American Psychological Association.

Degges-White, S., & Shoffner, M. F. (2002). Career counseling with lesbian clients: Using the theory of work adjustment as a framework. *Career Development Quarterly, 51,* 87–96.

Diamond, L. M. (2007). A dynamical systems approach to the development and expression of female same-sex sexuality. *Perspectives on Psychological Science, 2*(2), 142–161.

Diamond, L. M. (2008). Female bisexuality from adolescence to adulthood: Results from a 10-year longitudinal study. *Developmental Psychology, 44*(1), 5–14.

Docter, R. F. (1988). *Tranvestites and transsexuals: Toward a theory of cross-gender behavior*. New York: Plenum Press.

Ellis, A. L., & Mitchell, R. W. (2000). Sexual orientation. In L. T. Szuchman & F. Muscarella (Eds.), *Psychological perspectives on human sexuality* (pp. 196–231). New York: John Wiley & Sons.

Fields, J. (2004). Same-sex marriage, sodomy laws, and the sexual lives of young people. *Sexuality Research & Social Policy: A Journal of the NSRC, 1*(3), 11–23.

Flowers, P., & Buston, K. (2001). "I was terrified of being different": Exploring gay men's accounts of growing-up in a heterosexist society. *Journal of Adolescence, 24,* 51–65.

Frankowski, B. L. (2004). Sexual orientation and adolescents. *Pediatrics, 113,* 1827–1832.

Gamson, J. (2000). Sexualities, queer theory, and qualitative research. In N. K. Denzin & Y. S. Lincoln, *Handbook of Qualitative Research* (2nd ed., pp. 347–365). Thousand Oaks, CA: Sage.

Gergen, K. J. (1985). The social constructionist movement in modern psychology. *American Psychologist, 40*(3), 266–275.

Gergen, K. J. (2009). *An invitation to social construction* (2nd ed.). Thousand Oaks, CA: Sage.

Herdt, G. (1997). *Same sex, different cultures*. Boulder, CO: Westview Press.

Herring, R. D. (1998). *Career counseling in schools: Multicultural and developmental perspectives*. Alexandria, VA: American Counseling Association.

Hofstede, G. (1980). *Culture's consequences, international differences in work-related values (cross cultural research and methodology)*. Newbury Park, CA: Sage.

Itim International. (2009). *Geert Hofstede cultural dimensions*. Retrieved from www.geert-hofstede.com/.

Kitzinger, C., & Wilkinson, S. (1995). Transitions from heterosexuality to lesbianism: The discursive production of lesbian identities. *Developmental Psychology, 31,* 95–104.

Levine, S. B. (1993). Gender-disturbed males. *Journal of Sex & Marital Therapy, 19*(2), 131–141.

Logan, C. R, & Barret, R. (2005). Counseling competencies for sexual minority clients. *Journal of LGBT Issues in Counseling, 1*(1), 3–22.

Lorber, J. (2004). Preface. *Journal of Homosexuality, 46*(3–4), xxv–xxvi.

Matsumoto, D. (2000). *Culture and psychology* (2nd ed.). Belmont, CA: Wadsworth/Thompson Learning.

McCarthy, J. (2005). Individualism and collectivism: What do they have to do with counseling? *Journal of Multicultural Counseling and Development, 33*(2), 108–117.

McKirnan, D., Stokes, J., Doll, L., & Burzette, R. (1995). Bisexually active males: Social characteristics and sexual behavior. *Journal of Sex Research, 32,* 65–76.

Merriam Webster Dictionary. (2011). *Definition of gay*. Retrieved from www.merriam-webster.com/dictionary/gay.

Meyer, W., Bockting, W. O., Cohen-Kettenis, P., Coleman, E., DiCeglie, D., Devor, H., . . . Wheeler, C. C. (2001). *The Harry Benjamin International Gender Dysphoria Association's Standards of care for gender identity disorders* (6th ed.). Retrieved from www.wpath.org/publications_standards.cfm.

Minton, H. L. (1997). Queer theory: Historical roots and implications for psychology. *Theory & Psychology, 7*(3), 337–353.

Minton, H. L., & Mattson, S. R. (1998). Deconstructing heterosexuality: Life stories from gay New York, 1931–1941. *Journal of Homosexuality, 36*(1), 43–61.

Mosher, W. D., Chandra, A., & Jones, J. (2005, September 15). *Sexual behaviour and selected health measures: Men and women 15–44 years of age, United States, 2002*. Advance Data from Vital Health and Statistics. Number 362. Hyattsville, MD: U.S. Department of Health and Human Services, Centers for Disease Control and Prevention, National Center for Health Statistics. Retrieved from www.cdc.gov/nchs/data/ad/ad362.pdf.

Pedersen, P. B., Crethar, H. C., & Carlson, J. (2008). *Inclusive cultural empathy: Making relationships central in counseling and psychotherapy.* Washington, DC: American Psychological Association.

Prochaska, J. O., Norcross, J. C., & Diclemente, C. C. (1994). *Changing for good: A revolutionary six-stage program for overcoming bad habits and moving your life positively forward.* New York: Avon.

Rieger, G., Linsenmeier, J. A. W., Gygax, L., & Bailey, J. M. (2008). Sexual orientation and childhood gender nonconformity: Evidence from home videos. *Developmental Psychology, 44*(1), 46–58.

Roscoe, W. (1988). Making history: The challenge of gay and lesbian studies. *Journal of Homosexuality, 15,* 1–40.

Savin-Williams, R. C. (2005). *The new gay teenager.* Cambridge, MA: Harvard University Press.

Statistics Canada. (2009, September 22). *2006 census: Family portrait: Continuity and change in Canadian families and households in 2006: National portrait: Census families.* Retrieved from www12.statcan.ca/census-recensement/2006/as-sa/97-553/p4-eng.cfm.

Stein, T. S. (1996). The essentialist/social constructionist debate about homosexuality and its relevance for psychotherapy. In R. P. Cabaj & T. S. Stein (Eds.), *Textbook of homosexuality and mental health* (pp. 83–99). Washington, DC: American Psychiatric Press.

Stokes, J. P., Damon, W., & McKirnan, D. J. (1997). Predictors of movement toward homosexuality: A longitudinal study of bisexual men. *Journal of Sex Research, 34*(3), 304–312.

Sue, D. W., Arredondo, P., & McDavis, R. J. (1992). Multicultural counseling competencies and standards: A call to the profession. *Journal of Counseling and Development, 70,* 477–483.

Sue, D. W., Bernier, J. E., Durran, A., Feinberg, L., Pedersen, P., Smith, E. J., . . . Vasquez-Nutall, E. (1982). Position paper: Cross-cultural counseling competencies. *Counseling Psychologist, 10*(2), 45–52.

Sue, D. W., Carter, R. T., Casas, J. M., Fouad, N. A., Ivey, A. E., Jensen, M., . . . Vazquez-Nutall, E. (1998). *Multicultural counseling competencies: Individual and organizational development.* Thousand Oaks, CA: Sage.

Tyler, J. M., Jackman-Wheitner, L., Strader, S., & Lenox, R. (1997). A change-model approach to raising awareness of gay, lesbian, and bisexual issues among graduate students in counseling. *Journal of Sex Education & Therapy, 22*(2), 37-43.

Vanderburgh, R. (2009). Appropriate therapeutic care for families with pre-pubescent transgender/gender-dissonant children. *Child & Adolescent Social Work Journal, 26*(2), 135–154.

Vilain, E. J. N. (2008). Genetics of sexual development and differentiation. In D. L. Rowland &

L. Incrocci (Eds.), *Handbook of sexual and gender identity disorders* (pp. 329–353). Hoboken, NJ: John Wiley & Sons.

Wiederman, M. W. (1999). Volunteer bias in sexuality research using college student participants. *Journal of Sex Research, 36*(1), 59–66.

References for Chapter 2

Adam, P. C. G., de Wi, J. B. F., Toskin, I., Mathers, B. M., Nashkhoev, M., Zablotska, I., . . . Rugg, D. (2009). Estimating level of HIV testing, HIV prevention coverage, HIV knowledge, and condom use among men who have sex with men (MSM) in low-income and middle-income countries. *JAIDS Journal of Acquired Immune Deficiency Syndromes, 52*(Suppl 2), S143–S151.

Another Islamic scientific gift to civilization. (2009, August 22). Retrieved from http://islammonitor.org/index2.php?option=com_content&do_pdf=1&id=2719.

Answers.com. (2010). *Machismo definition.* Retrieved from www.answers.com/topic/machismo.

Araujo, M. A. L., Montagner, M. A., da Silva, R. M., Lopes, F. L., & de Freitas, M. M. (2009). Symbolic violence experienced by men who have sex with men in the primary health service in Fortaleza, Ceara, Brazil: Negotiating identity under stigma. *AIDS Patient Care and STDs,* 23(8), 663–668.

Associated Press. (2010, December 22). *Obama signs repeal of 'don't ask, don't tell.'* Retrieved from www.msnbc.msn.com/id/40777922/ns/politics-white_house/t/obama-signs-repeal-dont-ask-dont-tell/.

Avery, I. W. (1985). *Atlanta.* Atlanta, GA: Constitution. Page 5 retrieved from http://books.google.ca/books?id=pmdIAAAAYAAJ&pg=PA5&lpg=PA5&dq=population+of+atlanta+in+1855&source=bl&ots=o6riqH6FpA&sig=ZKs2KcZ8lcGWq_FXDGtN1g2SQp4&hl=en&ei=S8pXTpzCCIrhiAKO8ozACQ&sa=X&oi=book_result&ct=result&resnum=1&ved=0CCEQ6AEwAA#v=onepage&q=population%20of%20atlanta%20in%201855&f=false.

Bayer, R. (1981). *Homosexuality and American psychiatry.* New York: Basic.

Belkin, A., & McNichol, J. (2000–2001). Homosexual personnel policy in the Canadian Forces: Did lifting the ban undermine military performance? *JSTOR: International Journal, 56*(1), 73–88.

Bernstein, M. (1997). Celebration and suppression: The strategic uses of identity by the lesbian and gay movement. *American Journal of Sociology, 103*(3), 531–565.

Blumenfeld, W. J., & Raymond, D. (1993). *Looking at gay and lesbian life* (updated and expanded ed.). Boston: Beacon Press.

Brickell, C. (2006). Sexology, the homo/hetero binary, and the complexities of male sexual history. *Sexualities, 9*(4), 423–447.

Bronski, M. (2011). *A queer history of the United States.* Boston: Beacon Press.

Bruce-Jones, E., & Itaborahy, L. P. (2011, May). State-sponsored homophobia: A world survey of laws criminalising same-sex sexual acts between consenting adults. An ILGA report. *The International Lesbian, Gay, Bisexual, Trans and Intersex Association.* Retrieved from http://old.ilga.org/Statehomophobia/ILGA_State_Sponsored_Homophobia_2011.pdf.

Buhrich, N., & McConaghy, N. (1977). Clinical comparison of transvestism and transsexualism: An overview. *Australian and New Zealand Journal of Psychiatry, 11*(2), 83–86.

Bullough, V. L., & Bullough, B. (1993). *Cross dressing, sex, and gender.* Baltimore, MD: University of Pennsylvania Press.

Burnett, R. (2009, October 23). *Montreal's Sex Garage raid: A watershed moment.* Retrieved from www.xtra.ca/public/National/Montreals_Sex_Garage_raid_A_watershed_moment-7735.aspx.

Cabaj, R. P. (1988). New thinking on sexuality and homosexuality. *Psychiatric Annals, 18,* 11.

Cabaj, R. P. (1998). History of gay acceptance and relationships. In R. P. Cabaj & D. W. Purcell (Eds.), *On the road to same-sex marriage: A supportive guide to psychological, political, and legal issues* (pp. 1–28). San Francisco: Jossey-Bass.

Carael, M., Marais, H., Polsky, J., & Mendoza, A. (2009). Is there a gender gap in the HIV response? Evaluating national HIV responses from the United Nations General Assembly Special Session on HIV/AIDS country reports. *JAIDS Journal of Acquired Immune Deficiency Syndromes, 52*(Suppl 2), S111–S118.

Cardoso, F. L. (2009). Similar faces of same-sex sexual behavior: A comparative ethnographical study in Brazil, Turkey, and Thailand. *Journal of Homosexuality, 56*(4), 457–484.

CBC. (2009). *Trudeau's Omnibus Bill: Challenging Canadian taboos*. Retrieved from http://archives.cbc.ca/politics/rights_freedoms/topics/538/.

CBC News. (2002, December 20). *Bathhouse raid angers Calgary gay community*. Retrieved from www.cbc.ca/canada/story/2002/12/20/bathhouse_raid021220.html.

CBC News. (2007, March 1). *Same-sex rights: Canada timeline*. Retrieved from www.cbc.ca/news/background/samesexrights/timeline_canada.html.

Chauncey, G. (1995). *Gay New York, NY: The making of the gay male world 1890–1940*. London, UK: Flamingo.

Chibbaro, L. (2011, March 23). *Jury rejects hate crime charge in gay murder*. Retrieved from www.washingtonblade.com/2011/03/23/jury-rejects-hate-crime-charge-in-gay-murder/.

Chow, P. K.-Y., & Cheng, S.-T. (2010). Shame, internalized heterosexism, lesbian identity, and coming out to others: A comparative study of lesbians in mainland China and Hong Kong. *Journal of Counseling Psychology, 57*(1), 92–104.

CNN Interactive. (1998, February 3). *Researchers trace first HIV case to 1959 in the Belgian Congo*. Retrieved from www.cnn.com/HEALTH/9802/03/earliest.aids/.

Conger, J. J. (1975). Proceedings of the American Psychological Association for the year 1974: Minutes of the annual meeting of the Council of Representatives. *American Psychologist, 30,* 620–651.

D'Emilio, J. (1993). Gay politics and community in San Francisco since World War II. In L. D. Garnets & D. C. Kimmel (Eds.), *Psychological perspectives on lesbian and gay male experiences* (pp. 59–79). New York: Columbia University Press.

De Cecco, J. P. (1981). Definition and meaning of sexual orientation. *Journal of Homosexuality, 6,* 51–67.

Department of Justice, Canada. (2011, June 9). *Canadian Charter of Rights and Freedoms*. Retrieved from http://laws-lois.justice.gc.ca/eng/charter/.

Docter, R. F. (1988). *Transvestites and transsexuals: Toward a theory of cross-gender behavior*. New York: Plenum Press.

Dong, T. B. (1999). Foreword. *Journal of Homosexuality, 36*(3–4), xxiii–xxvi.

Douglas, A. (1894). Two loves (poem). *The Chameleon, 1*(1). Reprinted and retrieved from www.law.umkc.edu/faculty/projects/ftrials/wilde/poemsofdouglas.htm.

Dowsett, G. W. (2005). Review of beyond shame: Reclaiming the abandoned history of radical gay sexuality. *Sexualities, 8*(2), 255–256.

Drescher, J. (2008). A history of homosexuality and organized psychoanalysis. *Journal of the American Academy of Psychoanalysis & Dynamic Psychiatry, 36*(3), 443–460.

Drescher, J., & Merlino, J. P. (Eds.). (2007). *American psychiatry and homosexuality: An oral history*. Binghamton, NY: Harrington Park Press/Haworth Press.

Dyer, R. (2003). *Heavenly bodies: Film stars and society* (2nd ed.). New York: Routledge.

Dzelme, K., & Jones, R. A. (2001). Male cross-dressers in therapy: A solution-focused perspective for marriage and family therapists. *American Journal of Family Therapy, 29*(4), 293–305.

Feng, Y., Wu, Z., Detels, R., Qin, G., Liu, L., Wang, X., . . . Zhang, L. (2010). HIV/STD prevalence among men who have sex with men in Chengdu, China and associated risk factors for HIV infection. *JAIDS Journal of Acquired Immune Deficiency Syndromes, 53*(Suppl 1), S74–S80.

Fields, J. (2004). Same-sex marriage, sodomy laws, and the sexual lives of young people. *Sexuality Research & Social Policy: A Journal of the NSRC, 1*(3), 11–23.

Filax, G. (2006). *Queer youth in the province of the "severely normal."* Vancouver, BC: UBC Press.

Flacelière, R. (1962). *Love in ancient Greece* (J. Cleugh, Trans.). New York: Crown.

Fontaine, J. H. (2002). Transgender issues in counseling. In L. D. Burlew & D. Capuzzi (Eds.), *Sexuality counseling* (pp. 177–194). Hauppauge, NY: Nova Science.

Ford, C. S., & Beach, F. A. (1951). *Patterns of sexual behavior*. New York: Harper.

Froomkin, D. (2011, February 23). *Gay rights advocates celebrate Obama's DOMA turnaround*. Retrieved from www.huffingtonpost.com/2011/02/23/doma-unconstitutional-gay-rights-groups-celebrate_n_827355.html.

Furnham, A., & Saito, K. (2009). A cross-cultural study of attitudes toward and beliefs about, male homosexuality. *Journal of Homosexuality, 56*(3), 299–318.

Gallo, M. M. (2006). *Different daughters: A history of the Daughters of Bilitis and the rise of the lesbian rights movement*. New York: Carroll & Graf.

Garrett, M. T., & Barret, B. (2003). Two spirit: Counseling Native American gay, lesbian, and

bisexual people. *Journal of Multicultural Counseling and Development, 31*(2), 131–142.
Gilley, B. J. (2010). Native sexual inequalities: American Indian cultural conservative homophobia and the problem of tradition. *Sexualities, 13*(1), 47–68.
Grace, A. P., & Wells, K. (2005). The Marc Hall prom predicament: Queer individual rights v. Institutional church rights in Canadian public education. *Canadian Journal of Education, 28*(3), 237–270.
Grube, J. (1990). Natives and settlers: An ethnographic note on early interaction of older homosexual men with younger gay liberationists. *Journal of Homosexuality, 20*(3–4), 119–135.
Gruszczynska, A. (2009). Sowing the seeds of solidarity in public space: Case study of the Poznan March of Equality. *Sexualities, 12*(3), 312–333.
Halperin, D. M. (2002). *How to do the history of homosexuality.* Chicago: University of Chicago Press.
Halwani, R. (1998). Essentialism, social constructionism, and the history of homosexuality. *Journal of Homosexuality, 35*(1), 25–51.
Herdt, G. (1997). *Same sex, different cultures.* Boulder, CO: Westview Press.
Herek, G. M. (2006). Legal recognition of same-sex relationships in the United States: A social science perspective. *American Psychologist, 61*(6), 607–621.
Hooker, E. (1957). The adjustment of the male overt homosexual. *Journal of Projective Techniques, 21,* 18–31.
Horne, S. G., Ovrebo, E., Levitt, H. M., & Franeta, S. (2009). Leaving the herd: The lingering threat of difference for same-sex desires in postcommunist Russia. *Sexuality Research & Social Policy: A Journal of the NSRC, 6*(2), 88–102.
Hurley, M. C. (2005, September 14). *Bill C-38: The Civil Marriage Act.* Retrieved from www.parl.gc.ca/About/Parliament/LegislativeSummaries/bills_ls.asp?ls=c38&Parl=38&Ses=1.
Jeffries, W. L., IV. (2009). A comparative analysis of homosexual behaviors, sex role preferences, and anal sex proclivities in Latino and non-Latino men. *Archives of Sexual Behavior, 38*(5), 765–778.
Kapac, J. (1998). Culture/community/race: Chinese gay men and the politics of identity. *Anthropologica, 40*(2), 169–181.
Karkazis, K. A. (2003). Beyond treatment: Mapping the connections among gender, genitals, and sexuality in recent controversies over intersexuality. *Dissertation Abstracts International Section A: Humanities and Social Sciences, 63*(10-A), 3619.
Karlen, A. (1980). Homosexuality in history. In J. Marmor (Ed.), *Homosexual behaviour* (pp. 75–99). New York: Basic.
Koso-Thomas, O. (1987). *The circumcision of women: A strategy for eradication.* London, UK: Zed.
Lahey, K. A., & Alderson, K. (2004). *Same-sex marriage: The personal and the political.* Toronto: Insomniac Press.
Laurent, E. (2005). Sexuality and human rights: An Asian perspective. *Journal of Homosexuality, 48*(3/4), 163–225.
Leff, L. (2011, June 14). *California same-sex marriage ruling upheld: Court won't overturn Prop 8 decision because judge was* gay. Retrieved from www.huffingtonpost.com/2011/06/14/california-gay-marriage-proposition-8_n_876560.html.
Lubbers, M., Jaspers, E., & Ultee, W. (2009). Primary and secondary socialization impacts on support for same-sex marriage after legalization in the Netherlands. *Journal of Family Issues, 30*(12), 1714–1745.
Lwin, M. O., Stanaland, A. J. S., & Chan, D. (2010). Using protection motivation theory to predict condom usage and assess HIV health communication efficacy in Singapore. *Health Communication, 25*(1), 69–79.
Martin, J. I., & Yonkin, D. R. (2006). Transgender identity. In D. F. Morrow & L. Messinger (Eds.), *Sexual orientation & gender expression in social work practice: Working with gay, lesbian, bisexual, & transgender people* (pp. 105–128). New York: Columbia University Press.
McKinley, J., & Schwartz, J. (2010, August 4). Court rejects same-sex marriage ban in California. *New York Times.* Retrieved from www.nytimes.com/2010/08/05/us/05prop.html.
Mendes-Leite, R. (1993). A game of appearances: The "ambigusexuality" in Brazilian culture of sexuality. *Journal of Homosexuality, 25*(3), 271–282.
Noelle, M. (2002). The ripple effect on the Matthew Shepard murder: Impact on the assumptive worlds of members of the targeted group. *American Behavioral Scientist, 46*(1), 27–50.
O'Donohue, W., & Caselles, C. E. (1993). Homophobia: Conceptual, definitional, and value issues. *Journal of Psychopathology and Behavioral Assessment, 15*(3), 177–195.
Outhistory. (2009, October 7). *Stonewall Riot police reports, June 28, 1969. Newly obtained documents reveal name of woman arrestee and names of three men arrestees: Marilyn Fowler, Vincent DePaul, Wolfgang Podolski, and Thomas Staton.*

Retrieved from www.outhistory.org/wiki/Stonewall_Riot_Police_Reports,_June_28,_1969.

Paré, M. F. (2009). *History of gay Toronto and birth of Queer West Village*. Retrieved from http://queerwest.org/history.php.

Parkfor, J. (2011, May 2). *Man arrested over murder of US gay pride activist*. Retrieved from www.pinknews.co.uk/2011/05/02/man-arrested-over-murder-of-us-gay-pride-activist/.

Parks, C. A., Hughes, T. L., & Matthews, A. K. (2004). Race/ethnicity and sexual orientation: Intersecting identities. *Cultural Diversity and Ethnic Minority Psychology, 10*(3), 241–254.

Percy, W. A., III (1996). *Pederasty and pedagogy in archaic Greece*. Chicago: University of Illinois Press.

Ploderl, M., & Fartacek, R. (2009). Childhood gender nonconformity and harassment as predictors of suicidality among gay, lesbian, bisexual, and heterosexual Austrians. *Archives of Sexual Behavior, 38*(3), 400–410.

Pride Library at the University of Western Ontario. (n.d.). *History of the gay liberation in Canada, 1970s Climate and Timeline*. Retrieved from www.uwo.ca/pridelib/microsites/bodypolitic/gaylib/70stimeline.htm.

Rattachumpoth, R. (1999). Foreword. *Journal of Gay & Lesbian Social Services,* 9(2–3), xvii–xxiv.

Ross, M. W., Paulsen, J. A., & Stalstrom, O. W. (1988). Homosexuality and mental health: A cross-cultural review. *Journal of Homosexuality, 15,* 131–152.

Rothon, R. (2006, August 31). *In hindsight: The decriminalization of homosexuality*. Retrieved from www.xtra.ca/public/Vancouver/The_decriminalization_of_homosexuality-2057.aspx.

Ruan, S., Yang, H., Zhu, Y., Wang, M., Ma, Y., Zhao, J., . . . Raymond, H. F. (2009). Rising HIV prevalence among married and unmarried among men who have sex with men: Jinan, China. *AIDS and Behavior, 13*(4), 671–676.

Shafer, S. (2011, June 13). *When a gay judge rules on gay rights*. Retrieved from www.npr.org/2011/06/13/137109321/when-a-gay-judge-rules-on-gay-rights.

Shapiro, E. (2004). 'Trans'cending barriers: Transgender organizing on the Internet. *Journal of Gay & Lesbian Social Services: Issues in Practice, Policy & Research, 16*(34), 165–179.

Smith, A. D., Tapsoba, P., Peshu, N., Sanders, E. J., & Jaffe, H. W. (2009). Men who have sex with men and HIV/AIDS in sub-Saharan Africa. *Lancet, 374*(9687), 416–422.

Smith, M. (2005). The politics of same-sex marriage in Canada and the United States. *PS Political Science & Politics, 38*(2), 225–228.

Steiner, B. W. (1982). From Sappho to Sand: Historical perspective on crossdressing and cross gender. *Canadian Journal of Psychiatry/La Revue canadienne de psychiatrie, 26*(7), 502–506.

Sullivan, M. K. (2003). Homophobia, history, and homosexuality: Trends for sexual minorities. *Journal of Human Behavior in the Social Environment, 8*(2–3), 1–13.

Tafoya, T. (2003). Native gay and lesbian issues: The two-spirited. In L. D. Garnets & D. C. Kimmel (Eds.), *Psychological perspectives on lesbian, gay, and bisexual experiences* (2nd ed., pp. 401–409). New York: Columbia University Press.

Taylor, C. L. (1985). Mexican male homosexual interaction in public contexts. *Journal of Homosexuality, 11,* 117–136.

Teney, C., & Subramanian, S. V. (2010). Attitudes toward homosexuals among youth in multiethnic Brussels. *Cross-Cultural Research, 44*(2), 151–173.

Thing, J. (2010). Entre Maricones, Machos, y Gays: Globalization and the construction of sexual identities among queer Mexicanos. *Dissertation Abstracts International Section A: Humanities and Social Sciences, 70*(8-A), 3211.

Veyne, P. (1985). Homosexuality in ancient Rome. In P. Aries & A. Bejin (Eds.), *Western sexuality: Practice and precept in past and present times* (pp. 26–35). New York: Basil Blackwell.

Wagstaff, D. A., Abramson, P. R., & Pinkerton, S. D. (2000). Research in human sexuality. In L. T. Szuchman & F. Muscarella (Eds.), *Psychological perspectives on human sexuality* (pp. 3–59). New York: John Wiley & Sons.

Ward, K. M. (1995, August). *Court urged to just say NO to Colorado's amendment*. Retrieved from www.now.org/nnt/08-95/colorado.html.

Warner, T. (2002). *Never going back: A history of queer activism in Canada*. Toronto, ON: University of Toronto Press.

Whitam, F. L. (1980). The prehomosexual male child in three societies. *Archives of Sexual Behavior, 9*(2), 87–100.

Whitam, F. L. (1991). From sociology: Homophobia and heterosexism in sociology. *Journal of Gay & Lesbian Psychotherapy, 1*(4), 31–44.

Xiao, Y., Sun, J., Li, C., Lu, F., Allen, K. L., Vermund, S. H., & Jia, Y. (2010). Prevalence and correlates of HIV and syphilis infections among men who have sex with men in seven provinces in China with historically low HIV prevalence. *JAIDS Journal of Acquired Immune Deficiency Syndromes, 53*(Suppl 1), S66–S73.

Zucker, K. J., & Bradley, S. J. (1999). Gender identity disorder and transvestic fetishism. In S. D. Netherton, D. Holmes, & C. E. Walker (Eds.), *Child and adolescent psychological disorders: A comprehensive textbook* (pp. 367–396). New York: Oxford University Press.

References for Chapter 3

Adam, B. D. (2006). Relationship innovation in male couples. *Sexualities, 9*(1), 5–26.

Adam, B. D., Husbands, W., Murray, J., & Maxwell, J. (2008). Circuits, networks, and HIV risk management. *AIDS Education and Prevention, 20*(5), 420–434.

Alderson, K. (2000). *Beyond coming out: Experiences of positive gay identity*. Toronto, ON: Insomniac Press.

Alderson, K. (2002). *Breaking out: The complete guide to building and enhancing a positive gay identity for men and women*. Toronto, ON: Insomniac Press.

Alderson, K. G. (2003). The ecological model of gay male identity. *Canadian Journal of Human Sexuality, 12*(2), 75–85.

Alderson, K. G. (2004). A different kind of outing: Training counsellors to work with sexual minority clients. *Canadian Journal of Counselling, 38,* 193–210.

Alderson, K. G., & Jevne, R. F. J. (2003). Yin and yang in mortal combat: The psychic conflict beneath the coming-out process for gay males. *Guidance and Counselling, 18,* 128–141.

Alderson, K. G., Orzeck, T. L., Davis, S., & Boyes, M. (2011). *Sexual orientation: Defining and measuring it.* Manuscript in preparation.

Alexander, C. J. (1999). Reparative therapy for gays and lesbians. *Journal of Gay and Lesbian Social Services, 9*(4), 115–118.

Allen, D. J., & Oleson, T. (1999). Shame and internalized homophobia in gay men. *Journal of Homosexuality, 37*(3), 33–43.

Andersson, G. T., Noack, T., Seierstad, A., & Weedon-Fekjaer, H. (2006). The demographics of same-sex marriages in Norway and Sweden. *Demography, 43*(1), 79–98.

Anetzberger, G. J., Ishler, K. J., Mostade, J., & Blair, M. (2004). Gray and gay: A community dialogue on the issues and concerns of older gays and lesbians. *Journal of Gay & Lesbian Social Services: Issues in Practice, Policy & Research, 17*(1), 23–45.

Arredondo, P., Toporek, R., Brown, S. P., Sanchez, J., Locke, D., Sanchez, J., & Stadler, H. (1996). Operationalization of the multicultural counseling competencies. *Journal of Multicultural Counseling & Development, 24*(1), 42–78.

Associated Press. (2001, May 9). Study says some gays can switch. *Calgary Herald*, p. A5.

Aveline, D. (2006). "Did I have blinders on or what?": Retrospective sense making by parents of gay sons recalling their sons' earlier years. *Journal of Family Issues, 27*(6), 777–802.

AVERT. (2009, November 13). *Worldwide HIV & AIDS statistics commentary*. Retrieved from www.avert.org/worlstatinfo.htm.

Bagley, C., & Tremblay, P. (1998). On the prevalence of homosexuality and bisexuality, in a random community survey of 750 men aged 18 to 27. *Journal of Homosexuality, 36*(2), 1–18.

Barber, J. S., & Mobley, M. (1999). Counseling gay adolescents. In A. M. Horne, M. S. Kiselica, et al. (Eds.), *Handbook of counseling boys and adolescent males: A practitioner's guide* (pp. 161–178). Thousand Oaks, CA: Sage.

Barth, J., & Parry, J. (2009). Political culture, public opinion, and policy (non)diffusion: The case of gay and lesbian-related issues in Arkansas. *Social Science Quarterly, 90*(2), 309–325.

Bartholomew, K., Regan, K. V., Oram, D., & White, M. A. (2008). Correlates of partner abuse in male same-sex relationships. *Violence and Victims, 23*(3), 344–360.

Bartlett, N. H., Patterson, H. M., VanderLaan, D. P., & Vasey, P. L. (2009). The relation between women's body esteem and friendships with gay men. *Body Image, 6*(3), 235–241.

Bartlett, P. (2007). Killing gay men, 1976–2001. *British Journal of Criminology, 47*(4), 573–595.

Baunach, D. M., Burgess, E. O., & Muse, C. S. (2010). Southern (dis)comfort: Sexual prejudice and contact with gay men and lesbians in the south. *Sociological Spectrum, 30*(1), 30–64.

Beane, J. (1981). "I'd rather be dead than gay": Counseling gay men who are coming out. *Personnel and Guidance Journal, 60,* 222–226.

Bell, A. P., & Weinberg, M. S. (1978). *Homosexualities: A study of diversity among men and women*. New York: Simon and Schuster.

Berger, R. M., & Kelly, J. J. (2001). What are older gay men like? An impossible question? *Journal of Gay & Lesbian Social Services: Issues in Practice, Policy & Research, 13*(4), 55–65.

Betz, N. E., & Fitzgerald, L. F. (1993). Individuality and diversity: Theory and research in counseling psychology. *Annual Review of Psychology, 44,* 343–381.

Bieschke, K. J., Perez, R. M., & Debord, K. A. (Eds.). (2006). *Handbook of counseling and psychotherapy with lesbian, gay, bisexual, and transgender clients* (2nd ed.). Washington, DC: American Psychological Association.

Birken, L. (1997). Homosexuality and totalitarianism. *Journal of Homosexuality, 33*(1), 1–16.

Birkett, M., Espelage, D. L., & Koenig, B. (2009). LGB and questioning students in schools: The moderating effects of homophobic bullying and school climate on negative outcomes. *Journal of Youth and Adolescence, 38*(7), 989–1000.

Black, D., Gates, G., Sanders S., & Taylor, L. (2000). Demographics of the gay and lesbian population in the United States: Evidence from available systematic data sources. *Demography, 37*(2), 139–154.

Blanchard, R. (2008a). Review and theory of handedness, birth order, and homosexuality in men. *Laterality: Asymmetries of Body, Brain and Cognition, 13*(1), 51–70.

Blanchard, R. (2008b). Sex ratio of older siblings in heterosexual and homosexual, right-handed and non-right-handed men. *Archives of Sexual Behavior, 37*(6), 977–981.

Blanchard, R., & Lippa, R. A. (2008). The sex ratio of older siblings in non-right-handed homosexual men. *Archives of Sexual Behavior, 37*(6), 970–976.

Blumenfeld, W. J., & Raymond, D. (1993). *Looking at gay and lesbian life* (updated and expanded edition). Boston: Beacon Press.

Blumstein, P. W., & Schwartz, P. (1993). Bisexuality: Some social psychological issues. In L. D. Garnets & D. C. Kimmel (Eds.), *Psychological perspectives on lesbian and gay male experiences* (pp. 168–183). New York: Columbia University Press.

Bohan, J. S. (1996). *Psychology and sexual orientation: Coming to terms*. New York: Routledge.

Brady, S., & Busse, W. J. (1994). The gay identity questionnaire: A brief measure of homosexual identity formation. *Journal of Homosexuality, 26,* 1–22.

Bridgewater, D. (1992). A gay male survivor of antigay violence. In S. H. Dworkin & F. J. Gutierrez (Eds.), *Counseling gay men and lesbians: Journey to the end of the rainbow* (pp. 219–230). Alexandria, VA: AACD Press.

Brown, L. B., Alley, G. R., Sarosy, S., Quarto, G., & Cook, T. (2001). Gay men: Aging well! *Journal of Gay & Lesbian Social Services: Issues in Practice, Policy & Research, 13*(4), 41–54.

Brown, T. L., & Alderson, K. G. (2010). Sexual identity and heterosexual male students' usage of homosexual insults. *Canadian Journal of Human Sexuality, 19*(1–2), 27–42.

Buhrke, R. A., Ben-Ezra, L. A., Hurley, M. E., & Ruprecht, L. J. (1992). Content analysis and methodological critique of articles concerning lesbian and gay male issues in counseling journals. *Journal of Counseling Psychology, 39,* 91–99.

Burchell, A. N., Calzavara, L. M., Myers, T., Remis, R. S., Raboud, J., Corey, P., & Swantee, C. (2010). Stress and increased HIV infection risk among gay and bisexual men. *AIDS, 24*(11), 1757–1764.

Byne, W. (1997). Why we cannot conclude that sexual orientation is primarily a biological phenomenon. *Journal of Homosexuality, 34*(1), 73–80.

Cabaj, R. P. (1998). History of gay acceptance and relationships. In R. P. Cabaj & D. W. Purcell (Eds.), *On the road to same-sex marriage: A supportive guide to psychological, political, and legal issues* (pp. 1–28). San Francisco: Jossey-Bass.

Carragher, D. J., & Rivers, I. (2002). Trying to hide: A cross-national study of growing up non-identified gay and bisexual male youth. *Clinical Child Psychology and Psychiatry, 7,* 457–474.

Cass, V. C. (1979). Homosexual identity formation: A theoretical model. *Journal of Homosexuality, 4,* 219–235.

Cass, V. (1996). Sexual orientation identity formation: A Western phenomenon. In R. P. Cabaj & T. S. Stein (Eds.), *Textbook of homosexuality and mental health* (pp. 227–251). Washington, DC: American Psychiatric Press.

Centers for Disease Control and Prevention. (2009). *National Center for HIV, Viral Hepatitis, STD, and TB Prevention.* Retrieved from www.cdc.gov/nchhstp/.

Chan, E., & Cavacuiti, C. (2008). Gay Abuse Screening Protocol (GASP): Screening for abuse in gay male relationships. *Journal of Homosexuality, 54*(4), 423–438.

Chang, J., & Block, J. (1960). A study of identification in male homosexuals. *Journal of Consulting Psychology, 24,* 307–310.

Chen-Hayes, S. F. (2001). Counseling and advocacy with transgendered and gender-variant persons in schools and families. *Journal of Humanistic Counseling, 40*(1), 34–48.

Chesler, M. A., & Zuniga, X. (1991). Dealing with prejudice and conflict in the classroom: The pink triangle exercise. *Teaching Sociology, 19*(2), 173–181.

Chojnacki, J. T., & Gelberg, S. (1994). Toward a conceptualization of career counseling with gay/lesbian/bisexual persons. *Journal of Career Development, 21,* 3–10.

Chung, Y. B., & Harmon, L. W. (1994). The career interests and aspirations of gay men: How sex-role orientation is related. *Journal of Vocational Behavior, 45,* 223–239.

Clark, D. (1997). *Loving someone gay* (Rev. ed.). Berkeley, CA: Celestial Arts.

Cochran, B. N., & Cauce, A. M. (2006). Characteristics of lesbian, gay, bisexual, and transgender individuals entering substance abuse treatment. *Journal of Substance Abuse Treatment, 30*(2), 135–146.

Cochran, S. D. (2001). Emerging issues in research on lesbians' and gay men's mental health: Does sexual orientation really matter? *American Psychologist, 56,* 931–947.

Cody, P. J., & Welch, P. L. (1997). Rural gay men in northern New England: Life experiences and coping styles. *Journal of Homosexuality, 33*(1), 51–67.

Cole, S. W., Kemeny, M. E., Taylor, S. E., & Visscher, B. R. (1996). Elevated physical health risk among gay men who conceal their homosexual identity. *Health Psychology, 15,* 243–251.

Coleman, E. (1981–1982). Developmental stages of the coming out process. *Journal of Homosexuality, 7*(2–3), 31–43.

Conklin, W. (2000). Employee resource groups: A foundation for support and change. *Diversity Factor, 9*(1), 12–25.

Cook-Daniels, L. (2008). Living memory GLBT history timeline: Current elders would have been this old when these events happened . . . *Journal of GLBT Family Studies, 4*(4), 485–497.

Cooley, J. J. (1998). Gay and lesbian adolescents: Presenting problems and the counselor's role. *Professional School Counseling, 1*(3), 30–34.

Cooper, L. (2008). On the other side: Supporting sexual minority students. *British Journal of Guidance & Counselling, 36*(4), 425–440.

Corey, G. (2009). *Theory and practice of counseling and psychotherapy* (8th ed.). Belmont, CA: Brooks/Cole.

Cornett, C. (1995). *Reclaiming the authentic self: Dynamic psychotherapy with gay men.* Northvale, NJ: Jason Aronson.

Cox, S., & Gallois, C. (1996). Gay and lesbian identity development: A social identity perspective. *Journal of Homosexuality, 30*(4), 1–30.

Crawford, I., Allison, K. W., Zamboni, B. D., & Soto, T. (2002). The influence of dual-identity development on the psychosocial functioning of African-American gay and bisexual men. *Journal of Sex Research, 39*(3), 179–189.

Croteau, J. M., & Thiel, M. J. (1993). Integrating sexual orientation in career counseling: Acting to end a form of the personal-career dichotomy. *Career Development Quarterly, 42,* 174–179.

Croteau, J. M., Anderson, M. Z., Distefano, T. M., & Kampa-Kokesch, S. (2000). Lesbian, gay, and bisexual vocational psychology: Reviewing foundations and planning construction. In R. M. Perez, K. A. Debord, & K. J. Bieschke (Eds.), *Handbook of counseling and psychotherapy with lesbian, gay, and bisexual clients* (pp. 383–408). Washington, DC: American Psychological Association.

D'Augelli, A. R. (2006). Developmental and contextual factors and mental health among lesbian, gay, and bisexual youths. In A. M. Omoto & H. S. Kurtzman (Eds.), *Sexual orientation and mental health: Examining identity and development in lesbian, gay, and bisexual people* (pp. 37–53). Washington, DC: American Psychological Association.

D'Augelli, A. R., Grossman, A. H., & Starks, M. T. (2005). Parents' awareness of lesbian, gay, and bisexual youths' sexual orientation. *Journal of Marriage and Family, 67*(2), 474–482.

D'Augelli, A. R., Grossman, A. H., Starks, M. T., & Sinclair, K. O. (2010). Factors associated with parents' knowledge of gay, lesbian, and bisexual youths' sexual orientation. *Journal of GLBT Family Studies, 6*(2), 178–198.

D'Augelli, A. R., & Hershberger, S. L. (1993). Lesbian, gay, and bisexual youth in community settings: Personal challenges and mental health problems. *American Journal of Community Psychology, 21*(4), 421–448.

Dank, B. M. (1971). Coming out in the gay world. *Psychiatry, 34,* 180–197.

de Monteflores, C., & Schultz, S. J. (1978). Coming out: Similarities and differences for lesbians and gay men. *Journal of Social Issues, 34,* 59–72.

Devlin, P. K., & Cowan, G. A. (1985). Homophobia, perceived fathering, and male intimate relationships. *Journal of Personality Assessment*, *49*(5), 467–473.

Diamond, L. M. (2007). A dynamical systems approach to the development and expression of female same-sex sexuality. *Perspectives on Psychological Science, 2*(2), 142–161.

Diamond, L. M. (2008). Female bisexuality from adolescence to adulthood: Results from a 10-year longitudinal study. *Developmental Psychology, 44*(1), 5–14.

Dillon, F. R., Worthington, R. L., Savoy, H. B., Rooney, S. C., Becker-Schutte, A., & Guerra, R. M. (2004). On becoming allies: A qualitative study of lesbian-, gay-, and bisexual affirmative counselor training. *Counselor Education and Supervision*, *43*(2), 162–178.

Divisions of HIV/AIDS Prevention. (2009, February 26). *National Center for HIV/AIDS, Viral Hepatitis, STD, and TB Prevention Department of Health and Human Services, Centers for Disease Control and Prevention: Basic statistics*. Retrieved from www.cdc.gov/hiv/topics/surveillance/basic.htm.

Dobinson, C. (2004). Everyday acts of survival and unorganized resistance: Gay, lesbian and bisexual youth respond to oppression. In J. McNinch & M. Cronin (Eds.), *I could not speak my heart: Education and social justice for gay and lesbian youth* (pp. 49–80). Regina, SK: Canadian Plains Research Centre, University of Regina Press.

Dowsett, G. W. (2009). Dangerous desires and post-queer HIV prevention: Rethinking community, incitement and intervention. *Social Theory & Health, 7*(3), 218–240.

Drescher, J. (1998). I'm your handyman: A history of reparative therapies. *Journal of Homosexuality, 36*(1), 19–42.

Dunbar, E. (2006). Race, gender, and sexual orientation in hate crime victimization: Identity politics or identity risk? *Violence and Victims, 21*(3), 323–337.

Dworkin, S. H. (2000). Individual therapy with lesbian, gay, and bisexual clients. In R. M. Perez, K. A. Debord, & K. J. Bieschke (Eds.), *Handbook of counseling and psychotherapy with lesbian, gay, and bisexual clients* (pp. 157–182). Washington, DC: American Psychological Association.

Dworkin, S. H., & Gutierrez, F. (1989). Introduction to special issue. Counselors be aware: Clients come in every size, shape, color, and sexual orientation. *Journal of Counseling and Development, 68,* 6–8.

Eardley, E. (2002). "Queer's" near absence in academic and student service websites. *International Journal of Sexuality and Gender Studies, 7,* 39–50.

Ellis, A. L., & Mitchell, R. W. (2000). Sexual orientation. In L. T. Szuchman & F. Muscarella (Eds.), *Psychological perspectives on human sexuality* (pp. 196–231). New York: John Wiley & Sons.

Erikson, E. H. (1966). Eight ages of man. *International Journal of Psychiatry, 2*(3), 281–300.

Erikson, E. H. (1968). *Identity: Youth and crisis*. New York: Norton.

Eubanks-Carter, C., Burckell, L. A., & Goldfried, M. R. (2005). Enhancing therapeutic effectiveness with lesbian, gay, and bisexual clients. *Clinical Psychology: Science and Practice*, *12*(1), 1–18.

Fassinger, R. E. (1991). The hidden minority: Issues and challenges in working with lesbian women and gay men. *The Counseling Psychologist, 19,* 157–176.

Finkel, M. J., Storaasli, R. D., Bandele, A., & Schaefer, V. (2003). Diversity training in graduate school: An exploratory evaluation of the Safe Zone project. *Professional Psychology: Research & Practice, 34*(5), 555–561.

Flores, S. A., Mansergh, G., Marks, G., Guzman, R., & Colfax, G. (2009). Gay identity-related factors and sexual risk among men who have sex with men in San Francisco. *AIDS Education and Prevention, 21*(2), 91–103.

Flowers, P., & Buston, K. (2001). "I was terrified of being different": Exploring gay men's accounts of growing-up in a heterosexist society. *Journal of Adolescence, 24,* 51–65.

Floyd, F. J., & Stein, T. S. (2002). Sexual orientation identity formation among gay, lesbian, and bisexual youths: Multiple patterns of milestone experiences. *Journal of Research on Adolescence, 12,* 167–191.

Fontaine, J. H. (1998). Evidencing a need: School counselors' experiences with gay and lesbian students. *Professional School Counseling, 1*(3), 8–14.

Frable, D. E. S., Wortman, C., & Joseph, J. (1997). Predicting self-esteem, well-being, and distress in a cohort of gay men: The importance of cultural stigma, personal visibility, community networks, and positive identity. *Journal of Personality, 65*(3), 599–624.

Frost, D. M., & Meyer, I. H. (2009). Internalized homophobia and relationship quality among lesbians, gay men, and bisexuals. *Journal of Counseling Psychology, 56*(1), 97–109.

Galupo, M. P. (2007). Friendship patterns of sexual minority individuals in adulthood. *Journal of Social and Personal Relationships, 24*(1), 139–151.

Garnets, L., Herek, G. M., & Levy, B. (1990). Violence and victimization of lesbians and gay men: Mental health consequences. *Journal of Interpersonal Violence, 5,* 366–383.

Garnets, L., Herek, G. M., & Levy, B. (1992). Violence and victimization of lesbians and gay men: Mental health consequences. In G. M. Herek & K. T. Berrill (Eds.), *Hate crimes: Confronting violence against lesbians and gay men* (pp. 207–226). Newbury Park, CA: Sage.

Garnets, L. D., & Kimmel, D. C. (1993). Introduction: Lesbian and gay male dimensions in the psychological study of human diversity. In L. D. Garnets & D. C. Kimmel (Eds.), *Psychological perspectives on lesbian and gay male experiences* (pp. 1–51). New York: Columbia University Press.

Gastaldo, D., Holmes, D., Lombardo, A., & O'Byrne, P. (2009). Unprotected sex among men who have sex with men in Canada: Exploring rationales and expanding HIV prevention. *Critical Public Health, 19*(3–4), 399–416.

Godin, G., Naccache, H., Cote, F., Leclerc, R., Frechette, M., & Alary, M. (2008). Promotion of safe sex: Evaluation of a community-level intervention programme in gay bars, saunas and sex shops. *Health Education Research, 23*(2), 287–297.

Goellner, C. (2010, April 22). Archie Comics introduces openly gay character Kevin Keller. *Comics Alliance*. Retrieved from www.comicsalliance.com/2010/04/22/archie-introduces-an-openly-gay-character-kevin-keller/.

Gonsiorek, J. (1982a). An introduction to mental health issues and homosexuality. *American Behavioral Scientist, 25*(4), 367–384.

Gonsiorek, J. C. (1982b). Results of psychological testing on homosexual populations. *American Behavioral Scientist, 25,* 385–396.

Gonsiorek, J. C. (1993). Mental health issues of gay and lesbian adolescents. In L. D. Garnets & D. C. Kimmel (Eds.), *Psychological perspectives on lesbian and gay male experiences* (pp. 469–485). New York: Columbia University Press.

Gonsiorek, J. C. (2004). Reflections from the conversion therapy battlefield. *The Counseling Psychologist, 32*(5), 750–759.

Goodrich, K. M., & Luke, M. (2009). LGBTQ responsive school counseling. *Journal of LGBT Issues in Counseling, 3*(2), 113–127.

Grant, D., & Epp, L. (1998). The gay orientation: Does God mind? *Counseling and Values, 43*(1), 28–33.

Green, A. I. (2008). Health and sexual status in an urban gay enclave: An application of the stress process model. *Journal of Health & Human Behavior, 49*(4), 436–451.

Green, B. C. (1998). Thinking about students who do not identify as gay, lesbian, or bisexual, but . . . *Journal of American College Health, 47*(2), 89–91.

Grossman, A. H., D'Augelli, A. R., & O'Connell, T. S. (2001). Being lesbian, gay, bisexual, and 60 or older in North America. *Journal of Gay & Lesbian Social Services: Issues in Practice, Policy & Research, 13*(4), 23–40.

Grov, C., Bimbi, D. S., Nanin, J. E., & Parsons, J. T. (2006). Race, ethnicity, gender, and generational factors associated with the coming-out process among gay, lesbian, and bisexual individuals. *Journal of Sex Research, 43*(2), 115–121.

Haber, D. (2009). Gay aging. *Gerontology & Geriatrics Education, 30*(3), 267–280.

Haldeman, D. C. (1994). The practice and ethics of sexual orientation conversion therapy. *Journal of Consulting and Clinical Psychology, 62,* 221–227.

Halkitis, P. N. (2010). Reframing HIV prevention for gay men in the United States. *American Psychologist, 65*(8), 752–763.

Halkitis, P. N., Mattis, J. S., Sahadath, J. K., Massie, D., Ladyzhenskaya, L., Pitrelli, K., . . . Cowie, S.-A. E. (2009). The meanings and manifestations of religion and spirituality among lesbian, gay, bisexual, and transgender adults. *Journal of Adult Development, 16*(4), 250–262.

Hammersmith, S. K., & Weinberg, M. S. (1973). Homosexual identity: Commitment, adjustments, and significant others. *Sociometry, 36*(1), 56–78.

Han, C. S. (2006). Geisha of a different kind: Gay Asian men and the gendering of sexual identity. *Sexuality & Culture: An Interdisciplinary Quarterly, 10*(3), 3–28.

Han, C. S. (2007). They don't want to cruise your type: Gay men of color and the racial politics of exclusion. *Social Identities: Journal for the Study of Race, Nation and Culture, 13*(1), 51–67.

Hanley-Hackenbruck, P. (1988). 'Coming out' and psychotherapy. *Psychiatric Annals, 18,* 29–32.

Harris, G. E., & Alderson, K. (2007). An investigation of gay men's experiences with HIV counseling and peer support services. *Canadian Journal of Community Mental Health, 26*(1), 129–142.

Harris, G. E., & Alderson, K. G. (2006). Gay men living with HIV/AIDS: The potential for empowerment. *Journal of HIV/AIDS & Social Services, 5*(3–4), 9–24.

Harris, M. B., & Bliss, G. K. (1997). Coming out in a school setting: Former students' experiences and opinions about disclosure. *Journal of Gay and Lesbian Social Services, 7*(4), 85–100.

Hart, T. A., James, C. A., Purcell, D. W., & Farber, E. (2008). Social anxiety and HIV transmission risk among HIV-seropositive male patients. *AIDS Patient Care and STDs, 22*(11), 879–886.

Helminiak, D. A. (1994). *What the Bible really says about homosexuality*. San Francisco: Alamo Square Press.

Hencken, J., & O'Dowd, W. (1977). Coming out as an aspect of identity formation. *Gay Academic Union, 1,* 18–22.

Herdt, G. (1997). *Same sex, different cultures*. Boulder, CO: Westview Press.

Herek, G. M. (2009). Hate crimes and stigma-related experiences among sexual minority adults in the United States: Prevalence estimates from a national probability sample. *Journal of Interpersonal Violence, 24*(1), 54–74.

Herek, G. M., Gillis, J. R., & Cogan, J. C. (1999). Psychological sequelae of hate-crime victimization among lesbian, gay, and bisexual adults. *Journal of Consulting and Clinical Psychology, 67*(6), 945–951.

Hetrick, E. S., & Martin, A. D. (1987). Developmental issues and their resolution for gay and lesbian adolescents. *Journal of Homosexuality,* 14(1–2), 25–43.

Hewitt, C. (1995). The socioeconomic position of gay men: A review of the evidence. *American Journal of Economics and Sociology, 54,* 461–479.

Hill, R. J. (2006). What's it like to be queer here? *New Directions for Adult and Continuing Education, 112,* 7–16.

Hooker, E. (1957). The adjustment of the male overt homosexual. *Journal of Projective Techniques, 21,* 18–31.

Hubbard, J. (2010, October 3). Fifth gay teen suicide in three weeks sparks debate. Retrieved from http://abcnews.go.com/US/gay-teen-suicide-sparks-debate/story?id=11788128.

Ibanez, G. E., Van Oss Marin, B., Flores, S. A., Millett, G., & Diaz, R. M. (2009). General and gay-related racism experienced by Latino gay men. *Cultural Diversity and Ethnic Minority Psychology, 15*(3), 215–222.

Igartua, K. J., Gill, K., & Montoro, R. (2003). Internalized homophobia: A factor in depression, anxiety, and suicide in the gay and lesbian population. *Canadian Journal of Community Mental Health, 22,* 15–30.

Isay, R. A. (1996). *Becoming gay: The journey to self-acceptance*. New York: Pantheon.

Iwasaki, Y., & Ristock, J. L. (2007). The nature of stress experienced by lesbians and gay men. *Anxiety, Stress & Coping: An International Journal, 20*(3), 299–319.

Janoff, D. V. (2005). *Pink blood: Homophobic violence in Canada*. Toronto, ON: University of Toronto Press.

Johnson, R. (2011). *About.com: The rainbow (gay pride) flag*. Retrieved from http://gaylife.about.com/od/gaypride/p/rainbowflag.htm.

Jones, A. J. (1997). Truth and deception in AIDS information brochures. *Journal of Homosexuality, 32*(3–4), 37–75.

Jones, M. A., & Gabriel, M. A. (1999). Utilization of psychotherapy by lesbians, gay men, and bisexuals: Findings from a nationwide survey. *American Journal of Orthopsychiatry, 69,* 209–219.

Kaiser Family Foundation. (2001). *Inside-out: A report on the experiences of lesbians, gays and bisexuals in America and the public's views on issues and policies related to sexual orientation.* Retrieved from www.kff.org/kaiserpolls/3193-index.cfm.

Kalichman, S. C. (1998). *Understanding AIDS: Advances in research and treatment* (2nd ed.). Washington, DC: American Psychological Association.

Kamp Dush, C. M., & Amato, P. R. (2005). Consequences of relationship status and quality for subjective well-being. *Journal of Social and Personal Relationships, 22*(5), 607–627.

Kean, R. (2006). Understanding the lives of older gay people. *Gerontological Care and Practice, 18*(8), 31–36.

Kertzner, R. M., Meyer, I. H., Frost, D. M., & Stirratt, M. J. (2009). Social and psychological well-being in lesbians, gay men, and bisexuals: The effects of race, gender, age, and sexual identity. *American Journal of Orthopsychiatry, 79*(4), 500–510.

Kimmel, M. S. (Ed.). (2007). *The sexual self: The construction of sexual scripts*. Nashville, TN: Vanderbilt University Press.

Kimmel, M. S., & Mahler, M. (2003). Adolescent masculinity, homophobia, and violence: Random school shootings, 1982–2001. *American Behavioral Scientist, 46*(10), 1439–1458.

Kinnish, K. K., Strassberg, D. S., & Turner, C. W. (2005). Sex differences in the flexibility of sexual orientation: A multidimensional retrospective assessment. *Archives of Sexual Behavior, 34*(2), 173–183.

Kinsey, A. C., Pomeroy, W. B., & Martin, C. E. (1948). *Sexual behavior in the human male*. Philadelphia: W. B. Saunders.

Klein, F., Sepekoff, B., & Wolf, T. J. (1985). Sexual orientation: A multi-variable dynamic process. *Journal of Homosexuality, 11*(1–2), 35–49.

Klinger, R. L. (1995). Gay violence. *Journal of Gay & Lesbian Psychotherapy, 2*(3), 119–134.

Kosciw, J. G., Diaz, E. M., & Greytak, E. A. (2008). *The 2007 national school climate survey: The experiences of lesbian, gay, bisexual and transgender youth in our nation's schools.* A Report from the Gay, Lesbian and Straight Education Network (GLSEN). Retrieved from www.glsen.org/cgi-bin/iowa/all/library/record/2340.html?state=research&type=research.

Kosciw, J. G., Greytak, E. A., & Diaz, E. M. (2009). Who, what, where, when, and why: Demographic and ecological factors contributing to hostile school climate for lesbian, gay, bisexual, and transgender youth. *Journal of Youth and Adolescence, 38*(7), 976–988.

Kübler-Ross, E. (1969). *On death and dying*. New York: MacMillan.

Kunreuther, F. (1991). The Hetrick-Martin Institute: Services for youth. *Focal Point 5*(2), 10–11.

Kurdek, L. A. (2004). Are gay and lesbian cohabiting couples *really* different from heterosexual married couples? *Journal of Marriage and Family, 66,* 880–900.

Kurdek, L. A. (2005). What do we know about gay and lesbian couples? *Current Directions in Psychological Science, 14*(5), 251–254.

Kurdek, L. A. (2006). Differences between partners from heterosexual, gay, and lesbian cohabiting couples. *Journal of Marriage and Family, 68*(2), 509–528.

Lahey, K. A. (1999). *Are we 'persons' yet? Law and sexuality in Canada*. Toronto, ON: University of Toronto Press.

Lahey, K. A., & Alderson, K. (2004). *Same-sex marriage: The personal and the political.* Toronto, ON: Insomniac Press.

Lannutti, P. J. (2007). The influence of same-sex marriage on the understanding of same-sex relationships. *Journal of Homosexuality, 53*(3), 135–157.

LaSala, M. C. (2004a). Extradyadic sex and gay male couples: Comparing monogamous and nonmonogamous relationships. *Families in Society, 85,* 405–412.

LaSala, M. C. (2004b). Monogamy of the heart: Extradyadic sex and gay male couples. *Journal of Gay and Lesbian Social Services, 17,* 1–24.

Laumann, E. O., Gagnon, J. H., Michael, R. T., & Michaels, S. (1994). *The social organization of sexuality: Sexual practices in the United States.* Chicago: University of Chicago Press.

Lease, S. H., Horne, S. G., & Noffsinger-Frazier, N. (2005). Affirming faith experiences and psychological health for Caucasian lesbian, gay, and bisexual individuals. *Journal of Counseling Psychology, 52*(3), 378–388.

Lee, J. A. (1977). Going public: A study in the sociology of homosexual liberation. *Journal of Homosexuality, 3,* 49–78.

Leserman, J., DiSantostefano, R., Perkins, D. O., & Evans, D. L. (1994). Gay identification and psychological health in HIV-positive and HIV-negative gay men. *Journal of Applied Social Psychology, 24,* 2193–2208.

LeVay, S. (1991). A difference in hypothalamic structure between heterosexual and homosexual men. *Science, 253,* 1034–1037.

LeVay, S. (1993). *The sexual brain*. Cambridge, MA: MIT Press.

Lin, J. (2011, July 14). *California gay history law: Jerry Brown signs landmark bill*. Retrieved from www.huffingtonpost.com/2011/07/14/california-gay-history-law-jerry-brown_n_898745.html.

Mackey, R. A., Diemer, M. A., & O'Brien, B. A. (2004). Relational factors in understanding satisfaction in the lasting relationships of same-sex and heterosexual couples. *Journal of Homosexuality, 47*(1), 111–136.

Maguen, S., Floyd, F. J., Bakeman, R., & Armistead, L. (2002). Developmental milestones and disclosure of sexual orientation among gay, lesbian, and bisexual youths. *Journal of Applied Developmental Psychology, 23,* 219–233.

Malyon, A. K. (1982a). Biphasic aspects of homosexual identity formation. *Psychotherapy: Theory, Research, and Practice, 19,* 335–340.

Malyon, A. K. (1982b). Psychotherapeutic implications of internalized homophobia in gay men. *Journal of Homosexuality, 7*(2–3), 59–69.

Mao, L., McCormick, J., & Van de Ven, P. (2002). Ethnic and gay identification: Gay Asian men dealing with the divide. *Culture, Health & Sexuality, 4*(4), 419–430.

Marcia, J. E. (1966). Development and validation of ego-identity status. *Journal of Personality and Social Psychology, 3,* 551–559.

Marcia, J. E. (1994). The empirical study of ego identity. In H. A. Bosma, T. L. G. Graafsma, H. D. Grotevant, & D. J. de Levita (Eds.), *Identity and development: An interdisciplinary approach* (pp. 67–80). Thousand Oaks, CA: Sage.

Marinoble, R. M. (1998). Homosexuality: A blind spot in the school mirror. *Professional School Counseling, 1*(3), 4–7.

Marshal, M. P., Friedman, M. S., Stall, R., & Thompson, A. L. (2009). Individual trajectories of substance use in lesbian, gay and bisexual youth and heterosexual youth. *Addiction, 104*(6), 974–981.

Mays, V. M., & Cochran, S. D. (2001). Mental health correlates of perceived discrimination among lesbian, gay, and bisexual adults in the United States. *American Journal of Public Health, 91,* 1869–1876.

McCarn, S. R., & Fassinger, R. E. (1996). Re-visioning sexual minority identity formation: A new model of lesbian identity and its implications for counseling and research. *The Counseling Psychologist, 24*(3), 508–534.

McDonald, H. B., & Steinhorn, A. I. (1990). *Homosexuality: A practical guide to counseling lesbians, gay men, and their families*. New York: Continuum.

McFarland, W. P. (1993). A developmental approach to gay and lesbian youth. *Journal of Humanistic Education and Development, 32,* 17–29.

McKirnan, D. J., & Peterson, P. L. (1989). Alcohol and drug use among homosexual men and women: Epidemiology and population characteristics. *Addictive Behaviors, 14,* 545–553.

McWhirter, D. P., & Mattison, A. M. (1996). Male couples. In R. P. Cabaj & T. S. Stein (Eds.), *Textbook of homosexuality and mental health* (pp. 319–337). Washington, DC: American Psychiatric Press.

Meyer, I. H., & Wilson, P. A. (2009). Sampling lesbian, gay, and bisexual populations. *Journal of Counseling Psychology, 56*(1), 23–31.

Minton, H. L., & McDonald, G. J. (1983–1984). Homosexual identity formation as a developmental process. *Journal of Homosexuality, 9*(2–3), 91–104.

Minwalla, O., Rosser, B. R. S., Feldman, J., & Varga, C. (2005). Identity experience among progressive gay Muslims in North America: A qualitative study within Al-Fatiha. *Culture, Health & Sexuality, 7*(2), 113–128.

Miranda, J., & Storms, M. (1989). Psychological adjustment of lesbians and gay men. *Journal of Counseling and Development, 68,* 41–45.

Moradi, B., DeBlaere, C., & Huang, Y.-P. (2010). Centralizing the experiences of LGB people of color in counseling psychology. *The Counseling Psychologist, 38*(3), 322–330.

Morin, S. F., & Rothblum, E. D. (1991). Removing the stigma: Fifteen years of progress. *American Psychologist, 9,* 947–949.

Morrison, L. L., & L'Heureux, J. (2001). Suicide and gay/lesbian/bisexual youth: Implications for clinicians. *Journal of Adolescence, 24,* 39–49.

Morrison, T. G., & Whitehead, B. W. (2005). Strategies of stigma resistance among Canadian gay-identified sex workers. *Journal of Psychology & Human Sexuality, 17*(1–2), 169–179.

Morrow, S. L. (1997). Career development of lesbian and gay youth: Effects of sexual orientation, coming out, and homophobia. *Journal of Gay and Lesbian Social Services, 7*(4), 1–15.

Muller, A. (1987). *Parents matter: Parents' relationships with lesbian daughters and gay sons.* Tallahassee, FL: Naiad Press.

Murphy, T. (1992). Redirecting sexual orientation: Techniques and justifications. *Journal of Sex Research, 29,* 501–523.

Myers, T., Aguinaldo, J. P., Dakers, D., Fischer, B., Bullock, S., Millson, P., & Calzavara, L. (2004). How drug using men who have sex with men account for substance use during sexual behaviours: Questioning assumptions of HIV prevention and research. *Addiction Research & Theory, 12*(3), 213–229.

Napier, N. J. (1990). *Recreating yourself: Building self-esteem through imaging and self-hypnosis.* New York: Norton.

Nardi, P. M. (1999). *Gay men's friendships: Invincible communities*. Chicago: University of Chicago Press.

Natale, A. P. (2009). HIV/AIDS prevention: MSM wants, desires, and needs. *Journal of Gay & Lesbian Social Services: Issues in Practice, Policy & Research, 21*(1), 49–72.

Nauta, M. M., Saucier, A. M., & Woodard, L. E. (2001). Interpersonal influences on students' academic and career decisions: The impact of sexual orientation. *Career Development Quarterly, 49,* 352–362.

Nicolosi, J., Byrd, A. D., & Potts, R. W. (2000a). Beliefs and practices of therapists who practice sexual reorientation psychotherapy. *Psychological Reports, 86,* 689–702.

Nicolosi, J., Byrd, A. D., & Potts, R. W. (2000b). Retrospective self-reports of changes in homosexual orientation: A consumer survey of conversion therapy clients. *Psychological Reports, 86,* 1071-1088.

Omizo, M. M., Omizo, S. A., & Okamoto, C. M. (1998). Gay and lesbian adolescents: A phenomenological study. *Professional School Counselling, 1,* 35–37.

Operario, D., Han, C. S., & Choi, K. H. (2008). Dual identity among gay Asian Pacific Islander men. *Culture, Health & Sexuality, 10*(5), 447–461.

Otis, M. D., Rostosky, S. S., Riggle, E. D. B., & Hamrin, R. (2006). Stress and relationship quality in same-sex couples. *Journal of Social and Personal Relationships, 23*(1), 81–99.

Pachankis, J. E., Goldfried, M. R., & Ramrattan, M. E. (2008). Extension of the rejection sensitivity construct to the interpersonal functioning of gay men. *Journal of Consulting and Clinical Psychology, 76*(2), 306–317.

Pachankis, J. E., Westmaas, J. L., & Dougherty, L. R. (2011). The influence of sexual orientation and masculinity on young men's tobacco smoking. *Journal of Consulting and Clinical Psychology, 79*(2), 142–152.

Pathela, P., & Schillinger, J. A. (2010). Sexual behaviors and sexual violence: Adolescents with opposite-, same-, or both-sex partners. *Pediatrics, 126*(5), 879–886.

Pearson, Q. M. (2003). Breaking the silence in the counselor education classroom: A training seminar on counseling sexual minority clients. *Journal of Counseling and Development, 81*(2), 292–300.

Pedersen, P. B., Crethar, H. C., & Carlson, J. (2008). *Inclusive cultural empathy: Making relationships central in counseling and psychotherapy.* Washington, DC: American Psychological Association.

Peplau, L. A. (1993). Lesbian and gay relationships. In L. D. Garnets & D. C. Kimmel (Eds.), *Psychological perspectives on lesbian and gay male experiences* (pp. 395–419). New York: Columbia University Press.

Peplau, L. A., & Fingerhut, A. W. (2007). The close relationships of lesbian and gay men. *Annual Review of Psychology, 58,* 405–424.

Peplau, L. A., & Spalding, L. R. (2000). The close relationships of lesbians, gay men, and bisexuals. In C. Hendrick & S. S. Hendrick (Eds.), *Close relationships: A sourcebook* (pp. 111–123). Thousand Oaks, CA: Sage.

Pixton, S. (2003). Experiencing gay affirmative therapy: An exploration of clients' views of what is helpful. *Counselling & Psychotherapy Research, 3*(3), 211–215.

Plummer, K. (1975). *Sexual stigma: An interactionist account*. Boston: Routledge & Kegan Paul.

Poon, M. K.-L., Ho, P. T.-T., Wong, J. P.-H., Wong, G., & Lee, R. (2005). Psychosocial experiences of east and southeast Asian men who use gay Internet chatrooms in Toronto: An implication for HIV/AIDS prevention. *Ethnicity & Health, 10*(2), 145–167.

Pope, M. S., Prince, J. P., & Mitchell, K. (2000). Responsible career counseling with lesbian and gay students. In D. A. Luzzo (Ed.), *Career counseling of college students: An empirical guide to strategies that work* (pp. 267–282). Washington, DC: American Psychological Association.

Poteat, V. P., Espelage, D. L., & Koenig, B. W. (2009). Willingness to remain friends and attend school with lesbian and gay peers: Relational expressions of prejudice among heterosexual youth. *Journal of Youth and Adolescence, 38*(7), 952–962.

Prince, J. P. (1995). Influences on the career development of gay men. *Career Development Quarterly, 44,* 168–177.

Prince, J. P. (1997). Career assessment with lesbian, gay, and bisexual individuals. *Journal of Career Assessment, 5,* 225–238.

Prochaska, J. O., Norcross, J. C., & Diclemente, C. C. (1994). *Changing for good: A revolutionary six-stage program for overcoming bad habits and moving your life positively forward.* New York: Avon.

Public Health Agency of Canada. (2006, August). *HIV/AIDS Epi Update: HIV infections among MSM in Canada*. Centre for Infectious Disease Prevention and Control. Retrieved from www.phac-aspc.gc.ca/publicat/epiu-aepi/epi-06/pdf/epi06_e.pdf.

Radkowsky, M., & Siegel, L. J. (1997). The gay adolescent: Stressors, adaptations, and psychosocial interventions. *Clinical Psychology Review, 17*(2), 191–216.

Ramirez-Valles, J. (2007). "I don't fit anywhere": How race and sexuality shape Latino gay and bisexual men's health. In I. H. Meyer & M. E. Northridge (Eds.), *The health of sexual minorities: Public health perspectives on lesbian, gay, bisexual, and transgender populations* (pp. 301–319). New York: Springer Science + Business Media.

Ratner, E. F. (1993). Treatment issues for chemically dependent lesbians and gay men. In L. D. Garnets & D. C. Kimmel (Eds.), *Psychological perspectives on lesbian and gay male experiences* (pp. 567–578). New York: Columbia University Press.

Reback, C. J., & Larkins, S. (2010). Maintaining a heterosexual identity: Sexual meanings among a sample of heterosexually identified men who have sex with men. *Archives of Sexual Behavior, 39*(3), 766–773.

Reeves, T., Horne, S. G., Rostosky, S. S., Riggle, E. D. B., Baggett, L. R., & Aycock, R. A. (2010). Family members' support for GLBT issues: The role of family adaptability and cohesion. *Journal of GLBT Family Studies, 6*(1), 80–97.

Richardson, D. (1993). Recent challenges to traditional assumptions about homosexuality: Some implications for practice. In L. D. Garnets & D. C. Kimmel (Eds.), *Psychological perspectives on lesbian and gay male experiences* (pp. 117–129). New York: Columbia University Press.

Rieger, G., Linsenmeier, J. A. W., Gygax, L., & Bailey, J. M. (2008). Sexual orientation and childhood gender nonconformity: Evidence from home videos. *Developmental Psychology, 44*(1), 46–58.

Riggle, E. D. B., Rostosky, S. S., & Horne, S. G. (2010). Psychological distress, well-being, and legal recognition in same-sex couple relationships. *Journal of Family Psychology, 24*(1), 82–86.

Riggle, E. D. B., Whitman, J. S., Olson, A., Rostosky, S. S., & Strong, S. (2008). The positive aspects of being a lesbian or gay man. *Professional Psychology: Research and Practice, 39*(2), 210–217.

Ritter, K. Y., & Terndrup, A. I. (2002). *Handbook of affirmative psychotherapy with lesbians and gay men*. New York: Guilford Press.

Rodriguez, E. M., & Ouellette, S. C. (2000). Gay and lesbian Christians: Homosexual and religious identity integration in the members and participants of a gay-positive church. *Journal for the Scientific Study of Religion, 39*(3), 333–347.

Roisman, G. I., Clausell, E., Holland, A., Fortuna, K., & Elieff, C. (2008). Adult romantic relationships as contexts of human development: A multimethod comparison of same-sex couples with opposite-sex dating, engaged, and married dyads. *Developmental Psychology, 44*(1), 91–101.

Rosario, M., Schrimshaw, E. W., Hunter, J., & Braun, L. (2006). Sexual identity development among lesbian, gay, and bisexual youths: Consistency and change over time. *Journal of Sex Research, 43*(1), 46–58.

Ross, M. W., Paulsen, J. A., & Stalstrom, O. W. (1988). Homosexuality and mental health: A cross-cultural review. *Journal of Homosexuality, 15,* 131–152.

Rothblum, E. D. (1994). Introduction to the special section: Mental health of lesbians and gay men. *Journal of Consulting and Clinical Psychology, 62,* 211–212.

Rothblum, E. D. (2009). An overview of same-sex couples in relationships: A research area still at sea. In D. A. Hope (Ed.), *Contemporary perspectives on lesbian, gay, and bisexual identities* (pp. 113–139). New York: Springer Science + Business Media.

Rowen, C. J., & Malcolm, J. P. (2003). Correlates of internalized homophobia and homosexual identity formation in a sample of gay men. *Journal of Homosexuality, 43*(2), 77–92.

Russell, S. T., Seif, H., & Truong, N. L. (2001). School outcomes of sexual minority youth in the United States: Evidence from a national study. *Journal of Adolescence, 24,* 111–127.

Russell, T. G. (1989). AIDS education, homosexuality, and the counselor's role. *The School Counsellor, 36,* 333–337.

Ryan, C., Huebner, D., Diaz, R., & Sanches, J. (2009). Family rejection as a predictor of negative health outcomes in White and Latino lesbian, gay, and bisexual young adults. *Pediatrics, 123*(1), 346–352.

Sailer, D. D., Korschgen, A. J., & Lokken, J. M. (1994). Responding to the career needs of gays, lesbians, and bisexuals. *Journal of Career Planning and Employment, 54*(3), 39–42.

Sanchez, F. J., Westefeld, J. S., Liu, W. M., & Vilain, E. (2010). Masculine gender role conflict and negative feelings about being gay. *Professional Psychology: Research and Practice, 41*(2), 104–111.

Sapp, J. (2001). Self-knowing as social justice: The impact of a gay professor on ending homophobia in education. *Encounter: Education for meaning and social justice, 14*(4), 17–28.

Savage, T. A., & Harley, D. A. (2005). African American lesbian, gay, and bisexual persons. In D. A. Harley & J. M. Dillard (Eds.), *Contemporary mental health issues among African Americans* (pp. 91–105). Alexandria, VA: American Counseling Association.

Savin-Williams, R. C. (1998). The disclosure to families of same-sex attraction by lesbian, gay, and bisexual youths. *Journal of Research on Adolescence, 8*(1), 49–68.

Savin-Williams, R. C. (2001). *Mom, dad, I'm gay: How families negotiate coming out*. Washington, DC: American Psychological Association.

Savin-Williams, R. C. (2005). *The new gay teenager*. Cambridge, MA: Harvard University Press.

Savin-Williams, R. C., & Ream, G. L. (2007). Prevalence and stability of sexual orientation components during adolescence and young adulthood. *Archives of Sexual Behavior, 36*(3), 385–394.

Schmitt, J. P., & Kurdek, L. A. (1987). Personality correlates of positive identity and relationship involvement in gay men. *Journal of Homosexuality, 13*(4), 101–109.

Schnoor, R. F. (2009). Finding one's place: Ethnic identity construction among gay Jewish men. *Dissertation Abstracts International Section A: Humanities and Social Sciences, 69*(12-A), 4884.

Schope, R. D. (2005). Who's afraid of growing old? Gay and lesbian perceptions of aging. *Journal of Gerontological Social Work, 45*(4), 23–39.

Schuck, K. D., & Liddle, B. J. (2001). Religious conflicts experienced by lesbian, gay, and bisexual individuals. *Journal of Gay & Lesbian Psychotherapy, 5*(2), 63–82.

Sell, R. L. (2007). Defining and measuring sexual orientation for research. In I. H. Meyer & M. E. Northridge (Eds.), *The health of sexual minorities: Public health perspectives on lesbian, gay, bisexual, and transgender populations* (pp. 355–374). New York: Springer Science + Business Media.

SF AIDS Foundation. (2010, May 26). *How HIV is spread*. Retrieved from www.sfaf.org/aids101/transmission.html.

Shannon, J. W., & Woods, W. J. (1991). Affirmative psychotherapy for gay men. *The Counseling Psychologist, 19*(2), 197–215.

Shippy, R. A., Cantor, M. H., & Brennan, M. (2004). Social networks of aging gay men. *Journal of Men's Studies, 13*(1), 107–120.

Shively, M., & De Cecco, J. P. (1977). Components of sexual identity. *Journal of Homosexuality, 3,* 41–48.

Shuper, P. A., & Fisher, W. A. (2008). The role of sexual arousal and sexual partner characteristics in HIV+ MSM's intentions to engage in unprotected sexual intercourse. *Health Psychology, 27*(4), 445–454.

Simonsen, G., Blazina, C., & Watkins, C. E. (2000). Gender role conflict and psychological well-being among gay men. *Journal of Counseling Psychology, 47,* 85–89.

Slater, B. R. (1988). Essential issues in working with lesbian and gay male youths. *Professional Psychology: Research and Practice, 19*(2), 226–235.

Smith, S. D., Dermer, S. B., & Astramovich, R. L. (2005). Working with nonheterosexual youth to understand sexual identity development, at-risk behaviors, and implications for health care professionals. *Psychological Reports, 96*(3), 651–654.

Sophie, J. (1985–1986). A critical examination of stage theories of lesbian identity development. *Journal of Homosexuality, 12*(2), 39–51.

Sue, D. W., Arredondo, P., & McDavis, R. J. (1992). Multicultural counseling competencies and standards: A call to the profession. *Journal of Counseling & Development, 70,* 477–486.

Sue, D. W., Bernier, J. E., Durran, A., Feinberg, L., Pedersen, P., Smith, E. J., . . . Vasquez-Nutall, E. (1982). Position paper: Cross-cultural counseling competencies. *The Counseling Psychologist, 10*(2), 45–52.

Sue, D. W., Carter, R. T., Casas, J. M., Fouad, N. A., Ivey, A. E., Jensen, M., . . . Vazquez-Nutall, E. (1998). *Multicultural counseling competencies: Individual and organizational development*. Thousand Oaks, CA: Sage.

Sullivan, M. K. (2003). Homophobia, history, and homosexuality: Trends for sexual minorities. *Journal of Human Behavior in the Social Environment, 8*(2–3), 1–13.

Tan, P. P. (2005). The importance of spirituality among gay and lesbian individuals. *Journal of Homosexuality, 49*(2), 135–144.

Throckmorton, W. (1998). Efforts to modify sexual orientation: A review of outcome literature and ethical issues. *Journal of Mental Health Counseling, 20*(4), 283–304.

Totten, M., Quigley, P., & Morgan, M. (2004). CPHA safe school study. *Canadian Public Health Association and the National Crime Prevention Strategy*. Retrieved from www.cpha.ca/uploads/progs/_/safeschools/safe_school_study_e.pdf.

Townsend, J. M. (1998). *What women want—what men want: Why the sexes still see love and commitment so differently*. New York: Oxford University Press.

Troiden, R. R. (1979). Becoming homosexual: A model of gay identity acquisition. *Psychiatry, 42,* 362–373.

Tyler, J. M., Jackman-Wheitner, L., Strader, S., & Lenox, R. (1997). A change-model approach to raising awareness of gay, lesbian, and bisexual issues among graduate students in counseling. *Journal of Sex Education & Therapy, 22*(2), 37–43.

Vare, J. W., & Norton, T. L. (1998). Understanding gay and lesbian youth: Sticks, stones, and silence. *Clearing House, 71*(6), 327–331.

Vargo, M. E. (1998). *Acts of disclosure: The coming-out process of contemporary gay men.* Binghamton, NY: Harrington Park Press.

Walton, G. (2006). "Fag church": Men who integrate gay and Christian identities. *Journal of Homosexuality, 51*(2), 1–17.

Watson, S. C. A. (2003). Coping with the HIV and AIDS epidemic in HIV seronegative gay males in Montreal (Quebec). *Dissertation Abstracts International: Section B: The Sciences and Engineering, 63*(7-B), 3487.

Watters, A. T. (1986). Heterosexual bias in psychological research on lesbianism and male homosexuality (1979–1983) utilizing the bibliographic and taxonomic system of Morin (1977). *Journal of Homosexuality, 13,* 35–58.

Weinberg, M. S. (1970). Homosexual samples: Differences and similarities. *Journal of Sex Research,* 6, 312–325.

Weiten, W., & Lloyd, M. (2000). *Psychology applied to modern life: Adjustment at the turn of the century*. Stamford, CT: Wadsworth.

Wells, K., & Tsutsumi, L. M. (2005). *Creating safe and caring schools for lesbian, gay, bisexual, and trans-identified students: A guide for counsellors*. Edmonton, AB: The Society for Safe and Caring Schools and Communities. Retrieved from www.sacsc.ca/PDF%20files/Resources/LGBTQ%20guide%20for%20counsellors%20unbooked.pdf.

Westhaver, R. (2005). 'Coming out of your skin': Circuit parties, pleasure and the subject. *Sexualities, 8*(3), 347–374.

Wienke, C., & Hill, G. J. (2009). Does the "marriage benefit" extend to partners in gay and lesbian relationships? Evidence from a random sample of sexually active adults. *Journal of Family Issues, 30*(2), 259–289.

Williams, C. L., Giuffre, P. A., & Dellinger, K. (2009). The gay-friendly closet. *Sexuality Research & Social Policy: A Journal of the NSRC, 6*(1), 29–45.

Williams, T., Connolly, J., Pepler, D., & Craig, W. (2003). Questioning and sexual minority adolescents: High school experiences of bullying, sexual harassment and physical abuse. *Canadian Journal of Community Mental Health, 22,* 47–58.

Wills, G., & Crawford, R. (2000). Attitudes toward homosexuality in Shreveport-Bossier City, Louisiana. *Journal of Homosexuality, 38*(3), 97–116.

Witelson, S. F., Kigar, D. L., Scamvougeras, A., Kideckel, D. M., Buck, B., Stanchev, P. L., . . . Black, S. (2008). Corpus callosum anatomy in right-handed homosexual and heterosexual men. *Archives of Sexual Behavior, 37*(6), 857–863.

Wright, S. L., & Canetto, S. S. (2009). Stereotypes of older lesbians and gay men. *Educational Gerontology, 35*(5), 424–452.

Yip, A. K. T. (2002). The persistence of faith among nonheterosexual Christians: Evidence for the neosecularization thesis of religious transformation. *Journal for the Scientific Study of Religion, 41*(2), 199–212.

References for Chapter 4

Abbott, D., & Burns, J. (2007). What's love got to do with it?: Experiences of lesbian, gay, and bisexual people with intellectual disabilities in the United Kingdom and views of the staff who support them. *Sexuality Research & Social Policy: A Journal of the NSRC, 4*(1), 27–39.

Ackbar, S., & Senn, C. Y. (2010). What's the confusion about fusion?—Differentiating positive and negative closeness in lesbian relationships. *Journal of Marital and Family Therapy, 36*(4), 416–430.

Alderson, K. (2000). *Beyond coming out: Experiences of positive gay identity*. Toronto, ON: Insomniac Press.

Alderson, K. G. (2010). From madness to mainstream: Working with gay men today. In N. Arthur & S. Collins (Eds.), *Culture-infused counselling: Celebrating the Canadian mosaic* (2nd ed., pp. 395–422). Calgary, AB: Counselling Concepts.

Amadio, D. M., & Chung, Y. B. (2004). Internalized homophobia and substance use among lesbian, gay, and bisexual persons. *Journal of Gay & Lesbian Social Services: Issues in Practice, Policy & Research, 17*(1), 83–101.

Arndt, M., & Hewat, H. (2009). The experience of stress and trauma: Black lesbians in South Africa. *Journal of Psychology in Africa, 19*(2), 207–212.

Arnow, B. A., & Post, L. I. (2010). Depression. In D. McKay, J. S. Abramowitz, & S. Taylor (Eds.), *Cognitive-behavioral therapy for refractory cases: Turning failure into success* (pp. 183–210). Washington, DC: American Psychological Association.

Associated Press. (2009, March 5). *California high court weighs arguments in gay marriage ban*. Retrieved from www.foxnews.com/story/0,2933,505126,00.html.

Austin, S. B., Ziyadeh, N., Kahn, J. A., Camargo, C. A., Jr., Colditz, G. A., & Field, A. E. (2004). Sexual orientation, weight concerns, and eating-disordered behaviors in adolescent girls and boys. *Journal of the American Academy of Child & Adolescent Psychiatry, 43*(9), 1115–1123.

Avery, A., Chase, J., Johansson, L., Litvak, S., Montero, D., & Wydra, M. (2007). America's changing attitudes toward homosexuality, civil unions, and same-gender marriage: 1977–2004. *Social Work, 52*(1), 71–79.

Balsam, K. F. (2003). Traumatic victimization in the lives of lesbian and bisexual women: A contextual approach. *Journal of Lesbian Studies, 7*(1), 1–14.

Balsam, K. F., Beauchaine, T. P., Rothblum, E. D., & Solomon, S. E. (2008). Three-year follow-up of same-sex couples who had civil unions in Vermont, same-sex couples not in civil unions, and heterosexual married couples. *Developmental Psychology, 44*(1), 102–116.

Barber, J. S., & Mobley, M. (1999). Counseling gay adolescents. In A. M. Horne, M. S. Kiselica, et al. (Eds.), *Handbook of counseling boys and adolescent males: A practitioner's guide* (pp. 161–178). Thousand Oaks, CA: Sage.

Beals, K. P., & Peplau, L. A. (2001). Social involvement, disclosure of sexual orientation, and the quality of lesbian relationships. *Psychology of Women Quarterly, 25*(1), 10–19.

Bedard, K. K., & Marks, A. K. (2010). Current psychological perspectives on adolescent lesbian identity development. *Journal of Lesbian Studies, 14*(1), 16–25.

Black, D., Gates, G., Sanders, S., & Taylor, L. (2000). Demographics of the gay and lesbian population in the United States: Evidence from available systematic data sources. *Demography, 37*(2), 139–154.

Boehmer, U., Bowen, D. J., & Bauer, G. R. (2007). Overweight and obesity in sexual-minority women: Evidence from population-based data. *American Journal of Public Health, 97*(6), 1134–1140.

Boon, S. L., & Alderson, K. G. (2009). A phenomenological study of women in same-sex relationships who were previously married to men. *Canadian Journal of Human Sexuality, 18*(4), 149–168.

Bos, H. M. W., Gartrell, N. K., van Balen, F., Peyser, H., & Sandfort, T. G. M. (2008). Children in planned lesbian families: A cross-cultural comparison between the United States and the Netherlands. *American Journal of Orthopsychiatry, 78*(2), 211–219.

Bos, H. M. W., & Van Balen, F. (2008). Children in planned lesbian families: Stigmatisation, psychological adjustment and protective factors. *Culture, Health & Sexuality, 10*(3), 221–236.

Bowen, D. J., Balsam, K. F., & Ender, S. R. (2008). A review of obesity issues in sexual minority women. *Obesity, 16*(2), 221–228.

Bowleg, L., Brooks, K., & Ritz, S. F. (2008). "Bringing home more than a paycheck": An exploratory analysis of Black lesbians' experiences of stress and coping in the workplace. *Journal of Lesbian Studies, 12*(1), 69–84.

Bowleg, L., Huang, J., Brooks, K., Black, A., & Burkholder, G. (2003). Triple jeopardy and beyond: Multiple minority stress and resilience among Black lesbians. *Journal of Lesbian Studies, 7*(4), 87–108.

Bridges, S. K., Selvidge, M. M. D., & Matthews, C. R. (2003). Lesbian women of color: Therapeutic issues and challenges. *Journal of Multicultural Counseling and Development, 31*(2), 113–130.

Brittain, D. R., Baillargeon, T., McElroy, M., Aaron, D. J., & Gyurcsik, N. C. (2006). Barriers to moderate physical activity in adult lesbians. *Women & Health, 43*(1), 75–92.

Browning, C., Reynolds, A. L., & Dworkin, S. H. (1991). Affirmative psychotherapy for lesbian women. *The Counseling Psychologist, 19,* 177–196.

Buckroyd, J., & Rother, S. (2007). *Therapeutic groups for obese women: A group leader's handbook.* Chichester, UK: John Wiley & Sons.

Burch, B. (2008). Infidelity: Outlaws and in-laws and lesbian relationships. *Journal of Lesbian Studies, 12*(2–3), 145–159.

Butler, A. C. (2000). Trends in same-gender partnering, 1988–1998. *Journal of Sex Research, 37*(4), 333–343.

Butler, S. S. (2004). Gay, lesbian, bisexual, and transgender (GLBT) elders: The challenges and resilience of this marginalized group. *Journal of Human Behavior in the Social Environment, 9*(4), 25–44.

Button, S. B. (2004). Identity management strategies utilized by lesbian and gay employees: A quantitative investigation. *Group & Organization Management, 29*(4), 470–494.

Buxton, A. P. (2004). Works in progress: How mixed-orientation couples maintain their marriages after the wives come out. *Journal of Bisexuality, 4*(1–2), 57–82.

Cass, V. C. (1979). Homosexual identity formation: A theoretical model. *Journal of Homosexuality, 4,* 219–235.

Cass, V. (1996). Sexual orientation identity formation: A Western phenomenon. In R. P. Cabaj & T. S. Stein (Eds.), *Textbook of homosexuality and mental health* (pp. 227–251). Washington, DC: American Psychiatric Press.

Chen, Y., & Chen, Y. (2006). Lesbians in China's mainland: A brief introduction. *Journal of Lesbian Studies, 10*(3–4), 113–125.

Chesler, M. A., & Zuniga, X. (1991). Dealing with prejudice and conflict in the classroom: The pink triangle exercise. *Teaching Sociology, 19*(2), 173–181.

Chojnacki, J. T., & Gelberg, S. (1994). Toward a conceptualization of career counseling with gay/lesbian/bisexual persons. *Journal of Career Development, 21*, 3–10.

Chow, P. K.-Y., & Cheng, S.-T. (2010). Shame, internalized heterosexism, lesbian identity, and coming out to others: A comparative study of lesbians in mainland China and Hong Kong. *Journal of Counseling Psychology, 57*(1), 92–104.

Chrisler, J. C. (1989). Should feminist therapists do weight loss counseling? *Women & Therapy, 8*(3), 31–37.

Cochran, B. N., & Cauce, A M. (2006). Characteristics of lesbian, gay, bisexual, and transgender individuals entering substance abuse treatment. *Journal of Substance Abuse Treatment, 30*(2), 135–146.

Cochran, S. D., & Mays, V. M. (2007). Physical health complaints among lesbians, gay men, and bisexual and homosexually experienced heterosexual individuals: Results from the California Quality of Life Survey. *American Journal of Public Health, 97*(11), 2048–2055.

Cochran, S., Mays, V., Alegria, M., Ortega, A., & Takeuchi, D. (2007). Mental health and substance use disorders among Latino and Asian American lesbian, gay, and bisexual adults. *Journal of Consulting and Clinical Psychology, 75*(5), 785–794.

Cohn, T. J., & Hastings, S. L. (2010). Resilience among rural lesbian youth. *Journal of Lesbian Studies, 14*(1), 71–79.

Collins, S., & Oxenbury, J. (2010). Affirming women who love women: Principles for counselling lesbians. In N. Arthur & S. Collins (Eds.), *Culture-infused counselling: Celebrating the Canadian mosaic* (2nd ed., pp. 363–394). Calgary, AB: Counselling Concepts.

Colvin, R. (2009). Shared perceptions among lesbian and gay police officers: Barriers and opportunities in the law enforcement work environment. *Police Quarterly, 12*(1), 86–101.

Coren, J. S., Coren, C. M., Pagliaro, S. N., & Weiss, L. B. (2011). Assessing your office for care of lesbian, gay, bisexual, and transgender patients. *The Health Care Manager, 30*(1), 66–70.

Corliss, H. L., Cochran, S. D., Mays, V. M., Greenland, S., & Seeman, T. E. (2009). Age of minority sexual orientation development and risk of childhood maltreatment and suicide attempts in women. *American Journal of Orthopsychiatry, 79*(4), 511–521.

Corliss, H. L., Grella, C. E., Mays, V. M., & Cochran, S. D. (2006). Drug use, drug severity, and help-seeking behaviors of lesbian and bisexual women. *Journal of Women's Health, 15*(5), 556–568.

Croteau, J. M., Anderson, M. Z., Distefano, T. M., & Kampa-Kokesch, S. (2000). Lesbian, gay, and bisexual vocational psychology: Reviewing foundations and planning construction. In R. M. Perez, K. A. Debord, & K. J. Bieschke (Eds.), *Handbook of counseling and psychotherapy with lesbian, gay, and bisexual clients* (pp. 383–408). Washington, DC: American Psychological Association.

Croteau, J. M., & Hedstrom, S. M. (1993). Integrating commonality and difference: The key to career counseling with lesbian women and gay men. *Career Development Quarterly, 41*, 201–209.

Dahan, R., Feldman, R., & Hermoni, D. (2008). Is patients' sexual orientation a blind spot of family physicians? *Journal of Homosexuality, 55*(3), 524–532.

Daley, A. (2010). Being recognized, accepted, and affirmed: Self-disclosure of lesbian/queer sexuality within psychiatric and mental health service settings. *Social Work in Mental Health, 8*(4), 336–355.

Detenber, B. H., Cenite, M., Ku, M. K. Y., Ong, C. P. L., Tong, H. Y., & Yeow, M. L. H. (2007). Singaporeans' attitudes toward lesbians and gay men and their tolerance of media portrayals of homosexuality. *International Journal of Public Opinion Research, 19*(3), 367–379.

Diamant, A. L., Wold, C., Spritzer, K., & Gelberg, L. (2000). Health behaviors, health status and access to and use of health care: A population-based study of lesbian, bisexual and heterosexual women. *Archives of Family Medicine, 9*(10), 1043–1051.

Diamond, L. M. (2007). A dynamical systems approach to the development and expression of female same-sex sexuality. *Perspectives on Psychological Science, 2*(2), 142–161.

Diamond, L. M. (2008). Female bisexuality from adolescence to adulthood: Results from a 10-year longitudinal study. *Developmental Psychology, 44*(1), 5–14.

Diamond, L. M., & Savin-Williams, R. C. (2000). Explaining diversity in the development of same-sex sexuality among young women. *Journal of Social Issues, 56*, 297–313.

Dilley, J. A., Simmons, K. W., Boysun, M. J., Pizacani, B. A., & Stark, M. J. (2010). Demonstrating the importance and feasibility of including sexual orientation in public health surveys: Health disparities in the Pacific Northwest. *American Journal of Public Health, 100*(3), 460–467.

DiStefano, A. S. (2008). Suicidality and self-harm among sexual minorities in Japan. *Qualitative Health Research, 18*(10), 1429–1441.

Dwyer, D. (2010, August 4). Unconstitutional: Federal court overturns Proposition 8, gay marriage ban in California: Attorneys opposing same-sex marriage promise immediate appeal on proposition 8 ruling. *ABC News*. Retrieved from http://abcnews.go.com/Politics/california-gay-marriage-ruling-due-appeal-expected/story?id=11322255.

Embrick, D. G., Walther, C. S., & Wickens, C. M. (2007). Working class masculinity: Keeping gay men and lesbians out of the workplace. *Sex Roles, 56*(11–12), 757–766.

Enteen, J. (2007). Lesbian studies in Thailand. *Journal of Lesbian Studies, 11*(3–4), 255–263.

Erwin, T. M. (2007). Two moms and a baby: Counseling lesbian couples choosing motherhood. *Women & Therapy, 30*(1–2), 99–149.

Eubanks-Carter, C., Burckell, L. A., & Goldfried, M. R. (2005). Enhancing therapeutic effectiveness with lesbian, gay, and bisexual clients. *Clinical Psychology: Science and Practice, 12*(1), 1–18.

Fassinger, R. E. (1995). From invisibility to integration: Lesbian identity in the workplace. *Career Development Quarterly, 44*, 148–167.

Feldman, M. B., & Meyer, I. H. (2007). Eating disorders in diverse lesbian, gay, and bisexual populations. *International Journal of Eating Disorders, 40*(3), 218–226.

Fetner, T., & Kush, K. (2008). Gay–straight alliances in high schools: Social predictors of early adoption. *Youth & Society, 40*(1), 114–130.

Finkel, M. J., Storaasli, R. D., Bandele, A., & Schaefer, V. (2003). Diversity training in graduate school: An exploratory evaluation of the Safe Zone project. *Professional Psychology: Research & Practice, 34*(5), 555–561.

Flowers, P., & Buston, K. (2001). "I was terrified of being different": Exploring gay men's accounts of growing-up in a heterosexist society. *Journal of Adolescence, 24*, 51–65.

Fokkema, T., & Kuyper, L. (2009). The relation between social embeddedness and loneliness among older lesbian, gay, and bisexual adults in the Netherlands. *Archives of Sexual Behavior, 38*(2), 264–275.

Fredriksen-Goldsen, K. I., & Muraco, A. (2010). Aging and sexual orientation: A 25-year review of the literature. *Research on Aging, 32*(3), 372–413.

Frisell, T., Lichtenstein, P., Rahman, Q., & Langstrom, N. (2010). Psychiatric morbidity associated with same-sex sexual behaviour: Influence of minority stress and familial factors. *Psychological*

Medicine: A Journal of Research in Psychiatry and the Allied Sciences, 40(2), 315–324.

Galupo, M. P. (2007). Friendship patterns of sexual minority individuals in adulthood. *Journal of Social and Personal Relationships, 24*(1), 139–151.

Gastic, B., & Johnson, D. (2009). Teacher-mentors and the educational resilience of sexual minority youth. *Journal of Gay & Lesbian Social Services: Issues in Practice, Policy & Research, 21*(2–3), 219–231.

Gelbal, S., & Duyan, V. (2006). Attitudes of university students toward lesbians and gay men in Turkey. *Sex Roles, 55*(7–8), 573–579.

Glassgold, J. M. (2008). Bridging the divide: Integrating lesbian identity and orthodox Judaism. *Women & Therapy, 31*(1), 59–72.

Glover, J. A. (2009). The interpersonal lives of young adult women: A study of passionate friendship. *Dissertation Abstracts International: Section B: The Sciences and Engineering, 70*(3-B), 1982.

Goldberg, A. E. (2010). *Lesbian and gay parents and their children: Research on the family life cycle.* Washington, DC: American Psychological Association.

Goldberg, S., Sickler, J., & Dibble, S. L. (2005). Lesbians over sixty: The consistency of findings from twenty years of survey data. *Journal of Lesbian Studies, 9*(1–2), 195–213.

Gottman, J., & Levenson, R. (2010). The 12-year study. Gay and lesbian couples research: A case of similarities of same-sex and cross-sex relationships, differences between gay and lesbian couples. Manuscript submitted for publication. Retrieved from www.gottman.com/SubPage.aspx?spdt_id=2&sp_id=100842&spt_id=1.

Haas, A. P., Eliason, M., Mays, V. M., Mathy, R. M., Cochran, S. D., D'Augelli, A. R., . . . Clayton, P. J. (2011). Suicide and suicide risk in lesbian, gay, bisexual, and transgender populations: Review and recommendations. *Journal of Homosexuality, 58*(1), 10–51.

Halkitis, P. N., Mattis, J. S., Sahadath, J. K., Massie, D., Ladyzhenskaya, L., Pitrelli, K., . . . Cowie, S.-A. E. (2009). The meanings and manifestations of religion and spirituality among lesbian, gay, bisexual, and transgender adults. *Journal of Adult Development, 16*(4), 250–262.

Hall, M. (1987). Sex therapy with lesbian couples: A four stage approach. *Journal of Homosexuality, 14*(1–2), 137–156.

Hammers, C. (2009). An examination of lesbian/queer bathhouse culture and the social organization of (im)personal sex. *Journal of Contemporary Ethnography, 38*(3), 308–335.

Hastings, S. L., & Hoover-Thompson, A. (2011). Effective support for lesbians in rural communities: The role of psychotherapy. *Journal of Lesbian Studies, 15,* 197–204, 2011

Hatzenbuehler, M. L., McLaughlin, K. A., Keyes, K. M., & Hasin, D. S. (2010). The impact of institutional discrimination on psychiatric disorders in lesbian, gay, and bisexual populations: A prospective study. *American Journal of Public Health, 100*(3), 452–459.

Heath, M., & Mulligan, E. (2008). 'Shiny happy same-sex attracted woman seeking same': How communities contribute to bisexual and lesbian women's well-being. *Health Sociology Review, 17*(3), 290–302.

Henrickson, M. (2007). Lavender faith: Religion, spirituality and identity in lesbian, gay and bisexual New Zealanders. *Journal of Religion & Spirituality in Social Work, 26*(3), 63–80.

Herdt, G., & Kertzner, R. (2006). I do, but I can't: The impact of marriage denial on the mental health and sexual citizenship of lesbians and gay men in the United States. *Sexuality Research & Social Policy: A Journal of the NSRC, 3*(1), 33–49.

Herek, G. M. (2009). Hate crimes and stigma-related experiences among sexual minority adults in the United States: Prevalence estimates from a national probability sample. *Journal of Interpersonal Violence, 24*(1), 54–74.

Herrera, F. (2009). Tradition and transgression: Lesbian motherhood in Chile. *Sexuality Research & Social Policy: A Journal of the NSRC, 6*(2), 35–51.

Herrick, A. L., Matthews, A. K., & Garofalo, R. (2010). Health risk behaviors in an urban sample of young women who have sex with women. *Journal of Lesbian Studies, 14*(1), 80–92.

Hill, R. J. (2009). Incorporating queers: Blowback, backlash, and other forms of resistance to workplace diversity initiatives that support sexual minorities. *Advances in Developing Human Resources, 11*(1), 37–53.

Hollander, D. (2008). Teenagers' sexual identity may not reflect behavior; both are linked to risk. *Perspectives on Sexual and Reproductive Health, 40*(4), 239–240.

Hook, M. K., & Bowman, S. (2008). Working for a living: The vocational decision making of lesbians. *Journal of Lesbian Studies, 12*(1), 85–95.

Horie, Y. (2006). Possibilities and limitations of "Lesbian Continuum": The case of a protestant church in Japan. *Journal of Lesbian Studies, 10*(3–4), 145–159.

Horowitz, J. E., Galst, J. P., & Elster, N. (2010). Sperm donation and recipiency. In J. E. Horowitz, J. P. Galst, & N. Elster (Eds.), *Ethical dilemmas in fertility counseling* (pp. 107–127). Washington, DC: American Psychological Association.

Huang, Y.-P., Brewster, M. E., Moradi, B., Goodman, M. B., Wiseman, M. C., & Martin, A. (2010). Content analysis of literature about LGB people of color: 1998–2007. *The Counseling Psychologist, 38*(3), 363–396.

Hughes, M. (2009). Lesbian and gay people's concerns about ageing and accessing services. *Australian Social Work, 62*(2), 186–201.

Hutchinson, M. K., Thompson, A. C., & Cederbaum, J. A. (2006). Multisystem factors contributing to disparities in preventive health care among lesbian women. *Journal of Obstetric, Gynecologic, & Neonatal Nursing: Clinical Scholarship for the Care of Women, Childbearing Families, & Newborns, 35*(3), 393–402.

Iasenza, S. (2000). Lesbian sexuality post–Stonewall to post-modernism: Putting the "lesbian bed death" concept to bed. *Journal of Sex Education and Therapy, 25*(1), 59–69.

Igartua, K. J. (1998). Therapy with lesbian couples: The issues and the interventions. *Canadian Journal of Psychiatry / La Revue canadienne de psychiatrie, 43*(4), 391–396.

Igartua, K. J., Gill, K., & Montoro, R. (2003). Internalized homophobia: A factor in depression, anxiety, and suicide in the gay and lesbian population. *Canadian Journal of Community Mental Health, 22*(2), 15–30.

Johnston, L. B., & Jenkins, D. (2004). Coming out in mid-adulthood: Building a new identity. *Journal of Gay & Lesbian Social Services: Issues in Practice, Policy & Research, 16*(2), 19–42.

Kam, L. Y. L. (2006). Noras on the road: Family and marriage of lesbian women in Shanghai. *Journal of Lesbian Studies, 10*(3–4), 87–103.

Kamano, S. (2005). Entering the lesbian world in Japan: Debut stories. In E. Rothblum & P. Sablove (Eds.), *Lesbian communities: Festivals, RVs, and the Internet* (pp. 11–30). Binghamton, NY: Harrington Park Press/ Haworth Press.

Kasl, C. S. (2002). Special issues in counseling lesbian women for sexual addiction, compulsivity, and sexual codependency. *Sexual Addiction & Compulsivity, 9*(4), 191–208.

Kelleher, C. (2009). Minority stress and health: Implications for lesbian, gay, bisexual, transgender, and questioning (LGBTQ) young people. *Counselling Psychology Quarterly, 22*(4), 373–379.

Kimmel, D. C., & Yi, H. (2004). Characteristics of gay, lesbian, and bisexual Asians, Asian Americans, and immigrants from Asia to the USA. *Journal of Homosexuality, 47*(2), 143–171.

King, E. B., Reilly, C., & Hebl, M. (2008). The best of times, the worst of times: Exploring dual perspectives of "coming out" in the workplace. *Group & Organization Management, 33*(5), 566–601.

King, M., Semlyen, J., Tai, S. S., Killaspy, H., Osborn, D., Popelyuk, D., & Nazareth, I. (2008). A systematic review of mental disorder, suicide, and deliberate self-harm in lesbian, gay and bisexual people. *BMC Psychiatry, 8,* ArtID 70.

Kitzinger, C., & Wilkinson, S. (1995). Transitions from heterosexuality to lesbianism: The discursive production of lesbian identities. *Developmental Psychology, 31*(1), 95–104.

Koh, A. S., & Ross, L. K. (2006). Mental health issues: A comparison of lesbian, bisexual and heterosexual women. *Journal of Homosexuality, 51*(1), 33–57.

Krukowski, R. A., Harvey-Berino, J., & West, D. S. (2010). Obesity. In M. A. Cucciare & K. R. Weingardt (Eds.), *Using technology to support evidence-based behavioral health practices: A clinician's guide* (pp. 169–197). New York: Routledge/Taylor & Francis.

Kulkin, H. S. (2006). Factors enhancing adaptive coping and mental health in lesbian youth: A review of the literature. *Journal of Homosexuality, 50*(4), 97–111.

Kurdek, L. A. (2004). Are gay and lesbian cohabiting couples *really* different from heterosexual married couples? *Journal of Marriage and Family, 66,* 880–900.

Kurdek, L. A. (2006). Differences between partners from heterosexual, gay, and lesbian cohabiting couples. *Journal of Marriage and Family, 68*(2), 509–528.

Kurdek, L. A. (2008). Change in relationship quality for partners from lesbian, gay male, and heterosexual couples. *Journal of Family Psychology, 22*(5), 701–711.

Lahey, K. A., & Alderson, K. (2004). *Same-sex marriage: The personal and the political.* Toronto, ON: Insomniac Press.

Laird, J. (2000). Gender in lesbian relationships: Cultural, feminist, and constructionist reflections.

Journal of Marital and Family Therapy, 26(4), 455–467.

Lalande, V., & Laverty, A. (2010). Creating connections: Best practices in counselling girls and women. In N. Arthur & S. Collins (Eds.), *Culture-infused counselling: Celebrating the Canadian mosaic* (2nd ed., pp. 339–362). Calgary, AB: Counselling Concepts.

Laumann, E. O., Gagnon, J. H., Michael, R. T., & Michaels, S. (1994). *The social organization of sexuality: Sexual practices in the United States.* Chicago: University of Chicago Press.

Leedy, G., & Connolly, C. (2007). Out of the cowboy state: A look at lesbian and gay lives in Wyoming. *Journal of Gay & Lesbian Social Services: Issues in Practice, Policy & Research, 19*(1), 17–34.

Legenbauer, T., Vocks, S., Schafer, C., Schutt-Stromel, S., Hiller, W., Wagner, C., & Vogele, C. (2009). Preference for attractiveness and thinness in a partner: Influence of internalization of the thin ideal and shape/weight dissatisfaction in heterosexual women, heterosexual men, lesbians, and gay men. *Body Image, 6*(3), 228–234.

Lemoire, S. J., & Chen, C. P. (2005). Applying person-centered counseling to sexual minority adolescents. *Journal of Counseling & Development, 83*(2), 146–154.

Lepischak, B. (2004). Building community for Toronto's lesbian, gay, bisexual, transsexual and transgender youth. In Y. C. Padilla (Ed.), *Gay and lesbian rights organizing: Community-based strategies* (pp. 81–98). Binghamton, NY: Harrington Park Press/ Haworth Press.

Lev, A. I. (2008). More than surface tension: Femmes in families. *Journal of Lesbian Studies, 12*(2–3), 127–144.

Levinson, D. J. (1978). *The seasons of a man's life.* New York: Ballantine.

Levinson, D. J. (Speaker). (1990). *The seasons of a woman's life: Implications for women and men* (Cassette Recording No. APA 90-100). Aurora, CO: Sound Images.

Linehan, M. M. (2008). Suicide intervention research: A field in desperate need of development. *Suicide and Life-Threatening Behavior, 38*(5), 483–485.

Lyons, H. Z., Brenner, B. R., & Lipman, J. (2010). Patterns of career and identity interference for lesbian, gay, and bisexual young adults. *Journal of Homosexuality, 57*(4), 503–524.

Mallinckrodt, B. (2009). Advances in research with sexual minority people: Introduction to the special issue. *Journal of Counseling Psychology, 56*(1), 1–4.

Margolis, R. E. (2005). A new generation of lesbian Jewish activism. *Journal of Lesbian Studies, 9*(1–2), 161–168.

Marks, A. K., Powell, K., & Garcia Coll, C. (2009). Ethnic identity. In R. A. Shweder (Ed.), *The child: An encyclopedic companion* (pp. 321–324). Chicago: University of Chicago Press.

Marshal, M. P., Friedman, M. S., Stall, R., King, K. M., Miles, J., Gold, M. A., . . . Morse, J. Q. (2008). Sexual orientation and adolescent substance use: A meta-analysis and methodological review. *Addiction, 103*(4), 546–556.

Martin, J. I., & D'Augelli, A. R. (2003). How lonely are gay and lesbian youth? *Psychological Reports, 93*(2), 486.

Masini, B. E., & Barrett, H. A. (2007). Social support as a predictor of psychological and physical well-being and lifestyle in lesbian, gay, and bisexual adults aged 50 and over. *Journal of Gay & Lesbian Social Services: Issues in Practice, Policy & Research, 20*(1–2), 91–110.

Matthews, C. R., Lorah, P., & Fenton, J. (2006). Treatment experiences of gays and lesbians in recovery from addiction: A qualitative inquiry. *Journal of Mental Health Counseling, 28*(2), 110–132.

Matthews, C. R., & Selvidge, M. M. D. (2005). Lesbian, gay, and bisexual clients' experiences in treatment for addiction. *Journal of Lesbian Studies, 9*(3), 79–90.

Mays, V. M., Cochran, S. D., & Roeder, M. R. (2003). Depressive distress and prevalence of common problems among homosexually active African American women in the United States. *Journal of Psychology & Human Sexuality, 15*(2–3), 27–46.

McCarn, S. R., & Fassinger, R. E. (1996). Revisioning sexual minority identity formation: A new model of lesbian identity and its implications for counseling and research. *Counseling Psychologist, 24*(3), 508–534.

McDermott, E., Roen, K., & Scourfield, J. (2008). Avoiding shame: Young LGBT people, homophobia and self-destructive behaviours. *Culture, Health & Sexuality, 10*(8), 815–829.

McElwain, A. D., Grimes, M. E., & McVicker, M. L. (2009). The implications of erotic plasticity and social constructionism in the formation of female sexual identity. *Journal of Feminist Family Therapy: An International Forum, 21*(2), 125–139.

McKinley, J., & Schwartz, J. (2010, August 4). Court rejects same-sex marriage ban in California. *New York Times*. Retrieved from www.nytimes.com/2010/08/05/us/05prop.html.

McNair, R. P., & Hegarty, K. (2010). Guidelines for the primary care of lesbian, gay, and bisexual people: A systematic review. *Annals of Family Medicine, 8*(6), 533–541.

McQueeney, K. (2009). "We are God's children, y'all": Race, gender, and sexuality in lesbian and gay-affirming congregations. *Social Problems, 56*(1), 151–173.

McWhirter, J. J., McWhirter, B. T., McWhirter, E. H., & McWhirter, R. J. (2004). *At-risk youth: A comprehensive response* (3rd ed.). Belmont, CA: Thomson Brooks/Cole.

Meyer, I. H. (2010). Identity, stress, and resilience in lesbians, gay men, and bisexuals of color. *The Counseling Psychologist, 38*(3), 442–454.

Meyer, I. H., Dietrich, J., & Schwartz, S. (2008). Lifetime prevalence of mental disorders and suicide attempts in diverse lesbian, gay, and bisexual populations. *American Journal of Public Health, 98*(6), 1004–1006.

Mitchell, V. (2008). Lesbian family life, like the fingers of a hand: Under-discussed and controversial topics. *Journal of Lesbian Studies, 12*(2–3), 119–125.

Moradi, B., Mohr, J. L., Worthington, R. L., & Fassinger, R. E. (2009). Counseling psychology research on sexual (orientation) minority issues: Conceptual and methodological challenges and opportunities. *Journal of Counseling Psychology, 56*(1), 5–22.

Moradi, B., Wiseman, M. C., DeBlaere, C., Goodman, M. B., Sarkees, A., Brewster, M. E., & Huang, Y.-P. (2010). LGB of color and White individuals' perceptions of heterosexist stigma, internalized homophobia, and outness: Comparisons of levels and links. *The Counseling Psychologist, 38*(3), 397–424.

Morrison, M. A., Morrison, T. G., & Sager, C.-L. (2004). Does body satisfaction differ between gay men and lesbian women and heterosexual men and women? A meta-analytic review. *Body Image, 1*(2), 127–138.

Morrow, D. F. (2003). Cast into the wilderness: The impact of institutionalized religion on lesbians. *Journal of Lesbian Studies, 7*(4), 109–123.

Nawaz, H., & Katz, D. (2001). American College of Preventive Medicine practice policy statement: Weight management counseling of overweight adults. *American Journal of Preventive Medicine, 21*(1), 73–78.

Nelms, S. D. (2007). The Black lesbian experience: The intertwining of race and sexuality. *Dissertation Abstracts International: Section B: The Sciences and Engineering, 68*(5–B), 3451.

Nelson, F. (1999). Lesbian families: Achieving motherhood. *Journal of Gay & Lesbian Social Services: Issues in Practice, Policy & Research, 10*(1), 27–46.

Neustifter, R. (2008). Common concerns faced by lesbian elders: An essential context for couples therapy. *Journal of Feminist Family Therapy, 20*(3), 251–267.

Neville, S., & Henrickson, M. (2009). The constitution of "lavender families": A LGB perspective. *Journal of Clinical Nursing, 18*(6), 849–856.

Nichols, M. (1982). The treatment of inhibited sexual desire (ISD) in lesbian couples. *Women & Therapy, 1*(4), 49–66.

Nichols, M., & Shernoff, M. (2007). Therapy with sexual minorities: Queering practice. In S. R. Leiblum (Ed.), *Principles and practice of sex therapy* (4th ed., pp. 379–415). New York: Guilford Press.

Ohnstad, A. (2009). If I am not straight or gay, who am I? *Clinical Social Work Journal, 37*(4), 357–367.

Ortiz-Hernandez, L., & Granados-Cosme, J. A. (2006). Violence against bisexuals, gays and lesbians in Mexico City. *Journal of Homosexuality, 50*(4), 113–140.

Owens, G. P., Riggle, E. D. B., & Rostosky, S. S. (2007). Mental health services access for sexual minority individuals. *Sexuality Research & Social Policy: A Journal of the NSRC, 4*(3), 92–99.

Parikh, S. V., Segal, Z. V., Grigoriadis, S., Ravindran, A. V., Kennedy, S. H., Lam, R. W., & Patten, S. B. (2009). Canadian Network for Mood and Anxiety Treatments (CANMAT) clinical guidelines for the management of major depressive disorder in adults. II. Psychotherapy alone or in combination with antidepressant medication. *Journal of Affective Disorders, 117*(Suppl 1), S15–S25.

Parks, C. A., Hughes, T. L., & Matthews, A. K. (2004). Race/ethnicity and sexual orientation: Intersecting identities. *Cultural Diversity and Ethnic Minority Psychology, 10*(3), 241–254.

Peel, E., & Harding, R. (2008). Editorial introduction: Recognizing and celebrating same-sex relationships: Beyond the normative debate. *Sexualities, 11*(6), 659–666.

Peplau, L. A., & Fingerhut, A. W. (2007). The close relationships of lesbian and gay men. *Annual Review of Psychology, 58,* 405–424.

Peplau, L. A., Frederick, D. A., Yee, C., Maisel, N., Lever, J., & Ghavami, N. (2009). Body image satisfaction in heterosexual, gay, and lesbian adults. *Archives of Sexual Behavior, 38*(5), 713–725.

Peplau, L. A., Spalding, L. R., Conley, T. D., & Veniegas, R. C. (1999). The development of sexual orientation in women. *Annual Review of Sex Research, 10*, 70–99.

Peters, W. (2009). "It feels more like a parody": Canadian *Queer as Folk* viewers and the show they love to complain about. *Journal of Lesbian Studies, 13*(1), 15–24.

Phillips, J., & Marks, G. (2007). Ageing lesbians: Marginalising discourses and social exclusion in the aged care industry. *Journal of Gay & Lesbian Social Services: Issues in Practice, Policy & Research, 20*(1–2), 187–202.

Pixton, S. (2003). Experiencing gay affirmative therapy: An exploration of clients' views of what is helpful. *Counselling & Psychotherapy Research, 3*(3), 211–215.

Poland, S., & Lieberman, R. (2002). Best practices in suicide intervention. In A. Thomas & J. Grimes (Eds.), *Best practices in school psychology IV* (Vol. 1, Vol. 2, pp. 1151–1165). Washington, DC: National Association of School Psychologists.

Polders, L. A., Nel, J. A., Kruger, P., & Wells, H. L. (2008). Factors affecting vulnerability to depression among gay men and lesbian women in Gauteng, South Africa. *South African Journal of Psychology, 38*(4), 673–687.

Poon, C. S., & Saewyc, E. M. (2009). Out yonder: Sexual-minority adolescents in rural communities in British Columbia. *American Journal of Public Health, 99*(1), 118–124.

Poteat, V. P., Espelage, D. L., & Koenig, B. W. (2009). Willingness to remain friends and attend school with lesbian and gay peers: Relational expressions of prejudice among heterosexual youth. *Journal of Youth and Adolescence, 38*(7), 952–962.

Poulin, C., Gouliquer, L., & Moore, J. (2009). Discharged for homosexuality from the Canadian military: Health implications for lesbians. *Feminism & Psychology, 19*(4), 496–516.

Prokos, A. H., & Keene, J. R. (2010). Poverty among cohabiting gay and lesbian, and married and cohabiting heterosexual families. *Journal of Family Issues, 31*(7), 934–959.

Ravel, B., & Rail, G. (2006). The lightness of being "gaie": Discursive constructions of gender and sexuality in Quebec women's sport. *International Review for the Sociology of Sport, 41*(3–4), 395–412.

Rawsthorne, M. L. (2009). Just like other families? Supporting lesbian-parented families. *Australian Social Work, 62*(1), 45–60.

Read, M. M. (2009). Midlife lesbian lifeworlds: Narrative theory and sexual identity. In P. L. Hammack & B. J. Cohler (Eds.), *The story of sexual identity: Narrative perspectives on the gay and lesbian life course* (pp. 347–373). New York: Oxford University Press.

Renaud, M. T. (2007). We are mothers too: Childbearing experiences of lesbian families. *Journal of Obstetric, Gynecologic, & Neonatal Nursing: Clinical Scholarship for the Care of Women, Childbearing Families, & Newborns, 36*(2), 190–199.

Reynolds, A. L. (2003). Counseling issues for lesbian and bisexual women. In M. Kopala & M. A. Keitel (Eds.), *Handbook of counseling women* (pp. 53–73). Thousand Oaks, CA: Sage.

Rickards, T., & Wuest, J. (2006). The process of losing and regaining credibility when coming-out at midlife. *Health Care for Women International, 27*(6), 530–547.

Riggle, E. D. B., Rostosky, S. S., & Horne, S. G. (2009). Marriage amendments and lesbian, gay, and bisexual individuals in the 2006 election. *Sexuality Research & Social Policy: A Journal of the NSRC, 6*(1), 80–89.

Riskind, R. G., & Patterson, C. J. (2010). Parenting intentions and desires among childless lesbian, gay, and heterosexual individuals. *Journal of Family Psychology, 24*(1), 78–81.

Rivers, I., Poteat, V. P., & Noret, N. (2008). Victimization, social support, and psychosocial functioning among children of same-sex and opposite-sex couples in the United Kingdom. *Developmental Psychology, 44*(1), 127–134.

Rivett, M. (2001). The family therapy journals in 2000: A thematic review. *Journal of Family Therapy, 23*(4), 423–433.

Rodriguez, E. M. (2010). At the intersection of church and gay: A review of the psychological research on gay and lesbian Christians. *Journal of Homosexuality, 57*(1), 5–38.

Roisman, G. I., Clausell, E., Holland, A., Fortuna, K., & Elieff, C. (2008). Adult romantic relationships as contexts of human development: A multimethod comparison of same-sex couples with opposite-sex dating, engaged, and married dyads. *Developmental Psychology, 44*(1), 91–101.

Rosario, M. (2008). Elevated substance use among lesbian and bisexual women: Possible explanations and intervention implications for an urgent public health concern. *Substance Use & Misuse, 43*(8–9), 1268–1270.

Rosario, M., Schrimshaw, E. W., & Hunter, J. (2008). Predicting different patterns of sexual identity development over time among lesbian, gay, and bisexual youths: A cluster analytic approach. *American Journal of Community Psychology, 42*(3–4), 266–282.

Rosario, M., Schrimshaw, E. W., Hunter, J., & Levy-Warren, A. (2009). The coming-out process of young lesbian and bisexual women: Are there butch/femme differences in sexual identity development? *Archives of Sexual Behavior, 38*(1), 34–49.

Rose, S. (2000). Heterosexism and the study of women's romantic and friend relationships. *Journal of Social Issues, 56*(2), 315–328.

Rose, S. M., & Zand, D. (2002): Lesbian dating and courtship from young adulthood to midlife. *Journal of Lesbian Studies, 6*(1), 85–109.

Ross, L. E. (2005). Perinatal mental health in lesbian mothers: A review of potential risk and protective factors. *Women & Health, 41*(3), 113–128.

Ross, L., Epstein, R., Goldfinger, C., Steele, L., Anderson, S., & Strike, C. (2008). Lesbian and queer mothers navigating the adoption system: The impacts on mental health. *Health Sociology Review, 17*(3), 254–266.

Ross, L. E., Steele, L., Goldfinger, C., & Strike, C. (2007). Perinatal depressive symptomatology among lesbian and bisexual women. *Archives of Women's Mental Health, 10*(2), 53–59.

Rostosky, S. S., Otis, M. D., Riggle, E. D. B., Kelly, S., & Brodnicki, C. (2008). An exploratory study of religiosity and same-sex couple relationships. *Journal of GLBT Family Studies, 4,* 17–36.

Rostosky, S. S., Riggle, E. D. B., Savage, T. A., Roberts, S. D., & Singletary, G. (2008). Interracial same-sex couples' perceptions of stress and coping: An exploratory study. *Journal of GLBT Family Studies, 4*(3), 277–299.

Rothblum, E. D. (2009). An overview of same-sex couples in relation ships: A research area still at sea. In D. A. Hope (Ed.), *Contemporary perspectives on lesbian, gay, and bisexual identities* (pp. 113–139). New York: Springer Science + Business Media.

Russell, S. T., Clarke, T. J., & Clary, J. (2009). Are teens "post-gay"? Contemporary adolescents' sexual identity labels. *Journal of Youth and Adolescence, 38*(7), 884–890.

Ryan-Flood, R., & Rooke, A. (2009). Que(e)rying methodology: Lessons and dilemmas from lesbian lives: An introduction. *Journal of Lesbian Studies, 13*(2), 115–121.

Ryniker, M. R. (2008). Lesbians still face job discrimination. *Journal of Lesbian Studies, 12*(1), 7–15.

Saewyc, E. M., Poon, C. S., Homma, Y., & Skay, C. L. (2008). Stigma management? The links between enacted stigma and teen pregnancy trends among gay, lesbian, and bisexual students in British Columbia. *Canadian Journal of Human Sexuality, 17*(3), 123–139.

Sanchez, H. G. (2001). Risk factor model for suicide assessment and intervention. *Professional Psychology: Research and Practice, 32*(4), 351–358.

Sandfort, T. G. M., Bakker, F., Schellevis, F. G., & Vanwesenbeeck, I. (2006). Sexual orientation and mental and physical health status: Findings from a Dutch population survey. *American Journal of Public Health, 96*(6), 1119–1125.

Savin-Williams, R. C. (2005). *The new gay teenager.* Cambridge, MA: Harvard University Press.

Savin-Williams, R. (2008). Refusing and resisting sexual identity labels. In D. L. Browning (Ed.), *Adolescent identities: A collection of readings* (pp. 67–91). New York: Analytic Press/Taylor & Francis Group.

Savin-Williams, R. C., & Ream, G. L. (2007). Prevalence and stability of sexual orientation components during adolescence and young adulthood. *Archives of Sexual Behavior, 36*(3), 385–394.

Schope, R. D. (2005). Who's afraid of growing old? Gay and lesbian perceptions of aging. *Journal of Gerontological Social Work, 45*(4), 23–39.

Schwartz, J. (2009, May 26). *California high court upholds gay marriage ban.* Retrieved from www.nytimes.com/2009/05/27/us/27marriage.html.

Seaver, M. R., Freund, K. M., Wright, L. M., Tjia, J., & Frayne, S. M. (2008). Healthcare preferences among lesbians: A focus group analysis. *Journal of Women's Health, 17*(2), 215–225.

Selvidge, M. M. D., Matthews, C. R., & Bridges, S. K. (2008). The relationship of minority stress and flexible coping to psychological well being in lesbian and bisexual women. *Journal of Homosexuality, 55*(3), 450–470.

Senreich, E. (2010). The effects of honesty and openness about sexual orientation on gay and bisexual clients in substance abuse programs. *Journal of Homosexuality, 57*(3), 364–383.

Shafer, S. (2011, June 13). *When a gay judge rules on gay rights*. Retrieved from www.npr.org/2011/06/13/137109321/when-a-gay-judge-rules-on-gay-rights.

Share, T. L., & Mintz, L. B. (2002). Differences between lesbians and heterosexual women in disordered eating and related attitudes. *Journal of Homosexuality, 42*(4), 89–106.

Sinding, C., Barnoff, L., & Grassau, P. (2004). Homophobia and heterosexism in cancer care: The experiences of lesbians. *CJNR: Canadian Journal of Nursing Research, 36*(4), 170–188.

Sinding, C., Grassau, P., & Barnoff, L. (2007). Community support, community values: The experiences of lesbians diagnosed with cancer. *Women & Health, 44*(2), 59–79.

Skerven, K., & de St. Aubin, E. (2006). Lesbian self-development in context: Cohort analysis at two points in history. *Research in Human Development, 3*(4), 251–269.

Smith, M. (2005). The politics of same-sex marriage in Canada and the United States. *PS Political Science & Politics, 38*(2), 225–228.

Spitalnick, J. S., & McNair, L. D. (2005). Couples therapy with gay and lesbian clients: An analysis of important clinical issues. *Journal of Sex and Marital Therapy, 31*(1), 43–56.

Steele, L. S., Tinmouth, J. M., & Lu, A. (2006). Regular health care use by lesbians: A path analysis of predictive factors. *Family Practice, 23*(6), 631–636.

Stone, S. D. (Ed.). (1990). *Lesbians in Canada*. Toronto, ON: Between the Lines Press.

Stritof, S., & Stritof, B. (2009). Same-sex marriage FAQ—gender-neutral marriage laws. *About.com*. Retrieved from http://marriage.about.com/cs/samesexmarriage/a/samesex.htm.

Strock, C. (2008). *Married women who love women* (2nd ed.). New York: Routledge/Taylor & Francis.

Swami, V., & Tovee, M. J. (2006). The influence of body mass index on the physical attractiveness preferences of feminist and nonfeminist heterosexual women and lesbians. *Psychology of Women Quarterly, 30*(3), 252–257.

Tan, P. P. (2005). The importance of spirituality among gay and lesbian individuals. *Journal of Homosexuality, 49*(2), 135–144.

To, C. (2004). Towards equality through legal reform: Empowerment and mobilization of the Tongzhi (LGBT) community in Hong Kong. *Journal of Gay & Lesbian Social Services: Issues in Practice, Policy & Research, 16*(1), 65–74.

Townsend, J. M. (1998). *What women want—what men want: Why the sexes still see love and commitment so differently*. New York: Oxford University Press.

Tracy, J. K., & Junginger, J. (2007). Correlates of lesbian sexual functioning. *Journal of Women's Health, 16*(4), 499–509.

Trotter, E. C., & Alderson, K. G. (2007). University students' definitions of having sex, sexual partner, and virginity loss: The influence of participant gender, sexual experience, and contextual factors. *Canadian Journal of Human Sexuality, 16*(1–2), 11–29.

Twist, M., Murphy, M., Green, M. S., & Palmanteer, D. (2006). Therapists' support for gay and lesbian rights. *Guidance & Counseling, 21*(2), 107–113.

van Rosmalen-Nooijens, K. A. W. L., Vergeer, C. M., & Lagro-Janssen, A. L. M. (2008). Bed death and other lesbian sexual problems unraveled: A qualitative study of the sexual health of lesbian women involved in a relationship. *Women & Health, 48*(3), 339–362.

Vanita, R. (2007). Lesbian studies and activism in India. *Journal of Lesbian Studies, 11*(3–4), 245–253.

Veenvliet, S. G. (2008). Intrinsic religious orientation and religious teaching: Differential judgments toward same-gender sexual behavior and gay men and lesbians. *International Journal for the Psychology of Religion, 18*(1), 53–65.

Walker, J. A., & Prince, T. (2010). Training considerations and suggested counseling interventions for LGBT individuals. *Journal of LGBT Issues in Counseling, 4*(1), 2–17.

Warner, J., McKeown, E., Griffin, M., Johnson, K., Ramsay, A., Cort, C., & King, M. (2004). Rates and predictors of mental illness in gay men, lesbians and bisexual men and women: Results from a survey based in England and Wales. *British Journal of Psychiatry, 185*(6), 479–485.

Watzlawik, M. (2004). Experiencing same-sex attraction: A comparison between American and German adolescents. *Identity: An International Journal of Theory and Research, 4*(2), 171–186.

Waugh, T. (2006). *The romance of transgression in Canada: Queering sexualities, nations, cinemas*. Montreal, PQ, or Kingston, ON: McGill-Queen's University Press.

Weston, K. (2009). The lady vanishes: On never knowing, quite, who is a lesbian. *Journal of Lesbian Studies, 13*(2), 136–148.

Wheeler-Scruggs, K. S. (2008). Do lesbians differ from heterosexual men and women in Levinsonian phases of adult development? *Journal of Counseling & Development, 86*(1), 39–46.

Whitam, F. L., Daskalos, C. T., & Mathy, R. M. (1994). A cross-cultural assessment of familial factors in the development of female homosexuality. *Journal of Psychology & Human Sexuality, 7*(4), 59–76.

Whitam, F. L., Daskalos, C., Sobolewski, C. G., & Padilla, P. (1998). The emergence of lesbian sexuality and identity cross-culturally: Brazil, Peru, the Philippines, and the United States. *Archives of Sexual Behavior, 27*(1), 31–56.

Whitam, F. L., & Mathy, R. M. (1991). Childhood cross-gender behavior of homosexual females in Brazil, Peru, the Philippines, and the United States. *Archives of Sexual Behavior, 20*(2), 151–170.

White, W. S. (2009). Finding their way: A qualitative study of life course experiences of lesbian older adults with religion and spirituality. *Dissertation Abstracts International Section A: Humanities and Social Sciences, 70*(3-A), 1055.

Whitlock, R. U. (2009). "Them ol' nasty lesbians"—Queer memory, place, and rural formations of lesbian. *Journal of Lesbian Studies, 13*(1), 98–106.

Wienke, C., & Hill, Gr. J. (2009). Does the "marriage benefit" extend to partners in gay and lesbian relationships? Evidence from a random sample of sexually active adults. *Journal of Family Issues, 30*(2), 259–289.

Wieringa, S. E. (2007). "If there is no feeling . . . ": The dilemma between silence and coming out in a working-class butch/femme community in Jakarta. In M. B. Padilla, J. S. Hirsch, M. Munoz-Laboy, R. Sember, & R. G. Parker (Eds.), *Love and globalization: Transformations of intimacy in the contemporary world* (pp. 70–90). Nashville, TN: Vanderbilt University Press.

Williams, C. L., Giuffre, P. A., & Dellinger, K. (2009). The gay-friendly closet. *Sexuality Research & Social Policy: A Journal of the NSRC, 6*(1), 29–45.

Wilsnack, S. C., Hughes, T. L., Johnson, T. P., Bostwick, W. B., Szalacha, L. A., Benson, P., . . . Kinnison, K. E. (2008). Drinking and drinking-related problems among heterosexual and sexual minority women. *Journal of Studies on Alcohol and Drugs, 69*(1), 129–139.

Wilson, A. M. (2007). N'tacimowin inna nah': Coming in to two-spirit identities. *Dissertation Abstracts International Section A: Humanities and Social Sciences, 68*(6–A), 2341.

Worthington, R. L., Navarro, R. L., Savoy, H. B., & Hampton, D. (2008). Development, reliability, and validity of the Measure of Sexual Identity Exploration and Commitment (MOSIEC). *Developmental Psychology, 44*(1), 22–33.

Wright, S. L., & Canetto, S. S. (2009). Stereotypes of older lesbians and gay men. *Educational Gerontology, 35*(5), 424–452.

Zhao, Y., Montoro, R., Igartua, K., & Thombs, B. D. (2010). Suicidal ideation and attempt among adolescents reporting "unsure" sexual identity or heterosexual identity plus same-sex attraction or behavior: Forgotten groups? *Journal of the American Academy of Child & Adolescent Psychiatry, 49*(2), 104–113.

References for Chapter 5

Aggleton, P. (Ed.). (1996). *Bisexualities and AIDS: International perspectives*. Philadelphia: Taylor & Francis.

Alderson, K. (2000). *Beyond coming out: Experiences of positive gay identity*. Toronto, ON: Insomniac Press.

Alderson, K. G. (2003). The ecological model of gay male identity. *Canadian Journal of Human Sexuality, 12*(2), 75–85.

Arbaugh, T., Jr. (2002). Counseling the bisexual client. In L. D. Burlew & D. Capuzzi (Eds.), *Sexuality counseling* (pp. 111–127). Hauppauge, NY: Nova Science.

Association for Lesbian, Gay, Bisexual, and Transgender Issues in Counseling. (n.d.). *Competencies for counseling gay, lesbian, bisexual and transgendered (GLBT) clients*. Retrieved from www.algbtic.org/resources/competencies.

Auerback, S. (1987). Groups for the wives of gay and bisexual men. *Social Work, 32,* 321–325.

Balsam, K. F., & Mohr, J. J. (2007). Adaptation to sexual orientation stigma: A comparison of bisexual and lesbian/gay adults. *Journal of Counseling Psychology, 54*(3), 306–319.

Barker, M., Bowes-Catton, H., Iantaffi, A., Cassidy, A., & Brewer, L. (2008). British bisexuality: A snapshot of bisexual representations and identities in the United Kingdom. *Journal of Bisexuality, 8*(1–2), 141–162.

Barker, M., & Langdridge, D. (2008). II. Bisexuality: Working with a silenced sexuality. *Feminism & Psychology, 18*(3), 389–394.

Belanger, J. (2008). Training, knowledge, and attitudes about bisexuals among clinical psychology doctoral students. *Dissertation Abstracts International: Section B: The Sciences and Engineering, 69*(1-B), 663.

Bogaert, A. F., & Friesen, C. (2002). Sexual orientation and height, weight, and age of puberty: New tests from a British national probability sample. *Biological Psychology, 59*(2), 135–145.

Bowers, R., Minichiello, V., & Plummer, D. (2010). Religious attitudes, homophobia, and professional counseling. *Journal of LGBT Issues in Counseling, 4*(2), 70–91.

Boykin, K. (2005). *Beyond the down low: Sex, lies, and denial in Black America.* New York: Carroll & Graf.

Bradford, M. (2004). The bisexual experience: Living in a dichotomous culture. *Journal of Bisexuality, 4*(1–2), 7–23.

Brown, T. (2002). A proposed model of bisexual identity development that elaborates on experiential differences of women and men. *Journal of Bisexuality, 2*(4), 67–91.

Busseri, M. A., Willoughby, T., Chalmers, H., & Bogaert, A. R. (2006). Same-sex attraction and successful adolescent development. *Journal of Youth and Adolescence, 35*(4), 563–575.

Carver, P. R., Egan, S. K., & Perry, D. G. (2004). Children who question their heterosexuality. *Developmental Psychology, 40*(1), 43–53.

Chauncey, G. (1994). *Gay New York: Gender, urban culture, and the making of the gay male world, 1890–1940.* New York: Basic.

Chung, Y. B. (2003). Career counseling with lesbian, gay, bisexual, and transgendered persons: The next decade. *Career Development Quarterly, 52*(1), 78–85.

Cochran, B. N., & Heck, N. C. (2008). A useful resource regarding an often-overlooked population. [Review of the book *Affirmative psychotherapy with bisexual women and bisexual men*, by R. C. Fox, Ed.]. *Sex Roles, 58,* 597–598.

Cochran, S. D., & Mays, V. M. (2007). Physical health complaints among lesbians, gay men, and bisexual and homosexually experienced heterosexual individuals: Results from the California Quality of Life Survey. *American Journal of Public Health, 97*(11), 2048–2055.

Collins, J. F. (2000). Biracial-bisexual individuals: Identity coming of age. *International Journal of Sexuality and Gender Studi*es, *5*, 221–253.

Collins, J. F. (2004). The intersection of race and bisexuality: A critical overview of the literature and past, present, and future directions of the "borderlands." *Journal of Bisexuality, 4*(1–2), 99–116.

Collins, J. F. (2007). Counseling at the intersection of identities: Asian/Pacific American bisexuals. In B. A. Firestein (Ed.), *Becoming visible: Counseling bisexuals across the lifespan* (pp. 229–245). New York: Columbia University Press.

D'Augelli, A. R. (2002). Mental health problems among lesbian, gay, and bisexual youths ages 14 to 21. *Clinical Child Psychology and Psychiatry, 7*(3), 433–456.

Datti, P. A. (2009). Applying social learning theory of career decision making to gay, lesbian, bisexual, transgender, and questioning young adults. *Career Development Quarterly, 58*(1), 54–64.

Deacon, S. A., Reinke, L., & Viers, D. (1996). Expanding the realms of therapy. *American Journal of Family Therapy, 24*(3), 242–258.

deMause, L. (1998). The history of child abuse. *Journal of Psychohistory, 25*(3). Retrieved from www .psychohistory.com/htm/05_history.html.

Dengel, D. W. (2007). Examining biphobia in heterosexual, homosexual, and bisexual men and women. *Dissertation Abstracts International: Section B: The Sciences and Engineering, 68*(1-B), 619.

Dilley, J. A., Simmons, K. W., Boysun, M. J., Pizacani, B. A., & Stark, M. J. (2010). Demonstrating the importance and feasibility of including sexual orientation in public health surveys: Health disparities in the Pacific Northwest. *American Journal of Public Health, 100*(3), 460–467.

Dworkin, S. H. (2001). Treating the bisexual client. *Journal of Clinical Psychology, 57*(5), 671–680.

Dworkin, S. H. (2006). The aging bisexual: The invisible of the invisible minority. In D. Kimmel, T. Rose, & S. David (Eds.), *Lesbian, gay, bisexual, and transgender aging: Research and clinical perspectives* (pp. 36–52). New York: Columbia University Press.

Dysart-Gale, D. (2010). Social justice and social determinants of health: Lesbian, gay, bisexual, transgendered, intersexed, and queer youth in Canada. *Journal of Child and Adolescent Psychiatric Nursing, 23*(1), 23–28.

Earl, W. (1990). Married men and same-sex activity: A field study on HIV risk among men who do not identify as gay or bisexual. *Journal of Sex & Marital Therapy, 16,* 251–257.

Edser, S. J., & Shea, J. D. (2002). An exploratory investigation of bisexual men in monogamous, heterosexual marriages. *Journal of Bisexuality, 2*(4), 5–29.

Eliason, M. (2001). Bi negativity: The stigma facing bisexual men. *Journal of Bisexuality, 1*(2/3), 137–154.

Ferrer, L., & Gomez, L. A. J. (2007). Counseling bisexual Latinos: A minority within a minority. In B. A. Firestein (Ed.), *Becoming visible: Counseling bisexuals across the lifespan* (pp. 246–267). New York: Columbia University Press.

Finkel, M. J., Storaasli, R. D., Bandele, A., & Schaefer, V. (2003). Diversity training in graduate school: An exploratory evaluation of the Safe Zone project. *Professional Psychology: Research and Practice, 34*(5), 555–561.

Firestein, B. A. (Ed.). (2007). *Becoming visible: Counseling bisexuals across the lifespan.* New York: Columbia University Press.

Fox, R. C. (1996). Bisexuality: An examination of theory and research. In R. P. Cabaj & T. S. Stein (Eds.), *Textbook of homosexuality and mental health* (pp. 147–171). Washington, DC: American Psychiatric Association.

Fox, R. C. (Ed.). (2006). *Affirmative psychotherapy with bisexual women and bisexual men.* Binghamton, NY: Harrington Park Press.

Freud, S. (1925/1959). An autobiographical study. In J. Strachey (Ed. & Trans.), *The standard edition of the complete psychological works of Sigmund Freud* (Vol. 20, pp. 1–74). London, UK: Hogarth Press. (Original work published in 1925)

George, C., Alary, M., Hogg, R. S., Otis, J., Remis, R. S., Masse, B., . . . Schechter, M. T. (2007). HIV and ethnicity in Canada: Is the HIV risk-taking behaviour of young foreign-born MSM similar to Canadian born MSM? *AIDS Care, 19*(1), 9–16.

Guidry, L. L. (1999). Clinical intervention with bisexuals: A contextualized understanding. *Professional Psychology: Research and Practice, 30*(1), 22–26.

Herdt, G. (2001). Social change, sexual diversity, and tolerance for bisexuality in the United States. In A. R. D'Augelli & C. J. Patterson (Eds.), *Lesbian, gay, and bisexual identities and youth: Psychological perspectives* (pp. 267–283). New York: Oxford University Press.

Herek, G. M. (2002). Heterosexuals' attitudes toward bisexual men and women in the United States. *Journal of Sex Research, 39*(4), 264–274.

Hoburg, R., Konik, J., Williams, M., & Crawford, M. (2004). Bisexuality among self-identified heterosexual college students. *Journal of Bisexuality, 4*(1–2), 25–36.

Horner, E. (2007). Queer identities and bisexual identities: What's the difference? In B. A. Firestein (Ed.), *Becoming visible: Counseling bisexuals across the lifespan* (pp. 287–296). New York: Columbia University Press.

Hutchins, L. (2007). Playing with sacred fire: Building erotic communities. In B. A. Firestein (Ed.), *Becoming visible: Counseling bisexuals across the lifespan* (pp. 336–357). New York: Columbia University Press.

Isay, R. A. (1996). *Becoming gay: The journey to self-acceptance*. New York: Pantheon.

Israel, T., & Mohr, J. J. (2004). Attitudes toward bisexual women and men: Current research, future directions. *Journal of Bisexuality, 4*(1–2), 117–134.

Jackson, T. (2010). A qualitative study: Reflections on being a LGB adolescent in rural high school settings. *Dissertation Abstracts International: Section B: The Sciences and Engineering, 70*(12-B), 7900.

Jamil, O. B., Harper, G. W., & Fernandez, M. I. (2009). Sexual and ethnic identity development among gay-bisexual-questioning (GBQ) male ethnic minority adolescents. *Cultural Diversity and Ethnic Minority Psychology, 15*(3), 203–214.

Jeffries, W. L., IV, & Dodge, B. (2007). Male bisexuality and condom use at last sexual encounter: Results from a National Survey. *Journal of Sex Research, 44*(3), 278–289.

Jeffries, W. L., IV, Dodge, B., & Sandfort, T. G. M. (2008). Religion and spirituality among bisexual

Black men in the USA. *Culture, Health & Sexuality, 10*(5), 463–477.

Jorm, A. F., Korten, A. E., Rodgers, B., Jacomb, P. A., & Christensen, H. (2002). Sexual orientation and mental health: Results from a community survey of young and middle-aged adults. *British Journal of Psychiatry, 180*(5), 423–427.

Kelly, J. A., Amirkhanian, Y. A., McAuliffe, T. L., Granskaya, J. V., Borodkina, O. I., Dyatlov, R. V., . . . Kozlov, A. P. (2002). HIV risk characteristics and prevention needs in a community sample of bisexual men in St. Petersburg, Russia. *AIDS Care, 14*(1), 63–76.

Keppel, B., & Firestein, B. A. (2007). Bisexual inclusion in addressing issues of GLBT aging: Therapy with older bisexual women and men. In B. A. Firestein (Ed.), *Becoming visible: Counseling bisexuals across the lifespan* (pp. 164–185). New York: Columbia University Press.

Kimmel, D., Rose, T., Orel, N., & Greene, B. (2006). Historical context for research on lesbian, gay, bisexual, and transgender aging. In D. Kimmel, T. Rose, & S. David (Eds.), *Lesbian, gay, bisexual, and transgender aging: Research and clinical perspectives* (pp. 1–19). New York: Columbia University Press.

Kinsey, A. C., Pomeroy, W. B., & Martin, C. E. (1948). *Sexual behavior in the human male.* Philadelphia: W. B. Saunders.

Kinsey, A. C., Pomeroy, W. B., Martin, C. E., & Gebhard, P. H. (1953). *Sexual behavior in the human female.* Oxford, UK: Saunders.

Klein, F., Sepekoff, B., & Wolf, T. J. (1985). Sexual orientation: A multi-variable dynamic process. *Journal of Homosexuality, 11*(1–2), 35–49.

Kosciw, J. G., Greytak, E. A., & Diaz, E. M. (2009). Who, what, where, when, and why: Demographic and ecological factors contributing to hostile school climate for lesbian, gay, bisexual, and transgender youth. *Journal of Youth and Adolescence, 38*(7), 976–988.

Kumta, S., Lurie, M., Weitzen, S., Jerajani, H., Gogate, A., Row-kavi, A., . . . Mayer, K. H. (2010). Bisexuality, sexual risk taking, and HIV prevalence among men who have sex with men accessing voluntary counseling and testing services in Mumbai, India. *JAIDS Journal of Acquired Immune Deficiency Syndromes, 53*(2), 227–233.

Leaver, C. A., Allman, D., Meyers, T., & Veugelers, P. J. (2004). Effectiveness of HIV prevention in Ontario, Canada: A multilevel comparison of bisexual men. *American Journal of Public Health, 94*(7), 1181–1185.

Lever, J., Kanouse, D. E., Rogers, W. H., Carson, S., & Hertz, R. (1992). Behavior patterns and sexual identity of bisexual males. *Journal of Sex Research, 29*(2), 141–167.

Lewis, R. J., Derlega, V. J., Brown, D., Rose, S., & Henson, J. M. (2009). Sexual minority stress, depressive symptoms, and sexual orientation conflict: Focus on the experiences of bisexuals. *Journal of Social and Clinical Psychology, 28*(8), 971–992.

Liddle, B. J., Luzzo, D. A., Hauenstein, A. L., & Schuck, K. (2004). Construction and validation of the Lesbian, Gay, Bisexual, and Transgendered Climate Inventory. *Journal of Career Assessment, 12*(1), 33–50.

Logan, T. K., & Leukefeld, C. (2000). HIV risk behavior among bisexual and heterosexual drug users. *Journal of Psychoactive Drugs, 32*(3), 239–248.

Long, L. L., Burnett, J. A., & Thomas, R. V. (2006). *Sexuality counseling: An integrative approach.* Upper Saddle River, NJ: Pearson/Merrill Prentice Hall.

Mathy, R. M. (2002). Suicidality and sexual orientation in five continents: Asia, Australia, Europe, North America, and South America. *International Journal of Sexuality & Gender Studies, 7*(2–3), 215–225.

Matteson, D. R. (1995). Counseling with bisexuals. *Individual Psychology: Journal of Adlerian Theory, Research & Practice, 51*(2), 144–159.

Matteson, D. R. (1996). Psychotherapy with bisexual individuals. In R. P. Cabaj & T. S. Stein (Eds.), *Textbook of homosexuality and mental health* (pp. 433–450). Washington, DC: American Psychiatric Association.

Matteson, D. R. (1999). Intimate bisexual couples. In J. Carlson & L. Sperry (Eds.), *The intimate couple.* Philadelphia: Brunner/Mazel.

McLean, K. (2008). Inside, outside, nowhere: Bisexual men and women in the gay and lesbian community. *Journal of Bisexuality, 8*(1–2), 63–80.

Mead, M. (1975, January). Bisexuality: What's it all about? *Redbook, 144*(3), 29–31.

Meyer, I. H., & Ouellette, S. C. (2009). Unity and purpose at the intersections of racial/ethnic and sexual identities. In P. Hammack & B. J. Cohler (Eds.), *The story of sexual identity: Narrative perspectives on the gay and lesbian life course* (pp. 79–106). New York: Oxford University Press.

Mills, T. C., Paul, J., Stall, R., Pollack, L., Canchola, J., Chang, Y. J., . . . Catania, J. A. (2004). Distress and depression in men who have sex with men: The urban men's health study. *American Journal of Psychiatry, 161*(2), 278–285.

Ming Liu, W., Kenji Iwamoto, D., & Chae, M. H. (Eds.). (2010). *Culturally responsive counseling with Asian American men*. New York: Routledge/Taylor & Francis.

Mohr, J. J., & Rochlen, A. B. (1999). Measuring attitudes regarding bisexuality in lesbian, gay male, and heterosexual populations. *Journal of Counseling Psychology, 46,* 353–369.

Money, J. (1993). Sin, sickness, or status? Homosexual gender identity and psychoneuroendocrinology. In L. D. Garnets & D. C. Kimmel (Eds.), *Psychological perspectives on lesbian and gay male experiences* (pp. 130–167). New York: Columbia University Press.

Moore, D. L., & Norris, F. H. (2005). Empirical investigation of the conflict and flexibility models of bisexuality. *Journal of Bisexuality, 5*(1), 5–25.

Morrow, D. F., & Tyson, B. (2006). Religion and spirituality. In D. F. Morrow & L. Messinger (Eds.), *Sexual orientation & gender expression in social work practice: Working with gay, lesbian, bisexual, & transgender people* (pp. 384–404). New York: Columbia University Press.

Myers, M. F. (1991). Marital therapy with HIV-infected men and their wives. *Psychiatric Annals, 21*(8), 466–470.

Needham, B. L., & Austin, E. L. (2010). Sexual orientation, parental support, and health during the transition to young adulthood. *Journal of Youth and Adolescence, 39*(10), 1189–1198.

O'Leary, A., Purcell, D. W., Remien, R. H., Fisher, H. E., & Spikes, P. S. (2007). Characteristics of bisexually active men in the Seropositive Urban Mens' Study (SUMS). *AIDS Care, 19*(7), 940–946.

Ochs, R. (1996). Biphobia: It goes more than two ways. In B. A. Firestein (Ed.), *Bisexuality: The psychology and politics of an invisible minority* (pp. 217–239). Thousand Oaks, CA: Sage.

Ochs, R. (2001). Biphobia. In R. Ochs (Ed.), *Bisexual resource guide* (4th ed., pp. 45–51). Boston: Bisexual Resource Center.

Oswald, R. F., & Culton, L. S. (2003). Under the rainbow: Rural gay life and its relevance for family providers. *Family Relations: An Interdisciplinary Journal of Applied Family Studies, 52*(1), 72–81.

Oxley, E., & Lucius, C. A. (2000). Looking both ways: Bisexuality and therapy. In C. Neal & D. Davies (Eds.), *Issues in therapy with lesbian, gay, bisexual and transgender clients* (pp. 115–127). Maidenhead, UK: Open University Press.

Page, E. H. (2004). Mental health services experiences of bisexual women and bisexual men: An empirical study. *Journal of Bisexuality, 3*(3/4), 137–160.

Page, E. (2007). Bisexual women's and men's experiences of psychotherapy. In B. A. Firestein (Ed.), *Becoming visible: Counseling bisexuals across the lifespan* (pp. 52–71). New York: Columbia University Press.

Pitt, R. N., Jr. (2006). Downlow mountain? De/stigmatizing bisexuality through pitying and pejorative discourses in media. *Journal of Men's Studies, 14*(2), 254–258.

Poteat, V. P., Aragon, S. R., Espelage, D. L., & Koenig, B. W. (2009). Psychosocial concerns of sexual minority youth: Complexity and caution in group differences. *Journal of Consulting and Clinical Psychology, 77*(1), 196–201.

Potoczniak, D. J. (2007). Development of bisexual men's identities and relationships. In K. J. Bieschke, R. M. Perez, & K. A. DeBord (Eds.), *Handbook of counseling and psychotherapy with lesbian, gay, bisexual, and transgender clients* (2nd ed., pp. 119–145). Washington, DC: American Psychological Association.

Public Broadcasting Service Online. (n.d.). People & events: Conditions of antebellum slavery: 1830–1860. *Africans in American Resource Bank*. Retrieved from www.pbs.org/wgbh/aia/part4/4p2956.html.

Reich, D. B., & Zanarini, M. C. (2008). Sexual orientation and relationship choice in borderline personality disorder over ten years of prospective follow-up. *Journal of Personality Disorders, 22*(6), 564–572.

Rosario, M., Schrimshaw, E. W., & Hunter, J. (2008). Ethnic/racial disparities in gay-related stress and health among lesbian, gay, and bisexual youths: Examining a prevalent hypothesis. In B. C. Wallace (Ed.), *Toward equity in health: A new global approach to health disparities* (pp. 427–446). New York: Springer.

Rosario, M., Yali, A. M., Hunter, J., & Gwadz, M. V. (2006). Religion and health among lesbian, gay, and bisexual youths: An empirical investigation and theoretical explanation. In A. M. Omoto & H. S. Kurtzman (Eds.), *Sexual orientation and mental health: Examining identity and development in lesbian, gay, and bisexual people* (pp. 117–140). Washington, DC: American Psychological Association.

Rosenthal, A. M., Sylva, D., Safron, A., & Bailey, J. M. (2011). Sexual arousal patterns of bisexual men revisited. *Biological Psychology, 88*(1), 112–115.

Ross, L. E., Dobinson, C., & Eady, A. (2010). Perceived determinants of mental health for bisexual people: A qualitative examination. *American Journal of Public Health, 100*(3), 496–502.

Rotheram-Borus, M. J., Marelich, W. D., & Srinivasan, S. (1999). HIV risk among homosexual, bisexual, and heterosexual male and female youths. *Archives of Sexual Behavior, 28*(2), 159–177.

Russell, S. T., Driscoll, A. K., & Truong, N. (2002). Adolescent same-sex romantic attractions and relationships: Implications for substance use and abuse. *American Journal of Public Health, 92*(2), 198–202.

Rust, P. C. R. (2000). Review of statistical findings about bisexual behaviour, feelings, and identities. In P. C. R. Rust (Ed.), *Bisexual in the United States: A social science reader* (pp. 129–184). New York: Columbia University Press.

Rust, P. C. (2001a). Make me a map: Bisexual men's images of bisexual community. *Journal of Bisexuality, 1*(2–3), 47–108.

Rust, P. C. (2001b). Two many and not enough: The meanings of bisexual identities. *Journal of Bisexuality, 1*(1), 31–68.

Rust, P. C. (2003). Monogamy and polyamory: Relationship issues for bisexuals. In L. D. Garnets & D. C. Kimmel (Eds.), *Psychological perspectives on lesbian, gay, and bisexual experiences* (2nd ed., pp. 475–496). New York: Columbia University Press.

Saewyc, E. M., Homma, Y., Skay, C. L., Bearinger, L. H., Resnick, M. D., & Reis, E. (2009). Protective factors in the lives of bisexual adolescents in North America. *American Journal of Public Health, 99*(1), 110–117.

Scott, R. L. (2007). Addressing social invalidation to promote well-being for multiracial bisexuals of African descent. In B. A. Firestein (Ed.), *Becoming visible: Counseling bisexuals across the lifespan* (pp. 207–228). New York: Columbia University Press.

Sears, J. T. (Ed.). (2005a). *Youth, education, and sexualities: An international encyclopedia, Vol. 1: A–J.* Westport, CT: Greenwood Press.

Sears, J. T. (Ed.). (2005b). *Youth, education, and sexualities: An international encyclopedia, Vol. 2: K–Z.* Westport, CT: Greenwood Press.

Shechter, R. A. (2004). People in a world between: Psychodynamic themes in the treatment of bisexual patients. *Clinical Social Work Journal, 32*(3), 271–283.

Sheets, R. L., Jr., & Mohr, J. J. (2009). Perceived social support from friends and family and psychosocial functioning in bisexual young adult college students. *Journal of Counseling Psychology, 56*(1), 152–163.

Sherry, A., Adelman, A., Whilde, M. R., & Quick, D. (2010). Competing selves: Negotiating the intersection of spiritual and sexual identities. *Professional Psychology: Research and Practice, 41*(2), 112–119.

Singer, I., McLaughlin, J. F., Schechter, S., Greenstone, J. H., & Jacobs, J. (2002). Marriage. *Jewish Encyclopedia.* Retrieved from www.jewishencyclopedia.com/view.jsp?letter=M&artid=213.

Skegg, K., Nada-Raja, S., Dickson, N., Paul, C., & Williams, S. (2003). Sexual orientation and self-harm in men and women. *American Journal of Psychiatry, 160*(3), 541–546.

Smith, B., & Horne, S. (2007). Gay, lesbian, bisexual and transgendered (GLBT) experiences with earth-spirited faith. *Journal of Homosexuality, 52*(3–4), 235–248.

Snively, C. A. (2004). Building community-based alliances between GLBTQQA youth and adults in rural settings. *Journal of Gay & Lesbian Social Services: Issues in Practice, Policy & Research, 16*(3–4), 99–112.

Stobie, C. (2003). Reading bisexualities from a South African perspective. *Journal of Bisexuality, 3*(1), 33–52.

Stokes, J., McKirnan, D., & Burzette, R. (1993). Sexual behaviour, condom use, disclosure of sexuality, and stability of sexual orientation in bisexual men. *Journal of Sex Research, 30,* 203–213.

Storms, M. D. (1980). Theories of sexual orientation. *Journal of Personality and Social Psychology, 38*(5), 783–792.

Thomas, S. R., & Larrabee, T. G. (2002). Gay, lesbian, bisexual, and questioning youth. In J. Sandoval (Ed.), *Handbook of crisis counseling, intervention, and prevention in the schools* (2nd ed., pp. 301–322). Mahwah, NJ: Lawrence Erlbaum.

Traeen, B., Martinussen, M., Vitterso, J., & Saini, S. (2009). Sexual orientation and quality of life among university students from Cuba, Norway, India, and South Africa. *Journal of Homosexuality, 56*(5), 655–669.

Traeen, B., Stigum, H., & Sorensen, D. (2002). Sexual diversity in urban Norwegians. *Journal of Sex Research, 39*(4), 249–258.

Trotter, E. C., & Alderson, K. G. (2007). University students' definitions of having sex, sexual partner, and virginity loss: The influence of participant gender, sexual experience, and contextual factors. *Canadian Journal of Human Sexuality, 16*(1–2), 11–29.

Ueno, K., Gayman, M. D., Wright, E. R., & Quantz, S. D. (2009). Friends' sexual orientation, relational quality, and mental health among gay, lesbian, and bisexual youth. *Personal Relationships, 16*(4), 659–670.

van Griensven, F., Kilmarx, P. H., Jeeyapant, S., Manopaiboon, C., Korattana, S., Jenkins, R. A., . . . Mastro, T. D. (2004). The prevalence of bisexual and homosexual orientation and related health risks among adolescents in Northern Thailand. *Archives of Sexual Behavior, 33*(2), 137–147.

Ventegodt, S. (1998). Sex and the quality of life in Denmark. *Archives of Sexual Behavior, 27*(3), 295–307.

Vieira de Souza, C. T., Bastos, F. I., Lowndes, C. M., Landman Szwarcwald, C., Moreira dos Santos, E., Ayres de Castilho, E., . . . Oswaldo Cruz Foundation STD/HIV Prevention Group. (1999). Perception of vulnerability to HIV infection in a cohort of homosexual/bisexual men in Rio de Janeiro, Brazil. *AIDS Care, 11*(5), 567–579.

Walls, N. E. (2010). Religion and support for same-sex marriage: Implications from the literature. *Journal of Gay & Lesbian Social Services: The Quarterly Journal of Community & Clinical Practice, 22*(1–2), 112–131.

Ward, J. (2008). Dude-sex: White masculinities and "authentic" heterosexuality among dudes who have sex with dudes. *Sexualities, 11*(4), 414–434.

Weinberg, M. S., Williams, C. J., & Pryor, D. W. (1994). *Dual attraction: Understanding bisexuality*. New York: Oxford University Press.

Weinberg, M. S., Williams, C. J., & Pryor, D. W. (2001). Bisexuals at midlife: Commitment, salience, and identity. *Journal of Contemporary Ethnography, 30*(2), 180–208.

Weinrich, J. D., & Klein, F. (2002). Bi-gay, bi-straight, and bi-bi: Three bisexual subgroups identified using cluster analysis of the Klein Sexual Orientation Grid. *Journal of Bisexuality, 2*(4), 109–139.

Weiss, J. T. (2003). GL vs. BT: The archaeology of biphobia and transphobia within the U.S. gay and lesbian community. *Journal of Bisexuality, 3*(3–4), 25–55.

Weitzman, G. (2006). Therapy with clients who are bisexual and polyamorous. In R. C. Fox (Ed.), *Affirmative psychotherapy with bisexual women and bisexual men* (pp. 137–164). Binghamton, NY: Harrington Park Press.

Weitzman, G. (2007). Counseling bisexuals in polyamorous relationships. In B. A. Firestein (Ed.), *Becoming visible: Counseling bisexuals across the lifespan* (pp. 312–335). New York: Columbia University Press.

Wilson, A. (1996). How we find ourselves: Identity development and two-spirit people. *Harvard Educational Review, 66*(2), 303–317.

Wolf, T. J. (1985). Marriages of bisexual men. *Journal of Homosexuality, 11*(1–2), 135–148.

Wolf, T. J. (1987). Group psychotherapy for bisexual men and their wives. *Journal of Homosexuality, 14*(1–2), 191–199.

Zhao, Y., Montoro, R., Igartua, K., & Thombs, B. D. (2010). Suicidal ideation and attempt among adolescents reporting "unsure" sexual identity or heterosexual identity plus same-sex attraction or behavior: Forgotten groups? *Journal of the American Academy of Child & Adolescent Psychiatry, 49*(2), 104–113.

References for Chapter 6

Alderson, K. (2002). *Breaking out: The complete guide to building and enhancing a positive gay identity for men and women*. Toronto, ON: Insomniac Press.

Alderson, K. G. (2004). A different kind of outing: Training counsellors to work with sexual minority clients. *Canadian Journal of Counselling, 38*, 193–210.

Balsam, K. F., Lehavot, K., Beadnell, B., & Circo, E. (2010). Childhood abuse and mental health indicators among ethnically diverse lesbian, gay, and bisexual adults. *Journal of Consulting and Clinical Psychology, 78*(4), 459–468.

Balsam, K. F., & Mohr, J. J. (2007). Adaptation to sexual orientation stigma: A comparison of bisexual and lesbian/gay adults. *Journal of Counseling Psychology, 54*(3), 306–319.

Beaber, T. (2008). Well-being among bisexual females: The roles of internalized biphobia, stigma consciousness, social support, and self-disclosure.

Dissertation Abstracts International: Section B: The Sciences and Engineering, 69(4-B), 2616.

Bereket, T., & Brayton, J. (2008). "Bi" no means: Bisexuality and the influence of binarism on identity. *Journal of Bisexuality, 8*(1–2), 51–61.

Boehmer, U., Bowen, D. J., & Bauer, G. R. (2007). Overweight and obesity in sexual-minority women: Evidence from population-based data. *American Journal of Public Health, 97*(6), 1134–1140.

Bostwick, W. B., McCabe, S. E., Horn, S., Hughes, T., Johnson, T., & Valles, J. R. (2007). Drinking patterns, problems, and motivations among collegiate bisexual women. *Journal of American College Health, 56*(3), 285–292.

Bradford, M. (2006). Affirmative psychotherapy with bisexual women. In R. C. Fox (Ed.), *Affirmative psychotherapy with bisexual women and bisexual men* (pp. 13–25). Binghamton, NY: Harrington Park Press.

Brooks, K. D., & Quina, K. (2009). Women's sexual identity patterns: Differences among lesbians, bisexuals and unlabeled women. *Journal of Homosexuality, 56*(8), 1030–1045.

Brooks, L. M., Inman, A. G., Malouf, M. A., Klinger, R. S., & Kaduvettoor, A. (2008). Ethnic minority bisexual women: Understanding the invisible population. *Journal of LGBT Issues in Counseling, 2*(4), 260–284.

Burrill, K. G. (2002). Queering bisexuality. *Journal of Bisexuality, 2*(2–3), 95–105.

Case, P., Austin, S. B., Hunter, D. J., Manson, J. E., Malspeis, S., Willett, W. C., & Spiegelman, D. (2004). Sexual orientation, health risk factors, and physical functioning in the Nurses' Health Study II. *Journal of Women's Health, 13*(9), 1033–1047.

Coleman, E. (1985). Bisexual women in marriages. *Journal of Homosexuality, 11,* 87–100.

Collins, J. F. (2004). The intersection of race and bisexuality: A critical overview of the literature and past, present, and future directions of the "borderlands." *Journal of Bisexuality, 4*(1–2), 99–116.

Diamond, L. M. (2006). The evolution of plasticity in female–female desire. *Journal of Psychology & Human Sexuality, 18*(4), 245–274.

Diamond, L. M. (2007). A dynamical systems approach to the development and expression of female same-sex sexuality. *Perspectives on Psychological Science, 2*(2), 142–161.

Diamond, L. M. (2008). Female bisexuality from adolescence to adulthood: Results from a 10-year longitudinal study. *Developmental Psychology, 44*(1), 5–14.

Diamond, L. M., & Lucas, S. (2004). Sexual-minority and heterosexual youths' peer relationships: Experiences, expectations, and implications for well-being. *Journal of Research on Adolescence, 14*(3), 313–340.

Diamond, L. M., & Savin-Williams, R. C. (2000). Explaining diversity in the development of same-sex sexuality among young women. *Journal of Social Issues, 56,* 297–313.

Dilley, J. A., Simmons, K. W., Boysun, M. J., Pizacani, B. A., & Stark, M. J. (2010). Demonstrating the importance and feasibility of including sexual orientation in public health surveys: Health disparities in the Pacific Northwest. *American Journal of Public Health, 100*(3), 460–467.

Dixon, J. K. (1985). Sexuality and relationship changes in married females following the commencement of bisexual activity. *Journal of Homosexuality, 11*(1–2), 115–133.

Dodge, B., Reece, M., & Gebhard, P. H. (2008). Kinsey and beyond: Past, present, and future considerations for research on male bisexuality. *Journal of Bisexuality, 8*(3–4), 177–191.

Dworkin, S. H. (2006). The aging bisexual: The invisible of the invisible minority. In D. Kimmel, T. Rose, & S. David (Eds.), *Lesbian, gay, bisexual, and transgender aging: Research and clinical perspectives* (pp. 36–52). New York: Columbia University Press.

Ellis, L., & Wagemann, B. M. (1993). The religiosity of mothers and their offspring as related to the offspring's sex and sexual orientation. *Adolescence, 28,* 227–234.

Fairyington, S. (2008). Kinsey, bisexuality, and the case against dualism. *Journal of Bisexuality, 8*(3–4), 267–272.

Farmer, H. S. (2006). History of career counseling for women. In W. B. Walsh & M. J. Heppner (Eds.), *Handbook of career counseling for women* (2nd ed., pp. 1–44). Mahwah, NJ: Lawrence Erlbaum.

Feldman, M. B., & Meyer, I. H. (2007). Eating disorders in diverse lesbian, gay, and bisexual populations. *International Journal of Eating Disorders, 40*(3), 218–226.

Finkel, M. J., Storaasli, R. D., Bandele, A., & Schaefer, V. (2003). Diversity training in graduate school: An exploratory evaluation of the Safe Zone project. *Professional Psychology: Research and Practice, 34*(5), 555–561.

Firestein, B. A. (2007). Cultural and relational contexts of bisexual women: Implications for therapy. In K. J. Bieschke, R. M. Perez, & K. A. DeBord (Eds.), *Handbook of counseling and psychotherapy with lesbian, gay, bisexual, and transgender clients* (2nd ed., pp. 91–117). Washington, DC: American Psychological Association.

Ford, C. S., & Beach, F. A. (1951). *Patterns of sexual behavior*. New York: Harper.

Ford, J. A., & Jasinski, J. L. (2006). Sexual orientation and substance use among college students. *Addictive Behaviors, 31*(3), 404–413.

Fox, A. (1991). Development of a bisexual identity: Understanding the process. In L. Hutchins & L. Ka'ahumanu (Eds.), *Bi any other name: Bisexual people speak out* (pp. 29–36). Boston: Alyson.

Fox, R. C., Goetstouwers, L., & Pallotta-Chiarolli, M. (2008). International perspectives on bisexuality: An introduction. *Journal of Bisexuality, 8*(1–2), 3–8.

Gage Davidson, M. (2000). Religion and spirituality. In R. M. Perez, K. A. DeBord, & K. Bieschke (Eds.), *Handbook of counseling and psychotherapy with lesbian, gay, and bisexual clients* (pp. 409–433). Washington, DC: American Psychological Association.

Galupo, M. P., Sailer, C. A., & St. John, S. C. (2004). Friendships across sexual orientations: Experiences of bisexual women in early adulthood. *Journal of Bisexuality, 4*(1–2), 37–53.

Granello, D. H. (2010). A suicide crisis intervention model with 25 practical strategies for implementation. *Journal of Mental Health Counseling, 32*(3), 218–235.

Herdt, G. (2001). Social change, sexual diversity, and tolerance for bisexuality in the United States. In A. R. D'Augelli & C. J. Patterson (Eds.), *Lesbian, gay, and bisexual identities and youth: Psychological perspectives* (pp. 267–283). New York: Oxford University Press.

Hoburg, R., Konik, J., Williams, M., & Crawford, M. (2004). Bisexuality among self-identified heterosexual college students. *Journal of Bisexuality, 4*(1–2), 25–36.

Hooghe, M., Claes, E., Harell, A., Quintelier, E., & Dejaeghere, Y. (2010). Anti-gay sentiment among adolescents in Belgium and Canada: A comparative investigation into the role of gender and religion. *Journal of Homosexuality, 57*(3), 384–400.

Horowitz, J. L., & Newcomb, M. D. (1999, Fall). Bisexuality, not homosexuality: Counseling issues and treatment approaches. *Journal of College Counseling, 2*(2), 148–163.

Horowitz, S. M., Weis, D. L., & Laflin, M. T. (2003). Bisexuality, quality of lifestyle and health indicators. *Journal of Bisexuality, 3*(2), 5–28.

Israel, T., Gorcheva, R., Walther, W. A., Sulzner, J. M., & Cohen, J. (2008). Therapists' helpful and unhelpful situations with LGBT clients: An exploratory study. *Professional Psychology: Research and Practice, 39*(3), 361–368.

Ji, P., Du Bois, S. N., & Finnessy, P. (2009). An academic course that teaches heterosexual students to be allies to LGBT communities: A qualitative analysis. *Journal of Gay & Lesbian Social Services: Issues in Practice, Policy & Research, 21*(4), 402–429.

Kennedy, K. G., & Fisher, E. S. (2010). Bisexual students in secondary schools: Understanding unique experiences and developing responsive practices. *Journal of Bisexuality, 10,* 472–485.

Kinnish, K. K., Strassberg, D. S., & Turner, C. W. (2005). Sex differences in the flexibility of sexual orientation: A multidimensional retrospective assessment. *Archives of Sexual Behavior, 34*(2), 173–183.

Kinsey, A. C., Pomeroy, W. B., & Martin, C. E. (1948). *Sexual behavior in the human male*. Philadelphia: W. B. Saunders.

Kinsey, A. C., Pomeroy, W. B., Martin, C. E., & Gebhard, P. H. (1953). *Sexual behavior in the human female.* Oxford, UK: Saunders.

Koh, A. S., & Ross, L. K. (2006). Mental health issues: A comparison of lesbian, bisexual and heterosexual women. *Journal of Homosexuality, 51*(1), 33–57.

Laumann, E. O., Gagnon, J. H., Michael, R. T., & Michaels, S. (1994). *The social organization of sexuality: Sexual practices in the United States.* Chicago: University of Chicago Press.

Lease, S. H., Horne, S. G., & Noffsinger-Frazier, N. (2005). Affirming faith experiences and psychological health for Caucasian lesbian, gay, and bisexual individuals. *Journal of Counseling Psychology, 52*(3), 378–388.

Lewis, R. J., Derlega, V. J., Brown, D., Rose, S., & Henson, J. M. (2009). Sexual minority stress, depressive symptoms, and sexual orientation conflict: Focus on the experiences of bisexuals. *Journal of Social and Clinical Psychology, 28*(8), 971–992.

Lieppe, S. J. (2006). Vulnerability to distress and sexual orientation: A comparison of indicators of psychopathology in bisexual, homosexual, and heterosexual women. *Dissertation Abstracts International: Section B: The Sciences and Engineering, 67*(4-B), 2233.

Lourea, D. N. (1985). Psycho-social issues related to counseling bisexuals. *Journal of Homosexuality, 11*(1–2), 51–62.

Mathieson, C. M., Bailey, N., & Gurevich, M. (2002). Health care services for lesbian and bisexual women: Some Canadian data. *Health Care for Women International, 23*(2), 185–196.

Matteson, D. R. (1996). Psychotherapy with bisexual individuals. In R. P. Cabaj & T. S. Stein (Eds.), *Textbook of homosexuality and mental health* (pp. 433–450). Washington, DC: American Psychiatric Association.

McCabe, S. E., Hughes, T. L., & Boyd, C. J. (2004). Substance use and misuse: Are bisexual women at greater risk? *Journal of Psychoactive Drugs, 36*(2), 217–225.

McLaughlin, K. A., Hatzenbuehler, M. L., & Keyes, K. M. (2010). Responses to discrimination and psychiatric disorders among Black, Hispanic, female, and lesbian, gay, and bisexual individuals. *American Journal of Public Health, 100*(8), 1477–1484.

McLean, K. (2004). Negotiating (non)monogamy: Bisexuality and intimate relationships. *Journal of Bisexuality, 4*(1–2), 83–97.

McLean, K. (2008). Inside, outside, nowhere: Bisexual men and women in the gay and lesbian community. *Journal of Bisexuality, 8*(1–2), 63–80.

Meyer, C., Blissett, J., & Oldfield, C. (2001). Sexual orientation and eating psychopathology: The role of masculinity and femininity. *International Journal of Eating Disorders, 29*(3), 314–318.

Mohr, J. J., & Rochlen, A. B. (1999). Measuring attitudes regarding bisexuality in lesbian, gay male, and heterosexual populations. *Journal of Counseling Psychology, 46,* 353–369.

Moore, D. L., & Norris, F. H. (2005). Empirical investigation of the conflict and flexibility models of bisexuality. *Journal of Bisexuality, 5*(1), 5–25.

Moradi, B., & DeBlaere, C. (2010). Women's experiences of sexist discrimination: Review of research and directions for centralizing race, ethnicity, and culture. In H. Landrine & N. F. Russo (Eds.), *Handbook of diversity in feminist psychology* (pp. 173–210). New York: Springer.

Morgan, E. M., & Thompson, E. M. (2007). Young women's sexual experiences within same-sex friendships: Discovering and defining bisexual and bi-curious identity. *Journal of Bisexuality, 6*(3), 7–34.

Morris, J. F., Balsam, K. F., & Rothblum, R. D. (2002). Lesbian and bisexual mothers and nonmothers: Demographics and the coming-out process. *Journal of Family Psychology, 16,* 144–156.

Needham, B. L., & Austin, E. L. (2010). Sexual orientation, parental support, and health during the transition to young adulthood. *Journal of Youth and Adolescence, 39*(10), 1189–1198.

Nelson, C., Johnston, M., & Shrivastava, A. (2010). Improving risk assessment with suicidal patients: A preliminary evaluation of the clinical utility of the Scale for Impact of Suicidality—Management, Assessment and Planning of Care (SIS-MAP). *Crisis: The Journal of Crisis Intervention and Suicide Prevention, 31*(5), 231–237.

Onishenko, D., & Caragata, L. (2010). A theoretically critical gaze on the Canadian equal marriage debate: Breaking the binaries. *Journal of Gay & Lesbian Social Services: The Quarterly Journal of Community & Clinical Practice, 22*(1–2), 91–111.

Page, E. (2004). Mental health services experiences of bisexual women and bisexual men: An empirical study. *Journal of Bisexuality, 4*(1/2), 137–160.

Reinhardt, R. U. (2002). Bisexual women in heterosexual relationships. *Journal of Bisexuality, 2* (2–3), 163–171.

Reynolds, A. L. (2003). Counseling issues for lesbian and bisexual women. In M. Kopala & M. A. Keitel (Eds.), *Handbook of counseling women* (pp. 53–73). Thousand Oaks, CA: Sage.

Riggle, E. D. B., Rostosky, S. S., & Danner, F. (2009). LGB identity and eudaimonic well being in midlife. *Journal of Homosexuality, 56*(6), 786–798.

Roberts, M. K. (2003). Sexual orientation self-label, behavior, and preference: College students in Taiwan and the United States of America (China). *Dissertation Abstracts International: Section B: The Sciences and Engineering, 63*(9-B), 4384.

Ross, L., Epstein, R., Goldfinger, C., Steele, L., Anderson, S., & Strike, C. (2008). Lesbian and queer mothers navigating the adoption system: The impacts on mental health. *Health Sociology Review, 17*(3), 254–266.

Rothblum, E. D., & Factor, R. (2001). Lesbians and their sisters as a control group: Demographic and mental health factors. *Psychological Science, 12,* 63–69.

Russell, S. T., & Seif, H. (2002). Bisexual female adolescents: A critical analysis of past research, and results from a national survey. *Journal of Bisexuality, 2*(2–3), 73–94.

Rust, P. C. (2001). Two many and not enough: The meanings of bisexual identities. *Journal of Bisexuality, 1*(1), 31–68.

Rust, P. C. R. (1993). Coming out in the age of social constructionism: Sexual identity formation among lesbians and bisexual women. *Gender and Society, 7,* 50–77.

Rust, P. R. (2000). Heterosexual gays, homosexual straights. In P. R. Rust (Ed.), *Bisexuality in the United States: A social science reader* (pp. 279–306). New York: Columbia University Press.

Samji, T. (2008). Bi and in love: A phenomenological inquiry into the committed couple relationships of bisexual women. *Dissertation Abstracts International: Section B: The Sciences and Engineering, 68*(7-B), 4844.

Scales Rostosky, S., Riggle, E. D. B., Pascale-Hague, D., & McCants, L. E. (2010). The positive aspects of a bisexual self-identification. Psychology and Sexuality, *1*(2), 131–144.

Smiley, E. B. (1997). Counseling bisexual clients. *Journal of Mental Health Counseling, 19,* 373–382.

Stanley, J. L. (2004). Biracial lesbian and bisexual women: Understanding the unique aspects and interactional processes of multiple minority identities. In A. R. Gillem & C. A. Thompson (Eds.), *Biracial women in therapy: Between the rock of gender and the hard place of race* (pp. 159–171). New York: Haworth Press.

Steele, L. S., Ross, L. E., Dobinson, C., Veldhuizen, S., & Tinmouth, J. M. (2009). Women's sexual orientation and health: Results from a Canadian population-based survey. *Women & Health, 49*(5), 353–367.

Steinhouse, K. (2001). Bisexual women: Considerations of race, social justice and community building. *Journal of Progressive Human Services, 12*(2), 5–25.

Taub, J. (1999). Bisexual women and beauty norms: A qualitative examination. *Journal of Lesbian Studies, 3*(4), 27–36.

Thompson, E. M. (2007). Girl friend or girlfriend?: Same-sex friendship and bisexual images as a context for flexible sexual identity among young women. *Journal of Bisexuality, 6*(3), 47–67.

Tucker, J. S., Ellickson, P. L., & Klein, D. J. (2008). Understanding differences in substance use among bisexual and heterosexual young women. *Women's Health Issues, 18*(5), 387–398.

Volpp, S. Y. (2010). What about the "B" in LGT: Are bisexual women's mental health issues same or different? *Journal of Gay and Lesbian Mental Health, 14*(1), 41–51.

Vrangalova, Z., & Savin-Williams, R. C. (2010). Correlates of same-sex sexuality in heterosexually identified young adults. *Journal of Sex Research, 47*(1), 92–102.

Weinberg, M. S., Williams, C. J., & Pryor, D. W. (2001). Bisexuals at midlife: Commitment, salience, and identity. *Journal of Contemporary Ethnography, 30*(2), 180–208.

Welzer-Lang, D. (2008). Speaking out loud about bisexuality: Biphobia in the gay and lesbian community. *Journal of Bisexuality, 8*(1–2), 81–95.

Williams, M. J. K. (1999). *Sexual pathways: Adapting to dual sexual attraction.* Westport, CT: Praeger/Greenwood.

Wilsnack, S. C., Hughes, T. L., Johnson, T. P., Bostwick, W. B., Szalacha, L. A., Benson, P., . . . Kinnison, K. E. (2008). Drinking and drinking-related problems among heterosexual and sexual minority women. *Journal of Studies on Alcohol and Drugs, 69*(1), 129–139.

Wilson, A. (1996). How we find ourselves: Identity development and two-spirit people. *Harvard Educational Review, 66*(2), 303–317.

Zook, M. A. (2002). Psychotherapy experiences of women attracted to both men and women. *Dissertation Abstracts International: Section B: The Sciences and Engineering, 62*(11-B), 5400.

References for Chapter 7

Adshead, G. (1997). Transvestic fetishism: Assessment and treatment. In D. R. Laws & W. T. O'Donohue (Eds.), *Sexual deviance: Theory, assessment, and treatment* (pp. 280–296). New York: Guilford Press.

Alderson, K. (2002). *Breaking out: The complete guide to building and enhancing a positive gay identity for men and women.* Toronto, ON: Insomniac Press.

American Psychiatric Association. (2000). *Diagnostic and statistical manual of mental disorders* (4th ed., text rev.). Washington, DC: Author.

American Psychiatric Association. (2010a). *DSM-V development.* Retrieved from www.dsm5.org/

ProposedRevisions/Pages/proposedrevision.aspx?rid=189.

American Psychiatric Association. (2010b). *DSM-5 overview: The future manual*. Retrieved from www.dsm5.org/about/Pages/DSMVOverview.aspx.

American Psychiatric Association. (2010c). *Kenneth J. Zucker, Ph.D.* Retrieved from www.psych.org/MainMenu/Research/DSMIV/DSMV/MeettheTaskForce/KennethJZuckerPhD.aspx.

Bailey, J. M., & Zucker, K. J. (1995). Childhood sex-typed behavior and sexual orientation: A conceptual analysis and quantitative review. *Developmental Psychology, 31*(1), 43–55.

Bakshi, S. (2004). A comparative analysis of hijras and drag queens: The subversive possibilities and limits of parading effeminacy and negotiating masculinity. *Journal of Homosexuality, 46*(3–4), 211–223.

Balzer, C. (2004). The beauty and the beast: Reflections about the socio-historical and subcultural context of drag queens and tunten in Berlin. *Journal of Homosexuality, 46*(3–4), 55–71.

Bancroft, J. (1972). The relationship between gender identity and sexual behaviour: Some clinical aspects. In C. Ounsted & D. C. Taylor (Eds.), *Gender differences: Their ontogeny and significance*. London, UK: Churchill Livingstone.

Baqi, S., Shah, S. A., Baig, M. A., Mujeeb, S. A., & Memon, A. (1999). Seroprevalence of HIV, HBV and syphilis and associated risk behaviours in male transvestites (hijras) in Karachi, Pakistan. *International Journal of STD & AIDS, 10*(5), 300–304.

Barker, J. C. (1965). Behavior therapy for transvestism: A comparison of pharmacological and electrical aversion techniques. *British Journal of Psychiatry, 111*(472), 268–276.

Beatrice, J. (1985). A psychological comparison of heterosexuals, transvestites, preoperative transsexuals, and postoperative transsexuals. *Journal of Nervous and Mental Disease, 173*(6), 358–365.

Beigel, H. G. (1965). Three transvestites under hypnosis. *International Journal of Clinical and Experimental Hypnosis, 13*(2), 71–82.

Benestad, E. E. P. (2010). From gender dysphoria to gender euphoria: An assisted journey. *Sexologies: European Journal of Sexology and Sexual Health/ Revue europeenne de sexologie et de sante sexuelle, 19*(4), 225–231.

Benjamin, H. (1966). *The transsexual phenomenon*. New York: Julian Press.

Blackmore, C., Thorpe, J., Barker, J., Conway, C., & Lavin, N. (1963). The application of faradic aversion conditioning in a case of transvestism. *Behaviour Research and Therapy, 1*(1), 29–34.

Blanchard, R. (1989). The concept of autogynephilia and the typology of male gender dysphoria. *Journal of Nervous and Mental Disease, 177*(10), 616–623.

Boles, J., & Elifson, K. W. (1994). The social organization of transvestite prostitution and AIDS. *Social Science & Medicine, 39*(1), 85–93.

Bolin, A. (1988). *In search of Eve: Transsexual rites of passage*. New York: Bergin & Garvey.

Brierley, H. (1979). *Transvestism: Illness, perversion, or choice*. New York: Pergamon.

Brown, G. R. (1994). Women in relationships with cross-dressing men: A descriptive study from a nonclinical setting. *Archives of Sexual Behavior, 23*(5), 515–530.

Brown, G. R. (1996). Transvestism. In G. O. Gabbard & S. D. Atkinson (Eds.), *Synopsis of treatments of psychiatric disorders* (2nd ed., pp. 829–836). Washington, DC: American Psychiatric Association.

Brown, G. R., Wise, T. N., Costa, P. T., Herbst, J. H., Fagan, P. J., & Schmidt, C. W. (1996). Personality characteristics and sexual functioning of 188 cross-dressing men. *Journal of Nervous and Mental Disease, 184*(5), 265–273.

Buhrich, N. (1978). Motivation for cross-dressing in heterosexual transvestism. *Acta Psychiatrica Scandinavica, 57*(2), 145–152.

Buhrich, N. (1981). Psychological adjustment in transvestism and transsexualism. *Behaviour Research and Therapy, 19*(5), 407–411.

Buhrich, N., & Beaumont, T. (1981). Comparison of transvestism in Australia and America. *Archives of Sexual Behavior, 10*(3), 269–279.

Buhrich, N., & McConaghy, N. (1978). Parental relationships during childhood in homosexuality, transvestism and transsexualism. *Australian and New Zealand Journal of Psychiatry, 12*(2), 103–108.

Bullough, V. L. (1991). Transvestism: A reexamination. *Journal of Psychology & Human Sexuality, 4*(2), 53–67.

Bullough, V. L., & Bullough, B. (1993). *Cross dressing, sex, and gender*. Baltimore, MD: University of Pennsylvania Press.

Bullough, V., Bullough, B., & Smith, R. (1983). A comparative study of male transvestites, male-to-female transsexuals, and male homosexuals. *Journal of Sex Research, 19*(3), 238–257.

Caceres, C. F., & Cortinas, J. I. (1996). Fantasy island: An ethnography of alcohol and gender roles in a Latino gay bar. *Journal of Drug Issues, 26*(1), 245–260.

Cairns, K. V. (1997). Counselling the partners of heterosexual male cross-dressers. *Canadian Journal of Human Sexuality, 6*(4), 297–306.

Callender, C., & Kochems, L. M. (1983). The North American berdache. *Current Anthropology, 24*(4), 443–470.

Carroll, L., & Gilroy, P. J. (2002). Transgender issues in counselor preparation. *Counselor Education and Supervision, 41*(3), 233–242.

Carroll, R. A. (1999). Outcomes of treatment for gender dysphoria. *Journal of Sex Education & Therapy, 24*(3), 128–136.

Chapman, R., & Teed, L. (1990). Adolescent sexuality in offspring of parents living in "alternative" lifestyles. In M. E. Perry (Ed.), *Childhood and adolescent sexology* (pp. 317–322). New York: Elsevier Science.

Cole, S. S., Denny, D., Eyler, A. E., & Samons, S. L. (2000). Issues of transgender. In L. T. Szuchman & F. Muscarella (Eds.), *Psychological perspectives on human sexuality* (pp. 149–195). Hoboken, NJ: John Wiley & Sons.

Croughan, J. L., Saghir, M., Cohen, R., & Robins, E. (1981). A comparison of treated and untreated male cross-dressers. *Archives of Sexual Behavior, 10*(6), 515–528.

Davenport, C. W. (1986). A follow-up study of 10 feminine boys. *Archives of Sexual Behavior, 15*(6), 511–517.

de Vries, A. L. C., Cohen-Kettenis, P. T., & Delemarre-van de Waal, H. (2007). Clinical management of gender dysphoria in adolescents. *International Journal of Transgenderism, 9*(3–4), 83–94.

Devor, H. (1996). Female gender dysphoria in context: Social problem or personal problem. *Annual Review of Sex Research, 7,* 44–89.

Docter, R. F. (1988). *Transvestites and transsexuals: Toward a theory of cross-gender behavior*. New York: Plenum Press.

Docter, R. F., & Prince, V. (1997). Transvestism: A survey of 1032 cross-dressers. *Archives of Sexual Behavior, 26*(6), 589–605.

Dzelme, K., & Jones, R. A. (2001). Male cross-dressers in therapy: A solution-focused perspective for marriage and family therapists. *American Journal of Family Therapy, 29*(4), 293–305.

Ellis, A., & Grieger, R. (1977). *Handbook of rational-emotive therapy.* New York: Springer.

Ellis, K. M., & Eriksen, K. (2002). Transsexual and transgenderist experiences and treatment options. *Family Journal, 10*(3), 289–299.

Evans, N. J. (2002). The impact of an LGBT Safe Zone project on campus climate. *Journal of College Student Development, 43*(4), 522–539.

Faustman, W. O. (1976). Aversive control of maladaptive sexual behavior: Past developments and future trends. *Psychology: A Journal of Human Behavior, 13*(4), 53–60.

Fedoroff, J. P. (1988). Buspirone hydrochloride in the treatment of transvestic fetishism. *Journal of Clinical Psychiatry, 49*(10), 408–409.

Fineberg, N. A., & Craig, K. J. (2010). Pharmacotherapy for obsessive-compulsive disorder. In D. J. Stein, E. Hollander, & B. O. Rothbaum (Eds.), *Textbook of anxiety disorders* (2nd ed., pp. 311–337). Arlington, VA: American Psychiatric.

Freud, S. (1926). Inhibitions, symptoms and anxiety. *The complete psychological works of Sigmund Freud, vol. 20* (pp. 72–175). London, UK: Hogarth Press.

Freund, K., Steiner, B. W., & Chan, S. (1982). Two types of cross-gender identity. *Archives of Sexual Behavior, 11*(1), 49–63.

Freyer, T., Kloppel, S., Tuscher, O., Kordon, A., Zurowski, B., Kuelz, A.-K., . . . Voderholzer, U. (2011). Frontostriatal activation in patients with obsessive-compulsive disorder before and after cognitive behavioral therapy. *Psychological Medicine: A Journal of Research in Psychiatry and the Allied Sciences, 41*(1), 207–216.

Gattari, P., Spizzichino, L., Valenzi, C., Zaccarelli, M., & Rezza, G. (1992). Behavioural patterns and HIV infection among drug using transvestites practising prostitution in Rome. *AIDS Care, 4*(1), 83–87.

Gert, B. (1992). A sex-caused inconsistency in *DSM-III-R:* The definition of mental disorder and the definition of paraphilias. *Journal of Medical Philosophy, 17,* 155–171.

Glasser, M. (1992). The management of perversions, with special reference to transvestism. In R. Lincoln (Ed.), *Psychosexual medicine: A study of underlying themes* (pp. 49–60). Boca Raton, FL: Chapman & Hall/CRC.

Goodwin, L. J., & Peterson, R. G. (1990). Psychological impact of abuse as it relates to transvestism.

Journal of Applied Rehabilitation Counseling, 21(4), 45–48.

Grandi, J. L., Goihman, S., Ueda, M., & Rutherford, G. W. (2000). HIV infection, syphilis, and behavioral risks in Brazilian male sex workers. *AIDS and Behavior, 4*(1), 129–135.

Green, R., Roberts, C. W., Williams, K., Goodman, M., & Mixon, A. (1987). Specific cross-gender behaviour in boyhood and later homosexual orientation. *British Journal of Psychiatry, 151,* 84–88.

Greenberg, D. F. (1985). Why was the berdarche ridiculed? *Journal of Homosexuality, 11*(3–4), 179–189.

Greenberg, L. S. (2002). Lessons about anger and sadness from psychotherapy. In L. S. Greenberg (Ed.), *Emotion-focused therapy: Coaching clients to work through their feelings* (pp. 229–239). Washington, DC: American Psychological Association.

Hayes, S. C., Strosahl, K. D., & Wilson, K. G. (1999). *Acceptance and commitment therapy: An experiential approach to behavior change*. New York: Guilford Press.

Heinemann, E. (2000). Fakafefine; men who are like women: Incest taboo and transsexuality in Tonga (Polynesia). *Gender & Psychoanalysis, 5*(2), 155–183.

Herdt, G. (1997). *Same sex, different cultures*. Boulder, CO: Westview Press.

Inciardi, J. A., Surratt, H. L., Telles, P. R., & Pok, B. H. (1999). Sex, drugs, and the culture of travestismo in Rio de Janeiro. *International Journal of Transgenderism, 3*(1–2), 1–12.

Jani, S., & Rosenberg, L. A. (1990). Systematic evaluation of sexual functioning in eunuch-transvestites: A study of 12 cases. *Journal of Sex & Marital Therapy, 16*(2), 103–110.

Joesoef, M. R., Gultom, M., Irana, I. D., Lewis, J. S., Moran, J. S., Muhaimin, T., & Ryan, C. A. (2003). High rates of sexually transmitted diseases among male transvestites in Jakarta, Indonesia. *International Journal of STD & AIDS, 14*(9), 609–613.

Katz, J. (1976). *Gay American history: Lesbians and gay men in the U.S.A.* New York: Crowell.

Kulick, D. (1997). The gender of Brazilian transgendered prostitutes. *American Anthropologist, 99*(3), 574–585.

Lance, L. M. (2002). Acceptance of diversity in human sexuality: Will the strategy reducing homophobia also reduce discomfort of cross-dressing? *College Student Journal, 36*(4), 598–602.

Langstrom, N., & Zucker, K. J. (2005). Transvestic fetishism in the general population: Prevalence and correlates. *Journal of Sex & Marital Therapy, 31*(2), 87–95.

Larsson, S., & Bergstrom-Walan, M.-B. (1999). Multisexuality, cross-dressing and the multiplicity of mind. *Scandinavian Journal of Sexology, 2*(3), 141–161.

Lentz, R. S. (2004). Reconceptualizing transvestites: A grounded theory approach. *Dissertation Abstracts International: Section B: The Sciences and Engineering, 64*(11-B), 5790.

Lombardi, E. L., Wilchins, R. A., Priesing, D., & Malouf, D. (2001). Gender violence: Transgender experiences with violence and discrimination. *Journal of Homosexuality, 42*(1), 89–101.

Lothstein, L. M. (1979). Group therapy with gender-dysphoric patients. *American Journal of Psychotherapy, 33*(1), 67–81.

Lovitt, C. J. (2004). Transvestites might be the new outcasts. *BMJ: British Medical Journal, 328*(7445), 955.

Mageo, J.-M. (1996). Samoa on the Wilde side: Male transvestism, Oscar Wilde and liminality in making gender. *Ethos, 24*(4), 588–627.

Masand, P. S. (1993). Successful treatment of sexual masochism and transvestic fetishism associated with depression with fluoxetine hydrochloride. *Depression, 1*(1), 50–52.

McCune, J. Q., Jr. (2004). Transformance: Reading the Gospel in drag. *Journal of Homosexuality, 46*(3–4), 151–167.

McLelland, M. (2003). Living more & like oneself: Transgender identities and sexualities in Japan. *Journal of Bisexuality, 3*(3–4), 203–230.

Money, J., & Russo, A. J. (1979). Homosexual outcome of discordant gender identity/role in childhood: Longitudinal follow-up. *Journal of Pediatric Psychology, 4*(1), 29–41.

Money, J., & Russo, A. J. (1981). Homosexual vs. transvestite or transsexual gender-identity/role: Outcome study in boys. *International Journal of Family Psychiatry, 2*(1–2), 139–145.

Mostade, J. (2006). Affirmative counseling with transgendered persons. In C. C. Lee (Ed.), *Multicultural issues in counseling: New approaches to diversity* (3rd. ed., pp. 303–316). Alexandria, VA: American Counseling Association.

Nanda, S. (1985). The hijras of India: Cultural and individual dimensions of an institutionalized third gender role. *Journal of Homosexuality, 11*(3–4), 35–54.

Newring, K. A. B., Wheeler, J., & Draper, C. (2008). Transvestic fetishism: Assessment and treatment. In D. R. Laws & W. T. O'Donohue (Eds.), *Sexual deviance: Theory, assessment, and treatment* (2nd ed., pp. 285–304). New York: Guilford Press.

Oswald, R. F., & Culton, L. S. (2003). Under the rainbow: Rural gay life and its relevance for family providers. *Family Relations: An Interdisciplinary Journal of Applied Family Studies, 52*(1), 72–81.

Parkes, G., & Hall, I. (2006). Gender dysphoria and cross-dressing in people with intellectual disability: A literature review. *Mental Retardation, 44*(4), 260–271.

Parkes, G., Hall, I., & Wilson, D. (2009). Cross dressing and gender dysphoria in people with learning disabilities: A descriptive study. *British Journal of Learning Disabilities, 37*(2), 151–156.

Person, E., & Ovesey, L. (1974a). The transsexual syndrome in males: I. Primary transsexualism. *American Journal of Psychotherapy, 28*(1), 4–20.

Person, E., & Ovesey, L. (1974b). The transsexual syndrome in males: II. Secondary transsexualism. *American Journal of Psychotherapy, 28*(2), 174–193.

Person, E. S., & Ovesey, L. (1984). Homosexual cross-dressers. *Journal of the American Academy of Psychoanalysis, 12*(2), 167–186.

Pomeroy, W. B. (1975). The diagnosis and treatment of transvestites and transsexuals. *Journal of Sex & Marital Therapy, 1,* 215–224.

Prince, C. V. (2005/1957). Homosexuality, transvestism and transsexuality: Reflections on their etiology and differentiation. *International Journal of Transgenderism, 8*(4), 17–20.

Prince, V. C. (1967). *The transvestite and his wife*. Los Angeles, CA: Argyle.

Prince, V., & Bentler, P. M. (1972). Survey of 504 cases of transvestism. *Psychological Reports, 31*(3), 903–917.

Rekers, G. A., Rosen, A. C., Lovaas, O. I., & Bentler, P. M. (1978). Sex-role stereotypy and professional intervention for childhood gender disturbance. *Professional Psychology, 9*(1), 127–136.

Reynolds, A. L., & Caron, S. L. (2000). How intimate relationships are impacted when heterosexual men crossdress. *Journal of Psychology & Human Sexuality, 12*(3), 63–77.

Rhodes, T., Simic, M., Baros, S., Platt, L., & Zikic, B. (2008). Police violence and sexual risk among female and transvestite sex workers in Serbia: Qualitative study. *BMJ: British Medical Journal, 337*(7669), 1–6.

Richert, A. J. (1999). Some practical implications of integrating narrative and humanistic/existential approaches to psychotherapy. *Journal of Psychotherapy Integration, 9*(3), 257–278.

Rosario, V. A. (2004). "Que joto bonita!": Transgender negotiations of sex and ethnicity. *Journal of Gay & Lesbian Psychotherapy, 8*(1–2), 89–97.

Rosen, A. C., & Rehm, L. P. (1977). Long-term follow-up in two cases of transvestism treated with aversion therapy. *Journal of Behavior Therapy and Experimental Psychiatry, 8*(3), 295–300.

Rosen, R. C., & Kopel, S. A. (1977). Penile plethysmography and biofeedback in the treatment of a transvestite-exhibitionist. *Journal of Consulting and Clinical Psychology, 45*(5), 908–916.

Ruan, F. F., & Matsumura, M. (1991). *Sex in China: Studies in sexology in Chinese culture*. New York: Plenum Press.

Schacht, S. P. (2004). Beyond the boundaries of the classroom: Teaching about gender and sexuality at a drag show. *Journal of Homosexuality, 46*(3–4), 225–240.

Shaffer, J., Barclay, A., & Redman, S. (1989). Strategic therapy as a treatment approach in transvestism. *Psychotherapy in Private Practice, 7*(2), 91–102.

Shields, H., & Bredfeldt, G. (2001). *Caring for souls: Counseling under the authority of scripture*. Chicago: Moody Press.

Sifuentes-Jauregui, B. (2006). Review of unzipping gender: Sex, cross-dressing and culture. *Journal of Gender Studies, 15*(1), 95–97.

Smith, B., & Home, S. (2007) Gay, lesbian, bisexual and transgendered (GLBT) experiences with earth-spirited faith. *Journal of Homosexuality, 52*(3), 235–248.

Stayton, W. R. (1996). Sexual and gender identity disorders in a relational perspective. In F. W. Kaslow (Ed.), *Handbook of relational diagnosis and dysfunctional family patterns* (pp. 357–370). New York: John Wiley & Sons.

Steiner, B. W., Satterberg, J. A., & Muir, C. F. (1978). Flight into femininity: The male menopause? *Canadian Psychiatric Association Journal/La Revue de l'Association des psychiatres du Canada, 23*(6), 405–410.

Stoller, R. J. (1971). Transsexualism and transvestism. *Psychiatric Annals, 1*(4), 60–72.

Stoller, R. J. (1982). Transvestism in women. *Archives of Sexual Behavior, 11*(2), 99–115.

Stoller, R. J. (1996). The gender disorders. In I. Rosen (Ed.), *Sexual deviation* (3rd ed., pp. 111–133). New York: Oxford University Press.

Swales, M. A. (2009). Dialectical behaviour therapy: Description, research and future directions. *International Journal of Behavioral Consultation and Therapy, 5*(2), 164–177.

Tsang, D. C. (1995). Policing & perversions: Depo-Provera and John Money's new sexual order. *Journal of Homosexuality, 28*(3–4), 397–426.

Updike, T. L., Dawes, M. S., & Evans, A. R. (1987). Counseling guilt. *Psychology: A Journal of Human Behavior, 24*(1–2), 60–64.

Vanderwall, F. W. (1986). Guilt, Jesus, and spiritual counseling. *Studies in Formative Spirituality, 7*(2), 253–266.

Wallien, M. S. C., & Cohen-Kettenis, P. T. (2008). Psychosexual outcome of gender-dysphoric children. *Journal of the American Academy of Child & Adolescent Psychiatry, 47*(12), 1413–1423.

Weinberg, T. S., & Bullough, V. L. (1988). Alienation, self-image, and the importance of support groups for the wives of transvestites. *Journal of Sex Research, 24,* 262–268.

Wheeler, J., Newring, K. A. B., & Draper, C. (2008). Transvestic fetishism: Psychopathology and theory. In D. R. Laws & W. T. O'Donohue (Eds.), *Sexual deviance: Theory, assessment, and treatment* (2nd ed., pp. 272–284). New York: Guilford Press.

Wheelwright, J. (1989). *Amazons and military maids: Women who dressed as men in the pursuit of life, liberty and happiness*. London, UK: Pandora Press.

Whitam, F. L. (1997). Culturally universal aspects of male homosexual transvestites and transsexuals. In B. Bullough, V. L. Bullough, & J. Elias (Eds.), *Gender blending* (pp. 189–203). Amherst, NY: Prometheus.

Whitam, F. L., & Mathy, R. M. (1986). *Male homosexuality in four societies: Brazil, Guatemala, the Philippines, and the United States.* New York: Praeger.

Wise, T. N. (1979). Psychotherapy of an aging transvestite. *Journal of Sex & Marital Therapy, 5*(4), 368–373.

Wise, T. N. (1985). Coping with a transvestitic mate: Clinical implications. *Journal of Sex & Marital Therapy, 11*(4), 293–300.

Wise, T. N., & Meyer, J. K. (1980). The border area between transvestism and gender dysphoria: Transvestitic applicants for sex reassignment. *Archives of Sexual Behavior, 9*(4), 327–342.

Wolfe, R. W. (1992). Video aversive satiation: A hopefully heuristic single case study. *Annals of Sex Research, 5*(3), 181–187.

Woodhouse, A. (1985). Forgotten women: Transvestism and marriage. *Women's Studies: An International Forum, 8,* 583–592.

World Health Organization. (1992). *The ICD-10 classification of mental and behavioral disorders: Clinical descriptions and diagnostic guidelines*. Geneva, CH: Author.

Wright, A. D., & Humphreys, A. (1984). The use of hypnosis to enhance covert sensitisation: Two case studies. *British Journal of Experimental & Clinical Hypnosis, 1*(2), 3–10.

Wright, S. (2010). Depathologizing consensual sexual sadism, sexual masochism, transvestic fetishism, and fetishism. *Archives of Sexual Behavior, 39*(6), 1229–1230.

Wysocki, D. K. (1993). Construction of masculinity: V. A look into the lives of heterosexual male transvestites. *Feminism & Psychology, 3*(3), 374–380.

Zucker, K. J., & Blanchard, R. (1997). Transvestic fetishism: Psychopathology and theory. In D. R. Laws & W. T. O'Donohue (Eds.), *Sexual deviance: Theory, assessment, and treatment* (pp. 253–279). New York: Guilford Press.

Zuger, B. (1978). Effeminate behavior present in boys from childhood: Ten additional years of follow-up. *Comprehensive Psychiatry, 19*(4), 363–369.

References for Chapter 8

Abel, G. G. (1979). What to do when nontranssexuals seek sex reassignment surgery. *Journal of Sex & Marital Therapy, 5*(4), 374–376.

Alderson, K. (2007, June 7). Facilitating the transitioning process in the workplace settings of transsexual clients. *Canadian Psychological Association Annual Convention*, Ottawa, Ontario.

Alderson, K. G., & Cohen, J. N. (2011). *"Psychology works" fact sheet: Gender dysphoria in children.* Retrieved from www.cpa.ca/psychologyfactsheets/genderdysphoriachildren/.

Alegria, C. A. (2010). Relationship challenges and relationship maintenance activities following disclosure of transsexualism. *Journal of Psychiatric and Mental Health Nursing, 17*(10), 909–916.

American Psychiatric Association. (2010a). *DSM-V development: Gender dysphoria in adolescents or adults*. Retrieved from www.dsm5.org/ProposedRevisions/Pages/proposedrevision.aspx?rid=482.

American Psychiatric Association. (2010b). *DSM-V development: Gender dysphoria in children.* Retrieved from www.dsm5.org/ProposedRevisions/Pages/proposedrevision.aspx?rid=192.

American Psychological Association, Task Force on Gender Identity and Gender Variance. (2009). *Report of the Task Force on Gender Identity and Gender Variance*. Washington, DC: Author. Retrieved from www.apa.org/pi/lgbt/resources/policy/gender-identity-report.pdf.

Antoszewski, B., Kasielska, A., Jedrzejczak, M., & KrukJeromin, J. (2007). Knowledge of and attitude toward transsexualism among college students. *Sexuality and Disability, 25*(1), 29–35.

Bakker, A., Van Kesteren, P. J., Gooren, L. J., & Bezemer, P. D. (1993). The prevalence of transsexualism in the Netherlands. *Acta Psychiatrica Scandinavica, 87*(4), 237–238.

Banks, D. R. (2002). Personality characteristics of individuals seeking treatment for gender identity disorder. *Dissertation Abstracts International: Section B: The Sciences and Engineering, 62*(9B), 4208.

Barclay, J. M., & Scott, L. J. (2006). Transsexuals and workplace diversity: A case of "change" management. *Personnel Review, 35*(4), 487–502.

Bauer, G. R., Hammond, R., Travers, R., Kaay, M., Hohenadel, K. M., & Boyce, M. (2009). "I don't think this is theoretical; This is our lives": How erasure impacts health care for transgender people. *JANAC: Journal of the Association of Nurses in AIDS Care, 20*(5), 348–361.

Blanchard, R. (1989). The concept of autogynephilia and the typology of male gender dysphoria. *Journal of Nervous and Mental Disease, 177*(10), 616–623.

Blanchard, R. (2005). Early history of the concept of autogynephilia. *Archives of Sexual Behavior, 34*(4), 439–446.

Bockting, W. O. (2009). Transforming the paradigm of transgender health: A field in transition. *Sexual and Relationship Therapy, 24*(2), 103–107.

Bockting, W., Huang, C.-Y., Ding, H., Robinson, B., & Rosser, B. R. S. (2005). Are transgender persons at higher risk for HIV than other sexual minorities? A comparison of HIV prevalence and risks. *International Journal of Transgenderism, 8*(2), 123–131.

Borras, L., Huguelet, P., & Eytan, A. (2007). Delusional "pseudotranssexualism" in schizophrenia. *Psychiatry: Interpersonal and Biological Processes, 70*(2), 175–179.

Bradley, H. A. (2010). Transgender children and their families: Acceptance and its impact on well-being. *Dissertation Abstracts International: Section B: The Sciences and Engineering, 71*(1-B), 650.

Broad, K. L. (2002). GLB+T?: Gender/sexuality movements and transgender collective identity (de)constructions. *International Journal of Sexuality & Gender Studies, 7*(4), 241–264.

Brown, G. R., & McDuffie, E. (2009). Health care policies addressing transgender inmates in prison systems in the United States. *Journal of Correctional Health Care, 15*(4), 280–291.

Budge, S. L., Tebbe, E. N., & Howard, K. A. S. (2010). The work experiences of transgender individuals: Negotiating the transition and career decision-making processes. *Journal of Counseling Psychology, 57*(4), 377–393.

Burnes, T. R., Singh, A. A., Harper, A. J., Harper, B., Maxon-Kann, W., Pickering, D. L., . . . Hosea, J. (2010). American Counseling Association: Competencies for counseling with transgender clients. *Journal of LGBT Issues in Counseling, 4*(3–4), 135–159.

Canadian Psychological Association. (2010). *Policy and position statements: Gender identity in adolescents and adults*. Retrieved from www.cpa.ca/aboutcpa/policystatements/#Gender_Identity.

Caron, G. R., & Archer, R. P. (1997). MMPI and Rorschach characteristics of individuals approved for gender reassignment surgery. *Assessment, 4*(3), 229–241.

Carroll, L., & Gilroy, P. J. (2002). Transgender issues in counselor preparation. *Counselor Education and Supervision, 41*(3), 233–242.

Carroll, L., Gilroy, P. J., & Ryan, J. (2002). Counseling transgendered, transsexual, and gender-variant clients. *Journal of Counseling & Development, 80*(2), 131–138.

Cohen, J. N., & Alderson, K. G. (2011). *"Psychology works" fact sheet: Gender dysphoria in adolescents and adults*. Retrieved from www.cpa.ca/psychologyfactsheets/genderdysphoria/.

Cohen-Kettenis, P. T., Delemarrevan de Waal, H. A., & Gooren, L. J. G. (2008). The treatment of adolescent transsexuals: Changing insights. *Journal of Sexual Medicine, 5*(8), 1892–1897.

Cohen-Kettenis, P. T., & Gooren, L. J. (1992). The influence of hormone treatment on psychological functioning of transsexuals. *Journal of Psychology & Human Sexuality, 5*(4), 55–67.

Cohen-Kettenis, P. T., Owen, A., Kaijser, G. G., Bradley, S. J., & Zucker, K. J. (2003). Demographic characteristics, social competence, and behavior problems in children with gender identity disorder: A cross-national, cross-clinic comparative analysis. *Journal of Abnormal Child Psychology: An official publication of the International Society for Research in Child and Adolescent Psychopathology, 31*(1), 41–53.

Cole, C. M., O'Boyle, M., Emory, L. E., & Meyer, W. J. (1997). Comorbidity of gender dysphoria and other major psychiatric diagnoses. *Archives of Sexual Behavior, 26*(1), 13–26.

Cole, S. S., Denny, D., Eyler, A. E., & Samons, S. L. (2000). Issues of transgender. In L. T. Szuchman & F. Muscarella (Eds.), *Psychological perspectives on human sexuality* (pp. 149–195). Hoboken, NJ: John Wiley & Sons.

Coleman, E., Adler, R., Bockting, W., Botzer, M., Brown, G., Cohen-Kettenis, P., . . . Zucker, K. (2011). *Standards of care for the health of transsexual, transgender, and gender nonconforming people* (7th ed.). Word Professional Association for Transgender Health. Retrieved from www.thisishow.org/Files/soc7.pdf.

Connell, R. (2010). Two cans of paint: A transsexual life story, with reflections on gender change and history. *Sexualities, 13*(1), 319.

Cook-Daniels, L. (2006). Trans aging. In D. Kimmel, T. Rose, & S. David (Eds.), *Lesbian, gay, bisexual, and transgender aging: Research and clinical perspectives* (pp. 20–35). New York: Columbia University Press.

Cook-Daniels, L., & Munson, M. (2010). Sexual violence, elder abuse, and sexuality of transgender adults, age 50+: Results of three surveys. *Journal of GLBT Family Studies, 6*(2), 142–177.

Couch, M., Mulcare, H., Pitts, M., Smith, A., & Mitchell, A. (2008). The religious affiliation of gay, lesbian, bisexual, transgender and intersex Australians: A report from the private lives survey. *People and Place, 16*(1), 1–11.

Crosby, R. A., & Pitts, N. L. (2007). Caught between different worlds: How transgendered women may be "forced" into risky sex. *Journal of Sex Research, 44*(1), 43–48.

Dahl, M., Feldman, J. L., Goldberg, J. M., & Jaberi, A. (2007). Physical aspects of transgender endocrine therapy. *International Journal of Transgenderism, 9*(3–4), 111–134.

De Cuypere, G., T'Sjoen, G., Beerten, R., Selvaggi, G., De Sutter, P., Hoebeke, P., . . . Rubens, R. (2005). Sexual and physical health after sex reassignment surgery. *Archives of Sexual Behavior, 34*(6), 679–690.

De Cuypere, G., Van Hemelrijck, M., Michel, A., Carael, B., Heylens, G., Rubens, R., Hoebeke, P., & Monstrey, S. (2007). Prevalence and demography of transsexualism in Belgium. *European Psychiatry, 22*(3), 137–141.

De Cuypere, G., & Vercruysse, H., Jr. (2009). Eligibility and readiness criteria for sex reassignment surgery: Recommendations for revision of the WPATH Standards of Care. *International Journal of Transgenderism, 11*(3), 194–205.

De Sutter, P. (2009). Reproductive options for transpeople: Recommendations for revision of the WPATH's Standards of Care. *International Journal of Transgenderism, 11*(3), 183–185.

de Vries, A. L. C., & Cohen-Kettenis, P. T. (2009). Review of World Professional Association for Transgender Health's Standards of Care for children and adolescents with gender identity disorder: A need for change? *International Journal of Transgenderism, 11*(2), 100–109.

Denny, D. (2007). Transgender identities and bisexual expression: Implications for counselors. In B. A. Firestein (Ed.), *Becoming visible: Counseling bisexuals across the lifespan* (pp. 268–284). New York: Columbia University Press.

Devor, A. H. (2004). Witnessing and mirroring: A fourteen stage model of transsexual identity formation. In U. Leli & J. Drescher (Eds.), *Transgender subjectivities: A clinician's guide* (pp. 41–67). New York: Haworth Press.

Dhejne, C., Lichtenstein, P., Boman, M., Johansson, A. L. V., Langstrom, N., & Landen, M. (2011). Long-term follow-up of transsexual persons undergoing sex reassignment surgery: Cohort study in Sweden. *PLoS ONE, 6*(2), ArtID e16885.

Di Ceghe, D., Sturge, C., & Sutton, A. (1998). The Royal College of Psychiatrists: Gender identity disorders in children and adolescents: Guidance for management. *International Journal of Transgenderism, 2,* No Pagination Specified.

Dickey, R., & Steiner, B. W. (1990). Hormone treatment and surgery. In R. Blanchard & B. W. Steiner (Eds.), *Clinical management of gender identity disorders in children and adults* (pp. 139–158). Washington, DC: American Psychiatric Association.

Dixen, J. M., Maddever, H., Van Maasdam, J., & Edwards, P. W. (1984). Psychosocial characteristics of applicants evaluated for surgical gender reassignment. *Archives of Sexual Behavior, 13*(3), 269–276.

Docter, R. F. (1985). Transsexual surgery at 74: A case report. *Archives of Sexual Behavior, 14*(3), 271–277.

Docter, R. F. (1988). *Transvestites and transsexuals: Toward a theory of cross-gender behavior*. New York: Plenum Press.

Dysart-Gale, D. (2010). Social justice and social determinants of health: Lesbian, gay, bisexual, transgendered, intersexed, and queer youth in Canada. *Journal of Child and Adolescent Psychiatric Nursing, 23*(1), 23–28.

Eliason, M. J., Dibble, S., & DeJoseph, J. (2010). Nursing's silence on lesbian, gay, bisexual, and transgender issues: The need for emancipatory efforts. *Advances in Nursing Science, 33*(3), 206–218.

Emerson, S., & Rosenfeld, C. (1996). Stages of adjustment in family members of transgender individuals. *Journal of Family Psychotherapy, 7*(3), 1–12.

Erich, S., Tittsworth, J., Dykes, J., & Cabuses, C. (2008). Family relationships and their correlations with transsexual well-being. *Journal of GLBT Family Studies, 4*(4), 419–432.

Erich, S., Tittsworth, J., & Kersten, A. S. (2010). An examination and comparison of transsexuals of color and their white counterparts regarding personal wellbeing and support networks. *Journal of GLBT Family Studies, 6*(1), 25–39.

Erich, S., Tittsworth, J., Meier, S. L. C., & Lerman, T. (2010). Transsexuals of color: Perceptions of discrimination based on transsexual status and race/ethnicity status. *Journal of GLBT Family Studies, 6*(3), 294–314.

Estrada, S. (2008). An exploration of the life experiences of Latina male-to-female transsexuals. *Dissertation Abstracts International: Section B: The Sciences and Engineering, 69*(4B), 2623.

Ettner, R. (2008). Transsexual couples: A qualitative evaluation of atypical partner preferences. *International Journal of Transgenderism, 10*(2), 109–116.

Factor, R., & Rothblum, E. (2008). Exploring gender identity and community among three groups of transgender individuals in the United States: MTSs, FTMs, and genderqueers. *Health Sociology Review, 17*(3), 235–253.

Feldman, J., & Safer, J. (2009). Hormone therapy in adults: Suggested revisions to the sixth version of the Standards of Care. *International Journal of Transgenderism, 11*(3), 146–182.

Fontaine, J. H. (2002). Transgender issues in counseling. In L. D. Burlew & D. Capuzzi (Eds.), *Sexuality counseling* (pp. 177–194). Hauppauge, NY: Nova Science.

Fraser, L. (2009a). Depth psychotherapy with transgender people. *Sexual and Relationship Therapy, 24*(2), 126–142.

Fraser, L. (2009b). Etherapy: Ethical and clinical considerations for Version 7 of the World Professional Association for Transgender Health's Standards of Care. *International Journal of Transgenderism, 11*(4), 247–263.

Fraser, L. (2009c). Psychotherapy in the World Professional Association for Transgender Health's Standards of Care: Background and recommendations. *International Journal of Transgenderism, 11*(2), 110–126.

Garofalo, R., Deleon, J., Osmer, E., Doll, M., & Harper, G. W. (2006). Overlooked, misunderstood and at-risk: Exploring the lives and HIV risk of ethnic minority male-to-female transgender youth. *Journal of Adolescent Health, 38*(3), 230–236.

Garofalo, R., Osmer, E., Sullivan, C., Doll, M., & Harper, G. (2007). Environmental, psychosocial, and individual correlates of HIV risk in ethnic-minority male-to-female transgender youth. *Journal of HIV/AIDS Prevention in Children & Youth, 7*(2), 89–104.

Gehring, D., & Knudson, G. (2005). Prevalence of childhood trauma in a clinical population of transsexual people. *International Journal of Transgenderism, 8*(1), 23–30.

Gomez-Gil, E., Trilla, A., Salamero, M., Godas, T., & Valdes, M. (2009). Sociodemographic, clinical, and psychiatric characteristics of transsexuals from Spain. *Archives of Sexual Behavior, 38*(3), 378–392.

Gomez-Gil, E., Vidal-Hagemeijer, A., & Salamero, M. (2008). MMPI-2 characteristics of transsexuals requesting sex reassignment: Comparison of patients in prehormonal and presurgical phases. *Journal of Personality Assessment, 90*(4), 368–374.

Gonzalez, M., & McNulty, J. (2010). Achieving competency with transgender youth: School counselors as collaborative advocates. *Journal of LGBT Issues in Counseling, 4*(3–4), 176–186.

Green, E. R. (2006). Debating trans inclusion in the feminist movement: A transpositive analysis. *Journal of Lesbian Studies, 10*(12), 231–248.

Green, R. (1987). *The "sissy boy syndrome" and the development of homosexuality*. New Haven, CT: Yale University Press.

Green, R. (1996). Gender identity disorder in children. In G. O. Gabbard & S. D. Atkinson (Eds.), *Synopsis of treatments of psychiatric disorders* (2nd ed., pp. 837–841). Washington, DC: American Psychiatric Association.

Grossman, A. H., & D'Augelli, A. R. (2006). Transgender youth: Invisible and vulnerable. *Journal of Homosexuality, 51*(1), 111–128.

Gurvich S. E. (1992). The transsexual husband: The wife's experience. *Dissertation Abstracts International, 52*(8-A), 3089.

Haas, A. P., Eliason, M., Mays, V. M., Mathy, R. M., Cochran, S. D., D'Augelli, A. R., . . . Clayton, P. J. (2011). Suicide and suicide risk in lesbian, gay, bisexual, and transgender populations: Review and recommendations. *Journal of Homosexuality, 58*(1), 10–51.

Haberman, M. A., & Michael, R. P. (1979). Autocastration in transsexualism. *American Journal of Psychiatry, 136*(3), 347–348.

Hanssmann, C., Morrison, D., Russian, E., Shiu-Thornton, S., & Bowen, D. (2010). A community-based program evaluation of community competency trainings. *JANAC: Journal of the Association of Nurses in AIDS Care, 21*(3), 240–255.

Hegedus, J. K. (2009). When a daughter becomes a son: Parents' acceptance of their transgender children. *Dissertation Abstracts International: Section B: The Sciences and Engineering, 70*(3-B), 1982.

Herbst, J. H., Jacobs, E. D., Finlayson, T. J., McKleroy, V. S., Neumann, M. S., & Crepaz, N. (2008). Estimating HIV prevalence and risk behaviors of transgender persons in the United States: A systematic review. *AIDS and Behavior, 12*(1), 117.

Hill, D. B., Rozanski, C., Carfagnini, J., & Willoughby, B. (2007). Gender identity disorders in childhood and adolescence: A critical inquiry. *International Journal of Sexual Health, 19*(1), 57–75.

Hines, S. (2009). Forming gender: Social change and transgender citizenship. In E. H. Oleksy (Ed.), *Intimate citizenships: Gender, sexualities, politics* (pp. 79–99). New York: Routledge/Taylor & Francis.

Holman, C. W., & Goldberg, J. M. (2007). Ethical, legal, and psychosocial issues in care of transgender adolescents. *International Journal of Transgenderism, 9*(3), 95–110.

Imbimbo, C., Verze, P., Palmieri, A., Longo, N., Fusco, F., Arcaniolo, D., & Mirone, V. (2009). A report from a single institute's 14-year experience in treatment of male-to-female transsexuals. *Journal of Sexual Medicine, 6*(10), 2736–2745.

Israel, G. E., & Tarver, D. E., II. (2001). *Transgender care: Recommended guidelines, practical information and personal accounts*. Philadelphia: Temple University Press.

Johansson, A., Sundbom, E., Hojerback, T., & Bodlund, O. (2010). A five-year follow-up study of Swedish adults with gender identity disorder. *Archives of Sexual Behavior, 39*(6), 1429–1437.

Johnson, C. V., Mimiaga, M. J., & Bradford, J. (2008). Health care issues among lesbian, gay, bisexual, transgender and intersex (LGBTI) populations in the United States: Introduction. *Journal of Homosexuality, 54*(3), 213–224.

Jones, C. H. (2008). Religio-spirituality and the coming-out process. *Dissertation Abstracts International Section A: Humanities and Social Sciences, 69*(6-A), 2171.

Joslin-Roher, E., & Wheeler, D. P. (2009). Partners in transition: The transition experience of lesbian, bisexual, and queer identified partners of transgender men. *Journal of Gay & Lesbian Social Services: Issues in Practice, Policy & Research, 21*(1), 30–48.

Keiswetter, S., & Brotemarkle, B. (2010). Culturally competent care for HIV-infected transgender persons in the inpatient hospital setting: The role of the clinical nurse leader. *JANAC: Journal of the Association of Nurses in AIDS Care, 21*(3), 272–277.

Kessler, S. J., & McKenna, W. (2000). Gender construction in everyday life: Transsexualism. *Feminism & Psychology, 10*(1), 11–29.

Kirk, J., & Belovics, R. (2008). Understanding and counseling transgender clients. *Journal of Employment Counseling, 45*(1), 29–43.

Klein, C., & Gorzalka, B. B. (2009). Sexual functioning in transsexuals following hormone therapy and genital surgery: A review. *Journal of Sexual Medicine, 6*(11), 2922–2939.

Knudson, G., De Cuypere, G., & Bockting, W. (2010). Recommendations for revision of the *DSM* diagnoses of gender identity disorders: Consensus statement of the World Professional Association for Transgender Health. *International Journal of Transgenderism, 12*(2), 115–118.

Korell, S. C., & Lorah, P. (2007). An overview of affirmative psychotherapy and counseling with transgender clients. In K. J. Bieschke, R. M. Perez, &

K. A. DeBord (Eds.), *Handbook of counseling and psychotherapy with lesbian, gay, bisexual, and transgender clients* (2nd ed., pp. 271–288). Washington, DC: American Psychological Association.

Kosenko, K. A. (2011). Contextual influences on sexual risk-taking in the transgender community. *Journal of Sex Research, 48*(2–3), 285–296.

Kraemer, B., Delsignore, A., Schnyder, U., & Hepp, U. (2008). Body image and transsexualism. *Psychopathology, 41*(2), 96–100.

Lamble, S. (2008). Retelling racialized violence, remaking White innocence: The politics of interlocking oppressions in Transgender Day of Remembrance. *Sexuality Research & Social Policy: A Journal of the NSRC, 5*(1), 24–42.

Landen, M., & Innala, S. (2000). Attitudes toward transsexualism in a Swedish national survey. *Archives of Sexual Behavior, 29*(4), 375–388.

Langer, S. J., & Martin, J. I. (2004). How dresses can make you mentally ill: Examining gender identity disorder in children. *Child & Adolescent Social Work Journal, 21*(1), 5–23.

Lawrence, A. A. (2005). Sexuality before and after male-to-female sex reassignment surgery. *Archives of Sexual Behavior, 34*(2), 147–166.

Lawrence, A. A. (2008). Gender identity disorders in adults: Diagnosis and treatment. In D. L. Rowland & L. Incrocci (Eds.), *Handbook of sexual and gender identity disorders* (pp. 423–456). Hoboken, NJ: John Wiley & Sons.

Lennon, E., & Mistler, B. J. (2010). Breaking the binary: Providing effective counseling to transgender students in college and university settings. *Journal of LGBT Issues in Counseling, 4*(3–4), 228–240.

Lev, A. I. (2004). *Transgender emergence: Therapeutic guidelines for working with gender-variant people and their families*. New York: Haworth Clinical Practice Press.

Lev, A. I. (2007). Transgender communities: Developing identity through connection (pp. 147–175). In K. J. Bieschke, R. M. Perez, & K. A. DeBord (Eds.), *Handbook of counseling and psychotherapy with lesbian, gay, bisexual, and transgender clients* (2nd ed.). Washington, DC: American Psychological Association.

Levine, S. B. (2009). Real-life test experience: Recommendations for revisions to the Standards of Care of the World Professional Association for Transgender Health. *International Journal of Transgenderism, 11*(3), 186–193.

Levy, D. L., & Reeves, P. (2011). Resolving identity conflict: Gay, lesbian, and queer individuals with a Christian upbringing. *Journal of Gay & Lesbian Social Services: The Quarterly Journal of Community & Clinical Practice, 23*(1), 53–68.

Livingstone, T. (2008). The relevance of a person-centered approach to therapy with transgendered or transsexual clients. *Person-Centered and Experiential Psychotherapies, 7*(2), 135–144.

Lombardi, E., & Davis, S. M. (2006). Transgender health issues. In D. F. Morrow & L. Messinger (Eds.), *Sexual orientation & gender expression in social work practice: Working with gay, lesbian, bisexual, & transgender people* (pp. 343–363). New York: Columbia University Press.

Lombardi, E. L., & van Servellen, G. (2000). Building culturally sensitive substance use prevention and treatment programs for transgendered populations. *Journal of Substance Abuse Treatment, 19*(3), 291–296.

Long, L. L., Burnett, J. A., & Thomas, R. V. (2006). *Sexuality counseling: An integrative approach*. Upper Saddle River, NJ: Pearson/Merrill Prentice Hall.

Lynch, B. J. (2011). Affirmation of transgender students: Evaluation of a rural New England college. *Dissertation Abstracts International: Section B: The Sciences and Engineering, 71*(7-B), 4503.

Maguen, S., Shipherd, J. C., Harris, H. N., & Welch, L. P. (2007). Prevalence and predictors of disclosure of transgender identity. *International Journal of Sexual Health, 19*(1), 313.

Manners, P. J. (2009). Gender identity disorder in adolescence: A review of the literature. *Child and Adolescent Mental Health, 14*(2), 62–68.

Marks, I., Green, R., & Mataix-Cols, D. (2000). Adult gender identity disorder can remit. *Comprehensive Psychiatry, 41*(4), 273–275.

Menvielle, E. J., & Tuerk, C. (2002). A support group for parents of gendernonconforming boys. *Journal of the American Academy of Child & Adolescent Psychiatry, 41*(8), 1010–1013.

Meyenburg, B. (1999). Gender identity disorder in adolescence: Outcomes of psychotherapy. *Adolescence, 34*(134), 305–313.

Meyer, W., Bockting, W. O., Cohen-Kettenis, P., Coleman, E., DiCeglie, D., Devor, H. . . . Wheeler, C. C. (2001). *The Harry Benjamin International Gender Dysphoria Association's standards of care for gender identity disorders*

(6th ed.). World Professional Association for Transgender Health. Retrieved from www.wpath.org/publications_standards.cfm.

Meyer-Bahlburg, H. F. L. (2009). Variants of gender differentiation in somatic disorders of sex development: Recommendations for Version 7 of the World Professional Association for Transgender Health's Standards of Care. *International Journal of Transgenderism, 11*(4), 226–237.

Mizock, L., & Fleming, M. Z. (2011). Transgender and gender variant populations with mental illness: Implications for clinical care. *Professional Psychology: Research and Practice, 42*(2), 208–213.

Mizock, L., & Lewis, T. K. (2008). Trauma in transgender populations: Risk, resilience, and clinical care. *Journal of Emotional Abuse, 8*(3), 335–354.

Modestin, J., & Ebner, G. (1995). Multiple personality disorder manifesting itself under the mask of transsexualism. *Psychopathology, 28*(6), 317–321.

Mostade, J. (2006). Affirmative counseling with transgendered persons. In C. C. Lee (Ed.), *Multicultural issues in counseling: New approaches to diversity* (3rd. ed., pp. 303–316). Alexandria, VA: American Counseling Association.

Murad, M. H., Elamin M. B., Garcia, M. Z., Mullan, R. J., Murad, A., Erwin P. J., & Montori, V. M. (2010). Hormonal therapy and sex reassignment: A systematic review and meta-analysis of quality of life and psychosocial outcomes. *Clinical Endocrinology, 72*(2), 214–231.

Nuttbrock, L., Hwahng, S., Bockting, W., Rosenblum, A., Mason, M., Macri, M., & Becker, J. (2009). Lifetime risk factors for HIV/sexually transmitted infections among male-to-female transgender persons. *JAIDS Journal of Acquired Immune Deficiency Syndromes, 52*(3), 417–421.

Persson, D. I. (2009). Unique challenges of transgender aging: Implications from the literature. *Journal of Gerontological Social Work, 52*(6), 633–646.

Pinto, R. M., Melendez, R. M., & Spector, A. Y. (2008). Male-to-female transgender individuals building social support and capital from within a gender-focused network. *Journal of Gay & Lesbian Social Services: Issues in Practice, Policy & Research, 20*(3), 2008, 203–220.

Pitts, M. K., Couch, M., Mulcare, H., Croy, S., & Mitchell, A. (2009). Transgender people in Australia and New Zealand: Health, wellbeing and access to health services. *Feminism & Psychology, 19*(4), 475–495.

Rachlin, K. (2002). Transgender individuals' experiences of psychotherapy. *International Journal of Transgenderism, 6*(1), No Pagination Specified.

Reinsmith-Jones, K. (2009). Body and soul: Transformational journeys toward authenticity within the context of transsexuality. *Dissertation Abstracts International Section A: Humanities and Social Sciences, 69*(10A), 4142.

Rekers, G. A., Rosen, A. C., Lovaas, O. I., & Bentler, P. M. (1978). Sex-role stereotypy and professional intervention for childhood gender disturbance. *Professional Psychology, 9*(1), 127–136.

Rosenberg, M. (2002). Children with gender identity issues and their parents in individual and group treatment. *Journal of the American Academy of Child & Adolescent Psychiatry, 41*(5), 619–621.

Ross, M. W., Walinder, J., Lundstrom, B., & Thuwe, I. (1981). Cross-cultural approaches to transsexualism: A comparison between Sweden and Australia. *Acta Psychiatrica Scandinavica, 63*(1), 75–82.

Ruan, F., & Bullough, V. L. (1988). The first case of transsexual surgery in mainland China. *Journal of Sex Research, 25*(4), 546–547.

Ryan, C., Russell, S. T., Huebner, D., Diaz, R., & Sanchez, J. (2010). Family acceptance in adolescence and the health of LGBT young adults. *Journal of Child and Adolescent Psychiatric Nursing, 23*(4), 205–213.

Samons, S. L. (2009). Can this marriage be saved? Addressing male-to-female transgender issues in couples therapy. *Sexual and Relationship Therapy, 24*(2), 152–162.

Sanchez, F. J., & Vilain, E. (2009). Collective self-esteem as a coping resource for male-to-female transsexuals. *Journal of Counseling Psychology, 56*(1), 202–209.

Sangganjanavanich, V. F., & Cavazos, J., Jr. (2010). Workplace aggression: Toward social justice and advocacy in counseling for transgender individuals. *Journal of LGBT Issues in Counseling, 4*(3–4), 187–201.

Sausa, L. A., Keatley, J., & Operario, D. (2007). Perceived risks and benefits of sex work among transgender women of color in San Francisco. *Archives of Sexual Behavior, 36*(6), 768–777.

Schaefer, L. C., & Wheeler, C. C. (2004). Guilt in cross gender identity conditions: Presentations and treatment. In U. Leli & J. Drescher (Eds.), *Transgender subjectivities: A clinician's guide* (pp. 117–127). New York: Haworth Press.

Schilt, K., & Connell, C. (2007). Do workplace gender transitions make gender trouble? *Gender, Work and Organization, 14*(6), 596–618.

Schneider, M. S., & Dimito, A. (2010). Factors influencing the career and academic choices of lesbian, gay, bisexual, and transgender people. *Journal of Homosexuality, 57*(10), 1355–1369.

Schrock, D. P., Boyd, E. M., & Leaf, M. (2009). Emotion work in the public performances of male-to-female transsexuals. *Archives of Sexual Behavior, 38*(5), 702–712.

Seil, D. (2004). The diagnosis and treatment of transgendered patients. *Journal of Gay & Lesbian Psychotherapy, 8*(1–2), 99–116.

Shelley, C. A. (2009). Trans people and social justice. *Journal of Individual Psychology, 65*(4), 386–396.

Simon, L., Zsolt, U., Fogd, D., & Czobor, P. (2011). Dysfunctional core beliefs, perceived parenting behavior and psychopathology in gender identity disorder: A comparison of male-to-female, female-to-male transsexual and nontranssexual control subjects. *Journal of Behavior Therapy and Experimental Psychiatry, 42*(1), 38–45.

Smith, Y. L. S., van Goozen, S. H. M., Kuiper, A. J., & Cohen-Kettenis, P. T. (2005). Transsexual subtypes: Clinical and theoretical significance. *Psychiatry Research, 137*(3), 151–160.

Sohn, M., & Bosinski, H. A. G. (2007). Gender identity disorders: Diagnostic and surgical aspects. *Journal of Sexual Medicine, 4*(5), 1193–1208.

Stotzer, R. L. (2008). Gender identity and hate crimes: Violence against transgender people in Los Angeles county. *Sexuality Research & Social Policy: A Journal of the NSRC, 5*(1), 43–52.

Stotzer, R. L. (2009). Violence against transgender people: A review of United States data. *Aggression and Violent Behavior, 14*(3), 170–179.

Taher, N. S. (2007). Self-concept and masculinity/femininity among normal male individuals and males with gender identity disorder. *Social Behavior and Personality, 35*(4), 469–478.

Taylor, J. K. (2007). Transgender identities and public policy in the United States: The relevance for public administration. *Administration & Society, 39*(7), 833–856.

Toomey, R. B., Ryan, C., Diaz, R. M., Card, N. A., & Russell, S. T. (2010). Gender-nonconforming lesbian, gay, bisexual, and transgender youth: School victimization and young adult psychosocial adjustment. *Developmental Psychology, 46*(6), 1580–1589.

Travers, R., Guta, A., Flicker, S., Larkin, J., Lo, C., McCardell, S., & van der Meulen, E. (2010). Service provider views on issues and needs for lesbian, gay, bisexual, and transgender youth. *Canadian Journal of Human Sexuality, 19*(4), 191–198.

Vanderburgh, R. (2009). Appropriate therapeutic care for families with pre-pubescent transgender/gender-dissonant children. *Child & Adolescent Social Work Journal, 26*(2), 135–154.

Vasey, P. L., & Bartlett, N. H. (2007). What can the Samoan "fa'afafine" teach us about the Western concept of gender identity disorder in childhood? *Perspectives in Biology and Medicine, 50*(4), 481–490.

Vincent, L., & Camminga, B. (2009). Putting the 'T' into South African human rights: Transsexuality in the postapartheid order. *Sexualities, 12*(6), 678–700.

Vujovic, S., Popovic, S., Sbutega-Milosevic, G., Djordjevic, M., & Gooren, L. (2009). Transsexualism in Serbia: A twenty-year follow-up study. *Journal of Sexual Medicine, 6*(4), 1018–1023.

Walinsky, D., & Whitcomb, D. (2010). Using the ACA Competencies for counseling with transgender clients to increase rural transgender well-being. *Journal of LGBT Issues in Counseling, 4*(3–4), 160–175.

Wallien, M. S. C., & Cohen-Kettenis, P. T. (2008). Psychosexual outcome of gender-dysphoric children. *Journal of the American Academy of Child & Adolescent Psychiatry, 47*(12), 1413–1423.

Wallien, M. S. C., Swaab, H., & Cohen-Kettenis, P. T. (2007). Psychiatric comorbidity among children with gender identity disorder. *Journal of the American Academy of Child & Adolescent Psychiatry, 46*(10), 1307–1314.

Wester, S. R., McDonough, T. A., White, M., Vogel, D. L., & Taylor, L. (2010). Using gender role conflict theory in counseling male-to-female transgender individuals. *Journal of Counseling & Development, 88*(2), 214–219.

Weyers, S., Elaut, E., De Sutter, P., Gerris, J., T'Sjoen, G., Heylens, G., . . . Verstraelen, H. (2009). Long-term assessment of the physical, mental, and sexual health among transsexual women. *Journal of Sexual Medicine, 6*(3), 752–760.

White, T., & Ettner, R. (2004). Disclosure, risks and protective factors for children whose parents are undergoing a gender transition. In U. Leli & J. Drescher (Eds.), *Transgender subjectivities: A clinician's guide* (pp. 129–145). New York: Haworth Press.

Willging, C. E., Salvador, M., & Kano, M. (2006). Pragmatic help seeking: How sexual and gender minority groups access mental health care in a rural state. *Psychiatric Services, 57*(6), 871–874.

Williamson, C. (2010). Providing care to transgender persons: A clinical approach to primary care, hormones, and HIV management. *JANAC: Journal of the Association of Nurses in AIDS Care, 21*(3), 221–229.

Wilson, I., Griffin, C., & Wren, B. (2005). The interaction between young people with atypical gender identity organization and their peers. *Journal of Health Psychology, 10*(3), 307–315.

Winfeld, L. (2005). *Straight talk about gays in the workplace: Creating an inclusive, productive environment for everyone in your organization* (3rd ed.). New York: Harrington Park Press.

Winter, S. (2009). Cultural considerations for the World Professional Association for Transgender Health's Standards of Care: The Asian perspective. *International Journal of Transgenderism, 11*(1), 19–41.

Winter, S., Rogando-Sasot, S., & King, M. (2008). Transgendered women of the Philippines. *International Journal of Transgenderism, 10*(2), 79–90.

Wise, T. N., & Meyer, J. K. (1980). Transvestites who become gender dysphoric. *Archives of Sexual Behavior, 9,* 323–337.

Wren, B. (2002). 'I can accept my child is transsexual but if I ever see him in a dress I'll hit him': Dilemmas in parenting a transgendered adolescent. *Clinical Child Psychology and Psychiatry, 7*(3), 377–397.

Wylie, K. R., Fung, R., Jr., Boshier, C., & Rotchell, M. (2009). Recommendations of endocrine treatment for patients with gender dysphoria. *Sexual and Relationship Therapy, 24*(2), 175–187.

Yunger, J. L., Carver, P. R., & Perry, D. G. (2004). Does gender identity influence children's psychological well-being? *Developmental Psychology, 40*(4), 572–582.

Zamboni, B. D. (2006). Therapeutic considerations in working with the family, friends, and partners of transgendered individuals. *Family Journal, 14*(2), 174–179.

Zucker, K. J. (2006). Gender identity disorder. In D. A. Wolfe & E. J. Mash (Eds.), *Behavioral and emotional disorders in adolescents: Nature, assessment, and treatment* (pp. 535–562). New York: Guilford.

Zucker, K. J., & Bradley, S. J. (1999). Gender identity disorder and transvestic fetishism. In S. D. Netherton, D. Holmes, & C. E. Walker (Eds.), *Child and adolescent psychological disorders: A comprehensive textbook* (pp. 367–396). New York: Oxford University Press.

Zucker, K. J., & Cohen-Kettenis, P. T. (2008). Gender identity disorders in children and adolescence. In D. L. Rowland & L. Incrocci (Eds.), *Handbook of sexual and gender identity disorders* (pp. 376–422). Hoboken, NJ: John Wiley & Sons.

Zucker, K. J., & Spitzer, R. L. (2005). Was the gender identity disorder of childhood diagnosis introduced into *DSM-III* as a backdoor maneuver to replace homosexuality? A historical note. *Journal of Sex & Marital Therapy, 31*(1), 31–42.

References for Chapter 9

American Psychological Association. (2011). *Ethnic and racial minorities & socioeconomic status.* Retrieved from www.apa.org/pi/ses/resources/publications/factsheet-erm.aspx.

American Psychological Association, Task Force on Gender Identity and Gender Variance. (2009). *Report of the Task Force on Gender Identity and Gender Variance.* Washington, DC: Author. Retrieved from www.apa.org/pi/lgbt/resources/policy/gender-identity-report.pdf.

Bakker, A., Van Kesteren, P. J., Gooren, L. J., & Bezemer, P. D. (1993). The prevalence of transsexualism in the Netherlands. *Acta Psychiatrica Scandinavica, 87*(4), 237–238.

Blanchard, R. (2005). Early history of the concept of autogynephilia. *Archives of Sexual Behavior, 34*(4), 439–446.

Brown, N. R. (2010). The sexual relationships of sexual-minority women partnered with trans men: A qualitative study. *Archives of Sexual Behavior, 39*(2), 561–572.

Chen, S., McFarland, W., Thompson, H. M., & Raymond, H. F. (2011). Transmen in San Francisco: What do we know from HIV test site data? *AIDS and Behavior, 15*(3), 659–662.

Cohen-Kettenis, P. T., & Arrindell, W. A. (1990). Perceived parental rearing style, parental divorce and transsexualism: A controlled study. *Psychological Medicine: A Journal of Research in Psychiatry and the Allied Sciences, 20*(3), 613–620.

Cohen-Kettenis, P. T., & Gooren, L. J. (1992). The influence of hormone treatment on psychological functioning of transsexuals. *Journal of Psychology & Human Sexuality, 5*(4), 55–67.

Cole, S. S., Denny, D., Eyler, A. E., & Samons, S. L. (2000). Issues of transgender. In L. T. Szuchman & F. Muscarella (Eds.), *Psychological perspectives on human sexuality* (pp. 149–195). Hoboken, NJ: John Wiley & Sons.

Coleman, E., Adler, R., Bockting, W., Botzer, M., Brown, G., Cohen-Kettenis, P., . . . Zucker, K. (2011). *Standards of care for the health of transsexual, transgender, and gender nonconforming people* (7th ed.). World Professional Association for Transgender Health. Retrieved from www.thisishow.org/Files/soc7.pdf.

Cook-Daniels, L. (2006). Trans aging. In D. Kimmel, T. Rose, & S. David (Eds.), *Lesbian, gay, bisexual, and transgender aging: Research and clinical perspectives* (pp. 20–35). New York: Columbia University Press.

De Cuypere, G., T'Sjoen, G., Beerten, R., Selvaggi, G., De Sutter, P., Hoebeke, P., . . . Rubens, R. (2005). Sexual and physical health after sex reassignment surgery. *Archives of Sexual Behavior, 34*(6), 679–690.

De Cuypere, G., Van Hemelrijck, M., Michel, A., Carael, B., Heylens, G., Rubens, R., Hoebeke, P., & Monstrey, S. (2007). Prevalence and demography of transsexualism in Belgium. *European Psychiatry, 22*(3), 137–141.

Dickey, R., & Steiner, B. W. (1990). Hormone treatment and surgery. In R. Blanchard & B. W. Steiner (Eds.), *Clinical management of gender identity disorders in children and adults* (pp. 139–158). Washington, DC: American Psychiatric Association.

Djordjevic, M. L., Stanojevic, D., Bizic, M., Kojovic, V., Majstorovic, M., Vujovic, S., . . . Perovic, S. V. (2009). Metoidioplasty as a single stage sex reassignment surgery in female transsexuals: Belgrade experience. *Journal of Sexual Medicine, 6*(5), 1306–1313.

Drummond, K. D., Bradley, S. J., Peterson-Badali, M., & Zucker, K. J. (2008). A follow-up study of girls with gender identity disorder. *Developmental Psychology, 44*(1), 34–45.

Fleming, M., MacGowan, B., & Costos, D. (1985). The dyadic adjustment of female-to-male transsexuals. *Archives of Sexual Behavior, 14*(1), 47–55.

Fontaine, J. H. (2002). Transgender issues in counseling. In L. D. Burlew & D. Capuzzi (Eds.), *Sexuality counseling* (pp. 177–194). Hauppauge, NY: Nova Science.

Forshee, A. S. (2008). Transgender men: A demographic snapshot. *Journal of Gay & Lesbian Social Services: Issues in Practice, Policy & Research, 20*(3), 221–236.

Gomez-Gil, E., Trilla, A., Salamero, M., Godas, T., & Valdes, M. (2009). Sociodemographic, clinical, and psychiatric characteristics of transsexuals from Spain. *Archives of Sexual Behavior, 38*(3), 378–392.

Goodwin, S. (n.d.). Gender activities and exercises. Retrieved from http://jfmueller.faculty.noctrl.edu/crow/activitiesgender.htm.

Green, E. R. (2006). Debating trans inclusion in the feminist movement: A transpositive analysis. *Journal of Lesbian Studies, 10*(12), 231–248.

Green, J. (1994). *Getting real about FTM surgery*. Retrieved from www.gender.org/resources/getting_real.html.

Green, J. (2005). Part of the package: Ideas of masculinity among male-identified transpeople. *Men and Masculinities, 7*(3), 291–299.

Green, R. (1996). Gender identity disorder in children. In G. O. Gabbard & S. D. Atkinson (Eds.), *Synopsis of treatments of psychiatric disorders* (2nd ed., pp. 837–841). Washington, DC: American Psychiatric Association.

Hansbury, G. (2005). The middle men: Introduction to the transmasculine identities. *Studies in Gender and Sexuality, 6*(3), 241–264.

Hatzenbuehler, M. L., O'Cleirigh, C., Grasso, C., Mayer, K., Safren, S., & Bradford, J. (2011). Effect of same-sex marriage laws on health care use and expenditures in sexual minority men: A quasi-natural experiment. *American Journal of Public Health, e1–e7* [e-view ahead of print].

Hay, W. M., Barlow, D. H., & Hay, L. R. (1981). Treatment of stereotypic cross-gender motor behavior using covert modeling in a boy with gender identity confusion. *Journal of Consulting and Clinical Psychology, 49*(3), 388–394.

Herbst, J. H., Jacobs, E. D., Finlayson, T. J., McKleroy, V. S., Neumann, M. S., & Crepaz, N. (2008). Estimating HIV prevalence and risk behaviors of transgender persons in the United States: A systematic review. *AIDS and Behavior, 12*(1), 117.

Human Rights Campaign. (2011). *Corporate equality index: Rating American workplaces on lesbian, gay, bisexual and transgender equality*. Retrieved from http://sites.hrc.org/documents/CorporateEqualityIndex_2012.pdf.

Johansson, A., Sundbom, E., Hojerback, T., & Bodlund, O. (2010). A five-year follow-up study of Swedish adults with gender identity disorder. *Archives of Sexual Behavior, 39*(6), 1429–1437.

Kenagy, G. P., & Hsieh, C. M. (2005). The risk less known: Female-to-male transgender persons' vulnerability to HIV infection. *AIDS Care, 17*(2), 195–207.

Kidd, J. D., & Witten, T. M. (2008). Understanding spirituality and religiosity in the transgender community: Implications for aging. *Journal of Religion, Spirituality & Aging, 20*(12), 29–62.

Kins, E., Hoebeke, P., Heylens, G., Rubens, R., & de Cuypere, G. (2008). The female-to-male transsexual and his female partner versus the traditional couple: A comparison. *Journal of Sex & Marital Therapy, 34*(5), 429–438.

Korell, S. C., & Lorah, P. (2007). An overview of affirmative psychotherapy and counseling with transgender clients. In K. J. Bieschke, R. M. Perez, & K. A. DeBord (Eds.), *Handbook of counseling and psychotherapy with lesbian, gay, bisexual, and transgender clients* (2nd ed., pp. 271–288). Washington, DC: American Psychological Association.

Lawrence, A. A. (2008). Gender identity disorders in adults: Diagnosis and treatment. In D. L. Rowland & L. Incrocci (Eds.), *Handbook of sexual and gender identity disorders* (pp. 423–456). Hoboken, NJ: John Wiley & Sons.

Lev, A. I. (2007). Transgender communities: Developing identity through connection. In K. J. Bieschke, R. M. Perez, & K. A. DeBord (Eds.), *Handbook of counseling and psychotherapy with lesbian, gay, bisexual, and transgender clients* (2nd ed., pp. 147–175). Washington, DC: American Psychological Association.

Lobato, M. I., Koff, W. J., Schestatsky, S. S., Chaves, C. P. V., Petry, A., Crestana, T., . . . Henriques, A. A. (2008). Clinical characteristics, psychiatric co-morbidities and socio-demographic profile of transsexual patients from an outpatient clinic in Brazil. *International Journal of Transgenderism, 10*(2), 69–77.

Mahalingam, R. (2003). Essentialism, culture, and beliefs about gender among the Aravanis of Tamil Nadu, India. *Sex Roles, 49*(910), 489–496.

Mar, K. (2011). Female-to-male transgender spectrum people of Asian and Pacific Islander descent. *Dissertation Abstracts International: Section B: The Sciences and Engineering, 71*(8-B), 5134.

Mason, M. E. (2007). The experience of transition for lesbian partners of female-to-male transsexuals. *Dissertation Abstracts International: Section B: The Sciences and Engineering, 68*(5-B), 3403.

Matsumoto, Y., Sato, T., Ohnishi, M., Kishimoto, Y., Terada, S., & Kuroda, S. (2009). Stress-coping strategies of patients with gender identity disorder. *Psychiatry and Clinical Neurosciences, 63*(6), 715–720.

Meyer-Bahlburg, H. F. L. (2002). Gender identity disorder in young boys: A parent and peer-based treatment protocol. *Clinical Child Psychology and Psychiatry, 7*(3), 360–376.

Michel, A., Ansseau, M., Legros, J. J., Pitchot, W., & Mormont, C. (2002). The transsexual: What about the future? *European Psychiatry, 17*(6), 353–362.

Mostade, J. (2006). Affirmative counseling with transgendered persons. In C. C. Lee (Ed.), *Multicultural issues in counseling: New approaches to diversity* (3rd ed., pp. 303–316). Alexandria, VA: American Counseling Association.

Namaste, V. K. (1999). HIV/AIDS and female-to-male transsexuals and transvestites: Results from a needs assessment in Quebec. *International Journal of Transgenderism, 3*(12), No pagination specified.

Nanda, S. (2008). Cross-cultural issues. In D. L. Rowland & L. Incrocci (Eds.), *Handbook of sexual and gender identity disorders* (pp. 457–485). Hoboken, NJ: John Wiley & Sons.

Newfield, E., Hart, S., Dibble, S., & Kohler, L. (2006). Female-to-male transgender quality of life. *Quality of Life Research: An International Journal of Quality of Life Aspects of Treatment, Care & Rehabilitation, 15*(9), 1447–1457.

Pauly, I. B. (1974a). Female transsexualism: Part I. *Archives of Sexual Behavior, 3*(6), 487–507.

Pauly, I. B. (1974b). Female transsexualism: II. *Archives of Sexual Behavior, 3*(6), 509–526.

Pazos, S. (1999). Practice with female-to-male transgendered youth. *Journal of Gay & Lesbian Social Services: Issues in Practice, Policy & Research, 10*(3–4), 65–82.

Pfafflin, F. (1992). Regrets after sex reassignment surgery. In W. O. Bockting & E. Coleman (Eds.), *Interdisciplinary approaches in clinical management* (pp. 69–85). Binghamton, NY: Haworth Press.

Pfeffer, C. A. (2010). "Women's work"? Women partners of transgender men doing housework and emotion work. *Journal of Marriage & the Family, 72*(1), 165–183.

Schilt, K. (2006). Just one of the guys?: How transmen make gender visible at work. *Gender & Society, 20*(4), 465–490.

Seil, D. (1996). Transsexuals: The boundaries of sexual identity and gender. In R. P. Cabaj & T. S. Stein (Eds.), *Textbook of homosexuality and mental health* (pp. 743–762). Washington, DC: American Psychiatric Association.

Seil, D. (2004). The diagnosis and treatment of transgendered patients. *Journal of Gay & Lesbian Psychotherapy, 8*(1–2), 99–116.

Simon, L., Zsolt, U., Fogd, D., & Czobor, P. (2011). Dysfunctional core beliefs, perceived parenting behavior and psychopathology in gender identity disorder: A comparison of male-to-female, female-to-male transsexual and nontranssexual control subjects. *Journal of Behavior Therapy and Experimental Psychiatry, 42*(1), 38–45.

Smith, Y. L. S., Van Goozen, S. H. M., Kuiper, A. J., & Cohen-Kettenis, P. T. (2005). Sex reassignment: Outcomes and predictors of treatment for adolescent and adult transsexuals. *Psychological Medicine: A Journal of Research in Psychiatry and the Allied Sciences, 35*(1), 89–99.

Stephens, S. C., Bernstein, K. T., & Philip, S. S. (2011). Male to female and female to male transgender persons have different sexual risk behaviors yet similar rates of STDs and HIV. *AIDS and Behavior, 15*(3), 683–686.

Stoller, R. J. (1971). The term "transvestism." *Archives of General Psychiatry, 24,* 230–237.

Townsend, J. M. (1998). *What women want—what men want: Why the sexes still see love and commitment so differently*. New York: Oxford University Press.

Traish, A. M., & Gooren, L. J. (2010). Safety of physiological testosterone therapy in women: Lessons from female-to-male transsexuals (FMT) treated with pharmacological testosterone therapy. *Journal of Sexual Medicine, 7*(11), 3758–3764.

Van Borsel, J., De Cuypere, G., Rubens, R., & Destaerke, B. (2000). Voice problems in female-to-male transsexuals. *International Journal of Language & Communication Disorders, 35*(3), 427–442.

Vanderburgh, R. (2009). Appropriate therapeutic care for families with pre-pubescent transgender/gender-dissonant children. *Child & Adolescent Social Work Journal, 26*(2), 135–154.

van Trotsenburg, M. A. A. (2009). Gynecological aspects of transgender healthcare. *International Journal of Transgenderism, 11*(4), 238–246.

Vegter, V., & Alderson, K. G. (2011). *Conceptualizing masculinity in female-to-male trans-identified individuals*. Manuscript submitted for publication.

Winter, S., Webster, B., & Cheung, P. K. E. (2008). Measuring Hong Kong undergraduate students' attitudes towards transpeople. *Sex Roles, 59*(9–10), 670–683.

Wise, T. N., & Meyer, J. K. (1980). Transvestites who become gender dysphoric. *Archives of Sexual Behavior, 9,* 323–337.

Wylie, K. R., Fung, R., Jr., Boshier, C., & Rotchell, M. (2009). Recommendations of endocrine treatment for patients with gender dysphoria. *Sexual and Relationship Therapy, 24*(2), 175–187.

Zucker, K. J., & Cohen-Kettenis, P. T. (2008). Gender identity disorders in children and adolescence. In D. L. Rowland & L. Incrocci (Eds.), *Handbook of sexual and gender identity disorders* (pp. 376–422). Hoboken, NJ: John Wiley & Sons.

REFERENCES FOR CHAPTER 10

Alderson, J. (2004). Intersex: A sad postscript. *The Psychologist, 17*(11), 629.

Andersson, L. (1998). Loneliness research and interventions: A review of the literature. *Aging & Mental Health, 2*(4), 264–274.

Balsam, K. F., & Mohr, J. J. (2007). Adaptation to sexual orientation stigma: A comparison of bisexual and lesbian/gay adults. *Journal of Counseling Psychology, 54*(3), 306–319.

Boelen, P. A., de Keijser, J., van den Hout, M. A., & van den Bout, J. (2007). Treatment of complicated grief: A comparison between cognitive-behavioral therapy and supportive counseling. *Journal of Consulting and Clinical Psychology, 75*(2), 277–284.

Bostwick, J. M., & Martin, K. A. (2007). A man's brain in an ambiguous body: A case of mistaken gender identity. *American Journal of Psychiatry, 164*(10), 1499–1505.

Brinkmann, L., Schuetzmann, K., & Richter-Appelt, H. (2007a). Gender assignment and medical history of individuals with different forms of intersexuality: Evaluation of medical records and the patients' perspective. *Journal of Sexual Medicine, 4*(4i), 964–980.

Brinkmann, L., Schweizer, K., & Richter-Appelt, H. (2007b). Gender identity and psychological burden in adult intersexual persons. Results of the Hamburg Intersex Study. *Ergebnisse der Hamburger Intersex Studie. Zeitschrift fur Sexualforschung, 20*(2), 129–144.

Consortium on the Management of Disorders of Sex Development. (2006a). *Clinical guidelines for the management of disorders of sex development in childhood.* Intersex Society of North America. Retrieved from www.dsdguidelines.org.

Consortium on the Management of Disorders of Sex Development. (2006b). *Handbook for parents.* Intersex Society of North America. Retrieved from www.dsdguidelines.org.

Cook-Daniels, L. (2006). Trans aging. In D. Kimmel, T. Rose, & S. David (Eds.), *Lesbian, gay, bisexual, and transgender aging: Research and clinical perspectives* (pp. 20–35). New York: Columbia University Press.

Creighton, S., & Minto, C. (2001). Managing intersex. *BMJ: British Medical Journal, 323*(7324), 1264–1265.

Creighton, S. M., Minto, C. L., Liao, L. M., Alderson, J., & Simmonds, M. (2004). Meeting between experts: Evaluation of the first UK forum for lay and professional experts in intersex. *Patient Education and Counseling, 54*(2), 153–157.

Crocker, J., & Major, B. (1989). Social stigma and self-esteem: The self-protective properties of stigma. *Psychological Review, 96,* 608–630.

Cull, M. (2002). Treatment of intersex needs open discussion. *BMJ: British Medical Journal, 324*(7342), 919.

Currier, J. M., Neimeyer, R. A., & Berman, J. S. (2008). The effectiveness of psychotherapeutic interventions for bereaved persons: A comprehensive quantitative review. *Psychological Bulletin, 134*(5), 648–661.

Daaboul, J. J. (2003). A newborn infant with a disorder of sexual differentiation: Comment. *Journal of Developmental and Behavioral Pediatrics, 24*(2), 118–119.

Denver, K. N. (2005). A phenomenological study of the experience of being born and raised with an intersex condition. *Dissertation Abstracts International: Section B: The Sciences and Engineering, 65*(10-B), 5395.

Diamond, M., & Watson, L. A. (2004). Androgen insensitivity syndrome and Klinefelter's syndrome: Sex and gender considerations. *Child and Adolescent Psychiatric Clinics of North America, 13*(3), 623–640.

Erich, S., Tittsworth, J., Meier, S. L. C., & Lerman, T. (2010). Transsexuals of color: Perceptions of discrimination based on transsexual status and race/ethnicity status. *Journal of GLBT Family Studies, 6*(3), 294–314.

Erikson, E. H. (1968). *Identity: Youth and crisis.* New York: Norton.

Estrada Inda, L. (1983). Development of the life cycle in the human being. *Salud Mental, 6*(1), 21–25.

Gueniche, K., Jacquot, M., Thibaud, E., & Polak, M. (2008). Gender identity deadlock . . . A study of XY young adults born with a disorder of sex development and reared as female. *Neuropsychiatrie de l'Enfance et de l'Adolescence, 56*(6), 377–385.

Guth, L. J., Witchel, R. I., Witchel, S. F., & Lee, P. A. (2006). Relationships, sexuality, gender identity, gender roles, and self-concept of individuals who have congenital adrenal hyperplasia: A qualitative investigation. *Journal of Gay & Lesbian Psychotherapy, 10*(2), 57–75.

Hird, M. J. (2008). Queer(y)ing intersex: Reflections on counselling people with intersex conditions. In L. Moon (Ed.), *Feeling queer or queer feelings?: Radical approaches to counselling sex, sexualities and genders* (pp. 54–71). New York: Routledge/Taylor & Francis.

Holmes, M. (2002). Rethinking the meaning and management of intersexuality. *Sexualities, 5*(2), 159–180.

Holmes, M. M. (2008). Mind the gaps: Intersex and (re-productive) spaces in disability studies and bioethics. *Journal of Bioethical Inquiry, 5*(2–3), 169–181.

Hurtig, A. L., & Rosenthal, I. M. (1987). Psychological findings in early treated cases of female pseudohermaphroditism caused by virilizing congenital adrenal hyperplasia. *Archives of Sexual Behavior, 16*(3), 209–223.

Imperato, G. H., & Imperato, P. J. (2006). Beliefs and practices concerning twins, hermaphrodites, and albinos among the Bamana and Maninka of Mali. *Journal of Community Health: The Publication for Health Promotion and Disease Prevention, 31*(3), 198–224.

Inozemtseva, O., Matute, E., & Juarez, J. (2008). Learning disabilities spectrum and sexual dimorphic abilities in girls with congenital adrenal hyperplasia. *Journal of Child Neurology, 23*(8), 862–869.

Johnson, C. V., Mimiaga, M. J., & Bradford, J. (2008). Health care issues among lesbian, gay, bisexual, transgender and intersex (LGBTI) populations in the United States: Introduction. *Journal of Homosexuality, 54*(3), 213–224.

Kerry, S. (2009). Intersex individuals' religiosity and their journey to wellbeing. *Journal of Gender Studies, 18*(3), 277–285.

Kowalik, J., Weller, J., Venter, J., & Drachman, D. (2011). Cognitive behavioral therapy for the treatment of pediatric posttraumatic stress disorder: A review and meta-analysis. *Journal of Behavior Therapy and Experimental Psychiatry, 42*(3), 405–413.

Kuhnle, U., Bullinger, M., Schwartz, H. P., & Knorr, D. (1993). Partnership and sexuality in adult female patients with congenital adrenal hyperplasia. First results of a cross-sectional quality-of-life evaluation. *Journal of Steroid Biochemistry & Molecular Biology, 4,* 123–126.

Lee, P. A., Houk, C. P., Ahmed, S. F., & Hughes, I. A. (2006). Consensus statement on management of intersex disorders: International Consensus Conference on Intersex. *Pediatrics, 118*(2), e488–500.

Liakopoulou, M., Keramydas, D., Dracopoulou, M., & Dacou-Voutetakis, C. (2009). The dilemma of sex reassignment in an adolescent with 17beta -HSD-3 deficiency raised as a female: Ten-year follow-up. *Archives of Sexual Behavior, 38*(5), 615–618.

Looy, H. (2002). Male and female God created them: The challenge of intersexuality. *Journal of Psychology and Christianity, 21*(1), 10–20.

Looy, H., & Bouma, H., III. (2005). The nature of gender: Gender identity in persons who are intersexed or transgendered. *Journal of Psychology and Theology, 33*(3), 166–178.

MacKenzie, D., Huntington, A., & Gilmour, J. A. (2009). The experiences of people with an intersex condition: A journey from silence to voice. *Journal of Clinical Nursing, 18*(12), 1775–1783.

Margalit, M. (2010). *Lonely children and adolescents: Self-perceptions, social exclusion, and hope.* New York: Springer Science + Business Media.

Martin, J. I., & Yonkin, D. R. (2006). Transgender identity. In D. F. Morrow & L. Messinger (Eds.), *Sexual orientation & gender expression in social work practice: Working with gay, lesbian, bisexual, & transgender people* (pp. 105–128). New York: Columbia University Press.

Martin, J. L. (2008). Gendered violence on campus: Unpacking bullying, harassment, and stalking. In M. A. Paludi (Ed.), *Understanding and preventing campus violence* (pp. 3–26). Westport, CT: Praeger Publishers/Greenwood.

Mazur, T., Cohen-Kettenis, P. T., Meyer, W. J., III, Meyer-Bahlburg, H. F. L., & Zucker, K. J. (2008). Survey of HBIGDA membership on treatment of disorders of sex development (DSD). *International Journal of Transgenderism, 10*(2), 99–108.

Meyer-Bahlburg, H. F. L. (1998). Gender assignment in intersexuality. *Journal of Psychology & Human Sexuality, 10*(2), 1–21.

Meyer-Bahlburg, H. F. L. (2005). Introduction: Gender dysphoria and gender change in persons with intersexuality. *Archives of Sexual Behavior, 34*(4), 371–373.

Michel, A., Wagner, C., & Jeandel, C. (2008). The disclosure of an intersex condition: Psychological issues. *Neuropsychiatrie de l'Enfance et de l' Adolescence, 56*(6), 365–369.

Money, J. (1975). Ablatio penis: Normal male infant sex-reassigned as a girl. *Archives of Sexual Behavior, 4*(1), 65–71.

Money, J. (1991). Bibliography. *Journal of Psychology & Human Sexuality, 4*(2), 83–198.

Morgan, J. F., Murphy, H., Lacey, J. H., & Conway, G. (2005). Long-term psychological outcome for women with congenital adrenal hyperplasia: Cross sectional survey. *BMJ: British Medical Journal, 330*(7487), 340–341.

Morland, I. (2008). II. Intimate violations: Intersex and the ethics of bodily integrity. *Feminism & Psychology, 18*(3), 425–430.

Mostade, J. (2006). Affirmative counseling with transgendered persons. In C. C. Lee (Ed.), *Multicultural issues in counseling: New approaches to diversity* (3rd ed., pp. 303–316). Alexandria, VA: American Counseling Association.

Nielsen J., & Stradiot, M. (1987). Transcultural study of Turner's syndrome. *Clinical Genetics, 32*(4), 260–270.

O'Neil, D. (2011, August 13). *Sex chromosome abnormalities.* Retrieved from anthro.palomar.edu/abnormal/abnormal_5.htm.

Ostrer, H. (2009, September 15). *46,XY disorder of sex development and 46,XY complete gonadal dysgenesis.* Retrieved from www.ncbi.nlm.nih.gov/books/NBK1547/.

Pasterski, V. (2008). Disorders of sex development and atypical sex differentiation. In D. L. Rowland & L. Incrocci (Eds.), *Handbook of sexual and gender identity disorders* (pp. 354–375). Hoboken, NJ: John Wiley & Sons.

Piper, W. E., Ogrodniczuk, J. S., Joyce, A. S., Weideman, R., & Rosie, J. S. (2007). Group composition and group therapy for complicated grief. *Journal of Consulting and Clinical Psychology, 75*(1), 116–125.

Potoczniak, D. J., Aldea, M. A., & DeBlaere, C. (2007). Ego identity, social anxiety, social support, and self-concealment in lesbian, gay, and bisexual individuals. *Journal of Counseling Psychology, 54*(4), 447–457.

Preves, S. E. (2003). *Intersex and identity: The contested self.* New Brunswick, NJ: Rutgers University Press.

Rajon, A.-M. (2008). What we learn from parents of children with a genital ambiguity. *Neuropsychiatrie de l'Enfance et de l'Adolescence, 56*(6), 370–376.

Reiner, W., & Gearhart, J. (2004). Discordant sexual identity in some genetic males with cloascal exstrophy assigned to female sex at birth. *New England Journal of Medicine, 350*(4), 333–341.

Reis, E. (2009). *Bodies in doubt: An American history of intersex.* Baltimore, MD: Johns Hopkins University Press.

Richter-Appelt, H., Brinkmann, L., & Schutzmann, K. (2006). Parental bonding in childhood and psychological symptoms in a sample of adults with intersexuality. *Psychotherapie Psychosomatik Medizinische Psychologie, 56*(8), 325–335.

Rook, K. S. (1984). Interventions for loneliness: A review and analysis. In L. A. Peplau & S. E. Goldston (Eds.), *Preventing the harmful consequences of severe and persistent loneliness* (pp. 47–79). Washington, DC: National Institute of Mental Health (NIMH), Washington Government Printing Office.

Rosario, V. A. (2006). An interview with Cheryl Chase. *Journal of Gay & Lesbian Psychotherapy, 10*(2), 93–104.

Ross, J. L., St. Dennis-Feezle, L. K., & Weber, C. (2002). *Turner syndrome: Toward early recognition and improved outcomes.* Retrieved from www.medscape.org/viewarticle/445555.

Schober, J. M. (2001). Sexual behaviors, sexual orientation and gender identity in adult intersexuals: A pilot study. *Journal of Urology, 165,* 2350–2353.

Schweizer, K., & Richter-Appelt, H. (2010). Intersexuality and borderline personality disorder: Ambiguous body, ambiguous identity, insecure attachment. *PTT: Personlichkeitsstorungen Theorie und Therapie, 14*(3), 189–198.

Schweizer, K., Brunner, F., Schutzmann, K., Schonbucher, V., & Richter-Appelt, H. (2009). Gender identity and coping in female 46, XY adults with androgen biosynthesis deficiency (intersexuality/DSD). *Journal of Counseling Psychology, 56*(1), 189–201.

Sivapalan, H. (2009). Review of sexual and fertility issues in ill health and disability from early adolescence to adulthood. *International Review of Psychiatry, 21*(1), 88.

Slijper, F. M. E., Drop, S. L. S., Molenaar, J. C., & de Muinck Keizer-Schrama, S. M. P. F. (2000). Long-term psychological evaluation of intersex children: Reply. *Archives of Sexual Behavior, 29*(1), 119–121.

Slijper, F. M. E., Drop, S. L. S., Molenaar, J. C., & Scholtmeijer, R. J. (1994). Neonates with abnormal genital development assigned the female sex: Parent counseling. *Journal of Sex Education & Therapy, 20*(1), 9–17.

Stoller, R. (1968). *Sex and gender: On the development of masculinity and femininity.* London, UK: Hogarth Press.

Sutton, E. J., McInerney-Leo, A., Bondy, C. A., Gollust, S. E., King, D., & Biesecker, B. (2005). Turner syndrome: Four challenges across the lifespan. *American Journal of Medical Genetics, 139,* 57–66.

Tremain, S. (2001). On the government of disability. *Social Theory and Practice, 27*(4), 617–636.

Van Vliet, K. J. (2008). Shame and resilience in adulthood: A grounded theory study. *Journal of Counseling Psychology, 55*(2), 233–245.

Vilain, E. J. N. (2008). Genetics of sexual development and differentiation. In D. L. Rowland & L. Incrocci (Eds.), *Handbook of sexual and gender identity disorders* (pp. 329–353). Hoboken, NJ: John Wiley & Sons.

Warne, G. L., & Raza J. (2008). Disorders of sex development (DSDs), their presentation and management in different cultures. *Reviews in Endocrine & Metabolic Disorders, 9*(3), 227–236.

Weinstock, J. S. (2003). Lesbian, gay, bisexual, transgender, and intersex issues in the psychology curriculum. In P. Bronstein & K. Quina (Eds.), *Teaching gender and multicultural awareness: Resources for the psychology classroom* (pp. 285–297). Washington, DC: American Psychological Association.

Witten, T. M. (2003). Life course analysis—the courage to search for something more: Middle adulthood issues in the transgender and intersex community. *Journal of Human Behavior in the Social Environment, 8*(2–3), 189–224.

Zeiler, K., & Wickstrom, A. (2009). Why do "we" perform surgery on newborn intersexed children?

The phenomenology of the parental experience of having a child with intersex anatomies. *Feminist Theory, 10*(3), 359–377.

References for Chapter 11

Boykin, K. (2005). *Beyond the down low: Sex, lies, and denial in Black America.* New York: Carroll & Graf.

Eliason, M. (2011). Introduction to special issue on suicide, mental health, and youth development. *Journal of Homosexuality, 58*(1), 4–9.

Hetrick, E. S., & Martin, A. D. (1987). Developmental issues and their resolution for gay and lesbian adolescents. *Journal of Homosexuality,* 14(1–2), 25–43.

Konik, J., & Stewart, A. (2004). Sexual identity development in the context of compulsory heterosexuality. *Journal of Personality, 72*(4), 815–844.

Lahey, K. A., & Alderson, K. (2004). *Same-sex marriage: The personal and the political.* Toronto, ON: Insomniac Press.

Morrison, M. A., & Morrison, T. G. (Eds.). (2008). *The psychology of modern prejudice.* Hauppauge, NY: Nova Science.

Pedersen, P. (1990). The multicultural perspective as a fourth force in counseling. *Journal of Mental Health Counseling, 12*(1), 93–95.

Pedersen, P. (Ed.). (1999). *Multiculturalism as a fourth force.* New York: Brunner/Mazel.

Pedersen, P. B., Crethar, H. C., & Carlson, J. (2008). *Inclusive cultural empathy: Making relationships central in counseling and psychotherapy.* Washington, DC: American Psychological Association.

Savin-Williams, R. C. (2005). *The new gay teenager.* Cambridge, MA: Harvard University Press.

Index

Acquired immune deficiency syndrome (AIDS), 23. *See also* HIV/AIDS
ACT UP, 23
Adam, Barry, 49
Affectional orientation, 3, 55–56, 64
Affects, 55
Affirmation, 46, 86
Affirmative therapy, 85
Aging, 40
Aging bisexual men, counseling, 116
Aging bisexual women, counseling, 134
Aging female-to-male individuals, counseling, 200–201
Aging fetishistic crossdressing individuals, counseling, 156
Aging gay men, counseling, 61–62
Aging intersex individuals, counseling, 222
Aging lesbian women, counseling, 92
Aging male-to-female individuals, counseling, 182–183
AIDS (acquired immune deficiency syndrome), 23. *See also* HIV/AIDS
Ai nam ai nu, 216
Alcohol problems, and bisexual girls and women, 132–133
Alderson, Kevin, 38, 59, 247
Alexithymia, 69
American Psychiatric Association, 22, 141
Androgen resistance, 211
Association for Lesbian, Gay, Bisexual, and Transgender Issues in Counseling (ALGBTIC), vii
Attitudes and beliefs, challenging individual, 11
Autoandrophilia, 141
Autogynephilia, 141, 144, 190
Baker, Gilbert, 40
Barker, Meg, 107
Bed death, 72, 90
Belt, Elmer, 25
Bem Sex Role Inventory, 126
Benjamin, Harry, 25
Benkert, K. M. (Kertbeny), 20
Berdache, 41
Bereavement, 219–220
Beyond coming out, 39
Beyond Coming Out (Alderson), 38, 59
Bi-bi, 102
Bi-curious, 99
Bidell, Markus P., 253
Bi-gay, 102
Bi Men Network, 115
Binaries, 100
Biphilia, 3
Biphobia, 5
Bisexual, 56, 99. *See also* Bisexual boys and men; Bisexual girls and women
Bisexual boys and men, 97–120
  assumptions questions, challenging, 98–99
  Canada, recent research focused on, 106–107
  career and work, 105–106
  common concerns facing, 108–115
  counseling, 116–117
  counselors, implications for, 118–119
  exercises, classroom and individual, 119
  health (emotional and psychological, physical), 104–105
  identity confusion and labeling issues, 111–112
  internalized biphobia (IB), 112–113
  invisibility and its sequelae, 115
  life span development, 101–102

race and ethnicity, 102–103
reflections, 98–99
relationships (family, friendships, intimate romantic/sexual), 103–104, 113–114
research, 118–119
resources for, 117
roleplay scenarios, 108–110
sociopolitical realities, 106
spirituality and religion, 106
suicidality of, 104
support networks, finding, 114–115
Bisexual drug users, and HIV, 104
Bisexual girls and women, 121–137
alcohol problems and, 132–133
assumptions questions, challenging, 122–123
Canada, recent research focused on, 127–128
career and work, 126–127
common concerns facing, 128–133
community, lack of, 133
counseling, 133–135
counselors, implications for, 136
drug problems and, 132–133
exercises, classroom and individual, 136–137
health (emotional and psychological, physical), 126
identity confusion and fluidity of sexuality, 131–132
isolation, and, 133
life span development and, 124–125
mental health of, 132
race and ethnicity, 125
reflections, 122–123
relationships (family, friendships, intimate romantic/sexual), 125–127, 133
research, 135–136
resources for, 135
roleplay scenarios, 128–130
sociopolitical realities, 127
spirituality and religion, 127
suicidality, 132
Bisexual individuals, 4. *See also* Bisexual boys and men; Bisexual girls and women
Bisexual men. *See* Bisexual boys and men
Bisexual relationships, agreements in, 114
Bisexual women. *See* Bisexual girls and women
Bi-straight, 102
Blanchard, Ray, 147, 171
Breaking Out (Alderson), 54
Brown, Jerry, 48
Butch, 87
Career
bisexual boys and men, 105–106
bisexual girls and women, 126–127
fetishistic crossdressing children and adults, 146
gay boys and men, 45–46
intersex children and adults, 215
lesbian girls and women, 75–76
transsexual girls and transmen, 193
transsexual boys and transwomen, 168–169
Cass's model of gay and lesbian identity, stages of, 38
Catalysts, 38
Circuit parties, 49
Classification of Mental and Behavioral Disorders System (ICD-10) (World Health Organization), 141
Cognitions, 55
Cognitive behavior therapy (CBT), 89, 220
Collectivism, versus individualism, 8–9
Collectivist society, 9
Coming out, 37–40, 55–56
Congenital adrenal hyperplasia (CAH), 212
Contemplation, 11
Conversion therapy, 63–64
Core gender identity, 25, 162
Corporate Equality Index, 194
Counseling
aging bisexual men, 116
aging bisexual women, 134
aging female-to-male individuals, 200
aging fetishistic crossdressing individuals, 156
aging gay men, 61–62
aging intersex individuals, 222
aging lesbian women, 92
aging male-to-female transsexuals (MTF), 182–183
bisexual adolescent females, 134–135
bisexual boys and men, 116–117
bisexual female students, 134
bisexual male adolescents, 117
bisexual males living in rural communities, 116–117
bisexual male students, 117
bisexual women living in rural communities, 134
female-to-male adolescents, 201
female-to-male students, 201
feminist theory approach to, 85–85
fetishistic crossdressing adolescents, 156

fetishistic crossdressing individuals living in rural communities, 156
fetishistic crossdressing students, 156
four-step process for bisexual women, 131
gay adolescents, 62
gay men living in rural communities, 62
gay students, 62
intersex adolescents, 223
intersex individuals living in rural communities, 222
intersex students, 223
male-to-female transsexuals (MTF) adolescents, 183
male-to-female transsexuals (MTF) in rural communities, 183
male-to-female transsexuals (MTF) students, 183
Covert discrimination, 46, 86
Crossdressing individuals, vii, 4–5, 25, 142–143, 147, 156. *See also* Fetishistic crossdressing children and adults; Fetishistic crossdressing (FC) individuals, 5, 141;
Cross-sex hormones, 176–177
Current gender identity, 162

Daughters of Bilitis (DOB), 22
Defense of Marriage Acts (DOMAs), 78
DeLarverie, Stormé, 22
Disclosing, 38
Diagnostic and Statistical Manual of Mental Disorders Fourth Edition (Text Revision) *(DSM-IV-TR)* (American Psychiatric Association), 141
Discrimination, covert and overt, 46, 86
Disorders of sex development (DSD), 206
Divergence of sex development (DSD), 206, 212–213
DOMAs (Defense of Marriage Acts), 78
Don't Ask, Don't Tell, 24
Down low, 103
Drag kings, 5
Drag queens, 5, 148
Drug problems, and bisexual girls and women, 132–133
DSD. *See* Disorders of sex development; Divergence of sex development
During coming out, 38

Ecological theory of LGBTI development, 38
Ecological theory of LGBTI identity, 39 (figure)
Ego-dystonic crossdressing and/or compulsiveness, 154–155
Eisenhower, Dwight D., 22
Ellis, Albert, 104, 154
Essentialism, 68
social constructionism versus, 8–9
Essentialists, 8
Ethnicity, 41, 70–71, 102–103, 125
bisexual boys and men, 102–103
bisexual girls and women, 125
fetishistic crossdressing children and adults, 144
gay boys and men, 41
intersex children and adults, 214
lesbian girls and women, 70–71
transsexual girls and transmen, 191–192
transsexual boys and transwomen, 166
Existential well-being, 76
Explicitly out, 45
External homophobia, 60–61

Fa'afafine, 147
Fakafefine, 147
Family problems, and transsexual boys and transwomen, 180–181
Female-to-male transsexual (FTM), 141, 189
categories, 190
cross-sex hormones and sex reassignment surgery, 197–198
HIV infection, 193
Feminist theory approach to counseling, 85–85
Femme, 87
Fetishism, 141
Fetishistic crossdresser, 142
Fetishistic crossdressing children and adults, 138–159
assumptions questions, challenging, 139–140
career and work, 146
common concerns facing, 149–155
counselors, implications for, 158
ego-dystonic crossdressing and/or compulsiveness, 154–155
exercises, classroom and individual, 158–159
gender dysphoria, mild to moderate, 155
health (emotional and psychological, physical), 145–146
HIV infection, 145
life span development, 143–144
marital discord, 153–154
medications and, 151

race and ethnicity, 144
reflections, 139–140
relationships (family, friendships, intimate romantic/sexual), 145
research, 157
resources for, 156–157
roleplay scenarios, 149–150
sociopolitical realities, 147
spirituality and religion, 146–147
See also Crossdressing individuals
Fetishistic crossdressing (FC) individuals, 5, 141
aging, 156
information regarding (collecting), 152
living in rural communities, 156
with multiple nondominant identity statuses, 155–156
See also Crossdressing individuals
Fetishistic crossdressing students, counseling, 156
Fictive kin, 92
Fidelity concerns, 113–114
Freud, Sigmund, 19, 100
Fusion, 72

Gaie, 78–79
Garland, Judy, 22
Gay, 56
Gay adolescents, counseling, 62
Gay-affirmative therapists, 53
Gay boys and men, 34–65
affectional orientation confusion and self-identifying as gay, 55–56
aging, 40
assumptions questions, challenging, 35
Canada, recent research focused on, 48–50
career and work, 45–46
coming out, 37–40
common concerns facing, 50–59
counselors, implications for, 64
exercises, classroom and individual, 64–65
health (emotional and psychological, physical), 44–45
HIV/AIDS, 58–59
identity fragmentation, 56–57
internalized homophobia, 54–55
life span development, 35–40
race and ethnicity, 41
reflections, 35
relationships (family, friendships, intimate romantic/sexual), 41–44, 59–62
religious conflicts, 57–58
research, 63–64
resources for, 62–63
roleplay scenarios, 50–52
sociopolitical realities, 47–48
spirituality and religion, 46–47
stability versus fluidity of sexuality, 36–37
Gay identity, model of, 38
Gay kings, 29
Gay men, 3. *See also* Gay boys and men
Gay queens, 29
Gay students, counseling, 62
Gebhard, Paul, 123
Gender benders, 5
Gender dysphoria, 4–5, 143, 162, 179
adolescents or adults, 177
children, 177
mild to moderate, 155
Gender euphoria, 155
Gender identity, 25, 162
Gender identity disorder (GID), 152, 162–163
Genderqueers, 190
Gender-variant behavior, 178
Gender variation, 146
General Social Surveys, 70
Genotypes, 206
GID (gender identity disorder), 152, 162
Gonadal sex, 206
Goodridge, Hillary, 53
Goodridge, Julie, 53
Grieger, Russell, 154

HAART (highly active antiretroviral therapy), 23
Hall, Marc, 27
Harry Benjamin International Gender Dysphoria Association (HBIGDA), 183
Harry Benjamin International Standards of Care (SOC), 185
Hay, Harry, 22
Hermaphrodite, 206
Hermaphroditic identity, 221
Heterosexism, 5, 47
Heterosexism Inquirer, The (Yetman), 32
Heterosexist thinking, test of, 12–16
Heterosexual Questionnaire, The (Rochlin), 16
Highly active antiretroviral therapy (HAART), 23
Hijras, 148
Hindrances, 38
Hirschfeld, Magnus, 25

HIV/AIDS, 23, 45, 58–59, 104
Hombre, 144
Homonegativity, 5
Homophobia, 5, 47, 48
Homosexual, 8, 20, 80, 100
Homosexuality, 53
Homosexual orientation, 3, 8, 36, 42, 44, 49–50, 57, 80
Hooker, Evelyn, 22, 25
Hoover, J. Edgar, 22
Hostile Recognition, 42
Hypoactive sexual desire (HSD), 90–91

Ideal self, 56
Identity
  acceptance, 38
  achievement, 37
  comparison, 38
  confusion, 38, 111–112, 131–132
  diffusion, 37
  foreclosure, 37
  fragmentation, 56–57
  maintenance, 102
  moratorium, 37
  pride, 38
  synthesis, 38
  tolerance, 38
Implicitly out, 45
Individualism, versus collectivism, 8–9
Individualistic society, 9
Infidelity, 104
Internalized biphobia (IB), 112–113
Internalized homophobia, 39, 44, 54–55, 90
International Gender Dysphoria Association, 25
Interpersonal therapy (IPT), 89
Intersex, 206
Intersex children and adults, 204–225
  assumptions questions, challenging, 205–206
  bereavement, 219–220
  Canada, recent research focused on, 216
  career and work, 215
  common concerns facing, 217–222
  counselors, implications for, 224
  DSDs and, 207–213
  exercises, classroom and individual, 224
  family issues and support, 221
  health (emotional and psychological, physical), 214–215
  identity development, 221
  life span development, 213–214
  loneliness, secrecy, and feelings of isolation, 220–221
  posttraumatic reactions, 220
  race and ethnicity, 214
  reflections, 205–206
  relationships (family, friendships, intimate romantic/sexual), 214–216
  research, 223–224
  resources for, 223
  roleplay scenarios, 217–218
  shame and guilt, 220
  social support, 222
  sociopolitical realities, 215–216
  spirituality and religion, 215
Intersex identity, developing, 221
Intersex individuals, 4, 206, 222–223. *See also* Intersex children and adults
Intersex students, counseling, 223
Intervention, 56
Intimacy statuses, 36–37
Invisibility, 5–6
Isay, Richard, 103

Jorgensen, Christine, 25, 163
Jorgensen, George, 25, 163

Karyotype, 206
Kathoey, 147
Kertbeny. *See* Benkert, K. M. (Kertbeny)
Kinsey, Alfred, 47, 100
Kinsey Rating Scale, 132
Klein Sexual Orientation Grid, 56, 111
Klinefelter syndrome, 207, 217
Klippert, Everett, 25
Kramer, Larry, 23

Ladder, The, 22
Lady boys, 147
Lady Gaga, 226
Lawrence, Anne, 184
Lawrence v. Texas, 23
Lesbian, 3–4, 56, 80
Lesbian, Gay, Bisexual, and Transgendered Climate Inventory, 105
Lesbian clients, and assessing a potential work environment, 86–87
Lesbian girls and women, 66–96
  assumptions questions, challenging, 67–68

Canada, recent research focused on, 78–80
career and work, 75–76, 86–87
common concerns facing, 82–92
counseling, 85, 92–94
counselors, implications for, 95
depression and suicide risk, 88–89
exercise and, 73
exercises, classroom and individual, 96
feminist theory approach to counseling, 85–85
health (emotional and psychological, physical), 73–75
identity, 38, 79, 87–88
life span development, and, 68–70
parenthood issues, 91–92
race and ethnicity, 70–71
reflections, 67–68
relationships (family, friendships, intimate romantic/sexual), 71–73, 90–91
research , 94–95
resources for, 94
roleplay scenarios, 82–84
sociopolitical realities, 76–78
spirituality and religion, 76
substance abuse problems, 90
weight problems, 89–90
Lesbians in Canada (Stone), 80
Lesbian students, counseling, 93
Lesbian studies, 80
Lesbian women, 3–4. See also Lesbian girls and women
LeVay, Simon, 50
Leznoff, Maurice, 26
LGBT Aging Issues Network, 40
LGBTI (Lesbian, Gay, Bisexual, Transgender, and Intersex), 17–33
change-model approach, 11
common concerns facing, 10
contemporary perspectives, 21–32
counseling practice, conclusions for, 229–230
defining, 4–5
general conclusions, 226–229
groups, included in, 10–16
historical perspectives, 19–21
invisibility in research, 5–6
Iran, 27–28
issues identified, 227–228 (table)
research, 5–8
suicidality of, 73
terminology problems, 2–4
See also Bisexual boys and men; Bisexual girls and women; Fetishistic crossdressing children and adults; Gay boys and men; Intersex children and adults; Lesbian girls and women; Transsexual boys and transwomen; Transsexual girls and transmen
Life span development
bisexual boys and men, 101–102
bisexual girls and women, 124–125
fetishistic crossdressing children and adults, 143–144
gay boys and men, 35–40
intersex children and adults, 213–214
lesbian girls and women, 68–70
transsexual girls and transmen, 190–191
transsexual boys and transwomen, 164–166
Loving Denial, 42
Loving Open, 42
Loving Someone Gay (Clark), 47
Lyons, Phyllis, 22, 24

Machismo, 30
Mahu, 147
Maintenance stage, 11
Major depression, 88–89
Major depressive disorder (MDD), 88–89
Male-to-female transsexual (MTF), 141, 162
adolescents, 183
aging, 182–183
students, 183
living in rural communities, 183
cross-sex hormones and sex reassignment surgery, 176–177
HIV infection, 193
Marcia, James, 36
Marginal transvestites, 141. *See also* Transvestites
Maricón, 144
Marital discord, 153–154
Martin, Del, 22, 24
Mattachine Society, 22
Mead, Margaret, 100
Mental health, and bisexual girls and women, 132
Milk, Harvey, 23, 40
Minnesota Multiphasic Personality Inventory-2, 56
Minority stress, 44
Money, John, 25, 212, 223
Mosaic individuals, 206
Moscone, George, 23
MSM (men who have sex with men), 48
Muller, Ann, 42
Multicultural framework, 9–10

Multimodal Life History Inventory, 56
Myers-Briggs Type Indicator (MBTI), 56

Never Going Back (Warner), 18
Nonchromosomal DSDs, 208–212
Nuclear/periodic transvestites, 141. *See also* Transvestites

Obama, Barack, 63
Oppression, defining terms of, 5
Overt discrimination, 46, 86

Passing, 45
Pederasty, 19
Person of color, bisexual, and a dual identity, 102–103
Persons with nondominant sexualities, 3
Phenotype, 206
Phenotypic sex, 206
Philia, 3
Polyamorous, 104
Positive gay identity, 45
Poznan March, 30
Precontemplation, 11
Preparation stage, 11
Primary transsexual, 144
Pseudohermaphrodite, 206

Queer, 5, 64
Queer as Folk, 79
Queer theory, 2, 5, 8, 63–64, 124
Queer Theory of the United States, A (Bronski), 18

Race, 41, 70–71, 102–103, 125
  bisexual boys and men, 102–103
  bisexual girls and women, 125
  fetishistic crossdressing children and adults, 144
  gay boys and men, 41
  intersex children and adults, 214
  lesbian girls and women, 70–71
  transsexual girls and transmen, 191–192
  transsexual boys and transwomen, 166
Real self, 56
Reimer, Bruce, 212
Relationships
  lesbian girls and women, 90–91
  strain in, 113–114
  transsexual boys and transwomen, 180–181
Religion
  bisexual boys and men, 106
  bisexual girls and women, 127
  fetishistic crossdressing children and adults, 146–147
  gay boys and men, 46–47
  intersex children and adults, 215
  lesbian girls and women, 76
  transsexual boys and transwomen, 169–170
  transsexual girls and transmen, 193
Religious conflicts, 57–58
Religious well-being, 76
Research limitations, 7–8
Resentful Denial, 42
Robinson, Svend, 26
Rochlin, Martin, 12, 16
Rogers, Carl, 57
Roleplay
  scenarios, 50–52
  situations, 235–246
Romance of Transgression in Canada, The (Waugh), 80

Same-sex marriage (SSM), 30, 77 (table)
Same-sex passionate friendship, 71, 95
Sampling, nonrepresentative, 6
Self-identifying, 38
Services and Advocacy for Gay Elders, 40
Sex chromosomal DSDs, 207, 207–208 (table)
Sex development
  disorders of, 206
  divergence of, 206, 212–213
Sex reassignment surgery (SRS), 174, 176–177, 196–199
Sex-reversed, 212
Sexual Addiction Screening Inventory, 56
Sexual deviation, 146
Sexual identity, 4
Sexuality
  fluidity of, 131–132
  questionnaire, 247–252
  stability versus fluidity in, 36–37
Sexuality Questionnaire (Alderson), 64
Sexual minorities, 3
Sexual orientation, 3
Sexual Orientation Counselor Competency Scale, The (SOCCS) (Bidell), 253–258
Sexual variation, 146
She-males, 5
Shepard, Matthew, 23
Shively and De Cecco Scale, 56

Sexual Behavior in the Human Female (Kinsey, Pomeroy, Martin, and Gebhard), 123
Social constructionism, 68
  versus essentialism, 8–9
Social constructionists, 8
Social Readjustment Rating Scale, 56
Social support, and transsexual boys and transwomen, 182
Sociopolitics
  bisexual boys and men, 106
  bisexual girls and women, 127
  fetishistic crossdressing children and adults, 147
  gay boys and men, 47–48
  intersex children and adults, 215–216
  lesbian girls and women, 76–78
  transsexual boys and transwomen, 170
  transsexual girls and transmen, 193–194
Spirituality
  bisexual boys and men, 106
  bisexual girls and women, 127
  fetishistic crossdressing children and adults, 146–147
  gay boys and men, 46–47
  intersex children and adults, 215
  lesbian girls and women, 76
  transsexual boys and transwomen, 169–170
  transsexual girls and transmen, 193
SSM (same-sex marriage), 30, 77 (table)
Standards of Care for Gender Identity Disorders (SOC-6), 175
Standards of Care for the Health of Transsexual, Transgender, and Gender Nonconforming People (SOC-7), 175–176, 196
Stanfield, Robert, 26
Stealth, 182, 186, 189, 194
Stoller, Robert, 25
Stonewall Riots/Rebellion, 22, 193
Substance abuse, and lesbian girls and women, 90
Suicidality
  bisexual boys and men, 104
  bisexual girls and women, 132
Suicide risk, 88–89
Supporting Our Youth (Lepischak), 79
Support networks, 114–115
Symptom Checklist Revised, 56

Teine pepelo, 147
Tolerance, 46, 86
Tomboys, 147
Transgender Day of Remembrance, 170
Transgender individuals, 162
Transgenderism, 142
Transgenderist individual, 4–5
Transgender persons, 4
Transitioning, 163
Transmen, 4, 190. *See also* Transexual girls and transmen
Transphobia, 5
Transsexual, 25
Transsexual boys and transwomen, 160–186
  assumptions questions, challenging, 161–162
  Canada, recent research focused on, 170–171
  career and work, 168–169
  child and adolescent challenges, 178–179
  common concerns facing, 172–182
  counselors, implications for, 184–185
  exercises, classroom and individual, 186
  gender dysphoria, 179
  health (emotional and psychological, physical), and, 167–168
  life span development, and, 164–166
  multicultural competencies, 173–174
  race and ethnicity, 166
  reflections, 161–162
  relationships (family, friendships, intimate romantic/sexual), 166–170, 180–181
  research, 184
  resources for, 183–184
  roleplay scenarios, 172–173
  social support for, 182
  sociopolitical realities, 170
  spirituality and religion, 169–170
  transitioning, 179–182
Transsexual girls and transmen, 187–203
  assumptions questions, challenging, 188–189
  Canada, recent research focused on, 194
  career and work, 193
  common concerns facing, 195–200
  counselors, implications for, 202
  exercises, classroom and individual, 203
  gender scripts, learning new, 199
  health (emotional and psychological, physical), 192–193
  life span development, 190–191
  race and ethnicity, 191–192
  reflections, 188–189
  relationships (family, friendships, intimate romantic/sexual), 192–194

research, 202
resources for, 201–202
roleplay scenarios, 195–196
sex reassignment surgery, uncertainty about, 198–199
spirituality and religion, 193
Transsexual identity development, model of, 171
Transsexual individuals, 4–5, 25, 163–164, 166, 168–169
Transsexualism, 163
Transtheoretical model of change, 11, 12 (table)
Transvestic fetishism, 142
Transvestites, 25, 141, 148
Transwomen, 4, 162. *See also* Transsexual boys and transwomen
Triple jeopardy, 70
Troca-troca, 31
Trudeau, Pierre, 25, 27
Tunten, 148
Turner syndrome, 216
Two spirited, 20, 41, 103, 144

Waria, 147
Weight problems, and lesbian girls and women, 89–90
What the Bible Really Says About Homosexuality (Helminiak), 57
White, Dan, 23
Women who love women (WWLW), 80
Woodworkers, 190
Work
bisexual boys and men, 105–106
bisexual girls and women, 126–127
fetishistic crossdressing children and adults, 146
gay boys and men, 45–46
intersex children and adults, 215
lesbian girls and women, 75–76
transsexual boys and transwomen, 168–169, 181–182
transsexual girls and transmen, 193
Work environment heterosexism, levels of, 46, 86
World Health Organization, 141
World Professional Association for Transgender Health (WPATH), 25, 212
WWLW (women who love women), 80

Yetman, Lori, 13, 32
Yin-yang, 148

Zucker, Kenneth J., 147, 171, 216

About the Author

Kevin Alderson is an associate professor of counseling psychology at the University of Calgary. His areas of research interest include human sexuality and LGBTI studies. Throughout his 26 years as a practicing psychologist, Dr. Alderson has counseled hundreds of clients with LGBTI identities. He is the Editor in Chief of the *Canadian Journal of Counselling and Psychotherapy*, the national Canadian peer-reviewed journal in the counseling field.

Before joining the university in July 2001, Dr. Alderson was the Head of Counseling and Health Services at a community college in Calgary for several years. He writes a monthly column for *Outlooks Magazine*, the Canadian national queer tabloid. His seven published books include:

1. *Beyond Coming Out: Experiences of Positive Gay Identity* (2000)
2. *Breaking Out: The Complete Guide to Building and Enhancing a Positive Gay Identity for Men and Women* (2002)
3. *Same-Sex Marriage: The Personal and the Political* (co-authored with Dr. Kathleen Lahey, Queens University Law Professor, 2004)
4. *Grade Power: The Complete Guide to Improving Your Grades Through Self-Hypnosis* (2004)
5. *Breathe, Freedom: A Comprehensive and Hypnotic Approach to Quitting Smoking* (2011)
6. *Counselling: A Comprehensive profession* (Canadian edition, co-authored with S. T. Gladding, 2012)
7. *Breaking Out II: The Complete Guide to Building a Positive LGBTI Identity* (2012)

He recently authored the recent policy statement regarding *Gender Identity in Adolescents and Adults* for the Canadian Psychological Association (CPA) and co-authored the official fact sheets for CPA for *Gender Dysphoria in Adolescents and Adults* and for *Gender Dysphoria in Children.*

Dr. Alderson can be contacted through his website at www.kevinalderson.ca.

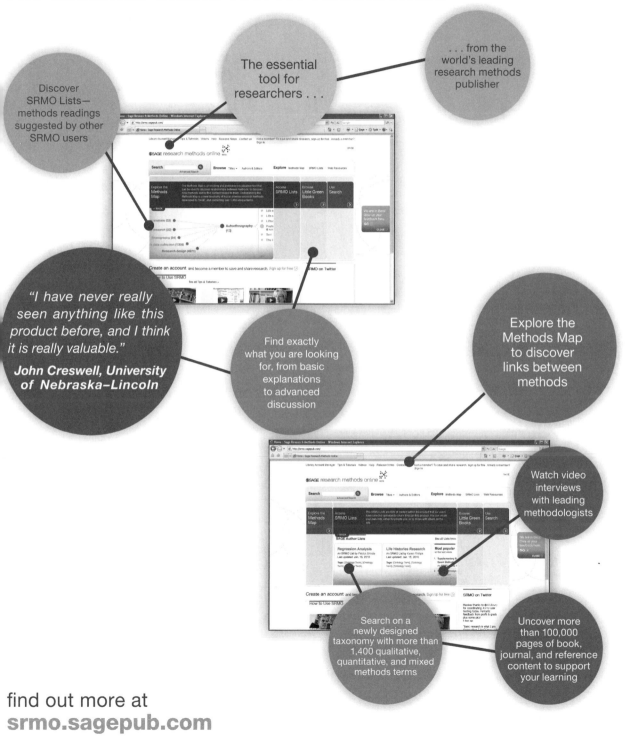